LECTURES ON PARALLEL COMPUTATION

Cambridge International Series on Parallel Computation: 4

LECTURES ON PARALLEL COMPUTATION

Edited by

ALAN GIBBONS
Department of Computer Science
University of Warwick

PAUL SPIRAKIS
Department of Computer Science
University of Patras

CAMBRIDGE UNIVERSITY PRESS
Cambridge, New York, Melbourne, Madrid, Cape Town, Singapore, São Paulo

Cambridge University Press
The Edinburgh Building, Cambridge CB2 2RU, UK

Published in the United States of America by Cambridge University Press, New York

www.cambridge.org
Information on this title: www.cambridge.org/9780521415569

First published 1993
This digitally printed first paperback version 2005

A catalogue record for this publication is available from the British Library

ISBN-13 978-0-521-41556-9 hardback
ISBN-10 0-521-41556-X hardback

ISBN-13 978-0-521-01760-2 paperback
ISBN-10 0-521-01760-2 paperback

The article by U. Vishkin is reproduced by permission of Springer-Verlag
from the Proceedings of 18th ICALP 1991, Lecture Notes in Computer Science,
Volume 510, edited by J. Leach Albert, B. Monien and M. Rodríguez.

Preface

One friend in a lifetime is much. Two are many. Three are hardly possible. Friendship needs a certain parallelism of life, a community of thought, a rivalry of aim.

Henry Brooks Adams

This volume is essentially based on a series of lectures delivered at the *Spring School of Parallel Computation* held at the University of Warwick. The School was organised under the general aegis of the *ALCOM (Algorithms and Complexity)* project of the *ESPRIT II Basic Research Actions* programme of the European Community. Invited lecturers of the school were:

David Evans (*Loughborough University of Technology*)
Alan Gibbons (*University of Warwick*)
Torben Hagerup (*Max Planck Institute, Saabrücken*)
Zvi Kedem (*Courant Institute of Mathematical Sciences, New York*)
David May (*Inmos Ltd., Bristol*)
William McColl (*University of Oxford*)
Colm Ó Dúnlaing (*Trinity College, Dublin*)
Vijaya Ramachandran (*The University of Texas at Austin*)
Paul Spirakis (*University of Patras*)
Gerard Tel (*University of Utrecht*)
Jacobo Torán (*Universitat Politècnica de Catalunya, Barcelona*)
Uzi Vishkin (*University of Maryland and Tel Aviv University*)
Harry Wijshoff (*University of Utrecht*)

Most of the invited speakers generously found the time to contribute to this volume, as have several additional authors who have helped to widen and enrich the material:

Andrew Chin (*Texas A&M University*)
Costas Iliopoulos (*King's College, London*)
Krishna Palem (*IBM Research Division, Yorktown Heights, New York*)
Arvind Raghunathan (*University of California, Davis*)

Almost exclusively, this book is concerned with the foundations of parallel computation. The pre-dominant interest is in the efficiency of computation. There has been some effort to ensure that the bulk of the contributed chapters form a coherent stream taking the reader from a position of having little prior knowledge of the subject to a position of being familiar with leading-edge material taken from a variety of contemporary research and preoccupations. For this reason, a few chapters are concerned with the presentation of basic material of broad interest, others present details of particular specialisations and yet others provide a ranging but advanced perspective. The book may therefore function at the same time as a source of teaching material and as a reference for researchers.

Unencumbered with engineering details, the *Parallel Random Access Machine* model of parallel computation (the so-called P-RAM) has played a central rôle in studies over the last decade or so of how inherent parallelism within problems can be exploited for efficient computation. The P-RAM, which is a shared-memory model, is therefore a significant vehicle for the enquiries of this volume. The initial chapters justify and define the model and subsequent chapters use it in the development of efficient parallel algorithmic design in a variety of application areas. Return visits to chapter 1 after those ensuing chapters which are concerned with detail will provide wider appreciation of its ranging perspective. Apart from the development of deterministic algorithms, there are also contributions which exploit randomisation and investigate algorithmic resilience in the face of processor failures. Some problems with efficient sequential solutions seem inherently to resist attempts at parallelisation and this intransigence is also studied.

The second half of the book extends our enquiries into distributed memory models of computation which bear a closer relationship to extant machines and machines that are likely to be built using current technology. For such machines, both special purpose network topologies (as exemplified by dedicated systolic arrays) and networks which have been advocated for general purpose computation are reviewed. The question of efficiently implementing P-RAM algorithms on general purpose networks is addressed as are the immensely interesting prospects for general purpose parallel computers. One important strand of the latter concerns efficient emulation of the P-RAM model by distributed memory machines in a machine independent way. Studies in this area show that there seems to be no hindrance to scalable, efficient and practical parallel computation by this means. The coherent approach thus provided from the basis of the P-RAM model further justifies its study. Today the P-RAM is generally accepted at least as a model of a programming environment for general purpose parallel machines.

We thank Lesley Sims, Somasundaram Ravindran, Ben Dessau and Nick Holloway who were energetic members of the local team organising the *ALCOM Spring School of Parallel Computation*. Jan van Leeuwen, of the University of Utrecht and the erstwhile co-ordinator of the *ALCOM* project, is to be thanked for the enabling of funds. We thank the invited lecturers who so generously gave of their time to make a success of the School. They and the additional authors are also to be thanked for their final and excellent contributions to this volume. We owe a special debt of gratitude to Toula Pantziou in Patras and especially to Nick Holloway in Warwick who worked hard on technical preparation prior to publication.

Alan Gibbons, *University of Warwick*
Paul Spirakis, *University of Patras*

August 1992.

Contents

Chapter 1

Structural Parallel Algorithmics

Uzi Vishkin *

Abstract

The first half of the chapter is a general introduction which emphasizes the central role that the PRAM model of parallel computation plays in algorithmic studies for parallel computers.

Some of the collective knowledge-base on non-numerical parallel algorithms can be characterized in a structural way. Each structure relates a few problems and technique to one another from the basic to the more involved. The second half of the chapter provides a bird's-eye view of such structures for: (1) list, tree and graph parallel algorithms; (2) very fast deterministic parallel algorithms; and (3) very fast randomized parallel algorithms.

1. Introduction

Parallelism is a concern that is missing from "traditional" algorithmic design. Unfortunately, it turns out that most efficient serial algorithms become rather inefficient parallel algorithms. The experience is that the design of parallel algorithms requires new paradigms and techniques, offering an exciting intellectual challenge. We note that it had not been clear that the design of efficient parallel algorithms for "enough" problems is at all possible. Specifically, I recall a discussion with a colleague in 1979. In a thought-off support of a skeptical position, he quoted [64], who proved that parallelism will be rather ineffective in the context of binary search; informally, they show that an increase in the number of processors from one to p may cut the time of binary search by a factor of at most $\log p$.

This review chapter relates to very introductory as well as rather advanced material on efficient parallel algorithmics. Only a very partial list of possible topics are touched upon. Preference was given to domains of parallel algorithms where more structure, in a sense that is explained later, was found. Omitted is a review of general NC algorithms and the wealth of fundamental results they offer (e.g., for more on this work see [33], [34] and [67]) It was impossible to give a self-contained presentation within the space limitations. An introduction to parallelism, PRAMs, and PRAM algorithms is followed by a review of list, tree and graph algorithms, most of which are not very recent. The last two chapters bring more recent very fast deterministic and randomized parallel algorithms. Our presentation emphasizes examples where the main contribution of a paper was not principally in the results it presented, but rather in a new idea, that provided new tools, and thereby evolutionized concepts as to what can be done efficiently in parallel. Frequently, this meant identifying and

---

*Partially supported by NSF grant CCR-8906949.

solving subtle key problems that had been previously unnoticed obstacles blocking further development in various areas. This distinction of idea-versus-result driven research is not an easy task, for a standard way of arguing that an idea is powerful is to show that it has many applications and leads to stronger results.

For over two decades there has been an understanding that fundamental physical limitations on processing speed will eventually force high performance computation to be targeted principally at the exploitation of parallelism. Today, just as the fastest cycle times are approaching these fundamental barriers, a second generation of moderately parallel machines is emerging, and a technology of processing elements and communication switches is appearing with sufficient power to accelerate the pace of experimental parallel machine research. At the same time, there has been a corresponding maturation in our understanding of interconnection networks and their performance costs, although the substantial evolution in this area shall doubtlessly continue. In the design of parallel algorithms, progress during the last decade has redirected the principal research focus from an effort to classify the problems that can be solved in $O(\log^k n)$ time on n^l processors, where l and k are constants (NC algorithms), to a growing body of research on how to design efficient algorithms exhibiting good speedup on parallel machines.

The question of how to model parallel computation is subtle, and has significant impact on both the design of parallel systems and the design of parallel algorithms. This problem has no single answer; indeed, investigations touched upon two aspects of the design question: *techniques for application-specific design*, and *general purpose design*.

Application specific problems include methodologies for designing algorithms on special purpose processing organizations. Their use is primarily justified by the enormous performance/cost benefits that can be attained for worthy problems that admit such solutions.

At the other end of the spectrum is the question of how to design general purpose parallel algorithms, which may not be targeted for a specific machine, and which may be too complex to be suitable for low level design. Our principal model for algorithmic design in this area is the PRAM (parallel random access machine), which is the focal point for the present report.

At first glance, the PRAM model of computation might not appear to be suitable as a general model for designing efficient parallel algorithms; indeed, even its original use by the theory community was not, for the most part, to design efficient algorithms. Yet the PRAM has now won fairly widespread acceptance in the theoretical community, as a model for efficient parallel computation.

Loosely speaking, the PRAM model of computation is an idealization that draws its power from three facts and consequences:

- It strips away levels of algorithmic complexity concerning synchronization, reliability, data locality, machine connectivity, and communication contention and thereby allows the algorithm designer to focus on the fundamental computational difficulties of the problem at hand. The result has been a substantial number of efficient algorithms designed in this model, and a growing number of design paradigms and utilities for designing such algorithms.

- Many of the design paradigms have turned out to be strikingly robust; as a consequence, they have applications in models outside the PRAM domain, including VLSI, where each wire element and gate is carefully accounted in the complexity cost.

- Recent advances have shown PRAM algorithms to be formally emulatable on high interconnect machines, and formal machine designs that support a large number of virtual processes can, in fact, give a speedup that approaches the number of processors for some sufficiently large problems. Some new machine designs are aimed at realizing idealizations that support pipelined, virtual unit time access PRAMs.

The following informal statement represents my belief on the future of general-purpose parallel computation: *Unless parallel machines are designed to support the PRAM, or a model of parallel computation which is very close to it, the design of parallel algorithms is doomed to be a very difficult (or even impossible) task*; to avoid misunderstand, it emphasized that computer designers should aspire to make their machine a virtual PRAM, and no statement is being made about the actual design.

In the rest of the chapter we take snapshots summarizing some chief characteristics of efficient parallel algorithms.

2. The PRAM Model

We start by reviewing the basics of the PRAM model. A PRAM employs p synchronous processors, all having unit time access to a shared memory. There are a variety of rules for resolving memory access conflicts. The most common are exclusive-read exclusive-write (EREW), concurrent-read exclusive-write (CREW), and concurrent-read concurrent-write (CRCW). An EREW PRAM does not allow simultaneous access by more than one processor to the same memory location for read or write purposes, while a CREW allows concurrent access for reads but not for writes, and a CRCW PRAM allows concurrent access for both reads and writes. (We shall assume that in a concurrent write model, the smallest numbered, among the processors attempting to write into a common memory location, actually succeeds). The survey paper [111] elaborates on the raison d'etre of the "PRAM approach". Survey papers specializing on the class NC are [33] and [34]. More recent review articles include [42], [67], and [69], as well as [10], which is devoted to parallel computational geometry. Books on the topic include [5], [54], [62], [85] and [93].

For sequential computation, it has been of considerable advantage to deal with an abstraction of the von-Neumann machine, namely the RAM or Random Access Machine (see a standard textbook, such as [3]). Two major advantages of such an abstraction are that it makes the algorithm designer's task less complex, and it eliminates obstacles to algorithm portability. A third reason for the success of the RAM model is that its cost complexity generally provides an accurate approximation of the running time on real sequential machines: by and large, efficient RAM algorithms translate into efficient programs on specific machines that are properly designed. Similar motivations justify the use of the PRAM model for parallel computation.

While the PRAM model is demonstrably simple, and provides a clean medium for expressing algorithms, its power depends equally on the wealth of high performance algorithms that have been inspired by the model.

Given two parallel algorithms for the same problem one is *more efficient* than the other if: (1) primarily, its time-processor product is smaller, and (2) secondarily (but important), its parallel time is smaller. *Optimal* parallel algorithms are those whose time-processor product is asymptotically equal to the serial complexity of the problem. They correspond to optimal (often linear) time sequential algorithms. A *fully-parallel* algorithm is a parallel algorithm that runs in constant time using an optimal number of processors. The notion of fully-parallel algorithm represents an *ultimate theoretical goal* for designers of parallel algorithms. Research on lower bounds for parallel computation indicates that this goal is unachievable for almost any interesting problem. These same results often preclude much weaker time bounds for the same problems. Consequences of the above discussion are: (1) the evolving theory of very fast parallel algorithms cannot benefit from the theory of not-as-fast parallel algorithms; and (2) any result that approaches the fully-parallel performance goal is somewhat surprising. The quest for fast and processor-efficient parallel algorithms has also contributed towards establishing a *tradition of excellence* similar to the one implied by the quest for fast serial algorithms.

While lower-bound techniques are not the focus of this chapter, we mention here several lower-bound results whose circumvention provided motivation for much of the research in sections 5 and 6: (1) $\Omega(\log n / \log \log n)$ time using a polynomial number of processors for the parity problem [18]; (2) for finding the maximum among n elements [109], and merging [17] on a parallel comparison model of computation; and (3) for CREW PRAM computation of the OR function of n bits [29].

As explained elsewhere (e.g., [67], [69] or [111]), the PRAM should be viewed as a virtual design-space for a parallel machine and not as a parallel machine, and improvement in the parallel running time of a PRAM algorithm can benefit us in reducing the actual running time. An important application area, where this is desired, is deadline-driven computing. Starting from the applications and trying to design very fast parallel algorithms for them is a natural approach. However, the fact that only few very fast algorithms are known makes this approach hard to pursue. How can one design a very fast parallel algorithm for a specific application without having some algorithmic paradigms that can be followed?! A knowledge-base of deadline-driven parallel algorithms is needed. We suggest the following first step towards building such a knowledge-base: develop a core of problems that can be computed very fast, as well as very fast computational paradigms. Another line of additional justification follows [69], [110] and [112] that advocate slackness in processors. Let us explain. Suppose we are given an efficient PRAM algorithm and a (real) parallel machine with p_1 processors, on which we wish to simulate the algorithm. Suppose that the PRAM algorithm is efficient for up to p_2 PRAM processors. In this case, *processor slackness* is defined as the ratio p_2/p_1. Informally, each of these three papers argues that even if p_1 is fixed, having a larger p_2 (and therefore larger processor slackness) leads to a more efficient simulation by the real machine.

Let us sum up. *Getting the fastest possible time by a processor-efficient algorithm is a primary intellectual challenge; the techniques developed are likely to have practical importance.*

3.   PRAM Algorithms

A considerable body of PRAM algorithms has been discovered over the past several years; many of them are for fundamental problems that have been recognized as classical in the theory of serial algorithms. The benefit from the PRAM model is not only in the extensive list of efficient and fast parallel algorithms that have been designed. Fundamental paradigms and design techniques have emerged, which are of use in many, if not all, models of physically available parallel machines. These techniques have led to efficient fast parallel algorithms in a diversity of areas, including computational geometry, graph problems, pattern matching, and comparison problems.

The PRAM was first proposed as a model for parallel computation in a joint complexity theoretic and algorithmic context in a 1979 thesis [119] and in a paper [44]; this original instance concerned the CREW PRAM model. [100] also advocated using a PRAM for studying the limits of parallel computation at around the same chronological time. [51] was the first to propose the CRCW PRAM model in a complexity theoretic context (he called it a SIMDAG). [86] identified and characterized the class NC. [103] suggested using the CRCW PRAM in an algorithmic context.

Figures 1-3 are a focal point for this short tutorial chapter. The figures illustrate some of the structure of PRAM algorithmics. The research itself seems to have been led by a desire to solve some involved problems; however, these figures reveals that in order to accomplish this, a variety of techniques, as well as solutions to more fundamental underlying problems, have been introduced. This structure of problems and techniques (from the basic to the more involved) adds *elegance* to parallel algorithmics. Such fine structure (or actually much finer) exists in a few classical fields of Mathematics, but is rather unique in combinatorics-related theories. The first observation that such interesting structures are possible was in the context of list, tree and graph problems; this particular structure is described in the next section, and illustrated in Figure 1. Most of this work was done between 1980 and 1988. We highlight structure-related issues of this work, primarily for background; an elaborate overview of most of this material can be found in [42] and [67]. The algorithms for most "target problems" in this figure (these are the more involved and known problems; usually, they are at the top or slightly below the top of the figure) run in logarithmic time. The other figures (and sections) are on doubly-logarithmic time, or faster algorithms; this work was done recently; while it was hard to anticipate the structure of Figure 1 beforehand, searching for a similar structure became one of the research goals for the later work.

4. List, Tree and Graph Algorithms

A basic routine that is used most often in parallel algorithms is undoubtedly that for the *prefix sums* problem [73]. The fact that the prefix-sums problem appears at the bottom of Figure 1 is meant to convey the basic role of this problem. A faster CRCW algorithm for prefix-sums also exists [39]. A generalization of this problem to pointer structures, the *list ranking* problem, was identified in [119]; list ranking has proven to be a key subroutine in parallel algorithms. In fact, obtaining optimal algorithms for list ranking and (undirected) graph connectivity proved to be central to obtaining optimal algorithms for a considerable number of list, tree and graph problems. First randomized, and later deterministic, optimal parallel algorithms for list ranking were given [113], [37], [36], [7] and [39]. The deterministic algorithms are based on a deterministic arbitration technique, dubbed *deterministic coin tossing* [37]. Extensions of this technique for sparse graphs and other applications were given [52], [40], and [58].

Key techniques for parallel algorithms on trees are reviewed next: (1) The *Euler tour* technique [108] reduces the computation of many tree problems to list ranking. (2) The *tree contraction* technique [76] led to a number of optimal randomized logarithmic-time algorithms for tree problems, including expression tree evaluation; optimal deterministic versions were also given [53], [38], [2] and [63]. Implicit use of tree contraction in a non-standard parallel algorithmic setting appeared in [22]. (3) *Centroid decomposition* of a tree, as implicitly used in [118] for $O(\log^2 n)$ time computations. Accelerating centroid decomposition was the motivation for the tree contraction version of [38].

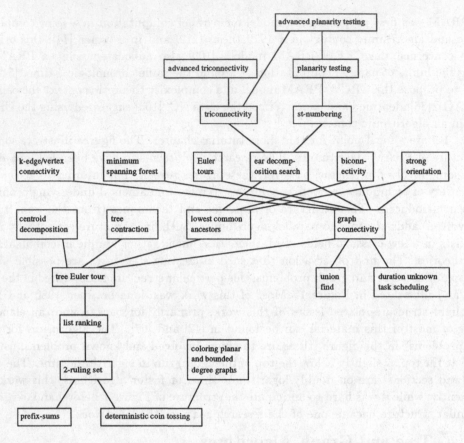

Figure 1. List, tree and graph algorithms

Two logarithmic time connectivity algorithms were given: (1) a deterministic one which is optimal on all except very sparse graphs [36]; (2) a randomized optimal one [46]. For Figure 1, the deterministic algorithms builds on a restricted *union find* problem, a scheduling problem, dubbed *duration unknown task scheduling*, and the Euler tour technique, as well as ideas from two previous connectivity algorithms [59] and [104]. It should be pointed out that the logarithmic time version of the deterministic connectivity algorithm requires the use of expander graphs and thus is highly impractical at present; however, a slightly less parallel version involves much smaller constants.

The graph connectivity problem turned out to be the main obstacle to deriving optimal logarithmic time algorithms for several graph problems, including: *biconnectivity* [108], *finding Euler tour in a graph* [11], [4] and *orienting the edges of an undirected graph to get a strongly connected digraph ("strong orientation)"* [114]. We also note some recent parallel algorithms for *k (edge and vertex) connectivity* problems [71] and [35].

The problem of achieving optimal speedups on sparse graphs for the strong orientation and biconnectivity problems turned out to depend on an efficient solution for yet another fundamental problem: preprocessing of a rooted tree so that a query requesting the *lowest common ancestor (LCA)* of any pair of nodes can be processed in $O(1)$ operations. Parallel algorithms for this problem [106] and [25] use the Euler tour technique.

Depth first search (DFS) is perceived by many as the most useful technique known for designing sequential algorithms for graph problems. Unfortunately, it is not known how to implement DFS efficiently in parallel. A technique called *ear decomposition search* (EDS) was suggested as a replacement for DFS in the context of efficient and fast parallel algorithms [81] and [77], after an earlier suggestion in [74] for computing EDS in parallel in a fast but inefficient manner. The EDS method implies alternative algorithms for *biconnectivity* and *strong orientation*. More powerful applications were for finding an *st-numbering* of a graph, again in [81], as well as for triconnectivity algorithms [78] and [98]. An *st*-numbering is used in the *planarity testing* algorithm of [68]. The most recent algorithms for triconnectivity [43] and planarity testing [95], are very nice examples of reaching target problems by building an even higher level in the structure of Figure 1, and using effectively many of the previous techniques.

5. Deterministic Fast Algorithms

Structure that was found in optimal doubly-logarithmic time (or faster), parallel algorithms is highlighted. Figure 2.1 discusses works that can be viewed as using the *doubly-logarithmic tree* paradigm, as per [13] . Doubly-logarithmic trees are rooted trees with $n = 2^{2^i}$ leaves for some integer $i > 0$. The root has $2^{2^{(i-1)}}$ children, each being the root of a doubly-logarithmic subtree with $2^{2^{(i-1)}}$ leaves. For $i = 0$ a doubly-logarithmic tree consists of a root and two children, which are leaves. Such structure guides the computation in optimal doubly-logarithmic parallel algorithms for finding the *maximum* among n elements [103] (using [109]), finding the *maximum relative to all prefixes* of an array of elements [101] and [23] (the *prefix-maxima* problem), *merging* two sorted lists [70] and [17], finding the *convex hull of a monotone polygon* [24], and finding *all nearest neighbors in a convex polygon* [107]. Note that all merging algorithms that are mentioned in this chapter may be implemented on a CREW PRAM. *String matching*: For some family of parallel algorithms it is sufficient to consider only non-periodic patterns [45]. A method for eliminating (at least) one among two potential occurrences of a non-periodic pattern string in a text string in [115] was observed in [15] to be similar to comparing two numbers in order to determine which one is larger and together with an algorithm for finding the maximum, led to an optimal doubly-logarithmic *string matching* algorithm; [16] showed recently a matching lower-bound for a parallel comparison model of computation. The *all nearest smaller values (ANSV)* problem is: given an array $(a_1, a_2...a_n)$, the ANSV problem is to find for each $1 \leq i \leq n$ the nearest j and l, such that a_j and a_l are smaller than a_i (that is, find the smallest $l > i$ such that $a_l < a_i$ and the largest $j < i$ such that $a_j < a_i$). While generalizing two problems - finding the maximum and merging - an optimal doubly-logarithmic algorithm for ANSV was still possible [23]. In the same paper, the ANSV algorithm is shown to lead to optimal doubly-logarithmic algorithms for the following *range-maxima* problem: preprocess an array of numbers $(a_1, a_2...a_n)$, so that for any pair of indices i and j, where $1 \leq i < j \leq n$, a *range-maximum* query requesting the maximum among $(a_i, a_{i+1}...a_j)$ can be processed in constant-time. More remotedly related to the doubly-logarithmic tree paradigm is a matrix searching algorithm [9]

Remark. Some of the problems mentioned in this section, particularly from here on, may have a rather specific flavor. However, they are still interesting since improvement on the more general problem is either impossible or apparently difficult.

The *surplus-log* approach: suppose the aim is designing a triply-logarithmic (or faster) optimal parallel algorithm; the surplus-log approach suggests the following first step: *design*

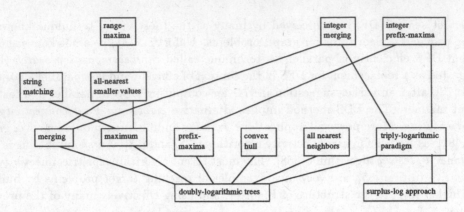

Figure 2.1. Doubly- and triply-logarithmic time algorithms

an algorithm with $n \log n$ *processors and constant-time.* Uses of the surplus-log approach come in two flavors: (1) As part of a global strategy. (2) As a rule-of-thumb (or "sorcery"); that is, it merely provides an insight that leads to further improvements; in other words, for some reason, which is not fully clear to us, it sometimes helps to follow the surplus-log approach.

A *triply-logarithmic paradigm* [19] uses the surplus-log approach, in conjunction with doubly-logarithmic algorithms for the same problems, as part of a global strategy. The strategy leads to optimal parallel algorithms for several problems whose running time is triply-logarithmic in the following sense: consider, for instance, the problem of merging two sorted lists of integers drawn from the domain $[1...s]$. The running time obtained is $O(\log \log \log s)$ [26]. There are also similar triply-logarithmic results for the prefix-maxima problem [19] (and thereby for finding the maximum among n elements).

Optimal *log-star* time (i.e., $O(\log^* n)$) time) parallel algorithms seem to be the hardest to fit into a strict structure of paradigms using presently available ideas. See Figure 2.2. However, using the surplus-log approach, as a rule-of-thumb, was helpful for several problems: (1) *String matching* for a preprocessed pattern [117]; (2) prefix-maxima [20]; there, this prefix-maxima algorithm is also the most time consuming step in an algorithm for routing around a rectangle - a VLSI routing problem ; and (3) for preprocessing a rooted tree, so that any *level-ancestor* query can be processed in constant-time [28]. The input for such query consists of a vertex v and an integer l; the output is the l'th ancestor of v, where the first ancestor of a vertex is its parent and the l'th ancestor is the parent of the $(l-1)$'st ancestor; the Euler tour of the tree is assumed to be given.

Optimal *inverse-Ackermann* time (i.e., $O(\alpha(n))$ time , where α is the inverse-Ackermann extremely slow growing function) parallel algorithms actually use the surplus-log approach in a methodological way, overviewed below. Benefiting from a construction on unbounded fan-in circuits in [30], the inverse-Ackermann paradigm [25] works by designing a series of algorithms; the first in the series should run in $O(1)$ time using $n \log n$ processors; then, in a certain way, slight increase in time implies significant decrease in the number of processors. The $\alpha(n)$'th algorithm in the series runs in $O(\alpha(n))$ time using $n\alpha(n)$ processors, and finally an optimal algorithm that uses $(n/\alpha(n))$ processors and $O(\alpha(n))$ time is derived. See Figure 2.3 for the sequel. The most basic problem that was solved using the inverse-Ackermann paradigm is for the *nearest-one* problem (see also [88], who calls it the *chaining problem*):

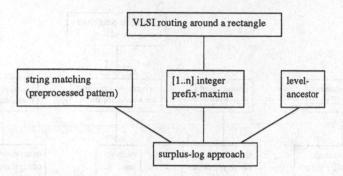

Figure 2.2. log-star time algorithms

given an array of bits $(a_1, ..., a_n)$, find for each $1 \leq i \leq n$, the two nearest j and l such that $a_j = a_l = 1$ (that is, find the smallest $j > i$ such that $a_j = 1$ and the largest $j < i$ such that $a_j = 1$). Inverse-Ackermann time for chaining is best possible in an "oblivious" model of parallel computation, even with n processors [31]. The nearest-one algorithm has been used to reduce a general version of the merging problem to the problem of finding all nearest neighbors (ANN) of vertices in a convex polygon; a consequence is that a doubly-logarithmic time lower-bound for merging extends to the ANN problem, resulting in a simpler proof than in [107]. Wherever reducibilities are more efficient than lower bounds they become promising tools for the theory of lower bounds. Before proceeding we make two comments: (1) in all problems below the input is assumed to come from the domain of integers $[1...n]$; (2) we avoid redefining problems that were defined earlier. Problems for which optimal inverse-Ackerman algorithms were given include: (1) the *all nearest smaller value* (ANSV) problem; this leads to: (2) *parentheses matching*: given the level of nesting for each parenthesis in a legal sequence of parentheses, find for each parenthesis its match; the last two results are in [27]; (3) the *nearest-one complementation* problem: given is an array of bits $(a_1, ..., a_n)$ and suppose for each $a_i = 1$, the two nearest indices j and l, such that $a_j = a_l = 1$, are known; find for each $a_i = 0$, $1 \leq i \leq n$, the two nearest j and l such that $a_j = a_l = 1$ (that is, find the smallest $j > i$ such that $a_j = 1$ and the largest $j < i$ such that $a_j = 1$); this leads to: (4) *merging* two sorted lists; the nearest-one complementation and the merging algorithms are for a CREW PRAM; the last two results are in [26].

The following two problems involve preprocessing and query retrieval: (1) preprocessing for *range-maxima* queries; the preprocessing is done by an optimal inverse-Ackermann parallel algorithm and processing a query takes inverse-Ackermann time; the series of algorithms obtained as part of the inverse-Ackermann paradigm also implies trading-off slightly slower, but still optimal, preprocessing for faster (e.g., constant-time) query retrieval; (2) preprocess a rooted tree so that a query requesting the *lowest-common-ancestor* (LCA) of any pair of vertices can be quickly processed; results are similar to the ones for range-maxima, assuming that the Euler tour of the tree is given; the algorithm is new, and interestingly also simpler than previous LCA algorithms [61] and [106].

6. Randomized Fast Algorithms

Randomization has shown to be very useful for both the simulation of PRAM-like shared memory models of parallel computation by other models of parallel machines (e.g., in [72],

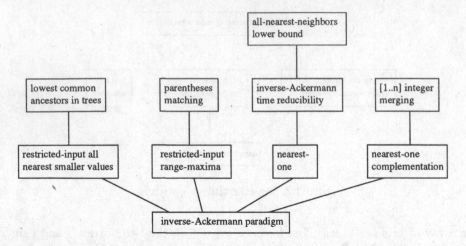

Figure 2.3. Inverse-Ackermann time algorithms

[69], [82], [91], [65] and [80]), and for the design of parallel algorithms (e.g., in [1], [8], [46], [48], [66], [75], [76], [83], [84], [94], [96], [92], [99], [102] and [113]).

All "target algorithms" in this section are randomized, and their running time is at the doubly-logarithmic level, or faster. By the *doubly-logarithmic level*, we mean $O(f(n) \log \log n)$ where the function $f(n)$ is $o(\log \log n)$.

Several constant-time optimal randomized algorithms were given: (1) for finding the maximum among n elements [92]; and its generalization (2) for linear programming in fixed dimension [8]; (3) for finding approximate median [102]; (4) for the nearest one problem (as in [25] and [88]), under the assumption that there is some upper bound on the number of ones, [89].

Several parallel deterministic and randomized algorithms, that run in time proportional to $\log n / \log \log n$ ("logarithmic level") or slower, were given for sorting [6], [12], [21], [32], [60] [87], [97], and [103], and integer sorting [14], [55], [56], [83], [84], [94], [89] and [90]. The lower-bound in [18] implies that faster algorithms are possible only by relaxing the definition of the problem: (1) [79] gave a doubly-logarithmic level result, assuming the input comes from a certain random source; the output is given in a "padded" representation; (2) [56] allows general integer inputs from the range $[1..n]$; the output is given in a linked list which is sorted in a non-decreasing order.

We proceed to Figure 3, the main structure in this section. At the most basic level, Figure 3 has the *d-polynomial approximate compaction (d-PAC)* problem (for $d = 3$ or 4). Given is an array of n cells; we know that only m of them contain one item each, and the rest are empty; the problem is to insert all items into an array of size m^d. A constant-time algorithm using n processors has been given for this fundamental problem in [88]. The *linear approximate compaction (LAC)* problem is harder: using the same input, the items are to be inserted into an array whose size is linear in m, say $4m$. An optimal randomized algorithm for LAC, whose running time is at the log-star level was given [84]. Unless mentioned otherwise, all log-star level results are from this chapter. The algorithm uses the d-PAC algorithm. A somewhat similar use of the d-PAC algorithm for a different problem can be found in [89]. Using the log-star-time deterministic algorithms for the nearest-one and

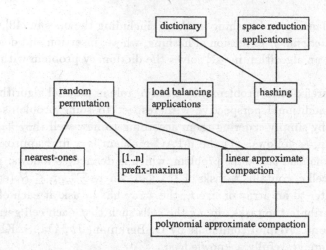

Figure 3. Very fast randomized algorithms

prefix-maxima problems, mentioned earlier, as well as the LAC algorithm, an optimal log-star level for *generating a random permutation* was given. Other methods for this problem are at the logarithmic level [76] and [94]; [57] gives a doubly-logarithmic level algorithm that produces random permutations in a non-standard representation. The LAC algorithm required a new algorithmic paradigm. This paradigm has been extended, within the same performance bounds, to cope with the more general and well-investigated problem of *hashing*: given a set of n input elements, build a linear size table that supports membership queries in constant-time. Logarithmic level hashing [83], and doubly-logarithmic level hashing [48] preceded this result. Some log-star level ideas for a non-standard algorithmic model, where cost of counting, as well as assignment of processors to jobs, are ignored were given in [50]. An $\Omega(\log^* n)$ time lower-bound using n processors is also given in [50]; the lower bound is for a model of computation that admits the log-star level algorithm. We mention here only one application of hashing; see [83] for reference to several parallel algorithms with excessive space requirements that become space-efficient by using parallel hashing; the penalties are increase in time (as required by the hashing algorithm) and switching from a deterministic to a randomized algorithm.

Assignment of processors to jobs is a typical concern in parallel algorithms; for instance, one of the most powerful methodologies for designing parallel algorithms is to have a first design in terms of total work and time; extending this first design into a "full PRAM" design is guided by a theorem due to [22]; the problem, however, is that the theorem holds only for a non-standard model of parallel computation, where assignment of processors to jobs can be done free of charge; the methodology was first used for the design of a PRAM algorithm in [105], and is elucidated in [116] and [62], who call it the *work-time* framework; typical applications of this methodology solve the processor assignment problem in an ad-hoc manner; however, sometimes proper processor assignment can be achieved using general methods for balancing loads among processors. Load balancing can be achieved by a simple application of a prefix-sums algorithm (e.g., [113]), with a logarithmic-level time overhead. A family of load balancing algorithms are treated in [47], with a doubly-logarithmic multiplicative overhead; [84] treats a more specific family, with log-star level additive overhead, using the LAC algorithm. Load balancing and hashing methods, including the ones in [48], led to a doubly-logarithmic level "*dictionary*" extension of hashing, where, insertion and deletion queries are also supported [49]; an algorithm in [41] solves the dictionary problem with running time of the form $O(n^\epsilon)$.

Routines for the prefix-sums problem play a major role in parallel algorithms, as indicated in Section 4. An additional perspective with respect to some problems in the previous paragraph is given by simply ordering them according to how well they "approximate" the prefix-sums problem, as follows: (1) the d-PAC problem is a first approximation; (2) the LAC problem; (3) the *load balancing* problem, which is defined as follows: given is an array of n cells $c_1, ..., c_n$; cell c_i contains t_i tasks, $1 \leq i \leq n$, where $\sum_{i=1}^{n} t_i \leq N$ (each cell i has the count t_i and a pointer to an array of size t_i; the array has a task at each of its entries); the problem is to redistribute the tasks among the cells such that each cell gets $O(N/n)$ tasks.

Acknowledgement. Helpful comments by O. Berkman, J. JáJá, S. Khuller, Y. Matias and R. Thurimella are gratefully acknowledged.

References

[1] N. Alon, L. Babai, and A. Itai. A fast and simple randomized parallel algorithm for the maximal independent set problem. *J. Algorithms*, 7:567–583, 1986.

[2] K. Abrahamson, N. Dadoun, D. A. Kirkpatrick, and T. Przytycka. A simple parallel tree contraction algorithm. Technical Report 87-30, The University of British Columbia, 1987.

[3] A. V. Aho, J. E. Hopcroft, and J. D. Ullman. *The design and analysis of computer algorithms.* Addison-Wesley, Reading, MA, 1974.

[4] B. Awerbuch, A. Israeli, and Y. Shiloach. Finding Euler circuits in logarithmic parallel time. In *Proc. of the 16th Ann. ACM Symp. on Theory of Computing*, pages 249–257, May 1984.

[5] S.G. Akl. *The Design and Analysis of Parallel Algorithms.* Prentice Hall, Engelwood Cliffs, New Jersey, 1989.

[6] M. Ajtai, J. Komlós, and E. Szemerédi. An $O(n \log n)$ sorting network. In *Proc. of the 15th Ann. ACM Symp. on Theory of Computing*, pages 1–9, 1983.

[7] R.J. Anderson and G.L. Miller. Optimal parallel algorithms for list ranking. In *3rd Aegean workshop on computing, Lecture Notes in Computer Science 319, 1988, Springer-Verlag*, pages 81–90, 1988.

[8] N. Alon and N. Megiddo. Parallel linear programming almost surely in constant time. In *Proc. of the 31st IEEE Annual Symp. on Foundation of Computer Science*, pages 574–582, 1990.

[9] M.J. Atallah. A faster algorithm for a parallel algorithm for a matrix searching problem. In *Proc. 2nd SWAT*, volume LNCS 447, pages 192–200. Springer-Verlag, 1990.

[10] M.J. Atallah. Parallel techniques for computational geometry. Technical Report CS-1020, Purdue University, 1990.

[11] M.J. Atallah and U. Vishkin. Finding Euler tours in parallel. *J. Comp. Sys. Sci.*, 29,3:330–337, 1984.

[12] K. Batcher. Sorting networks and their applications. In *AFIPS Spring Joint Computing Conference*, pages 307–314, 32(1968).

[13] O. Berkman, D. Breslauer, Z. Galil, B. Schieber, and U. Vishkin. Highly-parallelizable problems. In *Proc. of the 21st Ann. ACM Symp. on Theory of Computing*, pages 309–319, 1989.

[14] P.C.P. Bhatt, K. Diks, T. Hagerup, V.C. Prasad, T. Radzik, and S. Saxena. Improved deterministic parallel integer sorting. Technical Report TR 15/1989, Fachbereich Informatik, Universität des Saarlandes, D-6600 Saarbrücken, W. Germany, November 1989.

[15] D. Breslauer and Z. Galil. An optimal $O(\log\log n)$ parallel string matching algorithm. To appear in SIAM J. Comput., 1988.

[16] D. Breslauer and Z. Galil. A lower bound for parallel string matching. In *Proc. of the 23rd Ann. ACM Symp. on Theory of Computing*, 1991.

[17] A. Borodin and J.E. Hopcroft. Routing, merging, and sorting on parallel models of computation. *J. Computer and System Sciences*, 30:130–145, 1985.

[18] P. Beame and J. Hastad. Optimal bounds for decision problems on the CRCW PRAM. In *Proc. of the 19th Ann. ACM Symp. on Theory of Computing*, pages 83–93, 1987.

[19] O. Berkman, J. JáJá, S. Krishnamurthy, R. Thurimella, and U. Vishkin. Some triply-logarithmic parallel algorithms. In *Proc. of the 31st IEEE Annual Symp. on Foundation of Computer Science*, pages 871–881, 1990.

[20] O. Berkman, J. JáJá, S. Krishnamurthy, R. Thurimella, and U. Vishkin. Top-bottom routing is as easy as prefix minima. In preparation (a preliminary and partial version is part of Some Triply-logarithmic Parallel Algorithms, see above), 1991.

[21] G. Bilardi and A. Nicolau. Adaptive bitonic sorting: an optimal parallel algorithm for shared-memory machines. *SIAM J. Computing*, 18:216–228, 1989.

[22] R.P. Brent. The parallel evaluation of general arithmetic expressions. *J. Assoc. Comput. Mach.*, 21:302–206, 1974.

[23] O. Berkman, B. Schieber, and U. Vishkin. Some doubly logarithmic parallel algorithms based on finding all nearest smaller values. Technical Report UMIACS-TR-88-79, Univ. of Maryland Inst. for Advanced Computer Studies, 1988.

[24] O. Berkman, B. Schieber, and U. Vishkin. The parallel complexity of finding the convex hull of a monotone polygon. In preparation, 1991.

[25] O. Berkman and U. Vishkin. Recursive *-tree parallel data-structure. In *Proc. of the 30th IEEE Annual Symp. on Foundation of Computer Science*, pages 196–202, 1989.

[26] O. Berkman and U. Vishkin. On parallel integer merging. Technical Report UMIACS-TR-90-15, University of Maryland Inst. for Advanced Computer Studies, 1990.

[27] O. Berkman and U. Vishkin. Almost fully-parallel paretheses matching. In preparation, 1991.

[28] O. Berkman and U. Vishkin. Finding level-ancestors in trees. Technical Report UMIACS-TR-91-9, University of Maryland Institute for Advanced Computer Studies, 1991.

[29] S.A. Cook, C. Dwork, and R. Reischuk. Upper and lower time bounds for parallel random access machines without simultaneous writes. *SIAM J. Comput.*, 15:87–97, 1986.

[30] A.K. Chandra, S. Fortune, and R.J. Lipton. Unbounded fan-in circuits and associative functions. In *Proc. of the 15th Ann. ACM Symp. on Theory of Computing*, pages 52–60, 1983.

[31] S. Chaudhuri. Tight bounds for the chaining problem. preprint, December, 1990.

[32] R. Cole. Parallel merge sort. *SIAM J. Computing*, 17(4):770–785, 1988.

[33] S.A. Cook. Towards a complexity theory of synchronous parallel computation. *Ensign. Math.*, 27:99–124, 1981.

[34] S.A. Cook. A taxonomy of problems with fast parallel algorithms. *Information and Control*, 64:2–22, 1985.

[35] J. Cheriyan and R. Thurimella. Algorithms for parallel k-vertex connectivity and sparse certificates. In *Proc. of the 23rd Ann. ACM Symp. on Theory of Computing*, 1991.

[36] R. Cole and U. Vishkin. Approximate and exact parallel scheduling with applications to list, tree and graph problems. In *Proc. of the 27th IEEE Annual Symp. on Foundation of Computer Science*, pages 478–491, 1986.

[37] R. Cole and U. Vishkin. Deterministic coin tossing with applications to optimal parallel list ranking. *Information and Control*, 70:32–53, 1986.

[38] R. Cole and U. Vishkin. The accelerated centroid decomposition technique for optimal parallel tree evaluation in logarithmic time. *Algorithmica*, 3:329–348, 1988.

[39] R. Cole and U. Vishkin. Faster optimal parallel prefix sums and list ranking. *Information and Computation*, 81:334–352, 1989.

[40] R. Cole and O. Zajicek. An optimal parallel algorithm for building a data structure for planar point location. *J. Parallel and Distributed Computing*, 8:280–285, 1990.

[41] M. Dietzfelbinger and F. Meyer auf der Heide. An optimal parallel dictionary. In *Proc. 1st ACM Symposium on Parallel Algorithms and Architectures*, pages 360–368, 1989.

[42] D. Eppstein and Z. Galil. Parallel algorithmic techniques for combinatorial computation. *Ann. Rev. Comput. Sci.*, 3:233–283, 1988.

[43] D. Fussell, V.L. Ramachandran, and R. Thurimella. Finding triconnected components by local replacements. In *Proc. of 16th ICALP, Springer LNCS 372*, pages 379–393, 1989.

[44] S. Fortune and J. Wyllie. Parallelism in random access machines. In *Proceedings of the 10th Annual ACM Symposium on Theory of Computing*, pages 114–118, 1978.

[45] Z. Galil. Optimal parallel algorithms for string matching. *Information and Control*, 67:144–157, 1985.

[46] H. Gazit. An optimal randomized parallel algorithm for finding connected components in a graph. In *Proc. of the 27th IEEE Annual Symp. on Foundation of Computer Science*, pages 492–501, 1986.

[47] J. Gil. Fast load balancing on PRAM. Preliminary report; see also: Lower Bounds and Algorithms for Hashing and Parallel Processing, Ph.D. Thesis, Hebrew University, Jerusalem, Israel, 1990.

[48] J. Gil and Y. Matias. Fast hashing on a PRAM. In *Proc. of the 2nd Second ACM-SIAM Symposium on Discrete Algorithms*, pages 271–280, 1991.

[49] Y. Gil, Y. Matias, and U. Vishkin. A fast parallel dictionary. In preparation, 1990.

[50] Y. Gil, F. Meyer auf der Heide, and A. Wigderson. Not all keys can be hashed in constant time. In *Proc. of the 22nd Ann. ACM Symp. on Theory of Computing*, pages 244–253, 1990.

[51] L.M. Goldschlager. A universal interconnection pattern for parallel computers. *J. Assoc. Comput. Mach.*, 29:1073–1086, 1982.

[52] A. Goldberg, S. Plotkin, and G. Shannon. Parallel symmetry-breaking in sparse graphs. In *Proceedings 19th Annual ACM Symposium on Theory of Computing*, pages 315–324, 1987.

[53] A. Gibbons and W. Rytter. An optimal parallel algorithm for dynamic expression evaluation and its applications. In *Proceedings of the sixth Conference on Foundations of Software Technology and Theoretical Computer Science, Lecture Notes in Computer Science 241*, pages 453–469. Springer-Verlag, 1986.

[54] A. Gibbons and W. Rytter. *Efficient Parallel Algorithms*. Cambridge University Press, Cambridge, 1988.

[55] T. Hagerup. Towards optimal parallel bucket sorting. *Information and Computation*, 75:39–51, 1987.

[56] T. Hagerup. Constant-time parallel integer sorting. In *Proc. of the 23rd Ann. ACM Symp. on Theory of Computing*, 1991.

[57] T. Hagerup. Fast parallel generation of random permutations. In *Proc. of 18th ICALP*, 1991.

[58] T. Hagerup, M. Chrobak, and K. Diks. Parallel 5-coloring of planar graphs. In *Proc. of 14th ICALP*, pages 304–313, 1987.

[59] D.S. Hirschberg, A.K. Chandra, and D.V. Sarwate. Computing connected components on parallel computers. *Comm. ACM*, 22,8:461–464, 1979.

[60] D. S. Hirschberg. Fast parallel sorting algorithms. *Comm. ACM*, 21:657–661, 1978.

[61] D. Harel and R.E. Tarjan. Fast algorithms for finding nearest common ancestors. *SIAM J. Comput.*, 13(2):338–355, May 1984.

[62] J. JáJá. *Introduction to Parallel Algorithms*. Addison-Wesley, Reading, MA, 1991.

[63] S.R. Kosaraju and A.L. Delcher. Optimal parallel evaluation of tree-structured computations by ranking. In *Proc. of AWOC 88, Lecture Notes in Computer Science* No. 319, pages 101–110. Springer-Verlag, 1988.

[64] R.M. Karp and W.L. Miranker. Parallel minimax search for a maximum. *J. of Combinatorial Theory*, 4:19–34, 1968.

[65] Z.M. Kedem, K.V. Palem, and P.G. Spirakis. Efficient robust parallel computations. In *Proc. of the 22nd Ann. ACM Symp. on Theory of Computing*, pages 138–148, 1990.

[66] R.M. Karp and M.O. Rabin. Efficient randomized pattern-matching algorithms. *IBM J. of Research and Development*, 31:249–260, 1987.

[67] R.M. Karp and V. Ramachandran. A survey of parallel algorithms for shared-memory machines. Technical Report UCB/CSD 88/408, Computer Science Division (EECS) U. C. Berkeley, 1988. also, in Handbook of Theoretical Computer Science, North-Holland, to appear.

[68] P. Klein and J.H. Reif. An efficient parallel algorithm for planarity. *J. Comp. Sys. Sci.*, 37, 1988.

[69] C.P. Kruskal, L. Rudolph, and M. Snir. A complexity theory of efficient parallel algorithms. In *Proc. of 15th ICALP, Springer LNCS 317*, pages 333–346, 1988.

[70] C.P. Kruskal. Searching, merging, and sorting in parallel computation. *IEEE Trans. on Comp*, C-32:942–946, 1983.

[71] S. Khuller and B. Schieber. Efficient parallel algorithms for testing connectivity and finding disjoint s-t paths in graphs. In *Proc. of the 30th IEEE Annual Symp. on Foundation of Computer Science*, pages 288–293, 1989.

[72] A. Karlin and E. Upfal. Parallel hashing – an efficient implementation of shared memory. In *Proc. of the 18th Ann. ACM Symp. on Theory of Computing*, pages 160–168, 1986.

[73] R.E. Ladner and M.J. Fischer. Parallel prefix computation. *J. Assoc. Comput. Mach.*, 27:831–838, 1980.

[74] L. Lovasz. Computing ears and branching in parallel. In *Proc. of the 26th IEEE Annual Symp. on Foundation of Computer Science*, pages 464–467, 1985.

[75] M. Luby. A simple parallel algorithm for the maximal independent set problem. *SIAM J. Comput.*, 15:1036–1053, 1986.

[76] G.L. Miller and J.H. Reif. Parallel tree contraction and its application. In *Proc. of the 26th IEEE Annual Symp. on Foundation of Computer Science*, pages 478–489, 1985.

[77] G.L. Miller and V.L. Ramachandran. Efficient parallel ear decomposition and applications. unpublished manuscript, 1986.

[78] G.L. Miller and V.L. Ramachandran. A new graph triconnectivity algorithm and its parallization. In *Proc. of the 19th Ann. ACM Symp. on Theory of Computing*, pages 335–344, 1987.

[79] P.D. MacKenzie and Q.F. Stout. Ultra-fast expected time parallel algorithms. In *Proc. of the 2nd Second ACM-SIAM Symposium on Discrete Algorithms*, pages 414–424, 1991.

[80] C. Martel, R. Subramonian, and A. Park. Asynchronous PRAMs are (almost) as good as synchronous PRAMs. In *Proc. of the 31st IEEE Annual Symp. on Foundation of Computer Science*, pages 590–599, 1990.

[81] Y. Maon, B. Schieber, and U. Vishkin. Parallel ear-decomposition search (EDS) and st-numbering in graphs. *Theoretical Computer Science*, 47:277–298, 1986.

[82] K. Mehlhorn and U. Vishkin. Randomized and deterministic simulations of PRAMs by parallel machines with restricted granularity of parallel memories. *Acta Informatica*, 21:339–374, 1984.

[83] Y. Matias and U. Vishkin. On parallel hashing and integer sorting. In *Proc. of 17th ICALP, Springer LNCS 443*, pages 729–743, 1990. Also, in UMIACS-TR-90-13, Inst. for Advanced Computer Studies, Univ. of Maryland, Aug. 1990 (revised), and J. Algorithms, to appear.

[84] Y. Matias and U. Vishkin. Converting high probability into nearly-constant time - with applications to parallel hashing. In *Proc. of the 23rd Ann. ACM Symp. on Theory of Computing*, 1991.

[85] I. Parberry. *Parallel Complexity Theory*. Pitman, London, 1987.

[86] N. Pippenger. On simultaneous resource bounds. In *Proc. of the 20th IEEE Annual Symp. on Foundation of Computer Science*, pages 307–311, 1979.

[87] F. P. Preparata. New parallel sorting schemes. *IEEE trans. Computer*, C-27:669–673, 1978.

[88] P. Ragde. The parallel simplicity of compaction and chaining. In *Proc. of 17th ICALP, Springer LNCS 443*, pages 744–751, 1990.

[89] R. Raman. The power of collision: Randomized parallel algorithms for chaining and integer sorting. Technical Report TR-336 (revised version, January 1991), Computer Science Dept., Univ. of Rochester, 1990.

[90] R. Raman. Optimal sub-logarithmic time integer sorting on a CRCW PRAM (note). manuscript, 1991.

[91] A.G. Ranade. How to emulate shared memory. In *Proc. of the 28th IEEE Annual Symp. on Foundation of Computer Science*, pages 185–194, 1987.

[92] R. Reischuk. A fast probabilistic parallel sorting algorithm. In *Proc. of the 22nd IEEE Annual Symp. on Foundation of Computer Science*, pages 212–219, October 1981.

[93] J.H. Reif, editor. *Synthesis of Parallel Algorithms*. Morgan Kaufmann, San Mateo, California, 1991.

[94] S. Rajasekaran and J.H. Reif. Optimal and sublogarithmic time randomized parallel sorting algorithms. *SIAM J. Comput.*, 18:594–607, 1989.

[95] V.L. Ramachandran and J.H. Reif. An optimal parallel algorithm for graph planarity. In *Proc. of the 30th IEEE Annual Symp. on Foundation of Computer Science*, pages 282–287, 1989.

[96] J.H. Reif and S. Sen. Polling: a new random sampling technique for computational geometry. In *Proc. of the 21st Ann. ACM Symp. on Theory of Computing*, pages 394–404, 1989.

[97] J.H. Reif and L.G. Valiant. A logarithmic time sort for linear size networks. *J. Assoc. Comput. Mach.*, 34:60–76, 1987.

[98] V.L. Ramachandran and U. Vishkin. Efficient parallel triconnectivity in logarithmic parallel time. In *Proc. of AWOC 88, Lecture Notes in Computer Science* No. 319, pages 33–42. Springer-Verlag, 1988.

[99] J. Schwartz. Fast probabilistic algorithms for verification of polynomial identities. *JACM*, 27(4):701–717, 1980.

[100] J. T. Schwartz. Ultracomputers. *ACM Transactions on Programming Languages and Systems*, 2(4):484–521, 1980.

[101] B. Schieber. *Design and analysis of some parallel algorithms*. PhD thesis, Dept. of Computer Science, Tel Aviv Univ., 1987.

[102] S. Sen. Finding an approximate-median with high-probability in constant time. Manuscript, 1989.

[103] Y. Shiloach and U. Vishkin. Finding the maximum, merging, and sorting in a parallel computation model. *J. Algorithms*, 2:88–102, 1981.

[104] Y. Shiloach and U. Vishkin. An $O(\log n)$ parallel connectivity algorithm. *J. Algorithms*, 3:57–67, 1982.

[105] Y. Shiloach and U. Vishkin. An $O(n^2 \log n)$ parallel Max-Flow algorithm. *J. Algorithms*, 3:128–146, 1982.

[106] B. Schieber and U. Vishkin. On finding lowest common ancestors: simplification and parallelization. *SIAM Journal on Computing*, 17(6):1253–1262, 1988.

[107] B. Schieber and U. Vishkin. Finding all nearest neighbors for convex polygons in parallel: a new lower bounds technique and a matching algorithm. *Discrete Applied Math*, 29:97–111, 1990.

[108] R. E. Tarjan and U. Vishkin. Finding biconnected components and computing tree functions in logarithmic parallel time. *SIAM J. Computing*, 14:862–874, 1985.

[109] L.G. Valiant. Parallelism in comparison problems. *SIAM J. Comput.*, 4:348–355, 1975.

[110] L.G. Valiant. A bridging model for parallel computation. *Comm. ACM*, 33,8:103–111, 1990.

[111] U. Vishkin. Synchronous parallel computation - a survey. Technical Report TR 71, Dept. of Computer Science, Courant Institute, New York University, 1983.

[112] U. Vishkin. A parallel-design distributed-implementation (PDDI) general purpose computer. *Theoretical Computer Science*, 32:157–172, 1984.

[113] U. Vishkin. Randomized speed-ups in parallel computations. In *Proc. of the 16th Ann. ACM Symp. on Theory of Computing*, pages 230–239, 1984.

[114] U. Vishkin. On efficient parallel strong orientation. *Information Processing Letters*, 20:235–240, 1985.

[115] U. Vishkin. Optimal parallel pattern matching in strings. *Information and Computation*, 67,1-3:91–113, 1985.

[116] U. Vishkin. A parallel blocking flow algorithm for acyclic networks. Technical Report UMIACS-TR-90-11, University of Maryland Inst. for Advanced Computer Studies, 1990.

[117] U. Vishkin. Deterministic sampling - a new technique for fast pattern matching. *SIAM J. Comput.*, 20(1):22–40, February 1991.

[118] S. Winograd. On the evaluation of certain arithmetic expressions. *J. Assoc. Comput. Mach.*, 22,4:477–492, 1975.

[119] J. C. Wyllie. *The Complexity of Parallel Computations*. PhD thesis, Computer Science Department, Conell University, Ithaca, NY, 1979.

Chapter 2

PRAM Models and Fundamental Parallel Algorithmic Techniques: Part I*

Paul G. Spirakis   Alan Gibbons

Abstract

This chapter is intended to be an introduction to the field of efficient parallel algorithms and to fundamental parallel algorithmic techniques. The model of computation that we consider is the parallel random-access machine (PRAM) in which it is assumed that each processor has random access in unit time to any cell of a global memory. This model is an idealization that allows the algorithm designer to focus on the fundamental computational difficulties and on the logical structure of parallel computations required to solve the problem at hand. This is done in a context divorced from communication contention and machine specific issues.

We use the PRAM model in order to express and discuss several basic parallel algorithms for bookkeeping operations such as compacting an array or ranking a list, for expression evaluation, for problems on trees, for sorting and merging and for simulations among PRAM variations. These *fundamental techniques* are usually completely different from the best known sequential solutions to the same problems and indicate new paradigms for parallel algorithms design.

1. The PRAM: A Shared Memory Model

The PRAM (Parallel Random Access Machine) can be considered to be a parallel analog of the RAM or Random Access Machine (see e.g. [1]). It was first proposed in the thesis of Wyllie ([28]) and the paper of Fortune and Wyllie ([12]) (and in a complexity theoretic context in [17] and [24]). A PRAM consists of a number of sequential processors, each with its own private memory, working synchronously and communicating with one another through a *shared memory*. In one step each processor can access (either reading from it or writing to it) one memory location, or execute a single RAM operation. The processors synchronously execute the same program (through the central main control). Although performing the same instructions, the processors can be operating on different data. Hence, such a model is a single-instruction, multiple-data-stream (SIMD) model (see fig. 1).

The PRAM model hides levels of algorithmic and programming complexity concerning reliability, synchronization, data locality and message passing, interprocessor or processors-to-memory communication. The *simplicity* and *universality* of the model have lead to its wide acceptance by at least the theoretical community. In addition, recent advances have

---

*An introductory lecture delivered at the ALCOM Spring School of Parallel Computation, supported by the ESPRIT II Basic Research Actions Program of the EC under contract No 3075 (project ALCOM)

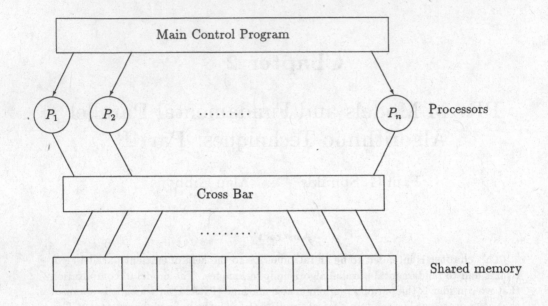

Figure 1. The organization of a PRAM

shown PRAM algorithms to be emulated in a satisfactory manner on realistic networked distributed memory machines. In fact, new machine designs are aimed in supporting a *virtual* PRAM or a shared memory virtual environment of parallel computation very close to it.

PRAMs can be classified according to the way memory access conflicts are resolved. An Exclusive Read Exclusive Write (EREW) PRAM is a PRAM where each global memory location can be accessed by at most one processor at any step. A Concurrent Read Exclusive Write (CREW) PRAM is one in which any memory location can be read simultaneously by many processors but can be written by at most one processor at any step (i.e. simultaneous reads are allowed but not simultaneous writes). A CRCW (Concurrent Read Concurrent Write) PRAM allows concurrent reads and writes. In this case, a *write conflict resolution rule* has to be provided. The most usual CRCW PRAM variations are the following:

COMMON: All processors writing into the same location write the same value.

ARBITRARY: Any one processor participating in a common write may succeed and the algorithm should work regardless of which one does.

PRIORITY: There is a linear order on the processors and the minimum numbered processor succeeds in writing.

The PRAM variations do not differ much in computational power. The following two results indicate this:

Fact 1 *([11] and also [26]) Any algorithm for a PRIORITY CRCW PRAM of P processors and running time T can be simulated by an EREW PRAM of P processors and time T ·* $O(\log P)$.

Fact 2 *([19]) Any algorithm for the PRIORITY CRCW PRAM of P processors with running time T, can be simulated by the COMMON CRCW PRAM in the same (parallel) time T, provided that $P' \gg P$ processors are available (actually $P' = O(P^2)$).*

Let us finally note that the SIMDAG machines of [17] are in fact CRCW PRAMs. Also, the name WRAM has been used to indicate CRCW PRAMs.

2. Work, Optimality and Efficiency

Let Π be a problem (input) of size n. Assume that Π can be solved on a PRAM by a parallel algorithm $\mathcal{A}$ in time $t(n)$ and by employing $p(n)$ processors. Then, the work of $\mathcal{A}$ is

$$w(n) = t(n) \cdot p(n)$$

Any PRAM algorithm that performs work $w(n)$ can be converted into a sequential algorithm of time $w(n)$. To do this, just put the sequential processor to simulate each parallel step of the PRAM in $p(n)$ time units.

Sometimes it is useful to *slowdown* a PRAM algorithm by (at the same time) *reducing* the number of processors. Any PRAM algorithm $\mathcal{A}$ running for parallel time $t(n)$ with $p(n)$ processors (and therefore performing work $w(n) = t(n) \cdot p(n)$) can be converted into a PRAM algorithm B for the same problem of work $O(w(n))$ and any number of processors $p \leq p(n)$, whose running time is $t(n) \cdot \lceil p(n)/p \rceil$. To justify this remark, just make each processor of B to do the computation of several processors of $\mathcal{A}$ *serially*, thus increasing the time of each step of $\mathcal{A}$ to $\lceil p(n)/p \rceil$ at most.

Define $polylog(n) = \bigcup_{k>0} O(\log^k n)$. Let Π be a problem of size n, as previously, and let $T(n)$ be the best (known) *sequential* time for the solution of Π. As Karp and Ramachandran in [18] remark, by Bloom's Speed up theorem there can be unnatural problems for which the notion of best sequential solution time is meaningless. For all practical purposes, however, $T(n)$ is well-defined and it is usually $\Omega(n)$ since any algorithm solving Π would have to look at all the input in the worst case. A PRAM algorithm $\mathcal{A}$ for Π, running in parallel time $t(n)$ with $p(n)$ processors is *optimal* if

(i) $t(n) = polylog(n)$ and

(ii) the work $w(n) = p(n) \cdot t(n)$ is $O(T(n))$.

A PRAM algorithm $\mathcal{A}$ for Π is *efficient* if $w(n) \leq T(n) \cdot polylog(n)$ and $t(n) = polylog(n)$. Note that, by Fact 1, the notion of efficiency is invariant with respect to the PRAM model used. It is a theoretical goal at least to discover optimal or efficient PRAM algorithms with $t(n)$ as small as possible. This goal is easier to achieve for the (stronger) CRCW PRAM as the reader will find out in this book.

Of course, the ultimate theoretical goal is to discover *fully parallel* algorithms i.e. running in constant time and using an optimal number of processors. Due to lower bounds that have been found, this goal is unachievable for almost any interesting problem.

Designers of highly parallel multiprocessors often measure the efficiency of parallel algorithms according to their "speedup", which resembles $T(n)/p(n)$ for a problem requiring sequential time $T(n)$. Thus, a parallel algorithm for such a problem is said to have *polynomial speedup* if it runs in parallel time $t(n)$ and for some $\beta < 1$,

$$t(n) = O(T(n^\beta))$$

Algorithms faster than this are said to have *super-polynomial speedup*.

3.   Constant parallel time for elementary operations in the CRCW PRAM

The concurrent-write ability of the CRCW PRAM often achieves $O(1)$ parallel time algorithms for some elementary problems. To see this, consider the problem of computing the OR of n boolean variables $x_1, \ldots, x_n$. Assume that the x_i's are stored in consecutive shared memory locations. The proposed algorithm employs a CRCW PRAM of n processors and is as follows:

Algorithm for $OR(x_1, \ldots, x_n)$ in constant time

Initialization: Let x be a shared memory location different from those of $x_1, \ldots, x_n$.

(0) Each processor p_i, $i = 1, \ldots, n$ writes "false" on x.

(1) Each processor p_i reads x_i.

(2) *For all $i = 1, \ldots, n$ in parallel do*
  if x_i = "true" then p_i writes "true" on x.

(3) Each processor p_i reads x.

The above algorithm works in all CRCW variations and uses four parallel steps to compute the $OR(x_1, \ldots, x_n)$. The reader will have no difficulty in describing a similar algorithm for the computation of the logical AND of n booleans. These algorithms are fully parallel.

By a similar approach (and by using $O(n^2)$ processors) a CRCW PRAM can compute in constant time the maximum or minimum of n numbers. To see this, let us show how to compute the minimum of n numbers, initially stored in the shared memory array C of dimension n. Let the array M (also shared, of dimension n) be used for intermediate storage. For simplicity we shall employ a CRCW PRAM of n^2 processors which we denote by P_{ij}, $1 \leq i, j \leq n$. The shared variable *minimum* will be used to keep the result. The algorithm is then as follows:

(1) Each P_{i1} (in parallel) sets $M(i) \leftarrow 0$ for $1 \leq i \leq n$.

(2) Each P_{ij}, $1 \leq i, j \leq n$, in parallel executes:
  if $C(i) < C(j)$ then $M(j) \leftarrow 1$

(3) Each P_{ij}, $1 \leq i, j \leq n$, in parallel executes:
  if $M(i) = 0$ and $i < j$ then $M(j) \leftarrow 1$

(4) Each P_{i1}, $1 \leq i \leq n$, in parallel executes:
  if $M(i) = 0$ then minimum $\leftarrow C(i)$

Such results were perhaps the starting point for the ultra-fast, sublogarithmic parallel time and yet efficient or optimal CRCW PRAM algorithms recently discovered for many fundamental operations. (See the chapter on Structural Parallel Algorithmics of this book.)

4. Processors Scheduling and Basic PRAM Techniques

4.1. Brent's Scheduling Principle

The following observation, due to Brent ([6]) is often useful for the design of efficient parallel algorithms:

Observation 1 *(Brent) Let $\mathcal{A}$ be a given algorithm with a parallel running time of t units. Suppose that $\mathcal{A}$ involves m computational operations (i.e. $work(\mathcal{A}) = m$). Then $\mathcal{A}$ can be implented to run on a p processors PRAM in $O(m/p + t)$ time.*

Proof: Let $m(i)$ be the work done in step i of $\mathcal{A}$. By employing p processors, this work can be achieved in time at most $m(i)/p + 1$. By summing over all i ($1 \leq i \leq t$) we have the result since $m = m(1) + m(2) + ... + m(t)$.   □

Note that the above simulation assumes that processor allocation *is not a problem*. In fact, it may often be difficult to partition $m(i)$ into p pieces.

4.2. Prefix Sums

Let $*$ be an associative operation over a domain D. The *prefix sums* problem is the following:
Given an array $x_1, ..., x_n$ of elements of D, compute the n prefix sums

$$S_i = x_1 * x_2 * ... * x_i \quad \left(= \sum_{j=1}^{i} x_j\right)$$

for $i = 1, ..., n$.

This problem has a lot of applications. For example consider the question of how to compact a sparse array: Given an array of n elements, many of which are zero, generate a new array containing nonzeros, in their original order. E.g. let us have the array:

7	0	0	9	0	1	0	0	0	3

We compute the position of each nonzero element by assigning 1 to each nonzero element's position and computing prefix sums with $* = +$

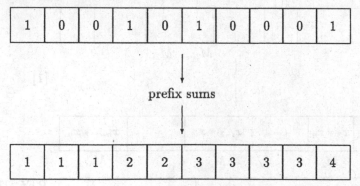

1	0	0	1	0	1	0	0	0	1

prefix sums

1	1	1	2	2	3	3	3	3	4

Another example is the problem of recognition of any regular language whose input size is restricted to n.

It is straightforward to compute all the S_i sequentially (by doing an incremental computation) in $n - 1$ steps.

4.2.1. Simple Prefix Sums

We first present a simple prefix sums parallel algorithm. Let n be a power of 2 for simplicity.

SIMPLE PARALLEL PREFIX ALGORITHM

INPUT: An array $\langle x_1, ..., x_n \rangle$ of elements from the domain D. Element x_i is in location M_i of shared memory. We employ an n processor EREW PRAM:

[0] if $n = 1$ then $S_1 \leftarrow x_1$

    else *begin*

        [1] For each $i = 1, ..., n/2$ compute $z_i \leftarrow x_{2i-1} * x_{2i}$

        and place it in location M_i.

        [2] Recursively compute prefix sums S_i, $i = 1, ..., n/2$, for the new

        array of length $n/2$.

        [3] for each $i = 1, ..., n$ set $S_i \leftarrow S_{i/2}$ if i is even

        else set $S_i = S_{(i-1)/2} * x_i$.

        end

Note that the above algorithm causes no conflicts in memory accesses. In order to show that the algorithm correctly computes the prefix sums, consider the array contents in each of the algorithm's stages:

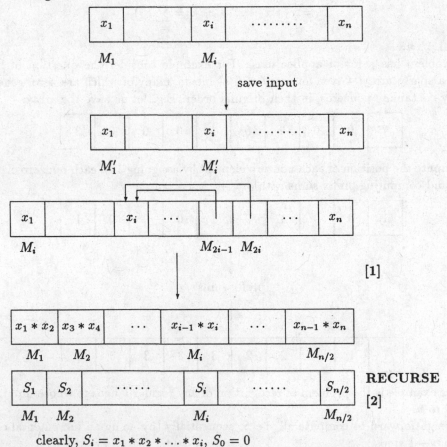

clearly, $S_i = x_1 * x_2 * ... * x_i$, $S_0 = 0$

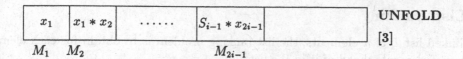

UNFOLD

[3]

To compute the time and work requirements of simple prefix sums just note that **[1]** and **[3]** take $O(1)$ time and $O(n)$ work. For **[2]** we have

$$t(n) = t(n/2) + O(1)$$

$$w(n) = w(n/2) + O(n)$$

with $t(1) = w(1) = 0$ implying $t(n) = O(\log n)$ and $w(n) = O(n)$.

4.2.2. Optimal Prefix Sums

By considering Brent's Scheduling Principle we expect an optimal Prefix Sums algorithm with processors $p(n) = n/\log n$. Processor allocation is easy to do in this case (in fact the following method is standard and is used in many cases).

OPTIMAL PREFIX SUMS

INPUT: An array $\langle x_1, ..., x_n \rangle$ of elements from the domain D. Element x_i is in location M_i of shared memory. We employ an EREW PRAM of $p \leq n/\log n$ processors. Let $q = \lceil n/p \rceil$.

Assign processor i to memory locations $(i-1)q + 1, (i-1)q + 2, ..., iq$ (for $i = 1, ..., p$). Processor i stores these values in its "local memory" and then it adds them and puts the result in M_i. (Time $O(n/p)$).

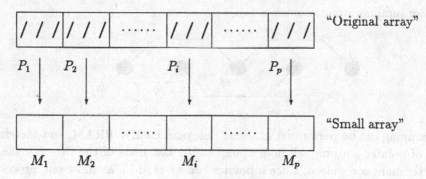

The algorithm then runs simple prefix sums on the shrinked array of p locations with p processors. This takes $O(\log n)$ time.

Finally, in an additional $O(n/p)$ time the ith processor computes prefix sums for its local array with S_{i-1} the first element.   □

The parallel time of the method is $O(n/p + \log n)$. For $p = n/\log n$ we get $t(n) = O(\log n)$ and $w(n) = O(n)$ i.e. optimal work.

On a CRCW PRAM this algorithm can be modified to optimally run in time $O(\log n/\log \log n)$ when $*$ is ordinary addition. (See [10]).

Note: It is *not easy* to obtain similar optimal parallel algorithms for elements stored in a list (the elements are *not indexed* as in the array case and processor allocation becomes highly not trivial).

4.3.   List Ranking

Given a linked list L of n elements, the list ranking problem is to obtain for each element the number of elements ahead of it in the list.

The problem is a special case of "Suffix list sums" for values $x_i = 1$. In fact its solution can be used to compute suffix list sums for x_i's in arbitrary domain D and associative operation $*$. The parallel suffix on a list is more difficult than parallel prefix on arrays since on the list there is no knowledge of any global structure. More explicitly, if we assume that the list is stored in the shared memory locations $M_1, ..., M_n$ then by "looking" at M_i only local information can be obtained.

4.3.1.   Pointer Jumping

Let the linked list be represented in two arrays, $c[1 : n]$ (the contents array) and $s[1 : n]$ (the successor array). The *pointer jumping* operation is the result of computing

$$s(i) \leftarrow s(s(i))$$

For example, the list:

in one pointer jumping step becomes:

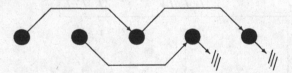

Pointer jumping can be performed in a unit time on a CREW PRAM, and therefore after $\log n$ steps of pointer jumping, all nodes point to the last node of the list. For the EREW model a little more is required, since a pointer can be read by at most one processor in a unit time. In each iteration of the pointer jumping on an EREW PRAM, the next to last processor in the list copies the value of the last processor, thus breaking the list into two lists (by pointing to itself). The next figure shows the state of the list after one pointer jumping step:

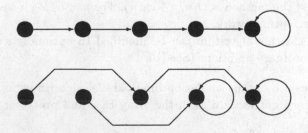

4.3.2.   List ranking by pointer jumping

Assume an EREW PRAM of n processors and a linked list stored in the arrays $c[1:n]$ and $s[1:n]$. The algorithm is as follows:

Repeat for $\lceil \log n \rceil$ iterations:
begin
    in parallel for each $i = 1..., n$ do
        $c(i) \leftarrow c(i) + c(s(i))$
        $s(i) \leftarrow s(s(i))$

Clearly, if initially $c(i) = 1$ for all i then at end $c(i)$ is the rank $r(i)$ of i (why?). To show this one needs to show that the following inductive hypothesis is preserved:
    "At start of each step $c(i)$ is the sum of elements in the list with ranks $r(i)$, $r(i) - 1, \ldots, r(s(i)) + 1$ for the current $s(i)$".
    After $\lceil \log n \rceil$ iterations, $s(i)$ becomes nil for all i.
    The parallel time of the list ranking by pointer jumping technique is $t(n) = O(\log n)$. Since $p(n) = n$ we get $w(n) = O(n \log n)$, which is not optimal since the sequential time to rank a list is $T(n) = n$. If we try to use the optimal prefix sum trick to optimally rank the list elements, we ran into problems since there is no obvious way to distinguish between the local environments of two elements in the list. In the array prefix sums computation, we could shrink the array size by two in constant time and the operation was *data independent* in the sense that the locations of the elements of the shrinked array are known in advance.

4.3.3.   A possible strategy for optimal list ranking

Let S be a set of at most $c \cdot n$ elements of the list L, with $c < 1$, such that the distance (in L) between any two consecutive elements of S is small.
    1. *(List Contraction)* The method creates a contracted list that links just the elements of S. The value of each such element is its own original value plus the sum of values of the elements that lie between it and its successor.
    Example (for $x_i = 1$):

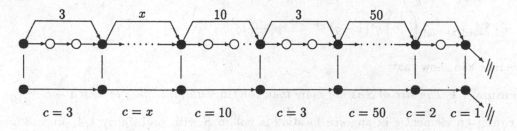

    2. *(Recursion)* Recursively solve the list ranking problem for the contracted list.
    3. *(Expansion)* Extend the solution to all elements of the original list (the time for this is proportional to the maximum distance between two elements of S).
    Clearly, the work of the above sketched strategy is proportional to the length of L (i.e. $O(n)$).

A variant of the above strategy is the following: Once a contracted list of length less than $n/\log n$ is obtained, list contraction is no longer used; instead the list ranking by pointer jumping is employed. This takes $O(\log n)$ time and $O(n)$ work for $p(n) = n/\log n$. The limited contraction phase is useful especially when S is constructed by *randomized* methods. Then we are concerned with the probability of error in each derivation of S. When the length of the list is large, the Law of Large Numbers essentially allows S to be quickly constructed with good properties.

4.3.4.   An optimal randomized algorithm for list ranking, of time $O(\log n)$

By our previous comments, the approach is as follows:

1. Use contraction (done probabilistically) until a contracted list of *length $\leq n/logn$* is obtained.

2. Then use the list ranking by pointer jumping.

3. Expand to produce ranks of all elements.

Note that 2 takes $O(\log n)$ time with work=$O(n)$ for $n/\log n$ processors. Also, 3 is at most bounded by the time and work of 1.

We need to specify how the contraction step is carried out. This means to provide a method for constructing S and to provide another method for "compacting" S so that its elements are placed in consecutive locations. We need this in order to prepare for the recursive solution of list ranking.

We propose to construct S by the *Random Mates* technique of [27] also [21]:

Random Mating: Each element chooses to be male or female with probability 1/2, independently.

An element e is not in S if and only if e is male and its predecessor in the list is female. To analyze the effect of Random Mating we need the following fact about Bernoulli tails:

Fact 3 *(Chernoff Bound's) [7]*
$\forall l, q, \beta$ *such that* $0 < q < 1$ *and* $0 < \beta < 1$

(i) $\sum_{k=0}^{\lfloor(1-\beta)lq\rfloor} \begin{pmatrix} l \\ k \end{pmatrix} q^k (1-q)^{l-k} \leq exp(-\frac{\beta^2}{2}lq)$

(ii) $\sum_{k=\lceil(1+\beta)lq\rceil}^{l} \begin{pmatrix} l \\ k \end{pmatrix} q^k (1-q)^{l-k} \leq exp(-\frac{\beta^2}{3}lq)$

We now can show that:

Lemma 4.1 *The size of S is not more than $15n/16$ with probability at least $1 - e^{-n/64}$.*

Proof: An element e in an *even* location is not in S with probability 1/4, since e must be male and its predecessor e' in odd position be female. Thus the number l of "possible" shortcuts is $n/2$, each with success probability $q = 1/4$. By applying the first Chernoff bound we get that:
Prob{following one iteration less than $n/8$ of the $n/2$ possible shortcuts are actually done} $\leq exp(-n/64)$ thus:
Prob{size of S is at most $15n/16$} $\geq 1 - exp(-n/64)$.   □

Also note that each element in S can find its successor in constant time, also with high probability. Thus $O(\log \log n)$ contractions are enough to shrink the list down to $O(n/\log n)$ size. The "total" probability of error is at most $O(\log \log n \cdot exp(-n/64))$ i.e. negligible.

To compact S each time, we must use the optimal $O(\log n/\log \log n)$ time deterministic prefix sums method which runs on COMMON PRAM. (We could also use an optimal $O(\log \log n)$ time *randomized* algorithm on an ARBITRARY PRAM, by Miller and Reif in [21], to approximately compact an array).

Thus, we get a *randomized* solution to list ranking of time $O(\log n)$ and work $O(n)$ and, by Brent's principle, of processors $n/\log n$.

4.3.5. Optimal $O(\log n)$ deterministic list ranking

From the exposition above it is clear that one way to a deterministic optimal method is to replace the random mating procedure by a deterministic technique of isolating a "contracted" set of element S. Cole and Vishkin ([9]) developed such a technique to break the local symmetry in the list, called *deterministic coin tossing*. We sketch the technique here:

Definition 1 *Given an n-element list, a subset S of elements is called an r-ruling set if no pair in S is adjacent on the list, and every element e not in S is at a distance no more than $\xi \cdot r$ on the list from an element in S, where ξ a constant.*

Let $\log^{(k)} n = \log \log \log ... \log n$ where log is iterated k times and put $r = \log^{(k)} n$. The algorithm *RULING*, first presented in [9], finds an r-ruling set of an n-element list with n-processors in $O(k)$ time. See also [16] for applications of the technique to sparse graphs.

ALGORITHM *RULING*
*Input:*An n-element list with successor pointers $s(i)$
    and predecessor pointers $s(i)$.
    1. For $i = 1, ..., n$ set $c(i) := i$
    2. For k iterations do
        for each i (in parallel) do
        begin
            find the rightmost bit position q such that
            the qth bit of $c(i)$ differs from the qth
            bit of $c(s(i))$. Let b be the qth bit of $c(i)$.
            Put $c(i) := b$ concatenated with the binary representation of q
        end
    3. For each i (in parallel) do
        if $c(p(i)) \leq c(i)$ and $c(s(i)) \leq c(i)$
        then i is into the ruling set.

Algorithm's correctness: The reader may think about coloring nodes. Initially each node has its own color. From the whole purpose of use of the ruling set S the following invariant must be kept:
(∗) No two adjacent nodes must have the same color.

After one iteration, the new colors $c(i)$ still satisfy $(*)$ but now they are represented by at most $\log\log n$ bits each (i.e. they are only $\lceil \log n \rceil$ in number). Thus the $c(i)$ of the jth iteration are represented by $B_j = O(\log^{(j)} n)$ bits each. Also, the distance between two local maxima at the jth iteration cannot be more than $2B_j$. Thus, at the end of algorithm $RULING$ any element in the list is within distance $O(\log^{(k)} n)$ of an element in the ruling set. □

If we now choose $k = \log^* n$ so that $\log^{(k)} n =$ e.g. 3, then in $O(\log^* n)$ time, with n processors, we get a 3-ruling set algorithm.

In constant time then, each element in the ruling set can find its successor by following list pointers. Thus we get a contracted list.

When the processors are only $n/\log n$ then each of them is responsible for $\log n$ nodes. Note that the nodes for which a given processor is responsible are not necessarily connected in the list. In this case, the processors will work on their $\log n$ nodes from left to right, eliminating them one at a time until they are all gone. The algorithm begins with each processor activating the first node on its list. Processors then check the nodes before and after their activated nodes in the linked list. If neither of the node's neighbours are activated, then the processor may safely eliminate the node from the linked list. This checking ensures that no two adjacent nodes are eliminated. Once a processor eliminates its activated node, it will proceed to activate the next node it is responsible for.

Those processors who could not eliminate their active nodes, color them using the $RULING$ technique. In $O(1)$ time they do a $\log\log n$ coloring of the "problem" nodes. This coloring is used to produce a "ruling set" of processors. Rulers are responsible for eliminating those colored nodes which form a monotonically decreasing color sequence forward and behind their active node. Since there are at most $\log\log n$ colors, each ruler is responsible for at most $2\log\log n$ nodes. Processors which are not in the ruling set may move on to activate the next node for which they are responsible. Once a ruler eliminates all the colored nodes he was assigned, he moves on to activate the next node in his original list. Note that each processor not in the ruling set moves on to activate a new node in constant time. The rulers activate a new node in $O(\log\log n)$ time. Now we only need to show that:

Claim 4.2 *After $O(\log n)$ steps, at most $n/\log n$ nodes remain to be removed from the linked list.*

Proof: To show the claim assign "credit" to all list nodes. The ith node should be credited with $(1 - 1/\log\log n)^i$ credits. Then, one can show (how?) that there exists a constant d such that at each step the algorithm eliminates at least $1/(d\log\log n)$ of the total remaining credit.

Once we have reached a stage where only $n/\log n$ nodes remain in the linked list, we can run the old parallel prefix on list (pointer doubling) which requires one processor per node.

This provides an optimal $O(\log n)$ time deterministic EREW PRAM algorithm for list ranking. □

5.   Sorting by comparisons and merging

The elements to be sorted have keys governing the sorting process. Assume we have n keys, stored in the array $key[1...n]$. We also assume that the keys are from a totally ordered domain.

5.1.   Batcher's bitonic merge-sort

5.1.1.   Introductory Comments

The *sorting network* of [3] is one of the earliest and classic parallel sorting methods. It can be easily implemented on an EREW PRAM. It is enough to assume that among the keys only comparisons are possible (no arithmetic). In the sequel we consider n to be a pouer of 2 (for simplicity) and let the keys be the leaves of a balanced binary tree. The operation at non-leaf nodes is a *merge* of two sorted sequences. The result in each non-leaf node is a sorted sequence of all the keys that are stored in leaf descendants of that node. Hence, the result at the root is the sorted sequence of all the keys.

If $M(n)$ is the time to merge two sorted sequences of n keys then, since the depth of the tree is $O(\log n)$, if we do in parallel all the merges of the same depth we get a parallel sorting time

$$t(n) = O(M(n) \cdot \log n)$$

The technique of Batcher ansures that $M(n) = O(\log n)$.

Example: A merge-sort tree:

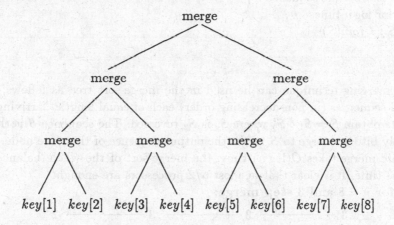

5.1.2.   Key ideas of bitonic merge

Let S_1, S_2 be two *sorted* sequences (in non-decreasing order), each of length $n/2$. Let S_2' be the sequence S_2 in reverse order. Let $S = S_1 \circ S_2'$ where $\circ$ stands for concatenation. The sequence S is called *unimodal*. A sequence is called *bitonic* if it is a cyclic shift of a unimodal sequence.

Lemma 5.1 *(Basic lemma [3]) Let $A = (a_1, a_2, ..., a_{2N})$ be a bitonic sequence of even length, of distinct elements in a linearly ordered set. Let the sequences $L(A)$ and $R(A)$ be*

$$L(A) = (min(a_1, a_{N+1}), min(a_2, a_{N+2}), \ldots, min(a_N, a_{2N}))$$

$$R(A) = (max(a_1, a_{N+1}), max(a_2, a_{N+2}), \ldots, max(a_N, a_{2N}))$$

Then $L(A), R(A)$ are both bitonic, and each element of $L(A)$ is less than each element of $R(A)$.

The above lemma inspires the following merging algorithm:

ALGORITHM *BITONIC MERGE*

Procedure *shuffle(S)*
begin
      1. Partition S into S_1, S_2 such that $S_1 =$ the first
          $n/2$ elements of S and $S_2 =$ the last $n/2$ elements of S.
      2. $S :=$ the interleaving of S_1, S_2.
end
Procedure *join(S)*
begin
      1. *shuffle(S)*.
      2. For all odd $i, 1 \leq i \leq n$, in parallel do
          if $key[i] > key[i+1]$ then swap them.
end
Main program *bitonic merge*
begin {Input is a bitonic sequence S}
      repeat for $\log n$ times
          $S := join(S)$
end

The above merging technique can be used in the merge-sort tree as follows: Let S_1, S_2 be two sorted sequences (in non-decreasing order) each of equal length, "arriving" at a tree node. We firts obtain $S = S_1 \circ S_2'$ where S_2' is S_2 reversed. The sequence S is then bitonic. Then we apply bitonic merge to S to get the output sequence of that tree node.

Since bitonic merge takes $O(\log n)$ time, the merge-sort of the whole balanced tree will take $O(\log^2 n)$ time. It is clear that at most $n/2$ processors are enough.

Example for $n = 8$ and 3 step merge:

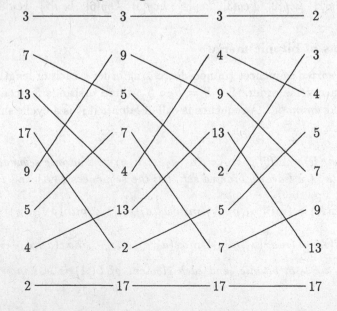

Another way to present the bitonic merge is a direct translation from Batcher's lemma (a recursive technique):

Recursive *Bitonic Merge*(S)
begin {Input is a bitonic sequence S}
if S is of length 1 *then* stop
else
    begin
    1. form $L(S)$, $R(S)$
    2. in parallel do $L(S) := Bitonic\ Merge(L(S))$
               and $R(S) := Bitonic\ Merge(R(S))$
    3. concatenate $L(S) \circ R(S)$
    end
end

Note that the bitonic sort can be implemented very neatly to run within these time/processor bounds on certain *fixed-degree* networks such as the butterfly or the shuffle-exchange.

5.2.   Comments on Optimal Sorting

Ajtai, Komlos and Szemeredi ([2]) first presented a sorting network of $O(n \log n)$ comparators, time= $O(\log n)$ and degree of parallelism $n/2$. The constants implied by the big O are so large that, despite the substantial improvements obtained later by M. Paterson, bitonic sort is preferable for all practical values of n. For an excellent presentation of the Ajtai, Komlos, Szemeredi network see [22]. Reif and Valiant (1983) were the first to provide a *randomized* optimal sorting on a PRAM running in $O(\log n)$ time and employing $O(n)$ processors. Cole, in [8] has given a practical *deterministic* method of sorting on an EREW PRAM which is optimal ie of $O(\log n)$ time and $O(n)$ processors. The algorithm can be viewed as a pipelined version of merge sort.

To get an idea of how Cole's algorithm works, suppose that we know how to merge two increasing sequences of lengths n, m in time $O(\log \log n)$ by using $n + m$ processors. (I.e. we can merge two sequences of length t in time $O(\log \log t)$ by using $2t$ processors.) Then, we can climb up the merge tree (by starting with $O(n)$ processors) and spend only at most $\log \log n$ time per level (with the obvious scheduling), thus getting a parallel sorting technique of time= $O(\log n \log \log n)$ and $O(n)$ processors. This is straight forward to implement on a CREW PRAM.

Cole's optimal sorting forces the algorithm to work on many tree levels at once, creating successively more refined approximations to the lists that the nodes must eventually produce. This is a pipelined merge-sort technique, since the sublists climb up the tree while they are merged. The method of approximation is chosen so that each approximation to the final list for a node can be obtained from the preceding approximation in constant time.

5.3.   How to merge in $O(\log \log n)$ time on a CREW PRAM

The following technique (see [4]) can be easily implemented on a CREW PRAM although processor allocations are not trivial.

$O(\log \log n)$ merging

Let $A = (a_1, ..., a_n)$ and $B = (b_1, ..., b_n)$ be two sorted sequences.

1. Divide A, B into $\sqrt{n}$ blocks of length $\sqrt{n}$ each.
2. Let f_i be the first element of the ith block of A.

   Let g_j be the first element of the jth block of B.

   In parallel compare each f_i with each g_i ($\sqrt{n} \times \sqrt{n} = n$ processors).
3. In parallel for each f_i let $k(i)$ be such that

   $g_{k(i)} < f_i < g_{k(i)+1}$ (Note $g_0 = -\infty$, $g_{\sqrt{n}+1} = +\infty$.)
4. Compare f_i with each element of the block of $g_{k(i)}$

At this point we know where each f_i fits into B. Thus the problem has been reduced to a set of disjoint problems each of which involves merging of of block of $\sqrt{n}$ elements of A with some consecutive piece of B. Recursively we solve these subproblems.

Clearly the parallel time $t(n)$ satisfies $t(n) \leq 2 + t(\sqrt{n})$ (if we charge only for comparison steps), implying

$$t(n) = O(\log \log n)$$

The n processors needed become $2n$ when we convert into CREW PRAM code due to some processor allocation problems. Borodin and Hopcroft in [4] proved a *matching* lower bound for parallel merging in the parallel comparison model: The time needed is $O(\log \log n)$ with $2n$ processors. Thus the presented technique is an optimal one.

6.   The Euler tour technique

The tree is a commonly occuring structure in computations of all kinds. Moreover, it is a recurring fact that within these computations the same subtasks for which we here describe efficient parallel solutions are frequently called upon. The efficiency which we are able to claim comes from the employment of a novel algorithmic technique introduced by Tarjan and Vishkin[25] and called the *Euler tour technique*.

An Eulerian circuit is a circuit in a graph which traverses every edge precisely once. By an elementary theorem, a directed connected graph contains an Eulerian circuit if and only if, for every vertex v, *in-degree*$(v) = $ *out-degree*(v). That is, if and only if the number of edges with v as an end-point and which are directed towards v is equal to the number of edges which have v as an end-point and are directed away from v. Given an undirected tree, the Euler tour technique proceeds by first replacing each edge of the tree by two anti-parallel edges and then by finding an Eulerian circuit (the so-called *Euler tour*) of the resulting directed graph. Consider the tree shown in (a) of the following figure. Given the so-called adjacency list representation of this graph (shown in (b)), the first task in the construction is to make each adjacency list circular by setting up a pointer from the final item to the first. This can easily be done by pointer jumping (as in the list ranking algorithms described earlier) so as to cause a pointer to be directed from the first item of each list to the final item. This pointer can then be employed to pass the address of the first item to the final item. Given the circular lists, the Euler tour is constructed by determining, for each edge (i,j), *tournext*(i,j) which is the edge following (i,j) on the Euler tour. Let *next*(j,i) be the edge following (j,i) on the adjacency list for node j. By this we mean that if on the adjacency list for node j, node k follows node i, then *next*(j,i) is (j,k). Then independently, for all directed edges (i,j), *tournext*(i,j) can be determined by executing: *tournext*$(i,j) \leftarrow$ *next*(j,i). For our example, the Euler tour is shown in (c). Notice that the effect is always to produce a circular list of edges which contains every edge. This is because (at any vertex) the choice of *tournext(i)* is such that, on successive approaches to that vertex, no edge is re-used until all other edges incident to the vertex have been used.

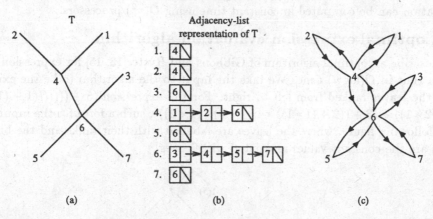

(a)   (b)   (c)

The Euler tour can easily be constructed by an optimal $O(\log n)$ time algorithm using pointer jumping described previously. If we break the Euler tour at an arbitrary tree node, we obtain a so-called *traversal list* for the tree. Traversal lists may be employed for many basic computations some of which we now describe. Perhaps the simplest of these is to construct a directed out- or in-tree rooted at an arbitrary vertex u given an undirected tree T. In an out-tree, all the edges are directed away from the root and in an in-tree all the edges are directed towards the root. We first construct an Euler tour of T and form a traversal list by breaking this at u. We then rank the edges of the traversal list (using a previously described optimal list-ranking algorithm). Given the ranks of edges, it is possible to mark each edge as either an *advance* edge or as a *retreat* edge because of two edges (i,j) and (j,i) the one of lowest rank is an advance edge and the one of highest rank is a retreat edge. Then an out-tree rooted at u simply consists of the set of advance edges and, conversely, an in-tree rooted at u consists of the set of retreat edges. All operations starting from the undirected tree are easily achieved by an optimal $O(\log n)$ time algorithm.

In particular applications we may wish to compute the number of descendents $nd(i)$ for each tree node i of a rooted tree. Given the traversal list of ranked edges, each $nd(i)$ can be computed independently as follows: $nd(i) \leftarrow [rank(i, parent(i)) - rank(parent(i), i) + 1]/2$. This is because, for every additional vertex in a subtree rooted at i, the number of edges in the traversal list is increased by two. It is therefore a trivial matter to contrive an optimal $O(\log n)$ time algorithm to compute $nd(i)$ for all i.

Another common task is that of obtaining a *preorder* numbering of the tree nodes. This can be achieved as follows. We again mark the advance edges of the traversal list which starts from the root of the tree. Now the sublist of advance edges is constructed by pointer doubling (in the list of edges, pointers are doubled as long as they do not yet point to a marked edge). The marked edges are then ranked by applying the list ranking algorithm to the sublist of marked edges. The preorder number, *preorder(i)*, of each node i can then be obtained independently by executing: $preorder(i) \leftarrow rank(parent(i), i)$, because in the traversal list advance edges (i,j) occur in preorder on j. Again, it is therefore a trivial matter to describe an optimal $O(\log n)$ time algorithm.

Finally, we consider the task of determining for all pairs of nodes, (i, j), of a rooted tree whether i is an ancestor, a descendent or neither of j. Node i is an ancestor of j if and only if the following inequalities hold: $preorder(i) \leq preorder(j) \leq preorder(i) + nd(i)$. Thus, if $preorder(i)$ and $nd(i)$ have been computed by the algorithms described earlier, the required binary relation can be computed in constant time using $O(n^2)$ processors.

7.   An optimal expression evaluation algorithm

Here we describe an optimal algorithm of Gibbons and Rytter[13, 15] for expression evaluation which runs in $O(\log n)$ time. We take the input to the algorithm to be the expression tree with the leaves ranked from left to right. For the expression $(5 + (((((((1 + (1 * 1)) * 3) + 2) * (2 * 1)) + (3 + ((2 + (1 * 1)) * 4))) + 3) * (1 * 2)))$, such a form for the input will be as in the following figure, where the leaves are labelled with their ranks and the bracketed quantities are the constant values associated with leaves.

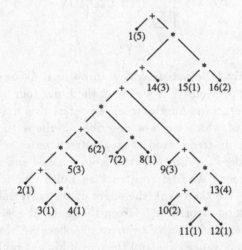

Note that the leaves of a rooted tree can be ranked by an optimal $O(\log n)$-time algorithm by employing the Euler tour technique of the previous section. Given the traversal list of the tree, the optimal list ranking algorithm described earlier can be applied to the sublist of leaves. The easy technical details are left to the reader. If the input is not in the form of an expression tree but in the form of a string of symbols (perhaps stored in an array), then Bar-On and Vishkin[5] have described an optimal algorithm running in $O(\log n)$ time which takes this input and produces the expression tree.

A crucial operation employed in the algorithm is that of *leaves-cutting*. The *cutting* of a single leaf of the tree, before any others have been cut, is summarised in the following figure:

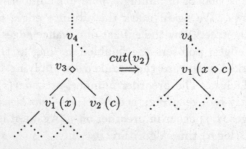

Here the leaf denoted by v_2 has been cut and the operation is denoted by $cut(v_2)$. By x we denote the value of the sub-tree rooted at v_1 and c is the (constant) value originally stored at v_2. The operaton $cut(v_2)$ involves both the local restructuring of the tree as indicated in the figure (which easily achieved in constant time with a single processor by adjusting tree pointers) and the association of a functional form $(x \diamond c)$. Here $\diamond$ is the arithmetic operation associated with the node v_3 and which we take, for the time being, to be one of the set $\{+,-,*,/\}$. If the restructed tree is employed to compute the expression and if, in the course of computation, the value represented by the functional form $(x \diamond c)$ is passed to node v_4, then this tree will compute the same value as the initial tree. Now consider cutting a number of leaves in sequential fashion. We regard each vertex v_i as having an associated functional form $f_i(x)$, where x is the value of the sub-tree rooted at v_i. The general rule for modifying the form of $f_i(x)$ after each leaves-cutting operation is then described with reference to the above figure. Initially, for all i, $f_i(x)$ is x. If, in a series of leaves-cutting operations, we perform the operation $cut(v_2)$ then $f_1(x)$ is reformulated to be $f_3(f_1(x) \diamond c)$. In this way, the tree with ever reducing numbers of leaves, continues to compute the same value.

It may seem at the moment that, if we proceed in the manner described, then we shall merely construct the arithmetic expression corresponding to the expression tree. However, the following crucial observation will confound this view. If the operator $\diamond$ is an element of $\{+,-,*,/\}$, then the new description of each functional form can be obtained in constant time and the functional form itself is of constant bounded length. Using normal rules of algebraic simplification it is easy to see, by a simple inductive argument which follows, that the most general form any of the $f_i(x)$ can attain is $f_i(x) = (ax + b)/(dx + c)$ where a, b, d and e are numerical constants and x represents the value of the sub-tree rooted at v_i. Thus, four constants are all that are needed to specify each functional form.

Before any leaves-cutting takes place, $a = e = 1$ and $b = d = 0$ and this provides a basis for the induction. In the operation $cut(v_2)$, we need to re-specify $f_1(x)$. Before the operation and by the induction hypothesis, we can take: $f_1(x) = (a_1x + b_1)/(d_1x + e_1)$ and $f_2(x) = (a_2x + b_2)/(d_2x + e_2)$. Then, after the operation $cut(v_2)$, $f_1(x)$ becomes $f_1(f_2 \diamond c)$. That this can be written in the form $(a_3x + b_3)/(d_3x + e_3)$, where $a_3 = ((a_1 \diamond c)a_2 + b_1d_1)$, $b_3 = ((a_1 \diamond c)b_2 + b_1e_2)$, $d_3 = ((d_1 \diamond c)a_2 + e_1d_2)$ and $e_3 = ((d_1 \diamond c)b_2 + e_1e_2)$, is easily seen and thus the induction step is proven. Each functional form can indeed always be represented by four numbers and these can be recomputed in constant time with a single processor.

What we have described so far may be viewed as a novel sequential algorithm in which leaves of the tree can be cut in any order. When the tree has been reduced to a pair of leaves one more sequential leaves cutting operation will finally evaluate the expression since the value of x for the functional form associated with the root of the tree will be known at that point. The sequential algorithm clearly takes runs in a time which is linear in the number of leaves of the tree. If we now think in terms of parallelising this algorithm, we need to ask which leaves can be cut simultaneously? Consider again the operation $cut(v_2)$ then, with reference to the previous figure, we define: $involved(v_2)=\{v_1, v_2, v_3\}$. We say that two operations $cut(v)$ and $cut(v')$ are independent if and only if $involved(v) \cap involved(v')$ is the empty set. Clearly, any set of pairwise independent cut operations can be performed in parallel.

A sufficient condition that $cut(v)$ and $cut(v')$ are independent is that v and v' are non-consecutively ranked leaves and that both are right children or both are left children. We therefore define the operation of *parallel leaves-cutting*, which consists of three substeps, as follows:

1. in parallel cut all odd ranked leaves which are left children

2. in parallel cut all odd ranked leaves which are right children

3. in parallel divide the rank of each leaf by two.

If we associate one processor with each odd ranked leaf, one parallel leaves-cutting operation clearly takes constant time. Each such operation halves the size of the tree (removes half the leaves) and so, after a logarithmic number of such operations, the associated expression will have been evaluated. Notice that after the first two substeps of the operation the remaining leaves will all be evenly numbered. The third substep is merely to restore a ranking to the leaves of the reduced tree.

We have described a parallel algorithm for expression evaluation which employs *tree contraction* and which runs in $O(\log n)$ time using $n/2$ processors. The number of processors can easily be reduced to $n/\log n$ by adding an initial phase to the algorithm in which each of these processors is assigned to its own logarithmic length segment of leaves. Each such processor (with all processors operating in parallel) cuts the leaves in its own segment in sequential fashion. This reduces the number of leaves in the tree to $O(n/\log n)$ and takes $O(\log n)$ time. Now the reduced tree is subjected to the original algorithm and overall we obtain an algorithm which is optimal in terms of its work measure. The following figure illustrates an application of the algorithm, without an initial phase for processor reduction, performed on the expression tree shown previously. The phases (a) through to (c) illustrate successive parallel leaves-cutting with result of each substep 1 and 2 illustrated. Where appropriate, nodes are labelled with their functional forms (elsewhere these forms may be presumed to correspond to their initial forms).

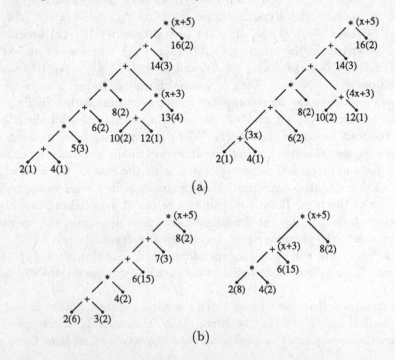

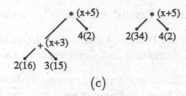

(c)

The algorithm, as we described it, works for arithmetic expressions with operators chosen from the set $\{+,-,*,/\}$. Clearly, if it can be shown that leaves-cutting can be achieved in constant bounded time for other operations then the area of application of the algorithm is extended. One such extension, for example, concerns the evaluation of expressions in algebras with constant bounded carriers (see [15]) and this in turn leads to the efficient parallel recognition of certain sub-classes of context free languages.

References

[1] J. Aho, J. Hopcroft and J. Ullman, "The Design and Analysis of Computer Algorithms", Addison-Wesley (1974).

[2] M. Ajtai, J. Komlos, E. Szemeredi, "Sorting in $c \log n$ parallel steps", Combinatorica, vol. 3, 1983, pp. 1-19.

[3] K. Batcher, "Sorting Networks and their applications", Proc. AFIPS Spring Joint Summer Computer Conf., vol. 32, 1968, pp. 307-314.

[4] A. Borodin, J.E. Hopcroft, "Routing, merging and sorting on parallel models of computation", J. Comp. Sys. Sci., vol. 30, 1985, pp. 130-145.

[5] I. Bar-On, U. Vishkin, "Optimal Parallel Generation of a Computation Tree Form", ACM Transactions on Programming Languages and Systems", vol. 7, 1985, pp. 348–57.

[6] R.P. Brent, "The parallel evaluation of general arithmetic expressions", JACM, vol. 21, 1974, pp. 201-206.

[7] H. Chernoff, "A measure of asymptotic efficiency of tests of a hypothesis based on the sum of observations", Annls Math. Statist. 23, pp. 493-509.

[8] R. Cole, "Parallel Merge Sort", SIAM J. Computing, vol. 17, 1988, pp. 770-785.

[9] R. Cole, U. Vishkin, "Deterministic coin tossing with applications to optimal paralllel list ranking", Inform. and Control, vol. 70, 1986, pp. 32-53.

[10] R. Cole, U. Vishkin, "Approximate and exact parallel scheduling with applications to list, tree and graph problems", Proc. 27th Annual IEEE Symp. on Foundations of Computer Science, 1986, pp. 478-491.

[11] D.M. Eckstein, "Parallel Processing using depth-first search and breadth-first search", PhD thesis, Dept of CS, Univ. of Iowa, Iowa City, Iowa, 1977.

[12] S. Fortune, J. Wyllie, "Parallelism in random access machines", Proc. 10th Annual ACM Symp. on Theory of Computing, 1978, pp. 114-118.

[13] A. Gibbons, W. Rytter, "An optimal parallel algorithm for dynamic expression evaluation and its applications", Proc. of the sixth Conference on Foundations of Software Technology and Theoretical Computer Science, Lecture Notes in Computer Science 241, Springer-Verlag, 1986, pp. 453-469.

[14] A. Gibbons, W. Rytter, "Efficient Parallel Algorithms", Cambridge Univ. Press, 1988.

[15] A. Gibbons, W. Rytter, "Optimal Parallel Algorithms for Dynamic Expression Evaluation and Context-Free Recognition", Information and Computation, vol. 81, 1989, pp. 32-44.

[16] A. Goldberg, S. Plotkin, G. Shannon, "Parallel symmetry-breaking in sparse graphs", Proc. 19th Annual ACM Symp. on Theory of Computing, 1987, pp. 315-324.

[17] L.M. Goldschlager, "A unified approach to models of synchronous parallel machines", JACM, vol. 29, 1982, pp. 1073-1086.

[18] R. Karp, V. Ramachandran, "Parallel Algorithms for shared Memory Machines", Handbook for the Computer Science, vol. I, Elsevier and MIT Press, 1991.

[19] L. Kucera, "Parallel Computation and conflict in memory access", Infor. Proc. Letters, vol. 14, 1982, pp. 43-96.

[20] T. Leighton, C. Leiserson, B. Maggs, S. Plotkin, J. Wein, "Theory of Parallel and VLSI Computation", MIT/LCS/RSS 1 Research Seminar Series, 1988.

[21] G. Miller, J. Reif, "Parallel tree Contraction and its applications", Proc. 26th Annual IEEE Symp. on Foundations of Comp. Sci., 1985, pp. 478-489.

[22] N. Pippenger, "Handbook for the Computer Science", vol. I, Elsevier and MIT Press, 1989.

[23] J. Reif, L. Valiant, "A logarithmic time sort for linear size networks", JACM, vol. 34, 1987, pp. 60-76.

[24] W.J. Savitch, M.J. Stimson, "Time Rounded random access machines with parallel processing", JACM, vol. 26, 79, pp. 103-118.

[25] R.E. Tarjan, U. Vishkin, "Finding biconnected components and computing tree functions in logarithmic parallel time", FOCS 1984, pp. 12-20, also SIAM Journal of Computing, vol. 14, 1985, pp. 862-74.

[26] U. Vishkin, "Implementation of Simultaneous memory address access in models that forbid it", J. Algorithms, vol. 4, 1983, pp. 45-50.

[27] U. Vishkin, "Randomized Speed-ups in Parallel Computation", Proc. 16th Annual ACM Symp. on Theory of Computing, 1984, pp. 230-239.

[28] J.C. Wyllie, "The complexity of parallel computations", PhD dissertation CS Dept. Cornell Univ. Ithaca, NY 1981.

Chapter 3

PRAM Models and Fundamental Parallel Algorithmic Techniques: Part II (Randomized Algorithms)*

Paul G. Spirakis

Abstract

There are many fields of algorithms design where probabilistic methods and randomization lead to appreciable gains. In fact, randomness has emerged as a fundamental tool in the design and analysis of algorithms. It is substantially easier to obtain algorithms for many problems if we allow the use of randomness as a resource. This has been demonstrated for parallel algorithms as well. In this chapter, we highlight some fundamental randomization techniques and also discuss the class RNC of problems efficiently solved by probabilistic parallel algorithms.

1. Randomized Parallel Algorithms and the class RNC

What does efficiency mean for a parallel algorithm? Roughly, we mean that it runs fast and uses not-too-many processors. This has been crystallized in the theoretical community in the notion of the complexity class NC, i.e. the class[1] of algorithms running in polylogarithmic (in the length of the input) time with polynomially many processors. Similarly, RNC (Randomized NC) is the class of NC algorithms whose processors are permitted to flip coins. Another way to think about RNC versus NC is the analogy between BPP and P: The class BPP can be defined as the class of all sets recognizable in polynomial time by a Probabilistic Turing Machnine with error probability at most 1/4. So, we could consider RNC to be the class of problems solvable in polylog parallel time by a randomized parallel algorithm, using a polynomially bounded number of processors.

Why do we consider randomized parallel algorithms? Among the many possible answers we stress that randomized solutions are simpler to design and that they provide intuition about deterministic, harder, solutions (e.g. compare the "random mates" technique with deterministic coin tossing). In addition, randomized algorithms are usually *more efficient* with respect to time and work and, in some cases, they are the "best we have" (e.g. in the matching problem). Also, the input to a randomized algorithm is assumed to be worst-case. The randomness appears only in the "truly" random choices that the algorithm makes.

---

*An introductory lecture delivered at the ALCOM Spring School of Parallel Computation, supported by the ESPRIT II Basic Research Actions Program of the EC under contract No 3075 (project ALCOM)
[1]See the appropriate chapter about NC in this book

A possible disadvantage of such algorithms is that they return a good solution only most of the time. More formally, consider a binary input-output relation $S(x, y)$ defined by a problem Π, where on input x the task is to find a y satisfying $S(x, y)$ if such a y exists. A randomized algorithm will output one of the following:

1. A suitable value for y.

2. Report that no such y exists.

3. It may report "failure" i.e. inability to find whether such a y exists or not.

We distinguish among **zero-error** (Z) algorithms (also known as Las Vegas algorithms) and algorithms with **one-sided** error (R), also known as Monte Carlo algorithms. If, on input x, there exists a y: $S(x, y)$ then both types are alike. Each will produce a suitable y with probability $> 1/2$, otherwise it will report failure. If, however, on an input x there is no y such that $S(x, y)$ then (1) Z will report "no such y exists" with probability $> 1/2$, else it will report "failure" while (2) R will always report "failure".

Note that we can define zero-error and one-sided error counterparts to each of the considered parallel complexity classes (e.g. ZNC versus RNC, $ZCREW(k)$ versus $RCREW(k)$ etc).

Randomized algorithms are not "self-sufficient". To be reliably implemented, they require the existence of a source of adequately random bits. In particular, in parallel computation we require a large number of random bits to be generated very quickly. These random bits may be assumed to come out of the support of special hardware: For randomized algorithms on PRAMS, each processor is assumed to have the ability to generate random $\log n$-bit numbers. For randomized circuit computations, an n-input circuit is allowed a polynomial number (on n) of additional random bits. These assumptions may imply the *expense* of building a random source into our hardware or a high-quality pseudo-random number generator. However, recently, quite general performance-preserving "derandomization" techniques have been developed which allow the transformation of a wide class of efficient randomized parallel algorithms into equivalent *deterministic* ones of comparable performance (see e.g. the thesis of Berger in [3]).

Also, let us note that, in the definitions of ZNC and RNC, the probability of error just needs to be bounded away from 1/2 by a number $c > 0$

$$\exists c > 0, Pr\{error\} \le \frac{1}{2} - c$$

because then one can reduce the probability of error by arranging a large number $M(n)$ of machines, each running the same algorithm in parallel, and take the majority of the answers.

For c constant, $M(n)$ must be at least $a \cdot \log n$ for some $a > 0$ (by Chernoff bounds). For $c \ge \frac{1}{2} - \frac{1}{n^\lambda}$, $\lambda > 0$, one can similarly show that $\exists \lambda'$: $M(n)$ must be at least $n^{\lambda'}$.

The class RNC can be formally defined in terms of circuit computations. The combinatorial circuit is, perhaps, the simplest model for measuring parallel time. A circuit can be viewed as a finite directed acyclic graph whose nodes are either *inputs* or *outputs* or *gates*. The complexity of a circuit α (we denote it by $c(\alpha)$) is the number of gates of α, and the depth of α (denote by $d(\alpha)$) is the length of the longest path in α.

Although the circuit depth to compute a set is a reasonable lower bound on the parallel time required, it is not a reasonable upper bound in general. Borodin in [5] proposed making

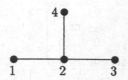

Figure 1. No perfect matching

it reasonable by requiring that the family $\{\alpha_n\}$ of circuits computing a set A (a circuit α_n for computing words of length n) to be uniform in some sense. Although there is no clearly correct choice for the definition of uniform circuits, we may adopt the following definition (see [6],[20]).

Definition 1 *A family $\{\alpha_n\}$ of circuits is uniform provided some deterministic Turing Machine can compute the transformation $1^n \longrightarrow \tilde{\alpha}_n$ in space $O(\log c(\alpha_n))$. Here $\tilde{\alpha}_n$ is a binary string encoding the circuit α_n in some reasonable fashion.*

We now can formally say that:

Definition 2 *A function f is in RNC^k iff it is computed by a uniform family $\{\alpha_n\}$ of probabilistic circuits (i.e. where gates are allowed random choice) with bitwise error probability at most $1/2 - c$ (c polynomially bounded away from 0), where $c(\alpha_n) = n^{O(1)}$ and $d(\alpha_n) = O(\log^k n)$.*

Although it is easy to show that $RNC \subseteq BPP$ however it is not known whether $RNC \subseteq NC$ or even if $RNC \subseteq P$. Among the theoretical community it is considered unlikely that $P \subseteq RNC$.

2.   The Matching Problem

2.1.   Matching reduces to symbolic determinants

Definition 3 *A perfect matching, in a graph G, is a set of edges M such that each vertex of G is incident with exactly one edge of M.*

Not all graphs have perfect matchings (see figure 1).

The matching problem is the problem of recognizing the graphs that have perfect matchings.

The following theorem, attributed to Tutte, reduces the matching problem to the problem of testing whether a symbolic determinant is nonzero:

Theorem 2.1 *([30]) Let G be a graph with vertex set $\{1, 2, ..., n\}$ and edge set E. Let $A = (\alpha_{ij})$ be the following $n \times n$ matrix, where x_{ij} are indeterminates:*

$$\alpha_{ij} = \begin{cases} x_{ij} & \text{if } \{i, j\} \text{ is in } E \text{ and } i < j \\ -x_{ij} & \text{if } \{i, j\} \text{ is in } E \text{ and } i > j \\ 0 & \text{if } \{i, j\} \text{ is not in } E \end{cases}$$

Then G has a perfect matching iff the determinant of A is not identically zero.

Example: In the graph of figure 1 the matrix

$$A = \begin{pmatrix} 0 & x_{12} & 0 & 0 \\ -x_{12} & 0 & x_{23} & x_{24} \\ 0 & -x_{23} & 0 & 0 \\ 0 & -x_{24} & 0 & 0 \end{pmatrix}$$

and the determinant of A is *identically* zero.

2.2.   How to test in RNC whether a symbolic determinant is nonzero

Theorem 2.2 *(Schwartz, [23]) Let $Q(x_1,...,x_n)$ be a polynomial of n indeterminates. Let $\tilde{Q}$ be the value of Q when each indeterminate is replaced by a random integer in the range $\{1,2,...,J\}$, where $J > n$. Then, if Q is not identically zero, then $Pr\{\tilde{Q} = 0\} \leq \frac{n}{J}$*

Note that, in fact, J relates to the degree of Q. To see this, consider $Q(x)$ of degree d. For at least $d+1$ of the numbers $-d, -d+1, ..., 0, 1, 2, ..., d$ the value of Q is nonzero (if Q is not identically zero) due to the fundamental theorem of Algebra. To prove the theorem we can then proceed by induction on the number of variables.

To apply the Theorem of Schwartz, in RNC, we can choose e.g. $J \geq 2n$. Then we can perform *in parallel* k random evaluations of Q. If Q is not identically zero, then about $k/2$ nonzeros will appear, with very high probability (due to the Chernoff bounds of the Bernoulli distribution, see Part I). Thus, we indeed have (see also [9])

Theorem 2.3 *For any class of polynomial expressions that can be evaluated by an algorithm in NC, an RNC algorithm can be constructed for testing whether a polynomial in that class is not identically zero.*

2.3.   Implications for the Matching Problem

From Tutte's and Schwartz's theorems and from the existence of an NC^2 algorithm for computing the determinant of an $n \times n$ matrix with integer entries in $[-n, n]$, we get an (one-sided error) RNC^2 algorithm for testing whether a graph has a perfect matching.

It is not obvious how to extend the above in order to construct the matching if one exists. This was first done in the work of Karp, Upfal and Wigderson (in [10]) where an RNC^3 algorithm was provided which also constructs the matching. The algorithm of Karp, Upfal and Wigderson proceeds as follows:

- From the Tutte Matrix of the graph $G(V, E)$, a rank function is implemented.

- The algorithm probabilistically "prunes out" edges from the graph G. The rank function guarantees that the remaining graph has a perfect matching.

- With high probability a constant fraction of the edges are pruned out at each stage.

- After $O(\log|V|)$ stages only a perfect matching remains.

This algorithm is also Monte Carlo in that it may fail to give a perfect matching. Using the Gallai-Edmonds Structure Theorem (see [14]) Karloff gave a complementary Monte Carlo (RNC^2) algorithm for bounding the size of a maximum matching from above, thus yielding a Las Vegas (ZNC) extension.

2.4.   An RNC^2 algorithm for Perfect Matching which also constructs the Matching

Mulmuley, Vazirani and Vazirani in [18], provided an elegant RNC^2 algorithm to directly find a perfect matching in a graph. The algorithm uses $O(n^{3.5}m)$ processors where n is the number of vertices and m the number of edges of the graph. Their algorithm is based on a key remark, the co-called **isolating lemma**.

2.4.1.   The Isolating Lemma

This key lemma of Mulmulay, Vazirani and Vazirani can be stated in a general way in terms of collections of subsets of a set:

Definition 4 *A set system (S, F) consists of a finite set S of elements $S = \{x_1, x_2, ..., x_n\}$ and a family F of subsets of S $F = \{S_1, S_2, ..., S_k\}$ with $S_j \subseteq S$, $1 \le j \le k$. Let us assign a weight w_j to each $x_j \in S$ and define $weight(S_j) = \sum_{x_i \in S_j} w_j$.*

Lemma 2.4 *(Isolating Lemma) Let (S, F) be a set system with integer weights chosen uniformly and independently from $[1, 2n]$. Then, with probability at least $1/2$, F contains a unique minimum weight set.*

Proof: Fix the weights of all elements except x_i. Define the threshold (x_i) to be the real number a_i such that:

1. If $w_i \le a_i$ then x_i belongs to some minimum weight set.

2. If $w_i > a_i$ then x_i is not in any minimum weight set.

Clearly if $w_i < a_i$ then x_i belongs in **all** minimum weight sets. The ambiguity appears when $w_i = a_i$ because then x_i belongs to some minimum weight set but not to some other minimum weight set. Then x_i is called **singular**.

But the threshold a_i was defined without reference to the weight w_i of x_i. It follows that a_i is independent of w_i. Since w_i is uniformly distributed in $\{1, 2, ..., 2n\}$ we get

$$Pr\{w_i = a_i\} \le \frac{1}{2n}$$

Since S has n elements $Prob\{there\ exists\ a\ singular\ element\} \le n \cdot \frac{1}{2n} = \frac{1}{2}$.

Thus with probability at least $1/2$ no element is singular. But there exists a unique minimum weight set iff no element is singular.   □

Note that by choosing the weights range to be $\{0, 1, 2, ..., 2n\}$ we make the probability of existence of a unique min weight set *strictly greater* than $1/2$. Note also that, by the same proof, the maximum weight will be unique with probability at least $1/2$ as well.

2.4.2.   The algorithm of Mulmuley, Vazirani and Vazirani

Let F be the set of perfect matchings of G with N edges. If each edge is given a random integer weight in $\{0, 1, 2, ..., 2N\}$ then by the isolating lemma

Prob{there is a unique perfect matching of minimum weight} > 1/2.

1. Assign edge weights as above.

2. Form the Tutte Matrix of G. Replace each x_{ij} by $2^{w_{ij}}$. Let B be the new matrix.

3. Compute in NC^2 the determinant of B and the adjoint of B (the entry ij^{th} of the adjoint of B is the minor $det(B_{ij})$).

4. Let 2^w be the highest power of 2 that divides $det(B)$. Then $w = $ *the weight of the unique perfect matching*.

5. In parallel for each $e \in E$ $e = \{i,j\}$ compute $\frac{|B_{ij}|2^{w_{ij}}}{2^w}$.

6. Let $M = $ *the set of edges for which the quantity of step 5 is odd*.

7. If M is a perfect matching then output M.

2.4.3.   The correctness of the algorithm for bipartite graphs

Instead of the Tutte Matrix of G, form B by replacing the 1's in the adjacency matrix of G by $2^{w_{ij}}$ where $w_{ij}=weight\ of\ edge\ \{i,j\}$.

For each permutation σ on $\{1,2,...,n\}$ define $value(\sigma)$ to be $\prod_{i=1}^{n} b_{i\sigma(i)}$, where $b_{ij} = 2^{w_{ij}}$ for edges $\{i,j\}$ and zero else. Clearly σ is a perfect matching iff $value(\sigma) \neq 0$.

By definition, $|B| = \sum_\sigma sign(\sigma) \cdot value(\sigma)$ (where $sign(\sigma) = +1$ if σ is even and -1 if σ is odd).

Assume now that the minimum weight perfect matching is unique and call it M. Then, if σ_M is the permutation corresponding to it, we have: $value(\sigma_M) = 2^w$ where $w = weight(M)$

The value of each of the remaining permutations is either 0 or a higher power of 2. Thus:

Remark: 2^w is the highest power of 2 that divides $|B|$.

So, by evaluating $|B|$ we can find the weight of the minimum weight matching.

In order to obtain the matching itself, consider the expression $C = \frac{|B_{ij}|2^{w_{ij}}}{2^w}$. Notice $|B_{ij}|2^{w_{ij}} = \sum_{\sigma:\sigma(i)=j} sign(\sigma) \cdot value(\sigma)$.

If $\{i,j\}$ belongs to M then $\exists \sigma : \sigma(i) = j$ and $value(\sigma) = 2^w$ and all other σ are either 0 or higher powers of two. Thus C is odd. Similarly, if $\{i,j\}$ is not in M then C is even.

The proof for general graphs is similar. The main difference is that we need to operate with the Tutte matrix of G.

Each execution of the algorithm produces a Perfect Matching with probability at least $1/2$ (if one exists). The only non-trivial computational effort required in the algorithm is the evaluation of $|B|$ and $|B_{ij}|$. We will use the algorithm of [19] which computes $|B|$ and the adjoint of B (whose $(i,j)^{th}$ entry is the minor $|B_{ij}|$) in order to find B^{-1}. It requires $O(\log^2 n)$ time and $O(n^{3.5}m)$ processors for inverting an $n \times n$ matrix whose entries are m-bit integers. Thus, the algorithm presented is in RNC^2 (and in ZNC^2 by Karloff's technique).

2.5.   Applications of Matching

The following problems were found to be in RNC^2, by applying the previous results:

1. Construct a perfect matching of maximum weight whose edge weights are in unary.
2. Find a maximum cardinality matching.

3. Find a maximum $s - t$ flow in a network with unary edge weights (i.e. of polynomial size in n).

4. Find an RNC approximation scheme for Maximum Flow with unrestricted weights (see [26]). The following chapter (see [27]) extends this result.

3. An RNC approximation scheme for Maximum Flow and Weighted Matching with arbitrary weights

3.1. Introduction

The area of combinatorial optimization includes many practical problems in which it is often necessary to solve instances of large size that include big numbers. While some combinatorial optimization problems do have fast parallel algorithms, others as Max Flow are P-complete. However, even assuming $P \neq NC$, parallelism may be of some use in obtaining fast parallel algorithms that give approximate solutions. It seems that the best kind of approximations, are the so called approximation schemes i.e. algorithms that take as input an instance of the problem and an $\epsilon > 0$ and output a candidate solution with absolute performance ratio at most $1 + 1/\epsilon$. We say that an approximation scheme is an NC (RNC) approximation scheme, if for each fixed $\epsilon > 0$ the derived approximation algorithm A_ϵ is an NC (RNC) algorithm. The scheme A is a fully NC (RNC) approximation scheme, if A is an NC (RNC) approximation scheme and furthermore A uses a polynomial number of processors and time polylog in the size of the input and ϵ. We examine here the existence of such an NC (RNC) approximation scheme for the Maximum Flow and the Maximum Weight Matching problems.

The Max Flow problem was shown to be P-complete in [7]. The P-completeness proof of Max Flow uses large capacities on the edges; in fact the values of some capacities are exponential in the number of network vertices. If the capacities are constrained to be no greater than some polynomial in the number of vertices, then there is an ZNC algorithm for Max Flow. Since the parallel complexity of Max Flow depends on the size of the numbers involved, Max Flow is not P-complete in the strong sense. Approximations in NC to strong P-complete problems were studied in [2], [12], [25], [24].

A much more involved version of the cardinality matching problem is the one in which we are given a graph $G = (V, E)$ and a number $w(e)$ for each edge $e \in E$, called the weight. The Maximum Weight Matching problem asks for a matching that has the largest possible sum of weights. It is easy to see that in the weighted matching problem, we can assume that the graph is always complete by letting the weights of those edges that were missing to zero. Furthermore, we can also assume that the graph has an even number of vertices - otherwise add a new vertex with edges of weight zero incidents upon it. Thus we can consider the problem of computing a perfect matching of maximum weight. The parallel complexity of the Maximum Weight Perfect Matching problem when the edge-weights are given in binary is as yet unresolved, when the weights are given in unary there is a RNC^2 algorithm by Mulmuley et al ([18]).

In this chapter we show that there is a fully RNC approximation scheme for the general Max Flow, the Maximum Weight Matching and the Maximum Weight Perfect Matching problems. In fact, we show that there is a fully NC approximation scheme for them if and only if there is an NC algorithm to construct a Maximum Cardinality Matching in a graph.

For the Max Flow problem we first study a restricted version, that is Max Flow restricted to networks for which the maximum flow is polynomially bounded in the number of network vertices. We prove that this restriction is NC equivalent to the Maximum Matching Problem for bipartite graphs, by showing an NC reduction from this restriction to another subproblem of Max Flow, namely Max Flow restricted to networks with polynomially bounded capacities. The later problem is known to be NC equivalent to Maximum Matching for bipartite graphs ([10]). Thus both Max Flow restrictions belongs to the class RNC. Note that in the weighted matching problems the weight of a matching is polynomially bounded only when the edge weights are polynomially bounded.

Finally, we develop a fylly RNC approximation scheme for the general Max Flow and the Maximum Weight Perfect Matching problems. Our method involves only one randomized "step" in which a Maximum Cardinality Matching is constructed for a given graph. Thus, if Maximum Cardinality Matching could be solved in NC, then our technique would become an NC approximation scheme.

3.2.   Definitions and Remarks

We use standard definitions for networks and flows.

A *network* $N = (G, s, t, c)$ is a structure consisting of a directed graph $G = (V, E)$, two distinguished vertices, $s, t \in V$ (called the source and the sink), and $c : E \longrightarrow Z^+$, an assignment of an integer capacity to each edge in E.

A *flow pattern* f is an assignment of a non-negative number to each edge of G (called the flow into the edge) such that

1. there is no edge for which the flow exceeds the capacity, and

2. for every vertex except possibly the source and the sink, the sum of the flows on its incoming edges equals the sum of the flows on its outgoing edges.

There might be a net flow out of s, in which case 2 above implies that there will be a net flow into t. Given the network N, we denote by $F(N)$ the value of the maximum possible net flow into the sink. The Max Flow problem is the following.

Max Flow Problem

Given a network $N = (G, s, t, c)$ compute a flow pattern such that the flow into the sink equals $F(N)$.

Theorem 3.1 *(Goldschlager, Shaw, Staples) Max Flow is P-complete.*

In the following given a network $N = (G, s, t, c)$ we will use the notation $n = |V|$, $m = |E|$ and $Max(N) = max_{e \in E}\{c(e)\}$. We now state one of the principal theorems of network flow theory which relates maximum flow with minimum cut. This theorem will be used later on.

Let $G = (V, E)$ be a directed graph, and s, t two vertices. A directed path from s to t, an $(s, t) - path$, is a sequence of edges from s to t. Vertices s and t are said to be connected if there exists an $(s, t) - path$. A subset $C \subseteq E$ is called an $(s, t) - cut$ set if in the graph $G' = (V, E - C)$ s and t are disconnected. Note that any $(s, t) - cut$ set C determines a partition of the vertices of the graph into two sets S and T, such that $s \in S$ and $t \in T$ for which C contains just those edges extending between S and T, conversely every partition S, T, as above, determines an $(s, t) - cut$ set. So, we can identify every $(s, t) - cut$ set with a partition S, T. We define the capacity of a given cut set $C = (S, T)$ as

$$c(C) = \sum c(e)$$

where the summation extends over all arcs $e = (u, v)$, such that $u \in S$ and $v \in T$.

Theorem 3.2 *(Max-Flow Min-Cut Theorem) The maximum value of an* $(s, t) - flow$ *is equal to the minimum capacity of an* $(s, t) - cut$.

The terminology and results about Maximum Matching for graphs, that we will use is the following. Let $G = (V, E)$ be an undirected graph. A subset $X \subseteq E$ is said to be a matching if no two edges in X are incident to the same vertex. The Maximum Cardinality Matching problem is,

Maximum Cardinality Matching Problem

Given a graph $G = (V, E)$ find a matching of maximum cardinality.

A much more involved version of the matching problem is the one in which we are given the graph $G = (V, E)$ and a number $w(e)$ for each edge $e \in E$, called the weight. The maximum weight matching problem is,

Maximum Weight Matching Problem

Given a weight graph $G = (V, E)$ find a matching of G with the largest possible sum of weights.

It is easy to see that in the weighted matching problem, we can assume that the graph is always complete by letting the weights of those edges that were missing to zero. Furthermore, we can also assume that G has an even number of vertices-otherwise add a new vertex with edges of weight zero incidents upon it. Thus we will consider the following problem:

Maximum Weight Perfect Matching Problem

Given a weighted graph $G = (V, E)$ find a perfect matching of G with the largest possible sum of weights.

The parallel complexity of the problem when the edge-weight are given in binary is as yet unresolved, when the weights are given in unary we have:

Theorem 3.3 *(Mulmuley, Vazirani, Vazirani) There is a randomized parallel algorithm to construct a maximum weight perfect matching for a weighted graph, whose edge weights are given in unary, that uses* $O(\log^2 n)$ *time and* $O(n^{3.5} mW)$ *processors, where* W *is the weight of the heaviest edge.*

The problems of Max Flow and Maximum Matching (on bipartite graphs) relate closely with respect to NC reductions: There is an NC reduction from Max Flow with polynomial capacities to Maximum Cardinality Matching (see [10]), and an NC reduction from Maximum Cardinality Matching to Max Flow (see [13]). I.e., we have

Lemma 3.4 *Max Flow restricted to networks with capacities bounded by a polynomial in the number of vertices is NC equivalent to Maximum Cardinality Matching for bipartite graphs.*

Further, we have the following result.

Theorem 3.5 *(Karp, Upfal, Wigderson) There is a randomized parallel algorithm to construct a maximum* $(s, t) - flow$ *in a directed network, such that the number of processors is bounded by a polynomial in the number of vertices and the time used is* $O((\log n)^k \log Max(N))$ *for some constant* k.

3.3.   Networks with polynomial maximum flow

In this section we show that the problem of constructing a maximum $(s,t) - flow$ in a network that has maximum flow polynomially bounded in the number of vertices is NC equivalent to the problem of constructing a Maximum Matching in a given bipartite graph. The proof is based in the construction (by an NC algorithm) of a second network which has the same maximum flow but for which the maximum flow and the maximum capacity in the network are polynomially related.

Lemma 3.6 Let $N = (G, s, t, c)$. Given any integer k, we can decide in NC whether $F(N) \geq k$ or $F(N) < km$ where $m = |E|$.

Proof: Given k we consider the network $M = (G_1, s, t, c_1)$ defined by

$$G_1 = (V, E_1)$$

$$E_1 = \{e \in E | c(e) \geq k\}$$

$$c_1(e) = c(e) \text{ for } e \in E_1$$

we have to consider two cases:

Case 1: s, t are disconnected in G_1, in this case the original network N must have a minimum $(s, t) - cut$ set C which involves no edge with capacity greater than or equal to k, so we have $c(C) < k|C| \leq km$ and then $F(N) < km$.

Case 2: s, t are connected in G_1, then there is an $(s, t) - path$ P in G formed by edges with capacity greater than or equal to k, led d be the minimum capacity along the path P, then the flow pattern

$$f(e) = \begin{cases} d & \text{if } e \in P \\ 0 & \text{otherwise} \end{cases}$$

is a valid flow pattern for N, thus $F(N) \geq k$.

So an algorithm to decide whether $F(N) \geq k$ or $F(N) < km$ has only to construct the graph G_1 and test whether s and t are connected, and this can be done in NC, provided that the comparisons between $c(e)$ and k (for all e) can be done in NC. These numbers, as inputs to the problem have to be recognized in NC. Thus, their length (in binary) is at most polynomial. Then the comparisons can be done fast in parallel by partitioning long numbers into consecutive strings of $\log n$ bits, doing (in parallel) local comparisons and suitably merging the results. $\square$

Since lemma 3.6 applies even to numbers that are exponential in size, we get:

Lemma 3.7 Let $N = (G, s, t, c)$ be a network. We can compute in NC an integer value k such that $2^k \leq F(N) < 2^{k+1}m$ where $m = |E|$.

Proof: Let $b = \log(Max(N))$, we can do in parallel the test stated in lemma 3.6 for the value $2^b, 2^{b-1}, ..., 2^0$. As $F(N)$ is at least zero and at most $2^b m$, there will be a unique k for which s, t are connected through edges with capacity at least 2^k and disconnected through edges with capacity at least 2^{k+1}. In this case we have $F(N) \geq 2^k$ and $F(N) < 2^{k+1}m$. Note that the values $2^b, 2^{b-1}, ..., 2^0$ are $b+1$ i.e., $\log(Max(N)) + 1$ i.e., at most polynomial in the input size. $\square$

The following lemma establishes the NC reduction from Max Flow with polynomial maximum flow to Max Flow with polynomial capacities:

Lemma 3.8 *Let $N = (G, s, t, c)$ be a network, we can construct in NC a second network $N_1 = (G, s, t, c_1)$ such that: $\log(Max(N_1)) \leq \log(F(N_1)) + O(\log n)$ and $F(N) = F(N_1)$.*

Proof: Let k be the value obtained in lemma 3.7, to define N_1 we only change the capacity assignment of G as follows

$$c_1(e) = \begin{cases} 2^{k+1}m & \text{if } c(e) \geq 2^{k+1}m \\ c(e) & \text{otherwise} \end{cases}$$

trivially, N_1 has the same min cuts as N, just note that no edge with capacity greater than $2^{k+1}m$ can be in a minimum cut for N, hence, $F(N_1) = F(N)$. By lemma 3.7 we then have $2^k \leq F(N_1) < 2^{k+1}m$ and $Max(N_1) \leq 2^{k+1}m$ i.e., $Max(N_1) \leq 2mF(N_1)$.   □

Lemma 3.8 shows that Max Flow restricted to networks with polynomially bounded maximum flow is NC reducible to Max Flow restricted to polynomially bounded capacities, the later problem is a simplification of the former one, so we immediately have,

Theorem 3.9 *For each polynomial p, the problem of constructing a maximum $(s, t) - flow$ in a network N such that $F(N) \leq p(n)$ is NC equivalent to the problem of constructing a Maximum Matching in a bipartite graph, and thus it is in RNC.*

Further using theorem 3.5 we have

Theorem 3.10 *There is a randomized parallel algorithm to construct a maximum $(s, t) - flow$ in a directed network, such that the number of processors is bounded by a polynomial in the number of vertices and the time used is $O((\log n)^\alpha \log F(N))$ for some constant α.*

3.4.   RNC approximations to Max Flow

We show here that the general Max Flow problem can be approximated by a (Las Vegas) randomized NC algorithm which, given a network N and an $\epsilon > 0$, outputs a solution F' such that $F(N)/F' \leq 1 + 1/\epsilon$. The algorithm uses a polynomial number of processors (independent of ϵ) and parallel time $O(\log^\alpha n(\log n + \log \epsilon))$, where α is independent of ϵ. Thus the algorithm is a RNC one as soon as ϵ is at most polynomial in n. (Actually ϵ can be $O(n^{\log^\beta n})$ for some β).

Lemma 3.11 *Let $N = (G, s, t, c)$ be a network. Let $k \geq 1$ be an integer, then we can construct in NC a network $M = (G, s, t, c_1)$ such that $kF(M) \leq F(N) \leq kF(M) + km$, where $m = |E|$.*

Proof: We consider the network M defined by

$$c_1(e) = \lfloor \frac{c(e)}{k} \rfloor, \text{ for all } e \in E$$

Then for a given $(s, t) - cut$ set C the following holds: $c(C) \leq kc_1(C) + k|C|$ (1), $kc_1(C) \leq c(C)$ (2).

Let A be a min cut for N and B a min cur for M, that is $c(A) = F(N)$ and $c_1(B) = F(M)$. Then we have,

• As B is a min cut for M, $c_1(B) \leq c_1(A)$ then $kc_1(B) \leq kc_1(A)$.

- Using (2) we have $kc_1(A) \le c(A)$.

- As A is a min cut for N, $c(A) \le c(B)$

- Using (1) we have $c(B) \le kc_1(B) + k|B| \le kc_1(B) + km$.

So we conclude $kc_1(B) \le c(A) \le kc_1(B) + km$ therefore $kF(M) \le F(N) \le kF(M) + km$. $\square$

Theorem 3.12 *Let $N = (G, s, t, c)$ be a network. Then, there is a Las Vegas Randomized NC algorithm such that for all $\epsilon > 0$ at most polynomial in the number of network vertices, the algorithm computes a legal flow of value F' such that*

$$\frac{F(N)}{F'} \le 1 + \frac{1}{\epsilon}$$

Furthermore, the algorithm uses a polynomial number of processors and runs in expected parallel time $O(\log^\alpha n(\log n + \log \epsilon))$, for some constant α, independent of ϵ.

Proof: The following algorithm satisfies the theorem:
Algorithm FAST-FLOW

(1) Compute k as in lemma 3.7.
   (i.e., $2^k \le F(N) \le 2^{k+1}m$)
(2) Construct a network N_1 as in lemma 3.8.
   (i.e., $\log(Max(N_1)) \le \log(F(N_1)) + O(\log n)$)
(3) Now, if it happens that 2^k is $\le (1 + \epsilon)m$ then $F(N) \le (1 + \epsilon)m^2$
   hence we can find the maxflow by using Maximum Matching, in ZNC.
   In such a case, the algorithm stops here.
   Else (i.e., now $2^k \ge (1 + \epsilon)m$).
   begin
   (4) Let $\beta = \lfloor \frac{2^k}{(1+\epsilon)m} \rfloor$. Clearly $\beta \ge 1$, is an integer.
      Construct N_2 from N_1 and β using the construction of lemma 3.11.
      Note that β itself can be constructed in NC, and
      $F(N_2) \le F(N)/\beta \le \frac{2^{k+1}m}{\beta} = O(\epsilon m^2)$,
      thus N_2 has polynomially bounded maximum flow.
   (5) Solve the Max Flow problem in N_2 as a Maximum Matching problem,
      using the ZNC algorithm of 9.
   (6) Output $F' = \beta F(M_2)$ and for all $e \in E$, $f'(e) = \beta f(e)$.
   end
end

The following two claims prove that the algorithm satisfies the performance bounds of the theorem.

Claim 3.13 *The processors and parallel time of FAST-FLOW satisfy the theorem.*

Proof: Steps (1), (2), (4) and (6) can be done in NC, independently of the actual value of ϵ.

In steps (3) and (5) the call to Maximum Matching uses a polynomial in n number of processors and expected parallel time $O(\log^\alpha n \log F(N))$ for some $\alpha > 1$, independent of ϵ, i.e., parallel time $(\log^\alpha n(\log n + \log \epsilon))$. $\square$

Claim 3.14 *The approximation ratio $r(\epsilon)$ of FAST-FLOW is less than or equal to $1 + 1/\epsilon$.*

Proof:

$$r(\epsilon) = \frac{F(N)}{F'} = \frac{F(N)}{\beta F(N_2)} .$$

But $F(N) \leq \beta F(N_2) + \beta m$ by lemma 3.11. Thus $r(\epsilon) \leq 1 + \frac{\beta m}{\beta F(N_2)}$.
Since $\beta F(N_2) \geq F(N) - \beta m$ and since $F(N) \geq 2^k$ we get $\beta F(N_2) \geq 2^k - \beta m$, thus

$$r(\epsilon) \leq 1 + \frac{\beta m}{2^k - \beta m}$$

But, $\beta \leq \frac{2^k}{(1+\epsilon)m}$ i.e., $\beta m \leq \frac{2^k}{1+\epsilon}$ and also

$$2^k - \beta m \geq 2^k - \frac{2^k}{1+\epsilon} = \frac{\epsilon 2^k}{1+\epsilon}$$

hence

$$\frac{\beta m}{2^k - \beta m} \leq 1/\epsilon$$

thus

$$r(\epsilon) \leq 1 + 1/\epsilon$$

$\square$

This completes the proof of the theorem. $\square$

3.5.   RNC approximations to Weighted Matching

In the Weighted matching problems the weight of a matching is polynomially bounded only when the edge weights are polynomially bounded. Thus we show directly that the Maximum Weight Perfect Matching problem with weights given in binary can be approximated by a RNC^2 algorithm which, given a weighted graph G and an $\epsilon > 0$, outputs a solution M' such that $M(G)/M' \leq 1 + 1/\epsilon$. The algorithm uses a polynomial (in n and ϵ) number of processors and parallel time $O(\log^2 n)$. Thus the algorithm is a RNC^2 one as soon as ϵ is at most polynomial in n.

Lemma 3.15 *Let $G = (V, E)$ be a graph with edge-weights given in binary. Let $k \geq 1$ be an integer, then we can construct in NC a weighted graph $G' = (V, E)$ such that $kM(G') \leq M(G) \leq kM(G') + kn/2$, where n denotes the number of vertices in G.*

Proof: We consider the graph G' defined by

$$w'(e) = \lfloor \frac{w(e)}{k} \rfloor$$

for all $e \in E$. Let X' be a maximum weight perfect matching in G', as X' is also a maximum weight perfect matching in G, we get

$$kM(G') \leq kw'(X') \leq w(X') \leq M(G)$$

Let X be a maximum weight perfect matching in G. We have

$$w(X) = \sum_{e \in X, w(e) \geq k} w(e) + \sum_{e \in X, w(e) < k} w(e)$$

$$\leq \sum_{e \in X, w(e) \geq k} k(\lfloor \frac{w(e)}{k} \rfloor + 1) + \sum_{e \in X, w(e) < k} w(e)$$

$$\leq w'(X) + k|X| \leq kM(G') + kn/2$$

So the lemma holds.   □

Theorem 3.16 *Let $G = (V, E)$ be a weighted graph. Then, there is a Las Vegas Randomized NC^2 algorithm such that for all $\epsilon > 0$ at most polynomial in the number of network vertices, the algorithm computes a perfect matching of weight M' such that*

$$\frac{M(G)}{M'} \leq 1 + \frac{1}{\epsilon}$$

Furthermore, the algorithm uses $O(n^{5.5} m^2 \epsilon)$ processors and runs in expected parallel time $O(\log^2 n)$.

Proof: Let W be the weight of the heaviest edge in G. The following algorithm satisfies the theorem:

Algorithm FAST-MATCHING

(1) Compute $k = \lfloor \log W \rfloor$.
   (i.e., $2^k \leq F(N) \leq 2^k n$)
(2) Now, if it happens that 2^k is $\leq (1 + \epsilon)n$ then $W \leq (1 + \epsilon)n^2$
   hence we can find the maximum weight perfect matching in ZNC.
   In such a case, the algorithm stops here.
   Else (i.e., now $2^k \geq (1 + \epsilon)n$)
   begin
   (3) Let $\beta = \lfloor \frac{2^k}{(1+\epsilon)n} \rfloor$. Clearly $\beta \geq 1$, is an integer.
      Construct G' from G and β using the construction of lemma 3.15.
      Note that β itself can be constructed in NC, and $W' \leq \frac{2^k n}{\beta} = O(\epsilon n^2)$,
      thus G' has polynomially bounded edge-weights.
   (4) Solve the Matching problem in G' using the ZNC algorithm
      of theorem 3.3.
   (5) Output $M' = \beta M(G')$ and X'
   end
end

Let us see that the algorithm satisfies the performance bounds of the theorem. The time and processors bounds follow from theorem 3.3. Using the same argument as in claim 2 of theorem 3.12, the approximation ratio $r(\epsilon)$ of FAST-MATCHING is less or equal to $1 + 1/\epsilon$.   □

3.6. NC approximations

An algorithm A is an NC approximation algorithm for an optimization problem if, given any instance x it finds a candidate solution whith value denoted by $A(x)$. And, the approximation ratio of A, denoted by $R_A(x)$ is defined as $R_A(x) = OPT(x)/A(x)$. Using the second part of the algorithm given in lemma 3.11, the remark given in step (1) of the FAST- MATCHING algorithm, and the reduction from maximum weight matching to maximum weight perfect matching, we have,

Lemma 3.17   *1. There is an NC approximation algorithm for the Maximum Flow problem such that $R_A = 2m$ where $m = |E|$.*

2. There is an NC approximation algorithm for the Maximum Weight Perfect Matching problem such that $R_A = n$ where $n = |V|$.

3. There is an NC approximation algorithm for the Maximum Weight Matching problem such that $R_A = n$ where $n = |V|$.

An NC (RNC) approximation scheme is an algorithm A which takes as input an instance of the problem an an $\epsilon > 0$, such that if for each fixed $\epsilon > 0$ the derived approximation algorithm A_ϵ is an NC (RNC) algorithm. The scheme A is a fully NC (RNC) approximation scheme if A uses itself a polynomial number of processors and time polylog in the size of the input and ϵ. Thus the results obtained in the previous sections give us,

Theorem 3.18   *1. There exists a fully RNC approximation scheme for Max Flow.*

2. There exists a fully RNC² approximation scheme for Maximum Weight Perfect Matching.

3. There exists a fully RNC² approximation scheme for Maximum Weight Matching.

Using the fact that when a problem is solvable by a pseudo NC algorithm, the subproblem obtained by restricting Π to only those instances which involve polynomially bounded numbers is solvable in NC, and that the problem Max Flow verifies these conditions we conclude:

Theorem 3.19 *There exists a fully NC approximation scheme for Max Flow, Maximum Weight Perfect Matching and Maximum Weight Matching if and only if there exists an NC algorithm to construct a Maximum Cardinality Matching in a graph.*

4. Fast Probabilistic Array Compaction

4.1. Motivation

A natural question to ask is whether randomization may lead to techniques which can use dynamic properties of the input (e.g., sparseness) in an effective way. For example, in the case of parallel addition (or multiplication) in shared memory models, we understand intuitively that we should not add (multiply) those inputs whose value is zero (one). Even if we manage to quickly estimate the number of nonzero inputs, we still must organize them in an appropriate manner (e.g., pack them in shared memory), in order to perform the addition. Our goal here is to devise such algorithms (by use of randomization) which are sensitive to such dynamic properties of the input and hence beat the known lower bounds (which hold for the general case).

We use the synchronous concurrent read-concurrent write (CRCW) model of parallel computation (called WRAM). This model assumes the presence of a (potentially unlimited number of processors with (potentially) unlimited local memory in each processor. We assume that our processors are capable of doing independent probabilistic choices on a fixed input. Different processors can read the same memory location at the same time. However, in the WRAM model, in the case of a simultaneous write attempt, exactly one processor succeeds. We make no assumption as to which one succeeds but we do assume that the failed ones are notified. This can be easily implemented by having processors read the result of the "write".

We first consider the fundamental problem of parallel addition of n numbers. Our technique first provides a probabilistic estimate of the count (m) of the nonzero inputs, and then uses a probabilistic method to lay them out in shared memory and add them. The whole algorithm takes $O(\log m)$ expected parallel time, uses $O(m)$ shared space, and involves only m processors. To our knowledge, deterministic WRAM algorithms for addition must take $\Omega(\log n)$ parallel time when at most n processors are used and n numbers are to be added.

For more details see [29].

4.2.   The case of parallel addition

4.2.1.   The Algorithm of Spirakis

Let the array M represent the shared memory. Let $\alpha \geq 4$ be a positive integer constant. Let each processor P_i be equipped with a local variable, $TIME_i$, intended to keep the current parallel step. Initially, each processor P_i ($1 \leq i \leq n$) holds locally a number x_i. The goal is to compute the sum of the x_i's. Let m be the number of the nonzero x_i's. We give the algorithm in two parts: Procedure ADDITION(m') actually performs the addition, assuming an estimate $m' = cm + d$, ($c, d > 1$ constants) known. Function ESTIMATION produces such an estimate. So, the whole algorithm has the following high level description:

begin
    m' ←—ESTIMATION
    ADDITION(m')
end

We provide the description of ESTIMATION first. In ESTIMATION, each P_i with $x_i \neq 0$ produces k estimates of m (k is a constant) through a probabilistic technique, and then does a variance-reduction process to get the final estimate. The actual value of k is determined in the analysis. The probabilistic technique, which produces the estimates of m, is described in the procedure PRODUCE-AN-ESTIMATE. In this procedure, the processors with nonzero x's (m in number) produce a Monte Carlo estimate of the maximum of m geometric random variables. This is achieved by having the m processors flip coins and see how long the last one gets heads. A detailed description of ESTIMATION follows:

Function ESTIMATION
Procedure PRODUCE-AN-ESTIMATE
begin

stage 1 (Initialization)

Processor P_1 initializes a special shared memory location
(CLOCK) to zero. Then, each P_i executes $TIME_i \longleftarrow 0$.

stage 2 (Estimate)

Processor P_i

if $x_i \neq 0$ **then**

  begin

    (1) Flip a fair coin (two-sided)

    (2) If the outcome is "tail" then

      begin

      (2a) $TIME_i \longleftarrow TIME_i + 1$

      (2b) CLOCK$\longleftarrow TIME_i$

      (2c) go to (1)

      end

  end

comment: The following is done by processors which
flipped a "head"

    (3) **if** $x_i \neq 0$ **then**

      begin

      (4) read CLOCK into a local variable R_1

      (5) wait for 5 steps

      (6) read CLOCK into a local variable R_2

      (7) if $R_1 \neq R_2$ then go to (4)

      end

comment: At this every P_i with $x_i \neq 0$ has flipped a "head"

    (8) Each P_i with $x_i \neq 0$ reads CLOCK and makes its
value to be the current estimate.

  end (of procedure PRODUCE-AN-ESTIMATE)

  begin (main part of ESTIMATION)

Each P_i with $x_i \neq 0$ runs procedure PRODUCE-AN-
ESTIMATE k times and produces estimates
$E_1, E_2, ..., E_k$. Then all compute

    (1) $E \longleftarrow (\log 2)\frac{E_1 + ... + E_k}{k}$

    (2) $m' \longleftarrow exp(2) \cdot exp(E) + d$ where $d \geq 1$ is a

constant. m' is the value returned by ESTIMATION.

We assume that it is written to a special shared memory
location, so that it is available to all processors.

    end (of function ESTIMATION)

We now provide a description of procedure ADDITION (m'). It has three stages. In the
first stage (initialization) a number (which is a multiple of m) of contiguous memory locations
is initialized to zero. In the second stage, all processors with nonzero x's write their x's in
these shared memory locations, a diferent location for each processor. (This stage is called
memory marking). Finally, the third stage performs a standard parallel addition of the
numbers stored in the above-mentioned shared memory locations. A detailed description of

each stage follows:

procedure ADDITION(m')

Stage 1 (Initialization)

In one parallel step, processors initialize $\alpha \cdot m' + 2$ shared memory locations to zero, by executing: "Processor P_j writes a zero to $M(j)$, if $j \leq \alpha m' + 2$. Then, they all execute $TIME_j \longleftarrow 0$.

Stage 2 (Memory Marking)

Processor P_j

if $x_j \neq 0$ then

  begin

  (1) Select y equiprobably at random from $\{1, 2, ..., \alpha m'\}$

  (2) $TIME_j \longleftarrow TIME_j + 1$

  (3) Read $M(y)$; $TIME_j \longleftarrow TIME_j + 1$

  (4) If $M(y) = 0$ then write x_j into $M(y)$

     Also, $TIME_j \longleftarrow TIME_j + 1$

  (5) If the "write" failed then

    begin

    (5a) write $TIME_j$ into $M(\alpha m' + 1)$

    (5b) go to (1)

    end

  end

Comment: The following part is executed by P_j with $x_j = 0$ and by "successful" P_j with $x_j \neq 0$.

  (6) Read $M(\alpha m' + 1)$ into a local variable R_1

  (7) Wait for 8 steps

  (8) Read $M(\alpha m' + 1)$ into a local variable R_2

  (9) If $R_1 \neq R_2$ then go to (6)

Comment: $R_1 = R_2$ means all processors with $x_j \neq 0$ succeeded in writing x_j in a shared memory location, different for each processor, among $M(1), ..., M(\alpha m')$. (If a processor was failing, the value of $M(\alpha m' + 1)$ would change).

Stage 3 (Addition)

(Processor P_j is assigned to location $M(j)$, $1 \leq j \leq \alpha m'$.)

¿From this point on, processors P_j (where $1 \leq j \leq \alpha m'$) perform a standard parallel addition of the numbers $M(1), ..., M(\alpha m')$. In the ith parallel step of the addition, processor P_j adds $M(j)$ and $M(j + 2^i)$ into $M(j)$, for $j = k \cdot 2^i + 1$, $k = 0, 1, ..., \alpha m'/2^i$. This is done in $O(m')$ space and $O(\log m')$ parallel time.

4.2.2.   Analysis of the Algorithm

Lemma 4.1 *At the end of each execution of procedure PRODUCE-AN-ESTIMATE, the variable CLOCK is a random variable, whose mean and variance satisfy:*

  1. $E(CLOCK) \cdot \log 2 \geq \log m + 0.5$

2. $(E(CLOCK) - 1) \cdot \log 2 \leq \log m + 0.5$

3. $var(CLOCK) \leq 4$

Proof: CLOCK is the maximum of m independent geometric random variables $X_1, ..., X_m$ (the number of coin flips until a head of the P_i's with $x_i \neq 0$) with density $Prob\{X_i = j\} = (1/2)^j$, $j \geq 1$. The rest is a relatively easy calculation, since $Prob\{CLOCK \leq j\} = (Prob\{X_1 \leq j\})^m$.   □

Lemma 4.2 *Given any* $\delta > 0$, *if we choose* $k \geq 4/\delta$ *then, with probability at least* $1 - \delta$, *we have*

1. $|E - \log m| \leq 2$ *and*

2. *The total running time of ESTIMATION is*

$$O(\frac{4}{\delta} \log m)$$

Proof: From Chebyshev inequality and Lemma 4.11 we get $Prob\{|E - \log m| \leq 1.2\} \geq 1 - 4/\delta$. Also note that the running time of ESTIMATION is $O(k \cdot E) = O(E_1 + ... + E_k)$.   □

Corollary: Given any $\delta > 0$, if we choose $k \geq 4/\delta$ then, with probability at least $1 - \delta$ we have

$$m \leq m' \leq m \cdot exp(4)$$

Proof: It follows immediately, by lemma 4.2.   □
In the following we assume $k \geq 4/\delta$ for a fixed small δ.

Lemma 4.3 *Conditioned on the event* $\epsilon = \{m \leq m' \leq m \cdot exp(4)\}$, *the time of stage 2 of procedure ADDITION* (m') *has an expected value of* $O(\log m)$. *Furthermore, the (conditional on* ϵ) *probability that the time of stage 2 exceeds* $\beta \cdot \log m$ *is* $\leq m^{-\beta \log \alpha + 1}$ *(and can be made arbitrarily small).*

Proof: It is easy to see that every time a processor P_j attempts to write its x_i, and if $g \leq m$ shared memory locations are already "occupied", the competitors of P_j are $m - g - 1$. Even if all of them manage to select different memory locations which were not occupied previously, the maximum number of locations that P_j must "avoid" is $g + m - g - 1 = m - 1$.

So P_j will succeed with probability at least

$$\frac{\alpha m' - (m - 1)}{\alpha m'} \geq \frac{\alpha m' - (m' - 1)}{\alpha m'} \geq \frac{\alpha - 1}{\alpha}$$

in each trial (and this holds for every P_j).

A generalization of the lemma 4.1 about the maximum of m geometrics with success probability $\geq 1 - 1/\alpha$ implies that the average number of parallel steps required for all m processors to succed is $O(\log m') = O(\log m)$.

The probability that there exists a processor which continues failing for at least $\log m$ rounds is

$$\leq m \cdot (\frac{1}{\alpha})^{\beta \log m} \leq m^{-\beta \log \alpha + 1}$$

□

It is easy to see that the algorithm uses $O(m')$ shared memory, $O(m')$ processors, and *performs the addition correctly*, because, at the end of stage 2 of $ADDITION(m')$ the m nonzero x_i's are placed one in each of m shared memory locations, and these locations are among $M(1), \ldots, M(\alpha m')$. The rest of these locations contain zeros. So, we have:

Theorem 4.4 *Given any $\delta \in (0, 1)$, we can choose $\beta > 0$ such that with probability at least $1 - max(\delta, m^{-\beta \log \alpha + 1})$, our algorithm performs the parallel addition in $O(\log m)$ time, and uses $O(m)$ shared space and $O(m)$ processors. Our algorithm never errs. With diminishingly small probability, it may choose a bad estiate m' of m and hence it may never exit the loop (6)-(9) of stage 2 of $ADDITION(m')$.*

4.3.   Linear approximate compaction

4.3.1.   The problem

Matias and Vishkin in [16] isolated the following subproblem whose solution was clearly needed in the previous result about parallel addition: Given is an array A of n cells, with a processor standing by each cell. In addition, at most m items are distributed among the cells. Each cell either contains one item or is empty. The *linear approximate compaction* (LAC) problem is to insert the items into an array $B[1..4m]$ (*linear* in m). Matias and Vishkin proved the following theorem:

Theorem 4.5 *([16]) Using n processors the LAC problem can be solved in $O(\log^* m)$ expected parallel time. The parallel time complexity of the same algorithm is also $O(\log^* m)$ with probability at least $1 - m^{-\alpha}$ for any constant $\alpha > 0$.*

4.3.2.   The Matias-Vishkin algorithm

An item will be identified by the index of its original cell. Initially each cell of B is empty (and this is marked by initializing it to zero). Throughout the algorithm more and more items are mapped to accomplish an one-to-one mapping into the array B. An unmapped item is called *active*. Once an item is mapped it becomes inactive. Initially all items are active.

The algorithm has $O(\log^* m)$ iterations. Let q_1 be a constant (to be set by analysis) and $q_{i+1} = 2^{q_i}$ for $i \geq 1$.

   High level description of iteration i:

   The main idea is to enhance the mapping of active items by reallocating many processors to them.

Input of iteration i: the number of active items is assumed to be at most m/q_i^6. The iteration consists of two basic steps:

   (allocation) Allocate $7q_i$ processors to each active item. For each active item, this allocation is accomplished with probability $\geq 1 - 2^{-7q_i}$. Each active item which indeed gets $7q_i$ processors is called *participating*.

   (mapping) Map each participating item to a different empty cell of B. For each participating item this mapping is accomplished with probability $\geq 1 - 2^{-7q_i}$.

Output of the iteration: The number of active items is at most $\frac{m}{(2^{q_i})^6} = \frac{m}{q_{i+1}^6}$ with high probability.

□

The probability-time conversion principle:

The main new idea that opened the opportunity for the $O(\log^* m)$ result here (and in many other results!) is in making the probability of success in mapping to depend exponentially on q_i. This provides exponential reduction in the number of active items, enabling q_{i+1} to be exponential in q_i. The allocation step reallocates enough processors that become available and thereby "exponential-ladder" acceleration is accomplished and results in $O(\log^* m)$ rounds. In the analysis we justify the above.

4.3.3. The steps in detail and the analysis

Let m_i be the number of active items at the end of iteration i. Iteration i *succeds* if $m_i \leq \frac{m}{q_{i+1}^6}$ and all its preceding iterations succeded. If all iterations succed then the series $\{m_i\}$ is as follows:

$$\frac{m}{q_1^6} \longrightarrow \frac{m}{2^{q_1^6}} \longrightarrow \frac{m}{2^{2^{q_1^6}}} \longrightarrow \cdots$$

So, after $\log^* m$ successful iterations all items are placed in B.

Important Note: Let us have an array of n cells and a processor standing by each item. Again, assume at most m cells contain one item each and the other cells are empty. The d-polynomial approximate compaction problem (d-PAC) is to insert the items into an array $[1..m^d]$. Radge in [21] gave a constant time *deterministic* algorithm (of n processors) for the 4-PAC problem. Matias and Vishkin use the 4-PAC method as a subroutine in the allocation step.

The allocation step:

The allocation step consists of two substeps. Partition A into subarrays of size $7q_i^5$ each. For each subarray with at most q_i active items, compact (by 4-PAC) all active items into the first q_i^4 cells. Since we can afford $7q_i$ processors for each of the first q_i^4 cells of each subarray, this results in assigning $7q_i$ processors to each such active item. The first substep of the allocation step will thin-out the number of active items in each subarray and thereby enable application of the 4-PAC method in the second substep.

First substep:

An auxiliary array with $m/7q_i$ cells is used, where each cell has $7q_i$ processors standing by. Each active item tries to occupy a cell of the auxiliary array: the item selects a random cell; if no other item selected the same cell, then the item occupies the cell; if the cell was selected by other items the item aborts. Each occupying item gets $7q_i$ processors and hence it becomes participating.

An active item will fail here with probability $\leq \frac{m/q_i^6}{m/7q_i} = 7q_i^{-5}$. In fact, one can prove that the number of the non-participating active elements after the present substep is $\geq q_i$ with probability $\leq 2^{-7q_i}$.

Second substep:

Separately for each subarray of size $7q_i^5$: apply 4-PAC for compacting the non-participating active items into the first q_i^4 cells. Since the 4-PAC method is deterministic, a compaction will *not* fail if the subarray contains $\leq q_i$ non-participating active items.

The mapping step:

First substep:

For each participating item, each of its allocated processors tries to occupy a cell in B (by selecting a random cell and ending up occupying it if it was empty and was not simultaneously selected by others). If one (or more) processors of a participating item occupied a cell the item is called *succesful*. The probability that a participating item is *not* succesful is $\leq 2^{-7q_i}$.

Second substep:

For each succesful participating item, one of the occupying processors is selected. The item is mapped to the cell occupied by this processor.

Completing the analysis

An active item may fail to become participating in the allocation step. A participating item may fail to be mapped in the mapping step. The probability of each of these failures is $\leq 2^{-7q_i}$. Thus, the number of active items at the end of the iteration becomes at most $m/(2^{q_i})^6$ with very high probability. (Here one must cope with minor probabilistic dependence among events that can happen.)

Finally, the Matias-Vishkin algorithm needs an initialization step in which the number of active items is decreased to at most $m/q_1{}^6$ with high probability.

5.   The Maximal Independent Set Problem

5.1.   Motivation and history

A Maximal Independent Set (MIS) in an undirected graph G is a *maximal* collection of vertices I such that no pair of vertices in I is adjacent.

History of parallel Solutions to MIS

Karp and Wigderson (in [11]) provided a randomized algorithm of expected running time $O(\log^4 n)$, n^2 processors. Also, a deterministic algorithm in NC^4.

Luby (in [15]) gave a randomized $O(\log^2 n)$ method of m processors, also a deterministic $O(\log^2 n)$ algorithm of $O(n^2 m)$ processors, through a derandomization process.

We shall describe here the method of Luby and will provide the main analysis points. In the sequel, let $G(V, E)$ be a graph of vertex set V and edge set E. I will be the current MIS. Let $d(v)$ be the degree of vertex v.

5.2.   Luby's Monte Carlo method

5.2.1.   The algorithm

begin
    $I \leftarrow \emptyset$
    $G'(V', E') \leftarrow G(V, E)$
    while $V' \neq \emptyset$ **do**
    begin
        $X \leftarrow \emptyset$
        in parallel $\forall v \in V'$
        randomly choose to add v to X with $prob = 1/2d(v)$
        (if $d(v) = 0$ always add v to X)
        $I' \leftarrow X$
        in parallel $\forall v \in X, w \in X$
            if $\{v, w\} \in E'$ **then**
            if $d(v) \leq d(w)$ **then** $I' \leftarrow I' - \{v\}$

else $I' \leftarrow I' - \{w\}$
(Note that I' is an independent set in G')
$I \leftarrow I' \cup I$
$Y \leftarrow I' \cup Neighbours(I')$
$G' = (V', E') \leftarrow$ induced subgraph on $V' - Y$

end
end

At termination, I is MIS. So, we must show that the while loop has a small expected number of executions.

Let m_1 be the number of edges in G' before execution of the body of the while loop.
Let m_2 be the number of edges in G' after execution of the body of the while loop.
Let m_3 be the number of edges eliminated from G' due to one execution of the while loop.
Then $m_2 = m_1 - m_3$.

Luby shows that $E(m_3) \geq 1/8m_1$. Thus, $E(m_2) \leq 7/8m_1$, implying that the expected number of the while loop is $O(\log n)$. Note that

$$E(m_2) \leq 7/8m_1 \implies \text{Fast progress with high probability.}$$

Proof: From the Markov inequality we have that

$$Pr\{m_2 \geq \alpha\} \leq \frac{E(m_2)}{\alpha}$$

i.e. $Pr\{m_2 \geq \frac{7.5}{8}m_1\} \leq \frac{7}{7.5} = \frac{14}{15}$.

Let "success" be when $m_2 < \frac{7.5}{8}m_1$ and "failure" else. So, $Pr\{success\} > 1/15$. Consider $N = k \cdot \log n$ repititions.

$$Pr\{\#successes \geq \frac{1}{2}k\log n\frac{1}{15}\} \geq 1 - exp(-\frac{1}{60}k\log n)$$

by Chernoff bounds. I.e. $Pr\{\text{Completion after } k\log n \text{ repetitions }\} \geq 1 - n^{-k/60}$.   □

5.2.2. Analysis of the algorithm

$\forall v \in V$ let $E_v =$"v is chosen in the random selection to be added to X". Let

$$P_v = Pr\{E_v\} = \frac{1}{2d(v)}$$

The events E_v are mutually independent. Let $sum_v = \sum p_w$, where w a neighbour of v.

Lemma 5.1 $Pr\{v \in Neighbours(I')\} \geq \frac{1}{4} \cdot min(sum_v, 1)$.

Proof: Just remark that $Pr\{v \in Neighbours(I')\} \geq Pr\{\bigcup_{i=n}^{d(v)}(\text{some adjacent vertex } i \text{ is in } I')\}$.

Without loss of generality, let the neighbours of v be $1,\ldots,d(v)$. Let $E'_1 = E_1$, $E'_i = (\bigcap_{j=1}^{i-1} \bar{E}_j) \cap E_i$. Let $A_i = \cap \bar{E}_z$: $d(z) \geq d(i)$ and z a neighbour of i. Then $Pr\{v \in$

$Neighbours(I')\} \geq \sum_{i=1}^{d(v)} Pr\{\acute{E}_i'\} \cdot Pr\{A_i/E_i'\}$

But $Pr\{A_i/E_i'\} \geq Pr\{A_i\} \geq 1 - \sum_{\{z,i\}\in E, d(z)\geq d(i)} p_z \geq 1/2$. Thus

$$Pr\{v \in Neighbours(I')\} \geq 1/2 \sum_{i=1}^{d(v)} Pr\{E_i'\}$$

Now notice that $\sum_{i=1}^{d(v)} Pr\{E_i'\} = Pr\{\cup_{i=1}^{d(v)} E_i\}$.

Luby noticed that $Pr\{\cup_{i=1}^{d(v)} E_i\} \geq 1/2 min(sum_v, 1)$ even when E_i are only pairwise independent. (See chapter 5.2.3.) Thus

$$Pr\{v \in Neighbours(I')\} \geq \frac{1}{4} min(sum_v, 1)$$

□

Now if $\forall W \subseteq V$ the set of edges "touching W" is $ET(W) = \{(v,w) \in E : v \in W \text{ or } w \in W\}$ then the progress done in one execution of the while loop is the edges in $F = ET(I' \cup Neighbours(I'))$.

Each $(v,w) \in F$ either because $v \in I' \cup Neighbours(I')$ or because w does.

Thus $E(m_3) \geq \frac{1}{2}\sum_{v\in V'} d(v)Pr\{v \in (I' \cup Neighbours(I'))\} \geq \frac{1}{2}\sum_{v\in V'} d(v)Pr\{v \in Neighbours(I')\}$.

Some calculations are now needed to get $E(m_3) \geq \frac{1}{8}m_1$.   □

Important Remark

The fact that the analysis can be carried out even when the events E_v are **pairwise** independent implies that we can use a much smaller sample space (of size $\leq n^2$) to do the vertex selections. But then one can sample all the space *quickly in parallel* and get a deterministic algorithm.

Berger and Rompel (in [4]) extended this to produce a simulation in NC of $\log^c n$-independence. A similar result was found by Motwani, Naor and Naor in [17]. Also see [28], [22], [1] and the PhD thesis [3].

5.2.3.   The pairwise independence lemma

Lemma 5.2 *Let $E_1, \ldots, E_n$ events such that $Pr(E_i) = p_i$ and $Pr(E_i \cap E_j) = p_i \cdot p_j$, $i \neq j$, $i,j \in \{1, \ldots, n\}$. Let $sum = \sum_i p_i$. Then $Pr\{\cup_i E_i\} \geq \frac{1}{2}min\{sum, 1\}$.*

Note: To apply inclusion-exclusion one needs the probabilities of all intersections, and this is a computationally demanding task. The lemma was proved by Luby ([15]) and has many applications.

   Proof: ([15]) W.l.o.g suppose that $p_1 \geq p_2 \geq \ldots \geq p_n$. Let $E_k' = \cup_{i=1}^k E_i$, $\alpha_k = \sum_{i=1}^k p_i$.

$\forall 1 \leq k \leq n$ $Pr\{E_n'\} \geq Pr\{E_k'\}$. But $Pr\{E_k'\} \geq \alpha_k - \sum_{1\leq i<j\leq k} p_i \cdot p_j$ (inclusion-exclusion plus pairwise independence). This becomes minimum when all $p_i = \frac{\alpha_k}{k}$, thus

$$Pr\{E_k'\} \geq \alpha_k(1 - \frac{\alpha_k(k-1)}{2k})$$

If $\alpha_n \leq 1 \implies Pr\{E_n'\} \geq \frac{\alpha_n}{2} = \frac{sum}{2}$. If $\alpha_n > 1$ let $\lambda = min\{k : \alpha_k \geq 1\}$. If $\lambda = 1 \implies Pr\{E_1'\} \geq 1$. Thus $\lambda \geq 2$. Then $\alpha_{\lambda-1} < 1 \leq \alpha_\lambda \leq \frac{\lambda}{\lambda-1}$ (because $p_1 \geq p_2 \geq \ldots \geq p_n$).

So $Pr\{E_\lambda'\} \geq \alpha_\lambda(1 - \frac{\alpha_\lambda(\lambda-1)}{2\lambda}) \geq \frac{1}{2}$ and $Pr\{E_n'\} \geq Pr\{E_\lambda'\}$.   □

References

[1] N. Alon, L. Babai, A. Itai, "A fast and simple randomized parallel algorithm for the maximal independent set problem", Journal of Algorithms,7: 567-583, 1987.

[2] R. Anderson, E. Mayr, "Parallelism and greedy algorithms" Advances in Computing Research, Vol. 24, JAI Press, 1987, pp. 17-38.

[3] B. Berger, "Using Randomness to Design Efficient Deterministic Algorithms" PhD Thesis, MIT, May 1990.

[4] B. Berger, J. Rompel, "Simulating $(\log^c n)$-wise independence in NC" Proc. 30th Annual Symposium on Foundations of Computer Science pp. 2-7, IEEE, Oct. 1989.

[5] A. Borodin, "On relating time and space to size and depth" SIAM Journal on Computing, Vol. 6, 1977, pp. 733-744.

[6] S.A. Cook, "Towards a complexity theory of synchronous parallel computation" En. Math., Vol. 27, 1981, pp. 99-124.

[7] L. Goldschlager, R.A. Shaw, J. Staples "The maximum flow problem is log space complete for P" Theoret. Comp. Sci., Vol. 21, 1982, pp. 105-111.

[8] H.J. Karloff "A Las Vegas RNC algorithm for maximum matching" Combinatorica, Vol. 6, 1986, pp. 387-392.

[9] R. Karp, V. Ramachandran, "Parallel Algorithms for Shared Memory Machines", Handbook of Computer Science, Vol. I, MIT Press, 1991.

[10] R. Karp, E. Upfal, A. Widerson, "Constructing a perfect matching is in RNC" Combinatorica, Vol. 6, 1986, pp. 35-48.

[11] R. Karp, A. Widerson, "A fast parallel algorithm for the maximal independent set problem", JACM Vol. 32, 1985, pp. 762-773.

[12] L. Kirousis, M. Serna, P. Spirakis, "The parallel complexity of the subgraph connectivity problem" in 30th Annual IEEE Symposium on Foundations of Computer Science, pp. 234-299, 1989.

[13] E. Lawler, "Combinatorial Optimization: Networks and Matroids", Holt, Rinehart and Winston,1976.

[14] L. Lovasz, "On Determinants, Matchings and Random Algorihtms" Fundamentals of Computing Theory, ed L. Budach, Akademia Verlag, Berlin, 1979.

[15] M. Luby, "A Simple Parallel Algorithm for the Maximal Independent Set Problem" STOC 1985 also SIAM Journal on Computing, Vol. 15, 1986, pp. 1036-1053.

[16] Y. Matias, U. Vishkin, "Converting High Probability into Nearly-Constant Time-with Applications to Parallel Hashing" 1991, ACM STOC, pp. 307-316.

[17] P. Motwani, J. Naor, M. Naor, "The Probabilistic Method Yields Deterministic Parallel Algorithms" 30th Annual IEEE Symposium on Foundations of Computer Science (FOCS 1989) pp. 8-13.

[18] K. Mulmuney, U. Vazirani, V. Vazirani, "Matching is as Easy as Matrix Inversion" 1987 ACM STOC, pp. 345-354.

[19] V. Pan, "Fast and efficient algorithms for the exact inversion of integer matrices", 5th Annual Foundations of Software Technology and Theoretical Computer Science Conference, 1985.

[20] N. Pippenger, "On Simulataneous resource bounds" Proc. 20th Annual IEEE Symp. on Foundations of Comp. Sci., 1979, pp. 307-311.

[21] P. Ragde, "The parallel simplicity of compaction and chaining" Proc. 17th ICALP, Springer LNCS, 443, pp. 744-751, 1990.

[22] P. Raghavan, 'Probabilistic construction of deterministic algorithms: approximating packing integer programs", J. Computer and System Sciences, 37(4) 130-143, Oct. 1988.

[23] J.T. Schwartz, "Fast probabilistic algorithms for verification of polynomial identities" JACM Vol. 27, 1980, pp. 701-717.

[24] M. Serna, "Approximating Linear Programming is log-space complete for P" Info Processing Letters 37: 233-236, 1991.

[25] M. Serna, P. Spirakis, "The approximability of problems complete for P" In International Symposium on Optimal Algorithms, LNCS Vol. 401, Springer, pp. 193-204, 1989.

[26] M. Serna, P. Spirakis, "Tight RNC approximations to Max Flow" STACS 91, LNCS Vol. 480, Springer, pp. 118-126.

[27] M. Serna, P. Spirakis, "Tight RNC approximation to Max Flow and Weighted Matching" CTI Tech. Report, 1992.

[28] J. Spencer, "Ten Lectures on the Probabilistic Method", SIAM, Philadelphia PA 1987.

[29] P. Spirakis, "Optimal Parallel Randomized Algorithms for Sparse Addition and Identification" Information and Computation, Vol. 76, No. 1, Jan 1988, pp. 1-12.

[30] W.T. Tutte "The Factorization of Linear Graphs" J. London Math. Soc. 22 (1947) pp. 107-111.

Chapter 4

Efficient Parallel Graph Algorithms

Vijaya Ramachandran *

Abstract

We present an overview of efficient parallel algorithms for problems on graphs. We describe a technique called ear decomposition that has proved to be very useful in the design of efficient parallel algorithms for several problems on undirected graphs. We also note the 'transitive closure bottleneck', a phenomenon that has been observed for problems on directed graphs, as a result of which it has proved to be difficult to get efficient parallel algorithms for problems on general directed graphs.

1. Introduction

Graphs are used very often as models of problems of practical importance and there has been a considerable amount of work over the past couple of decades in the design and analysis of efficient sequential algorithms for graph problems. More recently, with the advent of parallel machines, there has been a similar productivity in the design and analysis of parallel graph algorithms.

The design of efficient parallel algorithms for graph problems has presented a challenge since the traditional sequential graph search techniques of depth first search and breadth first search have resisted attempts to be parallelized efficiently. Most linear time sequential graph algorithms are based on depth-first search. These include some of the classical algorithms for fundamental graph problems such as graph biconnectivity [23], graph triconnectivity [8] and graph planarity ([9, 13]). Since depth first search is not known to be efficiently parallelizable, new techniques are needed to come up with good parallel algorithms for these problems.

In this chapter we shall survey the current status of efficient parallel algorithm design for graph problems. The model of computation that we will use is the Parallel Random Access Machine (or PRAM) (see, e.g., [12]). We describe this model in the next section, where we also describe the notion of a highly parallel algorithm being efficient or optimal.

In the following section we describe a method of searching undirected graphs called *ear decomposition* and a special type of ear decomposition called *open ear decomposition*. These decompositions can be computed efficiently in parallel and efficient parallel algorithms for several fundamental graph problems can be obtained based on these decompositions.

For directed graphs the situation is not as good. We describe a phenomenon known as the 'transitive closure bottleneck'; due to this phenomenon we currently do not have efficient

---

*This work was supported in part by NSF grants CCR-89-10707 and CCR-90-23057. Portions of this write-up appear in the invited article "A framework for algorithm design for undirected graphs," Optimal Algorithms, Springer-Verlag LNCS 401, pp. 33-40, 1989.

parallel algorithms for most problems on general directed graphs. In view of the transitive closure bottleneck most of our discussion will focus on parallel algorithms for undirected graphs.

2.   Model of Parallel Computation

The model of parallel computation that we will be using is the *Parallel Random Access Machine* or *PRAM,* which consists of several independent sequential processors, each with its own private memory, communicating with one another through a global memory. In one unit of time, each processor can read one global or local memory, execute a single RAM operation, and write into one global or local memory location. We will use the ARBITRARY CRCW PRAM in which concurrent reads and concurrent writes are permitted at a memory location and any one processor participating in a concurrent write may succeed.

Let S be a problem that, on an input of size n, can be solved on a PRAM by a parallel algorithm in parallel time $t(n)$ with $p(n)$ processors. The quantity $w(n) = t(n) \cdot p(n)$ represents the *work* done by the parallel algorithm. Any PRAM algorithm that performs work $w(n)$ can be converted into a sequential algorithm running in time $w(n)$ by having a single processor simulate each parallel step of the PRAM in $p(n)$ time units. More generally, a PRAM algorithm that runs in parallel time $t(n)$ with $p(n)$ processors also represents a PRAM algorithm performing $O(w(n))$ work for any processor count $P < p(n)$.

Define $polylog(n) = \bigcup_{k>0} O(\log^k n)$. Let S be a problem for which currently the best sequential algorithm runs in time $T(n)$. A PRAM algorithm for S, running in parallel time $t(n)$ with $p(n)$ processors is *optimal* if $t(n)$ is polylog(n) and the work $w(n) = p(n) \cdot t(n)$ is $O(T(n))$. The algorithm is *efficient* if $t(n) = polylog(n)$ and the work $w(n)$ is $T(n) \cdot polylog(n)$. An efficient parallel algorithm is one that achieves a high degree of parallelism and comes to within a polylog factor of optimal speed-up. A major goal in the design of parallel algorithms is to find optimal or efficient algorithms with $t(n)$ as small as possible. For more on the PRAM model and PRAM algorithms, see Karp & Ramachandran [12].

Several problems including the n-element prefix sums and list ranking problems and the computation of various tree functions on an n-node tree have optimal $O(\log n)$ time algorithms. The problem of sorting n integers, each of which has value polynomial in n, can be solved in $O(\log n / \log \log n)$ time while performing $O(n \cdot \log \log n)$ work [1]. For the problem of computing the connected components and a spanning forest of an undirected graph the first efficient parallel algorithm was obtained for the CREW PRAM by Hirschberg, Chandra, and Stockmeyer [7]. The most efficient algorithm currently known is the 'almost-optimal' logarithmic time algorithm of Cole & Vishkin [2]. This algorithm assumes that the input is available in adjacency lists. For other types of sparse inputs, e.g., unordered edge lists, the algorithm needs integer sorting and runs in logarithmic time on an ARBITRARY CRCW PRAM while performing $O((m+n) \cdot \log \log n)$ work, where m and n are the number of edges and vertices in the graph.

The algorithms we will survey in this chapter will use the above algorithms as subroutines.

3.   Ear Decomposition

An *ear decomposition* $D = [P_0, P_1, \ldots, P_{r-1}]$ of an undirected graph is a partition of its edge set into an ordered collection of simple paths called *ears* such that the first ear P_0 is a simple cycle and each P_i, $i > 0$ is a simple path (possibly closed), each of whose endpoints belongs to some P_j, $j < i$, and none of whose internal vertices belongs to any P_j, $j < i$. (There

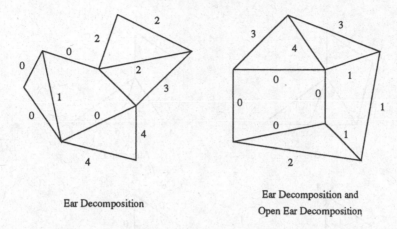

Ear Decomposition

Ear Decomposition and
Open Ear Decomposition

Figure 1. Ear Decompositions. (Ear numbers are indicated along edges).

are other variants of this definition that replace P_0 by two ears whose union forms a simple cycle.)

An *open ear decomposition* is an ear decomposition for which none of the P_i, $i > 0$ is a cycle.

Figure 1 gives an example of an ear decomposition and an open ear decomposition.

A *separating edge* of a graph G is an edge e such that G - e has at least two connected components. G is *2-edge connected* if it contains no separating edge.

A *separating vertex* or *cutpoint* of G is a vertex v such that $G - v$ has at least two connected components. G is *biconnected* if it contains no cutpoint.

The following two classical results relate ear decomposition to 2-edge connectivity and biconnectivity.

Lemma 3.1 [26] A graph is 2-edge connected if and only if it has an ear decomposition. □

Lemma 3.2 [26] A graph is biconnected if and only if it has an open ear decomposition. □

We now describe a simple algorithm for finding an ear decomposition in a 2-edge connected undirected graph G [14, 16, 15, 19].

1. Find a spanning tree T for G; root T at a vertex r and number the vertices in preorder.

2. Assign labels, starting with zero, to the nontree edges of G in nondecreasing order of the least common ancestors of the endpoints of the nontree edges. (These are the ear numbers of the nontree edges.)

3. Label each tree edge e by the label of the nontree edge with the smallest label whose fundamental cycle contains e. (These are the ear numbers of the tree edges.)

Figure 2 shows the construction of an ear decomposition in a 2-edge connected graph using this algorithm.

A proof by induction on ear number shows that this algorithm generates a sequence of paths satisfying the properties of an ear decomposition. Each of these steps can be performed

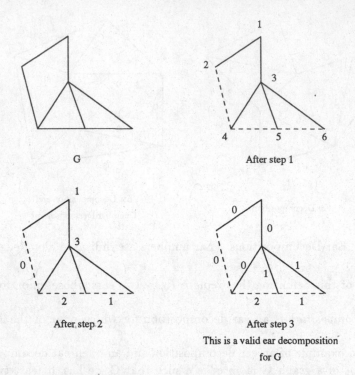

Figure 2. Constructing an Ear Decompositon

efficiently in $O(\log n)$ time using efficient parallel algorithms for finding a spanning tree [2], least common ancestors [22], tree functions [24], and integer sorting [1].

The above algorithm can be refined to give an open ear decomposition for a biconnected graph by modifying step 2. Note that in figure 2, we will get an open ear decomposition for the graph if we interchange the labels of the nontree edges with labels 1 and 2; this is still a legal labeling according to step 2 since the endpoints of these two nontree edges share the same least common ancestor. The algorithm for open ear decomposition uses the local connectivity information at each least common ancestor to further order the nontree edges with the same least common ancestor [16, 15, 19]. This in turn gives an efficient $O(\log n)$ time parallel algorithm for finding an open ear decomposition in an undirected biconnected graph. In case the input graph is not biconnected this algorithm will induce an open ear decomposition for each biconnected component of the graph.

4.   Open Ear Decomposition and Triconnectivity

A *separating pair* in a graph is a pair of vertices whose removal results in a graph with more than one connected component. A graph is *triconnected* if it has no separating pair.

The following claim, shown in [17], shows that an open ear decomposition serves to localize each separating pair on a single ear.

Claim 4.1 [17] Let D be an open ear decomposition of a graph G and let x, y be a separating pair in G. Then there exists an ear P in D such that x and y lie on P and the portion of P between x and y is separated from the rest of P in $G - x, y$.   □

Let G be a biconnected graph with an open ear decomposition D. A *bridge* of an ear

P (see e.g., [4]) is a maximal collection of edges in $G - P$ such that there exists a path in $G - P$ between any pair of edges in the collection. A bridge that consists of a single edge is a *trivial* bridge; otherwise it is a *nontrivial* bridge. In this section we will only be interested in those edges in a bridge of $G - P$ that are incident on P. Miller & Ramachandran [17] show that by finding the bridges of P and ascertaining their 'interlacement' pattern we can identify the separating pairs in G that lie on P. (Informally, two bridges of an ear P *interlace* if they cannot be placed on the same side of P in any planar embedding of G.) They also show that it suffices to compute certain approximations to the bridges of P (called the *nonanchor bridges* and the *anchoring star*) that are easy to compute. This leads to the following high-level description of the triconnectivity algorithm.

1. Find an open ear decomposition D of the input graph G.

2. Find the nonanchor bridges and the anchoring star of each ear.

3. Determine the interlacement pattern of the bridges of each ear as computed in step 2 and hence determine the set of separating pairs on each ear.

4. If no separating pair is identified in step 3 then report that G is triconnected.

The algorithm in [17] uses a divide and conquer technique to implement steps 2 and 3, resulting in an $O(\log^2 n)$ time algorithm with a linear number of processors (thus performing $O(n \cdot \log^2 n)$ work). This algorithm is improved in [21] where the time bound is reduced to $O(\log n)$ by pipelining the computation of [17] in step 2 and by reducing step 3 to the problem of determining connectivity in an auxiliary linear-sized graph.

An alternate strategy is used in [6] to further improve the performance of this algorithm. They use a technique called *local replacement* to eliminate the need for a divide and conquer approach for step 2. The local replacement technique removes the interaction between ears at their endpoints and allows the computation of step 2 to be performed simultaneously on all ears. This reduces the complexity of the entire triconnectivity algorithm to the the complexity of determining connectivity.

These results have been extended to the problem of finding the triconnected components of a graph. In the following we briefly describe this work.

Finding Triconnected Components

We first review some material from [25, 8] relating to the definition of triconnected components. While this definition may appear contrived at first, in reality it decomposes a biconnected graph into substructures that preserve the triconnected structure of G. In particular, questions relating to graph planarity and isomorphism between a pair of graphs can be mapped onto related questions regarding the tree of triconnected components.

This material deals with multigraphs. An edge e in a multigraph is denoted by (a, b, i) to indicate that it is the ith edge between a and b; the third entry in the triplet may be omitted for one of the edges between a and b.

We extend the definition of separating pairs to multigraphs. A pair of vertices a, b in a multigraph G is a separating pair if and only if there are two nontrivial bridges, or at least three bridges, one of which is nontrivial, of a, b in G. If G has no separating pairs then G is

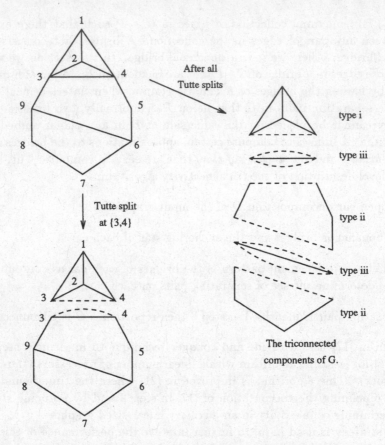

Figure 3. Tutte Splits and Triconnected Components

triconnected. The pair a, b is a *nontrivial* separating pair if there are two nontrivial bridges of a, b in G

Let a, b be a separating pair for a biconnected multigraph $G = (V, E)$. For any bridge X of a, b, let $\bar{X}$ be the induced subgraph on $(V - V(X)) \cup a, b$. Let B be a bridge of a, b in G such that both B and $\bar{B}$ have at least two edges, and either B or $\bar{B}$ is biconnected. We can apply a *Tutte split* $s(a, b, i)$ to G by forming G_1 and G_2 from G, where G_1 is $B \cup (a, b, i)$ and G_2 is the induced subgraph on $(V - V(B)) \cup a, b$, together with the edge (a, b, i). The graphs G_1 and G_2 are called *split graphs* of G with respect to a, b. The *Tutte components* of G are obtained by successively applying a Tutte split to split graphs until no Tutte split is possible. Every Tutte component is one of three types: i) a triconnected simple graph; ii) a simple cycle; or iii) a pair of vertices with at least three edges between them. The Tutte components of a biconnected multigraph G are the unique *triconnected components* of G. These definitions are illustrated in figure 3. Note that a Tutte split cannot be performed at separating pair 3,5 since for each bridge B of 3,5, neither B nor $\bar{B}$ is biconnected.

It is shown in [17] that an open ear decomposition gives a simple and natural method to perform Tutte splits. Each Tutte split $s(a, b, i)$ is made at an ear P that contains the separating pair a, b. An edge (a, b, i) is added to the component containing the portion of P that lies between a and b and another edge (a, b, i) is added to the component containing the rest of P.

It is possible that there are several separating pairs containing a vertex v and in such a case there will be several triconnected components containing a copy of vertex v. The algorithm in [17] uses a divide and conquer technique to generate the triconnected components in parallel without causing conflicts between different processors attempting to access the same vertex to generate different splits associated with that vertex. This leads to an $O(\log^2 n)$ time algorithm with a linear number of processors to obtain the triconnected components of a graph. Fussell, Ramachandran & Thurimella [6] use the local replacement technique to avoid the use of divide and conquer. A vertex is converted into a tree of copies of itself after the application of local replacement; a given copy can appear as a 'real' separating pair in at most one ear. Thus all of the Tutte splits can be performed simultaneously. This leads to an algorithm for finding triconnected components with the same complexity as that of finding connected components.

5. Four Connectivity

A vertex triple x, y, z is a separating triplet of a graph G if $G - x, y, z$ contains at least two connected components. If G contains no separating triplet then G is said to be *four connected*.

Kanevsky & Ramachandran [10] establish the following claim that relates each separating triplet in a triconnected graph G with an open ear decomposition D to a specific ear in D.

Claim 5.1 [10] Let G be a triconnected graph with an open ear decomposition D and let x, y, z be a separating triplet of G. Then there exists an ear P in D such that two of the vertices, say x and y, in x, y, z lie on P, and the portion of P between x and y is separated from the rest of P in $G - x, y, z$. Further, if z does not lie on P then z is a cutpoint in a bridge of P.   □

Given a triconnected graph G together with an open ear decomposition D, [10] represent any separating triplet of G by the notation $([x, y], z)$ where x and y represent an unordered pair of vertices that lie on a single ear and x, y, z is a separating triplet of G. They further classify separating triplets to be either Type 1 or Type 2. In a Type 1 separating triplet $([x, y], z)$, the vertex z belongs to the ear containing x and y; in a Type 2 separating triplet vertex z is a cutpoint in a bridge of that ear. Using this characterization [10] develop an algorithm for testing four connectivity and finding all separating triplets in a triconnected graph. This algorithm runs in $O(\log^2 n)$ parallel time with n^2 processors on an n node graph. A sequential version of the algorithm runs in $O(n^2)$ time which improves the asymptotic bounds obtained by previous algorithms for this problem on dense graphs by a linear factor. Very recently, the sequential time bound for this problem has been further improved in [11]; this algorithm is not known to be efficiently parallelizable.

6. Other Applications of Ear Decomposition

Ear decomposition can be used to obtain a very simple parallel algorithm for the *strong orientation* problem. In this problem we are asked to assign a direction to each edge in an undirected graph so that the resulting graph is strongly connected. It can be shown that an undirected graph has a strong orientation if and only if it is 2-edge connected. Given a 2-edge connected graph we can obtain a strong orientation for it by finding an ear decomposition for the graph and then orienting the edges in each ear, in parallel, as a directed path from any one endpoint to the other.

Ear decomposition can also be used as the starting point for algorithms for higher edge connectivity analogous to the use of open ear decomposition for higher vertex connectivity. The resulting algorithms tend to be simpler than the corresponding ones for vertex connectivity. For instance, using ear decomposition, we can obtain a simple linear time sequential algorithm and an efficient parallel one for 3-edge connectivity (e.g., [18]).

As shown in the earlier sections open ear decomposition is an useful starting point for algorithms for higher vertex connectivity. Other problems that have efficient parallel algorithms based on open ear decomposition include st-numbering [15] and planarity testing [20].

7. Parallel Algorithms for Directed Graphs

We have had considerably less success in the design and analysis of efficient parallel algorithms for problems on directed graphs. At present the most efficient highly parallel algorithm known for the basic problem of testing if one vertex is reachable from another in a directed graph computes the transitive closure of the adjacency matrix of the input graph and reads out the result from this matrix. This computation requires well in excess of a number of processors quadratic in the number of vertices in the input graph. Since this problem can be computed in linear time sequentially, this parallel algorithm is not efficient. As a result most problems on general directed graphs do not have efficient parallel algorithms at this time. This phenomenon is often called the *transitive closure bottleneck.*

The straightforward method of computing the transitive closure of an n by n matrix is to compute the nth power of the matrix by repeated squaring. This algorithm runs in logarithmic time using n^3 processors on a CRCW PRAM using the standard matrix multiplication algorithm. The faster matrix multiplication algorithms (see, e.g., [3]) can be parallelized to run in logarithmic time using n^α processors, where α is the 'matrix multiplication exponent'; currently α is around 2.376. While these algorithms work only for matrix multiplication over a ring, they can be adapted to work for the transitive closure problem. The resulting algorithm is quite complicated, however, and has a large constant factor in the running time, and hence the standard method still remains the algorithm of choice.

Several problems on directed graphs can be solved using the strategy of repeated matrix multiplication used in the transitive closure problem. These include strong components, topological sort, breadth first search (both directed and undirected), all pairs reachability, and all pairs shortest pairs. For the last two problems, the resulting parallel algorithms are efficient for dense graphs since the work they perform is within a polylog factor of the sequential algorithm.

8. Conclusion

In this chapter we have surveyed results in the design of efficient parallel algorithms for various problems on general graphs. For undirected graphs ear decomposition has proved to be a powerful tool in the design of sequential and parallel algorithms for various important problems such as higher connectivity of graphs, strong orientation, s-t numbering and planarity. It is to be anticipated that other algorithms based on ear decomposition will be developed. For directed graphs no such efficient parallel algorithms are known due to the transitive closure bottleneck. Developing techniques to circumvent this bottleneck is a challenging area for research.

References

[1] Bhatt, P.C.P., Diks, K., Hagerup, T., Prasad, V.C., Radzik, T., & Saxena, S. "Improved deterministic parallel integer sorting," tech. report 15/1989, Univ. of Saarbrucken, Germany, 1989.

[2] Cole, R. & Vishkin, U., "Approximate and exact parallel techniques with applications to list, tree and graph problems," *Proc. 27th Ann. IEEE Symp. on Foundations of Comp. Sci.,* 1986, pp. 478-491.

[3] Coppersmith, D. & Winograd, S. "Matrix multiplication via arithmetic progressions," *Proc. 19th Ann. ACM Symp. on Theory of Computing,* 1987, pp. 1-6.

[4] Even, S. *Graph Algorithms,* Computer Science Press, Potomac, MD, 1979.

[5] Even, S. & Tarjan, R. "Computing an st-numbering," *Theoretical Computer Science* 2, 1976, pp. 339-344.

[6] Fussell, D., Ramachandran, V. & Thurimella, R., "Finding triconnected components by local replacements," *Proc ICALP,* Italy, Springer-Verlag LNCS 372, July 1989, pp. 379-393.

[7] Hirschberg, D.S., Chandra, A.K., and Sarwate, D.V. "Computing connected components on parallel computers," *Comm. ACM,* vol. 22, 1979, pp. 461-464.

[8] Hopcroft, J.E. & Tarjan, R.E. "Dividing a graph into triconnected components," *SIAM J. Computing* 2, 1973, pp. 135-158.

[9] Hopcroft, J.E., & Tarjan, R.E. "Efficient planarity testing," *J. ACM,* vol. 21, 1974, pp. 549-568.

[10] Kanevsky, A. & Ramachandran, V., "Improved algorithms for graph four-connectivity," *Jour. of Computer and System Science,* vol. 42, 1991, pp. 288-306.

[11] Kanevsky, A., Tamassia, R., Di Battista & Chen, J. "On-line maintenance of the four-connected components of a graph," *Proc. 32nd Ann. IEEE Symp. on Foundations of Comp. Sci.,* 1991, pp. 793-801.

[12] Karp, R.M. & Ramachandran, V. "Parallel algorithms for shared-memory machines," *Handbook of Theoretical Computer Science,* North-Holland, 1990, pp. 869-941.

[13] Lempel, A., Even, S. & Cederbaum, I. "An algorithm for planarity testing of graphs," *Theory of Graphs: International Symposium,* Rome, July 1966, Gordon and Breach, New York, NY, pp. 215-232.

[14] Lovasz, L. "Computing ears and branchings in parallel," *26th Annual IEEE Symposium on Foundations of Computer Science,* 1985, pp. 464-467.

[15] Maon, Y., Schieber, B. & Vishkin, U. "Parallel ear decomposition search (EDS) and st-numbering in graphs," *Theoret. Comput. Sci.,* vol. 47, 1986, pp. 277-298.

[16] Miller, G.L. & Ramachandran, V. "Efficient parallel ear decomposition with applications," unpublished manuscript, MSRI, Berkeley, CA, January 1986.

[17] Miller, G.L. & Ramachandran, V. "A new graph triconnectivity algorithm and its parallelization," *Proc. 19th Annual ACM Symp. on Theory of Computing,* New York, NY, 1987, pp. 335-344.

[18] Ramachandran, V. Course notes on "Theory of Parallel Computation," Dept. of Computer Sciences, Univ. of Texas at Austin, Spring 1990.

[19] Ramachandran, V. "Parallel open ear decomposition with applications to graph biconnectivity and triconnectivity," in *Synthesis of Parallel Algorithms*, J. Reif, ed., Morgan-Kaufmann, to appear.

[20] Ramachandran, V. & Reif, J.H. "An optimal parallel algorithm for graph planarity," *Proc. 30th Ann. IEEE Symp. on Foundations of Comp. Sci.*, 1989, pp. 282-287; full version available as tech. report TR-90-15, Dept. of Computer Sciences, the Univ. of Texas at Austin.

[21] Ramachandran, V. & Vishkin, U. "Efficient parallel triconnectivity in logarithmic time," *VLSI Algorithms and Architectures*, Springer-Verlag LNCS 319, 1988, pp. 33-42.

[22] Schieber, B. & Vishkin, U. "On finding lowest common ancestors: simplification and parallelization," *VLSI Algorithms and Architectures*, Springer-Verlag LNCS 319, 1988, pp. 111-123.

[23] Tarjan, R. E. , "Depth first search and linear graph algorithms," *SIAM J. Comput.* 1, 1972, pp. 146-160.

[24] Tarjan, R.E. & Vishkin, U. "An efficient parallel biconnectivity algorithm," *SIAM J. Computing* 14, 1984, pp. 862-874.

[25] Tutte, W. T., *Connectivity in Graphs*, University of Toronto Press, 1966.

[26] Whitney, H. "Non-separable and planar graphs," *Trans. Amer. Math. Soc.* 34, 1930, pp. 339-362.

Chapter 5

Some Parallel Geometric Algorithms

Colm Ó Dúnlaing *

Abstract

These notes will review some techniques of computational geometry which parallelise well. Specifically, the construction of convex hulls in two dimensions and three dimensions and the Voronoi diagram for sets of points in two dimensions, and some methods for planar point-location, will be described. The theme will be the application of refined techniques to a few problems; the more abstract questions of parallel complexity will not arise; and for lack of space, some important methods, such as randomisation, will not be covered.

1. Introduction.

These notes, which are necessarily incomplete[1], introduce some problems in computational geometry, and survey some efficient parallel solutions. By 'computational geometry' we mean the maintenance of large volumes of simple geometric data. The combinatorial aspect of dealing with voluminous data is more weighty than the primitive geometric problems involved, which are usually rather simple. All the problems will be in two or three dimensions. Specifically, we consider the following:

- Given a finite set S of points in the plane, to compute their convex hull.

- Given a triangulated straight-line plane graph G, to build an efficient point-location structure for G.

- Given a finite set S of points in space, to compute their convex hull.

- Given a finite set S of line-segments in the plane, to verify that they don't intersect except at endpoints, and if they don't, to build the *trapezoidal partition* structure for S.

- Given a finite set S of points in the plane, to compute its *Voronoi diagram* Vor(S).

---

*Supported by the EEC under Esprit BRA 3075 (ALCOM). Electronic mail address: odunlain@maths.tcd.ie

[1]For instance, dynamic problems [4, 10, 11] are omitted, the model of computation is always a PRAM, with no consideration of more realistic architectures [14, 11], and only deterministic, not randomised [38] algorithms are reviewed.

The field has attracted researchers since about 1975 [40]. At roughly the same time the prospects of parallelisation began to engage the efforts of researchers; notable early papers on parallel algorithms were [12, 47]. Not surprisingly, the parallelisation of geometric algorithms was not considered at the time. A substantial dissertation on the subject was written by Chow in 1981 [14], but it remained largely isolated work, until the 1985 conference paper of Aggarwal et al. [1] returned to the subject.

At a first glance the better-known serial geometric algorithms seem hard to parallelise, because usually they either (i) process data sorted in some order, with the focus of attention necessarily developed in a strict order, or (ii) use divide-and-conquer recursions which seem hard to distribute effectively over many processors. As an illustration of (i) the useful *sweepline* approach (for 2-dimensional problems) is to imagine the data being swept over from left-to-right by a moving vertical line, occasionally reaching some geometric criticality where the structure is altered. While extremely useful for serial algorithms (see, e.g., [26]), it is usually hard to parallelise. It turns out that (ii) presents fewer difficulties.

1.1 Category of computing machine. The algorithms presented here will all be for PRAM machines, parallel random-access machines, where a system of identical processors read from and write to a shared random-access memory. There are three classes of such machine, depending on the kind of memory access contention tolerated. The weakest model, EREW (exclusive read/exclusive write), requires that at any time any memory cell should be accessed by at most one processor; this is insufficient or too inconvenient for our purposes. A stronger model, CREW (concurrent read/exclusive write) will allow any number of processors to read the same memory cell simultaneously, but not to write to the cell simultaneously. This is usually enough for our purposes: the shared read-access allows processors to use common data-structures together, while the operations are usually sufficiently 'local' to avoid memory-write conflicts. The strongest model we shall use will be the arbitrary CRCW machine, which allows simultaneous read and write access. If several processors attempt to write to the same location, then one of them succeeds, and the successful processor is chosen arbitrarily. (Stronger models, such as where the lowest-indexed processor succeeds, are not needed here.)

Each processor is assumed capable of exact rational and integer arithmetic in bounded time. In applications which use an r-ruling set (see 7.3, [18]), an unusual operation is assumed to have unit cost: namely, given two distinct bitstrings of length $\log_2(n)$, to find the index of the lowest-order bit where they differ.

1.2 Algorithmic techniques. The notes concentrate quite heavily on two themes. First, *divide-and-conquer* in parallel. All convex-hull constructions and Voronoi diagram constructions discussed here have the same pattern: to construct an object $B(S)$ from a set S of points in 2 or 3 dimensions:

1. Initially, the set S is sorted in some fixed direction (x- or z-direction). The algorithm then proceeds recursively; let P be the first $|S|/2$ points in this sorted order, and Q the remainder.

2. Construct $B(P)$ and $B(Q)$ recursively.

3. Construct the 'junction' $J(P,Q)$ between $B(P)$ and $B(Q)$. For the 2-dimensional convex hull problem, this is a common tangent; in three dimensions it is the 'collar'; and for the Voronoi diagram it is the 'contour.'

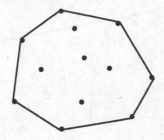

Figure 1. Convex Hull $H(S)$ of S.

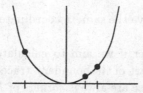

Figure 2. Reduction of sorting.

4. Combine $B(P)$, $J(P,Q)$, and $B(Q)$ to form $B(S)$. Part of the structures $B(P)$, $B(Q)$, will probably be discarded in this step.

The second theme, which will arise in implementing the various procedures in parallel, is that of *location*: either we use structures which enable a single processor to locate some geometric feature efficiently, or, more effectively, have several processors (typically $\sqrt{n}$) co-operate to identify the feature. This last technique may be dubbed *fast parallel location* [43, 48].

2. Convex hull in 2 dimensions.

Given a set S of n points in $\mathbb{R}^2$, their *convex hull* $H(S)$ is the smallest convex set enclosing S. To distinguish points in S from the infinitely many points not in S, we call them *sites*.

This section will consider the problem of constructing the convex hull $H(S)$ from S, both serially and in parallel. The output of the algorithm is to be a list of all the corners of $H(S)$ in anticlockwise order around its perimeter. This requirement suggests that the problem might be as hard as sorting and therefore require $\Omega(n\log(n))$ operations, where $n = |S|$. Indeed, a convex hull algorithm can be used to sort a list of n real numbers x_i. If one projects them onto the parabola $y = x^2$, then all the points (x_i, x_i^2) will be corners of their convex hull and appear in sorted order[2].

To introduce a typical divide-and-conquer approach to the convex hull problem, we review Shamos's serial technique [40].

2.1 For simplicity we assume (i) that S is in *general position*[3]: no three points in S are

---

[2]This is just a loose argument, since the $\Omega(n\log(n))$ lower bound on sorting assumes the comparison model which does not acknowledge the possibility of shortcuts by real-number calculations; however, the bound applies in the more realistic algebraic computation-tree model of Ben-Or's [7, 34, 42].

[3]It is common practice to make such assumptions in computational geometry, to simplify exposition; otherwise, definitions often need careful elaboration, with many special cases, whose analysis is repetitive and laborious.

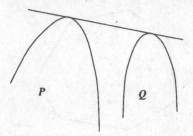

Figure 3. Illustrating step 3

collinear, and no two points in S have the same x-coordinate, and (ii) that the cardinality n of S is a power of 2.

It simplifies the exposition further if we aim to calculate, not the convex hull, but its *upper chain* UC(S). This is that part of its boundary traced by a clockwise path from the leftmost to rightmost sites in S (these are always corners of $H(S)$). To avoid special cases in the construction, the upper chain is terminated by infinite vertical lines descending from its leftmost and rightmost corners. The lower chain is defined similarly. It is trivial to construct $H(S)$ by combining the two chains.

2.2 The divide-and-conquer method of constructing UC(S) is as follows.

1. In a preprocessing step, an array is created containing the sites in S sorted by x-coordinate.

   Thereafter, the algorithm is recursive: the set S is divided by a vertical line L separating its two median elements into two sets P and Q to the left and right of L respectively, so $|P| = |Q| = n/2$.

2. The upper chains for P and Q are calculated recursively.

3. Then their *upper common tangent*, which is the unique line touching both UC(P) and UC(Q), necessarily at unique corners p and q respectively[4], is calculated.

4. Finally, an array is created, containing the sequence of corners of UC(P) from ℓ to p followed by the sequence of corners of UC(Q) from q to r, where ℓ and r are the leftmost and rightmost sites in P and Q respectively.

2.3 It is easy to implement the last step, and fairly easy to implement step 3, in linear time ($O(n)$, where $n = |S|$).

If we adjust the time-units so that the cost of steps 3 and 4 is bounded by n, then the cost of the the algorithm, *ignoring the preprocessing step*, is bounded by a quantity $T(n)$ satisfying

$$T(n) = n + 2T(n/2).$$

This implies that the runtime is $O(n \log(n))$.[5] Since initially sorting the sites has the same asymptotic cost, the overall cost is $O(n \log(n))$. As has already been mentioned, this is

---

[4]by the nondegeneracy assumptions (2.1).

[5]This is easily seen by writing u_k for $T(n)/n$ where $k = \log_2(n)$: then $u_k = 1 + u_{k-1}$, so $u_k = c + k$ for some constant c, and $T(n) = n(c + \log_2(n))$.

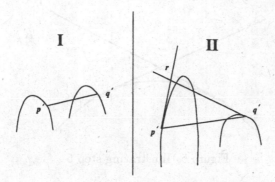

Figure 4. Search method described in [35].

optimal for the convex hull problem. However, supposing that the sites S were sorted in advance, it is possible that the recursive construction could be implemented more efficiently; indeed, it can, as we shall now see.

2.4   Overmars and van Leeuwen [35] showed that the upper common tangent could be located in time $O(\log(n))$. This yields a linear-time serial algorithm if the sites are presented in horizontally sorted order.

Their method keeps the corners of $UC(P)$ and $UC(Q)$ in balanced search-trees of logarithmic depth; for example, one could use red-black trees [46]. Let p and q denote the corners supporting the upper common tangent. The search for p and q is organised as follows.

The search keeps track of two nodes, call them u and v, in the trees for $UC(P)$ and $UC(Q)$ respectively, where the corners p and q are descendants of u and v respectively.

Let p' and q' be the corners stored at u and v. It is easy to maintain pointers in the search-trees to the corners adjacent to p' and q' in the respective upper chains: then a simple calculation tells one whether $p = p'$ and $q = q'$. If not, the line through these two corners cuts the boundaries of the two chains in three or four points, and several cases need to be considered, which are mostly covered by the accompanying sub-figures I and II.

In sub-figure I, p' is not the leftmost intersection point, and therefore p is to its left, so u can be replaced by its left child. In figure II, they are both outermost intersection points, and p and q can be on either side of p' and q', so a more careful local test needs to be applied. Observe that if q is not to the left of q' then p must be to the right of p' (this is the situation illustrated). Extend the side following p' into a line U, and the side preceding q' into a line W, and let r be the point of intersection. In the illustration, since q is not to the left of q', the line W intersects $UC(P)$ before it intersects U: therefore r is to the left of the leftmost site in Q, and in particular, to the left of the vertical separating line L. This information allows u to be replaced by its right child. If r is to the right of L then v is replaced by its left child.

Therefore the upper common tangent can be located in time proportional to the sum of the depths of the two trees, i.e., logarithmic time. A tree holding $UC(S)$ in sorted order can be formed in logarithmic time by splitting and joining [46].

2.5   This leads to the following recurrence for the runtime of the algorithm (excluding the preprocessing step):

$$T(n) = \log(n) + 2T(n/2).$$

Figure 5. Illustrating step 5

The solution to this is $O(n)$, following the method in 2.3, essentially because the series $\sum \frac{k}{2^k}$ is convergent.

2.6 Having seen a serial algorithm for constructing UC(S), we next see an optimal parallel algorithm from [1], with simplifications due to Stojmenović [44][6].

1. In a preprocessing step, the set S is sorted horizontally. This costs $O(\log(n))$ time (CREW) with n processors [2, 15]. The rest of the algorithm is recursive, based on separating S into $\sqrt{n}$ horizontally separated groups of size $\sqrt{n}$.[7]

2. For each group $S_i, 1 \leq i \leq \sqrt{n}$, recursively compute UC(S_i) with $\sqrt{n}$ processors, storing the result in a balanced tree.

3. Assign one processor to each of the $\binom{\sqrt{n}}{2}$ pairs $(S_i, S_j), i < j$, and let it calculate the tangent common to the two upper chains. Let T_{ij} denote this common tangent.

4. For $1 \leq k \leq \sqrt{n}$ let L_k be the line with minimal slope among the tangents $T_{1,k}, \ldots,$ $T_{k-1,k}$, and let R_k be the line with maximal slope among the tangents $T_{k,k+1}, \ldots, T_{k,\sqrt{n}}$. (Take L_1 and $R_{\sqrt{n}}$ as the vertical lines extending downwards from the leftmost and rightmost sites in S.)

   These lines L_k can be computed in parallel as follows: sort the $\binom{\sqrt{n}}{2}$ items $(k, T_{i,k}), 1 \leq i < k \leq \sqrt{n}$, by (slope of line) within (index k), thus extracting the lines L_k of minimal slope. The lines R_k are calculated similarly.

5. For each k, if the lines L_k and R_k cross one another, or meet at a common corner where they form a concave angle, then S_k does not contribute any corners to UC(S). Otherwise, it contributes all corners on UC(S_k) between the point where it meets L_k and the point where it meets R_k.

6. Now that the corners belonging to UC(S) have been identified, they can be counted and ranked using parallel prefix (7.1), and stored in sorted order in an array A.

7. The array A can be converted to a balanced binary tree in bounded parallel time.

---

[6]In [1], a criterion was applied in step 5 which was sufficient but not necessary for a corner to belong to UC(S). Stojmenović's strengthened criterion eliminates a few stages from the algorithm in [1].

[7]If n is not a perfect square, let there be $\sqrt{n/2}$ groups of size $\sqrt{2n}$.

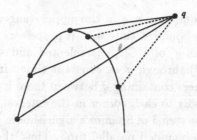

Figure 6. Tangent to UC(P) from q.

2.7 Let $T(n)$ measure the parallel cost of the recursive part of the above algorithm, with n processors available, excluding the initial preprocessing step. The techniques employed all run in $O(\log(n))$ parallel time: namely, for step 3 one uses the method described previously (2.4), for step 4 one uses an optimal sorting method, for step 6 one uses parallel prefix, and the last step is easily executed in bounded time.

This implies that $T(n)$, if measured in suitable units, satisfies the recurrence

$$T(n) = \log n + T(\sqrt{n}),$$

whence $T(n) = \log(n) + \log(n)/2 + \log(n)/4 \ldots < 2\log(n)$ is $O(\log(n))$.

2.8 The above algorithm, while fairly elaborate, achieves optimal parallel time [20] and optimal work, since the total number of operations is $O(n \log(n))$. As it happens, the straightforward serial algorithm (2.2) can be parallelised directly. This result is due to Wagener [48].

The serial algorithm performed the recursion by solving one upper common tangent (UCT) problem, in linear or logarithmic time, with one processor; the parallel algorithm of [1, 44] performed the recursion by solving roughly $n/2$ UCT problems in logarithmic time with n processors. Wagener's version solves one UCT problem in bounded time with n processors.

2.9 The method, exemplifying *fast parallel location* (1.2), is as follows. The corners of UC(P) and UC(Q) are stored in sorted order in arrays.

Let us focus first on UC(P) and consider a fixed point q to the right of P. We want to find the tangent through q to UC(P). That is, we want to find the corner p of UC(P) supporting this tangent. Suppose there are $\sqrt{n}$ processors available.

Imagine the sequence of lines from q through the corners of UC(P). Their slopes first decrease to a minimum — and the line of minimum slope is the tangent passing through p — and then they increase. Therefore, if one assigns just one processor to every $\sqrt{n}$-th corner of UC(P) then those processors can judge whether the slopes are locally decreasing or increasing and thus identify the unique pair (c_1, c_2) of such corners which have p between them. Re-assigning the processors to all the corners between c_1 and c_2, and performing the same local test, p can be located.

2.10 Thus: given a point q to the right of P, the tangent to UC(P) through q can be calculated in bounded time with $\sqrt{n}$ processors. It is fairly clear, actually, that this line can be calculated in time $O(1)$ with $n^{1/c}$ processors for any fixed c: of course, c affects the size of the constants in this estimate.

Now consider all corners q' of UC(Q) and the tangents from q' to UC(P). The slopes of these tangents increase until they reach their maximum at a corner q, then they decrease.

The tangent through this unique corner q is the upper tangent common to UC(P) and UC(Q). It can be calculated in bounded time with n processors as follows:

(i) First, every $\sqrt{n}$-th corner q' of UC(Q) is selected and $\sqrt{n}$ processors allocated to compute the tangent to UC(P) through q' in constant time. In this way, the unique pair (c_1, c_2) of adjacent sample corners containing q between them is identified.

(ii) Re-allocating $\sqrt{n}$ processors to each corner in the interval, q is identified.

Thus we see how to parallelise step 3 of Shamos's algorithm in bounded parallel time. It is easy to execute the last step in bounded parallel time. Thus, the cost $T(n)$ of the recursive part of the algorithm satisfies the recurrence

$$T(n) = O(1) + T(n/2)$$

so $T(n)$ is $O(\log(n))$. The preprocessing cost is the same.

2.11   Wagener [48] improves this algorithm further. Assuming that the preprocessing has been done — in other words, that the set S is presented in horizontally sorted order — he shows how to construct UC(S) in time $O(\log(n))$ using $n/\log(n)$ processors. As is often the case with such 'optimal speedup' methods, it is a hybrid method, with an 'early' strategy for small problems and a 'late' strategy for larger ones.

Write m for $n/\log(n)$. The improved method may be paraphrased as follows.

1. First divide S horizontally into m groups of size $\log(n)$ and, assigning one processor to each group, compute its upper chain in time $O(\log(n))$ (2.4).

2. The recursive step for combining upper chains continues, using balanced trees and just one processor per combination, until the problem size reaches $\log^2(n)$: each tree holds the upper chain for $\log(n)$ consecutive groups.

3. At this stage, upper chains have been computed for sets P of sites of size $\log^2(n)$. The associated upper chains U are stored in balanced trees. Assuming that with every node in the tree is stored the number of descendants of that node, it is straightforward for $\log(n)$ processors to identify every $\log(n)$-th corner of U, and copy a block of $\log(n)$ adjacent corners into an array. This takes time $O(\log(n))$.

   Thereafter, the upper chains U are maintained in sequences of groups of about $\log(n)$ corners. For definiteness, we require that each group contain between $\log_2(n)/2$ and $2\log_2(n)$ corners.

4. To calculate the upper chain of $P \cup Q$ where P and Q each contains $k\log_2(n)$ sites, and $k \geq \log_2(n)$, using k processors: let U and V be the respective upper chains. Take the first corners in each group in each side, extracting subsets U' and V', and apply the method of 2.10 to identify the groups containing the points p and q supporting the common tangent. Then apply the same method within the groups to locate the common tangent.

   Write $U = U_1 \cup U_2 \cup U_3$, where U_3 consists of all corners following p and therefore to be removed, U_2 consists of all corners up to p in the group containing p, and U_1 is the union of all groups preceding this group. Similarly, write $V = V_1 \cup V_2 \cup V_3$ where V_1 contains all corners to be removed, V_2 is a partial group, and V_3 is a union of groups. It is required to store $U_1 \cup U_2 \cup V_2 \cup V_3$ as a union of groups.

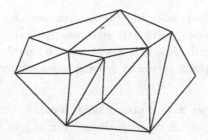

Figure 7. Triangulated plane graph

If $U_2 \cup V_2$ is of the correct size, let it form a group on its own; if it is too large, split it into two groups; if it is too small, take an adjacent group and combine with it, splitting if the result is too large.

All of this can be done in bounded parallel time with k processors.

2.12   The parallel runtime estimate for the above mixed algorithm is as follows: initally, computing the upper chains for groups of $\log(n)$ sites, is $O(\log(n))$; following the 'early' strategy up to a problem size $\log^2(n)$: $O(\log (\log^2(n))\log\log(n))$, which is $O(\log(n))$; and following the 'late' strategy with bounded time per recursion: $O(\log(n))$.

3.   Planar point location.

3.1   A *straight-line plane graph* consists of a finite set of points in the plane (vertices), some pairs of vertices being connected by straight line-segments (edges), with the proviso that distinct edges cannot intersect except at their vertex endpoints. One writes $G = (V, E)$ to indicate that G is such a graph with vertices V and edges E.

The union of all edges and vertices forms a closed set, by abuse of notation also denoted G, in the plane. The complement of this set is a disjoint union of connected open sets in the plane, called the *faces* of the graph G. Exactly one of the faces is unbounded. A plane graph is *triangulated* if all its bounded faces are triangular and the complement of its unbounded face is convex.

Given a (straight) plane-graph G and a point q, the *planar location problem* for q is to return the edge or face of G containing q.

PROPOSITION 3.2 (see [33]) (i) *Every straight-line plane graph can be triangulated by adding more straight edges if necessary;* (ii) (Euler's formula) *given a connected plane graph with f faces, e edges, and v vertices, $f - e + v = 2$;* (iii) *in any plane graph, $e < 3v$.*   □

COROLLARY 3.3 (i) *In a planar graph G, for any k, let J be the set of vertices of degree $\leq k$. Then $|J| > (k-5)n/(k+1)$, where n is the number of vertices in G.* (ii) *J contains an independent set I of at least $|J|/(k+1)$ vertices.*

Proof [23, 28, 33].   (i) The degree of a vertex is the number of edges incident to the vertex. Each edge contributes 2 to the total vertex degree, 1 to each of its incident vertices. Therefore the total vertex degree is $2e$ which is less than $6n$. Let M be the complement of J: then the total degree of all vertices in M is at least $(k+1)|M| < 6n$, so $|M| < 6n/(k+1)$ and $|J| > (k-5)n/(k+1)$.

(ii) Process J in any sequence, selecting the first vertex and thereafter selecting every vertex not adjacent to any vertex previously selected. Selection of a vertex obstructs the selection of at most k other vertices since it has at most k neighbours. This creates a subset I of J which is independent (each vertex in I being adjacent to no other vertex in I) and such that $(k+1)|I| \geq |J|$.   □

3.4   Based on these results, we have a planar point-location structure for a triangulated[8] plane graph G, called a 'Kirkpatrick decomposition.' Fix $k \geq 6$, and let

$$\mu = 1 - \frac{(k-5)}{(k+1)^2}.$$

The preprocessing constructs a sequence $G_0, G_1, \ldots G_r$ of triangulated plane graphs, with connections between the faces of consecutive graphs in the sequence. G_r has a bounded number b of vertices. By Corollary 3.3, $r \leq \log_{1/\mu}(n/b)$, so r is $O(\log(n))$.

It saves trouble if the entire graph G is enclosed in a 'frame,' just a rectangle, say, whose corners are added as new vertices. It is easy to triangulate the resulting graph by connecting the vertices on the outer face of G to the corners of the frame. We require that the frame remain part of *all* the graphs G_j, and $b = 4/(1-\mu)$, so the 'coarsest' graph G_r is just this rectangle with a few vertices inside it. Although the number r may be slightly increased, it remains $O(\log(n))$.

1. G_0 is obtained by framing G. The corners of the frame are denoted F. The remaining steps deal with constructing G_{j+1} from G_j.

2. Suppose G_j has vertex set V_j. Let J be the set of vertices of degree $\leq k$ in G_j, and let I be a large independent set in J.

3. Let $V_{j+1} = (V_j \backslash I) \cup F$. Let E consist of all edges of G_j both of whose ends are in V_{j+1}.

4. Let E_{j+1} be a set of edges containing E with whatever extra edges are needed to produce the triangulated plane graph $G_{j+1} = (V_{j+1}, E_{j+1})$.

5. Build pointer linkages so from every face of G_{j+1} the list of faces of G_j which intersect it can be accessed directly[9].

LEMMA 3.5 (i) *A Kirkpatrick decomposition for a triangulated plane graph G can be built in linear time $O(n)$ where n is the number of vertices in G.* (ii) *Any point query can be solved using the decomposition in logarithmic time.*

Proof. (i) It is easy to frame the graph G in linear time (because the outer face has convex complement). In each iterative step, calculating the independent set I and building the subgraph with vertices V_{j+1} can be executed in time $O(|V_j|)$. Triangulating the resulting graph is also easy, because the faces being either triangles or the union of at most k triangles with a common apex, have at most k bounding edges. Constructing the pointer linkages can

---

[8]Any straight-line plane graph can be triangulated in linear time [13], but the algorithm is very complicated.

[9]This is rather vague, but the details are not difficult.

be accomplished in linear time. Thus, the cost of forming the Kirkpatrick decomposition is proportional to the sum $\sum |V_j|$, which is $O(n)$, because $(|V_{j+1}| - 4)/|V_j| \leq \mu.$[10]

(ii) Given a query-point q, first locate it with respect to the coarsest graph G_r. If outside, then it is in the unbounded face of G. Otherwise, iteratively proceed (using the linkages supplied) from the face of G_{j+1} whose closure contains q to the face of G_j whose closure contains q. This takes bounded time per iteration. Thus q is located correctly with respect to G_0 (and hence G) in time $O(\log(n))$.   □

3.6 We turn to Dadoun and Kirkpatricks' parallel version of this algorithm [21, 22]. They show how to construct a 'large' independent set I in time $O(\log^*(n))$ with n processors.[11] The fraction of elements in such a 'large' independent set appears to be about 3^{1-2k} rather than about $1/k$ (which is a crude estimate of $1 - \mu$), so the constants hidden in the estimates are rather larger than before.

The parallel algorithm finding a large independent set in a plane graph G proceeds as follows.

1. Form a subgraph G' by deleting the nodes of degree $> k$. This uses one processor allotted to each vertex.[12] Let E be the set of edges of G'. The subsequent steps are repeated about $2k$ times to express G' as the union of at most $2k - 1$ *list graphs*, that is, directed graphs in which every vertex has at most one edge directed away from it and one edge directed into it. That is, the edge-set E is expressed as a union of t sets E_i, where $t < 2k$, each set E_i defining a list-graph on the nodes of G'. The union of the E_i contains one *oriented* copy of each edge in E.

2. To construct E_1, there are k rounds. There is a processor attached to each vertex. A vertex u 'proposes' to each adjacent vertex v in turn that the edge (u, v) be accepted for E_1. Then if u has any 'proposals' (w, u), it accepts exactly one.

   Once E_1 has been constructed, the edges are removed from G' and $E_2, \ldots E_t$ are constructed in the same way.

   It is possible that a vertex u have none of its proposals accepted during a round. Then all of its neighbours have accepted different proposals during the round. The number of rounds in which a node u is unsuccessful in naming an out-edge is bounded by $k - 1$, since after $k - 1$ such rounds its neighbours would have accepted all proposals except those from u. Hence after $2k - 1$ rounds u would have discarded all its edges, so $t < 2k$.

3. To construct the independent set I, the processors first choose a 2-*ruling set* I_1 from (V, E_1). This can be accomplished in $\log^*(n)$ parallel steps (7.3). Then they choose a 2-ruling set I_2 from (I_1, E_2) i.e., the nodes in I_1 linked by the directed edges in E_2. The procedure continues until I_t is constructed. By construction, I_t contains at least $n/3^{2k-1}$ nodes (vertices), and it is an independent set since no two nodes in I_t are connected by any edge in $E_1, E_2, \ldots E_t$.

---

[10]It follows that $|V_j| \leq A + (n - A)\mu^j$ where $A = 4/(1 - \mu)$.

[11]The iterated logarithm $\log^*$ is defined loosely in (7.5).

[12]Certainly, with one processor per vertex, the low-degree vertices can be identified in bounded parallel time. Forming the subgraph G' can be done efficiently if the graphs are represented in the manner proposed in [27].

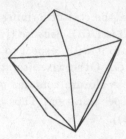

Figure 8. Convex hull in 3 dimensions.

By glossing over some details of the parallel implementation, the results of this section can be summarised as follows.

PROPOSITION 3.7 [21]. *Given a triangulated plane (straight-edge) graph G with n vertices, it is possible to build a Kirkpatrick decomposition of G in parallel time $O(\log(n)\log^*(n))$ with n processors [CREW], whereby a single processor can solve any point-location query in time $O(\log(n))$.*   □

4.   Convex hull in 3 dimensions.

The divide-and-conquer method of constructing the convex hull in 2 dimensions adapts naturally to the 3-dimensional problem. Here we are given a set S of n sites in space and we are required to compute the smallest convex set $H(S)$ containing all the sites. The output description will list the corners of $H(S)$, with adjacency information. This is more complicated than in two dimensions: the boundary of the hull is a planar graph, so we want a description of this graph, namely, for each corner, the list of corners connected to it by an edge of the convex hull, sorted anticlockwise around the corner.

4.1   Corresponding to the nondegeneracy assumptions (2.1) it is assumed that (i) no four sites in S are coplanar and (ii) the cardinality n of S is a power of 2. The divide-and-conquer approach may be outlined as follows:

1. Initially, S is sorted by z-coordinate. The description thereafter is recursive, assuming that $S = P \cup Q$ where P and Q are separated by a horizontal plane H, with P beneath and Q above.

2. Recursively calculate $H(P)$ and $H(Q)$.

3. Calculate the *collar*: this is a union of triangular faces, each face supporting a plane tangent to an edge of one hull and a corner of the other. We call such a plane a *common tangent plane* (CTP).[13]

   A side-effect of this calculation will be that each corner of $H(P)$ and $H(Q)$ is determined to be or not to be a corner of $H(S)$.

4. Having identified the corners, edges, and faces of $H(S)$, build a description of $H(S)$.

---

[13]The faces are triangular and the CTPs meet exactly three corners by the nondegeneracy assumptions.

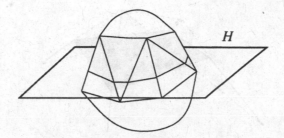

Figure 9. Collar joining two hulls.

This method, which was first described by Hong and Preparata [37], has certain difficulties of implementation. Imagine that the faces of $H(P)$ are green, those of $H(Q)$ red, and those of the collar are blue. One naturally expects that in $H(S)$ there should be a green base and a red cap, and between them a cylindrical blue collar. This picture lacks generality: the collar can have holes in it, so there can appear red and green islands.[14]

In [1] these details are handled fairly thoroughly and a complicated $O(\log^3(n))$ parallel algorithm is achieved. Chow [14] achieved the same runtime with a different approach which used Voronoi diagrams (on the sphere) to control the calculation. These diagrams were themselves calculated with subsidiary convex hull constructions.

4.2 In parallelising the Hong-Preparata algorithm, the focus of interest, of course, is implementing step 3. Its implementation in [1] is based on the following *line-query*:

> Given a line L and a convex polyhedron K, to determine if L intersects K, and, if not, to return the two planes through L tangent to K.

In [1] this query is solved in a complicated way, by decomposing the polyhedron K into what are there called 'seam polytopes,' and applying a search procedure which ultimately solves the query in serial time $O(\log^2(n))$. A much simpler and more efficient method is to use a Kirkpatrick decomposition of the polyhedron K to solve line-queries in $O(\log(n))$ serial time.

4.3 The planar graph decomposition method (3.4) can be applied to decompose a convex polyhedron to support line queries [23]. We work with the *dual graph* of the polyhedron. That is, we think of the polyhedron faces as corresponding to points of the graph, and two faces as adjacent if they share an edge in common. Think of the polyhedron as an intersection of half-spaces: when deleting an independent set of faces, we are implicitly removing the corresponding half-spaces from the scene, and the resulting polyhedron will be coarser. At the coarsest level, the polyhedron has bounded complexity; for example, it could be just a tetrahedron.

So we have a sequence $K_0, \ldots K_r$ of polyhedra, where K_r is a tetrahedron, K_0 is the original polyhedron, $K_j \subset K_{j+1}$, each face of each polyhedron is triangulated,[15] the data-structure has a record for each of these triangles, and there are linkages supplied from the triangles of K_{j+1} to those triangles of K_j which they intersect, and there are linkages from each corner

---

[14]Figure 9 does not convey the full picture.

[15]In our application K_0 is the convex hull of points in general position, so all its faces are triangles. This does not hold for the other polyhedra $K_1 \ldots K_r$.

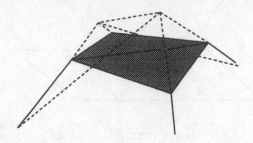

Figure 10. Face removed to coarsen the polyhedron

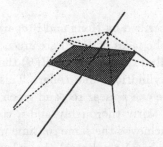

Figure 11. Line query, nonempty intersection, new bounding point.

of K_{j+1} to the same corner in K_j, if it exists, or to the bounded-degree face which cuts the corner off from K_{j+1}, if it doesn't.

4.4 The hierarchy can be used to solve any line-query (4.2) in serial time $O(\log(n))$ as follows.

(i) The faces of each K_j are triangulated. If a line L intersects K_j, let $[p,q]$ be the line-segment $L \cap K_j$. The points p and q are known, together with the triangles on the polyhedron boundary containing them. Figure 11 illustrates the next step.

(ii) There are connections between related triangles in faces of K_j and K_{j-1}. A triangle can be pruned to a hexagon at worst. If the bounding point p, say, is located in part of a triangle that is pruned, then one inspects the face or faces introduced to determine whether the intersection continues, and, if so, to revise the bounding point.

(iii) Once the intersection becomes empty (if it does), there are two tangent planes to K_j through L which are supported by two corners of the polyhedron. These planes change only when the supporting corners are removed, in which case they move to a corner of the adjacent low-degree face introduced. Figure 12 illustrates this.

Clearly, a single processor can use this structure as shown to solve line-queries in logarithmic time.

4.5 Let us review some of the details remaining in implementing the recursive procedure (4.1). One is given $H(P)$ and $H(Q)$, with hierarchical decompositions of these separate hulls. To each edge of each hull is alotted a processor.

Given an edge e, it is possible to determine whether e will be an edge of $H(S)$, and if so to calculate the two faces of $H(S)$ which meet at this edge. Let L be the line through an edge e of $H(P)$, say. Let the processor solve the line-query for L relative to $H(Q)$. If L penetrates the other hull, then e cannot be an edge of $H(S)$; otherwise, let T be one of the two planes through L, tangent to $H(Q)$ at a corner q. If T is tangent to $H(P)$ at e then it defines one of

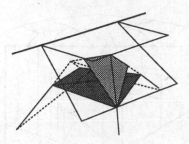

Figure 12. Line query, empty intersection, new tangent point.

the collar faces; if the triangle in T with e as base and q as apex passes through the interior of $H(P)$ then e is an edge of $H(S)$, but not on the collar; otherwise, e will not be an edge of $H(S)$.

Next, with one processor per edge, it is possible to search the edge list around each corner p of $H(P)$ to determine whether any edge remains as an edge of $H(S)$. These searches take logarithmic time. If not, then, except in the case where p is the *only* corner of $H(S)$ in P (and it has lowest z-coordinate), p will not be a corner of $H(S)$. Applying the same method to Q, we identify all corners of $H(S)$.

Suppose that e is an edge of $H(P)$ on the collar of $H(S)$. There are records available for two faces incident to e, and these can be re-used to define the faces of $H(S)$ incident to e. Records for edges incident to the old faces can be re-used for the edges incident to the new faces.

Linkages need to be supplied between collar faces which share a collar edge in common. The easiest way to do this is to use the hierarchical search structure for each edge $\{p, q\}$ of $H(S)$, $p \in P, q \in Q$, to identify the other two corners supporting the two tangent planes. These define edges of $H(P)$ or $H(Q)$ which can be located by binary search among the adjacency lists; having done this, one has the full linkage description among the faces and edges of $H(S)$, and from this it is straightforward to obtain the edge-list sorted around the corners of $H(S)$ by pointer doubling (7.2).

5.   Trapezoidal partitions in the plane.

Let S be a set of n closed line-segments in the plane. It is assumed that all $2n$ endpoints have different x-coordinates (therefore, in particular, that no segment is vertical). If the segments in S intersect only at their endpoints, then they are called *nonintersecting*.[16]

5.1   Let $I_0, \ldots, I_{2n}$ be the $2n + 1$ closed segments on the x-axis whose endpoints are the x-coordinates of the endpoints of the segments in S. The outer two intervals are unbounded. An *interval tree* T covering these intervals is a balanced binary tree which has one leaf for each interval I_j. In the present context T is also called a *segment tree*. Generally, if v is a node of T then I_v denotes the union of all segments associated with descendants of v in T. The *strip* Π_v associated with v is the vertical strip $I_v \times (-\infty, \infty)$. Say a segment s_1 is 'above' a different segment s_2 if there exists a vertical line-segment whose top and bottom endpoints are on s_1 and s_2 respectively [1, 5].

---

[16]Since the endpoints have different x-coordinates, they cannot intersect at the endpoints. This requirement eliminates almost all plane graphs for which the methods of this section could furnish another point-location structure; the restriction, however, simplifies the description.

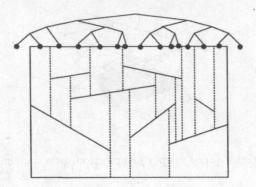

Figure 13. Segment tree, trapezoidal partition.

5.2 If the segments are nonintersecting, then the 'above' relation on line-segments is a partial order, that is, if s_1 is above s_2 then s_2 is not above s_1. In this case, the segment structure induces a *trapezoidal partition* of the plane: one adds, for each segment endpoint v, the vertical segment passing through v whose endpoints (where they exist) are on other segments in S and which otherwise intersect no segments in S. Let s be a segment, whose endpoints have x-coordinates $x_1 < x_2$. Then s *spans* a strip Π_v if $I_v \subseteq [x_1, x_2]$ and it *covers* v if it spans Π_v but not $\Pi_{\text{parent}(v)}$. Each segment covers at most two nodes at every level, so it covers $O(\log(n))$ nodes.

Given a point p in the plane, to *multilocate* p with respect to the segments in S is to list all nodes v such that Π_v contains p, and for each such v, to return the segment covering v which lies immediately above p (if it exists).

5.3 A multilocation structure on the set S, defined if S is nonintersecting, has several useful applications, such as planar-point location and polygon triangulation [1]. In [5] it is shown how to verify that S is nonintersecting, and, if so, build such a structure in $O(\log(n))$ time with n processors. This method is extended in [39] so the structure can deal efficiently with unexpected line-segment intersections, though the run-time depends, of course, on $(n + k)/p$ where k is the number of internal intersections and p is the number of processors available.

We describe in outline the method of [5], assuming that S is nonintersecting. The problem, essentially, is as follows: suppose that T is a (full and balanced) binary tree whose nodes support sorted sets $C(v)$ of items. We want a multilocation structure on T which will enable a single processor, given an item x, to traverse the tree from a leaf to the root and return for each node v encountered, the items in $C(v)$ bracketing x. (In [5] a more general problem is considered, where T is a directed graph, possibly with cycles.)

For each node v, a 'bridge list' $B(v)$ is built up in stages, as finer and finer samples, in the following way:

$$B_{s+1}(v) := C_s(v) \cup B'_{s+1}(\text{parent}(v)),$$

where $B'_{s+1}(w)$ consists of every 4th element of $B_s(w)$, and $C_s(v)$ consists of every 2^{k-s}-th element of $C(v)$. Here k is the maximum over all nodes v of $\log_2(|C(v)|)$ (rounded up), and $A \cup B$ is the *sorted* union (obtained by merging).

The merges proceed until all the sets $B_s(v)$ have reached their final value. It is not obvious how to perform the merges efficiently, but the method is closely related to the cascading merge algorithm described in the appendix (7.7). Ultimately, the bridge list $B(v)$ contains

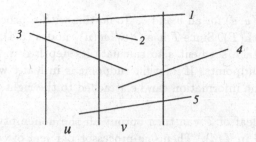

Figure 14. Strips for u and v with various segments.

about $1/4$ of $C(v)$, $1/16$ of $C(\text{parent}(v))$, and so on, and the linkages supplied enable a processor to pass from an item in v to the closest two adjacent items in $B(w)$, where w is the parent of v, in constant time: hence also to the closest adjacent items in $C(w)$.

With this structure, the multilocation is solved as follows: given an item x and a leaf ℓ of T, first locate x in $B(\ell)$, and then traverse the tree to locate x in $C(v)$ for all ancestors v of ℓ. One can use binary search to locate in $B(\ell)$: the overall cost then is $O(\log(N))$ where N is the sum of the cardinalities $|C(v)|$. With careful implementation the overall work, that is, (parallel time) $\times$ (number of processors), in forming the bridge-lists, is $O(N)$.

The phrase *fractional cascading* refers to this process of merging a sufficiently large sample from all ancestors of v into $B(v)$ to enable rapid multilocation.

5.4 Application to trapezoidal partition. To relate it to the segment-tree structure, following [5] one uses an interval tree T whose leaves cover not one interval but $\log_2(n)$ adjacent intervals. The slabs Π_v are defined as before. The sets $C(v)$ consist of all segments covering v (5.2).

For any node v, define

$$\text{END}(v) = \{s \in S : s \text{ has an endpoint interior to } \Pi_v\}.$$

By construction, for each leaf-node ℓ, $|\text{END}(\ell)| \leq \log_2(n)$. Define the *depth* of a segment s as the depth of the deepest node v such that Π_v contains s completely. Next, define

$$L(v) = \{\text{segments crossing left, not right, boundary of } \Pi_v\},$$

$$L(v, d) = \{s \in L(v) : \text{depth}(s) = d\},$$

with $R(v)$ and $R(v, d)$ being defined similarly for the right boundary of Π_v. The sets $L(v, d)$ and $R(v, d)$ are empty unless $d < \text{depth}(v)$. Various examples are illustrated in Figure 14. In the figure, segment 1 covers neither u nor v, segment 2 is in $\text{END}(v)$, segment 3 covers u and is in $L(v)$, segment 4 is in $R(v)$, and segment 5 covers v and is in $R(u)$.

PROPOSITION 5.5 [5] *Given a node w with left and right children u and v respectively,* (i) *for $d < \text{depth}(w)$, $L(w, d) = L(u, d) \cup L(v, d)$;* (ii) *$L(w)$ is the union of the $L(w, d)$ for all $d < \text{depth}(w)$;* (iii) *$L(w) = L(u) \cup L(v) \setminus L(v, \text{depth}(w))$;* (iv) *$C(u) = L(v) \setminus L(v, \text{depth}(w))$.* (v) *Similar relations hold among the $R(\dots)$ sets.* □

All the statements in this proposition follow easily from the definitions. The proposition allows formation of the various sets of items as described in $O(\log(n))$ parallel time with n processors. This is done as follows.

(1) Calculate the sets $L(v, d)$ for all v and d. To do this with n processors, let a copy $T(d)$ be made for each $d < \text{depth}(T)$. Since T has $O(n/log(n))$ nodes (5.4), the total size is $O(n)$. Assign one processor to each segment s to calculate its depth d in T, and the leaf nodes whose strips contain its endpoints. If its right endpoint is in leaf ℓ whose depth exceeds d, then s is in $L(\ell, d)$, and the information can be attached to the right endpoint; similarly for its left endpoint.

A single processor per leaf of T can then output all the nonempty $L(\ell, d)$ which can be attached to the copy of ℓ in $T(d)$. Then one processor per leaf of each $T(d)$ can attach a complete subtree to this leaf so that all items in $L(\ell, d)$ are attached to distinct leaves of $T(d)$. The overall size is still $O(n)$. Then the sets $L(v, d)$ can be calculated for all v in $T(d)$ whose depths exceed d, using cascading merge,[17] based on Proposition 5.5 (i).

(2) Now all sets $L(v, d)$ (and, symmetrically, $R(v, d)$) have been computed. For each non-root node v let $d_v = \text{depth}(\text{parent}(v))$. Find, for each non-root node v and each item in $L(v, d_v)$, the closest items from among all $L(v, d)$, $d < d_v$. This can be done in $O(\log(n))$ parallel time with n processors overall, by suitable application of a parallel merging algorithm [29]. The idea is to merge a copy of $L(v, d_v)$ with each relevant set $L(v, d)$, and then choose the closest items from the $2d_v$ possible candidates. The overall problem size is still $O(n)$.

(3) Using this ranking information, apply cascading merge, using part (iii) of Proposition 5.5, to calculate the sets $L(v)$ and $R(v)$. There is an interesting *aliasing* technique used here. Rather than explicitly deleting an element of $L(v, \text{depth}(w))$ from $L(v)$, it is mapped to the closest item following it in $L(v)\backslash L(v, \text{depth}(w))$. Thus a record for a deleted segment adopts the description of another segment as an alias.[18] This allows the cascading merge to go ahead without further adjustment. After the cascading merge has finished, the aliased records can be purged from the lists $L(v)$ by compression via parallel prefix (7.1).

(4) The sets $C(v)$ can be constructed by deleting $L(v, d_v)$ from a copy of $L(v)$ by compression via parallel prefix.

6.   Voronoi diagram in the plane.

6.1 We are given a finite set S of points in the plane, and as before we shall refer to them as 'sites.' Given a site p, the set of points in the plane which are as close to p as to any other site in S is called the *Voronoi cell* for p. Given another site q, the set of points as close to p as to q is a closed half-plane bounded by the perpendicular bisector of the line-segment pq. Hence the Voronoi cell is the intersection of $n - 1$ closed half-planes, where $n = |S|$, and therefore it is a closed convex set with polygonal boundary. The *Voronoi diagram* $\text{Vor}(S)$ is the union of these cell boundaries. The diagram may also be defined more directly: a point x belongs to $\text{Vor}(S)$ if there exists a disc centered at x, touching two or more sites in S, and containing no site in its interior. The radius of this disc is the distance of x to the closest sites in S, which we call the *sites adjacent to x*.

Clearly the diagram is a plane embedded graph whose edges are straight line-segments (possibly unbounded[19]), and whose faces are the Voronoi cells. Being planar, its descriptive complexity is linear in n (Proposition 3.2).

For a general survey of this structure and its variants, see [6].

---

[17]$T(d)$ doesn't conform to the simplified cascading merge (7.7) described in the appendix.

[18]One cannot simply leave a copy of the item without aliasing, because it would lead to attempted comparisons between incomparable line-segments.

[19]So technically it is a generalised form of planar graph.

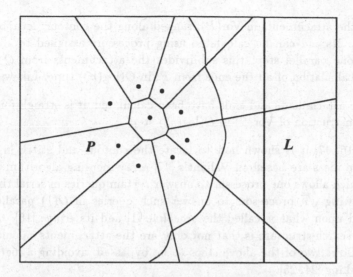

Figure 15. Vor(P), (P, L)-beachline and -fringe.

As with the convex hull problem, we make certain nondegeneracy assumptions. In addition to the assumptions stated in 2.1, we require that no four sites be concyclic. As an immediate consequence every vertex of Vor(S), being adjacent to at least three sites, is adjacent to exactly three, and has exactly three incident edges.

6.2 The techniques described here are based on the serial algorithm due to Hoey and Shamos [41]. The set of sites are initially sorted by x-coordinate; then the algorithm proceeds recursively:

- Partition the input set S of n sites into two sets P and Q of size $n/2$ by a vertical straight line L;

- compute the Voronoi diagrams of the left and right half-sets recursively, with $n/2$ processors assigned to each;

- compute the *contour*, the locus of all points in the plane equidistant from P and Q;

- *stitch* the diagrams together along the contour.

It was shown in [1] how to compute the contour and stitch the diagrams together in $\log(n)$ parallel time. This is done, roughly speaking, as follows.

- Each edge of Vor(P) can meet the contour at most twice; for simplicity let us assume at most once: using suitable data structures and one processor per edge of Vor(P), those edges which meet the contour are identified. Let us call such edges 'attachments,' and the points where they meet the contour (necessarily vertices of Vor(S)) their 'ends.' This takes $O(\log(n))$ parallel time. Likewise for Vor(Q).

- The edges of Vor(P) meeting the contour can be ranked and sorted according to the y-coordinates of their ends, without knowing these coordinates, in $O(\log(n))$ parallel steps.

- Among all the attachments in Vor(P), ranked along the contour, let e be the median attachment. Its end can be calculated using processors assigned to all attachments from Q in one parallel step; this subdivides the attachments from Q and permits, ultimately, calculation of all the ends from P, in $O(\log(n))$ time. Likewise for Q.

- Once all the attachments and ends have been calculated, it is straightforward to complete the construction of Vor(S) in $O(\log(n))$ steps.

In the papers [16, 17] it is shown how to locate the contour and stitch in $O(\log\log(n))$ parallel time. The ideas are based on Valiant's [47] array-merging algorithm. In place of a data-structure which allows one processor to answer certain queries in serial time $O(\log(n))$, we have one allowing $\sqrt{n}$ processors to answer such queries in $O(1)$ parallel time. The structure is based upon what is called the *beachline* [1] and its *fringe* [16]. An important advantage of the search-structure is that not only are the attachments calculated, but also the ends. This allows two of the above steps to be bypassed, avoiding a $\log(n)$ bottleneck caused by list-ranking [24, 25].

Another feature of the approach of [16, 17] is that a processor surplus is allowed. Thus, we can have a beachline B (which is a sorted array) 'covered' by a sorted array A of processors, the same entry in B being serviced perhaps by a block of several processors in A. This presents no essential difficulty (even for CREW machines) since all but the leftmost processor in each block of A can remain idle. This avoids the need for full compression of data between levels of recursion, for which the natural method is parallel prefix (7.1), another potential bottleneck [36].

Although the fringe structure is a fairly complex structure of complete binary trees, it is closely bound up with the structure of the beachline to which it is attached. Indeed, construction of the beachlines, which would be trivial in the serial case,[20] is a significant part of the algorithm. In [16], the beachlines were all precomputed independently in $O(\log(n))$ parallel steps using fractional cascading [5]. This allowed the algorithm to proceed without difficulty but was processor-inefficient, since the precomputed structures were built using $n\log(n)$ processors.

The improved method in [17] uses n processors to precompute not the beachlines but partial information about the beachlines. Specifically, given a set B of k points in the plane, sorted by y-coordinate, a *ruling* for B is a set of $O(k/\log(n))$ horizontal lines such that each horizontal strip contains $O(\log(n))$ points in B. With this information precomputed, the beachlines can be calculated between recursive levels in time $O(\log\log(n))$.

6.3 Beachline and Fringe. The (P, L)-beachline is the set of all points x in the plane whose distance to the closest site in P equals its distance from L. The (P, L)-fringe is that part of Vor(P) to the right of the beachline. The (Q, L)-beachline and fringe are defined in the same way: the two beachlines are piecewise parabolic segments, all with the same directrix L, and they are on opposite sides of L. Anything said about the (P, L)-fringe or beachline holds, of course, for the (Q, L)-fringe or beachline, allowance being made for their opposite orientation.

One can show the following facts: (i) The (P, Q)-contour is contained between the two beachlines; (ii) the (P, L)-fringe is a forest, that is, it is an acyclic graph; (iii) each con-

---

[20]The beachline structure is that of the simplest kind of Davenport-Schinzel sequence, which have been studied exhaustively in the serial and parallel settings [4, 10, 11, 45].

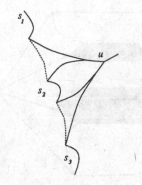

Figure 16. Orientation of fringe tree edges.

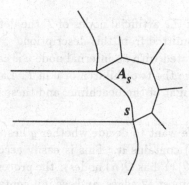

Figure 17. Region A_s owned by segment s.

nected component of the (P, L)-fringe contains exactly one unbounded edge, that edge being associated with two adjacent corners of the convex hull $H(P)$.

6.4 Fringe as search structure.

Each tree in the (P, L)-fringe can be oriented to make it a binary tree: namely, the leaves are ordered by descending y-coordinate along the beachline, and this ordering carries up to the internal nodes. See Figure 16. Following [17] one can introduce artificial nodes to combine all the fringe trees into the structure of a single full binary tree T.

Each beachline cusp is a leaf of T; and each beachline segment (except for the outer two unbounded segments) can be mapped to a unique node v of the tree: it is the lowest common ancestor of its bounding cusps u and w, and these three nodes, u, v, w, come consecutively with respect to the inorder traversal of the tree.

The fringe structure partitions that part of the plane to the right of the (P, L)-beachline into *regions*: each region A_s meets the beachline in a unique segment s (Figure 17), although the same cell of Vor(P) may contribute several regions. It is convenient also to extend these regions to the left of the beachline with infinite horizontal rays extending leftwards from the cusps: this furnishes a partition of the entire plane. To each node v of T is associated a simple region which we call a *tube* R_v: if v is a cusp then $R_v = \emptyset$. Otherwise, let u' and w' be its highest and lowest cusp descendants in T. If v is a voronoi vertex then the tube is the semi-infinite region bounded by edges $u'v$ and vw', and by the infinite rays extending leftwards from u' and w'. It is significant that the edges $u'v$ and vw' are entirely contained

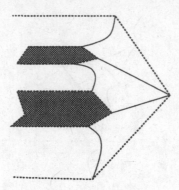

Figure 18. A pocket.

in cells of Vor(P). If v is one of the artificial nodes of T the definition needs to be modified in a simple way which will be omitted from this description.

The basic search region associated with an internal node v is called a T-*pocket*: it is defined as $R_v \backslash R_u \backslash R_w$ where u and w are the two children of v in T. Each pocket intersects at most three regions of Vor(P) to the right of the beachline, and these regions are separated by the line-segments uv and vw.

6.5 Let q be a query point. We want to decide whether q lies to the right of the beachline, and, if so, which cell of Vor(P) contains it. This is easily accomplished with n processors applied to the internal nodes of T (T has $O(n)$ nodes): the processor applied to v inspects the associated pocket, which has at most 12 edges, and see if it contains q. Exactly one processor locates q; it checks if q is to the right of the 3 beachline segments meeting the pocket, and, if so, determines which of the (at most) 3 cells of Vor(P) intersecting the pocket contains q.

We want to accomplish the same effect, following the method of 2.10, using just $\sqrt{n}$ processors. To do this we need to coarsen the partition of the plane, as follows: the beachline is stored, as an alternating sequence of segments and cusps, in an array, and the structure of T is attached to this array (by equating each bounded segment with a unique internal node of T as described above). Let us imagine a sampling of the leaves of T by selecting every $\sqrt{n}$-th array entry, and marking it if it is a cusp, or marking an adjacent cusp if it is a segment. Thus, roughly speaking, every $\sqrt{n}$-th cusp is marked. Define the *span* of an internal node v to be its set of marked descendants, and call a node of T a *splitting node* if *both* its children have nonempty span, and a *bottom node* if its parent but none of its descendants is a splitting node — every bottom node has a unique marked descendant.

The splitting nodes and bottom nodes together carry the structure of a binary tree T' which we call the *skeleton tree*. One defines the parent of a bottom or splitting node (whose span does not include all marked cusps) as its closest splitting-node ancestor. This defines a binary tree: the left child in T' of a splitting node v with left child u is u if it is a bottom node, and otherwise the deepest descendant u'' of u, necessarily a splitting node, which has the same span as u.

The notion of pocket applies as well to the tree T': if v is a node of T', its T'-*pocket* is just the tube R_v if it is a bottom node, or it is $R_v \backslash R_u \backslash R_w$ if it is a splitting node with children u and w in T'.

LEMMA 6.6 (i) *There are $O(\sqrt{n})$ T'-pockets, where n is the number of nodes in T, and* *each pocket contains $O(\sqrt{n})$ nodes of T. Each pocket of T is contained entirely in some pocket of T'. (ii) The structure of T' can be inferred in bounded time with n processors, where n is the number of nodes in T. (iii) Given a point q and $\sqrt{n}$ processors, q can be located in its correct fringe region in bounded time. (iv) Each pocket edge crosses the contour at most once, and the crossing-point can be calculated in bounded time with $\sqrt{n}$ processors.*

Proof (partial). For (i) and (ii), see [17]. For (iii), q is contained in a unique T'-pocket, which can be isolated by assigning one processor to each node of T'; then, reassigning the processors to the nodes within the pocket, q is located to a unique T-pocket, and the calculation is finished as described previously (6.5). (iv) Let e be a pocket edge in the p-cell of Vor(P). If it crossed the contour more than once, then it would cross it at two points, since these would be points on the boundary of the convex p-cell in Vor$(P \cup Q)$. But this would mean it meets the beachline to the right of the contour, which is impossible. To verify if a pocket edge crosses the contour, locate its endpoints[21] in the correct regions of the (Q, L)-fringe; if they are on opposite sides of the contour then the edge crosses the contour, and the crossing point can be identified in a 2-step process similar to (iii).   □

6.7 Contour identified by progressive refinement. Consider a fixed T'-pocket on the (P, L)-fringe. Allocating $\sqrt{n}$ processors, the points where its edges (at most 6) cross the contour are determined in constant parallel time. The pocket intersects the contour, therefore, in at most 3 connected intervals, called *contour fragments*. Using n processors overall, (the endpoints of) all T'-pocket fragments can be determined in bounded time: likewise for the (Q, L)-fringe.

The same idea can be repeated: now create a finer sample by marking every $\sqrt[4]{n}$-th beachline cusp, producing a skeleton tree with smaller pockets. With careful organisation, n processors can determine where the contour crosses the smaller pocket boundaries, thus refining the information about the contour. A fact crucial to the success of this method is that the contour is monotonic in the y-direction: although the contour crossing points are not sorted, this fact enables the different fragments to be processed in a coherent way, and, indeed, the process of subdividing fragments is modelled closely on Valiant's parallel merging algorithm [47]. Continuing the procedure $\log\log(n)$ times, the pockets are reduced to T-pockets, and all contour vertices have been determined.

6.8 Building the diagram. Granted that fringe structures are available at each stage, we have seen how to identify the contour vertices (and the non-contour edges meeting these vertices). It turns out not difficult to build up the diagram structure (with the structure of a plane graph, given appropriate pointer linkages) during the recursive construction. Details are given in [17].

6.9 Preprocessing: rulings for the beachlines. In order to support the recursive construction, it is necessary to have some information about the beachline available. Two beachlines can easily be merged in logarithmic parallel time, but that would be too slow for our purposes, and it is not obvious how to merge two beachlines faster than that. Also the beachline can be built in $O(\log(n))$ time with n processors, using a cascading merge technique [16], which, if the sites are not pre-sorted, is optimal; but it is not easy to exploit sorting information to speed up the process, and if we require all beachlines in advance, their

---

[21]The calculation is different, but simple, for an unbounded edge.

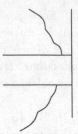

Figure 19. Ends of the (U, L)-beachline.

total size is $O(n \log(n))$, and one would expect to need an equivalent number of processors to do this.

In [17] these difficulties are avoided by producing in advance not all the beachlines but rather approximate information about the beachlines, namely, 'rulings' for the beachlines: a ruling for the (P, L)-beachline is a sequence of $O(|P|/\log(n))$ horizontal lines such that between adjacent lines there are $O(\log(n))$ beachline cusps. These enable the recursive stages of the Voronoi diagram algorithm to be implemented in parallel time $O(\log\log(n))$ on a CRCW machine. The beachline ruling for P can be constructed in time $O(\log(n) \log\log(n))$ using $k/\log(n)$ processors, where $k = |P|$. This allows all rulings to be precomputed in the given time using n processors. The model of computation is an arbitrary CRCW PRAM (1.1) [8].

6.10 The construction is outlined as follows. The data supplied are the sites P sorted both horizontally and vertically (the horizontal order is intrinsic to the algorithm; the vertical order can be supplied as a by-product of mergesort applied to all the sites together).

Write m for $k/\log_2(n)$. Let the plane be divided into m horizontal strips, $\log_2(n)$ sites in each strip, and let T be an interval tree for these horizontal strips (5.1). For each node v of T there is a horizontal 'slab' Π_v. (If v is a leaf node then we speak of its 'strip' rather than slab.) An important fact is that the contribution from within the slab to the beachline outside the slab is quite regular, though the pattern within the slab can be quite irregular. Given a horizontal slab Π, let $U = P \cap \Pi$: the *ends* of the (U, L) beachline are the two unbounded parts outside the slab.

PROPOSITION 6.11 [17] (i) *Each site in U owns at most one beachline segment in each end.* (ii) *The vertical ordering of cusps in each end (downward in the upper end, upward in the lower end) matches the horizontal ordering of sites in U.* (iii) *Given P horizontally sorted, the two ends can be calculated in linear time with one processor, or, optimally, in time $O(\log(n))$ with $|U|/\log_2(n)$ processors.*   □

The rather easy proof of this lemma is omitted from here. From parts (i) and (ii), each end corresponds to a subsequence of P. The linear-time and optimal parallel constructions are based on the principles used in (2.4, 2.11). It is not proposed to construct all the ends for all the slabs Π_v, since their total cardinality is roughly $k \log(k)$. What is needed is to *restrict* the range of the ends of the slab, to where it is relevant in forming the beachline outside the slab.

Consider a fixed strip Π_ℓ where ℓ is a leaf of T. Let A consist of all siblings of right-ancestors of ℓ, and let B consist of all siblings of all left-ancestors of ℓ (see 7.1). Within the strip, the

(P, L) beachline is formed from (i) the (U, L)-beachline; (ii) the lower ends of all slabs in A; and (iii) the upper ends of all slabs in B. If v is a node from A, then it is a left-sibling and ℓ is a descendant of its sibling; if v is from B then the reverse holds. Therefore for any left-sibling v, only that part of its lower end contained in its sibling's slab is relevant. The following lemma is stated without proof. The CRCW machine is used because minimisation is applied during the procedure [17].

LEMMA 6.12 *For all left- (resp. right-) sibling nodes v, the points where their lower (resp, upper) ends cross their siblings' slab boundaries can be calculated in time $O(\log(n) \log \log(n))$ on a CRCW machine with m processors.*   □

What is more relevant is that the *sites* whose segments cross the slab boundaries are identified. This enables the restricted ends of all slabs to be calculated in logarithmic parallel time with m processors: the overall size of the restricted ends is $O(k)$ rather than $k \log k$.

Now, returning to our leaf-node ℓ and the sets A and B: it is possible to identify and count the cusps contributed from slabs in A and B to the strip Π_ℓ and sort them in parallel using $O(\log \log(n))$ rounds of Valiant's merging algorithm [29, 47]. (Cusps are classified according to the strips they occur in by integer sorting [8].)

Finally the ruling is easily defined: choose a horizontal line through the strip boundaries and through every $\log_2(n)$-th cusp within each strip. The crucial point is that, while some cusps which could have been contributed from above or below the strip may have been missed, there were $O(\log(n))$ missing cusps, and therefore between two lines of the ruling there are $O(\log(n))$ cusps of the (P, L)-beachline.

7.   Appendix: miscellaneous techniques.

This appendix contains some parallel techniques which have proved useful in computational geometry (and elsewhere). See [32] for related methods and other details.

7.1 Parallel prefix [31, 30]. This is a parallel algorithm solving the following problem: given a list $x_1, \ldots x_k$ of numbers stored in an array, to compute all prefix sums $\sum_1^r x_i$, $1 \le r \le k$. It can be solved with in $O(\log(k))$ time with $k/\log(k)$ processors, essentially by covering the array with a balanced tree structure and calculating partial sums of subintervals covered by nodes of the tree [30].

More specifically, the method is as follows. Let the array of numbers x_i be separated into $k/\log_2(k)$ blocks of length $\log_2(k)$ each. The available processors first calculate the partial sums in each group. Then there is a balanced binary tree T placed over the array, whose leaves cover the groups of length $\log(k)$. A node u in the tree covers a certain union of adjacent groups of the array: the sum of all these group totals can be computed iteratively with the processors available, working level-by-level, up through the tree; when a node v is reached, the group totals for its two children u and w are available, and their sum is the group total for v.

If v is the r-th leaf node in this tree, let A be the set of left-siblings of those ancestors w of v which are right-children. The set A covers the first $r - 1$ groups of list elements, and the total of all these groups can be calculated by a single processor assigned to v (see Figure 20). Once this information is available, it is straightforward for the processors to output all k prefix sums in time $O(\log(k))$. This parallel runtime is more-or-less optimal [36].

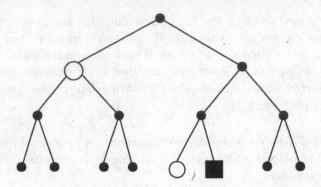

Figure 20. Prefix sum. Processor at square leaf adds numbers stored at empty circles.

7.2 List ranking. Let F be a linked list of n nodes. If $p = p_0, p_1, \ldots, p_r = q$ is a contiguous subsequence of nodes from the list, then r is the distance from p to q in the list: let us write $d(p, q)$ for this distance r. The *rank* of a node p in the list is $n - d(p, \ell)$ where ℓ is the last element of the list. If processors are assigned to every node in the list, the values of $d(\ldots, \ell)$ can be calculated in time $O(\log(n))$ as follows: there are about $\log_2(n)$ phases; in the $r + 1$-st phase all nodes at distance less than 2^r from the end of the list know their distance from the end, and the other nodes know the node at distance 2^r ahead of them in the list.

The synchronised $r + 1$-st step is as follows. Initially, the 'link' associated with each node p points to the next element of the list, and the last node ℓ in the list has its $d(\ell, \ell) = 0$, and the global variable R, containing 2^r, is initially 1.

```
FOR all nodes p in parallel DO
    IF p^.link is not null THEN BEGIN
       q:= p^.link;
       IF q^.link is null THEN
          p^.d := R + q^.d;
                    (* d is distance to the end of list *)
       ELSE
          p^.link := q^.link;
    END;
R:= 2*R;
```

This is a *pointer doubling* technique. The parallel time $O(\log(n))$ achieved by this algorithm is optimal for exclusive-write machines, as can be shown by a reduction from parity [25]. Of course, the work done, that is, (parallel time)×(processor count), is not optimal: a single processor traversing the list can calculate all ranks in time $O(n)$. Optimal parallel list-ranking algorithms exist [19, 3], but the problem is not easy.

In [18][22] a very nearly optimal algorithm, achieving $O(\log(n) \log^*(n))$ time with $O(n)$ work, is described ($\log^*(n)$, the iterated logarithm, is defined in (7.5) below). A component in this algorithm is the calculation of a *2-ruling set* for the list in time $O(\log^*(n))$. It is described

---

[22]The parallel machine involved is assumed capable of an unusual unit-cost operation as was stated in (1.1), since the bitstring representation of list-node addresses is exploited. Arguments justifying this model are presented in [18].

below (recall its use in extracting a large independent set from a bounded-degree graph (3.6)).

7.3 r-Ruling Set. Let F be a linked list. For convenience, the last element of F is linked to the first, making a circular linked list. Define an r-ruling of F to be a subset U of the nodes of F satisfying the following two conditions:

(i) No two nodes in U are adjacent; (ii) For each node p in F there is a node q in U where q is reached from p by a sequence of $\leq r$ links.

7.4 It will be assumed that the nodes are indexed from 0 to $n-1$, so the pointer-links can be assumed stored in an integer array (array entries represented in binary). $\text{SERIAL}_0[i] = i$ for all indexes i (the rationale for this definition will soon be clear).

For a fixed node indexed i let j index the next node in the list. The *D-bit* (for 'discriminating bit') for i is the rightmost (lowest-order) bit where the binary representations of i and j differ. The index r, between 0 and $\log_2(n)$, of i's D-bit, is denoted $\text{SERIAL}_1[i]$.

Let us call the index of a node's D-bit the 'height' of a node. If we visualise the nodes placed sequentially along the x-axis, with their heights plotted as a graph, then the heights wander up and down between 0 and $\log_2(n)$. A node is a *local minimum (maximum)* if it is no higher (no lower) than the two adjacent nodes[23]. It is an isolated local minimum (maximum) if it is lower (higher) than both adjacent nodes.

Note the following *alternating property*: if p, q are adjacent nodes at the same height, then their D-bits have opposite parity. This follows directly from the definitions.

7.5 A $\log_2(n)$-ruling set for F is computed using one processor per node, in two parallel steps:

(i) All local minima which are either isolated or whose D-bit is 1, are marked.

(ii) Then all local maxima which are either isolated or whose D-bit is 1 and which are not adjacent to marked nodes, are marked.

Let p be an unmarked node and consider the sequence of r nodes following p, where $r = \log_2(n)$. At least two nodes in this sequence have the same height. Taking a closest pair of nodes in the sequence having the same height, if they are not adjacent, then there is an isolated minimum or maximum between them, and if they are adjacent, then at least one has parity 1 and each is a minimum or a maximum. Hence at least one node in the sequence is marked, so the marking defines a $\log_2(n)$-ruling.

Now, having chosen such a ruling set, let all nodes in the ruling set be removed from the list, thereby breaking the list into many lists of length $< \log_2(n)$. Let F_1 be the resulting structure. Observe that if F had two adjacent nodes at the same height, then one of them was marked. Hence in F_1, no two successive nodes have the same height.

Therefore, we can repeat the procedure. Now, attached to each node p is the quantity $\text{SERIAL}_1(p)$, which is simply the index of its D-bit, and no two adjacent nodes agree on this quantity. Thus, we can redefine the D-bit of a node p which has a successor q in F_1 to be the lowest-order bit where $\text{SERIAL}_1(p) \neq \text{SERIAL}_1(q)$, and let $\text{SERIAL}_2(p)$ be the index of the D-bit. Note that $\text{SERIAL}_2(p)$, where defined, is in the range $0 \ldots \log \log(n)$. Essentially the same technique as in (7.5) can be applied to achieve a $\log \log(n)$ ruling; we ignore the small complication that the lists are not circular. The observations are as for the first iteration. Thus, after k iterations, a ruling set of size $(\log_2(\log_2 \ldots \log_2(n) \ldots))$ ($\log_2$ composed k times)

---

[23]The last node is adjacent to the first.

is achieved. In particular, with $k = \log^*(n)$, a 2-ruling set has been achieved.[24]

7.6 Forward chaining. The *forward chaining problem* is as follows. Suppose that A is an array of bits with one processor attached to each array entry. Suppose that each 1-bit is intended to mark the beginning of a subinterval of the array, so we will call the 1-bits the 'interval leaders.' The problem is to inform all the other processors of the correct interval leaders. When the interval leaders are linked together, it is possible to do this in $O(\log \log(n))$ time (CREW), as follows [17]. Consider A partitioned into $\sqrt{n}$ blocks of size $\sqrt{n}$.

We have the 'marked' processors, the interval leaders, and we have the processors at the beginning of each block, the block leaders. Each interval leader ascertains if there are any block leaders in its interval. If so, it informs the *leftmost* such block leader. All the processors in this block can consult the block leader, and then the interval leader, to ascertain the range of block leaders in the interval, and hence to inform them all (there are enough processors to do this).

Having done this, all processors in the same interval as their block leader or the leader of the next block can identify themselves by consulting the block leader. The only processors which remain in doubt are those in intervals which do not contain a block leader, and these can be informed by a recursive application of the same method within the blocks.   □

The same effect can be achieved by a subtle variation of these methods, on a CRCW machine, without using links between marked nodes. The technique is an important component of the fast integer sorting algorithm described in [8]. We state the result:

If A is an array of processors, some of them marked, in a CRCW machine, then in time $O(\log \log(n))$ the processors can attach to each array entry $A[j]$ indices i and k to the closest marked entries (if they exist) left and right of j.   □

7.7   Cascading merge. Valiant's [47] $O(\log \log(n))$ parallel merging technique allows the classical 'merge-sort' algorithm to be executed in parallel time $O(\log(n) \log \log(n))$ using $n/\log \log(n)$ processors [29]. The cost of merging two arrays of size n can be shown to require parallel time $\Omega(\log \log(n))$ with n processors [9]. Cascading is a method of taking successively larger samples of a set to circumvent this lower bound: results from one round of a computation can be used to speed up the next round. Its first application is an optimal parallel sorting algorithm [15]. It turns out useful in computational geometry [5].

In cascading merge and fractional cascading, all sets are comprised of items from a fixed universe of sortable items, they are maintained as sorted lists, and $B \cup C$ indicates the result of *merging* lists B and C. A *c-sample* of a sorted list $a_1, a_2 \ldots$ is the subsequence $a_c, a_{2c}, \ldots$ consisting of every c-th element. If a and b are items, $a \le b$, then $[a, b]$ is the closed interval $\{x \colon a \le x \le b\}$ and $(a, b]$ is the half-open interval $\{x \colon a < x \le b\}$.

A list A' is a *c-cover* for a list A if for any two adjacent items a, b in A', $A \cap (a, b]$ contains at most c items. Here default values $a = -\infty$ and $b = \infty$ are allowed to capture the 'ends' of the list A.

The following is a simplified version of a parallel sorting problem considered in [5]. Suppose that n is a power of 2, and T is a fully-balanced binary tree with n leaves, of height $\log_2(n)$. At each leaf of T is stored an item. The problem is to calculate for each internal node v of T the sorted list $U(v)$ of all items stored at leaf descendants of v. There are n processors available.

---

[24] This may be taken as a definition of $\log^*(n)$.

The strategy is broadly as follows. At each node v larger and larger subsets of $U(v)$ accumulate. Subsets available at one stage help calculating that at the next stage. Specifically, there are $3\log_2(n)$ stages.

At stage s, those nodes whose heights h are such that s is between $2h+1$ and $3h$ are *active*. $U_s(v)$ is the partial list stored at v at stage s. While v is active, and until the last 2 stages it is active, $U'_{s+1}(v)$ is the 4-sample of $U_s(v)$. In the last 3 stages, v has become *full*, that is, $U_s(v) = U(v)$. In the last 2 stages $U'_{s+1}(v)$ are chosen as a 2-sample, then the entire list $U_s(v)$, respectively. The merge step is as follows:

$$U_{s+1}(v) := U'_{s+1}(u) \cup U'_{s+1}(w),$$

where u and w are the children of v. An important key to its effective implementation is contained in the following lemma.

LEMMA 7.8 *Let $[a, b]$ intersect $k+1$ items in $U'_s(v)$. Then it intersects at most $8k+c$ in $U_s(v)$ for all $k, s \geq 1$, where c is bounded.*

Proof (Partial). By induction. We show the inductive step in certain cases. Let $[a, b]$ intersect $k+1$ items in $U'_{s+1}(v)$, which is a 4-sample of $U_s(v)$. Then $[a, b]$ intersects at most $4k+7$ items in $U_s(v)$. Writing $U_s(v)$ as $U'_s(u) \cup U'_s(w)$ where these are 4-samples attached to the children of v, suppose that $[a, b]$ intersects each part in $i+1$ and $j+1$ items, respectively. (We cover the case where both i and j are nonnegative.) By definition, $i+j \leq 4k+5$. By induction, $[a, b]$ intersects at most $8i+c$ items in $U_s(u)$ and $8j+c$ in $U_s(w)$. Hence at most $2i+c/4$ in $U'_{s+1}(u)$, similarly for the other side. Adding together, the size of $[a, b] \cap U_{s+1}(v)$ is at most $2(i+j)+c/2$. Substituting $4k+5$ for $i+j$, we get a bound of $8k+10+c/2$, so the result holds with $c = 20$.   □

The more complete proof in [5] shows the bound with $c = 8$, on the assumption that a and b actually belong to $U'_s(v) \cup \{\pm\infty\}$; the infinite values are defaults to cover the first and last subintervals of $U_s(v)$. Continuing the discussion in the lemma with $c = 8$, $[a, b]$ intersects at most $2k+2$ items in $U'_{s+1}(v)$. With $k = 1$, we are speaking of an adjacent pair, and conclude

COROLLARY 7.9 $U'_s(v)$ *is a 4-cover for* $U'_{s+1}(v)$ *for all stages s and nodes v.*   □

The following lemma, from [15], explains the steps in the merge-sort procedure. If A is a list and x is an item, then the *rank* of x in A is the number of items $< x$ in A. B is *ranked* in A if the ranks in A of the items from B have been tabulated. B and C are *cross-ranked* if B is ranked in C and C in B. For simplicity, let us assume that all items have distinct sort-keys.

LEMMA 7.10 *Suppose that A_s, A'_{s+1}, B'_s, B'_{s+1}, C'_s, C'_{s+1} are sorted lists where $A'_{s+1} \subset A_s$, B'_s and C'_s c-cover B'_{s+1} and C'_{s+1} respectively (c a constant), $A_s = B'_s \cup C'_s$, B'_s and C'_s are ranked in B'_{s+1} and C'_{s+1} respectively, and B'_s and C'_s are cross-ranked. Then the following can be computed in bounded time with a linear number of processors: (i) the cross-ranking between B'_{s+1} and C'_{s+1}; (ii) the merged list $A_{s+1} = B'_{s+1} \cup C'_{s+1}$; and (iii) the ranking of A'_{s+1} in A_{s+1}.*

Proof (sketch: The scenario is summarised in Figure 21.) (i) Consider two adjacent items x, y in B'_s. Say they are *close* if their ranks in C'_s differ by at most 1. In this case, their rank

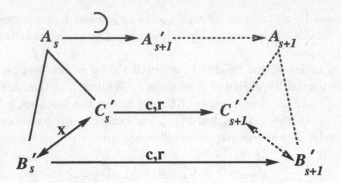

Figure 21. Relationships in Lemma 7.10

difference in C'_{s+1} is also bounded, and all (at most c) items z between them in B'_{s+1} are ranked in the same bounded interval of C'_{s+1}, which enables a single processor to calculate the rank in C'_{s+1} of all such items z in bounded time.

Furthermore, when the processor discovers two adjacent items z whose ranks differ in C'_{s+1}, it can enter the ranks (in B'_{s+1}) for the items in C'_{s+1} which separate them.

Reciprocally, the same can be done for close pairs of items in C'_s. From this, the full cross-ranking is available.

(ii) From the cross-ranking calculated in (i) the sorted list A_{s+1} has implicitly been produced: item of index i in B'_{s+1} with rank j in C'_{s+1} has index $i + j$ in A_{s+1}.

(iii) An easy by-product of this calculation supplies all items x in B'_s with their ranks in A_{s+1}; similarly for C'_s; hence for A_s and therefore A'_{s+1}.   □

References

[1] A. Aggarwal, B. Chazelle, L. Guibas, C. Ó Dúnlaing, and C. Yap (1985,1988). Parallel Computational Geometry. *Proc. 26th IEEE Symp. on Foundations of Computer Science*, Portland, Oregon, 468–477; also, *Algorithmica* **3**(3), 293–328.

[2] M. Ajtai, J. Komlós, and E. Szemerédi (1983). An $O(\log(n))$ sorting network. *Combinatorica* **3**, 1–19.

[3] R. Anderson and G. Miller (1988). Deterministic parallel list ranking. *Proc. 3rd Aegean Workshop on Computing*, 81–90.

[4] M. Atallah (1985). Some dynamic computational geometry problems. *Computers and Mathematics with Applications* **11**, 1171–1181.

[5] M. Atallah, R. Cole, and M. Goodrich (1989). Cascading divide-and-conquer: a technique For designing parallel algorithms. *SIAM J. on Comput.*, **18**(3), 499–532.

[6] F. Aurenhammer (1991). Voronoi diagrams – a survey of a fundamental geometric data structure. *ACM Computing Surveys* **23**, 345–404.

[7] M. Ben-Or (1983). Lower bounds for algebraic computation trees. *Proc. 15th ACM Symp. on the Theory of Computing*, 80–86.

[8] P. Bhatt, K. Diks, T. Hagerup, V. Prasad, T. Radzik, and S. Saxena (1991). Improved deterministic parallel integer sorting. *Information and Computation* **94**, 29–47.

[9] A. Borodin and J. Hopcroft (1985). Routing, merging, and sorting on parallel models of computation. *Journal of Computer and System Sciences* **30**, 130–145.

[10] L. Boxer and R. Miller (1989). Parallel dynamic computational geometry. *J. New Gener. Comput. Syst.* **2:3**, 227–246

[11] L. Boxer and R. Miller (1989). Dynamic computational geometry on Meshes and Hypercubes. *Journal of Supercomputing* **3**, 161–191.

[12] R. Brent (1974). The parallel evaluation of general arithmetic expressions. *J. ACM* **21**, 201–206.

[13] B. Chazelle (1991). A linear-time algorithm for triangulating a simple polygon. *Discrete and Computational Geometry* **6**, 485–524.

[14] A. Chow. Parallel Algorithms for Geometric Problems. Ph.D. thesis, Comp. Sci. Dept., Univ. of Illinois, 1980.

[15] R. Cole (1988). Parallel merge sort. *SIAM Journal on computing* **17**, 770–785.

[16] R. Cole, M. Goodrich, and C. Ó Dúnlaing (1990). Merging free trees in parallel for efficient Voronoi diagram construction. *Proc. 17th ICALP, Springer LNCS 443*, 432–445.

[17] R. Cole, M. Goodrich, and C. Ó Dúnlaing (1992). A nearly optimal deterministic parallel Voronoi diagram algorithm. Manuscript, in preparation.

[18] R. Cole and U. Vishkin (1986). Deterministic coin tossing with applications to optimal list ranking. *Information and Control*, 1(1986), 32–53. (See also *Proc. 18th ACM STOC, 1986*, 206–219.)

[19] R. Cole and U. Vishkin (1988). Approximate parallel scheduling. Part I: The basic technique with applications to optimal parallel list ranking in logarithmic time. *SIAM Journal on Computing* **17** 128-142.

[20] S. Cook, C. Dwork, and R. Reischuk (1986). Upper and lower time bounds for parallel random access machines without simultaneous writes. *SIAM Journal on Computing* **15:1**, 87–97.

[21] N. Dadoun and D. Kirkpatrick (1989). Parallel construction of subdivision hierarchies. *Journal of Computer and System Sciences* **39**, 153–165.

[22] N. Dadoun and D. Kirkpatrick (1990). Parallel algorithms for fractional and maximal independent sets in planar graphs. *Discrete Applied Mathematics* **27**, 69–83.

[23] D. Dobkin and D. Kirkpatrick (1983). Fast detection of polyhedral intersections. *Theoretical Computer Science* **27**, 241–253.

[24] F. Fich (1992). The complexity of computation on the parallel random access machine. in *Synthesis of Parallel Algorithms*, ed. J. Reif, Morgan Kaufmann, to appear.

[25] F. Fich and V. Ramachandran (1990). Lower bounds for parallel computation on linked structures. *Proc. Annual ACM Symp. on Parallel Algorithms and Architectures, Crete*, 109–116.

[26] S. Fortune (1987). A sweep-line algorithm for Voronoi diagrams. *Algorithmica*, **2**(2), 153–174.

[27] L. Guibas and J. Stolfi (1985). Primitives for the manipulation of general subdivisions and the computation of Voronoi diagrams. *ACM Transactions on Graphics* **4**, 74–123.

[28] D. Kirkpatrick (1983). Optimal search in planar subdivisions. *SIAM Journal on Computing* **12**, 28–35.

[29] C. Kruskal (1983). Searching, merging, and sorting in parallel computation. *IEEE Transactions on Computers*, **C-32**(10), 942–946.

[30] C. Kruskal, L. Rudolph, and M. Snir (1985). The power of parallel prefix. *1985 Int. Conf. on Parallel Processing*, 180–185.

[31] R. Ladner and M. Fischer (1980). Parallel prefix computation. *J. ACM*, October 1980, 831–838.

[32] E. Mayr (1990). Basic parallel algorithms in Graph Theory. In *Computational Graph Theory*, ed. Tinhofer, Mayr, Noltmeier, Syslo, and Albrecht, Springer Computing Supplementum 7.

[33] K. Mehlhorn (1984). *Data Structures and Algorithms* (3 volumes). EATCS mongraphs on Theoretical Computer Science, Springer.

[34] C. Ó Dúnlaing (1988). A tight lower bound for the complexity of path-planning for a disc. *Information Processing Letters* **28**, 165–170.

[35] M. Overmars and J. van Leeuwen (1981). Maintenance of configurations in the plane. *J. Computer and System Sciences* **23**, 166–204.

[36] Ian Parberry (1985). On the time required to sum n semigroup elements on a parallel machine with simultaneous writes. *Theoretical Computer Science* **51**, 239–247.

[37] F. Preparata and S. Hong (1977). Convex hulls of finite sets of points in two and three dimensions. *Comm. ACM* **20** 87–93.

[38] J. Reif and S. Sen (1992). Optimal parallel algorithms for 3-dimensional convex hulls and related problems. *SIAM Journal on Computing* **21:3**.

[39] C. Rüb (1988). Line segment intersection reporting in parallel. Technical Report, University of Saarbrücken; to appear, *Algorithmica*.

[40] M. Shamos (1978). Computational geometry. Ph.D. Thesis, Yale University, New Haven, Connecticut.

[41] M. Shamos and D. Hoey (1975). Closest-Point Problems. *Proc. 15th IEEE Symp. on Foundations of Computer Science*, 151–162.

[42] S. Smale (1987). On the topology of algorithms, 1. *Journal of Complexity* **3**, 81–89.

[43] M. Snir (1985). On parallel searching. *SIAM J. on Computing* **14**, 688–707.

[44] I. Stojmenović (1986, 1991). Private communication.

[45] E. Szemerédi (1974). On a problem by Davenport and Schinzel. *Acta Arithmetica* **25**, 213–224.

[46] R. Tarjan (1983). *Data structures and network algorithms.* CBMS-NSF regional conference series in applied mathematics, no. 44.

[47] L. Valiant (1975). Parallelism in comparison problems, *SIAM Journal on Computing,* **4:3**, 348–355.

[48] H. Wagener (1985). Optimally parallel algorithms for convex hull determination. Manuscript, Technical University of Berlin.

Chapter 6

Parallel Algorithms for String Pattern Matching

Costas S. Iliopoulos *

Abstract

This article presents fundamental parallel algorithms for string pattern-matching problems that naturally arise in many areas of science and information processing. Moreover consideration is given to parallel algorithms for related string problems.

1. Introduction

Strings of symbols are used extensively to code information, computer input and output, editing, transfer over noisy channels (error correction codes), compiling, storing data etc. It is often necessary to compare two or more sequences, or strings, or vectors etc and measure the extent to which they differ. String pattern matching occurs naturally as part of text editing, term rewriting, data compression and lexical analysis; many text editors and programming languages include string matching facilities.

In Molecular Biology, macromolecules of protein and nucleic acids can be considered as long sequences of subunits linked together sequentially in a chain. String matching and string analysis are central in the study of molecular sequences. These sequences are typically from tens to thousands of units long (ribonucleic acid) or millions of units long (deoxybonucleic acid). For example ARV-2DNA, the human retrovirus associated with AIDS disease, consist of about 10000 symbols.

Extensive use of string analysis can be found in gas chromatography (the components - as a function of time - of a gaseous mixture separated in experiments form a sequence - called chromatogram), bird songs (as means of communication, regional dialects of the same species, comparison of parent/children song), geology (stratigraphic sequences obtained from drill holes), dendrochronology (dating based on tree rings).

The string pattern matching problem is defined as follows: Given two strings x (the text) and y (the pattern) of n and m symbols respectively, check whether y occurs in x. One of the difficulties of this problem is its dependency on whether the alphabet which the symbols are chosen from, is of a fixed size or an unbounded (general) one. Variations of the problem include the computation of one or all occurrences of y, allowing/disallowing preprocessing of the pattern, the amount of the additional space used and also the way of computing the matches/mismatches (on-line/off-line algorithms).

---

*The author wishes to acknowledge the support of the UK Science and Engineering Research Council grant number GR/F 00898 during the course of this research. The author was also partially supported by NATO grant CRG 900293, a Royal Society grant JD/MDO and by the ESPRIT BRA grants for ALCOM II and ASMICS.

The Karp-Miller-Rosenberg algorithm [15] was one of the first efficient (almost linear) sequential algorithms for finding repeated patterns and string matching. It was soon superseded by more efficient algorithms , for instance the Knuth-Morris-Pratt [17] worst-case linear time algorithm, Boyer-Moore [4] (expected linear time), Crochemore-Perrin [5], Galil-Seiferas [11] etc. The Karp-Miller-Rosenberg algorithm is parallelizable ([1, 6]) and thus the basis of a first-attempt parallel algorithm; most of the remaining algorithms seem to be inherently sequential.

Galil's [10] algorithm was the first optimal parallel algorithm for sting matching; it requires $O(\log n)$ time and $O(n/\log n)$ processors for a fixed alphabet but it is not optimal over general alphabets requiring (the same time) $O(n)$ processors. Vishkin [23] introduced a new criterion - the *witness* idea- and a new optimal algorithm ($O(\log n)$ time) for general alphabets. Breslauer and Galil [2] adapted parallel techniques of *computing the maximum of a set* ([8] and [20]) in Vishkin's algorithm lowering the time bound to $O(\log \log n)$ using $O(n/\log \log n)$ processors. In [3] was shown that the $O(\log \log n)$ time was the best possible within a constant factor, matching the lower bound of the string matching problem, when preprocessing was not allowed. Furthermore Vishkin in [24] and Galil in [9] gave optimal algorithms of $O(\log^* n)$ and $O(1)$ respectively for the string matching problem, both requiring the same time $O(\log^2 m/\log \log m)$ for pattern preprocessing. All the algorithms above are based on the CRCW PRAM model of computation.

The chapter is organized as follows. Basic definitions and properties are outlined in the next section. Next we introduce some naive algorithms and then we study the suffix trees (a Karp-Rosenberg-Miller parallelization). In section 5, Galil's optimal algorithm for pattern matching over fixed alphabets is presented. In section 6, Vishkin extension of Galil's algorithms for general alphabets together with the Breslauer-Galil improvement of its time complexity is examined. In section 7 we give a brief account of algorithms that allow pattern preprocessing and in section 8 we consider lower bounds on the time complexity of pattern matching and open problems.

2.   Preliminaries

Let Σ be a finite alphabet, and let Σ^* be the set of strings generated under concatenation over Σ (including the empty one). Let $x = a_1...a_n$, with $a_i \in \Sigma$. The length n of the string x will be denoted by $|x|$. The i-th symbol of x can be denoted as x_i. A substring $z = a_j...a_{j+k}$ of x can be written as $x[j...j + k]$. We reserve the symbol \$ as a special symbol not included in the alphabet Σ.

A string u is a *period* of a string w, if w is a prefix u^k, for some k, or equivalently w is a prefix of uw. We call the shortest period of a string w *the period* of w. We say that w has period size p, if the length of the period of w is p. If w is at least twice longer than its period, we say that w is periodic.

Lemma 2.1 *Periodicity Lemma [18] If w has two periods of size p and q and $w \geq p + q$, then w has a period of size gcd (p, q).*   □

Lemma 2.2 *If u occurs at positions j and $j + \delta$ ($\delta \leq |u|/2$) of a string z, then*

(i) u is periodic with a period length δ

(ii) u occurs at $j + p$, where p is the period size.   □

Let $v = u^k u'$, $k > 1$, u the period of v, u' a proper prefix of v and $p = |u|$. Moreover let $L = lp$ with $l \in \{k, k+1\}$. Then the following lemmas hold:

Lemma 2.3 *If v occurs at j and $j + qp$, with $q \leq k$ then $u^{k+q}u'$ occurs at j.* $\square$

Lemma 2.4 *The string v occurs at j, $j + p$ and $j + L$ iff $u^{k+l}u'$ occurs at j.* $\square$

Lemma 2.5 *If v occurs at j and $j + \delta$, $\delta \leq |v| - p$, then δ is a multiple of p.* $\square$

Lemma 2.6 *If v occurs at r and s with $r > s$ and v does not occur at $r + p$ and $s + p$, then*

$$r - s > |v| - p.$$ $\square$

For proofs of the above lemmas the reader is referred to [10].

3. Trivial parallel algorithms for string matching

One can construct an CRCW PRAM algorithm that solves the pattern matching problem in constant time using $O(nm)$ processors. We assign with m processors - say p_{ij}, $1 \leq j \leq m$ - to every position i, $1 \leq i \leq n$ of the text x. Moreover processor p_{ij} is associated with the j-th symbol of the pattern y; processor p_{ij} marks the position $BB(i)$ (BB is initialized to unmarked) if and only if $x_{i+j-1} \neq y_j$. The unmarked positions of BB yield the starting positions of all the occurrences of the pattern in the text.

It is not difficult to design a CREW algorithm that solves the string-matching problem in $O(\log m)$ time using $O(nm/\log m)$ processors. We assign $r := \lceil m/s \rceil$ (with $s = \lceil \log m \rceil$) processors - say $p_{i1}, ..., p_{ir}$ - to each position $1 \leq i \leq n - m + 1$ of the text x. Processor p_{ij} has the responsibility to check whether, the s-length substring of x that starts at position i, matches the j-th block (s symbols long) of the pattern y; i.e. p_{ij} checks sequentially:

$$x_{i+js+1}....x_{i+(j+1)s} \neq y_{js+1}....y_{(j+1)s}$$

If a mismatch is found, then processor p_{ij} turns $switch(i,j)$ (initialized to 0) to 1. Then we re-allocate the processors to compute

$$switch(i) = \sum_{j=1}^{r} switch(i,j), \quad 1 \leq i \leq n \quad (Boolean\ AND)$$

using the standard optimal parallel addition algorithm. The pattern starts at i-th position of the text if only if $switch(i) = 0$.

4. Suffix trees

A parallel algorithm for constructing the suffix tree - a data structure with many string applications (including string matching) was presented in [1]; part of the construction is reminiscent of an early approach to subquadratic pattern matching [15]. The algorithm presented here is optimal, requiring $O(\log n)$ time and n processors. We define T_x, he *suffix tree* of the string x as follows (see Figure 1):

(i) The suffix tree is a rooted tree with labelled edges.

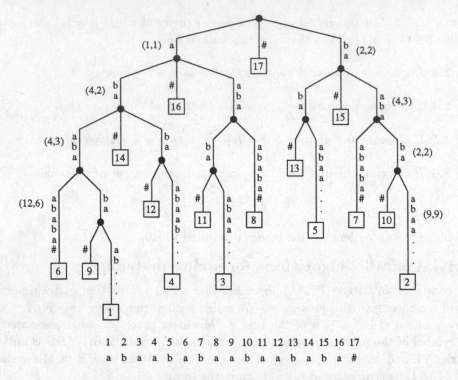

Figure 1. The suffix tree T_x with $x = abaababaabaaba$

(ii) Each edge is labelled with an identifier $ID(i, l)$, which represents the substring of x that starts at position i and has length l (this is a prefix of the suffix of x that starts at position i).

(iii) No two sibling edges have the same (non empty) prefix.

(iv) Each leaf is labelled with $[i]$, where i is a distinct position of x.

(v) The concatenation of the strings represented by the labels of the edges on a path from the root to leaf $[i]$ equals the suffix of x starting at position i.

The construction of suffix tree is done in two stages:First we construct an approximate version of the suffix tree of x - the skeleton tree and then we refine the skeleton tree, where necessary.

4.1.   The Skeleton Suffix Tree

The skeleton tree S_x (see Figure 2) is defined as follows:

(i) It is a rooted tree.

(ii) Each edge is labelled with an identifier $ID(i, 2^l)$, where l is the length of the path from the root to the node (nearest to the root) attached to the edge; the identifier represents the substring of x that starts a position i and has length 2^l.

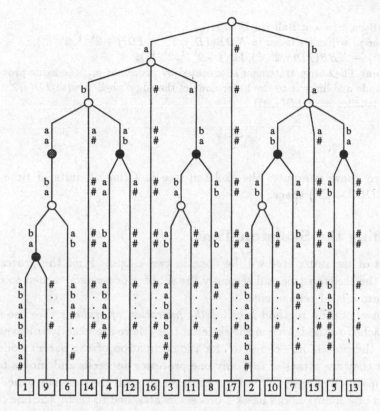

Figure 2. The skeleton suffix tree S_x with $x = abaababaabaaba$

(iii) No two sibling edges may have identical labels.

(iv) Each leaf is labelled with $[i]$, where i is a distinct position of the string x.

(v) The concatenation of the strings represented by the labels of the edges on a path from the root to leaf $[i]$ is the suffix of x starting at position i.

Processors handling suffixes match identical prefixes via their ID's which are uniquely defined by virtue of the write conflict rule of CRCW PRAMs. Furthermore the ID of a long string is initially combined from the pair of ID's of the two substrings created when we split the string in half; then using the concurrent write conflict mechanism, we replace the pair with a new unique value. (This is done in order to keep the length of the ID's constant.) The method is outlined as follows:

begin
Let BB be an $1 \times |\Sigma|$ Bulletin Board;
Processor p_j is associated with the j-th symbol of x;
forall j **pardo**
    processor p_j writes its index in $BB(x_j)$;
    $ID(j,1) \leftarrow BB(x_j)$;
    comment The creation of each ID is followed by the creation of a new node linked with the root as a child; the linking edge is labelled with the ID.
    for $k = 1$ **to** $\lceil \log n \rceil$ **do**

Let NBB be an $n \times n$ Bulletin Board.

processor p_j writes its index in $NBB(ID(j, 2^{k-1}), ID(j + 2^{k-1}, 2^{k-1}))$;

$ID(j, 2^k) \leftarrow NBB(ID(j, 2^{k-1}), ID(j + 2^{k-1}, 2^{k-1}))$;

comment The above statement is executed by processor p_{ij}; the same processor creates a new node and links it to the lower node of the edge labelled with $ID(j, 2^{k-1})$. The new edge is labelled with $ID(j, 2^k)$.

    od

  odpar

end   □

The procedure above computes the skeleton tree in $O(\log n)$ units of time using $O(n)$ processors and $O(n^2 + |\Sigma|)$ space.

4.2.   Refining the Skeleton Tree.

The refinement of the suffix tree will be done in two stages. First the processors will be distributed on the skeleton tree and secondly the set of processors attached to children of a node will perform a local refinement.

The processor allocation method is called *the migration of orphans*. We use n processors all initially attached to the leaves of the skeleton tree (there are exactly n leaves as many as suffixes). Now the processors "compete" for the occupation of the parent node (of the set of siblings that they are attached to); only one processor succeeds and moves to the parent node. The competition is repeated in the next level up until the root is reached. The result is that every set of k sibling nodes has k-1 processors attached to them; the one child without a processor is called an *orphan*. The $k - 1$ processors attached to the children of every node "elect" one processor (by concurrently writing in the same common memory location) to simulate the orphan node.

The skeleton tree needs to be refined in every node (except the root) that has two or more children; the labels of their outgoing edges are different but they might have a common prefix . The refinement at each node can be done independently; therefore we are presenting the refinement of just a portion of the skeleton tree consisting of a node and its children, i.e., *a local refinement*. The local refinement is done by means of binary search. Let n_z be a node of the skeleton tree and let $c_j, 1 \leq j \leq m$ be the children of n_z. Moreover let $z_j, 1 \leq j \leq m$ be the set of strings (all of the same length) that are represented by the labels of the edges $(n_z, c_j), 1 \leq j \leq m$. All but one (say c_m - orphan) node have one processor attached to them -a processor allocation produced by the migration of the orphans. Let $ID(q_j, |z_j|)$ be the already computed labels of these edges. The pseudo-code below outlines the method for refining this part of the tree.

  begin

  forall $1 \leq j \leq m - 1$ **pardo**

$l_j \leftarrow |z_j|$; $n_j \leftarrow n_z$;

comment Node n_j is used as a reference point of the processor allocation.

Processor p_j writes its index in $AUX(n_j)$;

Processor $p_{AUX(n_j)}$ is elected to simulate the "missing" processor p_m;

comment In the sequel we assume the existence of p_m for exposition purposes.

  while $l_j \neq 1$ **do**

$l_j \leftarrow l_j/2$;

processor p_j writes j in $BB(ID(q_j, l_j), n_j)$;

comment This competition establishes whether there are any common prefixes of size l_j among the strings represented by the labels.

if p_j is a "loser" ($j \neq BB(ID(q_j, l_j), n_j)$) **then**

Processor p_j writes j in $AUX(BB(ID(q_j, l_j), n_j))$;

$l_j \leftarrow AUX(BB(ID(q_j, l_j), n_j))$;

comment Processor p_j is a "loser"; that implies that at least another edge has a label with the same ID; p_{l_j} is elected as the leader of all the losers with the same ID. Note that several leaders may be elected concurrently.

$n_j \leftarrow n_{AUX(BB(ID(q_j, l_j), n_j))}$;

$q_j \leftarrow q_j + l_j$;

comment Processor p_{l_j} creates a new node n_j as the child of $n_{BB(ID(q_j, l_j), n_j)}$ and labels the edge between n_j and c_j with $ID(q_j, l_j)$. All edges with the same common prefix of length l_j have been replaced by one edge connecting the original parent node (of c_j) and the new node n_j (named by the leader of the "losers").

Processor p_{l_j} creates a new node c'_{l_j} as child of n_j;

Processor p_{l_j} labels the new edge with $ID(q_j, l_j)$;

else

comment Processor p_j is a "winner" if it succeeds in writing its index in BB.

$c_j \leftarrow n_{AUX(BB(ID(q_j, l_j), n_j))}$;

Processor p_j labels the edge (n_j, c_j) with $ID(q_j, l_j)$;

comment Now all "winners" have the task of refining all the labels of the edges descending from n_j. The node c_m is an orphan node.

od

odpar

end   □

Using the migration of orphans we can allocate the processors on the skeleton tree in $O(\log n)$ units of time and by using the procedure above we can refine it in $O(\log n)$ units of time using n processors.

Some applications of the parallel construction of the suffix tree in the design of efficient parallel algorithms are as follows:

(i) *On-line string matching.* Suppose that the text x is given in advance (for preprocessing). Answer as fast as possible (on-line) queries of the form: "Does the string y occur in x?" . This type of query takes $O(\log m)$ time, using $m/\log m$ processors; it makes use of the skeleton tree S_x - its preprocessing time is not included in the complexity of the query (see [1] for details). On-line queries can be extended to obtain additional information about y: What is the number of occurrences of y in x? In the case of more than one occurrence, what is the starting position of the first (or last or all) occurrence(s) of y in x? What is the longest prefix of y which occurs in x?

(ii) *Finding the longest repeated substring in a string.* Given a string x, find the longest substring which occurs in x more than once. This type of query can be executed in $O(\log n)$ units of time using n processors (see [1] for details).

(iii) *Approximate string matching.* Suppose a string x, a pattern y, and a parameter k are given. Find all occurrences of y in x with at most k differences. Using the serial algorithm presented in [19] (see also [21]) one can solve the approximate string matching problem in $O(k + \log n)$ time using $n + m$ processors.

Further applications of the parallel construction of the suffix tree can be found in the canonization of circular strings (see [14]), Lyndon factorization (see [7]) and superprimitivity testing (see [13]).

5.   Galil's algorithm for pattern matching

Galil's algorithm makes use of the doubling technique; it tests longer and longer (at least doubling the length) prefixes of the pattern y and finds its occurrences not only in the text x but also in the pattern y. The latter is done in order to discover periodicities. The algorithm requires $O(\log m)$ time on a CRCW PRAM using $O(n/\log m)$ processors; the input alphabet is of a fixed size.

Let $z = y\$x$, where y is the pattern and x is the text. Here we assume that $|y| = m$ and $|x| = 2m$, but the general case follows easily, for details see [10]. The output will be a Boolean array MATCH[i] , $1 \le i \le 3m + 1$; the pattern y occurs at position i if and only if MATCH[i] = 1. We shall use $3m + 1$ processors, each assigned to z_i and MATCH[i].

The initialization: Processor p_j tests whether $z_j z_{j+1} = x_1 x_2$, if it matches, then MATCH[j] becomes equal to one , otherwise $MATCH[j] := 0$. Also processor p_j (in the case of MATCH[j] = 1) assigns BLOCK[j] to j (note that the block-size of the next stage is one).

Consider the algorithm after the end of the i-th stage. The prefix $y^{(i)} := y[1, ..., 2^i]$ of the pattern has all of its occurrences in z computed. In fact the array MATCH is equal to 1 in position j if and only if $y^{(i)}$ occurs at j. The string z is divided into blocks (set of consecutive positions) of size 2^{i-2} as well as the array MATCH. Each block of MATCH contains exactly one 1 and the common-memory stored list BLOCK points to these 1's.

Now we proceed to the $i + 1$-stage. We double the size of the blocks and we consider the first block of MATCH, the sub-array MATCH[j], $1 \le j \le 2^{i-1}$; this block is indicative of the periodicity of $y^{(i)}$. If MATCH($p + 1$) = 1 for some $p \le 2^i$, then it follows from Lemma 2.2 (and the fact that MATCH[1] = 1 always) that $y^{(i)}$ is periodic with period size p. The processor p_{p+1}, recognizes this case by knowing that it belongs to the second block and that MATCH[$p + 1$] = 1; then p_{p+1} posts the period size p in the common memory location $PERIODSIZE$ (initialized to 0). The algorithm splits into two cases the *periodic* and the *regular* one.

5.1.   The Regular Case

This is the case that the first block of MATCH has only one 1 (the occurrence of $y^{(i)}$ at position 1). We now check the rest of the blocks. If a block has more than two ones, in positions j and $j + \delta$, then MATCH[j] becomes 0. The reason is that an occurrence $y^{(i)}$ is not the beginning of an occurrence of $y^{(i+1)}$; if $y^{(i+1)}$ occurred in j, then $y^{(i)}$ occurs in position δ ($y^{(i+1)}$ occurs at position 1 and $y^{(i)}$ is a substring of $y^{(i+1)}$ starting at position δ) and thus the first block has two 1's - a contradiction. This step can be executed as follows: all processors assigned to a MATCH which equals to 1 and their assigned position is in an "odd numbered BLOCK" check whether the next BLOCK points to an one or not (Note that the list BLOCK refers to blocks of size 2^{i-2}- it will be updated to the new size blocks in a few steps).

Now we check whether $y^{(i+1)}$ occurs at the unique position of a block- say j - that MATCH is one. This check can be done in one step by the processors assigned to position j to $j + 2^i$. If a processor found a mismatch, then it changes MATCH[j] to 0. This step is executed in parallel for each block.

5.2.   The Periodic Case

In this case we choose $y^{(i+1)}$ to be longer that 2^{i+1} in order to be able to use the criterion provided by lemma 2.4; in fact $y^{(i+1)}$ is a prefix of y with $|y^{(i+1)}| = 2^i + L$, where $L = \lceil 2^i/p \rceil$. We first check whether $y^{(i+1)}$ has the same period with $y^{(i)}$. This can be checked by processor p_1 in two units of time; the period remains the same if and only if MATCH$[p+1] = 1$ and MATCH$[L+1] = 1$ (it follows from lemma 2.4). This test splits the problem into two further cases : the one that the *period continues* and the one that the *period changes*

The period continues : Next we find all the occurrences of $y^{(i+1)}$ in z using the criterion of lemma 2.4. Processor p_j with MATCH$[j] = 1$, checks MATCH$[j+p]$ and MATCH$[j+L]$, if one of them is 0, then it changes MATCH$[j]$ to 0; $y^{(i+1)}$ cannot occur at j (lemma 2.4). Since $y^{(i+1)}$ is still periodic, we continue at the beginning of the periodic case.

The period changes: The period change was detected by the fact that either MATCH$[p+1] = 0$ or MATCH$[L+1] = 0$. In the case of MATCH$[p+1] = 0$, we have that the period of $y^{(i+1)}$ is not p and thus p_1 changes PERIODSIZE to 0 in the common memory. Otherwise if MATCH$[L+1] = 0$, then, again the period of $y^{(i+1)}$ is not the same with that of y^i. ¿From lemmas 2.5 and 2.6 follows that there is exactly one occurrence of $y^{(i+1)}$ at position j, with $1 \leq j \leq L+1-p$ such that $y^{(i+1)}$ does not occur at $j+p$. This occurrence can be found by each processor p_j, for all $1 \leq j \leq L+1-p$, testing whether MATCH$[j]$ and MATCH$[j+p]$ are both equal to one. The unique processor p_j that succeed posts the new period PERIODSIZE$=j-1$ in the common memory.

Next every processor p_r with MATCH$[r] = 1$, checks whether MATCH$[r+j-1] = 1$ and MATCH$[r+j-1+p] = 0$. If the check fails p_r assigns MATCH$[r]$ to 0; this follows from the fact that $y^{(i+1)}$ cannot occur at r, since $y^{(i)}$ does not occur at $r+j-1+p$. From lemma 2.6 follows that each block of MATCH exactly one 1 and thus we now update the common memory list BLOCK; If MATCH$[j] = 1$ and j belongs to the q-th block, then processor p_j writes BLOCK$[q] = j-1$). Further more we check whether $y^{(i+1)}$ occurs at the unique position of a block- say j - that MATCH is one. This check in one step by the processors assigned to position j to $j+2^i$. If one processor finds a mismatch then it changes MATCH$[j]$ to 0. This step is executed in parallel for each block. We continue with the next stage.

The algorithm as it is described above requires $O(\log m)$ units of time and $O(n)$ processors, but using the *Four Russians trick* and packing blocks of length $\log m$ into single words, the number of processors required can be reduced to $O(n/\log m)$ (see [10] for details). The packing is possible because the alphabet is of fixed size. Also the CRCW PRAM used, is the weakest one; it resolves a write conflict by allowing several processors to concurrently write 1 (no other values allowed) in the same memory location.

6.   Vishkin's and Breslauer-Galil Algorithms

Vishkin in [23] (see also [12]) introduced a new important criterion, which enable us to eliminate many possible occurrences of the pattern in $O(1)$ time; this novel technique used in conjunction with the periodicity criteria introduced by Galil in [10] lead into an $O(\log m)$ optimal algorithm for string pattern matching over general alphabets. Vishkin precomputes some information about the pattern y, which is called WITNESS(1...m) and uses it in the analysis of the text.

Let v and u be the a prefix and a period of the pattern y respectively. If $|u|$ does not divide v and $|v| \leq max\{|u|, |y| - |u|\}$, then y is not a prefix of vy and thus we can find an index k such that

$$y_k \neq y_{k-|v|}$$

We call this k, a witness to the mismatch of y and vy and we define

$$WITNESS(|v| + 1) = k$$

Having computed the WITNESS array one can eliminate "close" possible occurrences by implementing a *duel*. Suppose that we suspect that the pattern may start at position i and j of the text, where $0 \leq j - i \leq |u|$. We have computed $WITNESS(j - i + 1) = r$, which implies that

$$y_r \neq y_{r-j+i}$$

which in turn implies that at most one of the i and j can be the starting point of an occurrence of the pattern, since either $y_r = x_{r-i-1}$ or $y_{r-j+i} = x_{r+i-1}$. Therefore one can eliminate one of two occurrences in constant time.

Breslauer and Galil in [2] combined the WITNESS idea with the observation that the computation of the duels is very similar to computing the maximum. They adapted the Shiloach-Vishkin ([20]) and Fich et al ([8]) algorithms for finding the maximum to the duel computation, and this resulted to an $O(\log \log n)$ optimal algorithm. Next we give a brief description of the Breslauer-Galil algorithm.

Assume that we have already computed $WITNESS(2...r)$ for $r = min\{p, \lceil m/2 \rceil\}$ (for this preprocessing see [2]). Recall that p and m are the lengths of the period u and of the pattern y respectively. We will first partition the text into blocks of length r, and in each block eliminate all but one possible occurrences of y; this will be done with the help of WITNESS. Next, in the non-periodic case we verify all surviving occurrences and in the periodic case we have to further divide the text into blocks of length $n = 2m - p$ and then verify the occurrences using additional criteria(see below).

Elimination: Initially every position in the text is a possible starting point of an occurrence of the pattern. We partition the text into n/r blocks of r consecutive symbols each. Each block is partitioned into sub-blocks of size $r^{1/2}$ and repeat recursively. The desired result would be that each block of size $r^{1/2}$ has at most one possible occurrence or $r^{1/2}$ possible occurrences altogether. The basic step of the recursion is described next.

We have $r^{1/2}$ possible occurrences, thus we can form r pairs of these. We assign a processor to each pair of positions and we perform a duel (using WITNESS) in $O(1)$ time; we are using r processors. Since in every pair at least one position loses, at the end we are left with at most one possible occurrence in the block. The processor performing the duel marks an array SURVIVOR $[j]$ (initialized to unmarked), if j is a loosing (the duel) position. Then we assign r processors to SURVIVOR. The one unmarked position is reported by the processor attached to it. Now we have n/r blocks with at most one possible occurrence of the pattern in each.

The recursion above requires $O(r)$ processors and $O(\log \log r)$ time per block. We can optimize the above recursive procedure by first partitioning the text into blocks of size $O(\log \log r)$ and then sequentially eliminate all but one of the suspect occurrences (using WITNESS). Then proceed with the recursive procedure having $O(r/\log \log r)$ suspect occurrences and equal amount of processors. The overall time will be $O(\log \log r)$ using $O(n/\log \log r)$ processors.

The non-periodic case In this case we verify all possible occurrences using the m processors at each candidate position. This can be done in $O(1)$ time using $mn/r = O(n)$ processors.

The periodic case Let $y = u^k u'$, u' a prefix of u. In this case, we first verify at each possible occurrence only of the prefix uu of the pattern y (u is the period of y). This can be done in $O(1)$ time using n processors. Note that we cannot verify all suspect occurrences of y, because $r = p$ can be very small and the number of suspect occurrences can be very large due to the periodicity (we will need mn/p processors).

Next we divide the text into (overlapping) blocks of length $n = 2m - p$. In each block we assign m processors and compute the following:

(i) The largest position i of an occurrence of uu in the block such that $i \leq m - p$ and uu does not occur in position $i - p$. The reason is that y cannot occur in the block at any $i > m - p$ (not enough symbols) and any occurrence of uu prior to i cannot be an occurrence of y (lemma 2.6). We will call i, the *prime suspect* position. This can be done easily in constant time on an m processor PRIORITY CRCW-PRAM, which in this case can be simulated by a weak CRCW PRAM using the [8] algorithm (see also [2]).

(ii) We verify a possible occurrence of u' at position $i + kp$, using $|u'| < p$ processors and $O(1)$ unit of time (see also [2]).

(iii) We check that occurrences of uu follow i at positions $i + lp$, $1 \leq l < k - 1$ (in $O(1)$ time and $O(m/p)$ processors). This check together with the verification of u' confirms an occurrence of y (see also [2]).

7. Pattern Matching and Preprocessing

The time complexity of the string matching problem is constituted by the pattern analysis (in [23] the computation of the array WITNESS) and the text analysis. There are several instances where the pattern is available in advance and there is no pressure to process it fast, while it is important to process the text immediately. Ukkonen in [22] gave a (worst-case) exponential time algorithm for pattern processing but its text analysis (approximate string matching) was linear. In both [2] and [23], both text and pattern analysis required the same amount of time asymptotically.

In [24] Vishkin introduced an $O(\log^* n)$ optimal algorithm for text analysis while using an $O(\log^2 m/\log \log m)$ optimal algorithm for preprocessing the pattern (Note $\log^* n$ is the smallest k such that $\log^{(k)} \leq 2$, where $\log^{(1)} = \log n$ and $\log^{(i+1)} n = \log(\log^{(i)} n)$. Recently, Galil, in [9], reduced the time required for text analysis to $O(1)$ (preserving optimality). Both algorithms where inspired from the Karp-Rabin ([16]) randomised algorithm and in particular their use of *signatures*.

The main idea of Vishkin's (and used by Galil in [9]) algorithm was use of *deterministic sampling* of the pattern; there exists a set Δ of at most $\log m$ positions in the pattern such that if we compare them with positions $i + \Delta$ of the text for all i in any block of size $m/2$, we can get a match for at most one i. The existence of such a set implies that a new constant time algorithm for string matching: Compare Δ for each possible start (using $n \log m$ processors), thus having at most one survivor per block (of size $m/2$) which can be verified by m processors. The reader is referred to [24] and [9] for a detailed description of methods.

8.   Lower bounds on string-pattern matching and open problems

Let y be a pattern string of length m and x be the text of length $2m$ both over a general (unbounded alphabet Σ. It was shown in [3] that the parallel complexity of computing occurrences of y in the text x using p processors over a general alphabet is as follows:

$$\Omega(1) \quad if \quad p \geq m^2$$

$$\Omega(\log \log_{2p/m} m) \quad if \quad m \leq p \leq m^2$$

$$\Omega(\log \log m) \quad if \quad m/\log \log m \leq p \leq m$$

$$\Omega(m/p) \quad if \quad p \leq m/\log \log m$$

The first lower bound is matched by the constant-time $O(m^2)$ naive parallel algorithm presented in section 3. All the latter three bounds can be matched by the worst-case time complexity of the Breslauer-Galil algorithm [3] ; the first bound by slightly modifying the algorithm, the second lower bound is matched directly, and the last one can also be matched by slowing down the algorithm.

There are still several open questions (see [9]):

(i) What are the lower bounds of string-pattern matching over fixed alphabets? Can we speed up the string-matching over fixed alphabets? The lower bounds given above do not hold over fixed alphabets.

(ii) What are the lower bounds of the string matching problems for long text strings? The above lower bounds do not hold, if the text string is much longer that the pattern.

(iii) Can we reduce the preprocessing time of Galil's constant time algorithm to $O(\log \log n)$ in order to match the given lower bound?

(iv) What is the parallel complexity of the string pattern matching on CREW and EREW PRAM? The only algorithm known for these models are obtained by slowing down the CRCW PRAM algorithms.

References

[1] Apostolico, A., Iliopoulos, C., Landau, G., Schieber, B., Vishkin, U., Parallel construction of the suffix tree with applications, Algorithmica 3, 347-365 (1988)

[2] Breslauer, D., Galil, Z., An optimal $O(\log \log n)$ parallel string matching algorithm, *SIAM J. Comp.* 19:6, 1051-1058 (1990)

[3] Breslauer, D., Galil, Z.,A lower Bound for Parallel String Matching, *Proc. 23rd ACM Symp. on Theory of Computation,* 439-443 (1991)

[4] Boyer, R.S., and Moore, J.S, A fast string searching algorithm, CACM 20, 762-772 (1977)

[5] Crochemore, M., and Perrin, D., Two way pattern matching *Journal of ACM* to appear

[6] Crochemore, M., and Rytter, W., Usefulness of the Karp-Miller-Rosenberg algorithm in parallel computations on strings and arrays, manuscript (1990)

[7] Daykin, J.W., Iliopoulos, C.S., Smyth, W.F., Parallel algorithms for factorizing strings over an ordered alphabet, submitted.

[8] Fich, F.E., Radge, R.L., and Wigderson, A., Relations between concurrent-write models of parallel computation, *Proc 3rd ACM Symp. on Principles of Distributed Computing*, 179-189 (1984)

[9] Galil, Z., Hunting Lions in the Desert Optimally or a Constant time Optimal parallel string -matching algorithm, manuscript, (August 1991)

[10] Galil, Z., Optimal parallel algorithms for string matching, *Information and Control*, 67, 144-157 (1985)

[11] Galil, Z., Seiferas, J., Time-space optimal string matching, *J. Comput. Syst. Sci.* 26, 280-294 (1983)

[12] Gibbons, A.M., Rytter, W., Efficient parallel Algorithms, *Cambridge Univ. Press* (1988)

[13] Iliopoulos, C.S., Moore, D.W.G. , Algorithms for the general superprimitivity problem, (on preparation) (1991)

[14] Iliopoulos, C.S., Smyth, W.F. Optimal algorithms for computing the Canonical form of a circular string, to appear Theor. Comp.Sc. (1991).

[15] Karp, R., Miller, R., Rosenberg, A., Rapid identification of repeated patterns in strings arrays and trees, *STOC 4* 125-136 (1972)

[16] Karp, R., Rabin, M., Efficient pattern matching algorithms, *IBM Journal of Res and Dev. 31* 249-260 (1987)

[17] Knuth, D.E., Morris, J.H. and Pratt, V.R., Fast pattern matching in strings, *SIAM J. Comput.* 6, 322-350 (1977)

[18] Lyndon, R.C., Schutzenberger, M.P., The equation $a^M = b^N c^P$ in a free group, *Michigan Math. J.* 9, 289-298 (1962).

[19] Landau G.M. and Vishkin U., Introducing efficient parallelism into approximate string matching, *Proc. of the 18-th STOC*, pp 314-325 (1986)

[20] Shiloach,Y. and Vishkin, U., Finding the maximum, merging and sorting in a parallel computation model, *J. Algorithms* 2 88-102 (1981)

[21] Schieber, B., and Vishkin, U., Parallel computation of lowest common ancestor in trees, TR-63/87, Tel Aviv University, (1987)

[22] Ukkonen, E., Finding approximate patterns in strings, *J.Algorithms* 6 , 132-137 (1985)

[23] Vishkin, U., Optimal pattern matching in string, *Information and Control* 67, 91-113 (1985)

[24] Vishkin, U., Deterministic sampling- A new technique for fast pattern matching, *Proc 22nd ACM Symp. on Theory of Computation* 1990, 170-179 (1990)

Chapter 7

Design of Parallel Matrix Algorithms

D. J. Evans

Abstract

In this chapter a variety of topics concerned with the efficient design of matrix algorithms for parallel computers are discussed. Initially, the basic issues in developing matrix algorithms in block form as opposed to point form are outlined and these are then applied to the block tridiagonal matrices that occur frequently in Finite Element analyses. Then a new algorithm is developed in explicit form suitable for parallel implementation.

Further, a class of parallel direct and iterative methods for matrix equations is outlined, i.e. the Quandrant Interlock (Q.I.) or Butterfly method for point form and which can be easily extended to block form by the recently introduced BLAS3 subroutine software library which is illustrated by an example i.e. Block LU matrix factorisation.

Finally an extension of the well known odd/even algorithm for solving special forms of tridiagonal equations which occur in ordinary and partial differential equations is given. By developing recurrence relations with a larger stride it is shown that a more efficient Strides Reduction algorithm can be developed. The Stride of 3 Reduction algorithm as presented is thus the fastest method developed so far for this problem.

1. Direct Methods with Block Matrices

The development of direct algorithms for solving sparse matrix problems in point form is well known. What factors are likely to be important when we consider the linear matrix equation in block form for parallel computers?

The classical procedure for solving,

$$Ax = b; A := [a_{ik}], A \in \mathbb{R}^{n \times n}, x, b \in \mathbb{R}^n, \tag{1}$$

falls into three main steps:

- triangularization of A

- backward substitution

- iterative refinement of accuracy

The decomposition of A yields,

$$A := PLUQ, \tag{2}$$

where P and Q are permutation matrices, L is a lower and U is an upper triangular matrix of the following form:

$$
L := \begin{bmatrix} 1 & & & & \\ & \ddots & & 0 & \\ & & \ddots & & \\ & 1_{ik} & & \ddots & \\ & & & & 1 \end{bmatrix}, U := \begin{bmatrix} u_{11} & & & & \\ & \ddots & & u_{ik} & \\ & & \ddots & & \\ & 0 & & \ddots & \\ & & & & u_{nn} \end{bmatrix}.
$$

The solution of (1) is obtained by the following easily solvable subsystems:

$$
\begin{aligned}
Px^{(1)} &= b, \\
Lx^{(2)} &= x^{(1)}, \\
Ux^{(3)} &= x^{(2)}.
\end{aligned}
\tag{3}
$$

Equation (1) includes $(n-1)$ elimination steps.

Now if A is sparse, the permutation matrices are chosen such that L and U are sparse too. For the reason of finite storage only nonzero elements are stored so that data structures used need to be considered carefully. In order to preserve sparseness in the Guass decomposition monitoring of stability is of course necessary.

Another way of solving (1) is by partitioning into block matrices. For this reason the following system of linear equations is considered:

$$
A = b; A := [a_{ik}], A \in \mathbb{R}^{n \times n}, x, b \in \mathbb{R}^n,
\tag{4}
$$

where A is symmetric, positive definite and has a banded structure.

Now the system (4) is partitioned into block matrices $A_{ik} \neq 0$ of the following form:

$$
\begin{bmatrix}
A_{11} & A_{21}^T & & & \\
A_{21} & A_{22} & A_{32}^T & & 0 \\
& A_{32} & A_{33} & A_{43}^T & \\
& & \ddots & \ddots & \ddots \\
0 & & & \ddots & \ddots \\
& & & & A_{mm}
\end{bmatrix}
\cdot
\begin{bmatrix} x_1 \\ x_2 \\ x_3 \\ \vdots \\ \vdots \\ x_m \end{bmatrix}
=
\begin{bmatrix} b_1 \\ b_1 \\ b_3 \\ \vdots \\ \vdots \\ b_m \end{bmatrix}.
\tag{5}
$$

Then A is a tridiagonal block matrix with block matrices $A_{ik} \in \mathbb{R}^{r \times r}$ and partial vectors $x_i, b_i \in \mathbb{R}^r, i = 1, 2, \ldots, m$. Since A is positive definite and symmetric $(A = A^T)$ the diagonal block matrices A_{ii} are symmetric too, i.e. $A_{ii} = A_{ii}^T$ and A_{ii} is positive definite.

So for the 1st block system,

$$
A_{11}x_1 + A_{21}^T x_2 = b_1,
$$

follows. According to the assumption, A_{11}^{-1} exists and hence,

$$
x_1 + C_{21}^T x_2 = d_1,
\tag{6}
$$

where,

$$
C_{21}^T := A_{11}^{-1} A_{21}^T \text{ and } d_1 := A_{11}^{-1} b_1.
$$

By using (6) x_1 is eliminated from the 2nd block system and consequently,

$$\hat{A}_{22}x_2 + \hat{A}_{32}^T x_3 = \hat{b}_2, \tag{7}$$

where,

$$\hat{A}_{22} := A_{22} - A_{21}C_{21}^T, \hat{b}_2 := b_2 - A_{21}d_1.$$

At this point C_{21}^T, $\hat{A}_{22}$, d_1, $\hat{b}_2$ are efficiently determinable and the following system is obtained:

$$\begin{bmatrix} I & C_{21}^T & & & \\ & A_{22} & A_{32}^T & & \mathbf{0} \\ & A_{32} & A_{33} & A_{43}^T & \\ & & & \ddots & \\ \mathbf{0} & & & & \ddots \end{bmatrix} \cdot \begin{bmatrix} x_1 \\ x_2 \\ x_3 \\ \vdots \\ \vdots \end{bmatrix} = \begin{bmatrix} d_1 \\ \hat{b}_2 \\ b_3 \\ \vdots \\ \vdots \end{bmatrix}. \tag{8}$$

This elimination process may be continued recursively, and after m steps, the system,

$$\begin{bmatrix} I & C_{21}^T & & & & \\ & I & C_{32}^T & & \mathbf{0} & \\ & & I & C_{43}^T & & \\ & & & \ddots & & \\ \mathbf{0} & & & & \ddots & \\ & & & & & I \end{bmatrix} \cdot \begin{bmatrix} x_1 \\ x_2 \\ x_3 \\ \vdots \\ \vdots \\ x_m \end{bmatrix} = \begin{bmatrix} d_1 \\ d_2 \\ d_3 \\ \vdots \\ \vdots \\ d_m \end{bmatrix}. \tag{9}$$

is obtained. So the partial vector sought is,

$$x_m := d_m.$$

The remaining partial vectors are determined in reverse order by,

$$x_i := d_i - C_{i+1,i}^T x_{i+1}, i = m-1, \ldots, 1. \tag{10}$$

In order to avoid the direct calculation of the inverse $\hat{A}_{ii}^{-1}$ in (6) a certain number of linear equation systems with respectively different righthand sides are solved for determining the block matrices $C_{i+1,1}^T$ in (9).

Since $det \hat{A}_{ii} \neq 0$,

$$\left. \begin{array}{l} \hat{A}_{ii}C_{i+1,i}^T = A_{i+1,i}^T \\ \hat{A}_{ii}d_i = \hat{b}_i \end{array} \right\} \text{ for } i = 1, 2, \ldots, m-1, \tag{11}$$

where,

$$\hat{A}_{11} = A_{11} \text{ and } \hat{b}_{-1} = b.$$

Hence for large m and r, the number of operations is significantly reduced against the normal number of calculations of the inverse.

Number of operations to determine the inverse: $\sim 3(m-2)r^3$.

Number of equation systems: $\sim 5/3(m-1)r^3$.

An alternative method is the application of the Cholesky decomposition to the individual block systems. The decomposition

$$A_{11} := L_{11}L_{11}^T,$$

and
$$A_{11}x_1 + A_{21}^T x_2 = b_1,$$

yields
$$L_{11}^T x_1 + L_{21}^T x_2 = h_1 \qquad (12)$$

Thus the equations,
$$L_{11} L_{21}^T = A_{21}^T$$
$$L_{11} h_1 = b_1 \qquad (13)$$

Since $A_{21} = L_{21} L_{11}^T$ yields,
$$\hat{A}_{22} x_2 + \hat{A}_{32}^T x_3 = \hat{b}_2, \qquad (14)$$

where,
$$\hat{A}_{22} := A_{22} - L_{21} L_{21}^T, \hat{b}_2 = b_2 - L_{21} h_1,$$

by multiplication of L_{21} and subtraction from the 2nd block equation analogous to (7).

After further reduction, the system, $L_x = h$, i.e.

$$\begin{bmatrix} L_{11}^T & L_{21}^T & & & \\ & L_{22}^T & L_{32}^T & & \text{\Large 0} \\ & & L_{33}^T & L_{43}^T & \\ & & & \ddots & \ddots \\ \text{\Large 0} & & & & \ddots \\ & & & & & L_{mm}^T \end{bmatrix} \cdot \begin{bmatrix} x_1 \\ x_2 \\ x_3 \\ \vdots \\ \vdots \\ x_m \end{bmatrix} = \begin{bmatrix} h_1 \\ h_2 \\ h_3 \\ \vdots \\ \vdots \\ h_m \end{bmatrix} \qquad (15)$$

is obtained. The coefficient matrix L is a block matrix decomposition of the given matrix A (Cholesky decomposition). At this point of the algorithm the partial vector x_m follows from,

$$L_{mm}^T x_m = h_m. \qquad (16)$$

The remaining partial vectors are obtained recursively from,

$$L_{ii}^T x_i = h_i - L_{i+1,i}^T x_{i+1}, i = m - 1, \ldots, 1. \qquad (17)$$

Here for large m, r the number of operations is reduced to $\sim 7/6(m-1)r^3$ compared with the process treated above.

2.   Block Tridiagonal Equations

A variant of the direct block process can be applied to tridiagonal block matrices. For this purpose the system of linear equations,

$$Ax = b; A := [a_{ik}], A \in \mathbb{R}^{n \times n}, x, b \in \mathbb{R}^n, A \text{ nonsingular}, \qquad (18)$$

partitioned into block matrices of the following form, is considered:

$$\begin{bmatrix} A_1 & C_1 & & & & \\ B_2 & A_2 & C_2 & & \text{\Large 0} & \\ & B_3 & A_3 & C_3 & & \\ & & \ddots & \ddots & \ddots & \\ \text{\Large 0} & & & B_{m-1} & A_{m-1} & C_{m-1} \\ & & & & B_m & A_m \end{bmatrix} \cdot \begin{bmatrix} x_1 \\ x_2 \\ x_3 \\ \vdots \\ \vdots \\ x_m \end{bmatrix} = \begin{bmatrix} b_1 \\ b_2 \\ b_3 \\ \vdots \\ \vdots \\ b_m \end{bmatrix}. \qquad (19)$$

A is a tridiagonal block matrix, where

$$
\begin{aligned}
A_i &\in \mathbb{R}^{r_i \times r_i}, \quad i = 1, 2, \ldots, m \quad \text{(square matrices)} \\
B_i &\in \mathbb{R}^{r_i \times r_{i-1}}, \quad i = 2, \ldots, m \quad \text{(rectangular matrices)}
\end{aligned}
\tag{20}
$$

If $r_i = r$, $i = 1, 2, \ldots, m$, then all blocks A_i, B_i, C_i are square matrices of order r (see previous process). Then the matrix A in (19) is of band structure with bandwidth given by A_i, B_i, C_i.

In the special case $A_i, B_i, C_i \in \mathbb{R}^{1 \times 1}$ the matrix A in (19) is a tridiagonal matrix with bandwidth 3.

For the partial vectors $x_i, b_i \in \mathbb{R}^{r_i}, i = 1, 2, \ldots, m$,

$$
x_i := [x_1, \ldots, x_{r_i}]_i^T, i = 1, 2, \ldots, m,
$$

and

$$
b_i := [b_1, \ldots, b_{r_i}]_i^T, i = 1, 2, \ldots, m.
$$

Now the system $Ax = b$ is transformed into an upper block triangular system,

$$
Cx = d,
\tag{21}
$$

where C, d are assumed to be,

$$
C := \begin{bmatrix}
F_1 & C_1 & & & \\
 & F_2 & \ddots & & \mathbf{0} \\
 & & \ddots & \ddots & \\
\mathbf{0} & & & \ddots & C_{m-1} \\
 & & & & F_m
\end{bmatrix}, d := \begin{bmatrix}
d_1 \\
d_2 \\
\vdots \\
\vdots \\
d_m
\end{bmatrix}.
\tag{22}
$$

For the new blocks F_i and d_i respectively, the following algorithm is obtained recursively:

$$
\begin{aligned}
F_1 &:= A_1, \\
d_1 &:= b_1, \\
F_i &:= A_i - B_i F_{i-1}^{-1} C_{i-1} \\
d_i &:= b_i - B_i F_{i-1}^{-1} d_{i-1}
\end{aligned}
\left.\vphantom{\begin{aligned}F\\d\end{aligned}}\right\}, i = 2, 3, \ldots, m.
\tag{23}
$$

According the assumption $det(A) \neq 0$ and,

$$
det(A) = det(C) = \prod_{i=1}^{m} det(F_i) \neq 0.
\tag{24}
$$

Hence the diagonal blocks F_i are nonsingular; consequently the algorithm may be carried out without pivoting. In practice the order of the diagonal blocks is generally small.

For calculating the inverse F_i^{-1} special numerically efficient algorithms are used. In order to avoid the direct calculation of the inverse, Gaussian elimination, for example, is used for solving the equation systems,

$$
D_i := B_i F_{i-1}^{-1} \Leftrightarrow F_{i-1}^T D_i^T = B_i^T.
\tag{25}
$$

Here D_i^T is the solution matrix of the system of equations (25).

So by the algorithm (23) the system $Cx = d$ is obtained; finally the following partial systems have to be solved:

$$F_m x_m = d_m,$$
$$F_i x_i = d_i - C_i x_{i+1}, i = m - 1, \ldots, 1. \tag{26}$$

The partial systems (26) are generally solved by LU decomposition or, in the case of $F_i = F_i^T$, by Cholesky decomposition:

$$(L_m U_m) x_m = d_m,$$
$$(L_i U_i) x_i = f_i = d_i - C_i x_{i+1}, i = m - 1, \ldots, 1. \tag{27}$$

Thus the corresponding triangular systems are solved.

Partial pivoting or complete pivoting in general lead to a reduction of rounding errors and instabilities (cancellation effect).

3.   Explicit Solution of Block Matrix Equations

In the solution of the finite element discretisation of a two-point boundary value problem, the solution of the following block tridiagonal system occurs:

$$Az = K;$$

here,

$$A = \begin{bmatrix} B_1 & C_1 & & & & \\ A_2 & B_2 & C_2 & & \mathbf{0} & \\ & \ddots & \ddots & \ddots & & \\ & & \ddots & \ddots & \ddots & \\ \mathbf{0} & & \ddots & \ddots & C_{N-1} \\ & & & & A_N & B_N \end{bmatrix},$$

where $A_i, B_i, C_i, i = 1, 2, \ldots, N$, with $A_1 = C_N = 0$, are 2×2 submatrices.

The usual solution procedure is the following Gaussian elimination procedure (without pivoting) given by the recursion formula,

$$W_1 = B_1^{-1} C_1, W_i = (B_i - A_i W_{i-1})^{-1} C_i, \quad 2 \le i \le N, \tag{28}$$

and

$$G_1 = B_1^{-1} K_1, G_i = (B_i - A_i W_{i-1})^{-1} (K_i - A_i G_{i-1}), \quad 2 \le i \le N, \tag{29}$$

with the vector components Z_i of the solution given by,

$$Z_N = G_N, Z_i = G_i - W_i Z_{i+1}, \quad N - 1 \ge i \ge 1. \tag{30}$$

Explicit Solution

Since the submatrices A_i, B_i, C_i are simple 2×2 matrices, the recursion formulae (28)-(30) can be expressed in explicit form as follows.

Let us denote,

$$B_i = \begin{bmatrix} b_{11}^i & b_{12}^i \\ b_{21}^i & b_{22}^i \end{bmatrix}, C_i = A_{i+1}^T = \begin{bmatrix} c_{11}^i & c_{12}^i \\ c_{21}^i & c_{22}^i \end{bmatrix}, K_i = \begin{bmatrix} k_1^i \\ k_2^i \end{bmatrix}, i = 1, 2, \ldots, n, \tag{31}$$

where the elements in block matrix index i are denoted by a superior i. Then, by definition we have,

$$B_i^{-1} = \frac{1}{d^1} \begin{bmatrix} b_{22}^i & -b_{12}^i \\ -b_{21}^i & b_{11}^i \end{bmatrix}, \text{ where } d^i = b_{11}^i b_{22}^i - b_{12}^i b_{21}^i, \tag{32}$$

and from (28) we have,

$$W_i = B_1^{-1} C_1 = \frac{1}{d^1} \begin{bmatrix} b_{22}^1 c_{11}^1 - b_{12}^1 c_{21}^1 & b_{22}^1 c_{12}^1 - b_{12}^1 c_{22}^1 \\ b_{11}^1 c_{21}^1 - b_{21}^1 c_{11}^1 & b_{11}^1 c_{22}^1 - b_{21}^1 c_{12}^1 \end{bmatrix} \tag{33}$$

Now,

$$A_i W_{i-1} = \begin{bmatrix} c_{11}^{i-1} & c_{21}^{i-1} \\ c_{12}^{i-1} & c_{22}^{i-1} \end{bmatrix} * \frac{1}{d^{i-1}} \begin{bmatrix} b_{22}^1 c_{11}^1 - b_{12}^1 c_{21}^1 & b_{22}^1 c_{12}^1 - b_{12}^1 c_{22}^1 \\ b_{11}^1 c_{21}^1 - b_{21}^1 c_{11}^1 & b_{11}^1 c_{22}^1 - b_{21}^1 c_{12}^1 \end{bmatrix}^{i-1}$$

$$= \frac{1}{d^{i-1}} \begin{bmatrix} s_1^{i-1} & s_2^{i-1} \\ s_3^{i-1} & s_4^{i-1} \end{bmatrix}, \tag{34}$$

where,

$$\begin{aligned} s_1^{i-1} &= (b_{22} c_{11}^2 - b_{12} c_{11} c_{21} + b_{11} c_{21}^2 - b_{21} c_{21} c_{11})^{i-1}, \\ s_2^{i-1} &= (b_{22} c_{11} c_{12} - b_{12} c_{11} c_{22} + b_{11} c_{21} c_{22} - b_{21} c_{21} c_{12})^{i-1}, \\ s_3^{i-1} &= (b_{22} c_{12} c_{11} - b_{12} c_{12} c_{21} + b_{11} c_{21} c_{22} - b_{21} c_{11} c_{22})^{i-1}, \\ s_4^{i-1} &= (b_{22} c_{12}^2 - b_{12} c_{12} c_{22} + b_{11} c_{22}^2 - b_{21} c_{22} c_{12})^{i-1}. \end{aligned}$$

Hence,

$$B_i - A_i W_{i-1} = \frac{1}{d^{i-1}} \begin{bmatrix} d^{i-1} b_{11}^i - s_1^{i-1} & d^{i-1} b_{12}^i - s_2^{i-1} \\ d^{i-1} b_{21}^i - s_3^{i-1} & d^{i-1} b_{22}^i - s_4^{i-1} \end{bmatrix}, \tag{35}$$

$$(B_i - A_i W_{i-1})^{i-1} = \frac{1}{D^{i-1}} \begin{bmatrix} d^{i-1} b_{22}^i - s_4^{i-1} & s_2^{i-1} d^{i-1} b_{12}^i \\ s_3^{i-1} - d^{i-1} b_4^i & d^{i-1} b_{11}^i - s_1^{i-1} \end{bmatrix}, \tag{36}$$

where,

$$D^{i-1} = d^{i-1} \left[(d^{i-1} b_{11}^i - s_1^{i-1})(d^{i-1} b_{22}^i - s_4^{i-1}) - (d^{i-1} b_{22}^i - s_2^{i-1})(d^{i-1} b_{21}^i - s_3^{i-1}) \right].$$

Hence, from (1) we have,

$$W_i = (B_i - A_i W_{i-1})^{i-1} C_i, 2 \le i \le N,$$

expressed in explicit form as,

$$W_i = \frac{1}{D^{i-1}} \times$$

$$\begin{bmatrix} (d_1^i b_{22} - s_4^{i-1}) c_{11}^i + (s_2^{i-1} - d^{i-1} b_{12}^i) c_{22}^i & (d^{i-1} b_{22} - s_4^{i-1}) c_{12}^i + (s_2^{i-1} - d^{i-1} b_{12}^i) c_{22}^i \\ (s_3^{i-1} - d^{i-1} b_{21}^i) c_{11}^i + (d^{i-1} b_{11} - s_1^{i-1}) c_{21}^i & (s_3^{i-1} - d^{i-1} b_{21}^i) c_{12}^i + (d^{i-1} b_{11} - s_1^{i-1}) c_{22}^i \end{bmatrix}. \tag{37}$$

Again, from (29) we have,

$$G_1 = B_1^{-1} K_1 = \frac{1}{d^1} \begin{bmatrix} b_{22}^1 & -b_{12}^1 \\ -b_{21}^1 & b_{11}^1 \end{bmatrix} \begin{bmatrix} k_1^1 \\ k_2^1 \end{bmatrix} = \frac{1}{d^1} \begin{bmatrix} b_{22}^1 k_1^1 - b_{12}^1 k_2^1 \\ b_{11}^1 l_2^1 - b_{21}^1 k_1^1 \end{bmatrix}. \tag{38}$$

Also, we have,

$$A_i G_{i-1} = \begin{bmatrix} c_{11}^{i-1} & c_{21}^{i-1} \\ c_{12}^{i-1} & c_{22}^{i-1} \end{bmatrix} * \frac{1}{d^{i-1}} \begin{bmatrix} b_{22}^{i-1} k_1^{i-1} - b_{12}^{i-1} k_2^{i-1} \\ b_{11}^{i-1} k_2^{i-1} - b_{21}^{i-1} k_1^{i-1} \end{bmatrix} = \frac{1}{d^{i-1}} \begin{bmatrix} p_1^{i-1} \\ p_2^{i-1} \end{bmatrix},$$

where,

$$p_1^{i-1} = c_{11}(b_{22} k_1 - b_{12} k_2) + c_{21}(b_{11} k_2 - b_{21} k_1)^{i-1},$$

$$p_2^{i-1} = c_{12}(b_{22} k_1 - b_{21} k_2) + c_{22}(b_{11} k_2 - b_{21} k_1)^{i-1}.$$

Then,

$$K_i - A_i G_{i-1} = \frac{1}{d^{i-1}} \begin{bmatrix} d^{i-1} k_1^i - p_1^{i-1} \\ d^{i-1} k_2^i - p_2^{i-1} \end{bmatrix}. \tag{39}$$

By substitution in,

$$G_i = (B_i - A_i W_{i-1})^{-1}(K_i - A_i G_{i-1}),$$

we have, in explicit form,

$$G_i = \frac{1}{D^{i-1} d^{i-1}} \times$$
$$\begin{bmatrix} (d^{i-1} b_{22}^i - s_4^{i-1})(d^{i-1} k_1^i - p_1^{i-1}) + (s_2^{i-1} - d^{i-1} b_{12}^i)(d^{i-1} k_2^i - p_2^{i-1}) \\ (s_3^{i-1} - d^{i-1} b_{21}^i)(d^{i-1} k_1^i - p_1^{i-1}) + (d^{i-1} b_{11}^i - s_1^{i-1})(d^{i-1} k_2^i - p_2^{i-1}) \end{bmatrix}, \tag{40}$$
$$2 \le i \le N.$$

Finally from (30) the solution is recursively given by,

$$Z_N = G_N = \frac{1}{D^{N-1} d^{N-1}} \times$$
$$\begin{bmatrix} (d^{N-1} b_{22}^N - s_4^{N-1})(d^{N-1} k_1^N - p_1^{N-1}) + (s_2^{N-1} - d^{N-1} b_{12}^N)(d^{N-1} k_2^N - p_2^{N-1}) \\ (s_3^{N-1} - d^{N-1} b_{21}^N)(d^{N-1} k_1^N - p_1^{N-1}) + (d^{N-1} b_{11}^N - s_1^{N-1})(d^{N-1} k_2^N - p_2^{N-1}) \end{bmatrix}, \tag{41}$$

followed by

$$Z_i - G_i - W_i Z_{i+1}, 1 \le i \le N-1.$$

It can be noticed that the above formula encompasses the following cases:

1. Tridiagonal form, where $c_{11} = c_{12} = 0$.

2. Quindiagonal form, where $c_{22} = 0$.

3. Septadiagonal form (special) form.

The equations (41) now in explicit form are suitable for parallel solution, (Evans & Yousif, 1987).

4.   Butterfly Methods for Solving Linear Equations

In this section we compare direct methods of solving linear equations with new parallel quadrant interlocking (QI) (methods), (Evans & Yousif, 1983).

Given a matrix A, i.e.,

$$\begin{bmatrix} a_{11} & a_{12} & a_{13} & a_{14} \\ a_{21} & a_{22} & a_{23} & a_{24} \\ a_{31} & a_{32} & a_{33} & a_{34} \\ a_{41} & a_{42} & a_{43} & a_{44} \end{bmatrix} \quad \det A^{-1} \neq 0 \text{ non-singular.}$$

We can attempt to find matrix factors L and U if the form:

$$L = \begin{bmatrix} 1 & & & 0 \\ l_{21} & 1 & & \\ l_{31} & l_{32} & 1 & \\ l_{41} & l_{42} & l_{43} & 1 \end{bmatrix} \text{ and } U = \begin{bmatrix} u_{11} & u_{12} & u_{13} & u_{14} \\ & u_{22} & u_{23} & u_{24} \\ & & u_{33} & u_{34} \\ 0 & & & u_{44} \end{bmatrix},$$

such that $A \equiv LU$.

Equating coefficients we can obtain the following relations to determine the coefficients of L and U.

$$u_{11} = a_{11}, \ u_{12} = a_{12}, \ u_{13} = a_{13}, \ u_{14} = a_{14},$$
$$l_{21}u_{11} = a_{21}, \ l_{21}u_{12} + u_{22} = a_{22}, \ l_{21}u_{13} + u_{23} = a_{23}, \ l_{21}u_{14} + u_{24} = a_{24},$$
$$l_{31}u_{11} = a_{31}, \ l_{31}u_{12} + l_{32}u_{22} = u_{32}, \ l_{31}u_{13} + l_{32}u_{23} + u_{33} = a_{33}, \text{ etc.}$$

Similarly for the last row. These essentially are all sequential relations, since each of the unknowns $l_{i,j}$ and $u_{i,j}$ are bought into the above relations one at a time and then determined.

The reason why such a factorisation is sought in L.U. form is that to obtain the solution of the linear system,

$$Ax = b, \tag{42}$$

then by making use of the substitution $A = LU$ the problem reduces to the solution of the coupled system,

$$Ly = b, \tag{43}$$

and

$$Ux = y, \tag{44}$$

where y is an intermediate vector.

The systems (42) and (43) are easily solvable systems and can be solved by forward or backward substitution processes, i.e. in the following manner,

$$Ly = b,$$
$$\begin{bmatrix} 1 & & & 0 \\ l_{21} & 1 & & \\ l_{31} & l_{32} & 1 & \\ l_{41} & l_{42} & l_{43} & 1 \end{bmatrix} \begin{bmatrix} y_1 \\ y_2 \\ y_3 \\ y_4 \end{bmatrix} = \begin{bmatrix} b_1 \\ b_2 \\ b_3 \\ b_4 \end{bmatrix}, \tag{45}$$

can be solved as follows,

$$
\begin{aligned}
y_1 &= b_1 & &\rightarrow & y_1 &= b_1 \\
l_{21}y_{21} + y_2 &= b_2 & &\rightarrow & y_2 &= b_2 - l_{21}y_1 \\
l_{31}y_1 + l_{32}y_2 + y_3 &= b_3 & &\rightarrow & y_3 &= b_3 - l_{31}y_1 - l_{32}y_2 \\
l_{41}y_1 + l_{42}y_2 + l_{43}y_3 + y_4 &= b_4 & &\rightarrow & y_4 &= b_4 - l_{41}y_1 - l_{42}y_2 - l_{43}y_3
\end{aligned}
\tag{46}
$$

Similarly for $Ux = y$.

These are again all sequential processes since they have to be solved in the manner indicated.

Can we find a factorisation that is more suitable for parallel computation?

Quadrant Interlocking Methods

Consider now a factorization of A of the form,

$$
A = WZ, \tag{47}
$$

where

$$
W = \begin{bmatrix} 1 & 0 & & 0 \\ w_{21} & 1 & 0 & w_{24} \\ w_{31} & 0 & 1 & w_{34} \\ 0 & & 0 & 1 \end{bmatrix}, \text{ and } Z = \begin{bmatrix} z_{11} & z_{12} & z_{13} & z_{14} \\ 0 & z_{22} & z_{23} & 0 \\ & z_{32} & x_{34} & \\ z_{41} & z_{42} & z_{43} & z_{44} \end{bmatrix}. \tag{48}
$$

Thus in general W and Z have the form,

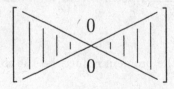   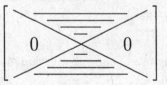

and are termed quadrant interlocking factors (Q.I.F.) which have a Butterfly shape.

To determine the coefficients of W and Z we equate coefficients. Thus,

I
$$
z_{11} = a_{11}, z_{12} = a_{12}, z_{13} = a_{13}, z_{14} = a_{14}. \tag{49}
$$

IV
$$
z_{41} = a_{41}, z_{42} = a_{42}, z_{43} = a_{43}, z_{44} = z_{44}. \tag{50}
$$

II

(1)   (2)
$$
w_{21}z_{11} + w_{24}z_{41} = a_{21}; \quad w_{21}z_{12} + z_{22} + w_{24}z_{42} = a_{22}
$$
$$
\tag{51}
$$

(3)   (4)
$$
w_{21}z_{13} + z_{23} + w_{24}z_{43} = a_{23}; \quad w_{21}z_{14} + w_{24}z_{44} = a_{24}.
$$

In (51) eliminate (1) and (4) to obtain w_{21} and w_{24}. Substitute in (2) and (3) to obtain z_{22} and z_{23}.

III

$$
\begin{array}{cc}
(1) & (2) \\
w_{31}z_{11} + w_{34}z_{41} = a_{31}; & w_{31}z_{12} + z_{32} + w_{34}z_{42} = a_{32} \\
\end{array}
\tag{52}
$$

$$
\begin{array}{cc}
(3) & (4) \\
w_{31}z_{13} + z_{33} + w_{34}z_{43} = a_{33}; & w_{31}z_{14} + w_{34}z_{44} = a_{34}.
\end{array}
$$

In (52) eliminate (1) and (4) to obtain w_{31} and w_{34}. Substitute in (2) and (3) to obtain z_{32} and z_{33}.

Thus, we can see that the first and last rows of Z are given immediately.

Then, (2×2) sets of linear equations are solved to obtain the $w_{i,1}$ and $w_{i,4}$, for $i = 2, 3$. Thus the calculation proceeds as follows,

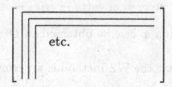

the outermost elements of the matrices W and Z are obtained. Then, the calculation proceeds on the innermost next layer of elements. Thus, only $\left(\frac{(n-1)}{2}\right)$ stages are required to compute all the elements of W and Z. For $n = odd$ - special consideration has to be provided to cope with the centre element separately. In comparison, the LU decomposition is given as,

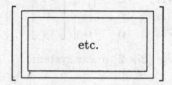

Solution of the Linear Systems

Using the relationship,

$$
A = WZ,
\tag{53}
$$

then the linear system,

$$
Ax = b,
$$

can be reformulated as the solution of 2 related linear systems,

$$
Wy = b \quad \text{and} \quad Zx = y.
\tag{54}
$$

To solve $Wy = b$ we proceed as follows,

$$
\begin{bmatrix}
1 & 0 & 0 & \\
w_{21} & 1 & 0 & w_{24} \\
w_{31} & 0 & 1 & w_{34} \\
0 & 0 & & 1
\end{bmatrix}
\begin{bmatrix}
y_1 \\
y_2 \\
y_3 \\
y_4
\end{bmatrix}
=
\begin{bmatrix}
b_1 \\
b_2 \\
b_3 \\
b_4
\end{bmatrix} .
$$

We see immediately that,

$$y_1 = b_1 \text{ and } y_4 = b_4, \tag{55}$$

then,

$$w_{21}y_1 + y_2 + w_{24}y_4 = b_2 \text{ and } w_{31}y_1 + y_3 + w_{34}y_4 = b_3, \tag{56}$$

or,

$$y_2 = \tilde{b}_2 = (b_2 - w_{21}y_1 - w_{24}y_4), \tag{57}$$

and

$$y_3 = \tilde{b}_3 = (b_3 - w_{31}y_1 - w_{34}y_4). \tag{58}$$

The solutions for y are obtained in pairs working from the Top and Bottom of the vector.

Once a vector y has been determined then to solve $Zx = y$ we proceed as follows,

$$\begin{bmatrix} z_{11} & z_{12} & z_{13} & z_{14} \\ 0 & z_{22} & z_{23} & 0 \\ & z_{32} & x_{34} & \\ z_{41} & z_{42} & z_{43} & z_{44} \end{bmatrix} \begin{bmatrix} x_1 \\ x_2 \\ x_3 \\ x_4 \end{bmatrix} = \begin{bmatrix} y_1 \\ y_2 \\ y_3 \\ y_4 \end{bmatrix}.$$

Starting at the centre we solve the (2×2) linear system,

$$\begin{aligned} z_{22}x_2 + z_{23}x_3 &= y_2 \\ z_{32}x_2 + z_{33}x_3 &= y_3, \end{aligned} \tag{59}$$

for x_2 and x_3. Then, we proceed outwards and solve the (2×2) linear system,

$$\begin{aligned} z_{11}x_1 + z_{14}x_4 &= y_1 = (y_1 - z_{12}x_2 - z_{13}x_3) \\ z_{41}x_1 + z_{44}x_4 &= y_4 = (y_4 - z_{42}x_2 - z_{43}x_3), \end{aligned} \tag{60}$$

for x_1 and x_3. Thus, the solution x can be obtained in $O(n)$ stages on a Parallel SIMD computer with n^2 processors.

Finally, it can be confirmed that the WZ method is a permuted (2×2) block form of the familiar LU method.

5.   Parallel Iterative Methods for Solving Linear Systems

Given a matrix A,

$$\begin{bmatrix} a_{11} & a_{12} & a_{13} & a_{14} \\ a_{21} & a_{22} & a_{23} & a_{24} \\ a_{31} & a_{32} & a_{33} & a_{34} \\ a_{41} & a_{42} & a_{43} & a_{44} \end{bmatrix} \quad \det A^{-1} \neq 0 \; non - singular.$$

Then the standard interactive approach is to assume the splitting,

$$A = D + L + U, \tag{61}$$

where,

$$D = \begin{bmatrix} a_{11} & & & 0 \\ & a_{22} & & \\ & & a_{33} & \\ 0 & & & a_{44} \end{bmatrix},$$

$$L = \begin{bmatrix} & & & 0 \\ a_{21} & & & \\ a_{31} & a_{32} & & \\ a_{41} & a_{42} & a_{43} & \end{bmatrix} \quad \text{and } U = \begin{bmatrix} & a_{12} & a_{13} & a_{14} \\ & & a_{23} & a_{24} \\ & & & a_{34} \\ 0 & & & \end{bmatrix}.$$

Then the Gauss or Jacobi method can be written as,

$$Dx^{(n+1)} = -Lx^{(n)} - Ux^{(n)} + b, \tag{62}$$

and the Guass-Seidel method as,

$$Dx^{(n+1)} = -Lx^{(n+1)} - Ux^{(n)} + b,$$

or

$$(D + L)x^{(n+1)} = -Ux^{(n)} + b.$$

This is a sequential equation. Or

$$\begin{aligned}
a_{11}x_1^{(n+1)} &= -a_{12}x_2^{(n)} - a_{13}x_3^{(n)} - a_{14}x_4^{(n)} + b_1, \\
a_{22}x_2^{(n+1)} &= -a_{21}x_1^{(n+1)} - a_{23}x_3^{(n)} - a_{24}x_4^{(n)} + b_2, \\
a_{33}x_3^{(n+1)} &= -a_{13}x_1^{(n+1)} - a_{32}x_2^{(n+1)} - a_{34}x_4^{(n)} + b_3, \\
a_{44}x_4^{(n+1)} &= -a_{41}x_1^{(n+1)} - a_{42}x_2^{(n+1)} - a_{43}x_3^{(n+1)} + b_4.
\end{aligned} \tag{63}$$

Can we apply the Quadrant Interlocking approach to derive a parallel method?

Quadrant Interlocking Splitting (Q.I.S.) Method

Suppose we write A in the form,

$$A = X + W + Z, \tag{64}$$

where X is defined as,

$$\begin{bmatrix} a_{11} & & & a_{14} \\ & a_{22} & a_{23} & \\ & a_{32} & a_{33} & \\ a_{41} & & & a_{44} \end{bmatrix}, \tag{65}$$

and,

$$W = \begin{bmatrix} & & & 0 \\ a_{21} & & a_{24} \\ a_{31} & & a_{34} \\ 0 & & & \end{bmatrix}, \quad \text{and } Z = \begin{bmatrix} & a_{12} & a_{13} & \\ 0 & & & 0 \\ & & & \\ & a_{42} & a_{43} & \end{bmatrix}. \tag{66}$$

Then, an iterative method can be written as,

$$Xx^{(n+1)} = -Wx^{(n)} - Zx^{(n)} + b, \tag{67}$$

similar to Jacobi form, and

$$Xx^{(n+1)} = -Wx^{(n+1)} - Zx^{(n)} + b, \tag{68}$$

or

$$(X + W)x^{(n+1)} = -Zx^{(n)} + b.$$

Similar to Gauss-Seidal form,

$$a_{11}x_1^{(n+1)} + a_{14}x_4^{(n+1)} = -a_{12}x_2^{(n)} - a_{13}x_3^{(n)} + b_1,$$

or

$$a_{41}x_1^{(n+1)} + a_{44}x_4^{(n+1)} = -a_{42}x_2^{(n)} - a_{43}x_3^{(n)} + b_4,$$

followed by,

$$a_{22}x_2^{(n+1)} + a_{23}x_3^{(n+1)} = -a_{21}x_1^{(n+1)} - a_{34}x_4^{(n+1)} + b_2,$$
$$a_{32}x_3^{(n+1)} + a_{33}x_3^{(n+1)} = -a_{31}x_1^{(n+1)} - a_{34}x_4^{(n+1)} + b_3. \tag{69}$$

This again requires the solution of (2×2) linear systems.

For $n = odd$ we need special consideration to cope with the centre element separately.

6.   Block LU Factorisation

With the assumption that the matrix A is a block matrix of general form,

$$A = \begin{bmatrix} A_{11} & A_{12} & \cdots & A_{1m} \\ A_{21} & A_{22} & \cdots & A_{2m} \\ \vdots & \vdots & \ddots & \vdots \\ A_{m1} & A_{m2} & \cdots & A_{mm} \end{bmatrix}, \tag{70}$$

where A_{ij} is a $\ell \times \ell$ matrix and $n = \ell m$ we now consider a block LU factorisation procedure. For simplicity we assume that the matrix A has a uniform block size ℓ and that n is divisible by ℓ. We further assume that A_{11} is invertible (non-singular), and define the $n \times \ell$ matrix $L^{(1)}$,

$$L^{(1)} = \begin{bmatrix} I_\ell \\ L_2^{(1)} \\ L_3^{(1)} \\ \vdots \\ L_m^{(1)} \end{bmatrix}, \tag{71}$$

where,

$$L_i^{(1)} = A_{i1}A_{11}^{-1}, \tag{72}$$

is a $\ell \times \ell$ matrix and I_ℓ is the identity matrix of order ℓ. We also introduce the $\ell \times n$ matrix $U^{(1)}$ as,

$$U^{(1)} = (U_1^{(1)}, U_2^{(1)}, \ldots, U_m^{(1)}), \tag{73}$$

where $U_i^{(1)} = A_{1i}$ is a $\ell \times \ell$ matrix. Then,

$$A = L^{(1)}U^{(1)} + \tilde{A}^{(1)},$$

where

$$\tilde{A}^{(1)} = \begin{bmatrix} 0 & 0 & \cdots & 0 \\ 0 & \tilde{A}_{22}^{(1)} & \cdots & \tilde{A}_{2m}^{(1)} \\ \vdots & \vdots & \ddots & \vdots \\ 0 & \tilde{A}_{m2}^{(1)} & \cdots & \tilde{A}_{mm}^{(1)} \end{bmatrix}, \tag{74}$$

with the zeros representing block $\ell \times \ell$ zero matrices, and for $i, j = 2, 3, \ldots, m$,

$$\tilde{A}_{ij}^{(1)} = A_{ij} - A_{i1} A_{11}^{-1} A_{1j}, = A_{ij} - L_i^{(1)} A_{1j}, \tag{75}$$

is also of order $(\ell \times \ell)$.

This process can now be repeated on the non-zero blocks of $\tilde{A}^{(1)}$. After $k - 1$ stages of the block elimination procedure we have the partially eliminated matrix,

$$\tilde{A}^{(k-1)} = \begin{bmatrix} 0 & 0 & \cdots & 0 & \cdots & \cdots & 0 \\ 0 & 0 & & \vdots & & & \vdots \\ \vdots & & \ddots & \vdots & & & \vdots \\ 0 & \cdots & \cdots & 0 & \cdots & \cdots & 0 \\ \vdots & & & \vdots & \tilde{A}_{kk}^{(k-1)} & \cdots & \tilde{A}_{km}^{(k-1)} \\ \vdots & & & \vdots & \vdots & & \vdots \\ 0 & \cdots & \cdots & 0 & \tilde{A}_{mk}^{(k-1)} & \cdots & \tilde{A}_{mm}^{(k-1)} \end{bmatrix}, \tag{76}$$

and the kth stage, which eliminates the next block of ℓ columns, is described by,

$$\tilde{A}^{(k-1)} = L^{(k)} U^{(k)} + \tilde{A}^{(k)}, \tag{77}$$

where $L^{(k)}$ and $U^{(k)}$ are $n \times \ell$ and $\ell \times n$ matrices respectively, with $L_i^{(k)} = U_i^{(k)} = 0$, for $i \leq k - 1$, $L_k^{(k)} = I_\ell$ and $\tilde{A}_{ij}^{(k)} = 0$ for $i \leq k$ or $j \leq k$. Assuming that $\tilde{A}_{kk}^{(k-1)}$ is non-singular we have,

$$L^{(k)} = \begin{bmatrix} 0 \\ \vdots \\ 0 \\ I_\ell \\ L_{k+1}^{(k)} \\ \vdots \\ L_m^{(m)} \end{bmatrix}, U^{(k)} = (0, \ldots, 0, \tilde{A}_{kk}^{(k-1)}, \ldots, \tilde{A}_{km}^{(k-1)}),$$

and

$$\tilde{A}^{(k)} = \begin{bmatrix} 0 & 0 & \cdots & 0 & \cdots & \cdots & 0 \\ 0 & 0 & & \vdots & & & \vdots \\ \vdots & & \ddots & \vdots & & & \vdots \\ 0 & \cdots & \cdots & 0 & \cdots & \cdots & 0 \\ \vdots & & & \vdots & \tilde{A}_{k+1,k+1}^{(k)} & \cdots & \tilde{A}_{k+1,m}^{(k)} \\ \vdots & & & \vdots & \vdots & & \vdots \\ 0 & \cdots & \cdots & 0 & \tilde{A}_{m,k+1}^{(k)} & \cdots & \tilde{A}_{mm}^{(k)} \end{bmatrix},$$

where, for $i = k + 1, k + 2, \ldots, m$,

$$L_i^{(k)} = \tilde{A}_{ik}^{(k-1)} (\tilde{A}_{kk}^{(k-1)})^{-1}, \tag{78}$$

and for $i, j = k + 1, k + 2, \ldots, m$,

$$\begin{aligned} \tilde{A}_{ij}^{(k)} &= \tilde{A}_{ij}^{(k-1)} - \tilde{A}_{ik}^{(k-1)} (\tilde{A}_{kk}^{(k-1)})^{-1} \tilde{A}_{kj}^{(k-1)}, \\ &= \tilde{A}_{ij}^{(k-1)} - L_i^{(k)} \tilde{A}_{kj}^{(k-1)} \end{aligned} \tag{79}$$

For m stages of the elimination procedure we find that,

$$
\begin{aligned}
A &= L^{(1)}U^{(1)} + \tilde{A}^{(1)} \\
&= L^{(1)}U^{(1)} + L^{(2)}U^{(2)} + \tilde{A}^{(2)} \\
&\;\;\vdots \\
&= L^{(1)}U^{(1)} + L^{(2)}U^{(2)} + \cdots + L^{(m)}U^{(m)} + \tilde{A}^{(m)}
\end{aligned}
\tag{80}
$$

where $\tilde{A}^{(m)}$ is the null matrix. Hence,

$$
A = \sum_{k-1}^{m} L^{(k)}U^{(k)} = LU,
\tag{81}
$$

where $L = (L^{(1)}, L^{(2)}, \ldots, L^{(n)})$ is a block, unit diagonal, lower triangular matrix, and

$$
U = \begin{bmatrix} U^{(1)} \\ U^{(2)} \\ \vdots \\ U^{(2)} \end{bmatrix},
$$

is block upper triangular.

The recent introduction of the BLAS3 software library enables elementary block matrix computation schemes to be easily programmed. The computation of LU factorisation is decomposed into calls to BLAS3. It is sufficient to consider the first stage of the elimination procedure, i.e. equations (71)-(75) as subsequent stages involving similar computations.

The block matrices $L_i^{(1)}$ are defined in terms of A_{11}^{-1}. However, we do not explicitly invert A_{11}. Instead its LU factors are formed,

$$
A_{11} = L_{11}U_{11},
\tag{82}
$$

where L_{11} is a unit diagonal lower triangular matrix and U_{11} is upper triangular. The computation forming the LU factors of A_{11} cannot be performed by making explicit calls to BLAS3 and require a call to a high level linear algebra routine which computes the LU factors of a submatrix. Now for $i = 2, 3 \ldots, m$,

$$
L_i^{(1)} = A_{i1}U_{11}^{-1}L_{11}^{-1} = Z_i L_{11}^{-1},
\tag{83}
$$

where

$$
Z_i = A_{i1}U_{11}^{-1}.
$$

The computation of each Z_i is a BLAS3 operation, as is the computation of each $L_i^{(1)} = Z_i L_{11}^{-1}$. This each of the block matrices $L_i^{(1)}$, $i = 2, 3, \ldots, m$, can be constructed using two calls to BLAS3. Further, the construction of each $L_i^{(1)}$ is independent so all the $L_i^{(1)}$ can be constructed concurrently.

Alternatively, if $L^{(1)} = \begin{bmatrix} I_b \\ \tilde{L}^{(1)} \end{bmatrix}$, where,

$$
\tilde{L}^{(1)} = \begin{bmatrix} L_2^{(1)} \\ L_3^{(1)} \\ \vdots \\ L_m^{(1)} \end{bmatrix},
$$

is of size $(m-1)\ell \times \ell$, then (72) can be expressed as,

$$\tilde{L}^{(1)} = A^{(1)} A_{11}^{-1}, \tag{84}$$

where

$$A^{(1)} = \begin{bmatrix} A_{21} \\ A_{31} \\ \vdots \\ A_{m1} \end{bmatrix},$$

is also $(m-1)\ell \times \ell$. Hence $\tilde{L}^{(1)}$ may also be computed using only two calls to BLAS3 where there are also now $(m-1)\ell$ right-hand sides and where any parallelism must be exploited within BLAS3. However, whichever strategy we adopt, the newly generated matrices overwrite the first block row and first block column of A.

The remainder of the first stage of the algorithm forms the matrix $\tilde{A}^{(1)}$ defined by (74) and (75). Noting that,

$$\tilde{A}_{ij}^{(1)} = A_{ij} - L_i^{(1)} A_{1j},$$

the $(m-1) \times (m-1)$ non-zero blocks of $\tilde{A}^{(1)}$ can be computed (concurrently) again using calls to the BLAS3 operation. Alternatively, since,

$$\tilde{A}^{(1)} = A - L^{(1)} U^{(1)},$$

we can compute the whole of $\tilde{A}^{(1)}$ using a single BLAS3 call.

7. The Cyclic Odd-Even Reduction Method
The Symmetric Constant-Diagonal Case

In this section we examine the tridiagonal equations solvers, operating on a set of n linear equations of the form,

$$A.\underline{x} = \underline{y}, \tag{85}$$

where A is a tridiagonal matrix of the form,

$$A = \begin{bmatrix} b & a & & & & \\ a & b & a & & 0 & \\ & a & b & a & & \\ & & \ddots & \ddots & \ddots & \\ 0 & & & \ddots & \ddots & a \\ & & & & a & b \end{bmatrix},$$

which, in shorthand notation, we denote as the $(\ldots, a, b, a, \ldots)$ case.

We now explore a technique known as *cyclic odd-even reduction*, which posseses advantages for transforming a sequential calculation into a highly parallel one, and appears to be the best algorithm for the *symmetric constant-tridiagonal* case, (Buzbee et al, 1970).

In the following discussion, we assume that n can take any of the following values, i.e. $2^m - 1$, 2^m, $2^m + 1$, where m is any positive integer.

The general procedure for the *cyclic odd-even reduction* algorithm, is the following; let us consider three adjacent rows of A, i.e.,

$$
\begin{array}{ccccc}
i-1 & a & b & a & \\
i & & a & b & a \\
i+1 & & & a & b & a
\end{array}
\qquad (86)
$$

A multiple of the middle row i is added to the summation of the $i-1$, $i+1$ rows, this obtaining the form $(\ldots, a', 0, b', 0, a', \ldots)$. This operation creates a tridiagonal system consisting of $2^{m-1} - 1$ or 2^{m-1} or $2^{m-1}+$ only, *even* or *odd* rows of the original matrix A.

For example, if we consider that, originally, the number of equations is: $n = 2^m - 1$, and the new system consists of the *even* rows of the original matrix A, $2^{m-1} - 1$ the number, then although the *odd* rows have been eliminated, the *odd* unknowns can be computed from the *even* unknowns, by a back substitution process. Repeating this process to the new system of $2^{m-1} - 1$ equations, involving just the *even* unknowns, we can eliminate every other row, thus obtaining a set of $2^{m-2} - 1$ equations involving unknowns with subscripts multiples of 4. We can repeat this process, until we obtain a single equation for $x_{2^{m-1}}$. which can be easily solved.

Then, *back-substituting*, we can compute the eliminated unknowns in the reverse order in which they were eliminated.

The *cyclic odd-even reduction* algorithm reached a significant speed increase when the a coefficients are initially equal to *unity*, i.e., the shorthand notation now has the form $(\ldots, 1, b, 1, \ldots)$, which remain equal to unity throughout the computation, thus reducing the number of additions and multiplications per iteration.

The *symmetric constant-diagonal* system, given in (85), can be *normalized* in the $(\ldots, 1, b, 1, \ldots)$ form, dividing by a, to normalize b and y, to produce the *symmetric constant-diagonal form*.

This can be done simultaneously, in most of the parallel computers, since the diagonal elements are a constant number.

More specifically, to describe the algorithm, let us consider the case that $n = 2^m - 1$, where $m = 3$, i.e., the original matrix A consists of 7 equations. In this case the matrix equation, given in (85) has the form,

$$
\begin{array}{c}
1 \\ 2 \\ 3 \\ 4 \\ 5 \\ 6 \\ 7
\end{array}
\begin{bmatrix}
b & 1 & & & & & \\
1 & b & 1 & & & 0 & \\
& 1 & b & 1 & & & \\
& & 1 & b & 1 & & \\
& & & 1 & b & 1 & \\
0 & & & & 1 & b & 1 \\
& & & & & 1 & b
\end{bmatrix}
\begin{bmatrix}
x_1 \\ x_2 \\ x_3 \\ x_4 \\ x_5 \\ x_6 \\ x_7
\end{bmatrix}
=
\begin{bmatrix}
y_1 \\ y_2 \\ y_3 \\ y_4 \\ y_5 \\ y_6 \\ y_7
\end{bmatrix}
.
\qquad (87)
$$

When, the procedure described previously, is applied, (e.g. for the *even* rows), we multiply equations 2,4,6 by $-b$, adding the two adjacent rows to each of them. Then, the system (87) becomes,

$$
\begin{array}{c}
1 \\ 2 \\ 3 \\ 4 \\ 5 \\ 6 \\ 7
\end{array}
\begin{bmatrix}
b & 1 & & & & & \\
0 & b^{[2]} & 0 & 1 & & \mathbf{0} & \\
 & 1 & b & 1 & & & \\
 & 1 & 0 & b^{[2]} & 0 & 1 & \\
 & 1 & & b & 1 & & \\
 & 1 & & 0 & b^{[2]} & 0 & \\
 & & \mathbf{0} & & & 1 & b
\end{bmatrix}
\begin{bmatrix}
x_1 \\ x_2 \\ x_3 \\ x_4 \\ x_5 \\ x_6 \\ x_7
\end{bmatrix}
=
\begin{bmatrix}
y_1 \\ y_2^{[2]} \\ y_3 \\ y_4^{[2]} \\ y_5 \\ y_6^{[2]} \\ y_7
\end{bmatrix}.
\tag{88}
$$

where,

$$
b^{[2]} = 2 - b^2,
\tag{89}
$$

$$
y_j^{[2]} = y_{j-1} - b.y_j + y_{j+1}, \quad \text{for } j = 2, 4, 6.
\tag{90}
$$

Since the *even* rows 2,4,6 in the system (88) are independent of the *odd* rows, they may be separated as follows:

$$
\begin{array}{c}
1(2) \\ 2(4) \\ 3(6)
\end{array}
\begin{bmatrix}
b^{[2]} & 1 & 0 \\
1 & b^{[2]} & 1 \\
0 & 1 & b^{[2]}
\end{bmatrix}
\cdot
\begin{bmatrix}
x_2 \\ x_4 \\ x_6
\end{bmatrix}
=
\begin{bmatrix}
y_2^{[2]} \\ y_4^{[2]} \\ y_6^{[2]}
\end{bmatrix}.
\tag{91}
$$

Applying the above process, once more, to the system (91), i.e. multiplying the second row of the system by $-b^{[2]}$, and adding the first and third rows, the system (91) becomes,

$$
\begin{array}{c}
1(2) \\ 2(4) \\ 3(6)
\end{array}
\begin{bmatrix}
b^{[2]} & 1 & 0 \\
0 & b^{[3]} & 0 \\
0 & 1 & b^{[2]}
\end{bmatrix}
\cdot
\begin{bmatrix}
x_2 \\ x_4 \\ x_6
\end{bmatrix}
=
\begin{bmatrix}
y_2^{[2]} \\ y_4^{[3]} \\ y_6^{[2]}
\end{bmatrix}.
\tag{92}
$$

where,

$$
b^{[3]} = 2 - (b^{[2]})^2,
\tag{93}
$$

$$
y_4^{[3]} = y_2^{[2]} - b^{[2]}.y_4^{[2]} + y_6^{[2]}.
\tag{94}
$$

Separating again the second row of the (92) system we obtain,

$$
b^{[3]}.x_4 = y_4^{[3]},
\tag{95}
$$

which can be easily solved, thus finding x_4.

By a process of *back-substitution*, and in terms of x_4, the first and third rows of the system (92), may be written as,

$$
b^{[2]}.x_2 = y_2^{[2]} - x_4,
\tag{96}
$$

$$
b^{[2]}.x_6 = y_6^{[2]} - x_4.
\tag{97}
$$

Therefore, we can easily calculate x_2 and x_6.

Continuing the back-substitution, in the same way, to the system (88), we can calculate x_1, x_3, x_5, x_7 in terms of x_2, x_4, x_6, thus finding the solution of the matrix equation (87), (see Figure 1).

The above described process, can be applied to any of the values for n, (i.e. $2^m - 1$, 2^m, $2^m + 1$, where m is any integer), choosing each time, the *even* or *odd* rows of the system to work with.

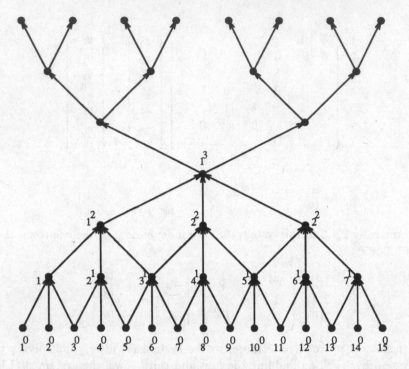

Figure 1. The communication topology of odd-even cyclic reduction

Stride of 3 Cyclic Reduction Algorithm

In the previous section it can be seen that the Cyclic Reduction algorithm consists of successive reductions of the system (85) to similar reduced systems in a 'stride of 2'.

Similarly we can consider forming a C.R. algorithm with reduced systems in a 'stride of 3' in the following way, (Evans, 1991).

We now consider the reduced C.R. algorithm given by equation (91). Thus we have the equations,

$$x_1 + b^{[2]}x_3 + x_5 \qquad = y_3^{[3]} \tag{98}$$

$$x_3 + b^{[2]}x_5 + u_7 = y_5^{[2]}. \tag{99}$$

In addition we have the equation,

$$x_3 + bx_4 + x_5 = y_4, \tag{100}$$

from equation (87).

By adding equations (98) and (99) we obtain,

$$x_1 + (1 + b^{[2]})x_3 + (1 + b^{[2]})x_5 + x_7 = y_3^{[2]} + y_5^{[2]}. \tag{101}$$

Then by multiplying (100) by $(1 + b^{[2]})$ and subtracting from (101) we obtain the final equation,

$$x_1 - b(1 + b^{[2]})x_4 + x_7 = y_3^{[2]} + y_5^{[2]} - (1 + b^{[2]})y_4. \tag{102}$$

If we now rewrite equation (102) in the form,

$$x_1 \bar{b}^{[2]}x_4 + x_7 = y_4^{[2]}, \tag{103}$$

which is the representative equation for a Stride of 3 in the C.R. algorithm, where,

$$\bar{b}^{[2]} = -b(1 + b^{[2]}) = b(b^2 - 3),$$

and

$$
\begin{aligned}
\bar{y}_4^{[2]} &= y_3^{[2]} + y_5^{[2]} - (3 - b^2)y_4 \\
&= y_2 + y_4 - by_3 + y_4 + y_6 - by_5 - (3 - b^2)y^4 \\
&= y_2 + y_6 - b(y_3 + y_5) - (1 - b^2)y_4.
\end{aligned}
\tag{104}
$$

So the solution procedure for $n = 3^p - 1$, for $p = 2$, i.e. $n = 8$ is as follows: the system

$$Ax = y.$$

i.e.,

$$
\begin{bmatrix}
b & 1 & & & & & & \\
1 & b & 1 & & & 0 & & \\
& 1 & b & 1 & & & & \\
& & 1 & b & 1 & & & \\
& & & 1 & b & 1 & & \\
& & & & 1 & b & 1 & \\
0 & & & & & 1 & b & 1 \\
& & & & & & 1 & b
\end{bmatrix}
\begin{bmatrix}
x_1 \\ x_2 \\ x_3 \\ x_4 \\ x_5 \\ x_6 \\ x_7 \\ x_8
\end{bmatrix}
=
\begin{bmatrix}
y_1 \\ y_2 \\ y_3 \\ y_4 \\ y_5 \\ y_6 \\ y_7 \\ y_8
\end{bmatrix},
\tag{105}
$$

is reduced to $A^{[2]}x^{[2]} = y^{[2]}$,

$$
\begin{bmatrix}
b^{[2]} & 1 \\
1 & b^{[2]}
\end{bmatrix}
\begin{bmatrix}
x_3 \\ x_6
\end{bmatrix}
=
\begin{bmatrix}
\bar{y}_3^{[2]} \\ \bar{y}_6^{[2]}
\end{bmatrix}.
\tag{106}
$$

which can be solved from x_3 and x_6, i.e.,

$$x_3 = (\bar{y}_3^{[2]} - b^{[2]}\bar{y}_6^{[2]})/(1 - b^{[2]^2}), x_6 = (\bar{y}_6^{[2]} - b^{[2]}\bar{y}_3^{[2]})/(1 - b^{[2]^2}).
\tag{107}$$

Then, the remaining elements of the solution vector x can be obtained by solving the 3 subsystems,

$$
\begin{bmatrix}
b & 1 \\
1 & b
\end{bmatrix}
\begin{bmatrix}
x_1 \\ x_2
\end{bmatrix}
=
\begin{bmatrix}
y_1 \\ y_2 - x_3
\end{bmatrix},
\tag{108a}
$$

$$
\begin{bmatrix}
b & 1 \\
1 & b
\end{bmatrix}
\begin{bmatrix}
x_4 \\ x_5
\end{bmatrix}
=
\begin{bmatrix}
y_4 - x_3 \\ y_5 - x_6
\end{bmatrix},
\tag{108b}
$$

and,

$$
\begin{bmatrix}
b & 1 \\
1 & b
\end{bmatrix}
\begin{bmatrix}
x_7 \\ x_8
\end{bmatrix}
=
\begin{bmatrix}
y_7 - x_6 \\ y_9
\end{bmatrix},
\tag{108c}
$$

again by Cramer's rule, (see Figure 2).

A comparison of the 'Stride of 3' and the Cyclic Odd Even algorithms for the solution of n equations is given by the ratio,

$$\log 3 / \log 2 = 1.585.
\tag{109}$$

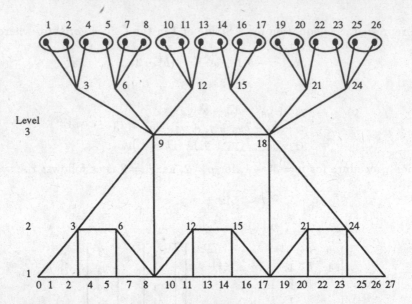

Figure 2. Communication topology Stride of 3 for $n = 3^3 - 1$ (26)

Stride of 5 Cyclic Reduction Algorithm

In a similar manner we can derive a C.R. algorithm with a stride of 5. Consider again the reduced system given by the equations,

$$x_1 + b^{[2]}x_3 + x_5 \qquad\qquad\qquad = y_3^{[2]} \qquad\qquad (110)$$

$$x_3 + b^{[2]}x_5 + x_7 \qquad\qquad = y_5^{[2]} \qquad\qquad (111)$$

$$x_5 + b^{[2]}x_7 + x_9 \qquad = y_7^{[2]} \qquad\qquad (112)$$

$$x_7 + b^{[2]}x_9 + x_{11} = y_9^{[2]}. \qquad\qquad (113)$$

Now we multiply equation (110) by $-b^{[2]}$ and add to equation (111) to yield,

$$x_1 + (1 - b^{[2]^2})x_5 - b^{[2]}x_7 = y_3^{[2]} - b^{[2]}y_5^{[2]}. \qquad\qquad (114)$$

Similarly we can multiply equation (112) by $-b^{[2]}$ and add to equation (113) to yield,

$$- b^{[2]}x_5 + (1 - b^{[2]^2})x_7 + x_{11} = y_9^{[2]} - b^{[2]}y_7^{[2]}. \qquad\qquad (115)$$

Now we add equations (114) and (115) to give,

$$x_1 + (1 - b^{[2]^2} - b^{[2]})x_5 + (1 - b^{[2]^2} - b^{[2]})x_7 + x_{11} = y_3^{[2]} + y_9^{[2]} - b^{[2]}(y_5^{[2]} + y_7^{[2]}). \qquad (116)$$

In addition, we have the equation from equation (87),

$$x_5 + bx_6 + x_7 = y_6. \qquad\qquad (117)$$

Now we eliminate x_5 and x_7 from equations (116) and (117) by multiplying equation (117) by $-(1 - b^{[2]^2} - b^{[2]})$ and add to equation (116). This produces the Stride of 5 version of the C.R. algorithm, i.e.,

$$x_1 + b(1 - b^{[2]^2} - b^{[2]})x_6 + x_{11} = y_3^{[2]} + y_9^{[2]} - b^{[2]}(y_5^{[2]} + y_7^{[2]}) - (1 - b^{[2]^2} - b^{[2]})y_6, \qquad (118)$$

or in the usual form,

$$x_1 + \bar{\bar{b}}^{[2]} x_6 + x_{11} = \bar{\bar{y}}^{[6]},$$

where

$$\bar{\bar{b}}^{[2]} = -b(1 - b^{[2]^2} - b^{[2]}) = b(b^4 - 5b^2 + 5), \tag{119}$$

and

$$\begin{aligned}
\bar{\bar{y}}_6^{[2]} &= y_3^{[2]} + y_9^{[2]} - b^{[2]}(y_5^{[2]} - y_7^{[2]}) - (1 - b^{[2]^2} - b^{[2]})y_6 \\
&= y_2 + y_4 - by_3 + y_8 + y_{10} - by_9 \\
&\quad - (2 - b^2)(y_4 + y_6 - by_5 + y_6 + y_8 + by_7) + (b^4 - 5b^2 + 5)y_6 \\
&= y_2 + y_{10} - b(y_3 + y_9) - (1 - b^2)(y_4 + y_8) \\
&\quad\quad + (2 - b^2)b(y_5 + y_7) + (b^4 + 3b^2 + 1)y_6.
\end{aligned} \tag{120}$$

Similarly the solution procedure for $n = 5^p - 1$ with $p = 2$, i.e. $n = 24$ is as follows: the system

$$Ax = y,$$

i.e.

$$\begin{bmatrix}
b & 1 & & & & & \\
1 & b & 1 & & \text{\Large 0} & & \\
& \ddots & \ddots & \ddots & & & \\
& & \ddots & \ddots & \ddots & & \\
\text{\Large 0} & & & \ddots & \ddots & 1 & \\
& & & & 1 & b
\end{bmatrix}
\begin{bmatrix}
x_1 \\ x_2 \\ \vdots \\ x_{23} \\ x_{24}
\end{bmatrix}
=
\begin{bmatrix}
y_1 \\ y_2 \\ \vdots \\ y_{23} \\ y_{24}
\end{bmatrix}, \tag{121}$$

is reduced to,

$$A^{[2]} x^{[2]} = z^{[2]},$$

i.e.,

$$\begin{bmatrix}
b^{[2]} & 1 & & \text{\Large 0} \\
1 & b^{[2]} & 1 & \\
& 1 & b^{[2]} & 1 \\
\text{\Large 0} & & 1 & b^{[2]}
\end{bmatrix}
\begin{bmatrix}
x_5 \\ x_{10} \\ x_{15} \\ x_{20}
\end{bmatrix}
=
\begin{bmatrix}
\bar{\bar{y}}_5^{[2]} \\ \bar{\bar{y}}_{10}^{[2]} \\ \bar{\bar{y}}_{15}^{[2]} \\ \bar{\bar{y}}_{20}^{[2]}
\end{bmatrix}. \tag{122}$$

The inverse of the matrix $A^{[2]}$ is given by,

$$\{A^{[2]}\}^{-1} = \Delta^{-1}
\begin{bmatrix}
b(b^2 - 2) & 1 - b^2 & b & -1 \\
1 - b^2 & b(b^2 - 1) & -b^2 & b \\
b & -b^2 & b(b^2 - 1) & 1 - b^2 \\
-1 & b & 1 - b^2 & b(b^2 - 2)
\end{bmatrix}, \tag{123}$$

where $\Delta = (b^4 - 3b^2 + 1)$, $b = b^{[2]}$.

Then the remaining elements of the solution vector x can be obtained by solving the 5 subsystems,

$$\begin{bmatrix}
b & 1 & & \text{\Large 0} \\
1 & b & 1 & \\
& 1 & b & 1 \\
\text{\Large 0} & & 1 & b
\end{bmatrix}
\begin{bmatrix}
x_1 \\ x_2 \\ x_3 \\ x_4
\end{bmatrix}
=
\begin{bmatrix}
y_1 \\ y_2 \\ y_3 \\ y_4 - x_5
\end{bmatrix}, \tag{124a}$$

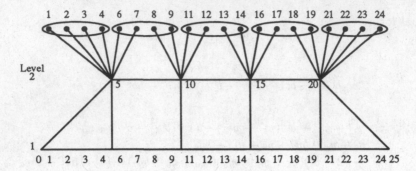

Figure 3. Communication topology Stride of 5 for $n = 5^2 - 1$ (24)

$$\begin{bmatrix} b & 1 & & 0 \\ 1 & b & 1 & \\ & 1 & b & 1 \\ 0 & & 1 & b \end{bmatrix} \begin{bmatrix} x_6 \\ x_7 \\ x_8 \\ x_9 \end{bmatrix} = \begin{bmatrix} y_6 - x_5 \\ y_7 \\ y_8 \\ y_9 - x_{10} \end{bmatrix},$$ (124b)

$$\begin{bmatrix} b & 1 & & 0 \\ 1 & b & 1 & \\ & 1 & b & 1 \\ 0 & & 1 & b \end{bmatrix} \begin{bmatrix} x_{11} \\ x_{12} \\ x_{13} \\ x_{14} \end{bmatrix} = \begin{bmatrix} y_{11} - x_{10} \\ y_{12} \\ y_{13} \\ y_{14} - x_{15} \end{bmatrix},$$ (124c)

$$\begin{bmatrix} b & 1 & & 0 \\ 1 & b & 1 & \\ & 1 & b & 1 \\ 0 & & 1 & b \end{bmatrix} \begin{bmatrix} x_{16} \\ x_{17} \\ x_{18} \\ x_{19} \end{bmatrix} = \begin{bmatrix} y_{16} - x_5 \\ y_{17} \\ y_{18} \\ y_{19} - x_{20} \end{bmatrix},$$ (124d)

and,

$$\begin{bmatrix} b & 1 & & 0 \\ 1 & b & 1 & \\ & 1 & b & 1 \\ 0 & & 1 & b \end{bmatrix} \begin{bmatrix} x_{21} \\ x_{22} \\ x_{23} \\ x_{24} \end{bmatrix} = \begin{bmatrix} y_{21} - x_{20} \\ y_{22} \\ y_{23} \\ y_{24} - x_{25} \end{bmatrix},$$ (124e)

which are solved in a similar manner as previously, (see Figure 3).

A comparison of the 'Stride of 5' and the Cyclic Odd Even Algorithm for the solution of n equations is given by the ratio,

$$\log 5 / \log 2 = 2.322.$$ (125)

References

[1] D.J. Evans, *New Parallel Algorithms in Linear Algebra*, in 1st Colloque Int. sur le Methodes Vectorielles et Paralleles en Calcul Scientifiqure, ed. A. Bossavit, E.D.F. Bull. de la Direction des Etudes et Recherches, Series C. Math. Informatique, No. 1, (1983), pp.61-70.

[2] D.J. Evans and W.S. Yousif, *Explicit Solution of Block Tridiagonal Systems*, Inform. Proc. Lett., 24(1987), pp.627-656.

[3] Buzbee, B.L., Golub, G.H. and Nielson, C.W., *On Direct Methods for Solving Poisson's Equation*, SINUM 7 (1970), pp.627-656.

[4] D.J. Evans, *The Strides Reduction Algoriths for Solving Tridiagonal Linear Systems*, Int. Jour. Comp. Maths., Vol. 42, 1991 (in press).

Chapter 8

Resilient Parallel Computing on Unreliable Parallel Machines*

Z. M. Kedem[†]   K. V. Palem   A. Raghunathan[‡]   P. G. Spirakis[§]

Abstract

With hardware becoming cheaper, "massively parallel systems" with large numbers of processors are fast becoming a technological reality. They are proving to be especially attractive since they offer increasingly faster computational speeds, at relatively low cost. Unfortunately, these massively parallel machines tend to become increasingly fault-prone. For example, the larger the number of processors, the greater the probability of some of them failing. As a consequence, programs designed oblivious of such failures will run erroneously, as the parallel machine degrades due to processor failures. An obvious approach to coping with this problem is to explicitly design programs keeping failures in the parallel machine in mind. While such an approach might be of interest in limited settings, it is unrealistic to expect programmers of parallel machines to be burdened with this issue always. In fact, given that parallel program (or algorithm) design is a complicated task in its own right, it is typically performed in the context of an *ideal parallel machine* that is unencumbered by failures or other "imperfections" intrinsic to its realistic counterpart. The resulting ideal programs will not run correctly on real implementations of parallel machines, which are fault-prone.

There has been considerable recent activity addressing this important issue. The main concerns of these efforts fall into two categories. *First*, research has been directed towards the design of *general* strategies for deriving resilient computations, that work *independent* of any particular parallel program. *Second*, these strategies are extremely efficient in that the overhead they introduce into the resilient computation, relative to the ideal program from which it is derived, is provably small. Furthermore, this overhead *scales* in proportion to the degree of parallelism in the given computation. Most importantly, these strategies are *fully automatic* and can be applied as compile-time transformations to the ideal program. Therefore, the programmer is freed of concerns arising from the unreliable behavior of the parallel machine, and its impact on the execution of the program.

The aim of this chapter is to survey these recent developments and describe strategies designed to yield *resilient* (correct) execution of parallel programs on *fault-prone*

---

*This research was partially supported by the National Science Foundation under grant numbers CCR-89-6949 and CCR-91-03953 and by the EEC ESPRIT Basic Research Actions Project ALCOM (No 3075).

†This author's research was conducted while he was visiting the IBM Research Division at the T. J. Watson Research Center and the Institute for Advanced Computer Studies at the University of Maryland.

‡Part of this author's research was conducted while he was visiting New York University.

§This author's research was conducted while he was visiting New York University.

parallel machines. We will sketch the techniques used to cope with the important case of processor failures, in some detail. The canonical fault-prone machine on which our programs will actually be executing, is one in which the set of resources (including processors) that are assigned to the program fluctuate *dynamically* during its execution. These fluctuations could be induced by phenomena such as *failures* and *repairs*, or due to *rescheduling* by the operating system.

In the sequel, we will sketch transformation for deriving resilient computations automatically. Then, we will discuss approaches to making resiliency not only feasible, but also extremely efficient as well. All of the above results are aimed at target parallel machines prone to processor failures. Techniques aimed at coping with asynchronous processors, faulty memories, or interconnection networks that fail when the parallel machine has a distributed memory architecture, will be discussed briefly as well.

During the process of designing a parallel algorithm of program, the programmer typically does not view the resources (notably processors) to be fluctuating from one step of the computation to the next. In other words, there is an assumption that the resource assignment is static. Now, if the target machine on which the program will be actually executing were to preserve this assumption, the well-known Brent's Lemma [6] can be used to scale the program, by adapting it to execute on a number of processors that is (possibly) smaller than that for which the program was originally designed. The reason is that this lemma embodies a processor rescheduling strategy for handling *static availability patterns*, that is, the situation in which the number of processors can change across instances of the computation, but the number of processors available during each instance of the computation is *predetermined* before it starts. In effect, the program can be transformed *off-line* to adapt itself to the number of available processors. In contrast, the problem we are faced with is much more demanding since with dynamic processor fluctuations, we need to develop techniques to handle availability patterns that are only available *on-line*. Consequently, the constructions and techniques to be described in this chapter collectively yield a generalization of Brent's lemma to the case where processor availability patterns are only revealed dynamically, as the computation is executing.

1.   Introduction

Historically, fault tolerance and parallel algorithm design have been separate fields. Fault tolerant algorithms have used redundancy to achieve *resiliency* in the face of failures. Typically, redundancy is used to duplicate the computation and storage. The intuition is of course that by replicating the computation in this fashion, eventually, we are bound to increase the chances of survival of one if its incarnations. In contrast, parallel algorithms have been concerned with the tradeoffs between multiple *resources*, usually processors, and *performance*, usually time. But more importantly, the redundancy in a parallel machine is used to perform strictly *different* parts of a computation to yield better performance. Viewed from this perspective (of rendundancy), the goals of achieving fault tolerance and those of efficient parallel computation are conflicting. The methods described in this chapter judiciously balance out these conflicting concerns by using redundancy for fault tolerance only when it is (dynamically) determined to be absolutely necessary. In the absence of such a need, they allow the multiplicity of processors and resources to effectively work in parallel thereby achieving the desired efficiency whenever possible.

Our goal is to describe general strategies supporting the execution of parallel computations that were originally designed to run in an "ideal" fault-free environment, in a setting that is "fault-prone". Our main concerns will be two-fold. First, we would like to develop strategies that work *independent* of the particular parallel computation that we are given. Second, any such strategy must introduce *negligible slowdowns*, while making the given computation resilient. Of course, all of the methods that we describe are *fully automatic* in that they can be applied to the given ideal program without the knowledge of the programmer or algorithm designer using the fault-prone parallel machine on which the resulting resilient programs are going to be executing. In other words, the transformations to be described below are resilient as well.

This presentation is divided into two distinct parts. The first part can be read without any prior knowledge of the results in the area. For completeness, it restates some of the results presented in [17], where a general strategy for automatically deriving resilient parallel programs from their ideal counterparts was first described. Its goal is to provide a detailed description of this general strategy for *resilient computing*. Further extensions to this general strategy that yield resiliency with small *constant* time overhead, compared to the execution of the same computation on an ideal machine, even under very pessimistic assumptions on failures (from [19]), will also be described here. These methods and techniques will be presented in the context of a parallel machine with (possibly transient) processor failures. (We note that such a machine is a generalization of the fail-stop parallel machine originally introduced in [15], and the reader is referred to Section 8. for a summary of the evolution of these and other models. Note that in [15], several beautiful resilient algorithms are presented for solving specific problems, including the *Write-All* problem; this problem plays a role in the subsequent sections of this chapter. The reader is also referred to Section 8., for a discussion of recent developments where the techniques from [17] have been adapted to the more demanding case of *asynchronous machines* [10, 22].) The strategy is based on utilizing several algorithms, which we will classify as *definite* and *tentative*. The presentation in the first part chooses them rather arbitrarily, to simplify the understanding of the fundamental issues involved.

The second part, which starts with Section 6 is more technical in nature. We present some specific tentative and definite algorithms that can be used in our strategy, and describe their complexity. This section assumes the knowledge of some of the previous work. Historical remarks including a discussion of how these methods extend to the distributed memory setting can be found in Section 8.. Finally, some concluding remarks are given in Section 9..

2.   The models of the PRAMs

In this section we will specify our assumptions on both the *ideal* and the *fault-prone* PRAMs. The underlying model is that the program is written for the ideal PRAM, and it is our job to execute it correctly on the fault-prone PRAM.

As the ideal PRAM, we take a standard Concurrent-Read/Concurrent-Write PRAM. It is not necessary for us to repeat the standard formal definitions and for convenience we make certain simplifying assumptions. There are n processors: $P_1, \ldots, P_n$ operating *synchronously* with *no local memory*; all memory is *global* and *fully shared*[1].

There is a vector of instructions[2] $INST[1..last]$, stored inside unbounded memory $M[1..\infty)$. There is a vector $PC[1..n]$ of *program counters* initialized to 1; $PC[i]$ is the program counter

---

[1]We are not completely precise here. The processor has local memory, but its status is lost between steps.

[2]We could have assumed that each processor has a different program.

Algorithm 1

1. read $PC[i]$;
2. **if** $PC[i] \neq 0$ **then**
3.   **begin**
4.   read and decode $INST[PC[i]]$;
5.   read appropriate locations of M, if any;
6.   compute and write $M[loc]$ if loc is defined for $INST[PC[i]]$;
7.   compute and write $PC[i]$
8.   **end**
9. **else**
10.   halt;

Figure 1. Internal program run by P_i, during the execution of a single step of the ideal PRAM

for P_i. Process P_i obtains its instruction by examining $PC[i]$, and modifies $PC[i]$ during the execution of its instruction.[3] We can assume that the instructions themselves are not modified during the execution. Execution of an instruction by P_i entails its reading of $PC[i]$ and of a finite number of memory locations, say 2 at most, modifying $PC[i]$ and at most a single memory location.[4]

Thus, we could describe a "generic" instruction I as executing the following sequence:

1. Reading $PC[i]$

2. Reading (and decoding) $INST[1..last]$

3. Reading at most 2 memory locations

4. Writing new value of $PC[i]$

5. Writing the new value of some memory location $M[loc]$; in case no memory location needs to be written we will sometimes denote it by stating that in this case $loc = 0$

Such an execution of a single instruction is defined by Algorithm 1 in Fig. 1, which describes the internal program run by the PRAM. In the sequel, we will refer to programs written for such a machine and their executions as *ideal*.

We still assume the machine to be synchronous. However a processor can fail *at any point* (but not in the middle of executing a single write. It can then be restarted at the *beginning* of any subsequent step. If a processor is alive throughout the step, we will refer to it as *active*, otherwise we will refer to it as *idle*. If a processor is alive at the beginning of the step and dies in the middle we will refer to it as idle during the step.

---

[3]We can assume the P_i is aware of its serial number, i.

[4]We do not address *randomized* algorithms explicitly here. However, one could add an instruction *RAND*, which would choose a random number (from an appropriate distribution) and store it in some meory location. This, is in effect, what is done in [21] in the context of parallel computations.

> Processor P_i executes the program:
>
> 1. $x[i] := 1;$

Figure 2. Program solving the Write-All problem

3.   The fail-stop PRAM and the Write-All problem

Our fault-prone PRAM is a generalization of the fail-stop PRAM first described in[15]. We have discussed some of this in Section 1.. More details can be found in Section 8.. As noted before, in [15], a deterministic and resilient algorithm for solving the *Write-All* problem in the fail-stop PRAM is presented. The problem itself is trivial. We are given n processors and an array $x[1..n]$ initialized to 0. The job is to write the value 1 in each location of the array. The one-step program to do so on a PRAM is given in Fig. 2.

However, the algorithm for executing this program on the fail-stop machine is by no means trivial. As processors can fail, the algorithm of [15] detects which locations might not have been written and determines which processors might be available to do the required work.[5] Then the processors are reassigned.

4.   Execution of single-step programs

4.1.   A difficulty

We start by describing one of the difficulties encountered while trying to executed an ideal program on the fault-prone machine. We could refer to it in a more general context as implementing a virtual ideal machine on the fault-prone machine.

A naive attempt to implement an ideal machine on the fault-prone machine based on simple reassignment of active processors will run into a number of difficulties. For a trivial example, consider an ideal program for exchanging the values of two locations $x[1]$ and $x[2]$ in a single step. P_1 executes $x[1] := x[2]$ and simultaneously P_2 executes $x[2] := x[1]$. If, say, P_1 is idle, the original value of $x[2]$ is lost, and the computation cannot be completed by another processor.

In [17], a *Two-Phase Idempotent Execution Strategy* (or *TIES* for short) was introduced. For completeness and for fixing notation that will be needed later, we will review its major points. We will do it by stages, as needed. We will start by describing the strategy for the ideal machine, that although it is not necessary to do so for executions on such machine.[6] We do it, however, as such execution can later be easier adapted to run on the fault-prone machine.

---

[5] We use the word "might," as due to failures, only estimates of the state are in general possible.

[6] Technically, however, it is needed if one wants to use Brent's Lemma to slow-down the execution by running the program on a smaller number of processors than the one for which the program was originally written.

Phase	P_1	P_2	P_3	P_4
1	$\phi_1^{(1)}$	$\phi_2^{(1)}$	$\phi_3^{(1)}$	$\phi_4^{(1)}$
2	$\phi_1^{(2)}$	$\phi_2^{(2)}$	$\phi_3^{(2)}$	$\phi_4^{(2)}$

Table 1. The two-phase execution of a single step on a 4-processor ideal PRAM

4.2.   Two-phase execution strategy

At a very gross level, we can view the execution of any one step of an arbitrary ideal parallel program as a transformation of the state of the ideal machine, which we assume to be completely described by (some of) the values stored in the locations of the global memory. We could modify the execution of the machine so such a transformation is done in two phases.

The *first phase* creates the changes to the state in temporary "scratch" storage. This is done by computing the new values of the variables to be modified and storing them in temporary storage.[7] The *second phase* copies the changes from the temporary storage to create the new state, by writing the new values of the variables into their original locations.

We now proceed with the description of the implementation of the two-phase execution. We assume the existence of three additional vectors: $LOC[1..n]$, $VAL[1..n]$ and $NEXT[1..n]$.[8] Using these vectors the execution of a single step of PRAM can be achieved by *rewriting* it as two phases. We execute in succession:

1. Algorithm 2 defined in Fig. 3, which executes the first phase, $\phi_i^{(1)}$, of the current instruction of processor P_i. It stores in temporary storage the new values of the variables to be written and the new values of the program counters (of the program being executed).

2. Algorithm 3 defined in Fig. 4, which executes the second phase, $\phi_i^{(2)}$, of the current instruction of processor P_i. It stores the new values of the variables and the program counters in the correct locations.

We will assume in the sequel that each such phase requires one clock unit of the PRAM; or more importantly, the machine is synchronized between phases.[9]

Thus, we can describe the execution of the single instruction of the PRAM of 4 processors as shown in Table 1. There, for each of the processors, P_1, P_2, P_3, P_4, we show that during the first "substep" P_i executes the first phase of its instruction, and during the second "substep" it executes the second phase of its instruction.

4.3.   Extension to fault-prone PRAMs

Consider now *in isolation* the execution of phase 1 of some processor. The execution is *idempotent* in the sense that the same results are obtained no matter how many times this

---

[7]Jumping ahead, doing this in the fault-prone machine, allows processors that have been allocated to do the work of processors that failed, to access the original values of the variables *in situ*.

[8]In Section 5.2.1. we will also maintain trace information about the old values; we will then for uniformity maintain both the old values and the new values in a single structure. In this section, however, we decided to keep as closely as possible to the exposition used in [17].

[9]Note also, although this is of no relevance now, that each phase consists of a reading sub-phase followed by a writing subphase.

```
Algorithm 2

1.    read PC[i];
2.    if PC[i] ≠ 0 then
3.       begin
4.       read and decode INST[PC[i]];
5.       read appropriate locations of M if any;
6.       compute PC[i] and write it in NEXT[i];
7.       compute loc and write it in LOC[i] if loc is defined, else write 0 in LOC[i];
8.       if LOC[i] ≠ 0 then
9.          compute M[LOC[i]] and write it in VAL[i]
10.      end
11.   else
12.      halt;
```

Figure 3. Definition of $\phi_i^{(1)}$, the execution of phase 1 of the current instruction of processor P_i

```
Algorithm 3

1.    read NEXT[i];
2.    read LOC[i];
3.    if LOC[i] ≠ 0 then
4.       begin
5.       read VAL[i];
6.       write VAL[i] in M[LOC[i]]
7.       end;
8.    write NEXT[i] in PC[i];
```

Figure 4. Definition of $\phi_i^{(2)}$, the execution of phase 2 of the current instruction of processor P_i

Phase	time	P_1	P_2	P_3	P_4
1	1	$\phi_1^{(1)}$			$\phi_3^{(1)}$
	2	$\phi_2^{(1)}$		$\phi_4^{(1)}$	$\phi_4^{(1)}$
	3	$\phi_3^{(1)}$			
	4	$\phi_4^{(1)}$			
2	1	$\phi_1^{(2)}$		$\phi_3^{(2)}$	$\phi_4^{(2)}$
	2				
	3	$\phi_2^{(2)}$		$\phi_4^{(2)}$	$\phi_3^{(2)}$

Table 2. A two-phase execution of a PRAM step with repetitions and idle processors

particular phase is executed.[10] This follows from the fact that the input set and the output set for Algorithm 2 are disjoint. The same property holds for phase 2 of any processor.

We can generalize this observation even further. Let us consider the execution in a fault-prone machine. There we allow processors not just to execute a phase of an instruction assigned to them. In general, they could be idle (fail) in a time clock, "take over" the work of other processors to substitute for them, etc. There are a few technicalities that should be addressed to show how such substitution can be done. In order not to increase the number of tedious details, we will not be precise about such specification here, but only indicate one possible approach. Assume the existence of a vector $ID[1..n]$. In the normal course of events, $ID[i] = i$ for each i. Processor P_i consults $ID[i]$ and then executes the current instruction for processor $P_{ID[i]}$. Thus if $ID[i] = j$, P_i executes the current instruction for P_j. Processors, can cause processors to substitute for processors by modifying ID appropriately. We will not pursue the low level technical details of such implementations any further here, but will concentrate on the challenging question of how to decide which processors substitute for which processors.

Examine now the execution described in Table 2. Here, the execution takes 7 time units of the PRAM, and we have numbered the time units within each phase. Logically, a single instruction of the PRAM program is executed. To assure that the instruction is executed correctly, it was enough to assure that the execution is divided into two non-overlapping phases, such that:

1. In phase 1, in each step each processor P_i was either idle or executed some $\phi_j^{(1)}$. Furthermore, each $\phi_j^{(1)}$, for $j = 1, 2, \ldots, n$, is executed (to completion) at least once.

2. In phase 2, in each step each processor P_i was either idle or executed some $\phi_j^{(2)}$. Furthermore, each $\phi_j^{(2)}$, for $j = 1, 2, \ldots, n$, was executed (to completion) at least once.

Again, this execution is correct, because in each phase the input-set and the output-set are disjoint.

---

[10]Note the connection between our work and dependable transaction processing systems. Our strategy is reminiscent of the redo/no-undo recovery mechanism, used in database operating systems; for more on database operating systems, see e.g. the monographs [5] and [9]. However, we need to handle a different scenario, and use a novel synchronization primitive we proposed.

Algorithm 4

During phase 1 of the round, processor P_i executes the program:

1. execute $\phi_i^{(1)}$;
2. execute $\phi_{i\hat{+}1}^{(1)}$;

During phase 2 of the round, processor P_i executes the program:

1. execute $\phi_i^{(2)}$;
2. execute $\phi_{i\hat{+}1}^{(2)}$;

Figure 5. The conga execution of a single round

4.4. Some algorithms for processor assignment to execute a single step

Until now, we have looked at a particular execution of an ideal PRAM step on a fault-prone PRAM and formulated a condition assuring that it was correct. We are however, interested in specifying algorithms for processors' behavior so that the execution of a step is either guaranteed to be a correct, or is correct with high probability under certain assumptions on failures processors.

We now describe two representative processor algorithms to guarantee or attempt correct execution of just a single ideal PRAM step in a fault-prone PRAM. We do not claim that these algorithms are "best," although this may be the case under some conditions. Their purpose is to illustrate the various issues involved and motivate further development.

Let the term *round* refer to the program executing a single step of the ideal PRAM, or execution of such a program. Such execution will take several (maybe many) steps on the fault-prone PRAM.

4.4.1. A tentative execution using the conga algorithm

We will start with the *conga execution* of a round. In this algorithm, each processor is responsible for executing steps of two processors; its own step and the step of the processor ahead of it, that is, to its right (the array is considered circular with 1 being to the right of n).[11] To specify various algorithms formally, it will be convenient, to define addition in the set $\{1, \ldots, n\}$ with 1 following n. We denote such addition by $\hat{+}$, thus $a \hat{+} b = (a + b - 1 \mod n) + 1$. The two phases are described in Algorithm 4 in Fig. 5. Table 3 shows a typical conga execution of a round.

The conga execution of a round is guaranteed to be a correct if, for instance during the round at most one processor can be idle. However, if two neighboring processors are idle

---

[11] Thus in our version of the conga dance, there is no leader; the processors are holding their hands on the waists of the processors ahead of them in a circular list.

Phase	time	P_1	P_2	P_3	P_4
1	1	$\phi_1^{(1)}$	$\phi_2^{(1)}$	$\phi_3^{(1)}$	$\phi_4^{(1)}$
	2	$\phi_2^{(1)}$		$\phi_4^{(1)}$	$\phi_1^{(1)}$
2	1	$\phi_1^{(2)}$		$\phi_3^{(2)}$	$\phi_4^{(2)}$
	2	$\phi_2^{(2)}$	$\phi_3^{(2)}$	$\phi_4^{(2)}$	

Table 3. A possible trace of the conga execution of one round in a fault-prone machine

during the round, the execution in general will not be correct. We will refer to this algorithm as *tentative*. This term is supposed to imply that:

1. If all processors are active during the round the execution will be correct.

2. Under "realistic" assumptions on the failures' occurrences, the execution will be correct "often enough."

Clearly, item 2 needs to be better specified. One needs a good model of the processors' active/idle behavior to decide whether the conga execution will be correct often enough. Probabilistic behavior of various tentative algorithm will be studied in Section 7.1.. Furthermore, we will also need to decide if the execution was correct and what to do if it was not; this will be dealt with in Section 5.2..

4.4.2.   A definite execution using the pointer shortcutting algorithm

In [17] a *pointer shortcutting algorithm*[12] was introduced. We restate it here using a somewhat different notation and refer the reader to [17] for additional details.

For now, our goal is to execute one round, which correctly executes one step of the ideal PRAM as long as there are sufficiently large number of time units in which a processor is active. (It does not have to be the same processor.) We assume the existence of two vectors $s^{(1)}[1..n]$ and $s^{(2)}[1..n]$ initialized to 0 and two boolean variables $DONE^{(1)}$ and $DONE^{(2)}$ initialized to *FALSE*. We first describe the pointer shortcutting execution and then briefly explain why it is correct. It is defined in Algorithm 5 in Fig. 6.

We refer to this type of algorithm as *definite*. This term implies that the execution *will be correct* as long as there are sufficiently many time units in which there is an active processor.

Theorem 1 *The pointer shortcutting execution of a round is definite.*

Proof: Consider first phase 1 of Algorithm 5. The following can be easily verified:

1. The invariant: "if $s^{(1)}[i] > 0$ then $\phi_i^{(1)}, \phi_{i\dotplus1}^{(1)}, \ldots, \phi_{i\dotplus(s^{(1)}[i]-1)}^{(1)}$ have been executed" is true.

2. If processor P_i is active during some step, then $s^{(1)}[i]$ is incremented during that step.

Similar statements hold for phase 2 of Algorithm 5. From these, our claim follows. □

---

[12]It is essentially the simple pointer-doubling algorithm on a circular list with parallel time of $\log n$ while using n processors on the ideal PRAM, modified to for idle processors.

Algorithm 5

During phase 1 of the round processor P_i executes the program:

1. **while not** $DONE^{(1)}$ **do**
2.   **begin**
3.   **if** $s^{(1)}[i \hat{+} s^{(1)}[i]] = 0$ **then**
4.   **begin**
5.   execute $\phi^{(1)}_{i \hat{+} s^{(1)}[i]}$;
6. $s^{(1)}[i] := s^{(1)}[i] + 1$
7.   **end**
8.   **else** $s^{(1)}[i] := s^{(1)}[i] + s^{(1)}[i \hat{+} s^{(1)}[i]]$;
9.   **if** $s^{(1)}[i] \geq n$ **then**
10. $DONE^{(1)} := TRUE$
11.   **end**;

During phase 2 of the round processor P_i executes the program:

1. **while not** $DONE^{(2)}$ **do**
2.   **begin**
3.   **if** $s^{(2)}[i \hat{+} s^{(2)}[i]] = 0$ **then**
4.   **begin**
5.   execute $\phi^{(2)}_{i \hat{+} s^{(2)}[i]}$;
6. $s^{(2)}[i] := s^{(2)}[i] + 1$
7.   **end**
8.   **else** $s^{(2)}[i] := s^{(2)}[i] + s^{(2)}[i \hat{+} s^{(2)}[i]]$;
9.   **if** $s^{(2)}[i] \geq n$ **then**
10. $DONE^{(2)} := TRUE$
11.   **end**;

Figure 6. The pointer shortcutting execution of a single round

4.4.3.   Comparison of the two algorithms

The tentative algorithm we described, Algorithm 4, will take $\Theta(1)$ time units to execute a round. However the execution may not be correct.[13] The definite algorithm we described, Algorithm 5, will take $\Omega(\log n)$ units and the execution will be correct. An immediate question occurs: Could we provide better definite algorithms?

Any definite algorithm needs $\Omega(\log n)$ time units to execute a single round even if in the particular execution all the processors were continuously active. Thus, using a definite algorithm requires at least a logarithmic slowdown. We will show in Section 5.2. how to combine tentative and definite executions to speed up performance.

5.   Execution of multi-step programs

We now proceed to consider the execution of the whole application program $\mathcal{P}$. The execution will be divided into *rounds*. During each round the fault-prone PRAM will attempt to execute correctly a single step of the ideal PRAM. Each round will consist of two phases. We might use the tentative conga execution for each round. There is no difficulty in doing this, and as long as the execution of each round is correct, the whole execution of $\mathcal{P}$ is correct too. Recall however, that conga execution will not be correct under many scenarios. Thus, we might consider the definite pointer shortcutting execution for each round. Such application of pointer shortcutting, however, introduces another difficulty.

5.1.   Pointer shortcutting execution of several steps

Repeated pointer shortcutting execution requires careful treatment of the auxiliary data structures. The pointer shortcutting execution needs auxiliary data structures $s^{(1)}$, $s^{(2)}$, $DONE^{(1)}$, $DONE^{(2)}$ suitably initialized, for both the reassignment of processors and termination checking. At the end of one round's execution, these data structures are "dirty." Providing dedicated clean copies of the data structures for each round is impractical, and therefore the obvious approach is to re-initialize the original data structure.

The simplistic way to do so is to execute an (ideal) PRAM program storing the appropriate values in the data structures. However, this initialization has to be done on a fault-prone machine. Thus, initializing the data structures requires running one or more rounds. To do that on the fault-prone machine requires additional copies of the data structures, properly initialized, etc., leading to a meaningless infinite reduction.

It was shown in [17] how to overcome this difficulty. The idea is to reinitialize the structures used in phase 2 while executing phase 1, and to reinitialize the structures used in phase 1 while executing phase 2. We only assume that the structures are properly initialized at the beginning of the execution of the first round. This allows execution of an arbitrary number of rounds by means of of Algorithm 6 in Fig. 7.

5.2.   Combining tentative and definite executions

In this section we show how to combine tentative and definite executions. As we have seen, tentative executions, say, using conga execution, may be fast but incorrect; definite

---

[13]Actually, in this case it takes $\Omega(\log n)$ time just to check whether the execution (which itself took $\Theta(1)$ time) was correct.

Algorithm 6

During phase 1 processor P_i executes the program:

1. $DONE^{(2)} := FALSE$;
2.   **while not** $DONE^{(1)}$ **do**
3.   **begin**
4.   **if** $s^{(1)}[i \hat{+} s^{(1)}[i]] = 0$ **then**
5.   **begin**
6.   execute $\phi^{(1)}_{i \hat{+} s^{(1)}[i]}$;
7. $s^{(2)}[i \hat{+} s^{(1)}[i]] = 0$;
8. $s^{(1)}[i] := s^{(1)}[i] + 1$
9.   **end**
10.   **else** $s^{(1)}[i] := s^{(1)}[i] + s^{(1)}[i \hat{+} s^{(1)}[i]]$;
11.   **if** $s^{(1)}[i] \geq n$ **then**
12. $DONE^{(1)} := TRUE$
13.   **end**;

During phase 2 processor P_i executes the program:

1. $DONE^{(1)} := FALSE$;
2.   **while not** $DONE^{(2)}$ **do**
3.   **begin**
4.   **if** $s^{(2)}[i \hat{+} s^{(2)}[i]] = 0$ **then**
5.   **begin**
6.   execute $\phi^{(2)}_{i \hat{+} s^{(2)}[i]}$;
7. $s^{(1)}[i \hat{+} s^{(2)}[i]] = 0$;
8. $s^{(2)}[i] := s^{(2)}[i] + 1$
9.   **end**
10.   **else** $s^{(2)}[i] := s^{(2)}[i] + s^{(2)}[i \hat{+} s^{(2)}[i]]$;
11.   **if** $s^{(2)}[i] \geq n$ **then**
12. $DONE^{(2)} := TRUE$
13.   **end**;

Figure 7. The pointer shortcutting execution of an arbitrary round

executions, say using pointer shortcutting execution, are slow but correct. It is our goal to use tentative executions and *audit* them using definite executions.

5.2.1.   Using definite executions to audit tentative executions

We assume the existence of global *round counter* ρ.[14] It is initialized to 1 at the beginning of the computation and is incremented by 1 at the end of each round. There are two vectors of counters, $c^{(1)}[1..n]$ and $c^{(2)}[1..n]$ initialized to 0.

Again, during each round there are two phases. The execution of a round is defined by Algorithm 7 in Fig. 8. Basically, while the executions proceeds, counters indicate how many steps of the application program assigned to each processor have been executed. Let the execution proceed for some number R of rounds. Then if

$$c^{(2)}[1] = c^{(2)}[2] = \ldots = c^{(2)}[n] = R \tag{1}$$

then the execution was correct. Eq. 1 can be tested by executing the simple program defined by Algorithm 8 in Fig. 9 running on the ideal PRAM.

If Algorithm 8 is executed on the fault-prone PRAM, in a way that guarantees that the execution was correct, by employing say the definite Algorithm 6, then if *GOOD* is set to *TRUE*, we know that the execution was correct.

However, we also have to be ready to handle the situation in which the execution of the application program $\mathcal{P}$ was not guaranteed to be correct, that is, after Algorithm 8 is executed *GOOD = FALSE*. In this case, we need to throw out (abort) the whole computation and restart it. A trivially obvious way of doing it is to create a copy of the whole application's memory before the execution is initiated and then restart the computation from the beginning. This is quite inefficient. Furthermore, even a single failure of a tentative execution of any round will require restarting the computation. Thus, if the computation is long enough, it may never finish. We will, therefore, present a different approach.

Basically, before a location of the memory is updated, the old value of that location is stored so that the state of the memory can be reconstructed as necessary. Furthermore, we will limit the number of steps that the computation needs to be rolled back.[15]

We will now specify different executions of the two phases in each round. These alternative specifications will be denoted by $\Phi_i^{(1)}$ and $\Phi_i^{(2)}$, respectively. $\Phi_i^{(1)}$ is specified in Algorithm 9 and Fig. 10, and $\Phi_i^{(2)}$ is specified in Algorithm 10 and Fig. 11. $\Phi_i^{(1)}$ is obtained from $\phi_i^{(1)}$ by adding instructions to create trace information and $\Phi_i^{(2)}$ is just a rewriting of $\phi_i^{(2)}$ using the new data structures. The data structures employed are: $TRACE\_PCOLD[1..n, 1..\infty)$, $TRACE\_PCNEW[1..n, 1..\infty)$, $TRACE\_LOC[1..n, 1..\infty)$, $TRACE\_VALOLD[1..n, 1..\infty)$, and $TRACE\_VALNEW[1..n, 1..\infty)$. Some of these correspond to the structures defined in Section 4.2.. Specifically, $TRACE\_PCNEW$ corresponds to $NEXT[i]$, $TRACE\_LOC[1..n, 1..\infty)$ corresponds to $LOC[i]$, and $TRACE\_VALNEW[1..n, 1..\infty)$ corresponds to $VAL[i]$.[16]

Now, if the execution was not correct, it is possible to restore the old values of the memory

---

[14]Round counters were also used by [21], but for a much restricted purpose. It also seems, that because of the assumption of *loose atomicity*, defined and employed there, it might be possible to replace them by two boolean flags, as employed in [17], and denoted in this report by $DONE^{(1)}$ and $DONE^{(2)}$.

[15]Our strategy will be reminiscent of the *no-redo/undo* mechanism in database operating systems.

[16]Our choice of the data structures was not most frugal possible, but one that is most easy to treat uniformly.

Algorithm 7

During phase 1, processor P_i executes the program:

1.   **if** $c^{(2)}[i] = \rho - 1$ **then**
2.   **begin**
3.   execute $\phi_i^{(1)}$;
4. $c^{(1)}[i] := \rho$
5.   **end**;
6.   **if** $c^{(2)}[i \hat{+} 1] = \rho - 1$ **then**
7.   **begin**
8.   execute $\phi_{i\hat{+}1}^{(1)}$;
9. $c^{(1)}[i \hat{+} 1] := \rho$
10.   **end**;

During phase 2, processor P_i executes the program:

1.   **if** $c^{(1)}[i] = \rho$ **then**
2.   **begin**
3.   execute $\phi_i^{(2)}$;
4. $c^{(2)}[i] := \rho$
5.   **end**;
6.   **if** $c^{(1)}[i \hat{+} 1] = \rho$ **then**
7.   **begin**
8.   execute $\phi_{i\hat{+}1}^{(2)}$;
9. $c^{(2)}[i \hat{+} 1] := \rho$
10.   **end**;

Figure 8. The conga execution of one round while updating counters

Algorithm 8

Processor P_i executes the program:

1.   **if** $c^{(2)}[i] \neq R$ **then**
2. $GOOD := FALSE$;

Figure 9. The ideal PRAM program determining whether the execution of the R rounds was correct assuming $GOOD$ was initialized to $TRUE$

```
Algorithm 9

1.   read PC[i];
2.   write PC[i] in TRACE_PCOLD[i, ρ];
3.   if PC[i] ≠ 0 then
4.      begin
5.      read and decode INST[PC[i]];
6.      read appropriate locations of M if any;
7.      compute PC[i] and write it in TRACE_PCNEW[i, ρ];
8.      compute loc and write it in TRACE_LOC[i, ρ] if loc is defined,
            else write 0 in TRACE_LOC[i, ρ];
9.      if TRACE_LOC[i, ρ] ≠ 0 then
10.        begin
11.        write M[TRACE_LOC[i, ρ]] in TRACE_VALOLD[i, ρ];
12.        compute M[TRACE_LOC[i, ρ]] and write it in TRACE_VALNEW[i, ρ]
13.        end
14.     end
15. else
16.     begin
17.     write 0 in TRACE_LOC[i, ρ];
18.     halt
19.     end;
```

Figure 10. Definition of $\Phi_i^{(1)}$, the execution of phase 1 of the current instruction of processor P_i, while creating trace information

```
Algorithm 10

1.   read TRACE_PCNEW[i, ρ];
2.   read TRACE_LOC[i, ρ];
3.   if TRACE_LOC[i, ρ] ≠ 0 then
4.      begin
5.      read TRACE_VALNEW[i, ρ];
6.      write TRACE_VALNEW[i, ρ] in M[TRACE_LOC[i, ρ]]
7.      end;
8.   write TRACE_PCNEW[i, ρ] in PC[i]; in M[TRACE_LOC[i, ρ]];
```

Figure 11. Definition of $\Phi_i^{(2)}$, the execution of phase 2 of the current instruction of processor P_i, while using trace information

by "rolling back" through the arrays $TRACE\_LOC$ and $TRACE\_VAL$ and also restoring the original $TRACE\_PC$. One could minimize the amount of rollback, by rolling back to the round whose number is the smallest in the vectors $c^{(1)}$ and $c^{(2)}$, but we will improve the scheme in a different way.

The obvious shortcoming of our scheme is the fact that we need trace memory proportional to R per processor. We will now show how the amount of trace memory can be limited to being proportional to the amount of time needed to a definite execution of one round, $O(\log n)$ per processor under realistic assumptions on the behavior of the system. Furthermore, the counters $c^{(1)}$ and $c^{(2)}$ will not need to store large numbers.

Essentially we run our uncertified execution using Algorithm 7. In parallel, we run Algorithm 8 for certain intermediate points of the execution of $\mathcal{P}$. These intermediate points, or *audit points*, are selected dynamically, as will be described shortly.

5.2.2.   The DOER, the UNDOER, and the AUDITOR

The systems will consist of three modules, the *DOER*, the *UNDOER*, and the *AUDITOR*. We will also need two copies of of the structures ρ, $GOOD$, $TRACE\_PC$, $TRACE\_LOC$, $TRACE\_VAL$ and several copies (three are sufficient) of the structures $c^{(1)}$ and $c^{(2)}$. The execution of $\mathcal{P}$ will be always in one of two modes: the *DO-mode* and the *UNDO-mode*.

We will describe the behavior of the system while using three variables, α, β, and γ, ranging over steps of the ideal program $\mathcal{P}$, or informally equivalently over the rounds of the execution on the fault-prone PRAM. We will always have $\alpha \leq \beta$. γ may be undefined at certain instances, which we denote by writing $\gamma = \perp$. If it is defined, then $\beta \leq \gamma$. Let l denote some chosen, intuitively short, length of time. (It could be $\Theta(\log n)$.) Initially, $\alpha = \beta = 0$, and $\gamma = \perp$.

We now define the two modes informally. They operate by employing a tentative algorithm and a definite algorithm in tandem. For ease of presentation, we will assume the conga and the pointer shortcutting algorithms.

The DO-mode.   By inductive assumption, steps $1, 2, \ldots, \alpha$ of $\mathcal{P}$ have been executed, audited, and determined to be correct. The steps $\alpha + 1, \alpha + 2, \ldots, \beta$ have been executed by means of a tentative algorithm. The values of appropriate set of counters $c^{(2)}$ can be used to audit the execution of these steps. (Recall that there are several sets of counters $c^{(1)}$ and $c^{(2)}$.) The *DOER* and the *AUDITOR* execute in parallel (or we could say "concurrently," as even though they execute on a parallel machine they do not interact with each other). We describe the execution of the two modules:

1. The *DOER* executes steps $\beta + 1, \beta + 2, \ldots$ using the tentative conga algorithm for each round. (Recall that a round executes a step of the ideal program.) As shown in Fig. 8, counters (which we assume are initialized to 0) are being updated to monitor the execution. Furthermore, trace information is maintained, as shown in Fig. 10.

   The execution of the *DO-mode* ends with the termination of the execution of the *AUDITOR*, which is described later. If the *AUDITOR* was not active, the execution terminates after the *DOER* ran for l rounds. In any case γ is defined to be the number of the last step whose round was supposed to be executed by the *DOER*.

2. The *AUDITOR* examines the values of the counters produced by the the previous execution of the *DO-mode*, in which the *DOER* was supposed to execute steps $\alpha+1, \alpha+2, \ldots$ of $\mathcal{P}$. The *AUDITOR* returns *GOOD* as *TRUE* if the counters values guarantee that all the rounds are executed, which is the case if Eq. 1 holds with $R = \beta - \alpha$. The *AUDITOR* executes a variant of Algorithm 8 using the definite pointer shortcutting algorithm. If $\alpha = \beta$, the *AUDITOR* is not active and *GOOD* is returned as *TRUE*.

We now decide how to proceed.

1. If the *AUDITOR* returned *GOOD* as *TRUE*, then we reset: $\alpha \leftarrow \beta$, $\beta \leftarrow \gamma$, and $\gamma \leftarrow \perp$. Then we start the *DO-mode* again, with a different set of auxiliary structures (counters, trace structures, etc.).

2. If the *AUDITOR* returned *GOOD* as *FALSE*, then we start the *UNDO-mode*.

This ends the description of the *DO-mode*.

The UNDO-mode.   By inductive assumption, steps $1, 2, \ldots, \alpha$ of $\mathcal{P}$ have been executed, audited, and determined to be correct. However, the execution of steps $\alpha + 1, \alpha + 2, \ldots \gamma$ is likely to be incorrect[17], and we have to roll it back. We proceed in two stages:

1. In the first stage, the *UNDOER* rolls back the execution from step γ back to step α. This is done by means of tentative execution of a trivial PRAM program copying the values from the trace structures to the appropriate locations in the memory. Counters, are being updated to monitor the progress of the tentative execution, similarly to the way it is done in the *DO-mode*. When the first stage ends, the second stage begins.

2. In the second stage, the *AUDITOR* examines the values of the counters produced by the the execution of the *UNDO-mode*. Again, it does it by means of executing a variant of Algorithm 8 using a definite execution.

We now decide how to proceed.

1. If the *AUDITOR* returned *GOOD* as *TRUE*, then we reset: $\beta \leftarrow \alpha$ and $\gamma \leftarrow \perp$. Then we start the *DO-mode* again, with a different set of auxiliary structures (counters, trace structures, etc.).

2. If the *AUDITOR* returned *GOOD* as *FALSE*, then we repeat the *UNDO-mode*.

This ends the description of the *UNDO-mode*.

Of course, the auxiliary structures are reinitialized as appropriate, so that they can be re-used. We do not go into these and many other necessary tedious details here.

---

[17]If the *AUDITOR* returns $GOOD = TRUE$, the execution is guaranteed to be correct, however if it returns $GOOD = FALSE$ the execution may still be correct.

5.2.3. An assessment

We should now discuss under what conditions such a strategy of combining tentative executions with audits using definite executions is valuable. This issue can only be addressed if one knows what are the probabilities that various processors are idle during any step. However a general comment can be made.

If the algorithms used for tentative and definite executions are such that "most of the time" the audit returns the value of $GOOD$ as $TRUE$, then in effect, the audit does not slow down the computation by more than a constant factor. If also the tentative executions are fast, ideally constant with high probability and in in the average case, then the execution of P on the fault-prone machine is within constant factor of time of the execution on the ideal machine.

It remains to discuss the space requirements of the strategy. Each round executed by a tentative algorithm requires small constant space per processor. Thus, the space requirement per processor is proportional to the number of steps to be executed in the DO-mode. This will be $\Omega(\log n)$ and generally it can be expected (see Section 7.1.) to be indeed proportional to $\log n$. Of course, one can also use the simple scheme in which no trace information is maintained, the state at step 0 is kept (possibly input only) and the counters are audited at completion only. In this case there is only constant space overhead per processor, in addition to the space required to store the initial state. However, such execution is feasible only if each round in the whole computation is likely to execute a parallel step correctly.

6. Efficiency Issues in General Resilient Computations

So far, we have emphasized the "feasibility" aspect only. The resulting strategies might not be necessarily efficient. In particular, *all* of the results related to realizing resilient computations, either in general settings as reported in [17] or in more specific settings as well, invariably imply a slowdown of the original computation by a factor of $\log n$ at least. While this might be theoretically satisfactory, this factor is too big to tolerate in a real system. It was shown in [19] by Kedem, Palem, Raghunathan, and Spirakis, that this factor of $\log n$ is indeed *intrinsic* to any strategy that guarantees certifiably correct execution on a step-by-step basis.

Theorem 2 *Consider any non-trivial step of an n-wide ideal parallel program I. Any resilient execution of such a step on a fault-prone machine with any number of processors requires time $\Omega(\log n)$.*

This slowdown is true *even if no processor fails* in the fault-prone machine. This is because [19] show that global knowledge about the correct termination of a step can never be acquired in less than $\Omega(\log n)$, independent of the techniques used. So, the slowdown is not a function of any specific program used in realizing resiliency, but is intrinsic to any program that guarantees correct execution of every step through local (per-step) resiliency. In order to realize resiliency with extremely low (small constant) overhead despite this bottleneck, [19] have reengineered the strategy as outlined below.

7. Algorithms for Certified-Write-All

In this section, we describe and analyze algorithm for tentative and definite executions. For historical reasons and ease of description, we will actually discuss algorithms for solving the problem of Certified-Write-All. This is the same problem as the Write-All problem described in Section 3., with the proviso that at the end of the execution some flag variable indicates that the execution completed. As shown in [17] the complexity of solving this problem is equivalent to that of executing an arbitrary step of an ideal program.

For the purpose of the analysis, we will assume that once a processor becomes idle (or dies) it will remain idle.

In this section it is necessary for us to assume that the reader has detailed knowledge of the algorithm due to Kanellakis and Shvartsman [15]. We will refer to this algorithm in the sequel as the *K-S algorithm*.

7.1.   Tentative algorithms

As followed from the discussion above, it is important that we choose those tentative algorithms, whose execution is fast (ideally constant time) under reasonable probabilistic assumption on the processor faults. In this section we analyze the probabilistic behavior of two tentative algorithms, both also based on the K-S algorithm.

The model is that of random independent failures with failure probability $f \leq q/\log n$ per processor per step, where q is any positive constant.

We will assume that the processors are arranged linearly, and numbered $1, 2, \ldots, n$. At any time during the execution of our algorithm, a run of failed processors is a set of consecutive processors $i, i+1, \ldots, j$ that have all failed. Let L_m represent the length of the longest run of failed processors after the execution of the first step of the algorithm. We first derive a simple upper bound on L_m. The probability that there exists a run of length L_b starting at position i is given by f^{L_b}. Then an upper bound on the probability that there exists a run of length L_b is at most $n(f)^{L_b}$. If we set this equal to $\frac{1}{n^\sigma}$ for $\sigma \geq 2$, we then have that for

$$L_b = -(\sigma + 1)\frac{\log n}{\log f}$$

the probability of having a run of length L_b is at most $\frac{1}{n^\sigma}$. Thus, $L_m \leq L_b$ with probability at least $1 - \frac{1}{n^\sigma}$.

7.1.1.   A non-adaptive algorithm

Given a set of m processors, the K-S algorithm builds a binary tree of height $\log m$ with the m processors as leaves. The K-S algorithm repeatedly performs the following block step until the work of all processors has been done. One block step of the algorithm can be roughly interpreted to work as follows.

1. Each alive processor marks its position.

2. All alive processors go up the $\log m$ levels of the binary tree to compute the list of positions unmarked in the first step. (This could potentially lead to an overestimate of the number of unmarked positions, since processors could fail as they go up the tree. However, the list contains no more than the set of processors that have failed upto the time all processors meet at the root of the tree.)

3. Processors that are alive at this point descend down the tree to redistribute themselves on the unmarked positions. (The redistribution has the following property: If the number of unmarked positions U is greater than P_a, the number of processors that are still alive, each alive processor is assigned to a unique unmarked position. Otherwise, each unmarked position gets P_a/U processors.)

4. Each processor now marks its new position.

Using the fact that the failure (and repair) patterns are independent Bernoulli trials, and using Chernoff bounds to estimate the tails of the resulting distributions of, contiguous "runs" of failures[18], we get:

Theorem 3 *If the failure probability $f \leq \frac{q}{\log^2 n}$ is known in advance, the above algorithm will terminate in time $O(k \log L_b)$, which is at most $O(k(\log(\sigma+1) + \log\log n - \log\log(\frac{1}{f})))$, where k and σ are constants, with $k, \sigma \geq 3$. Further, the above algorithm terminates incorrectly with probability at most $\frac{2}{n^{\sigma-2}}$.*

Corollary 1 *The above theorem specializes in the following way.*

1. *When $f = O(n^{-\epsilon})$ for any $\epsilon > 0$, the above algorithm runs in constant time .*

2. *When $1/\log^{2+\epsilon} n \leq f \leq q/\log^2 n$ (any $\epsilon > 0$, $q > 0$) then this algorithm has parallel time $\theta(\log\log n)$.*

7.1.2.   An adaptive algorithm

The algorithm of the previous subsection required prior knowledge of f, which is an unreasonable assumption. However, it is easy to get around this problem. One obvious way around it is to repeat the algorithm for progressively increasing values of L. Each time the above algorithm is run, we test (in constant time) whether every location was marked. This step is called *anticertification*. If not, we increase L and repeat. We will now discuss how the value for L is increased.

At first glance, it appears that one should double our guess for L. On closer examination, we see that squaring L leads to a faster algorithm. Initially, we set $L = l_1 = 1$. Then we run the above algorithm. This is referred to as stage 1. In general, having run the algorithm for our guess of $L = l_i$ (stage i), we anticertify. If anticertification indicates that some location is still unmarked, we set $L = l_{i+1} = l_i^2$, and go to stage $i + 1$. When L becomes as big as L_b^2, the theorem above tells us that with high probability, every location is marked. In this case, there will be no more stages, since anticertification will indicate that every location is marked, and the algorithm terminates. Thus, the algorithm terminates with $L \leq L_b^2$ with probability at least $1 - \frac{2}{n^{\sigma-2}}$.

The parallel running time of this algorithm is (with high probability) at most

$$k \log l_1 + k \log l_2 + \ldots + k \log L_b^2$$

which is no bigger than $4k \log L_b$, since $\log l_i = \frac{\log l_{i+1}}{2}$.

What is the probability that this algorithm terminates correctly? The probability of terminating incorrectly is the probability of the event that at the end of some stage i, there was an unmarked location, but anticertification indicated that all locations were marked. We now estimate the probability that we terminate incorrectly at the end of stage i. For this, we need to provide our anticertification algorithm. In the discussion below, we act like the n processors are arranged in a ring. Thus, the processor referred to as $i + j$ is the processor numbered $(i + j) \bmod n$. During anticertification, each processor i (that is alive) checks whether processors $i + 1, i + 2, \ldots, i + \phi$ are marked. Here, $\phi \geq 4$ is an absolute constant, to be specified later. If there exists an unmarked location j, what is the probability that processors $j - 1, j - 2, \ldots j - \phi$ have all failed? This probability is at most $(4k \log(L_b)f)^\phi \leq f^{\phi-1}$, for appropriately chosen ϕ. The probability of terminating incorrectly at the end of any of the $\log \log L_b$ stages is at most $f^{\phi-1} \log \log L_b \leq f^{\phi-2}$.

Theorem 4 *The above algorithm will run in parallel time $O(k \log L_b)$, which is at most $O(k(\log(\sigma + 1) + \log \log n - \log \log(\frac{1}{f})))$, with probability at least $1 - \frac{2}{n^{\sigma-2}}$, where $k, \sigma \geq 3$. Furthermore, it will terminate incorrectly with probability at most $f^{\phi-2}$, $\phi \geq 4$.*

Corollary 2 *The above theorem specializes as follows.*

1. When $f = O(\frac{1}{n^\epsilon})$ for any $\epsilon > 0$, then this algorithm stops in constant time with probability $\geq 1 - \frac{2}{n^{\sigma-2}}$. Furthermore, it terminates incorrectly with probability at most $O(\frac{1}{n^{\epsilon(\phi-2)}})$

2. When $1/\log^{2+\epsilon} n \leq f \leq q/\log^2 n$ (any $\epsilon > 0$, $q > 0$) then this algorithm has parallel time $\theta(\log \log n)$ with probability $\geq 1 - \frac{2}{n^{\sigma-2}}$. Furthermore, it terminates incorrectly with probability at most $\frac{1}{(\log n)^{2(\phi-2)}}$.

7.2.   A deterministic Certified-Write-All algorithm of worst case work $O(n \log^2 n / \log \log n)$.

7.2.1.   Introductory comments and definitions

The worst case work of the K-S algorithm is $\Theta(n \log^2 n)$. Here we present a modification of the algorithm so that the worst case work is $\Theta(n \log^2 n / \log \log n)$.

Let P_1, U_1 be the initial number of processors and the initial number of unwritten positions (i.e. the array size). The algorithm's execution is a sequence of stages $i = 1, 2, \ldots$. Each stage is performed in a synchronous way by all live (active) processors.

Let t_i $(i = 1, 2, \ldots)$ be the time instances of the start of stage i of the algorithm. Let P_{t_i}, U_{t_i} be the numbers of live processors and unwritten cells at the beginning of stage i.

The algorithm uses four full binary trees, stored as heaps in shared memory, in each stage. In addition, each processor, in each stage, constructs and uses two *lists*. The use of the fours heaps is as in the algorithm W of [15].

In fact, the new algorithm is like algorithm W, but in addition, when $P_{t_i} < U_{t_i}$, then the algorithm's design guarantees that each processor writes a whole sublist of previously unwritten leaves and each processor works alone on its sublist. Each processor writes its corresponding sublist by pointer shortcutting. Furthermore, processors in each stage maintain a list of (an overestimate of) live processors and adapt the heap which has the live processors as leaves.

7.2.2.   Stage description

Each stage i consists of two parts: part 1 and part 2. Part 1 has two subparts: 1a and 1b.

Part 1a (list maintenance)   The processor employ four "current" heaps (as in [15]). When the processors go up the trees they calculate an overestimate of the surviving processors. This is done by using a standard $O(\log P_{t_i})$ parallel time version of a CRCW summation algorithm. Also, during their traversal upwards, the surviving processors calculate new processor numbers for themselves (based on the same sums, as in [15]).

During the traversal upwards, each processor maintains a list of unwritten positions. The list is constructed at the same time the number of surviving processors is calculated. A list of surviving processors is also constructed in the same way. To see how the list of unwritten positions is constructed, assume that at some node v of the tree, two lists have already been constructed (keeping the unwritten locations in the left and right subtrees of v) and that their head and tail pointers have been stored at v. Then, each processor *concatenates the lists* and thus maintains a pointer to the list of all the unwritten positions (at the end of the previous stage) in the subtree of root v. A *splitting pointer* is stored at v (and also kept by each processor passing through v) which points to the "concatenation point" of the new list (i.e. the beginning of the sublist of the right tree).

Part 1b (redistribution)   All surviving processors start at the root of the heaps. They traverse the heaps down and get rescheduled dynamically according to the work to be done in the subtrees of each node (as in [15]). Here divide-and-conquer is used. The existence of the splitter pointer guarantees that when processors arrive at the leaves, each of them can start on *the beginning* of a sublist of unwritten positions, nonoverlapping with sublists of other processors. The tails of the sublists are also known to the corresponding processors.

Since processors have new numbers and new starting positions for writing, they *redefined* the heaps superimposed on them as new full binary tress of height $\log P_{t_i}$ and P_{t_i} leaves.

Part 2 (writing)   Each processor writes its corresponding sublist (by pointer shortcutting) until it meets its tail pointer. Surviving processors at the end of the writing of sublists are now ready to go up the new trees (created in part 1b) in order to start stage $i + 1$.

Using this extension to the K-S algorithm, we get an overall work bound of $O(n \log^2 n / \log \log n)$ as summarized below:

7.2.3.   The algorithm's work

Theorem 5 *At the end of the algorithm all array positions are written provided that at least one processor survives. The worst case work is $O(U_1 + P_1 \log P_1 \log U_1 / \log \log U_1)$. Thus when $P_1 = U_1 = n$, the work is $O(n \log^2 n / \log \log n)$.*

8.   Historical Remarks

Kedem, Palem, and Spirakis [17] were the first to present a general stratey, referred to as the TIES strategy, for deriving resilient computations from ideal parallel programs. They presented the TIES strategy in the context of the fail-stop PRAM, which was proposed by Kanellakis and Shvartsman[15]. Since then the TIES strategy from [17] has been made significantly more efficient[19] even when processors reenter the computation synchronously, as described in the previous sections of this chapter. Further applications of TIES in the presence of "processor restarts"[16], as well as results on achieving resiliency in the presence of delays were also presented subsequently[7].

Martel, Subramonian, and Park [21] have applied the TIES strategy to derive resilient executions from arbitrary ideal computations in a model with *limited asynchrony*. More specifically, they assumed that processors can issue a *Fetch-Test-Store* instruction that is *guaranteed* to complete before a total work of $O(n)$ is done by other processors, where n is the number of processors. This instruction is used by them to test whether a processor "has fallen too far behind," and if its current execution must be interrupted. In this way, they in effect assume that a processor can be resynchronized once during an execution of each step or so of the application program. Finally, Kedem, Palem, Rabin and Raghunathan[18] have shown that ideal parallel programs can be executed "resiliently" (referred to as *progressive* computations) on a completely asynchronous shared-memory machine using *only* read and write instructions as primitives; this approach does not depend on postulating the existence of powerful read-modify-write primitives such as the Fetch-Test-Store instruction described above, in the asynchronous target machine. For a more detailed history of this and related work, please see [17].

In the fail-stop PRAM introduced by Kanellakis and Shvartsman [15], processors can fail at any time; once a processor fails, it is never restored. They also introduced a notion of work in this model and presented a very clever deterministic algorithm for solving the Write-All problem robustly in $O(n \log^2 n / \log \log n)$ work. (For the problem's definition see Section 3..) They also described robust algorithms for solving important and specific problems, such as list ranking. Subsequently and independently, Shvartsman [25] showed how to execute correctly certain classes of algorithms in that model.

Cole and Zajicek [10, 11] and Gibbons[13] studied versions of the asynchronous PRAM (APRAM). They analyzed the complexity of several important algorithms in this setting. Nishimura [22] critically reviewed the criteria for judging models of asynchronous machines, and introduced complexity notions an asynchronous model. We refer the reader to that paper for a detailed comparison of several asynchronous PRAM models and related issues. Martel, Park, and Subramonian [20] studied a completely asynchronous model and showed how to compute the maximum and related functions in it.

In parallel computational system, there could be failures both in the *memory* as well as in the *communication systems*. In addition, there could be processors with *local memory*, which is irretrievably lost when the corresponding processor fails. Here, processor failures effectively lead to memory failures. Rabin has a very elegant approach to solving these problems through *information dispersal* [23]. By using dispersal, one can "reconstruct" lost information with very high probability using extremely low amounts of replication of the original information. This replication is of course appropriately encoded and decoded, at low cost. Aumann and Ben-Or [1] have presented techniques for deriving reliable parallel computations in distributed memory settings. Their approach use techniques discussed above and presented in [17] and [23].

9.   Conclusions

We have described a strategy for deriving resilient executions of programs on a PRAM in which processors can fail at any time instance and can be restarted at the beginning of a subsequent step.[18] The strategy is based on the interplay of executions by means of tentative and definite algorithms. The tentative algorithms produce the computation, which may be incorrect with low probability. The definite algorithms, which themselves are guaranteed to execute correctly, audit the computation to check if it was correct. If it was not correct, then the traces left during the execution of the tentative algorithms are used to roll back the computation, which is then restarted from an appropriate intermediate (check) point. We also briefly sketched how the strategy can be modified to handle asynchronous behavior.

Efficiency is the fundamental reason for using tentative algorithms to execute an application program, as opposed to using definite algorithms for this purpose. In particular, definite algorithms used in isolation, cannot yield extremely efficient resilient computations. As discussed in this chapter, this fact follows form the lower bound of $\Omega(\log n)$ on time required by a fault-prone PRAM to execute a single step of an ideal n-processor PRAM using a definite algorithm. Therefore, by using definite executions alone, we would be introducing a slowdown of $\Omega(\log n)$. We have, however, shown, that under reasonable assumptions on processor failures a tentative execution of a step will take time of $\Theta(1)$, and under extremely pessimistic assumptions, it will take time $O(\log \log n)$. To complete the discussion, we also need to consider how frequently a rollback, which takes time $\Omega(\log n)$ may be required. It is possible to show, that under reasonable assumptions, it will happen sufficiently rarely so that the asymptotic behavior will not change. To summarize, we can state that the strategy is likely to require only a $\Theta(1)$ amortized time slowdown with additional space of $\Theta(\log n)$ required per processor.[19]

While the model used here was derived from a PRAM of n processors, it is easy to see that this scenario can be generalized, so that there are n virtual processors, with a possibly different number of actual processors. Although we did not discuss this specifically here, the strategies can be implemented in software, assuming all memory is shared. Shasha and Turek [26] have applied some of the ideas presented here, among others, to a transaction processing application.

References

[1] Y. Aumann and M. Ben-Or, "Asymptotically Optimal PRAM Emulation on Faulty Hyper-cube," *Proc. 32nd IEEE Symp. on Foundations of Computer Science*, pp. 440-446, 1991.

[2] Y. Aumann and M. Ben-Or, "Computing with Faulty Arrays," *Proc. 24th ACM Symposium on Theory of Computing*, 162–169, 1992.

[3] A. Aggarwal, A. Chandra, and M. Snir, "Hierarchical Memory with Block transfer," *Proc. 28th IEEE Symp. on Foundations of Computer Science*, pp. 204–216, 1987.

[4] A. Aho, J. Hopcroft, and J. Ullman, "The Design and Analysis of Computer Algorithms," Addison-Wesley, 1974.

[5] P. Bernstein, V. Hadzilacos, and N. Goodman, *Concurrency Control and Recovery in Database Systems*, Addison-Wesley, 1987.

[6] R. Brent, "The Parallel Evaluation of General Arithmetic Expressions," *JACM*, vol. 21, no. 3, pp. 201–206, 1974.

---

[18]Although in our presentation we assumed that they can be restarted only at the beginning of rounds, this condition can be relaxed.

[19]As we have also stated, under "optimistic" assumptions on processors' failures, smaller space overhead may be possible using a simplified variant of the scheme presented here.

[7] J. Buss, P. Kanellakis, P. Ragde and A. Shvartsman, "Parallel Algorithms with Processor Failures and Delays," *Tech. Rep. CS-92-23*, Brown Univ., August, 1991.

[8] S. Cook, C. Dwork, and R. Reischuk, "Upper and Lower time Bounds for Parallel Random Access Machines without Simultaneous Writes," *SIAM J. Computing,* vol. 15, no. 1, pp. 87–97, 1986.

[9] W. Cellary, E. Gelenbe, and T. Morzy, *Concurrency Control in Distributed Database Systems,* North-Holland, 1988.

[10] R. Cole and O. Zajicek, "The APRAM: Incorporating Asynchrony into the PRAM Model," *Proc. 1989 ACM Symp. on Parallel Algorithms and Architectures*, pp. 170–178, 1989.

[11] R. Cole and O. Zajicek, "The Expected Advantage of Asynchrony," *Proc. 2nd Annual ACM Symp. on Parallel Algorithms and Architectures*, pp. 85–94, 1990.

[12] S. Fortune and J. Wyllie, "Parallelism in Random Access Machines," *Proc. 10th ACM Symp. on Theory of Computing*, pp. 114–118, 1978.

[13] P. Gibbons, "A More Practical PRAM Model," *Proc. 1989 ACM Symp. on Parallel Algorithms and Architectures*, pp. 158–168, 1989.

[14] D. Jefferson, "Virtual Time II: Storage Management in Distributed Simulation," *Proc. 9th ACM Symp. on Principles of Distributed Computing*, pp. 75–89, 1990.

[15] P. Kanellakis and A. Shvartsman, "Efficient Parallel Algorithms Can be Made Robust," *Tech. Rep. CS-89-35*, Brown Univ., pp. 1–28, October 24, 1989. (Initial version appeared in *Proc. 8th ACM Symp. on Principles of Distributed Computing*, pp. 211–222, 1989.)

[16] P.C. Kanellakis and A.A. Shvartsman, "Efficient Parallel Algorithms on Restartable Fail-Stop Processors," *Proc. 10th ACM Symp. on Principles of Distributed Computing*, pp. 23–36, 1991

[17] Z. Kedem, K. Palem and P. Spirakis, "Parallel Computing on Faulty Shared Memory Machines (Part I)," *submitted for publication*, (Initial version appeared as "Efficient Robust Parallel Computations," *Proc. 22nd ACM Symp. on Theory of Computing*, pp. 138–148, 1990.)

[18] Z. Kedem, K. Palem, M. Rabin, A. Raghunathan, "Efficient Program Transformations for Resilient Parallel Computation via Randomization," *Proc. 24th ACM Symposiium on Theory of Computing*, 306–317, 1992.

[19] Z. Kedem, K. Palem, A. Raghunathan and P. Spirakis, "Combining Tentative and Definite Algorithms for Very Fast Dependable Parallel Computing," *Proc. 23nd ACM Symp. on Theory of Computing*, 381–390,1991.

[20] C. Martel, A. Park, and R. Subramonian, "Fast Asynchronous Algorithms for Shared Memory Parallel Computers," *Tech. Rep. CSE-89-8*, Univ. of California–Davis, pp. 1–17, July 25, 1989.

[21] C. Martel, R. Subramonian, and A. Park, "Asynchronous PRAMs are (Almost) as Good as Synchronous PRAMs," *Proc. 32nd IEEE Symp. on Foundations of Computer Science,*, pp. 590–599, 1990.

[22] N. Nishimura, "Asynchronous Shared Memory Parallel Computations," *Tech. Rep. 253/91* pp. 1–118, July, 1991.

[23] M. Rabin, "Efficient Dispersal of Information for Security, Load Balancing and Fault Tolerance," *JACM,* vol. 36, no. 2, pp. 335–348, 1989.

[24] A. Ranade, "How to Emulate Shared Memory," *Proc. 28th IEEE Symp. on Foundations of Computer Science,* pp. 185–194, 1987.

[25] A. Shvartsman, "Achieving Optimal CRCW Fault-tolerance," *Tech. Rep. CS-89-49*, Brown Univ., pp. 1–8, December 22, 1989.

[26] D. Shasha and J. Turek, "Beyond Fail-stop: Wait-free Serializability and Resiliency in the Presence of Slow-down Failures," *Tech. Rep. 514*, Dept. of Computer Science, New York Univ., pp. 1–22, September, 1990.

[27] L. Valiant, "A Bridging Model for Parallel Computation," *CACM,* vol. 33, no. 8, pp. 103–111, 1990.

Chapter 9

P-Completeness

Jacobo Torán

Abstract

In this chapter we consider a class of problems that are be feasable to compute by sequential algorithms but do not seem to be efficiently parallelizable. This notion is formalized in the concept of P-completeness. We present examples of this kind of problems and show that for some of them it is possible to obtain efficiently approximate solutions using parallel algorithms.

1. Introduction

It is widely accepted that a problem can be well-parallelized if it can be computed very quickly by an algorithm which uses a feasible amount or processors. Usually the bounds considered for these two complexity measures are poly-logarithmic time and polynomial number of processors, both measured with respect to the size of the input. These problems form the complexity class NC and can be computed efficiently in practice. It is natural to ask what kind of problems can be well parallelized.

By the definition of NC we know that every problem in the class belongs to P, the class of problems that can be solved sequentially in deterministic polynomial time, i.e. NC ⊆ P. From this inclusion follows that one cannot try to obtain efficient parallel algorithms for problems that are not computable in polynomial time. What about the problems in P? It is strongly believed that the inclusion in the other direction does not hold, but until now, no proof of this conjecture has been obtained. In fact, the question NC$\overset{?}{=}$P is one of the most important open problems in the area of parallel complexity.

As we have mentioned, most researchers believe that there are problems in P which do not belong to NC. Based on this fact a good way to give evidence that a problem is not well-parallelizable is to show that if it were in NC, then every problem in P would be in NC. This gives rise the concept of P-completeness. Intuitively a problem is P-complete if it has this property. More formally, we shall say that a problem is P-complete if it belongs to P and every other problem in this class can be efficiently transformed of reduced to it in a sense that will be explained later. P-complete problems are therefore the hardest problems in P and the best candidates for not being efficiently parallelizable; these problems are generally considered *inherently sequential*.

The P-completeness concept and its role in the NC versus P setting can be viewed analogously to the better known concept of NP-completeness [6] and its relation to the P$\overset{?}{=}$NP question. Like in the case of NP, there are literally hundreds of problems known to be P-complete. Extensive lists of such problems can be found in [11] and [23].

In this chapter, we will present some well known examples of P-complete problems from different areas such as graph theory, optimization or formal languages. We consider also the question of whether there exist problems in P which are neither in NC nor P-complete. Finally in a last section we discuss the approximability within NC of some of the studied P-complete problems.

To show P-completeness results we will use the standard many-one reducibility concept; a problem A is reducible to a problem B iff there exists a total fuction f such that for every input string x, $x \in A$ iff $f(x) \in B$. For every P-complete problem A we want to be able to say that if A is in NC then NC=P. Therefore we will require that the reducibility function f must be computed in NC. Usually logarithmic space reducibilities are used to show P-completeness. Since every function which can be computed in logspace can also be computed by a uniform family of circuits with polynomial size and $\log^2$ depth [3] (NC$_2$), the class of logspace functions suffices for our purpuses and will be used for our proofs. However it can be seen that all the reductions we give could be also performed by NC$_1$ circuits. In fact we will omit the details in the analysis of the complexity of the reductions. From the constructions should be clear that they can be done very *locally* using in every step very little information from the input, and therefore they can be computed in logarithmic parallel time or logarithmic space.

2.   Some Examples of P-complete Problems

2.1.   Circuit Value Problems

The first example of a P-complete problem we present deals with the evaluation of combinatorial circuits. More specifically it consists in deciding whether a given circuit with values assigned to the input gates produces value 1 as output. This problem is known as the Circuit Value Problem (CVP) and was shown to be P-complete by Ladner in [19]. As we will see, changing the restrictions imposed on the circuits one can obtain different versions of the problem which in many cases are also P-complete. These variations are very helpful to show the P-completeness of many other problems.

We start giving the formal definition of a combinatorial circuit. Let B_2 the set of two-input boolean functions, $B_2 = \{f : \{0,1\}^2 \to \{0,1\}\}$.

Definition 2.1 *A circuit α over the basis $B \subseteq B_2$ is a sequence $(\alpha_1, \ldots, \alpha_n)$ where each α_i is either a variable x_i (input), or $f(\alpha_j, \alpha_k)$ for some $f \in B$ (gate), with $j, k < i$. The size of the circuit is n. The value $v(\alpha_i)$ of a gate α_i in the circuit α, is defined as follows: If α_i is the input gate x_i then $v(\alpha_i) = v(x_i)$ and if $\alpha_i = f(\alpha_j, \alpha_k)$ then $v(\alpha_i) = f(v(\alpha_j), v(\alpha_k))$. We define the value of the circuit, $v(\alpha)$, to be $v(\alpha_n)$.*

The fact that every gate is connected only to gates with a smaller number prevents feedback loops. Clearly this definition can be generalized to circuits in which the number of inputs of the gates (fan-in) is greater than two. In the original paper in which the Circuit Value Problem was introduced [19] the circuits considered had gates over the complete basis $\{\wedge, \neg\}$. We consider therefore

Circuit Value Problem (CVP): Given a circuit α over the basis $(\wedge, \neg)$, decide whether $v(\alpha) = 1$.

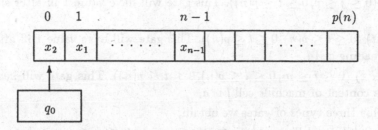

Figure 1: Initial configuration of the Turing machine.

We will show the P-completeness of this problem. The proof of ths result can be easily transformed to show the P-completeness for the evaluation of circuits over any other complete basis in B_2. It was shown by Goldschlager [7] that the problem remains P-complete if the circuits considered are restricted to be monotone i.e. only with AND and OR gates.

Monotone Circuit Value Problem (MCVP): Given a circuit α over the basis $(\wedge, \vee)$, decide whether $v(\alpha) = 1$.

To prove that every problem in P is logspace reducible to **CVP** it will be useful to consider also circuits in which the gates might have an unbounded number of inputs.

Unbounded Fan-in Circuit Value Problem (UCVP): Given a circuit α with unbounded fan-in AND and OR gates decide whether $v(\alpha) = 1$.

Observe that in the specification of **UCVP** negation gates are not allowed. Clearly the three problems considered belong to P since evaluating all the gates in order starting at the inputs one can compute the value of the circuit in at most quadratic time in the number of gates (this bound can be improved encoding the gates properly).

Using a generic reduction we will show that **UCVP** is P-complete and then we will reduce this problem to the other two. In our first reduction we prove that every language L in P is logspace reducible to **UCVP**. We follow the ideas of the proof presented in [24].

Theorem 2.2 *UCVP is P-complete.*

Proof. We have already explained that the problem belongs to P. For the hardness part we give a reduction for any set L in P to **UCVP**, which given an input string x will construct a circuit α that evaluates to 1 if and only if $x \in L$.

Let L be a problem in P computed by a standard one-tape deterministic Turing machine M (cf. [12]) with alphabet $\Sigma = \{a_0, \ldots, a_m\}$ (a_0 is the blank symbol), set of states $Q = \{q_0, \ldots, q_r\}$, transition function $\delta : Q \times \Sigma \to Q \times \Sigma \times \{L, R\}$, initial·state q_0 and unique acepting state q_r. The running time of M is bounded by a polynomial p; we can assume that on input x of length n M makes exactly $p(n)$ steps. In its initial configuration the machine is in state q_0 with string $x = x_0 x_1 \ldots x_{n-1}$ ($x_i \in \Sigma$) written at the beginning of its tape and with its head reading the leftmost cell (figure 1).

Given the input string x of length n we construct a circuit with the following gates:

• $State(j,t)$ $(0 \leq j \leq r, 0 \leq t \leq p(n))$. This gate will have value 1 iff after step t M is in state q_j.

• $Position(l,t)$ $(0 \leq l \leq p(n), 0 \leq t \leq p(n))$. This gate will have value 1 iff after step t the head of M is reading cell l.

• $Content(i,l,t)$ $(0 \leq i \leq m, 0 \leq l \leq p(n), 0 \leq t \leq p(n))$. This gate will have value 1 iff after step t the content of machine cell l is a_i.

Combining this three types of gates we obtain,

• $CSP(i,j,l,t)$ (Content,State,Position), $(0 \leq i \leq m, 0 \leq j \leq r, 0 \leq l \leq p(n), 0 \leq t \leq p(n))$. This gate will have value 1 iff after step t M is in state q_j reading cell l and its content is a_i.

Observe that the gate $CSP(i,j,l,t)$ is just an AND-gate with the inputs $State(j,t)$, $Position(l,t)$ and $Content(i,l,t)$.

There are $O(p^2(n))$ gates and therefore the size of the circuit is polynomial in x. We show now how to connect the defined gates. It is helpful to consider them placed in different levels depending on the value of t. The gates with $t = 0$ are the inputs of the circuit. From the description of how the connections are made, it should be clear that the function producing the circuit uses only logarithmic space.

Level 0: (Inputs)

$State(j,0) = 1 \Leftrightarrow j = 0$. The initial state is q_0

$Position(l,0) = 1 \Leftrightarrow l = 0$. Initialy the head is in cell number 0.

$Content(i,l,0) = 1 \Leftrightarrow (l < n$ and $x_l = a_i)$ or $(l \geq n$ and $i = 0)$. The content of the tape is x followed by blank symbols.

Level t+1:

$State(j,t+1)$ is an OR-gate which has as inputs the set of gates $\{CSP(i,k,l,t) : \delta(q_k,a_i) = (q_j,*,*)\}$. (Symbol $*$ denotes any possible value in the adequate range). After step $t + 1$ the machine is in state j if the transition function moves to q_j from the previous configuration.

$Position(l,t+1)$ is an OR-gate which has as inputs $\{CSP(i,k,l-1,t) : \delta(q_j,a_i) = (*,*,R)\} \cup \{CSP(i,k,l+1,t) : \delta(q_j,a_i) = (*,*,L)\}$. After step $t+1$ the head is in position l if it was either in position $l - 1$ at the previous stage and is moved to the right or it was in position $l + 1$ and is moved to the left.

$Content(i,l,t+1)$ is an OR-gate which has as inputs the set of gates $\{CSP(i,k,l,t) : \delta(q_j,a_k) = (*,a_i,*)\}$ plus a two-input AND-gate with inputs $Content(i,l,t), \neg Position(l,t)$. The content of cell l after step $t + 1$ is a_i if either the machine writes this symbol in cell l in this step or the position of the head in step t is not l and a_i was already the content of cell l. Observe that this is the only case in which we have used a negation, but this can be avoided since the value of the gate $\neg Position(i,t)$ is equal to the value of an OR-gate which receives as inputs the set of gates $\{Position(i',t) : i' \neq i\}$.

We can define one last gate, $Accept$, which is an OR with inputs $\{CSP(i,r,l,p(n)) : 0 \leq i \leq m, 0 \leq l \leq p(n)\}$. It can be easily proved by induction on the levels that the gates behave as the descriptions given above. The gate $Accept$ has value 1 iff after $p(n)$ steps machine M on input x is in the final state r. Therefore $x \in L$ iff the circuit evaluates to 1.   □

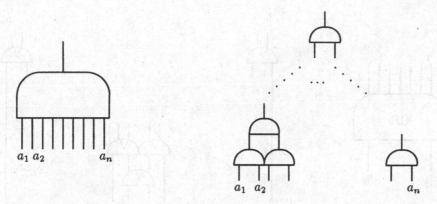

Figure 2

The P-completeness of **CVP** and **MCVP** can now be easily proved. To reduce **UMVP** to **MCVP** we explain how a circuit with unbounded fan-in AND and OR gates can be transformed into one in which the gates have fan-in two. The idea is to transform each gate α with n inputs into $n-1$ gates $\beta_1, \ldots \beta_{n-1}$ of the same type but with just two inputs. The new gates will be connected forming a binary tree (see figure 2). The tranformation can be performed in logarithmic space and the new circuit has at most quadratic size with respect to the first one. As a corollary we obtain,

Corollary 2.3 *MCVP is P-complete.*

In the definition of the Circuit Value Problem we required the circuit to have only AND and NOT gates. **MCVP** can be easily reduced to **CVP** using DeMorgan laws and transforming every two-input OR gate α of a monotone circuit into a group of AND and NOT gates in the intuitive way.

Corollary 2.4 *CVP is P-complete.*

Goldschlager and Parberry [10] have shown that for any basis $B \subseteq B_2$ the Circuit Value Problem over basis B remains P-complete except in the cases when B consists either of trivial functions, it consists only of the OR or the AND function (in this case the problem is complete for nondeterministic logarithmic space), or B consists only of the PARITY function. The problem is also P-complete if the circuits considered are planar [7]. However, if the circuit is planar and monotone at the same time then its evaluation problem can be solved in NC [8]. Mayr and Subramanian [22] have consider a class of circuits with certain fan-out restrictions for which the evaluation problem does not seem to be P-complete.

We will reduce the Monotone Circuit Value Problem to some other problems to show that they are also P-complete. For this it will be useful to consider circuits in the following "normal form".

1. The circuit is monotone and has only AND and OR gates of fan-in two.

2. Each input gate has fan-out one.

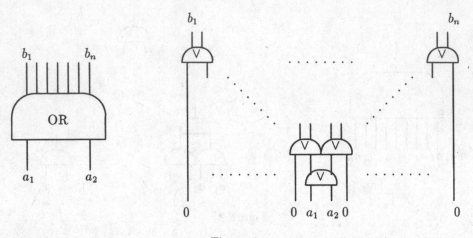

Figure 3

3. Each gate has fan-out smaller than or equal to two.

4. The circuit is alternating, i.e. AND gates have only outputs connected to OR gates and vice-versa.

5. Two different gates cannot have as input the same gates.

6. The output gate is an OR gate.

We have already justified that the Value Problem for circuits with restriction 1 is P-complete. Every circuit can be transformed into an equivalent one fulfilling the rest of the restrictions in the following way: For restriction 2 one can add new input variables to simulate those with fan-out greater than one. To fulfill restriction 3 each gate α with fan-out $n > 2$ can be transformed into $n - 1$ gates $\beta_1 \ldots \beta_{n-1}$ connected as in figure 3. Gate i has as inputs gate $\lfloor i/2 \rfloor$ and either an input gate with value 1 if α is an AND-gate or an input gate with value 0 if it is an OR-gate. Each of the new gates produces exactly two outputs. One can add dummy OR or AND gates its input connected to a gate of the previous level in order to satisfy restriction 4. A transformation for restrictions 5 and 6 can be done in a similar way.

The new circuit has polynomial size with respect to the number of gates of the original one and all the tranformation can be done using only logarithmic space. From now on, whenever we mention the **MCVP** we will consider the evaluation problem for circuits fulfilling the above restrictions.

2.2.   Other examples of P-complete problems

We reduce now **CVP** and **MCVP** to many other problems from different areas to show that they are also P-complete. The first example we consider is an algebraic problem which was proved to be P-complete by Jones and Laaser in [14].

Generability (GEN): Given a set X, a binary operator $\bullet$ (defined on X), a subset $S \subseteq X$ and an element $x \in X$ decide whether x belongs to the closure of S with respect to $\bullet$.

Theorem 2.5 *GEN is P-complete.*

Proof. It is easy to see that the problem can be computed in polynomial time using the following algorithm to compute the closure of S. $S \bullet S$ denotes the set $\{a \bullet b \ : \ a, b \in S\}$.

```
begin
    S_1 := S;
    repeat
        S_2 := S_1;
        S_1 := S_1 ∪ (S_1 • S_1);
    until S_1 = S_2;
    Closure(S) := S_1
end.
```

To show that GEN is P-hard, we show a reduction from Monotone Circuit Value Problem. Let $\alpha = (\alpha_1, \ldots, \alpha_n)$ be a monotone circuit with the restrictions considered in the previous section. From α we construct an instance $(X, \bullet, S, x)$ of GEN.

$$X := \{\alpha_i^0, \alpha_i^1 \ : \ \alpha_i \in \alpha\}$$

$$S := \{\alpha_i^0 \ : \ \alpha_i \text{ is an input node with value } 0\}$$

$$\cup \{\alpha_i^1 \ : \ \alpha_i \text{ is an input node with value } 1\}$$

$$x := \alpha_n^1 \quad (\alpha_n \text{ is the output gate})$$

The function $\bullet$ is defined as

$$\alpha_j^a \bullet \alpha_k^b := \begin{cases} \alpha_i^c & \text{if } \alpha_i = \text{AND}(\alpha_j, \alpha_k) \\ \alpha_i^d & \text{if } \alpha_i = \text{OR}(\alpha_j, \alpha_k) \\ \text{undefined} & \text{otherwise.} \end{cases}$$

where $a, b \in \{0, 1\}$, $c = a \wedge b$ and $d = a \vee b$.

Observe that by the restrictions imposed on the circuits we are considering, a pair of gates α_j, α_k can be the inputs of at most one gate α_i, and therefore the function $\bullet$ is well defined. Also the transformation can be done locally from the description of circuit α.

It is straightforward to show by induction on the gate numbers that for every i

$$v(\alpha_i) = a \iff \alpha_i^a \in Closure(S) \quad (a \in \{0, 1\}).$$

therefore we have

$$\alpha \in \mathbf{MCVP} \iff v(\alpha_n) = 1 \iff \alpha_n^1 \in Closure(S) \iff (X, \bullet, S, x) \in \mathbf{GEN}.$$

$\square$

The next example we give is a parsing problem from the area of formal languages.

Context-Free Language Membership (CFL-Member): Given a context-free grammar $G = (V, T, P, S)$ and a string $w \in T^\star$, decide whether $x \in L(G)$.

This problem was shown to be P-complete in [14]. We follow here the proof given there. It is intersting to observe that for any fixed context-free grammar G the membership problem in $L(G)$ can be computed in NC [25]. The problem becomes P-complete when the grammar is considered to be part of the input.

Theorem 2.6 *CFL-Member is P-complete.*

Proof. The standard parsing algorithms (for example the Cocke-Kasami-Younger algorithm, see e.g. [12]) run in polynomial time in the size of the input; this shows that the problem belongs to P. To prove that the problem is hard for the class we perform a reduction from **GEN**. Let $(X, \bullet, S, x)$ be an instance of the Generability problem. From it one can construct using only logarithmic space a grammar $G = (V, T, P, S)$ and a string $w \in T^*$ in the following way: w is the empty string λ, the set of variables V is equal to X, there is only one terminal symbol a, the initial variable S is the element x and the set of productions is

$$P := \{x \longrightarrow yz \; : \; y \bullet z = x\} \cup \{x \longrightarrow \lambda \; : \; x \in S\}.$$

We claim that for every y

$$y \in Closure(S) \Longleftrightarrow \lambda \text{ can be generated from variable } y \text{ in } G.$$

The proof of this claim follows from left to right by induction in the "closure level" of S, and in the other direction by induction on the number of steps of the derivation.   □

We present now some graph theoretical problems. The first one, Max-Flow (or Network-Flow), is one of the best known P-complete problems. It consists of computing the maximum flow that can circulate through a given network. Max-Flow was shown to be P-complete in [9]. This problem is different from the rest of examples we have seen in the sense that it is not a decisional problem but a function. In [9] the authors go around this problem showing that a decisional version of the problem, computing the last bit of the Max-Flow function, is P-complete. We present a proof of the result which uses some ideas from the one given in [2]. From this result follows that the existence of NC circuits computing the Max-Flow function would imply NC=P. We start defining the problem formally.

Definition 2.7 *A network $N = (G, s, t, c)$ is a directed graph $G = (V, E)$ with two distinguished nodes s and t (source and sink) and with a positive integer associated with each edge (the capacity function) $c : E \to \mathbb{N}$.*

Definition 2.8 *A network flow (or just a flow) is a function $f : E \to \mathbb{N}$ which assigns a non-negative integer to each edge in such a way that,*

1. *For every edge e, $f(e) \leq c(e)$, i.e, the flow of an edge is smaller or equal than its capacity.*

2. *For every node except s and t the sum of the flow in the incoming edges is equal to the sum of the flow of the outgoing edges (conservation of flow).*

Definition 2.9 *The value of the flow f in a network $N = (G, s, t, c)$ is equal to the outgoing flow from s minus the incoming flow to s. By the conservation of flow, this is equal to the incoming flow to t minus the outgoing flow from t.*

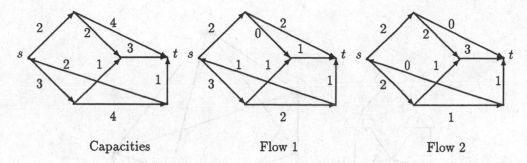

| Capacities | Flow 1 | Flow 2 |

Figure 4: Different flows in the same network.

The maximum flow problem is,

Max-Flow: Given a network N, compute the maximum value of a flow in N.

We consider the following decisional version of the problem

Odd-Max-Flow: Given a network N decide whether the maximum flow in N has odd value.

Theorem 2.10 *Odd-Max-Flow is P-complete.*

Proof. The maximum flow of a network can be computed in polynomial time using the well-known Ford-Fulkerson algorithm. To show that the problem is P-hard we give a logarithmic space reduction from **MCVP**. Let α be a monotone alternating circuit. For technical reasons we will consider the gates of α numbered in the inverse way as usually $\alpha = (\alpha_n, \alpha_{n-1}, \ldots, \alpha_0)$, i.e. every gate receives as inputs gates with a higher number and α_0 is the output gate (recall that we can suppose α_0 to be an OR-gate). From α we construct the network $N = (G, s, t, c)$. G is the graph with set of nodes $V := \{n, \ldots 0\} \cup \{s, t\}$, i.e. there is one node for every gate in α plus two special ones which will be the source and the sink. The edges of the graph are the connections of the circuit plus edges going from the source to every "input-node", edges going from every "AND-node" and from the "output-node" to the sink, and edges going from every "OR-node" to the source.

$$
\begin{aligned}
E := \ & \{(j,i),(k,i) \ : \ \alpha_i = \text{AND}(\alpha_j, \alpha_k) \text{ or } \alpha_i = \text{OR}(\alpha_j, \alpha_k)\} \cup \\
& \{(s,i) \ : \ \alpha_i \text{ is an input}\} \cup \\
& \{(i,t) \ : \ \alpha_i \text{ is an AND-gate or } i = 0 \text{ (output gate)}\} \cup \\
& \{(i,s) \ : \ \alpha_i \text{ is an OR-gate}\}
\end{aligned}
$$

In order to express the capacities of the edges, let us define the *surplus* function s on the gates of α. For a gate α_i with inputs gates α_j, α_k and m_i outputs ($m_i \leq 2$), $s(i) := 2^k + 2^j - m_i 2^i$. Now the capacities of the edges are defined as:

If i, j are not the source or the sink then $c(i,j) = 2^i$.

If α_i is an input gate then $c(s,i) = 2^i$ if $v(\alpha_i) = 1$ and $c(s,i) = 0$ if $v(\alpha_i) = 0$.

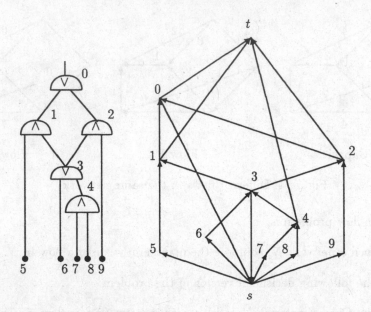

Figure 5: Transformation of a circuit into a graph.

If α_i is an AND-gate then $c(i,t) = s(i)$.

If α_i is an OR-gate then $c(i,s) = s(i)$.

$c(0,t) = 1$.

Observe that $(0,t)$ is the only edge with odd capacity. We will show that the maximum flow in the constructed network is odd if and only if $v(\alpha) = 1$.

To calculate the maximum flow f in N the idea is to send from each node in the direction of the sink as much flow as allowed by the capacities. Edges going directly to the sink have highest priority while edges leading to the source have lowest priority. The flow f is assigned according to the following pattern:

1. If i is an "input node" then f sends through (s,i) as much flow as allowed by the capacity.

2. If i is an "AND-node" leading to nodes j,k and to the sink t then from the incoming flow f sends through (i,t) as much flow as allowed by the capacity of this edge, and sends the rest of the incoming flow from i through the other edges.

3. If i is an "OR-node" leading to nodes j,k and to the source t then from the incoming flow f sends through (i,j) and through (i,k) as much flow as allowed by the capacity of these edges and sends the rest of the incoming flow from i through (i,s).

From the definition of f it follows that it is a correct flow assignment. We will show that this assignment generates the maximum flow on the network. For this we need a lemma which relates the outgoing flow from the nodes in N to the value of the gates in the circuit.

Lemma 2.11 *For every node* i, $0 \leq i \leq n$, *if* α_i *is an AND-gate then*

$v(\alpha_i) = 0 \Rightarrow$ *From node* i f *sends flow only to the sink (if any).*

$v(\alpha_i) = 1 \Rightarrow$ *From node* i f *sends as much flow as the outgoing capacity of the node.*

If α_i *is an OR-gate then*

$v(\alpha_i) = 0 \Rightarrow$ *Node* i *does not get any flow (and therefore* f *cannot send any flow from* i).

$v(\alpha_i) = 1 \Rightarrow$ *From node* i f *sends sends through all the edges* (i,j), $j \neq s$, *as much flow as allowed by its capacity.*

Proof. It follows by an easy induction on the number of the nodes. We prove it first for the case of the "AND-nodes". Let $\alpha_i = \text{AND}(\alpha_j, \alpha_k)$, with $k > j > i$.

If $v(\alpha_i) = 0$ then either $v(\alpha_j) = 0$ or $v(\alpha_k) = 0$. By induction hypothesis the incoming flow in node i is at most 2^k, but the capacity of edge (i,t) is $c(i,t) = s(i) \geq 2^j + 2^k - 2^{i+1} \geq 2^k$. Therefore all the outgoing flow from node i goes through edge (i,t).

If $v(\alpha_i) = 1$ then $v(\alpha_j) = v(\alpha_k) = 1$, and the incoming flow in i is equal to $2^j + 2^k$, the capacity of the edges going out of node i.

We consider now the case of "OR-nodes". Let $\alpha_i = \text{OR}(\alpha_j, \alpha_k)$, with $k > j > i$.

If $v(\alpha_j) = 0$ then $v(\alpha_j)$ and $v(\alpha_k)$ are equal to 0. By induction hypothesis f does not send any flow from nodes j and k to node i.

If $v(\alpha_i) = 1$ then $v(\alpha_j) = 1$ or $v(\alpha_k) = 1$. The incoming flow in i is then at least 2^j, which is greater than or equal to 2^{i+1}, the maximum capacity of the edges going from i to nodes which are not the source.   □

Lemma 2.12 *The function* f *described above assigns the maximum flow to* N.

Proof. Since there is no edge going out of the sink, the maximum flow cannot exceed the sum of the flow in the edges leading directly to t. The "input nodes" with value 0 cannot get any flow (its incoming capacity is 0), and because the circuit is monotone, no node corresponding to an OR-gate with value 0 can get any incoming flow and no node corresponding to an AND-gate with value 0 can get more flow than the capacity of the edge going from the node to t. Therefore the maximum flow cannot exceed the sum of the flow from two types of edges going to t: the edges from nodes corresponding to gates with value 1, and the edges from nodes corresponding to AND-gates with value 0 (but with an input with value 1) . By the previous lemma, f assigns to the first type of such edges as much flow as its capacity. The second type of edges get from f all the flow that arrives at the "AND-node", which is the maximum incoming flow any assignment can produce. This last point follows because of the alternating structure of circuit α the two nodes sending flow to the "AND-node" must be "OR-nodes". One of them has value 0 (and therefore cannot send any flow) and the other has value 1 and by the lemma sends as much flow as its outgoing capacity. This two facts show that f assigns the maximum flow.   □

Now it is easy to prove that the reduction works as desired. Since f by lemma 2.11 assigns to every edge going to t except possibly to $(0,t)$ an even amount of flow, the maximum flow is odd iff $f(0,t) = 1$ but again by the same lemma this is true iff $v(\alpha_0) = 1$. Therefore $v(\alpha) = 1$ iff $N \in$ **Odd-Max-Flow**. This proves the theorem.   □

Observe that in the reduction we use capacities with are exponential in the size of the network. In [16] it is shown that the problem restricted to networks with polynomial capacities is in Random-NC. Also if the networks are required to be planar graphs then the problem belongs to the class NC [13]. In [21] it is proven that a different decisional version of the **Max-Flow** problem, $\{\langle N, k\rangle$: the maximum flow of $N \geq k\}$, is also P-complete.

We present another problem from the area of graph theory. It was shown to be P-complete by Anderson and Mayr in [1]. We will follow the original proof. In the next section it will be shown that an optimization version of the problem can be approximated in NC.

High Degree Subgraph Problem (HDSP): Given a graph $G(V, E)$ and an integer k, decide whether G contains an induced subgraph with minimum degree at least k.

Theorem 2.13 *HDSP is P-complete.*

Proof. To show that the problem in in P, consider an algorithm which on input (G, k) deletes from G all the nodes of degree smaller than k (and the edges connected to them) and repeats the process until either there are no nodes left $((G, k) \notin$ **HDSP**$)$ or the only remaining nodes have degree greater than or equal to k $((G, k) \in$ HDSP$)$.

To prove that the problem is P-hard we give a reduction from **MCVP**. Given a monotone circuit $\alpha = (\alpha_1, \ldots, \alpha_n)$, the reduction constructs a graph G which has an induced subgraph of degree 3 iff α has value 1. Every gate α_i generates one of the subgraphs in G shown in figure 6. The a and b-nodes correspond to the inputs of the gates while the c and d-nodes correspond to their outputs. There are edges connecting the subgraphs in G in the same way as the gates are connected in α. In G the reduction constructs also another subgraph in the shape of a binary tree whose leaves are the input nodes of the subgraphs corresponding to input gates with value 1 and whose root is the output node corresponding to the output gate. The purpose of this subgraph is to connect the output node with the inputs with value 1 forcing these nodes to have degree at least three.

The reduction uses only logarithmic space. To show that it works properly we use the same greedy algorithm described above to prove that HDSP is in P. The algorithm on input $(G, 3)$ will initially delete the a and b-nodes corresponding to the input gates with value 0, which are the only nodes with degree smaller than three and then it will remove the whole subgraphs from the 0-input gates. It is easy to see reasoning inductively on the number of the gates that the algorithm will delete all the subgraphs corresponding to gates with value 0. For example, if an OR-gate has value 0 then by the inductive argument the edges connected to the a and b-nodes of its subgraph have been deleted, but then these nodes have only degree two and are also deleted propagating the deletion to the whole subgraph. It follows that if α has value 0 then the subgraph corresponding to the output gate on α is removed, then the binary tree connecting the output node to the input gates of value 1 is also deleted. This leaves the input nodes from these gates with only two neighbours and they are deleted, and this implies that the whole graph is deleted by the algorithm. On the other hand, if the value of α is 1 then the subgraph induced by the set of nodes corresponding to gates with value 1

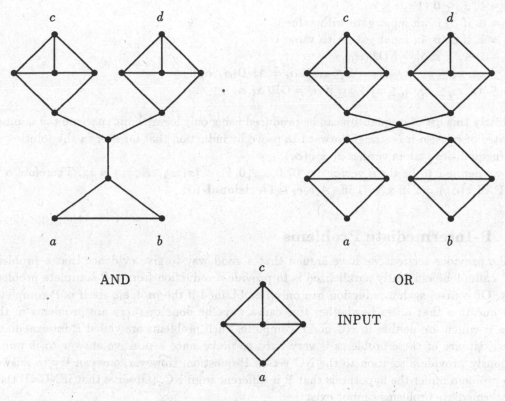

Figure 6

plus the binary tree connecting the input nodes with value 1 has degree at least three in all its nodes.   □

The last example of a P-complete problem we give, Linear Programming, is also well-known. The proof of its P-hardness is due to [4] and is not difficult. On the contrary the existence of a polynomial time algorithm for the problem was an open question for many years. Khachian [17] provided the first polynomial time method to compute Linear Programming.

Linear Programming (LP): Given an integer $m \times n$ matrix A, an integer m-vector b and an integer n-vector c, compute a rational n-vector x such that $Ax \le b$ and $c^T x$ is maximized.

We will prove that a decisional version of the problem (**Decisional-LP**) which asks whether the last component of vector x is equal to 1 is P-complete.

Theorem 2.14 *Decisional-LP is P-complete.*

Proof. We just show that the problem is P-hard by giving a reduction from **CVP**. Let α be a circuit with n gates $(\alpha_1, \ldots, \alpha_n)$. The reduction generates the following list of inequalities which form the matrix A and the vector b.

For every gate α_i the following inequalities are generated,

$x_i \leq 1, x_i \geq 0 \ (1 \leq i \leq n)$.

$x_i = 0$, if α_i is an input gate with value 0.

$x_i = 1$, if α_i is an input gate with value 1.

$x_i = 1 - x_j$, if $\alpha_i = \text{NOT}(\alpha_j)$.

$x_i \leq x_j, x_i \leq x_k, x_j + x_k - 1 \leq x_i$, if $\alpha_i = \text{AND}(\alpha_j, \alpha_k)$.

$x_j \leq x_i, x_k \leq x_i, x_i \leq x_j + x_k$, if $\alpha_i = \text{OR}(\alpha_j, \alpha_k)$.

Clearly this list of inequalities can be produced using only logarithmic space on the number of gates of α. Also it is straightforward to prove by induction that for every i the solution of the inequalities system verifies $x_i = v(\alpha_i)$.

If we define c to be the n vector $c = (0, 0, \ldots, 0, 1)$, $c^T(x_1, x_2, \ldots, x_n) = x_n$. Therefore $\alpha \in$ **CVP** iff $v(\alpha_n) = 1$ iff $x_n = 1$ iff $(A, b, c) \in$ **Decisional-LP**. $\square$

3. P-Intermediate Problems

In the previous sections we have argued that a good way to give evidence that a problem in P cannot be efficiently parallelized is to provide a reduction from a P-complete problem to it. Of course, such a reduction can only be obtained if the problem itself is P-complete. The question that arises is whether this can always be done or there are problems in the class P which are neither in NC nor P-complete. Such problems are called P-intermediate. The existence of these problems is very hard to prove since a positive answer to it would obviously provide a solution to the NC versus P question. However, one can try to answer this problem under the hypothesis that P is different from NC. (Observe that if NC=P then P-intermediate problems cannot exist).

The analogous question in the NP setting was solved by Ladner [20]. He showed that if P$\neq$NP then there are sets in NP which are neither in P nor NP-complete. The proof of the result uses a complicated diagonalization technique which was simplified by Schöning in [27]. Schmidt [26] translated the results to complexity classes bellow P and showed that if P is not included in LOGSPACE then there are languages which are neither P-complete nor in LOGSPACE. Building on these techniques Serna [28] and Vollmer [30] have recently obtained the following results:

Theorem 3.1 *If* NC$\neq$P *then there exists a language which is neither* P*-complete nor in* NC.

Moreover, if the classes are different then there are infinitely many problems between P and NC, each one with a different complexity.

Theorem 3.2 *If* NC$\neq$P *then there are* $\aleph_0$ *many degrees in* P-NC *(with respect to either logspace or* NC$_1$ *reducibility).*

The P-intermediate languages from these results are obtained through diagonalization and therefore they are artificial languages. No natural P-intermediate problem is known, even under the hypothesis NC$\neq$P. There are however some problems in P which are not known to be either P-complete nor in NC and are therefore candidates for being P-intermediate. The following are three examples of such problems taken from a list given by Karp and Ramachandran in [15].

Two variable linear progaming: Given an $m \times n$ rational matrix A with at most two non-zero elements in each row, and a rational m-vector b, compute a feasible solution of the system $Ax \leq b$.

Integer Greatest Common Divisor: Given integers a and b, compute the greatest common divisor of a and b.

Modular Integer Exponentiation: Given integers a, b and c, compute $a^b \mod c$.

4. NC approximations of P-complete Problems

We have seen that unless NC=P one cannot solve P-complete problems using efficient parallel algorithms. In this section we study the possibility to obtain approximate solutions for these problems within NC. For this we will consider certain optimization functions whose decisional version is P-complete and investigate whether is it possible to compute within NC a value which is close to the value of the function. It is an interesting fact that the functions associated to P-complete problems behave in very different ways with respect to its NC approximability; some of then can be well approximated by NC circuits while others cannot be approximated within any factor unless NC=P. To our knowledge the first NC approximation algorithm for a P-complete problem was given by Anderson and Mayr [1]. They showed that the optimization version of **HDSP** can be approximated in NC within a factor $\varepsilon < \frac{1}{2}$, but it cannot be approximated for $\varepsilon > \frac{1}{2}$ unless NC=P. We present the original proof of this result. Serna [28] has developed a theory related to the approximation of P-complete optimization functions; she considers different types of approximation and approximation schemes. Here we will just use a simple definition of approximation. Let us start approximating the High Degree Subgraph Problem which was shown to be P-complete in section 2. Its optimization version is,

Opt-HDSP: Given a graph G, find the largest k such that there is an induced subgraph with minimum degree k.

Let us denote the largest degree of a subgraph in G by $h(G)$. Opt-HDSP belongs to a class of optimization problems with a "threshold" approximation behaviour, i.e., there is a constant t such that for $\varepsilon < t$ there is an NC algorithm A which on input G produces an approximation of h, $A(G)$ with $\varepsilon h(x) \leq A(x) \leq h(x)$; however, for $\varepsilon > t$ the problem cannot be approximated in NC by an ε factor unless NC=P. The proof of this result uses the following combinatorial lemma from [5] that can be easily proved by induction on the number of nodes of the graph.

Lemma 4.1 *Every graph $G = (V, E)$ has an induced subgraph with minimum degree at least $\lceil \frac{|E|}{|V|} \rceil$.*

Theorem 4.2 *For any constant $\varepsilon < \frac{1}{2}$, there is an NC algorithm A such that for every graph G, $\varepsilon h(G) \leq A(G) \leq h(G)$.*

Proof. We present an NC algorithm that uses the following procedure which depends on ε:

```
procedure Test(G, k)
begin
    while G ≠ ∅ do begin
        Vₖ := {nodes in V of degree smaller than  k in G};
        if |Vₖ| < (1 − 2ε)|V| then return (true)
        else delete from G all the nodes in Vₖ
    end;
    return (false)
end
```

The algorithm on input $G = (V, E)$ runs this procedure in parallel for every k, $1 \leq k \leq |V|$, then selects $m := \max\{k : Test(G, k, \varepsilon) = \text{true }\}$ and outputs the value $m\varepsilon$.

This algorithm needs $O(\log^2(|G|))$ running time using a polynomial number of processors. First observe that the while loop in the procedure makes at most $\log_{2\varepsilon}(\frac{1}{|V|})$ iterations, since every time it is executed a $(1 - 2\varepsilon)$ fraction of the remaining nodes is removed. Notice that the number of iterations depend on the value of ε and that it is needed $\varepsilon < \frac{1}{2}$.

For every iteration the algorithm has to determine the degree of each of the remaining nodes and delete some of them. This can be done in logarithmic time with $|V| \times |E|$ processors.

We claim

i. if $Test(G, k, \varepsilon) = \text{true} \Rightarrow h(G) \geq \lceil \varepsilon k \rceil$, and

ii. if $Test(G, k, \varepsilon) = \text{false} \Rightarrow h(G) < k$.

Suppose that $Test(G, k, \varepsilon)$ is true and let $G' = (V', E')$ be the graph in the stage just before the procedure comes out of the while loop. Then $|V'_k| < (1 - 2\varepsilon)|V'|$. This means that there are in G' at least $2\varepsilon|V'|$ edges of degree at least k and therefore $|E'| \geq k\varepsilon|V'|$. By lemma 4.1, G' has an induced subgraph of degree at least $\lceil \varepsilon k \rceil$.

On the other hand if $h(G) \leq k$ then $Test(G, k, \varepsilon)$ never returns "false" since in the worst case the procedure deletes everything until there are only nodes of degree at least k and then $|V_k| = 0$.

The algorithm approximates $h(G)$ in the desired way since it outputs the value $\lceil \varepsilon k \rceil$ for the maximum k for which $Test(G, k, \varepsilon)$ is true, and by the two parts of the claim follows

$$\varepsilon h(G) \leq \varepsilon k \leq \lceil \varepsilon k \rceil \leq h(G).$$

□

We show that the above approximation is in some sense optimal.

Theorem 4.3 *If* NC$\neq$P *then Opt-HDSP cannot be approximated by a factor* $\varepsilon > \frac{1}{2}$.

Proof. The Monotone Circuit Value Problem can be reduced to HDSP in such a way that depending on the value of the circuit there can be a large difference in the degree of the subgraphs constructed in the transformation. For any $k \geq 3$, there is a logarithmic space reduction which given a monotone circuit α produces a graph G such that $h(G)$, the largest degree of an induced subgraph in G is $2k$ if the value of α is 1, and $h(G) = k + 1$ if the value

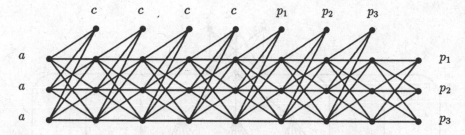

$$c \quad\quad c \quad\quad c \quad\quad c \quad\quad p_1 \quad\quad p_2 \quad\quad p_3$$

Figure 7: Expander with 3 inputs and 4 outputs.

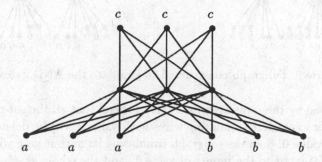

Figure 8: Subgraph constructed to simulate the OR gates.

of α is 0. Observe that this implies the result since making a reduction from **MCVP** to a graph G for a k satisfying $\frac{2k}{\varepsilon} > k+1$ and applying an approximation algorithm with factor $\varepsilon > \frac{1}{2}$ one could distinguish between the two cases and therefore solve the Circuit Value Problem.

The reduction is similar to the one in theorem 2.13 but uses more complicated subgraphs. The figures we present are for the case $k = 3$, but they can be easily generalized for every k. In the reduction from theorem 2.13 edges simulate wires of the circuit. Now the edges are substituted by "expanders" like the one shown in figure 7. The two vertices labelled p_i, $(i \in \{1,2,3\})$ are the same vertex (they are represented this way just to make the figure clearer). Nodes marked a are the input nodes while nodes marked c are outputs. In the simulation of the circuits all these nodes will propagate the same value. The expander represented in the figure has three inputs and four outputs. Adding more layers the expander can be modified to have as many output nodes as desired. In the construction we will use expanders with k inputs and with a number of outputs which is a multiple of k. Expanders are used to propagate the output values of the gates to other gates. Subgraphs simulating AND and OR gates are represented in figures 8 and 9.

Their inputs are a and b, each one repeated several times. One has to consider that there is an expander whose outputs are the a's and another one producing the b's.

The outputs of the AND and OR gates (k times c) are connected to inputs of an expander which in turn have its outputs connected to inputs of other gates. The outputs of the output gate in the circuit are connected to the inputs of an expander. This expander has outputs connected to the inputs of the subgraph simulating the input gates of value 1.

Consider the greedy algorithm from theorem 2.13 to delete nodes of degree smaller than

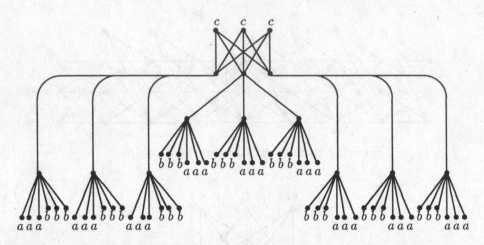

Figure 9: Subgraph constructed to simulate the AND gates.

$k+2$. It can be proved by the same arguments given there, that all the subgraphs simulating gates with value 0 or expanders simulating wires with value 0 will be deleted.

If the circuit had value 0, then the subgraph simulating its output gate will be deleted, the deletion will be propagated to the inputs of value 1, and the whole graph will be removed. Therefore in this case $h(G) \leq k+1$. Since the expanders have always a subgraph of degree $k+1$ it follows $h(G) = k+1$.

If the circuit had value 1, then the subgraphs simulating gates with value 1 and the expanders connecting these subgraphs will not be removed. This leaves a subgraph with degree 2k.   □

Kirousis, Serna and Spirakis give in [18] other examples of P-complete problem related to graph connectivity whose approximation presents a "threshold" behaviour similar to the one from **Opt-HDSP**. We end this section presenting a negative result from [29] which shows that Linear Programming cannot be approximated within NC for any value of ε unless NC=P. This holds even if we do not require the approximated value to be the cost of a possible solution of the problem.

To prove this fact we need a lemma stating that the function g_1 computing the number or gates with value 1 in a circuit cannot be approximated in NC within any factor.

Lemma 4.4 *If* NC$\neq$P *then for any constant* $\varepsilon > 0$ *there is no function f in NC such that for every circuit* α $\varepsilon g_1(\alpha) \leq f(\alpha) \leq g_1(\alpha)$.

Proof. A circuit α of size n can be transformed into a new circuit α' such that if $v(\alpha) = 1$ then $g_1(\alpha') > \lceil \frac{n}{\varepsilon} \rceil$, and if $v(\alpha) = 0$ then $g_1(\alpha') < n$. This can be easily achieved connecting the output gate of α to a chain of $\lceil \frac{n}{\varepsilon} \rceil$ OR-gates in which each gate has as inputs the outputs of the previous gate in the chain. Observe that if an NC ε-approximation for g_1 existed, one could compute the value of a circuit α in NC using the following procedure: Transform α into α' (this clearly can be done in NC), and run the approximation algorithm on α'. The value of α is 1 iff the value produced is greater than or equal to n.   □

Theorem 4.5 *If* NC$\neq$P *then for any constant* $\varepsilon > 0$ *there is no approximation algorithm which given an integer* $m \times n$ *matrix* A *an integer* m-*vector* b *and an integer* n-*vector* c *produces a value* v *such that* $\varepsilon c^T x \leq v \leq c^T x$, *where* x *is a rational* n *vector such that* $Ax \leq b$ *and* $c^T x$ *is maximized.*

Proof. In the proof of the P-completeness of LP (theoren 2.14), from a monotone circuit α, a matrix A and a vector b were constructed such that the unique solution vector $x = (x_1, \ldots, x_n)$ of the system $Ax \leq b$ had as many 1-component as gates in α with value 1. If the reduction is transformed to produce also the n-vector $c = (1, \ldots, 1)$, $c^T x$ is equal to the number of gates in α with value 1, and by the previous lemma, this value cannot be approximated in NC. $\square$

Aknowledgements: The author would like to thank José L. Balcázar and Birgit Jenner for many helpful comments.

References

[1] R. ANDERSON AND E. MAYR, A P-complete problem and approximations to it. Tech. Report Stanford University (1986).

[2] A. GIBBONS AND W. RYTTER, *Efficient Parallel Algorithms.* Cambridge University Press (1988).

[3] A. BORODIN, On relating time and space to size and depth. *SIAM Journal of Computing* **6** (1977), 733–744.

[4] D. DOBKIN, R. LIPTON AND S. REISS, Linear programming is log-space hard for P. *Information Processing Letters* **9** (1979), 96–97.

[5] P. ERDÖS, On the structure of linear graphs. *Israel Journal of Mathematics* **1** (1963), 156–160.

[6] M. GAREY AND D. JOHNSON, *Computers and Intractability.* W.H. Freeman (1979).

[7] L. GOLDSCHLAGER, The monotone and planar circuit value problems are log space complete for P. *SIGACT News* **9**, 2 (1977), 25–29.

[8] L. GOLDSCHLAGER, A space efficient algorithm for the monotone planar circuit value problem. *Information Processing Letters* **10**, 1 (1980), 25–27.

[9] L. GOLDSCHLAGER, L. SHAW AND J. STAPLES, The maximum flow problem is log space complete for P. *Theoretical Computer Science* **21** (1982), 105–111.

[10] L. GOLDSCHLAGER AND I. PARBERRY, On the construction of parallel computers from various bases of boolean functions. *Theoretical Computer Science* **43** (1986), 43–58.

[11] R. GREENLAW, H. HOOVER AND W. RUZZO, A compendium of problems complete for P. Technical Report TR-91-05-01 University of Washington (1991). Manuscript, (1984).

[12] J. HOPCROFT AND J. ULLMAN, *Introduction to Automata Theory, Languages and Computation.* Addison-Wesley (1979).

[13] D. JOHNSON, Parallel algorithms for minimum cuts and maximum flows in planar networks. *Journal of the ACM* **34** (1987), 950–967.

[14] N. JONES AND W. LAASER, Complete problems for deterministic polynomial time. *Theoretical Computer Science* **3** (1977), 105–117.

[15] R. KARP AND V. RAMACHANDRAN, Parallel algorithms for shared memory machines. In the *Handbook of Theoretical Computer Science*, vol 1. (Edited by J. van Leeuwen) Elsevier, (1990) 869–943.

[16] R. KARP, E. UPFAL AND A. WIGDERSON, Constructing a perfect matching in Random NC. *Proc. 17th ACM STOC* (1985), 22–32.

[17] L. KHACHIAN, A polynomial time algorithm for linear programming. *Doklady Akad. Nauk SSSR* **224** (1979), 1093–1096. Translated in *Soviet Math. Doklady* **20**, 191–194.

[18] L. KIROUSIS, M.J. SERNA AND P. SPIRAKIS, The parallel complexity of the subgraph connectivity problem. *Proc. 30th Symposium on Foundations of Computer Science* IEEE (1989), 294–299.

[19] R. LADNER, The Circuit Value Problem is log space complete for P. *SIGACT News* **7**, 1 (1975), 18–20.

[20] R. LADNER, On the structure of polynomial time reducibility, *Journal of the ACM* **22**, 1 (1975), 155–171.

[21] T. LENGAUER AND K. WAGNER, The correlation between the complexities of the non-hierarchical and hierarchical versions of graph problems, *Proc. STACS 87* Lecture Notes in Computer Science **247**, Springer-Verlag (1987), 100–113.

[22] E. MAYR AND A. SUBRAMANIAN, The complexity of circuit value and network stability. *Proc. 4th Structure in Complexity Theory Conference* IEEE (1989), 114–124.

[23] S. MIYANO, S. SHIRAISI AND T. SHOUDAY, A list of P-complete problems. Tech. Report RIFIS-TR-CS-17, RIFIS, Kyushu University (1990).

[24] I. PARBERRY, *Parallel Complexity Theory*. Pitman (1987).

[25] L. RUZZO, Tree-size bounded alternation. *Journal of Computers and System Sciences* **21** (1980), 218–235.

[26] D. SCHMIDT, The recursion theoretic structure of complexity classes. *Theoretical Computer Science* **38** (1985), 143–156.

[27] U. SCHÖNING, A uniform approach to obtain diagonal sets in complexity classes. *Theoretical Computer Science* **18** (1982), 95–103.

[28] M.J. SERNA, The parallel approximability of P-complete problems. Ph.D. Thesis, Universitat Politècnica de Catalunya (1990).

[29] M.J. SERNA, Approximating linear programming is log-space complete for P. *Information Processing Letters* **37** (1991), 233–236.

[30] H. VOLLMER, The Gap-Language-Technique revisited. To appear in *Proc. Computer Science and Logic 91* Lecture Notes in Computer Science, Springer-Verlag (1991).

Chapter 10

An Introduction to Distributed Memory Models of Parallel Computation*

Alan Gibbons

Abstract

This chapter is an introduction to distributed memory models of parallel computation and, in certain aspects, paves the way towards later chapters. Communication networks that have been advocated for general purposes are described and the problem of parallel routing within these networks is addressed through the *permutation routing* paradigm. A number of basic techniques are briefly introduced for efficient implementation of P-RAM algorithms on distributed memory models of parallel computation. These include techniques which are dependent on network topology or algorithmic structure, such as *graph embedding* and the method of *compress and iterate* as well as techniques with less specific application such as the employment of *hashing* and the use of *parallel slackness* to hide network *latency*.

1. Introduction

The P-RAM model of parallel computation (see [10] for example) assumes constant-length data paths from every processor to every memory cell. In current technology, this quickly becomes physically unrealisable as we scale up the number of processors and the size of the shared memory. In practical large scale parallel computers, packing constraints such as this force the inevitability of employing communication networks with non-constant time communication delays between co-operating processors (network *latency*) and restricted connection density at the nodes of the network (the processor sites). The need for such networks may be obviated in the long term by the appearance of new technologies (optical communication provides one such hope), but for the foreseeable future we will have to contend with the complication of networks with latency and restricted message passing density (*bandwidth*). In section 2 we catalogue some of the communication networks that currently have been proposed. The networks we consider are those that have been proposed for general purposes. We therefore omit consideration of special purpose hardware such as dedicated systolic arrays ([23]).

The main problem that must be addressed in respect of communication networks is that of parallel message passing. Perhaps the most useful paradigm is that of *permutation routing* which is the problem of each processor simultaneously sending one (constant length) message to another processor in such a way that each processor is to receive precisely one

---

*An introductory lecture delivered at the ALCOM Spring School of Parallel Computation supported by the Esprit II Basic Research Action Program of the EC under contract No. 3075 (project ALCOM).

message. In section 3 we address the problem of permutation routing on the two most popular communication networks, square meshes and hypercubes.

Algorithmic studies in the P-RAM model have provided a wealth of knowledge concerning the exploitation of inherent parallelism in problems. It is therefore natural that we should draw on this background when solving problems on distributed memory machines. Indeed, many researchers would argue that P-RAM simulation provides the only coherent way forward at present for the hope of scalable parallel computation. In sections 4 and 5 we variously describe a number of techniques which assist in the efficient implementation of P-RAM algorithms on distributed memory machines. The techniques that we describe were (historically) obtained in the process of problem by problem implementation of algorithms on distributed memory models and so, although they individually can be applied to wide classes of problems, they are not always of universal applicability. The question, for example, of emulating the P-RAM model by distributed memory machines is properly captured in enquiries of general purpose parallel computation which is covered in [24]. Some of the notions we briefly introduce are nevertheless components in particular of these enquiries (for example, the idea of *hashing* the memory space and the employment of *parallel slackness* to hide network latency) whereas others are network topology dependent or dependent upon the algorithmic structure in hand (for example, the use of *graph embedding* or the employment of the *compress and iterate* technique). In some contexts, such techniques as the latter may well be hidden from the programmer by system software in due course.

2.   Communication Networks

Our model of a realistic computer consists of a number of processing elements each located at the node of a graph. A processing element is a sequential computer with associated memory and the ability to route messages to adjacent nodes of the graph. To reflect realistic packaging constraints we require that the number of edges of the graph attached to any node (the *degree* of the graph) is small, preferably constant or growing slowly (for example, logarithmically) with the size of the graph. On the other hand, for speed of computation, we require that the network be of small diameter because then messages will have short routes between any pair of nodes. Moore graphs, which are graphs of minimum diameter for fixed network size and degree, have been extensively studied (see [13] for example). However, additional considerations (particularly the need to able to support high parallel message passing density) may dictate a little away from optimality in the Moore sense. There are also advantages to be gained from graph homogeneity (as exhibited by vertex- or edge-transitive graphs for example) which can (amongst other things) ease algorithmic description. Also, we may advantageously use recursively decomposable graphs which not only naturally support recursive algorithms but can also aid physical construction and size enhancement. Here we introduce networks that have been proposed for general purposes and do not describe dedicated systolic networks which are the subject of another area of the literature (see [23], for example).

In the following catalogue, n is the number of nodes of a network and in all cases we consider the graphs to be undirected (each edge being thus regarded as bi-directional). Sources of this material include [3, 18, 25, 29, 37]

2.1.   The binary hypercube

A hypercube is a graph with n nodes, where $n = 2^d$ for some positive integer d called the *dimension* of the hypercube. The nodes are labelled from 0 to $n - 1$ in binary notation and there is an edge between two nodes iff their binary labels differ in exactly one bit. Edges which connect nodes whose labels differ in the ith bit are called edges of the ith dimension. Figure 1 shows the i-dimensional hypercubes for $1 \leq i \leq 4$.

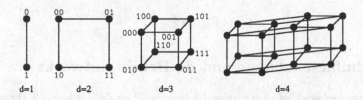

Figure 1.

The hypercube of dimension $(i + 1)$ is inductively constructed from two hypercubes each of dimension i by adding the edges of the $(i + 1)^{th}$ dimension between corresponding nodes of the smaller hypercubes. It is easy to see that the diameter of a hypercube is $\log_2 n$ and that the vertex degree is $\log_2 n$. Hypercubes are bipartite graphs.

2.2.   The cube-connected cycles and butterfly networks

Both the cube-connected cycles and the butterfly network can be regarded as constant-degree variations of the hypercube.

A cube connected cycles network is a d-dimensional hypercube in which each of the 2^d nodes has been replaced by a cycle of length d in such a way that the edge of the ith dimension originally incident with the hypercube node is now made incident with the ith node of the cycle. Every node is now of degree 3. For the cube-connected cycles network, $n = d2^d$. Figure 2(a) shows the network for $d = 3$. It is easy to see that the diameter of a cube-connected cycles network is $2\log_2 n$.

Figure 2(b) shows the butterfly of dimension 3. In general, a butterfly of dimension d has $(d + 1)$ *ranks* with 2^d nodes in each rank. Hence $n = (d + 1)2^d$. Figure 2(b) indicates the numbering of the ranks from 0 to d. Each node of a butterfly corresponds to a pair (r, c), where r is the rank the node and c is a d-bit binary number denoting the *column* of the node. An edge connects nodes (r, c) and (r', c') iff $r = r' + 1$ and either $c = c'$ or c and c' only differ in the rth bit. There is a self-evident recursive construction of the $(d + 1)$-dimensional butterfly from two d-dimensional butterflies for $d > 1$. A hypercube is obtained from a butterfly by collapsing each column of nodes. The diameter of a butterfly is $2\log_2 n$ and the (maximum) vertex-degree is 4.

The hypercube and its derivatives just described have been extensively and favourably reviewed as useful networks because they exhibit many of the desirable properties described earlier. Perhaps to a lesser extent, the same is true for the shuffle-exchange and de Bruijn networks.

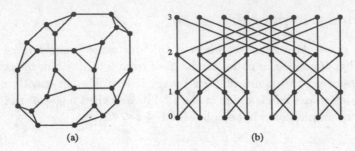

Figure 2.

2.3.   The shuffle-exchange and de Bruijn networks

A shuffle-exchange network of dimension d has $n = 2^d$ nodes. Figure 3 shows the shuffle-exchange network for $d = 3$. The nodes are labelled from 0 to $n - 1$ in binary notation. An edge connects two nodes iff either their labels differ precisely in their least significant bit (in which case the edge is called an *exchange* edge) or the label of one node is a cyclic shift (either left or right) of the other (in which case the edge is called a *shuffle* edge).

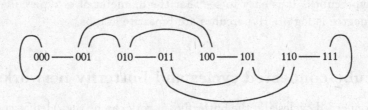

Figure 3.

A useful property of the shuffle-exchange network which we shall employ later is described as follows. Exchange edges connect nodes whose binary labels differ in their least significant digit and by cycling stored items using the shuffle edges we can cause pairs of items (all such pairs simultaneously) originally stored at nodes whose labels differ in their i^{th} bit ($i = 1, 2, ..., d$ in turn) to occupy nodes at opposite ends of an exchange edge.

The diameter of a shuffle-exchange network is $2 \log_2(n - 1)$ and the vertex degree is 3. The name *shuffle-exchange* derives from the fact that the network mimics (in one parallel use of the shuffle edges followed by one parallel employment of the exchange edges) the shuffle-exchange operation commonly employed in the classical sorting networks of Batcher (see [15], for example).

A de Bruijn network is similar to the shuffle-exchange network except that the exchange edges are replaced by *exchange-shuffle* edges. If we denote by x a binary string of $(d - 1)$ bits, then an exchange-shuffle edge connects nodes labelled xa and bx where a and b are binary bits ($a \neq b$). An alternative definition is that the de Bruijn network of dimension d is obtained from the shuffle-exchange network of dimension $(d + 1)$ by contracting all the exchange edges. Figure 4 shows the de Bruijn network for $d = 3$. De Bruijn networks have $\log_2 n$ diameter and vertex degree 4.

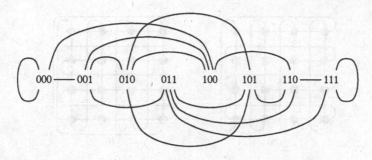

Figure 4.

2.4.   Meshes

Meshes are class of network that have received wide attention. Although generally speaking they suffer from having large diameter, their uniform structure and (if of low dimension) ease of construction make them attractive. A d-dimensional mesh (of dimensions $a_1, a_2, \ldots, a_d$) has nodes which are d-tuples $(z_1, z_2, \ldots, z_d)$, $(1 \le z_i \le a_i)$. Here z_i is called the ith co-ordinate and such a mesh is called a $(a_1 \times a_2 \times \ldots \times a_d)$ mesh. Edges connect d-tuples which differ by one in exactly one co-ordinate. The diameter of a d-dimensional mesh is $((a_1 - 1) + (a_2 - 1) + \ldots + (a_d - 1))$ and it has (maximum) degree of $2d$ (provided each $a_i \ge 3$). For fixed n and d a minimum diameter is achieved when all dimensions are equal. Figure 5 shows some meshes. Notice that the $(2 \times 2 \times 2 \times 2)$ mesh is the hypercube of dimension 4. Every hypercube is a mesh.

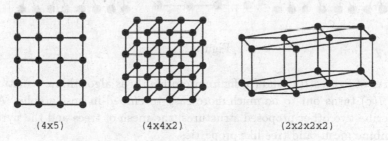

(4x5)   (4x4x2)   (2x2x2x2)

Figure 5.

Meshes sometimes feature additional edges to reduce the diameter. For example, figure 6(a) shows a $(4 \times 4 \times 4)$ mesh with *wrap-around* connections and figure 6(b) shows the same mesh with *toroidal* connections. In both cases, the additional edges reduce the diameter by a small constant factor and do not therefore have a significant functional impact for algorithmic complexity. Other connections might (the edges of figure 8 for example), but at the same time may significantly affect the mesh-like nature of the network.

2.5.   Tree structured networks

Trees figure prominently as an algorithmic structure in (P-RAM) parallel solutions to problems. It is natural therefore that there have many proposals (often for specific applications) for networks based on trees. We shall also be interested later in the question of whether the networks described already are able to efficiently embed these algorithmic structures.

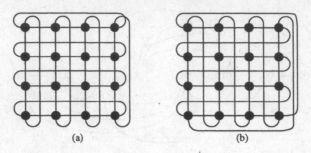

Figure 6.

A *complete* binary tree of height h has $n = 2^{(h+1)} - 1$ nodes. The set of nodes may be described as the set of all binary strings of length $\leq h$, including the empty string. Then edges only connect a string x to a string xa where a is 0 or 1. Such a tree of height 3 is shown in figure 7(a). Clearly, the complete binary tree has diameter $2h = 2\log_2(n + 1) - 2$ and (maximum) vertex degree of 3. Variations of the complete binary tree are x-trees (the x-tree of height 3 is shown in figure 7(b)) and double rooted complete binary trees (the double rooted complete binary tree of height 3 is shown in figure 7(c)).

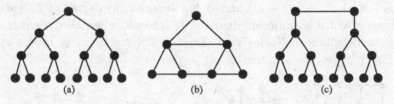

Figure 7.

The structures of figures 7(a) and (b) figure prominently as algorithmic structures whereas that of figure 7(c) turns out to be much more easy to embed in host graphs. As networks we briefly describe two other proposed structures, the mesh of trees and the pyramid. Both structures combine mesh- and tree-like properties.

Given a set of nodes laid out as in a d-dimensional $(N \times N \times \ldots \times N)$ mesh, a *mesh of trees* of dimension d is constructed by making the N nodes of each one-dimensional *row* the leaves of a complete binary tree. Clearly, we require that $N = 2^m$ for some positive integer m. For a mesh of trees, $n = N^d + dN^d - dN^{d-1}$ and the diameter is $2d\log_2 N = O(\log n)$. Figure 8 shows the mesh of trees for $d = 2$ and $N = 4$. The mesh of trees has some nice properties and has been proposed as a processor network for general purpose applications ([17]).

A pyramid of height h has $n = (4^{(h+1)} - 1)/3$ nodes. Figure 9 shows pyramids (viewed from above) of heights 1 and 2. The cental node in each of the diagrams of this figure is the apex of its pyramid. Nodes are triples (i, x, y), $1 \leq i \leq h$ and $1 \leq x, y \leq 2^i$. Edges connect (i, x, y) with vertices in $\{(i + 1, u, v) \mid u$ is $2x$ or $2x - 1$ and v is $2y$ or $2y - 1$ $\}$ as well as (i, a, b) such that (x, y) and (a, b) are adjacent nodes in the $2^i \times 2^i$ mesh for all i, $0 \leq i \leq n$ and all x, y, $1 \leq x, y \leq 2^i$. A pyramid has diameter $= 2h - 1 = 2log_4(3n - 1)$ and (maximum) degree of 9. The pyramid is also called the *quad-tree* by the engineering fraternity and is currently employed in much image processing work.

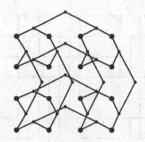

Figure 8.

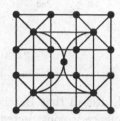

Figure 9.

3. Sorting and Routing

In a distributed memory model of parallel computation we take the processing elements to be indexed according to some natural scheme. When sorting in such a model, we suppose that the items to be sorted are distributed across the network, one located at each processing element. The object of the sorting process is to route the item which would be the ith (in a sorted list of the items) to the processing element with index i. The most useful paradigm of the parallel routing problem on communication networks is *permutation routing*. In permutation routing we are required to send exactly one message (of constant bounded length) from each processing element in such a way that each processing element is to receive precisely one message. Clearly this is the same problem as sorting on the destination addresses.

We consider sorting on three models: the (2-dimensional) mesh, the hypercube and the perfect shuffle network. We show that a classic sorter of Batcher (based on bitonic merge)

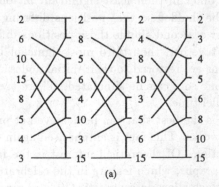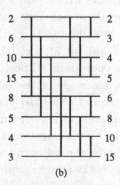

Figure 10.

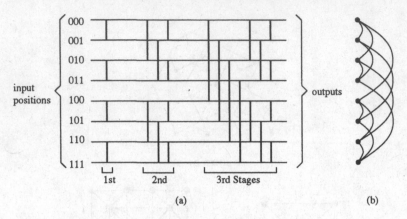

Figure 11.

can be readily simulated. Recall that Batcher's bitonic merge takes two sorted sequences from which a bitonic sequence is constructed. From this a sorted sequence is produced by applying (a logarithmic number of times) the operations of shuffle and compare-exchange. Figure 10 illustrates a bitonic merge (emphasising the shuffle operations in (a) and showing a more conventional view in (b)). Such a merge takes $O(\log k)$ time, where k is the size of the input. In order to sort n numbers (where n is a power of 2) we construct a complete binary tree (of height $\log n$), place the numbers at the leaves and a merge network at each internal nodes. In a natural leaves-to-root parallel computation, the numbers become sorted in $O(\log^2 n)$ time. Such a complete sorting network (for $n = 8$) is illustrated in figure 11. Notice that if we label the inputs from top to bottom in binary (as in figure 11) then elements whose positions differ in their least significant bit are compared in all $(\log^2 n)$ stages, those which differ in their second most significant digit of their position are compared in the last $(\log^2 n) - 1$ stages and so on. It is only in the final stage that elements differing in the most significant digit of their position are compared.

Bitonic sort can be simulated on the shuffle exchange network in $O(\log^2 n)$ parallel time. When compare-exchanging two elements, they are brought together so as to occupy network nodes at opposite ends of the same exchange edge. In order to see how the simulation works we recall the following property of the shuffle exchange network. Initially the shuffle exchange edges connect elements whose positions differ in their least significant bit only. After one parallel shuffle step these positions can be shuffled so that positions differing in their most significant bit are brought together, after a second shuffle those positions differing in their second most significant bit are brought together, then third most signicant bit and so on. After $\log_2 n$ shuffle operations all positions are restored to their initial nodes. Hence, within $O(\log n)$ time any one stage of the bitonic sort can be simulated. There are $\log_2 n$ stages and so overall we require $O(\log^2 n)$ parallel time.

For practical purposes, $O(\log^2 n)$ time is the best that can be achieved at present for permutation routing on communication networks. This fact is emphasised again on connection with the hypercube in the following section. Of theoretical interest is the fact that there exists a class of networks (the *expander* graphs, which feature in the celebrated logarithmic depth sorter of [2], see also [28, 21, 38]) which allow deterministic $O(\log n)$ permutation routing. However, they are not at present known to be of real use. Little is known concerning

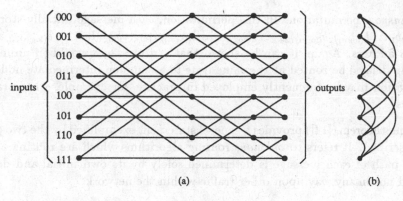

inputs

outputs

(a)   (b)

Figure 12.

the construction of expanders of practical size.

3.1. Permutation Routing on the hypercube

We first consider the following natural *greedy* algorithm for permutation routing on the hypercube. The addresses of hypercube nodes and the destination addresses of messages are presumed to be in binary form. In each step of the algorithm, at every node, the next queued message at that node is routed as follows. In the ith routing step for that message, the ith bit of the destination address of each message is compared with the ith bit of its current address and, if these do not correspond, they are made to correspond by routing the message to a neighbouring node along the edge of the ith dimension. In the algorithm, each message clearly follows a shortest (logarithmic length) route to its destination. Delays may be incurred because, in general, such a scheme will lead to queues of messages at nodes. We address this question shortly.

A convenient way of visualising this greedy algorithm is illustrated in figure 12. For the purposes of this figure, we imagine that permutation routing is conducted on the hypercube of dimension 3 of figure 12(b). Figure 12(a) can then be employed to trace the individual routes of messages in time in a left to right sweep. Messages are initially located at the left hand column of nodes and in the first step are routed either along a horizontal edge (which corresponds to the message remaining at its current address on the hypercube) or along an edge corresponding to the first dimension of the hypercube. Subsequent similar steps ultimately results in all messages reaching their destinations. Notice that the topology of figure 12 (a) is that of a butterfly network and that a horizontal contraction of the figure naturally reproduces the hypercube of figure 12(b).

Certain permutations of inputs to outputs of the butterfly provide particularly bad examples of routing congestion. Consider two cases:

- The *bit-reversal* permutation. For this permutation, the destination address of each message is the address of its initial location read backwards. In other words, a message initially at the binary address $b_0 b_1 \ldots b_{\log n}$ has destination $b_{\log n} b_{(\log n)-1} \ldots b_0$. Clearly, if $\log_2 n$ is even, then all $\sqrt{n}$ messages with destination addresses of the form $b_0 b_1 \ldots b_{(\log n)/2} 00 \ldots 0$ would (if unimpeded by queueing delays) be located at address $00 \ldots 0$ half way through execution of the algorithm.

- The *transpose* permutation. In this permutation, each message initially stored at address $b_0 b_1 \ldots b_{(\log n)/2} b_{(\log n)/2+1} \ldots b_{\log n}$ has $b_{(\log n)/2+1} \ldots b_{\log n} b_0 b_1 \ldots b_{(\log n)/2}$ as its destination address. Again, it can be shown that $\sqrt{n}$ messages would (if unimpeded by queueing delays) be routed at the same time to a common intermediate node. Such a permutation may be frequently employed in practise, for example, when transposing matrices.

The following theorem ([14]) provides a general statement exemplified by the two particular cases just described. It refers to *oblivious* routing algorithms which are routing algorithms in which the path of each message is determined solely by its own initial and destination addresses and not in any way upon other traffic within the network.

Theorem 3.1 *If G is any n-node, degree d network, then for any oblivious routing algorithm there is a permutation routing problem which will take at least $(\sqrt{n})/2d$ steps to complete.*

A natural lower bound for the running time of permutation routing algorithms on the hypercube is $O(\log n)$, provided by the diameter of the network. In this light, the greedy algorithm performs rather badly in the worst cases. On the other hand, there are permutations for which this lower bound is achieved. For example, if each message has a destination address which is the complement of its initial address, then the algorithm executes in exactly $\log_2 n$ steps. It is interesting therefore to ask what the average case behaviour is like. It turns out that the average case performance is very close to the best case performance. The fraction of all possible permutations leading to worst case queue lengths is *extremely* small. In fact, the average congestion is $o(\log n)$ leading to $\log n + o(\log n)$ expected running time. This fact forms the basis for algorithms with good performance.

The problem case permutations, although rare in the space of all permutations are nevertheless likely to be met fairly frequently in practice. This is because they tend to be structured in a regular manner like the bit-reversal and the transpose permutations. Two different approaches have been advocated to make all cases behave (with high probability) like the average case. The first of these approaches, making use of *hashing* is perhaps the most intuitively obvious. Instead of locating data at an address A, say, it is caused to be located at address $H(A)$ where $H(A)$ is a random map onto the address space. We briefly return to the topic of hashing at the end of section 4 and concentrate here on the second approach, that of employing so-called *two-phase randomised* routing.

It is not known at present whether there exists a distributed $O(\log n)$-time *deterministic* algorithm for permutation routing on the hypercube. That $O(\log n)$-time permutation routing is at all possible was discovered around 1980. The celebrated two-phase randomised routing approach was first conceived by Valiant and developed by him and Brebner ([40, 41, 39]). Leaving aside for the moment the question of queueing disciplines, the two-phase randomised routing algorithm can be very briefly described as follows. In the first phase, each message is greedily routed to a randomly chosen address. This is done by choosing (with equal probability) each bit of the destination address to be 0 or 1. In the second phase, each message is greedily routed to its true destination. Since only one message per edge is allowed at any time, there needs to be a facility for queueing messages. Notice that several initial addresses may route to the same initially chosen random address. The probability is very small [43] (dropping exponentially with d, the dimension of the cube) that all messages will arrive in more than kd steps, where k is a small integer constant. Thus the probability rapidly drops to zero (as d increases) that more than kd routing steps are required. It has been shown in [32] that the running time of the algorithm is remarkably invariant under a wide class of queueing disciplines including first-in, first-out and last-in, first-out.

If we define an *h-relation* to be a routing problem where each processor is to send at most h messages and to receive at most h messages then a permutation routing problem is a 1-relation. We have described how a 1-relation can be realised with high probability using two-phase randomised routing on the hypercube in a time proportional to the network diameter. In fact, an essentially similar approach applied to the cube-connected cycles, butterfly and the two-dimensional mesh yields similarly optimal results for these fixed degree networks. Moreover, the following stronger result for the hypercube (with logarithmically growing vertex degree) can be proved (as in [43]). Using two-phase randomised routing, a d-relation can be realised with high probability on a degree d hypercube in time $O(d)$.

Randomised routing has several advantages over the use of hashing. The need to compute $H(A)$ complicates the addressing mechanism. In addition, the use of hashing destroys any notion of advantageously placing logically dependent data in the same locality of the storage space. It is also true that bad cases can still (on rare occasions) be invoked for both the hashing and the randomised routing approaches. However, randomised routing has the advantage that a second attempt to solve some permutation routing problem is very unlikely to invoke a bad case that a first attempt may have invoked. Thus, randomised routing avoids the stated disadvantages of hashing although it is generally slower because *two* (average case) greedy permutation routing steps are involved.

We return now to deterministic permutation routing on the hypercube. For all practical purposes, the best known deterministic algorithms run in $O(\log^2 n)$ time. Several such algorithms are based upon simulations of the classical sorters of Batcher including, for example, the bitonic sorter. From the earlier description of bitonic sorting, we know that whenever two elements are compare-exchanged their binary addresses differ in precisely one bit and because, in the hypercube, nodes are connected which differ in precisely one bit, bitonic sort is easily and naturally simulated on the hypercube. Routing for each (parallel) compare-exchange step clearly takes $O(1)$ time and since there are $O(\log^2 n)$ such steps, bitonic sort can be simulated in $O(\log^2 n)$ time on the hypercube. At this time, the fastest algorithm known for permutation routing on the hypercube is due to Cypher and Plaxton [6]. Their algorithm runs in $O(\log n(\log \log n)^2)$ time or $O(\log n(\log \log n))$ time with a substantial amount of off-line computation. Although, asymptotically, this is an improvement over the the $O(\log^2 n)$ algorithm already described, because of the large constants hidden by the notation Cypher and Plaxton's algorithm only becomes competitive for hypercubes of dimension greater than 20. The algorithm is too complicated to be described here and the reader is referred to the excellent presentation in [20].

There is continuing strong interest to answer the difficult question whether an $O(\log n)$ time deterministic algorithm exists for permutation routing on the hypercube. It is interesting to observe that no impediment arises from the need to have $O(\log n)$ length paths for any permutation such that, in any given parallel routing step, no two messages occupy the same edge. The existence of such path sets is easily established by considering so-called Beneš networks which we now do. The following establishes the existence of an off-line deterministic algorithm for permutation routing on the hypercube which runs in $O(\log n)$ time. Indeed, it establishes such an algorithm for 2-relations.

A Beneš network of dimension d is constructed from two d-dimensional butterflies connected back-to-back. Figure 13(a) shows the Beneš network of dimension 3. The network consists of a set of inputs (on the left, with two inputs per butterfly input node) and a set of outputs (on the right, with two outputs per buterfly output node). Each node of the network is a switch by which two inputs are routed to two output edges. As we shall see, by suitably setting all the switches, any permutation of the inputs to the outputs of the network is possible. The switches in figure 13(a) are set for the permutation $(1 \to 7, 2 \to 5, 3 \to 2, 4 \to 8, 5 \to 3, 6 \to 6, 7 \to 1, 8 \to 4)$. It is interesting to observe that every edge of the network will be employed for any permutation. That a suitable setting of the switches exists for any permutation can be seen from the following inductive argument. As figure 13(b) indicates, the Beneš network of dimension d can be inductively constructed from two Beneš networks of dimension $(d - 1)$, the figure illustrates the case for $d = 3$. We inductively set switches within the constraints that paths from inputs $2i - 1$ and $2i$ must use the different sub-networks of dimension $(d - 1)$ as must the paths to outputs $2i - 1$ and $2i$. Thus in our example, we first set the switches which are visible in figure 13(b). We route the input from 1 through the upper network on the left which requires the output to 7 to come from the upper network. This in turn causes the output to 8 to be directed from the lower network. Thus the input from 4 must go to the lower network causing the input from 3 to be directed to the upper network. We continue in this fashion, alternating from one side of the network to the other. The reader will easily verify that such a process will meet the aforementioned constraints. Having set the switches of figure 13(b), we proceed to set all other switches inductively and in like manner. Notice that for n inputs, all paths from an input to an output are of length $2 \log n$.

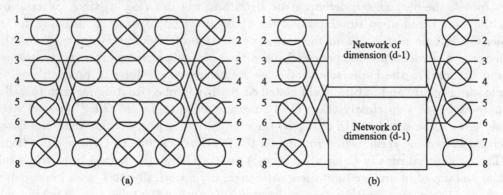

Figure 13.

We have seen that any permutation of inputs to outputs can be realised on the Beneš network. Like the network for bitonic sorting, if we contract all horizontal edges in our figures, the Beneš network transforms to a hypercube (both Beneš network and hypercube are of the same dimension). It follows that (taking each hypercube edge to be two antiparallel edges) there exists sets of paths by which, for any permutation, we can route *two* messages from each hypercube node such that each node is the destination for two such messages in time $O(\log n)$. Notice that at each step, every node is host to two messages and then in message passing, no more than one message occupies an edge. It may happen that certain messages wait at nodes to synchronise with the simulated Beneš routing. Our original goal was less ambitious, we wished to establish the existence of path sets to route one message from and to each node. An alternative way of dealing with this precise question is to observe that, for any permutation, we can route single messages from each initial Beneš node to the outputs along node disjoint paths (the previous solution only guaranteed edge-disjointness). We can set switches in precisely the same manner as before, except that we are now required to observe the constraints that inputs i and $(i+2^{d-1})$ must be routed to different subnetworks of dimension $(d-1)$ and, similarly, outputs i and $(i+2^{d-1})$ must come from the different subnetworks. For example, figure 14 shows such a set of paths for $d = 4$ and for the permutation employed in figure 13.

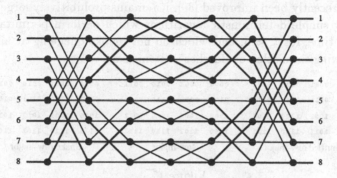

Figure 14.

3.2.   Permutation routing on the square mesh

We first consider the following natural *greedy* algorithm. In the first step of the algorithm each message moves along its row until it reaches its destination column. In the second step each message moves along its column to its destination address. Of course, in each time step, any processor transmits at most a single message and, of the queued messages, the furthest from their destinations have priority. It is easy to see that after at most $(2\sqrt{n} - 2)$ routing steps this algorithm will terminate. This is optimal in terms of numbers of routing steps. However, as is easily proved, it is possible for the algorithm to generate queues of length $(2\sqrt{n}/3 - 3)$ and so we require the undesirable feature of local storage which is not of constant bounded size. In addition, the time-complexity is degraded by a logarithmic factor because of the need to identify queued items of highest priority (by employing, for example, a priority queue at each node).

The average case behaviour of the greedy algorithm is much better than the worst case. If each processor sends a message to a random location (each location being chosen with equal probability and thus more than one message may be destined for the same location) then, as [20] shows, the probability that a message is delayed by δ time steps due to congestion is $O(e^{-\delta/6})$. In fact, with very high probability, no more than four messages are queued at any node. Any message traversing d mesh steps arrives at its destination in $d + O(\log n)$ time with probability $1 - O(n^{-1})$. Although the average behaviour of the algorithm is good, many of the permutation routing problems met in practise are more likely to invoke performances which are nearer to the worst case. We could therefore naturally adopt a randomised routing approach similar to that employed in the hypercube case. That is, we can first route each message to a randomly chosen address and then route this message to its true destination.

It can be shown that such an algorithm runs in $O(\sqrt{n})$ time and invokes queues of length $O(\log n)$ with high probability. In fact using a much more intricate algorithm, based on the same premise, it is possible (with high probability) to solve the problem in $2\sqrt{n} + O(\log n)$ time with constant sized queues [20].

Although randomised algorithms promise the best expected performance they are still, in principle, prone to rare bad behaviour. Considering deterministic algorithms, there are in fact several which perform rather well. For example, it is actually possible to solve such problems in $2\sqrt{n} - 2$ time using queues of constant bounded size [19]. However, although this constant has recently been improved [30], it remains prohibitively large.

There are many simple deterministic algorithms which perform permutation routing on the mesh in $k\sqrt{n}$ time, for $k \approx 6$, and which do not invoke queueing at all. For example, consider the following simulation of Batcher's bitonic sort.

0000	0001	0100	0101		0000	0001	0010	0011		0000	0001	0010	0011
0010	0011	0110	0111		0100	0101	0110	0111		0111	0110	0101	0100
1000	1001	1100	1101		1000	1001	1010	1011		1000	1001	1010	1011
1010	1011	1110	1111		1100	1101	1110	1111		1111	1110	1101	1100

Shuffled row-major	Row-major	Snake row-major

Figure 15.

We take the processing elements to be indexed according to shuffled row-major order which is illustrated in figure 15 (which, in passing, illustrates two other commonly employed schemes as well) for the 4×4 mesh. In this indexing scheme, if we recursively divide the square mesh into sub-squares then the nodes contained in each sub-square are always consecutively numbered. Now, with one item to be routed per mesh node, notice that in comparing elements whose positions differ in the ith most significant bit, all routing paths are horizontal (if i is odd) or all vertical (i even) and compare-exchange can be executed simultaneously without interference. In mesh steps, the routing path required to compare elements whose position differs in the jth bit is of length $2^{\lfloor k(j-1)/2 \rfloor}$. Thus the total time required for routing is:

$$\sum_{i=1}^{\log n} \sum_{j=1}^{i} 2^{\lfloor (j-1)/2 \rfloor} = 7\sqrt{n} - 2\log_2 n - 7 \approx 7\sqrt{n}$$

The total number of (constant-time) comparison steps is:

$$\sum_{i=1}^{\log n} i = O(\log^2 n)$$

When discussing permutation routing on the hypercube we described on off-line method to determine the routes of messages so that all messages can be delivered in optimal $O(\log n)$ deterministic time. Although we have on-line deterministic algorithms running in $O(\sqrt{n})$ time for the mesh, it is interesting to ask if off-line pre-computation can help to speed-up the actually routing. In this respect [1] have described such an algorithm and its application to a variety of networks, including the mesh. On this network, the algorithm routes messages in $3\sqrt{n} - 3$ time with no queueing. The idea is to permute the messages in each mesh row so that precisely one message in each column is intended for each row. How precisely to do this constitutes the off-line calculation. Clearly, the routing time bound is then easily attained (and without incurring queues) by first routing each message along its row to a column position determined by the off-line computation, then along the column to its correct row and finally along the row to its final destination. We leave the details of the off-line computation as an interesting excercise for the reader.

The literature is rich in the area of permutation routing on the mesh. A small selection of papers is [35, 36, 27, 39, 16, 26].

4.   Techniques for efficient implementation of P-RAM algorithms on distributed memory models of parallel computation

Our model of a distributed memory parallel computer consists of a number of processors each placed at the nodes of a communication network. Each processor has associated local workspace and a pro rata proportion of the shared memory. If, for a given P-RAM algorithm, we associate (in one-to-one correspondence) a P-RAM processor with each network processor then the P-RAM algorithm can be implemented on the distributed memory machine in a time equivalent to the P-RAM complexity except that each constant time required for simultaneous memory accesses by the P-RAM processors is replaced by the time to solve an equivalent routing problem on the network. Suppose that the P-RAM algorithm has been designed within the exclusive-read, exclusive-write model (the EREW P-RAM) and suppose that it is possible to arrange matters (in an implementation of the algorithm on a distributed memory model) such that for all instances of simultaneous memory accesses (in the SIMD P-RAM algorithm) at most one accessed word of the shared memory is located at any network node. In this case, each routing problem to be solved is equivalent to a permutation routing problem and algorithms described in the previous section may be employed. A surprisingly large proportion of P-RAM algorithms can be contrived to fall within this category.

As a simple example, consider the problem of evaluating, at $x = h$, the general polynomial $p(x)$ of degree n: $p(x) = a_0 + a_1 x + a_2 x^2 + ... + a_n x^n$. For ease of presentation assume that $n = 2^k - 1$ for some integer $k > 1$. We could adopt a recursive approach by observing that: $p(x) = p'(x) + x^{(n+1)/2} p''(x)$ where $p'(x)$ and $p''(x)$ are both polynomials of degree $2^{k-1} - 1$. The following EREW P-RAM algorithm provides the iterative equivalent. Given n processors (indexed from 0 to $(n-1)$), the ith processor (for all i in parallel) executes:

$$x \leftarrow h$$
$$d \leftarrow (n-1)/2$$
repeat until $d = 0$
       if $0 \leq i \leq d$ **then begin**
                $a_i \leftarrow a_{2i}$
                $a_i \leftarrow a_i + x a_{2i+1}$
                $x \leftarrow x^2$
                $d \leftarrow (d-1)/2$
       end

At the end of the computation, as is trivially verified, the required result is stored in a_0. The body of the repeat statement takes $O(1)$ time to execute and since there are a logarithmic number of iterations this is an $O(\log n)$ time computation. On a distributed memory machine we might adopt the following approach. Initially, for all i, store a_i at the ith processing element (PE_i), also we provide each PE_i with the values of h and n. Now each processor in parallel and synchronously executes the above algorithm. As before, the body of the repeat statement is executed $O(\log n)$ times. Consider the cost of one such execution. The recomputation of h and d takes $O(1)$ time. On the other hand, before recomputing a_i, each PE_i must first receive a_{2i} from PE_{2i} and then a_{2i+1} from PE_{2i+1}. This can be achieved by two successive applications of permutation routing. Therefore, whatever the network, we have described an implementation that runs in $O((\log n)pr(n))$ time, where $pr(n)$ is the permutation routing time for the network employed.

The above rather simple example illustrates the use of permutation routing. We might ask, however, whether the running time can be improved. A lower bound on networks where the algorithm has to combine values stored at all processing elements is naturally provided by the diameter, $D(n)$, of the network. We shall show, specifically for the mesh and the hypercube, that this lower bound can be attained for the problem. In both cases the complexity can be reduced to $O(D(n))$ by employing network topology dependent methods which exploit data locality. In this regard we will briefly describe two such methodologies, the technique of *compress and iterate* and the use of *graph embedding*. The time complexities of many other algorithmic implementations may be improved by these techniques.

Notice that each iteration of the repeat statement in our simple example reduces the the number of processors that need to be active by a factor of $1/2$. This fact can be employed advantageously. For example, consider implementation on the $\sqrt{n} \times \sqrt{n}$ mesh and suppose that the processing elements are numbered in shuffled row major order. In this case, our convention of associating a_i with PE_i ensures that the *active* processors always occupy a region of the mesh which reduces in area as the computation proceeds as figure 16 schematically shows. This means that routing takes place over shorter and shorter distances with successive iterations. In fact, the total time required for routing is now a sum of $(\log n)$ terms (each term corresponding to a permutation routing problem over a square area of shrinking dimensions) of the form:

$$O(\sqrt{n} + \sqrt{n} + \sqrt{n}/2 + \sqrt{n}/2 + \sqrt{n}/4 + \sqrt{n}/4 + \sqrt{n}/8 + \sqrt{n}/8 + \ldots) = O(\sqrt{n})$$

The overall time required for actual computation at the processing elements is only $O(\log n)$ and so, overall, this implementation runs in $O(\sqrt{n})$ time as required for optimality.

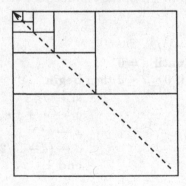

Figure 16.

For similar examples on the mesh, the value of the running time can be obtained by solving a recurrence relation of the form:

$$T(n) = T(n/2) + O(c(n)), n > 1$$
$$T(1) = O(1)$$

Here $c(n)$ is the cost of creating the smaller problem and its *compression*. The solution when $c(n) = O(\sqrt{n})$ is, as we saw $T(n) = O(pr(n))$. For other problems, where a similar recurrence applies, we need to keep the cost of smaller problem creation and compression within the same bounds of $O(pr(n))$ if (overall) an $O(pr(n))$ algorithm is to be obtained. In the example we easily contrived this condition, in general it is often necessary to be more creative.

The above simple example illustrates a generally useful method of enhancing the complexity by the technique of *compress and iterate*. This technique is very often applicable when a problem P is recursively reduced to m similar problems, $1 \leq m \leq b$, each of size $(\lceil n/b \rceil + c)$ where $b \leq 2$ and $c \leq 0$ are integer constants. For a fuller elaboration of the technique on the mesh see [11]. An underlying assumption in this recursive approach to problem solution is that the processor network employed is recursively decomposable.

We come now to the employment of graph embedding. Because our simple example can be solved by a recursive computation, we can think of a solution in which the algorithmic structure is the complete binary tree. In section 5, we show how to embed such a binary tree in both the mesh and the hypercube. The nodes of the tree correspond to processor sites in the communication network. In the course of the computation, a processor corresponding to an internal node of the tree computes $p(x) = p'(x) + Hp''(x)$ on receiving $p'(x)$ from its left child and $Hp''(x)$ from its right child. If it is a left child (respectively, right child) it then transmits $p(x)$ $(Hp(x))$ to its parent node. Here H is a power of h obtained by successive squaring in each step of the computation. All tree nodes at the same height perform their constant time computations at the same time. The overall time complexity is now dominated by the routing time. This is determined by the maximum path length (in terms of host network steps) from a leaf to the root of the embedded tree. The embeddings of section 5 provide asymptotically optimal values of $\sqrt{n}$ for the $\sqrt{n} \times \sqrt{n}$ mesh and $\log n$ for the n-node hypercube. Thus, for our example, we obtain $O(D(n))$ implementations for the recursively expressed P-RAM algorithm for polynomial evaluation. Clearly, since many efficient P-RAM algorithms employ the complete binary tree (either explicitly or implicitly), the methodology described has wide application and might be usefully automated.

We have been concerned with implementing EREW P-RAM algorithms on (in particular) mesh and hypercube topologies such that fast running time are obtained. In fact, employing these and similarly special techniques, we can often obtain faster implementations that would be afforded by the use of quite general P-RAM emulation on similar architectures. However, it is not always the case that shaving logarithmic factors off the running time is as important as, for example, running as large a problem size as possible on fixed size network in reasonable time. In this context we now briefly consider problems of size greater than n on networks of n processors.

If we employ the graph embeddings described in the next section, then we can view this question in a way similar to that in which processor number reduction is frequently attained in P-RAM algorithms. For example, suppose that we are to evaluate the expression $c_1 \oplus c_2 \oplus \ldots \oplus c_n$, where $\oplus$ is an associative binary operation. Using the obvious complete binary tree approach, a naive P-RAM algorithm would do this in $O(\log n)$ time using n processors. However, by employing a precomputation in which each of $n/\log n$ processor sequentially computes disjoint subexpressions of length $\log n$ in $O(\log n)$ time, the problem is now reduced so that the naive algorithm can be deployed to solve the problem on a tree with $n/\log n$ leaves. Thus overall the expression can be evaluated in $O(\log n)$ time using $n/\log n$ processors. The same idea can be deployed on the mesh so that each processor first sequentially evaluates a subexpression of length $\sqrt{n}$ in about $\sqrt{n}$ time. The resultant values are then combined by placing them at the leaves of an embedded complete binary tree. Thus such an expression of length $n\sqrt{n}$ is evaluated in about $2\sqrt{n}$ time on a $\sqrt{n} \times \sqrt{n}$ mesh. We therefore get a nice trade-off of raising the problem size to the power of 3/2 at the small expense of roughly doubling the running time compared with the naive algorithm on the same mesh. On the hypercube, the same idea enables us to solve such a problem of size $n\log_2 n$ on the n node network in about $2\log_2 n$ time.

In a more general vein, it is quite likely that we should want to simulate a P-RAM algorithm using n P-RAM processors on a network with p nodes where $n \gg p$. In this case, it makes sense to allocate about n/p P-RAM processors to each actual network processor. A network processor then sequentially simulates the activity of n/p P-RAM processors in the course of the computation. For example, let us return to our first solution to the problem of *polynomial evaluation*. Instead of a single a_i being allocated to each processing element, we now (for simplicity assume that $p/n = k$, where k is an integer) allocate the values a_j for $ik \le j \le (i+1)k - 1$ to PE_i. In the course of executing the code detailed earlier, we can (in principle) cause each processor to pipeline its k requests to access other processing elements in an up-date of its a_j values. Notice that it is a trivial matter (given the convention adopted for allocating the $a'_j s$ to processing elements) for each processing element to know the addresses of the other processing elements that need to be accessed. If there is sufficient *parallel slackness* (that is, if the ratio n/p is sufficiently large), then it is possible that the first request of those pipelined is returned before the last is transmitted. In this way, the *latency* of the network (that is the routing time) may be masked by the parallel slackness and will not therefore figure in the time-complexity of the implementation. We presuppose here that there is some additional facility which enables message throughput at nodes without interruption to normal processor activity. Depending upon the *bandwidth* of the network (that is, the density of traffic it can support) we may anticipate certain gains. For example, for the hypercube network, in $O(\log n)$ time every processing element may receive and send $\log n$ messages. Thus, if the parallel slackness is also $O(\log n)$, then the pipelined requests can *all* be achieved in $O(\log n)$ time. Thus, in principle, we can solve an expression evaluation problem of size n in $O(\log^2 n)$ time on $n/\log n$ processors. In fact, this is an optimal implementation of the P-RAM algorithm in terms of the *work* measure (that is, in terms of the processor, time product). Such optimality can be achieved by many implementations employing parallel slackness in this way to hide the network latency. In this setting, success depends on being able to dynamically locate data so that addresses are known and uniformly distributed across the communication network. This may invoke particular methods for particular problems.

The idea of employing parallel slackness to hide network latency has been advocated in quite general emulation of P-RAMs on distributed memory models of parallel computation. There is then a difficulty of how to distribute memory accesses uniformly so as to invoke requests for h-relational routing problems on the hypercube, for example, without reference to the particular overall problem to be solved. Naturally, the idea of hashing the address space then comes into its own. In order that such an approach be effective it is essential that there exists hash functions which are efficiently computable. Suitable hash functions have been described in [22], see also [7, 8]. Notice that if hashing is employed, it is not necessary to employ randomised routing since (with high probability) greedy routing will perform like the average case. Hashing and parallel slackness have been effectively combined to demonstrate, for example, that the exclusive-read, exclusive-write P-RAM can be emulated on the hypercube (see [43], for example) so as to preserve the work measure (at the expensive of a logarithmic slow-down in computation).

Until now, we have avoided the problem of concurrent access to processors on distributed memory machines. The details of proposed solutions are beyond the scope of this introductory chapter. However, we cite two solutions. The first employs a so-called *combining* network, that is, a network which allows the combination and replication of messages as well as delivering them in point-to-point manner. In this way, Ranade ([31, 33]) has shown that the concurrent-read, concurrent-write P-RAM may be efficiently emulated on the butterfly network. Secondly, by the employment of software techniques only, Valiant (in [43] for example) has shown that by employing sufficient parallel slackness (along with the use of rapid *integer sorting*) concurrent accesses can be supported optimally (in terms of the work measure) on the hypercube.

5. Embeddings

The classical definition of graph *embedding* is as follows. If G_1 and G_2 are two graphs, an embedding of G_1 into G_2 is a mapping of edges of G_1 into paths of G_2 such that each vertex of G_1 maps to a single vertex of G_2. G_1 is called the *guest* graph and G_2 is the *host*. Qualities of an embedding have traditionally been measured by the following parameters:

- *Dilation.* The dilation of an embedding is the maximum length of any path in the host to which an edge of the guest is mapped.

- *Expansion.* The expansion of an embedding is the ratio of the number of nodes in the host graph to the number of nodes in the guest graph.

- *Congestion.* The congestion of an embedding is the maximum number of paths (mappings of edges of the guest) using any edge of the host graph.

The preceding sections show that our interest in graph embeddings derives both from the idea of embedding (P-RAM) algorithmic structures in communication networks and from the need to assess the efficiency with which one distibuted machine may simulate another. We restrict our attention to embeddings which involve the commonest communication network topologies, the (mainly, two-dimensional) mesh and the hypercube. In the following subsection, concerned with embeddings in which at most one node of the guest is associated with a single node of the host, we characterise embeddings with the values of their dilation, expansion and congestion. In the final subsection we allow more than one node of the guest to be associated with a node of the host and also we adjust the parameters by which we judge the quality of an embedding. These modifications are appropriate in the context of embedding the complete binary tree (an important P-RAM algorithmic structure) in communication networks of which the mesh and hypercube will be of particular focus.

5.1.   Some well-known embedding results concerning meshes and hypercubes

Here we briefly state some well-known results concerning meshes and hypercubes, mostly without proof. In the following subsection we provide a detailed description of dense edge-disjoint embeddings of the complete binary tree in the mesh and in the hypercube. Embeddings of such a tree in these common network topologies is of particular importance when it comes to implementing P-RAM algorithms on distributed memory machines. Thus, we are justified in fully detailing these embeddings. Here we use the following shorthand: $d = dilation$, $e = expansion$ and $c = congestion$. Two excellent sources of primary references for many results in this area are [25, 20].

As a host graph, the hypercube is particularly rich in the number of other classes of graph that may be efficiently embedded in it. It is well-known that the double rooted binary tree with n nodes embeds in the n node hypercube with $d = 1$, $e = 1$, $c = 1$ [4]. See also section 5.2. The pyramid can be embedded in its *optimum* hypercube with $d = 2$ and $c = 2$ Here, and elsewhere, by *optimum* hypercube we mean the hypercube with n' nodes and no other hypercube exists with n'' nodes such that $n \leq n'' < n'$, where n is the number of nodes of the guest graph. The x-tree of height h embeds in the hypercube of dimension $h + 1$ with $d = 2$ and $e = 2$ for all $h > 0$. The mesh of trees of dimension d embeds in the hypercube of dimension $2d+2$ with $d = 2$ and $c = 1$. The butterfly is a subgraph of its optimum hypercube. The cube connected cycles network embeds in its optimum hypercube with $d = 2$ and $c = 1$. The following theorem concerns the embedding of meshes in hypercubes.

Theorem 5.1 *Any mesh with n nodes whose dimensions are each a power of two is a subgraph of its optimum hypercube.*

Proof :   By induction on n'. The following illustrates the inductive step. The hypercube with 2^3 nodes contains as subgraphs the following meshes: (2×2), (2×4) and $(2 \times 2 \times 2)$. Take two copies of this hypercube with the same subgraph mesh marked (in the same orientation for constructing the larger hypercube). We can construct an embedding in the hypercube with 2^4 nodes which contains a marked subgraph which is a mesh with one dimension doubled in size compared with the marked meshes of the smaller hypercube by simply also marking the appropriate edges of the new dimension. Also, the hypercube with 2^4 nodes is isomorphic to the $(2 \times 2 \times 2 \times 2)$ mesh. Thus the hypercube with 2^4 nodes has as subgraphs the following meshes: (2×8), (4×4), $(2 \times 2 \times 4)$ and $(2 \times 2 \times 2 \times 2)$. □

Theorem 5.1 also implies that many other meshes are subgraphs of their optimum hypercubes (for example, the (6×7) mesh is a subgraph of the (8×8) mesh whose optimum hypercube has 2^6 nodes).

Complete binary tree can be embedded in the two dimensional mesh using the well-known H-tree construction (see for example [37] page 84). However, see section 5.2 also. The complete binary trees of height h is also a subgraph of the de Bruijn network of dimension h, and can be embedded in the shuffle exchange network of dimension h with $d = 2$.

A long-standing open question concerning embeddings in the hypercube is as follows. Can the shuffle exchange and de Bruijn networks be embedded with $O(1)$ dilation and $O(1)$ expansion in the hypercube? Note that the shuffle exchange network can be embedded in the de Bruijn network with $d = 2$. Therefore, an embedding of the de Bruijn graph will resolve both questions. A recent paper in this respect is [5].

5.2. Dense edge-disjoint embeddings of the complete binary tree in the mesh and in the hypercube

Suppose that a particular algorithmic structure frequently occurs in the design of P-RAM algorithms. Such a structure might be usefully embedded in the communication network of the distributed-memory machine upon which we might wish to implement any of the P-RAM algorithms employing this structure. Indeed such a strategy might be usefully automated. Perhaps the most commonly occurring structure in this regard is the complete binary tree. It is precisely because this logarithmic depth structure is used (either explicitly or implicitly) that polylogarithmic time complexities are attained for many P-RAM algorithms.

In the P-RAM model, the complete binary tree is most usually employed as follows. Data for a problem (or sub-problem) are placed at the leaves, and the required result is obtained by performing computations at the internal nodes in one or more sweeps up and down the tree, so that computations at the same depth are performed in parallel. It should be noted however that some algorithms may require simultaneous computation at an arbitrary number of nodes at different depths of the tree. If we are to embed the complete binary tree in some host topology of a distributed memory machine, we therefore need to observe the following requirements to achieve an *efficient* embedding:

1. *All tree nodes at the same depth should be mapped into disjoint hypercube nodes if (as in the P-RAM computation) computations are to be performed in parallel at these nodes. In addition, P-RAM algorithms may require computation at nodes of the tree which are of different depth. Thus for greatest utility, the embedding should map at most a constant number of tree nodes to any node of the host graph.*

2. *Tree edges at the same depth should correspond to edge-disjoint paths in the hypercube if the commonest types of P-RAM algorithm employing this technique are to be simulated. For greatest flexibility, all tree paths should be mapped to disjoint paths in the host graph.*

3. *The maximum distance from the root to a leaf of the tree (in terms of edges of the host graph) should be minimised in order that the routing time is minimised.*

4. *Consistent with satisfying the above points, the size of the host graph should be a minimum in the interests of processor economy.*

We will show later that how the complete binary tree may be embedded in the two-dimensional mesh so as to optimise the above efficiency requirements [9]. For that embedding, each mesh edge is regarded as two anti-parallel directed edges. However, we first describe how the complete binary tree can be embedded with similar efficiency in the undirected hypercube. To this end we describe an edge-disjoint embedding of the complete binary tree with $n > 8$ leaves in the n node hypercube such that the maximum distance from a leaf to the root is $\log_2 n + 1$ (which is optimally short) [34]. Indeed, in every respect, this embedding fulfills the above efficiency requirements.

Other embeddings in the hypercube have been described which, in various ways, full short of the efficiency requirements stated above, for example:

1. The embedding of [4] meets all the efficiency requirements except that the host graph is twice as large as it need be. In fact [4] embeds the n leaf complete binary tree in the hypercube with $2n$ nodes. This embedding is, however, vertex-disjoint.

2. In [20] (pages 407-410), an embedding is described in which the n leaf tree is embedded in the n node hypercube. However, in this embedding, up to $\log_2 n$ tree nodes of different depths are mapped to a single node of the hypercube. Although the embedding is such as to facilitate the efficient implementation of most P-RAM algorithms, there may be difficulties in the exceptional cases when simultaneous computation is required to take place at an arbitrary number of different levels within the tree.

The embedding in the hypercube is described in theorem 5.2. For the proof of that theorem we require to define layouts of nodes of those hypercubes with 16 and 32 nodes. For $n = 32$, we adopt the scheme of figure 17(a). Nodes occur at the corners of the squares defined by the straight horizontal and vertical lines. The labels of nodes in the top left-hand quarter of the figure are shown. The first two binary bits of the labels of nodes in the other quarters are shown at the centre of their quarter of the figure. The last three binary bits of such an address will be the same as the corresponding node in the top left-hand quarter. Generally speaking, figures will only shown some edges of the hypercube, just those that are of interest. Dashed edges happen to correspond to certain hypercube edges but are used merely as an aid in locating nodes in the layout. For $n = 16$, the hypercube layout corresponds to the top half of figure 17(a).

Theorem 5.2 *For $n \geq 16$, there exists an embedding of the complete binary tree with n leaves in a hypercube with n nodes having the following properties:*

1. *Each hypercube node is assigned exactly one leaf of the tree.*

2. *Each hypercube node, except one, is also assigned exactly one internal node of the tree.*

3. *Distinct tree edges are mapped onto edge-disjoint (possibly null) paths in the hypercube.*

4. *The length of the image in the hypercube of a tree path from a leaf to the root is at most $\log_2 n + 1$ hypercube edges.*

Proof : We first prove the theorem for $n > 16$. For these values of n, we embed the *double-rooted complete binary tree* (denoted by DRCB tree) in the hypercube. The DRCB tree is a complete binary tree in which the path (of length 2) connecting the two sons of the root is replaced by a path of length 3. Either of the two internal nodes of this path may be regarded as the root of an embedded complete binary tree.

We inductively construct the embedding starting with the base case of $n = 32$. For clarity, we employ two figures (17(a) and 17(b)) to describe this case. Figure 17(a) shows the embedding of those tree edges which have leaves as end-points. For clarity, some embedded tree edges point towards that endpoint which is a leaf of the tree. Some tree edges are mapped to null paths which are indicated by loops. Figure 17(b) shows the embedding of all other tree edges. Notice that hashed edges are used for the path of length 3 on which full circles denote possible roots of the embedded complete binary tree. Also, notice that the three edges on this path belong to three different dimensions of the hypercube. In figure 17(b), the internal nodes are drawn with increasing size and the tree edges are drawn

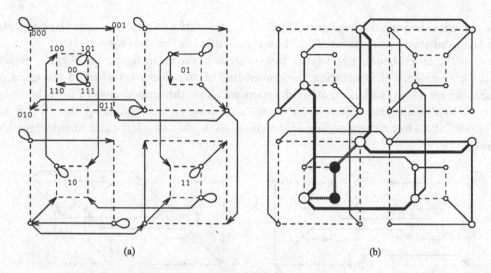

Figure 17.

with increasing boldness the nearer they are to the root. It is easy to see that this base case satisfies the theorem in all respects, in particular the maximum root to leaf distance is 6 hypercube edges.

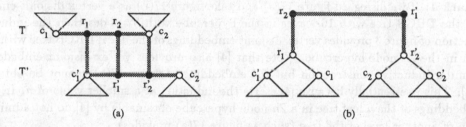

Figure 18.

Figure 18 illustrates the inductive step in the construction of the embedding of the DRCB tree with n leaves in the hypercube with n nodes from two embeddings of $n/2$ leaf DRCB trees in hypercubes with $n/2$ nodes. These two embeddings are denoted by T and T' in figure 18(a). The hashed vertical edges in that figure are edges of the new dimension of the constructed hypercube. The hashed horizontal paths $((c_1, r_1, r_2, c_2)$ and $(c'_1, r'_1, r'_2, c'_2))$ are the paths of length 3 which have as internal nodes the possible roots of the embedded complete binary trees with $n/2$ leaves. The triangular shapes attached to children of these possible roots represent the embedded subtrees rooted at these children. The two smaller hypercubes are orientated so that r_1 and c'_1 are made to correspond, then the dimension corresponding with the edge (r_1, r_2) is made to correspond with the dimension of the edge (r'_1, r'_2). In this way, the nodes r_2 and r'_1 are made to correspond. Similarly, the dimension of (r_2, c_2) is made to correspond with the dimension of (r'_2, c'_2) and so node c_2 is brought into correspondence with r'_2. This is always possible given the edge transitivity of the hypercube and given that each of the horizontal hashed paths of length 3 has three edges of different dimension. Figure 18(b) shows the embedding of the DRCB tree with n leaves and unit dilation in the constructed hypercube with n nodes. The labelling of nodes in this figure makes clear its derivation from figure 18(a). It is straightforward to see that the properties of the theorem statement are satisfied. The theorem is thus proved for $n > 16$.

For $n = 16$, an embedding satisfying the theorem is shown in figure 19. Again, we have used the convenience of illustrating the embedding of tree edges attached to leaves in one diagram (figure 19(a)) and in another diagram we show the embeddings of all other edges (figure 19(b)). Note that for $n = 16$ we do not show an embedding of the DRCB tree with unit dilation but an embedding of the complete binary tree for which three edges have dilation 2.   ☐

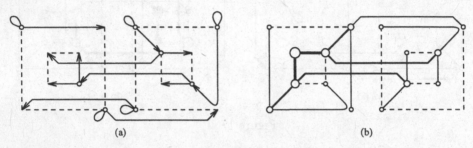

(a)   (b)

Figure 19.

Remark 1: If we disregard figure 17(a) and take figure 17(b) as a vertex disjoint embedding of the DRCB tree with 16 leaves in the hypercube with 32 nodes then the inductive construction of figure 3 provides vertex disjoint embeddings of the n leaf DRCB tree with unit dilation in the $2n$ node hypercube. Note that [4] also provides vertex disjoint embeddings by a similar inductive construction but the embedding of figure 17(b) cannot be obtained from [4]. This is essentially because [4] starts the induction at a smaller value of n. In fact, the embeddings of the n leaf tree in a $2n$ node hypercube obtainable by [4] do not admit the addition of another level of the tree (such as figure 17(a) provides).

Remark 2: Using the inductive construction of theorem 5.2, it is not possible to take the base of the induction for n smaller than 32. This is because (as is trivially proved) for $n = 16$ the n leaf DRCB tree cannot be embedded in the n node hypercube with unit dilation so as to satisfy the conditions of theorem 5.2. In addition and by a trivial proof, for $n = 4$ and $n = 8$ it is not possible to embed the n leaf complete binary tree in the n node hypercube so as to satisfy the same conditions.

Remark 3: The maximum leaf to root distance of $\log_2 n + 1$ provided by theorem 5.2 is optimal. If an embedding existed satisfying the conditions of theorem 1 except that this distance be $\log_2 n$, then this would imply that a unit dilation embedding of the complete binary tree (perhaps with some leaf to father edges mapped to null paths) was possible in the hypercube. Consider the mapping of the subtree consisting of all edges other than leaf to father edges. An embedding of this subtree would have to be vertex disjoint with every edge being mapped to a hypercube edge, this is not possible because this graph is not a subgraph of the hypercube. It is easy to see that it is not such a subgraph because both this subtree and the hypercube are bipartite graphs. In the case of the hypercube both halves of the bipartition contain the same number of nodes, this is not the case for the subtree and (with

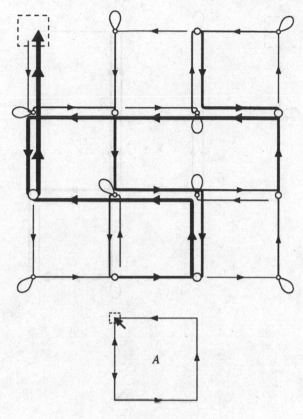

Figure 20.

each subtree edge mapped precisely to an edge of the hypercube) this would force more than one node of the subtree to be embedded in a single node of the host.

We now come to embedding the complete binary tree in the two-dimensional mesh. The mesh is assumed to have a pair of anti-parallel directed edges between each pair of adjacent nodes. The complete binary trees which are to be mapped into the mesh have their edges directed towards their root. The following theorem describes the embedding.

Theorem 5.3 *For all* $m \geq 1$, *there are embeddings of the complete binary trees with* 2^{2m} *and* 2^{2m+1} *leaves, in a* $2^m \times 2^m$ *mesh and a* $2^m \times 2^{m+1}$ *mesh respectively, with the following properties:*

1. *each mesh node is assigned exactly one leaf node of the tree,*

2. *each mesh node, except one, is also assigned exactly one internal node of the tree,*

3. *distinct tree edges are mapped onto edge-disjoint (possibly null) directed paths in the mesh,*

4. *the length of the image in the mesh of the tree path from a leaf to the root is at most* $2^m + O(m)$ *mesh steps for the* 2^{2m}-*leaf tree, and* $\frac{3}{2}2^m + O(m)$ *for the* 2^{2m+1}-*leaf tree.*

Proof :   We begin with the embedding in a square for trees with 2^{2m} leaves. The case $m = 1$ is easy. For $m = 2$, figure 20 shows one possible embedding in the 4×4 mesh. In this

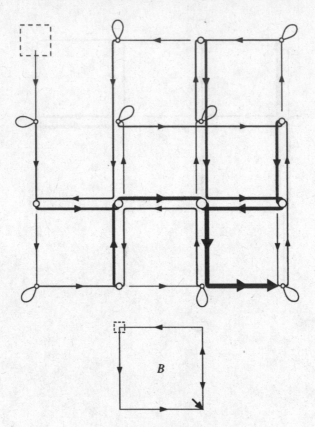

Figure 21. Layout B_2

figure, the internal tree nodes and the paths corresponding to the tree edges are drawn with increasing boldness from leaves to root. The leaf nodes are not shown explicitly since there is one at each mesh node. Note that some tree edges, incident with the leaves, are mapped to null paths, indicated by loops in the figure. The root is embedded on the left side, but the heavy path shown from this to the top-left corner is used later in larger embeddings. The node distinguished with a dotted square in the figure is that unique node which has not yet been assigned an internal tree node. The small diagram underneath gives the salient features of this embedding, A_2, for use in the recursive construction. The arrows on the perimeter indicate the usage so far of the outside edges, and show that all the clockwise outside edges on three of the sides are as yet unused.

We also require an alternative 4×4 embedding, B_2, shown in figure 21. The root here is embedded in the interior of the square but there is an outgoing path from it to the lower-right corner. This time, all the clockwise edges on the top, left and bottom sides are free.

The next stage of the construction, the embeddings for $m \geq 3$, is shown in figure 22. Three A_{m-1}'s and one B_{m-1} are combined to give embeddings of the 2^{2m}-leaf tree in a $2^m \times 2^m$ mesh. The three new internal tree nodes required are shown by white and black circles, and are connected by paths of appropriate weight. For the recursion, the embedding is continued in two different ways. The black root node can be connected to the top-left corner by one of the hatched paths shown, or joined to the lower-right corner by another hatched path. The first alternative yields an embedding A_m which has the edge characteristics of type A given by the small diagram in figure 20, while the second similarly yields B_m in figure 21. The arrangement shown in figure 22 therefore represents a recursive step by which the construction can be continued indefinitely. The third path illustrated, with different hatching, to the lower-left corner, will be used in the 2^{2m+1}-leaf embedding.

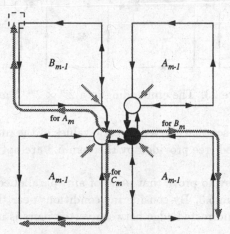

Figure 22. The recursive construction using A_{m-1} and B_{m-1}

We will show that the maximum distance, $D(m)$, from a leaf to the root of the tree is $2^m + O(m)$ mesh steps. It is a trivial matter to construct an embedding for $m = 1$ for which this distance is 2. For $m = 2$, we see by inspection of the embedding B_2 of figure 21 that this maximum distance is 6 mesh steps and so we have $D(2) = 6$. For $m > 2$ the proof proceeds by induction on m. Consider square meshes with $n = 2^{2m}$ nodes, $m \geq 2$. Let $A(m)$, $B(m)$, and $C(m)$, be the maximum distances from a leaf to the output from the top-left corner of pattern A_m, the lower-right corner of pattern B_m and the lower-left corner of pattern C respectively, for the $2^m \times 2^m$ array. From figures 20 and 21, we see that $A(2) = 10$ and $B(2) = 8$. A corresponding layout C_2 with $C(2) = 9$ is easy to derive from B_2. We can verify from figure 22 the following recurrence equations for $m \geq 3$:

$$
\begin{aligned}
A(m) &= D(m) + 2^m \\
B(m) &= D(m) + 2^m - 2 \\
C(m) &= D(m) + 2^m - 1 \\
D(m) &= \max\{A(m-1) + 2, B(m-1) + 2\} = D(m-1) + 2^{m-1} + 2.
\end{aligned}
$$

The solution to these equations is:

$$
D(m) = 2^m + 2m - 2, \text{ for } m \geq 1.
$$

For the case $n = 2^{2m+1}$, if $m \geq 3$ we can connect seven copies of A_{m-1} with one copy of C_{m-1} as shown in figure 23. Let $D'(m)$ be the corresponding maximal leaf-to-root distance. We may verify in figure 23 that $D'(m) = \max\{A(m-1) + 4, C(m-1) + 3\} + 2^{m-1}$ and so, $D'(m) = 3 \cdot 2^{m-1} + O(m)$. The cases where $m < 3$ are simple. $\square$

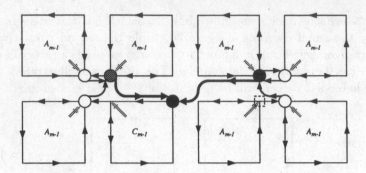

Figure 23. The embedding in a $2^m \times 2^{m+1}$ mesh

Remark 4: It is easy to see that the asymptotic values of the maximum path length from leaf to root of the embedded tree provided by theorem 5.3 are optimally short.

Remark 5: It is also easy to prove that pairs of anti-parallel edges are necessary for the dense embedding of theorem 5.3. By considering conditions near the boundary of the mesh, we can see that a simple undirected edge between vertex pairs is not sufficient.

References

[1] F. Annexstein and M. Baumslag. A unified approach to off-line permutation routing on parallel networks. *Proceedings of the 2nd Annual ACM Symposium on Parallel Algorithms and Architectures*, 398-406, July 1990.

[2] M. Ajtai, J. Komlós and E. Szemerédi. Sorting in C log N parallel steps, *Combinatorica*, 3:1-19, 1983.

[3] S.G. Akl. *The Design and Analysis of Parallel Algorithms*. Prentice Hall International Editions, 1989.

[4] S. N. Bhatt and I. C. F. Ipsen. How to Embed Trees in Hypercubes. *Report Yale/DCS/RR-443*, Department of Computer Science, Yale University (1985).

[5] M. Baumslag, M. C. Heydemann, J. Opatrny and D. Sotteau. Embedding of shuffle-like graphs in hypercubes, *Proceedings of PARLE 91*, Eindhoven, 1991.

[6] R. Cypher and C. G. Plaxton. Deterministic Sorting in Nearly Logarithmic Time on the Hypercube and Related Computers. *Proceedings of the 22nd ACM Symposium on Theory of Computing*, 193–203.

[7] M. Dietzfelbinger. On limitations of the performance of universal hashing with linear functions. *Forschungbereich Nr.84*, Fachbereich 17, Universität-GH, Paderborn, June 1991.

[8] M. Dietzfelginger, J. Gil, Y. Matias and N. Pippenger. Polynomial hash functions are reliable, *Proceedings of the 19th International Colloquium on Automata, Languages and Programming*, Lecture notes in Computer Science, Springer-Verlag, 1992.

[9] A.M. Gibbons and M.S. Paterson. Dense Edge-Disjoint Embedding of Binary Trees in the Mesh. *Proceedings of the 4th Annual ACM Symposium on Parallel Algorithms and Architectures*, June 1992, San Diego, California, 257-263.

[10] A.M. Gibbons and W. Rytter. *Efficient Parallel Algorithms*. Cambridge University Press, Cambridge, 1988. Paperback, 1990.

[11] A.M. Gibbons and Y.N. Srikant. A class of problems efficiently solvable on the mesh-connected computer including dynamic expression evaluation. *Information Processing Letters*, 32:305–311, 1989.

[12] A.M. Gibbons and R. Ziani. The balanced binary tree technique on mesh-connected computers. *Information Processing Letters*, 37:101–109, 1991.

[13] M.R. Jerrum and S. Skyum. Families of fixed degree graphs for processor interconnection. *IEEE Transactions on Computing*, 33:190–194, 1984.

[14] C. Kaklamanis, D. Krizanc and T. Tsantalis. Tight bounds for oblivious routing on the hypercube. In *Proceedings of the 2nd Annual ACM Symposium on Parallel Algorithms and Architectures*, 31-36, 1990.

[15] D. E. Knuth. *Sorting and Searching*, The Art of Computer Programming, volume 3, Addison Wesley (1973).

[16] D. Krizanc, S. Rajeskaran and T. Tsantilas. Optimal routing algorithms for mesh processor arrays. *Proc. Aegean Workshop on Computing (AWOC 89)*, Vol 319, Lecture Notes in Computer Science, Springer Verlag, 411–422, 1988.

[17] C.E. Leiserson. Fat trees: universal network for hardware efficient supercomputing. In *International Conference on Parallel Processing*, 393–402, 1985.

[18] J. van Leeuwen (Ed.) *Handbook of theoretical Computer Science, Volume A : Algorithms and Complexity*, Elsevier Science Publishers, 1990.

[19] T. Leighton, F. Makedon and I Tollis. A $2N - 2$ step algorithm for routing in an $N \times N$ mesh. *Proceedings of the 1989 Symposium on Parallel Algorithms and Architectures*, 328-335, June 1989.

[20] F. Thomson Leighton, *Introduction to Parallel Algorithms and Architectures: Arrays·Trees·Hypercubes*, Morgan Kaufmann Publishers, San Mateo, California (1992).

[21] T. Leighton and B. Maggs. Expanders might be practical. In *30th IEEE Annual Symposium on Foundations of Computer Science*, pages 384–389, 1989.

[22] K. Melhorn and U. Vishkin. Randomised and deterministic simulations of P-RAMs by parallel machines with restricted granularity of parallel memories, *Acta Informatica*, 21:339-374.

[23] W. F. McColl. Special purpose parallel computing. *Chapter 12 of this volume*.

[24] W. F. McColl. General purpose parallel computing. *Chapter 13 of this volume*.

[25] B. Monien and H. Sudborough. Comparing interconnection networks, volume 324 of *Lecture Notes in Computer Science*, pages 139–153. Springer-Verlag, 1988.

[26] D. Nassimi and S. Sahni. An Optimal Algorithm for Routing for Mesh-connected Parallel Computer, *Journal of the ACM*, Vol 27, No. 1, January 1980, 6–29.

[27] D. Nassimi and S. Sahni. Data broadcasing on SIMD Computers, *IEEE transactions on Computers*, Vol. C-30, February 1981, 282–288.

[28] M. S. Paterson. Improved sorting networks with $O(\log n)$ depth, *Algorithmica*, 5(1):75-92, 1990.

[29] M.J. Quinn. *Designing Efficient Algorithms for Parallel Computers*. McGraw-Hill International Editions, 1988.

[30] S. Rajasekaran and R. Overholt. Constant queue routing on a mesh. *Proceedings of the 8th Annual Symposium on Theoretical Aspects of Computer Science*, Lecture notes in Computer Science 480, Springer-Verlag, 444-455, 1991.

[31] A.G. Ranade. How to emulate shared memory, *Proceedings of the 28th Annual IEEE Symposium on Foundations of Computer Science*, 185-194, 1897.

[32] A.G. Ranade. Equivalence of message scheduling algorithms for parallel sorting algorithms, *Technical Report YALEU/DCS/TR-512*, Department of Computer Science, Yale University, New haven, CT, 1987.

[33] A.G. Ranade. *Fluent Parallel Computation*. Ph.D. thesis, Department of Computer Science, Yale University, 1989.

[34] Somasundaram Ravindran and Alan Gibbons. Dense edge-disjoint embedding of complete binary trees in the hypercube, *Research Report 223*, Department of Computer Science, University of Warwick, Coventry CV4 7AL (July, 1992). Submitted to *Information Processing Letters*.

[35] C. P. Shnorr and A. Shamir. An optimal Sorting Algorithm for Mesh-Connected Computers, *Proceedings 18th ACM Symposium on Theory of Computing*, 1986, 255–263.

[36] C. D. Thompson and H. T. Kung. Sorting on a Mesh-connected Parallel Computer, *Communications of the ACM*, Vol. 20, No. 4, April 1977, 263–277.

[37] J.D. Ullman. *Computational Aspects of VLSI*. Computer Science Press, 1984.

[38] E. Upfal. An O(log n) deterministic packet routing scheme. In *21st ACM Symposium on the Theory of Computing*, pages 241–250, 1989.

[39] L. G. Valiant and G. J. Brebner. Universal Schemes for Parallel Communication, *Proceedings 13th ACM Symposium on Theory of Computing*, 1981, 263–277.

[40] L. G. Valiant. Experiments with a parallel communication scheme, *Proceedings of the 18th Allerton Conference on Communication, Control and Computing* (1980) 861-811.

[41] L. G. Valiant. A scheme for fast parallel communication, *SIAM Journal of computing*, 11 (1982) 350-361.

[42] L. G. Valiant, A Bridging Model for Parallel Computation, *Communications of the ACM* (August, 1990) Vol.33, No.8, 103-111.

[43] L.G. Valiant. *Handbook of Theoretical Computer Science : Algorithms and Complexity*, volume A, chapter 18. Elsevier Science Publishers, J. van Leeuwen edition, 1990.

Chapter 11

Network Orientation

Gerard Tel *

Abstract

This chapter analyses how the symmetry of a processor network influences the existence of a solution for the network orientation problem. The orientation of hypercubes and tori is the problem of assigning labels to each link of each processor, in such a way that a sense of direction is given to the network. In this chapter the problem of network orientation for these two topologies is studied under the assumption that the network contains a single leader, under the assumption that the processors possess unique identities, and under the assumption that the network is anonymous. The distinction between these three models is considered fundamental in distributed computing.

It is shown that orientations can be computed by deterministic algorithms only when either a leader or unique identities are available. Orientations can be computed for anonymous networks by randomized algorithms, but only when the number of processors is known. When the number of processors is not known, even randomized algorithms cannot compute orientations for anonymous processor networks.

Lower bounds on the message complexity of orientation and algorithms achieving these bounds are given.

1. Introduction

In this chapter the problem of orienting processor networks is considered for hypercubes and tori. The orientation of cliques is considered in an early version of this chapter [30]. The orientation problem concerns the assignment of different labels ("directions") to the edges of each processor, in a globally consistent manner. The label of an edge indicates in which direction in the network this edge leads, and this information is useful for purposes of routing and traversal of networks.

The results obtained for this problem serve to illustrate a number of fundamental results in distributed computing obtained during the last decade. The chapter treats issues of symmetry in networks of processors in depth; the results in this area have to do with deterministic versus randomized algorithms, election and name assignment, and the computational power of anonymous networks. The chapter includes brief discussions of some of the most challenging problems in distributed computing, including fault–tolerance, synchronism, and termination detection.

*The work of the author is supported by the ESPRIT II Basic Research Actions Program of the EC under contract no. 3075 (project ALCOM).

1.1.   Computing Orientations

It was demonstrated by Santoro [25] that the availability of an orientation decreases the message complexity of important computations in networks of several topologies. (A formal definition of orientations is deferred to subsection 2.1.). For example, an $\Omega(N \log N)$ lower bound was proved (see Korach et al. [12]) on the message complexity of electing a leader in an unoriented clique of N processors. For oriented cliques an algorithm using $O(N)$ messages exists; see Loui et al. [18]. Kranakis and Krizanc's algorithm for computing boolean functions on hypercubes [15] assumes that an orientation of the hypercube is available. Similarly, Beame and Bodlaender's algorithm for computing boolean functions on torus networks [3] assumes that an orientation of the torus is available. For both network topologies it is not known, whether the same complexity (for computing arbitrary boolean functions) is achievable in unoriented networks. It is known though [15] that the collection of computable functions is larger for oriented networks.

Surprisingly, although the importance of orientations is well known, only few papers have addressed the question how orientations can be computed in networks where no orientation is available. Peterson [22] has presented an efficient election algorithm for oriented tori, and claimed that this algorithm can be adapted to work on unoriented tori, thus avoiding the question of computing an orientation. Korfhage and Gafni [14] have presented an algorithm to orient *directed* tori. (In this chapter only undirected tori are considered.) There has been considerable interest in the problem of orienting a ring network [10, 26].

1.2.   Network Symmetry

A fundamental notion in the study of distributed algorithms is the issue of the required *symmetry* of a solution. In this chapter the orientation problem is studied under three different symmetry assumptions: all processors execute a different algorithm, namely a standard algorithm parametrized by the name of a processor (*named* network); one processor executes a different algorithm, all others execute the same algorithm (*leader* network); all processors execute the same algorithm (*anonymous* network). (These assumptions will be presented more precisely in subsection 2.2..) The class of deterministically computable functions is the same for leader networks and for named networks. It was shown by Angluin [1] that anonymous networks can deterministically compute strictly less functions than leader networks. It was later shown by Itai and Rodeh [11] that anonymous networks can simulate leader networks with a randomized algorithm when the number of processors is known. Also, when the number of processors is not known, anonymous networks can randomizedly compute strictly less function than leader networks. The results in this chapter illustrate these fundamental results by analyzing the solvability of orientation as a function of the required symmetry.

About this chapter.   This chapter is organized as follows. In section 2. the orientation problem and the three symmetry models are defined, lower bounds are proved, and impossible cases are identified. In section 3. the problem is considered for hypercubes, and in section 4. for tori. Section 5. contains conclusions and general remarks, and discusses some important problems in the area of distributed computing.

2.   Preliminary Results

In subsection 2.1. the formal definitions of the considered network topologies are given, and the formal definitions of labelings and orientations. In subsection 2.2. leader networks, named networks, and anonymous networks are defined, and some algorithms are given to simulate one type of network on the other. In subsection 2.3. a lower bound on the complexity of network orientation is proved. In subsection 2.4. it is proved that the problem cannot be solved on anonymous networks using deterministic algorithms.

2.1.   Definitions of Networks and Orientations

Processor networks are identified with graphs, where the nodes are the processors and an edge between two nodes exists if the corresponding processors are connected by a communication channel. For each topology a labeling will be defined as an assignment, in each node, of labels to the edges of each node. An orientation is defined as a labeling where the labels satisfy an additional global consistency property.

The Hypercube.   The n–dimensional *hypercube* $(n > 0)$ is a network consisting of $N = 2^n$ nodes, where each node can be assigned a unique name from the set $\{(b_0, ..., b_{n-1}) : b_i = 0, 1\}$, in such a way that node $b = (b_0, ..., b_{n-1})$ is connected to the nodes $(b_0, ..., \bar{b}_i, ..., b_{n-1})$, $i = 0...n - 1$. The n–dimensional hypercube has $\frac{1}{2}nN$ edges, and every node has degree n. A *labeling* of the hypercube is an assignment in every node of different labels from the set $\{0, 1, .., n - 1\}$ to the edges incident to that node. An *orientation* of the hypercube is a labeling, for which each node v can be assigned a unique name $\mathcal{N}(v) = (b_0, ..., b_{n-1})$, in such a way that the edge connecting nodes v and w is labeled i in both v and w if $\mathcal{N}(v)$ and $\mathcal{N}(w)$ differ in bit i.

The Torus.   The $n \times n$ *torus* is a network consisting of $N = n^2$ nodes, where each node can be assigned a unique name from the set $\mathbb{Z}_n \times \mathbb{Z}_n$, in such a way that node (i, j) is connected to the four nodes $(i, j + 1)$, $(i, j - 1)$, $(i + 1, j)$, and $(i - 1, j)$. (Addition and subtraction here is mod n.) The $n \times n$ torus has $2n^2$ edges, and every node has degree 4. A *labeling* of the torus is an assignment in every node of different labels from the set $\{up, \ down, \ right, \ left\}$ to the edges incident to that node. An *orientation* of the torus is a labeling, for which each node v can be assigned a unique name $\mathcal{N}(v) = (i, j)$, such that the edge (v, w) is labeled up ($down, \ right, \ left$) in v if $\mathcal{N}(w) = (i, j + 1)$ $((i, j - 1), (i + 1, j), (i - 1, j))$.

For a labeling $\mathcal{L}$, let $\mathcal{L}_u(v)$ be the label assigned to edge (u, v) in node u. A network is said to be *labeled* if a labeling is known to the processors in that network, and *oriented* if an orientation is known. To allow a processor to distinguish between its links, it is assumed that a labeling $\mathcal{L}$ of the network is given initially. The aim of an orientation algorithm (for hypercubes or tori, respectively) is to terminate in each node v with a *permutation* π_v (of $\{0, ..., n - 1\}$, or $\{up, \ down, \ right, \ left\}$, respectively), such that the labeling $\mathcal{O} = \pi(\mathcal{L})$, defined by $\mathcal{O}_v(w) = \pi_v(\mathcal{L}_v(w))$, is an orientation.

2.2.   Network Models

In this chapter it is assumed that processors and communication are *asynchronous* and *reliable*. The time between two steps of one processor may be arbitrarily large (but is always finite) and messages that are sent will be received after an arbitrarily large, but finite delay, and unaltered. It is not assumed that messages, sent over the same link, will be received in the order in which they were sent. The number of processors is denoted by N and the number of links by E. The complexity of a distributed algorithm is expressed as the number of messages exchanged in an execution of the algorithm. A more precise measure is the *bit complexity*, which is expressed as the total number of bits transmitted in the messages together.

A distributed algorithm consists of a local algorithm for each processor. Different assumptions about the required *symmetry* of the algorithm are considered.

Leader Network. A network is called a *leader network* or said to *contain a leader* if there is exactly one processor which knows that it is "the leader". The availability of a leader can be exploited by providing a distinguished local algorithm for it, while all other processors execute the same local algorithm (which is different from the leader algorithm).

Named Network. A network is called a *named network* if each processor is assigned a unique *name* (an identification number). The name of a processor is known to that processor, but not to other processors.

Besides uniqueness no assumptions about the names may be used to prove the correctness of the algorithm (such as, that the numbers are taken from a certain bounded range $\{1, ..., M\}$). For the analysis of the bit complexity of algorithms, however, it is usually assumed that a name is represented in $O(\log N)$ bits.

Anonymous Network. A network is called an *anonymous network* if all processors execute the same algorithm and no names are known.

The Power of Leader and Named Networks.   It has turned out that leader networks and named networks are equivalent in terms of the computations that can be carried out on these networks. Each of the two models can be simulated by the other, because in a leader networks unique names can be assigned, and in named networks a leader can be elected. Algorithms for this purpose will be given in subsection 2.2.1..

Deterministic and Randomized Algorithms.   In order to express the computational power of anonymous networs, as compared to leader or named networks, it is necessary to distinguish between *deterministic* and *randomized* algorithms. The execution model of asynchronous distributed systems is a *non–deterministic* one. This means that the next step in a computation is in general not uniquely defined by the (global) state of a computation. As an example one may consider the situation where two processors have sent a message to a third processor v. As v is usually able to receive a message from any of its links, the next step in the.computation is chosen by the run–time system, which defines which of the two messages will be received first. Thus in general a distributed algorithm (even if v's reaction to the receipt of a message is specified precisely and deterministically) describes a *class of possible executions* rather than a single execution.

An algorithm is deterministic if the processors terminate in *each* possible execution of this class. For a randomized algorithm it is not required that the processors terminate in *each* execution of the algorithm, but only that this happens with a high probability (1 usually). (A probability distribution on the class of executions must be defined.) Thus, although infinite executions of a randomized algorithm may exist (and usually do exist), the algorithm is correct if the probability of such an execution is 0.

Note that an algorithm being a deterministic algorithm does not imply that its output is completely determined by its input; the non–determinism of the execution model may result in a large number of different executions, each with different outcome. For example, the Echo algorithm (to be described later; see algorithm 1) is a deterministic algorithm, but every spanning tree of the network is a possible outcome of the algorithm. The determinism of the algorithm refers to the fact that each of the possible executions terminates, not that there exists only one execution or that all executions yield the same result.

The Power of Anonymous Networks. Anonymous networks are weaker than leader and named networks in terms of the computations that they can perform. Leader and named networks can simulate anonymous networks (namely, by making the leader algorithm equal to the non–leader algorithm, or by not using the name, respectively). On the other hand, Angluin [1] has shown that no deterministic algorithms exists to elect a leader in anonymous networks. With arguments similar to hers it will be shown that no deterministic algorithms for orienting anonymous networks exist. As deterministic orientation algorithms do exist for leader and named networks, it follows that anonymous networks can compute strictly less functions than leader or named functions when deterministic algorithms are used. Consequently, randomized algorithms must be used for election, orientation, and other tasks in anonymous networks.

A leader can be elected in an anonymous network by a randomized algorithm, provided that N is known to the processors (theorem 2.11). This implies that a leader can be elected in anonymous hypercubes, because the size of those networks N can be computed from the degree of a node. The algorithm will be presented in subsection 2.2.2.. It was shown by Itai and Rodeh [11] that there exists no randomized election algorithm (for rings) when the number of nodes is unknown[1]. With an argument similar to theirs it will be shown (see subsection 4.3.) that there exists no randomized algorithm to orient anonymous tori of unknown size. As orientation algorithms do exist for leader and named tori of unknown size (see section 4.), it follows that anonymous networks can compute strictly less functions than leader or named networks, even when randomization is allowed.

2.2.1. Leader Networks and Named Networks

In this subsection an algorithm is described to elect a single processor as a leader in a named network, which uses (at most) $O(EN)$ messages. Subsequently an algorithm is described to assign unique names in a leader network, which uses $2E + N - 1$ messages. These algorithms prove the following two theorems.

---

[1]As a technical detail it should be noted here that according to our definitions only *processor terminating* algorithms are considered; see also subsection 5.3..

Processor v is the initiator:
    begin $rcvd_v := 0$;
        for $l = 1$ **to** dgr_v **do** send $\langle$**name**, $name_v\rangle$ via link l ;
        while $rcvd_v < dgr_v$ **do**
            begin receive msg via link l ;
                $rcvd_v := rcvd_v + 1$
            end
    end .

Processor v is not the initiator:
    begin $rcvd_v := 0$;
        while $rcvd_v < dgr_v$ **do**
        begin receive msg via link l ;
            if $rcvd_v = 0$ **then**
                (* First message defines the spanning tree *)
                begin $father_v := l$;
                        forall links $k \neq l$ **do** send msg via k
                end ;
            $rcvd_v := rcvd_v + 1$
        end ;
        send msg through link $father_v$
    end .

Algorithm 1. The Echo algorithm.

Theorem 2.1 *If a problem can be solved using M messages on a leader network, it can be solved using $M + O(NE)$ messages on a named network.*

Theorem 2.2 *If a problem can be solved using M messages on a named network, it can be solved using $M + 2E + N - 1$ messages on a leader network.*

The problem of electing a leader (in a named network) has received considerable attention during the last decade, and more efficient solutions than the one described here are known. The Spanning Tree algorithm proposed by Gallager, Humblet, and Spira [9] can be used to elect a leader using $O(N \log N + E)$ messages, which implies the following, stronger result.

Theorem 2.3 *If a problem can be solved using M messages on a leader network, it can be solved using $M + O(N \log N + E)$ messages on a named network.*

Electing a Leader in a Named Network.   The algorithm to elect a leader in a named network uses as a building block an algorithm known as the *Echo algorithm*. Using the Echo algorithm (algorithm 1) a single processor can flood its name over the network and eventually receive a confirmation that *all* processors have received its identity.

The flooding of the processor's name is initiated by sending a message to all neighbors. Processors receiving the name for the first time forward it, and record the link on which they first received the name, thus defining a spanning tree in the network. A processor confirms

```
begin rcvd_v := 0 ; larnm_v := name_v ; ldrc_v := 0
    for l = 1 to dgr_v do send ⟨name, name_v⟩ via link l ;
    while ldrc_v < dgr_v do
        begin receive message msg via link l ;
            if msg = ⟨leader, n⟩ then
                begin if ldrc_v = 0 then
                            (* First ⟨leader, n⟩ message, forward *)
                            forall k = 1..dgr_v do send ⟨leader, n⟩ via k ;
                        ldrc_v := ldrc_v + 1 ; leader_v := n
                end
            else (* a ⟨name, n⟩ message *)
                begin
                    if n > larnm_v then
                        (* Larger name, this implies first receipt! *)
                        begin larnm_v := n ; rcvd_v := 0 ; father_v := l ;
                            forall k ≠ l do send ⟨name, n⟩ via k
                        end ;
                    if n ≥ larnm_v then
                        begin rcvd_v := rcvd_v + 1 ;
                            if rcvd_v = dgr_v then
                                if n = name_v
                                    then forall k do send ⟨leader, name_v⟩ via k
                                    else send ⟨name, n⟩ via father_v
                        end
                    (* If n < larnm_v the message is ignored. *)
                end
        end
    (* Processor v is the leader iff leader_v = name_v *)
end .
```

Algorithm 2. Leader election with the Echo algorithm.

that all processors in its subtree have received the name by "echoing" the name to its father in the tree. The initiator terminates after receipt of a message (either an echo or a flooding message) from all of its neighbors. When this happens, all processors have confirmed the receipt of the initiator's identity (as proved, for example, in [29, Thm 3.5]).

The variables for each processor v are: $name_v$ and dgr_v, the name of v and number of links of v (constants for v actually); $rcvd_v$, the number of messages that v has received; and $father_v$, the link over which v first received a message. The name n of the initiator is transmitted in a ⟨name, n⟩ message.

The algorithm for leader election (algorithm 2) is obtained from the Echo algorithm through the application of a mechanism called *extinction* (cf. [29, Sec. 4.3]); see also below. To elect a leader, each processor initiates the flooding of its own identity using the Echo algorithm. However, processor v processes ⟨name, n⟩ messages only if $n \geq name_v$. Moreover, if v has ever received a ⟨name, n⟩ message (with $n \geq name_v$), it processes ⟨name, n'⟩ messages only if $n' \geq n$. To this end, processor v maintains a variable $larnm_v$, which is the

Processor v is the leader:

```
begin rcvd_v := 0 ;
      for l = 1 to dgr_v do send ⟨forward⟩ via link l ;
      while rcvd_v < dgr_v do
         begin receive msg via link l ; rcvd_v := rcvd_v + 1 ;
               if msg = ⟨son, s⟩ then subtr_v[l] := s
                                  else subtr_v[l] := 0
         end ;
      (* Start phase 2 *)
      name_v := 0 ; given := 0 ;
      for l = 1 to dgr_v do
         if subtr_v[l] > 0 then
            begin send ⟨interval, given + 1, given + subtr_v[l]⟩ via l ;
                  given := given + subtr_v[l]
            end
      (* given now equals the number of processors *)
end .
```

Algorithm 3. Assigning names in a leader network (leader algorithm).

largest name n that v has seen.

As a result, only the flood initiated by the processor with the largest name (w say) is processed by all other processors, and thus only processor w terminates the Echo algorithm. When this happens, w floods $\langle \textbf{leader}, name_w \rangle$ messages to all processors to inform them about the leader. The processors terminate the election when they have received a $\langle \textbf{leader}, n \rangle$ message via every link. To this end, processor v maintains a variable $ldrc_v$ to count the number of $\langle \textbf{leader}, n \rangle$ messages it has received. Upon termination v considers itself leader iff $leader_v = name_v$. The processor with the largest name, and only this processor, considers itself leader.

The properties of the algorithm are summarized in the following theorem.

Theorem 2.4 *There exists a deterministic algorithm to elect a leader in a named network. The algorithm exchanges $O(EN)$ messages.*

Assigning Names in a Leader Network. The algorithm to assign names in a leader network, algorithm 3/4, consists of two global phases, each initiated by the leader. The first phase, which again relies on the Echo algorithm, constructs a spanning tree in the network and computes, for each node, the size of the subtree of each of its children. In its echo, processor v reports the size of its subtree. In the second phase the leader assigns itself the number 0, and distributes the remainder of the set $\{0, .., N-1\}$ over its children, where each child receives as many numbers as there are nodes in its subtree. Each node, upon receipt of an interval of numbers from its father, assigns itself the smallest number and distributes the remainder of the interval over its children in a similar manner.

The algorithm uses three types of messages, namely $\langle \textbf{forward} \rangle$, $\langle \textbf{son}, s \rangle$, and $\langle \textbf{interval}, a, b \rangle$ messages. The variables of processor v are: $rcvd_v$, dgr_v, and $father_v$ as in the Echo algorithm; $subtr_v[1..dgr_v]$, the size of the subtree of each child; and $name_v$, the

Processor v is not the leader:

> **begin** $rcvd_v := 0$;
>> **while** $rcvd_v < dgr_v$ **do**
>>> **begin** receive msg via link l ;
>>>> **if** $rcvd_v = 0$ **then**
>>>>> (* The first message defines the spanning tree *)
>>>>> **begin** $father_v := l$;
>>>>>> **forall** links $k \neq l$ **do** send $\langle$**forward**$\rangle$ via k
>>>>> **end** ;
>>>> $rcvd_v := rcvd_v + 1$;
>>>> **if** $msg = \langle$**son**$, s\rangle$ **then** $subtr_v[l] := s$
>>>>> **else** $subtr_v[l] := 0$
>>> **end** ;
>>> (* Report to the father in the tree *)
>>> $size := 1 + \sum_{l=1}^{dgr_v} subtr_v[l]$;
>>> send $\langle$**son**$, size\rangle$ via link $father_v$;
>>> (* Phase 2 *)
>>> receive $\langle$**interval**$, a, b\rangle$;
>>> $name_v := a$; $given := a$;
>>> **for** $l = 1$ **to** dgr_v **do**
>>>> **if** $subtr_v[l] > 0$ **then**
>>>>> **begin** send $\langle$**interval**$, given + 1, given + subtr_v[l]\rangle$ via l ;
>>>>> $given := given + subtr_v[l]$
>>>> **end**
> **end** .

Algorithm 4. Assigning names in a leader network (non–leader algorithm).

---

name that v will be assigned by the algorithm. The algorithm terminates in each processor, and when processor v terminates, $name_v$ is an integer in $\{0, .., N-1\}$, different from $name_w$ for every $w \neq v$.

The properties of the naming algorithm are summarized in the following theorem.

Theorem 2.5 *There exists a deterministic algorithm to assign names in a leader network. The algorithm exchanges exactly $2E + N - 1$ messages.*

It is interesting to note, that the processors do not start phase 2 simultaneously, but rather each processor does so at its own time. A similar algorithm, which sends echo's also in the second phase and therefore has a message complexity of $2E + 2(N-1)$ was given by Bouabdallah and Naimi [5].

Extinction. To apply an algorithm for a leader network to a named network it is not necessary to pass through a separate election phase as described in algorithm 2 or [9]. It is possible to combine the election with an algorithm for a leader network by applying the extinction principle to this algorithm directly. To be more precise about this construction, let *LNA* be an algorithm that solves some network problem for a leader network. (*LNA* stands for "leader network algorithm".) The following two assumptions are made about *LNA*.

1. *LNA* is initiated only by the leader.

2. All processors are involved in every possible execution of *LNA* and have terminated before the leader terminates.

These assumptions hold for most algorithms for leader networks, but are not implied by the definition of a leader network. Every leader algorithm, however, can be modified (in a straight–forward way and at the expense of at most $2E$ extra messages) so as to satisfy these assumptions.

An algorithm *NNA* for a named network is constructed as follows. (*NNA* stands for "named network algorithm".) Each processor v has all the variables of algorithm *LNA* (those of the leader as well as those of the non–leaders), and a variable $larnm_v$, which is initialized to $name_v$. Each processor initiates algorithm *LNA* (as if it were the leader), but tags all messages with its name. When a message of *LNA* is received, the name n contained in it is compared with $larnm_v$. If $n < larnm_v$ the message is simply ignored. If $n = larnm_v$ the message is processed as in algorithm *LNA* (the leader part if $n = name_v$, the non–leader part if $n > name_v$). If $n > larnm_v$, v resets the variables of *LNA* to their initial value, sets $larnm_v := n$, and processes the message as in (the non–leader part of) *LNA*.

Let w be the processor for which $name_w > name_v$ for all $v \neq w$. No processor $v \neq w$ succeeds to terminate the execution of *LNA* it initiated, as w does not cooperate in this execution (use assumption 2). Eventually, all processors cooperate the execution of *LNA* which was initiated by w. When this execution terminates, the network problem is solved by this execution of *LNA*. The construction of algorithm *NNA* proves the following result.

Theorem 2.6 *If a problem can be solved using M messages on a leader network, it can be solved using $O(NM)$ messages in the worst case on a named network.*

Regardless of the function computed by *LNA*, algorithm *NNA* implicitly performs an election, because exaclty one processor (w) succeeds to terminate its own execution of *LNA*. The number of messages sent by algorithm *NNA* is usually much higher than the number stated in theorem 2.3. The extinction construction compares more favorable with the earlier result when the time complexity is considered. The election algorithm referred to in theorem 2.3 uses time proportional to N (in the worst case), so that the separate election stage adds $\Omega(N)$ time to the time needed by algorithm *LNA*. The extinction construction results in an algorithm that runs in the same amount of time as the original algorithm (when time is measured from the moment that all processors have started).

Furthermore, in several particular cases it has been observed that the *average case* complexity of the resulting algorithm is much better than its worst case complexity. Chang and Roberts [6] proposed an election algorithm where extinction is applied to an algorithm in which the leader sends a message on a *ring* of processors and receives it back after N steps. They proved that the worst case complexity of their algorithm is $O(N^2)$, and that the average case complexity is $O(N \log N)$. Mattern [20] has shown that the average complexity of algorithm 2 is $O(E \log N)$. These results suggest the following (open) question.

Open Question 2.7 *Is it in general the case that the average case complexity of algorithm NNA equals $\log N$ times the complexity of algorithm LNA?*

```
begin
    phase_v := 0 ; ldrc_v := 0 ; Newphase ;
    while ldrc_v < dgr_v do
        begin
            receive message msg via link l ;
            if msg = ⟨leader, n⟩ then
                begin if ldrc_v = 0 then
                        forall k = 1..dgr_v do send ⟨leader, n⟩ via k
                        ldrc_v := ldrc_v + 1 ; leader_v := n ;
                end
            else (* a ⟨name, n⟩ or ⟨son, n, s⟩ message *)
                begin
                    if n > larnm_v then
                    (* Larger name, this implies first receipt.
                        Processor v is defeated forever. *)
                    begin larnm_v := n ; rcvd_v := 0 ;
                            father_v := l ; subtr_v[l] := 0;
                            forall k ≠ l do send ⟨name, n⟩ via k
                    end ;
                    if n ≥ larnm_v then
                    begin rcvd_v := rcvd_v + 1 ;
                            if msg = ⟨son, n, s⟩
                                then subtr_v[l] := s else subtr_v[l] := 0 ;
                            if rcvd_v = dgr_v then
                                if n = name_v then
                                    if 1 + Σ_{k=1}^{dgr_v} subtr_v[l] = N
                                        then forall k do send ⟨leader, name_v⟩ via k
                                        else Newphase
                                    else send ⟨son, n, 1 + Σ_{k=1}^{dgr_v} subtr_v[l]⟩ via father_v
                    end
                end
        end
end .
```

Algorithm 5. Election for anonymous networks.

2.2.2. Randomized Algorithms for Anonymous Networks

In this subsection an algorithm (based on an algorithm by Matias and Afek [19]) is presented to elect a leader in an anonymous network of which the number of processors is known to each processor. The algorithm operates in phases, each of which is very similar to the election algorithm for named networks.

Each processor starts as a candidate in phase 1; see algorithm 5. To start a phase, each candidate selects a name using a random function, and initiates the flooding of this name using the Echo algorithm. Due to the possibility that different processors select the same name, a processor may terminate the Echo algorithm as the root of a tree which does not cover all processors. To detect this situation, the echos report the number of processors in

---

Procedure *Newphase*:
    begin $phase_v := phase_v + 1$; $tmp := rand$;
            $name_v := (phase_v, tmp)$; $rcvd_v := 0$; $larnm_v := name_v$;
            for $l = 1$ **to** dgr_v **do** send ⟨**name**, $name_v$⟩ via link l
    end

Algorithm 6. Procedure *Newphase* (see algorithm 5).

---

each subtree (as in algorithm 3/4). When a processor terminates the Echo algorithm as the root of a tree of N processors, it becomes the leader. When the number of processors in the tree is smaller than N, the processor proceeds to the next phase as a candidate.

To allow for a more compact coding of the algorithm, the phase number is made part of the name of a processor. Crucial for the correctness of this algorithm is, that whenever a processor has sent an echo (⟨**son**, n, s⟩) it will thereafter never be a candidate and never be elected. This is because after the sending of such a message by v, $larnm_v > name_v$ continues to hold, so v will never process a message carrying $name_v$.

Lemma 2.8 *If a processor starts phase k, no processor is elected in phase $k' < k$.*

Proof. Assume processor w starts phase k, then processor w has never sent and will never send a ⟨**son**, n, s⟩ message for a phase $k' < k$. To become elected in phase k', processor v must become the root of a tree of N nodes, all except the root having send a ⟨**son**, $name_v, s$⟩ message. □

Lemma 2.9 *If processor v becomes elected in phase k, $name_v$ in phase k is larger than all other names selected in phase k.*

Proof. To become elected, processor v first becomes the root of a tree of N processors, which implies that all processors have sent a ⟨**son**, $name_v, s$⟩ message. The sending of such a message by processor u implies $name_u < larnm_u$, which continues to hold thereafter. □

Lemma 2.10 *Algorithm 5 terminates with probability 1 in all processors, and when processor v terminates $leader_v = name_w$, the largest name of any processor. This name is the name of exactly one processor.*

Proof. Assume phase k is started by one or more processors. Assuming no processor starts phase $k + 1$, the processor(s) with largest name in phase k all the echo's to pass through the Echo algorithm in phase k. In that case, if there is a single processor with the largest name it will be elected, and if there are more processors with the largest name they will start phase $k + 1$, which is a contradiction. Thus, once phase k is started, either a processor becomes elected in that phase, or phase $k + 1$ will be started.

There is a positive constant ρ (depending on the probability distribution of the *rand* function) such that, if more than one processor starts phase k, at least one processor will become defeated in phase k with probability at least ρ. This implies that with probability 1 eventually all processors except one become defeated.

The remaining processor w becomes elected and floods ⟨**leader**, $name_w$⟩ messages over the network, which cause all processors v to terminate with $leader_v = name_w$. □

Theorem 2.11 *There exists a randomized algorithm for election in anonymous networks of known size, which terminates with probability 1.*

The expected message complexity depends on the probability distribution of the *rand* function. It is left as an open problem to the reader to obtain a complexity as low as possible.

2.3. Lower Bounds for Network Orientation

Let N denote the number of processors and E the number of links in the network. In this subsection a lower bound of $\Omega(E)$ messages is shown on the message complexity of orientation algorithms, for the topologies considered in this chapter.

Theorem 2.12 *Any algorithm for the orientation of hypercubes or tori exchanges at least $E - \frac{1}{2}N$ messages in every execution.*

Proof. For a labeling $\mathcal{L}$, let $\mathcal{L}^{u,v,w}$ (where v and w are neighbors of u) be the labeling defined by $\mathcal{L}_u^{u,v,w}(v) = \mathcal{L}_u(w)$, $\mathcal{L}_u^{u,v,w}(w) = \mathcal{L}_u(v)$, and all other labels of $\mathcal{L}^{u,v,w}$ are as in $\mathcal{L}$. ($\mathcal{L}^{u,v,w}$ is obtained by exchanging $\mathcal{L}_u(w)$ and $\mathcal{L}_u(v)$.) It can be verified that for every orientation $\mathcal{O}$ (of a hypercube or torus), and every v, u, and w, $\mathcal{O}^{u,v,w}$ is *not* an orientation.

Consider an execution of an orientation algorithm, with initial labeling $\mathcal{L}$, that terminates with a permutation π_v for each node (where $\mathcal{O} = \pi(\mathcal{L})$ is an orientation). Assume furthermore that in this execution some node u did not send nor receive any message to or from its two neighbors v and w. As u has not communicated with v, nor with w, the same execution is possible if the network is initially labeled with $\mathcal{L}^{u,v,w}$, and all processors terminate with the same permutation. However, $\mathcal{O}' = \pi(\mathcal{L}^{u,v,w}) = \mathcal{O}^{u,v,w}$ is *not* an orientation, and the algorithm is not correct.

It follows, that in every execution every node must communicate with at least all its neighbors except one.   □

Corollary 2.13 *The orientation of the n–dimensional hypercube requires the exchange of $\Omega(n2^n)$ messages. The orientation of the $n \times n$ torus requires the exchange of $\Omega(n^2)$ messages.*

Along the same line a lower bound on the bit (and/or time) complexity can be derived. A generalization of the argument used in the proof of theorem 2.12 derives an incorrect result if the communication patterns on (u, v) and (u, w) are identical (but not necessarily empty in both cases). This means that the same messages are exchanged on (u, v) and (u, w) (and at the same time, if time is considered). The argument then shows that for each u there are at least $\delta(u)$ different patterns of communication. ($\delta(u)$ denotes the degree of u, and as the considered networks are regular, we henceforth write δ instead.) If only one message is sent per link (and no information is coded in the *time* at which it is sent), it contains at least $\log \delta$ bits, and the bit complexity is $\Omega(E \log \delta)$. When the time of sending a message is used to code information, a lower bit complexity may be achievable.

2.4. Deterministic Orientation of Anonymous Networks

In this subsection it will be shown that the orientation problem cannot be solved for anonymous networks by using deterministic algorithms. This result is obtained by providing symmetric initial labelings that cannot be turned into an orientation by a deterministic algorithm.

Definition 2.14 *A labeling $\mathcal{L}$ (of a hypercube or torus) is* symmetric *if there exists a permutation σ (of $\{0, .., n - 1\}$ or $\{up, down, right, left\}$) such that for all links (u, v), $\mathcal{L}_u(v) = \sigma(\mathcal{L}_v(u))$.*

Equivalently, $\mathcal{L}$ is symmetric if for all nodes u, v, , u', v', $\mathcal{L}_u(v) = \mathcal{L}_{u'}(v')$ implies $\mathcal{L}_v(u) = \mathcal{L}_{v'}(u')$. A labeling is a pre–orientation if it can be turned into an orientation by application of the same permutation in every node.

Definition 2.15 *A labeling $\mathcal{L}$ is a* pre–orientation *if there exists a single permutation π_0 such that with $\pi_v = \pi_0$ for all v, $\pi(\mathcal{L})$ is an orientation.*

Theorem 2.16 *If, for an anonymous network, there exists a symmetric labeling which is not a pre–orientation, then this network cannot be oriented by a deterministic algorithm.*

Proof. Let $\mathcal{L}$ be a symmetric labeling, and assume a deterministic algorithm is started in a network with initial labeling $\mathcal{L}$. There is an execution E of this algorithm in which every processor executes exactly the same sequence of steps.

To see this, consider the environment of a processor consisting of its (local) state and the contents of its incoming links. Initially all processors have an identical environment (namely, where the state is the initial one and all links are empty). If at any moment the processors are in identical environments, if a step is enabled in one processor, the same step is enabled in all processors. Assume this step is executed in all processors. After the step all processors are again in the same state. If the step included the receipt of a message msg via link l, this message is removed from the incoming link l of every processor. If the step included the sending of a message msg via link l, this message is added to the incoming link $\sigma(l)$ of every processor, because $\mathcal{L}$ is symmetric. Thus, after the execution of the step in every processor, the processors are in identical environments again.

By assumption, the algorithm terminates. Because every processor has executed the same sequence of steps, it terminates with the same permutation π_0 in every processor. Because $\mathcal{L}$ is not a pre–orientation, $\pi_0(\mathcal{L})$ is not an orientation, and the algorithm is incorrect. $\square$

It remains to show that there exist symmetric labelings that are not pre–orientations. Suitable labelings are easily found for hypercubes and tori of even size because their bipartiteness can be employed.

Corollary 2.17 *There exists no deterministic algorithm to orient an anonymous hypercube.*

Proof. For convenience, label the nodes with bitstrings of length n as in the definition of the hypercube. Call a node *even* if it has an even number of 1's in its bitstring and *odd* if it has an odd number of 1's. For v labeled with $(b_0, ..., b_{n-1})$ and u labeled with $(b_0, ..., \bar{b}_i, ..., b_{n-1})$, set $\mathcal{L}_u(v) = i$ when u is even, and $\mathcal{L}_u(v) = n - 1 - i$ when u is odd.

To show that $\mathcal{L}$ is symmetric, observe that $\mathcal{L}_u(v) + \mathcal{L}_v(u) = n - 1$ always (because every link connects an even node with an odd node).

To show that $\mathcal{L}$ is not a pre–orientation, observe that for an orientation $\mathcal{O}$ of the hypercube, for every u and v, $\mathcal{O}_u(v) = \mathcal{O}_v(u)$. As permuting the labels of all links does not change this property, the same holds for pre–orientations.

Labeling $\mathcal{L}$, however, does not satisfy this property (for $n > 1$), as is easily verified. $\square$

Corollary 2.18 *There exists no deterministic algorithm to orient an anonymous torus of even size.*

Proof. For convenience, label the nodes with elements of $\mathbb{Z}_n \times \mathbb{Z}_n$, as in the definition of the torus. Call the node labeled with (i, j) *even* if $2|(i + j)$, and *odd* otherwise. For node v labeled with (i, j) and u labeled with $(i, j+1)$ $((i, j-1), (i+1, j), (i-1, j))$, let $\mathcal{L}_v(u) = up$ (*down, right, left*) if v is even, and $\mathcal{L}_v(u) = down$ (*up, left, right*) if v is odd.

To show that $\mathcal{L}$ is symmetric, observe that $\mathcal{L}_u(v) = \mathcal{L}_v(u)$ for every link (u, v) (as one of them is even and the other is odd).

To show that $\mathcal{L}$ is not a pre–orientation, observe that for an orientation $\mathcal{O}$ of the torus, for every u and v, $\mathcal{O}_u(v) \neq \mathcal{O}_v(u)$. As permuting the labels of all links does not change this property, the same holds for pre–orientations. Labeling $\mathcal{L}$ does not satisfy this property as observed above.   □

3.   The Orientation of Hypercubes

In this section algorithms for the orientation of hypercubes will be given. Subsection 3.1. presents an algorithm for a leader hypercube, which uses exactly $2E$ messages. It follows from theorem 2.3 and corollary 2.13 that a message optimal algorithm is obtained by preceding this algorithm with an efficient election algorithm. In subsection 3.2. a different solution is analyzed, namely the algorithm obtained when extinction is applied to the algorithm in subsection 3.1.. Subsection 3.3. considers the problem for anonymous hypercubes.

3.1.   Leader Hypercubes

In this subsection an algorithm is proposed, which extends the initial labeling of the leader's links to an orientation. The initial labeling and the availability of a leader uniquely define an orientation as expressed in the following theorem (given here without proof).

Theorem 3.1 *Let $\mathcal{L}$ be a labeling of the hypercube and w be a designated node. There exists exactly one orientation $\mathcal{O}$ which satisfies $\mathcal{O}_w(v) = \mathcal{L}_w(v)$ for each neighbor of w.*

The algorithm computes exactly this orientation, and, moreover, a corresponding labeling of the nodes with bitstrings of length n, where the leader is labeled with $(0, ..., 0)$. This node labeling is also uniquely defined. The algorithm uses three types of messages. The leader sends to each of its neighbors the label of the connecting link in $\langle \mathbf{dim}, i \rangle$ messages. Non–leaders send their node label to other processors in $\langle \mathbf{i\text{–}am}, (b_0, ..., b_{n-1}) \rangle$ message. Non–leaders inform their neighbors about the label of connecting links in $\langle \mathbf{label}, i \rangle$ messages.

The algorithm is given as algorithm 7 (for the leader) and algorithm 8 (for non–leaders). It consists of two phases, where in the first phase messages flow away from the leader, and in the second phase messages flow towards the leader. In the sequel, let w denote the leader processor. A *predecessor* of node v is a neighbor u of v for which $d(u, w) < d(v, w)$, and a *successor* of node v is a neighbor u of v for which $d(u, w) > d(v, w)$. In a hypercube node v has no neighbor u for which $d(u, w) = d(v, w)$ and a node at distance d from the leader has d predecessors and $n - d$ successors.

The leader initiates the algorithm by sending a $\langle \mathbf{dim}, i \rangle$ message over the link labeled i. When a non–leader processor v has learned its distance $dist_v$ to the leader and has received $dist_v$ messages from its predecessors, v is able to compute its node label. Processor v forwards

begin $rcvd_v := 0$; $dist_v := 0$; $label_v := (0, ..., 0)$;

    for $l = 0$ **to** $n - 1$ **do** (* Send for phase 1 *)

      begin send $\langle$**dim**, $l\rangle$ via link l ;

          $\pi_v[l] := l$

    end ;

    while $rcvd_v < n$ **do** (* Receive for phase 2 *)

      begin receive $\langle$**label**, $l\rangle$ (* necessarily via link l *)

          $rcvd_v := rcvd_v + 1$

      end

end .

Algorithm 7. Orientation of leader hypercube (leader algorithm).

this label in an $\langle$**i–am**, $(b_0, ..., b_{n-1})\rangle$ message to its successors. To show that v is indeed able to do so, first consider the case where v receives a $\langle$**dim**, $i\rangle$ message via link l. As the message is sent by the leader, $dist_v = 1$, and all other neighbors are successors. The node label of v is $(b_0, ..., b_{n-1})$, where $b_i = 1$, and the other bits are 0. (The label of link l becomes i in this case.) Thus v forwards $\langle$**i–am**, $(b_0, ..., b_{n-1})\rangle$ via all links $k \neq l$.

Next, consider the case where v receives an $\langle$**i–am**, $(b_0, ..., b_{n-1})\rangle$ message. The distance d of the sender of this message to the leader is derived from the message (the number of 1's in $(b_0, ..., b_{n-1})$). $\langle$**i–am**, $label\rangle$ messages are sent only to successors, thus the sender is a predecessor of v and $dist_v = d + 1$. As v has $dist_v$ neighbors at distance d, v waits until $dist_v$ $\langle$**i–am**, $label\rangle$ messages have been received. By then v computes its node label as the logical disjunction of the received node labels, and forwards it to the neighbors from which no $\langle$**i–am**, $label\rangle$ was received, as these are the successors.

In the first phase, each non–leader processor v computes its node label. In the second phase, each non–leader processor v learns from its successors the orientation of the links to the successors, and computes the orientation of the links to the predecessors. This information is sent over the link in $\langle$**label**, $i\rangle$ messages. A processor sends $\langle$**label**, $i\rangle$ messages to its predecessors as soon as it has received these messages from all successors, and then terminates. The leader terminates when $\langle$**label**, $i\rangle$ messages have been received from all neighbors.

The variables for processor v are: $rcvd_v$, the number of messages already received; $dist_v$, the distance to the leader (computed when the first message arrives, initialized to $n + 1$); $label_v$, the node label computed by v; $neigh_v[0..n - 1]$, an array holding the node labels of the predecessors of v; and π_v, to store the orientation.

Lemma 3.2 *The algorithm terminates in every processor.*

Proof. Using induction on d it is easily verified that all processors at distance at most d eventually send the messages for phase 1. For $d = 0$, only the leader itself has distance d to the leader and it may send the messages without receiving other messages first. Assume all processors at distance d to the leader send all messages for phase 1, and consider a processor v at distance $d + 1$ from the leader. As all predecessors of v eventually send the phase 1 messages to v, v eventually receives one of these messages, and sets $dist_v := d + 1$. When v

```
begin rcvd_v := 0 ; dist_v := n + 1 ; label_v := (0, ..., 0) ;
      forall l do neigh_v[l] := nil ;
      while rcvd_v < dist_v do (* Receive for phase 1 *)
         begin receive msg via link l ; rcvd_v := rcvd_v + 1 ;
               (* msg is a ⟨dim, i⟩ or ⟨i-am, (b_0, ..., b_{n-1})⟩ message *)
               if msg is ⟨dim, i⟩ then
                  begin dist_v := 1 ;
                        neigh_v[l] := (0, ..., 0) ; label_v[i] := 1
                        (* So now label_v = (0, .., 1, .., 0), with one 1 *)
                  end
               else
                  begin dist_v := 1 + # of 1's in (b_0, ..., b_{n-1}) ;
                        label_v := (label_v or (b_0, ..., b_{n-1})) ;
                        neigh_v[l] := (b_0, ..., b_{n-1})
                  end
         end ;
      (* Send for phase 1 *)
      forall l with neigh_v[l] = nil do
            send ⟨i-am, label_v⟩ via link l ;
      while rcvd_v < n do (* Receive for phase 2 *)
         begin receive ⟨label, i⟩ via link l ;
               rcvd_v := rcvd_v + 1 ; π_v[l] := i
         end ;
      (* Send for phase 2 *)
      forall l with neigh_v[l] ≠ nil do
         begin π_v[l] := bit in which label_v and neigh_v[l] differ ;
               send ⟨label, π_v[l]⟩ via link l
         end
end .
```

Algorithm 8. Orientation of leader hypercube (non–leader algorithm).

has received the phase 1 messages from all of its $d+1$ predecessors, v sends phase 1 messages itself (to its successors).

Similarly it is shown that all processors send the messages of phase 2 and terminate. □

Lemma 3.3 *After termination* $\mathcal{O} = \pi(\mathcal{L})$ *is an orientation. For neighbors* v *and* u, *label$_v$ and label$_u$ differ exactly in bit* $\mathcal{O}_v(u)$ *(which is equal to* $\mathcal{O}_u(v)$).

Proof. According to theorem 3.1 there exists exactly one orientation $\mathcal{O}$ and one corresponding node labeling $\mathcal{N}$ such that $\mathcal{O}_w(v) = \mathcal{L}_w(v)$ and $\mathcal{N}(w) = (0, .., 0)$.

In phase 1 the processors compute the node labeling $\mathcal{N}$, as is seen by using induction on the distance to the leader. Node w sets $label_w$ to $(0, ..., 0)$, which is $\mathcal{N}(w)$. Neighbor v of w sets $label_v$ to $(b_0, ..., b_{n-1})$, where b_i is 1 if the link from w to v is labeled i in w, and 0 otherwise. Thus $label_v = \mathcal{N}(v)$.

Now assume all nodes u at distance d from w compute $label_u = \mathcal{N}(u)$ and consider node v at distance $d+1$ from w. $\mathcal{N}(v)$ is a string of $d+1$ 1's and $n - d - 1$ 0's. Node v has $d+1$

predecessors, and $\mathcal{N}(u)$ is found for predecessor u by changing one 1 in $\mathcal{N}(v)$ into a 0. Thus the conjunction of the $d+1$ labels $\mathcal{N}(u)$ is indeed $\mathcal{N}(v)$.

After phase 1, for predecessor u of v, $neigh_v[l] = label_u$ with $l = \mathcal{L}_v(u)$. In phase 2, v computes $\pi_v[l]$ as the bit in which $label_v$ and $neigh_v[l]$ differ, so that $label_v$ and $label_u$ differ exactly in bit $\pi_v[l]$, which is $\mathcal{O}_v(u)$ as required. The same label is used by u for the link, after u receives v's $\langle label, \pi_v[l] \rangle$ message. $\square$

The properties of algorithm 7/8 are summarized in the following theorem.

Theorem 3.4 *There exists a deterministic algorithm to orient leader hypercubes, which exchanges the asymptotically optimal number of $2E$ messages.*

The bit complexity. As the $\langle i\text{--}am, label \rangle$ messages of the algorithm consist of a node label, they contain a string of n bits. It will now be shown that the algorithm can be implemented using only messages of $O(\log n)$ bits. The $\langle dim, i \rangle$ and $\langle label, i \rangle$ messages contain a number between 0 and $n-1$ and thus contain $O(\log n)$ bits.

The algorithm does not need all information contained in the $\langle i\text{--}am, label \rangle$ messages. It suffices to transmit the number of 1's, the smallest index at which there is a 1, and the sum modulo n of the indexes for which there is a 1. For a node label $label = (b_0, ..., b_{n-1})$ define the weight, low, and index sum as $weight(label) = \#\{i \ : \ b_i = 1\}$; $low(label) = \min\{i \ : \ b_i = 1\}$; $ixsum(label) = (\sum_{b_i=1} i) \bmod n$. Finally, the *summary* is the tuple $smmry(label) = (weight(label), low(label), ixsum(label))$. The summary of a node is the summary of its node label.

Lemma 3.5 *Let v be a node at distance $d+1 \geq 2$ from w.*
(1) $dist_v = d+1$ can be derived from one summary of a predecessor of v.
(2) The summary of v can be computed from the $d+1$ summaries of v's predecessors.
(3) The node label of v can be computed from the summary of v and the $d+1$ summaries v's predecessors.
(4) The node label of a predecessor u of v can be computed from the node label of v and the summary of u.

Proof. (1) The computation of $dist_v$ is trivial as $weight(\mathcal{N}(u))$ equals $d(u, w)$.

(2) Now let $d+1$ summaries of predecessors of v be given. d of the $d+1$ summaries have low equal to $low(\mathcal{N}(v))$, while one summary has a higher low (the predecessor whose label is found by flipping the *first* 1 in $\mathcal{N}(v)$). This gives $low(\mathcal{N}(v))$, but also identifies the index sum $ixsum_0$ of a node label which differs from $\mathcal{N}(v)$ in position low. Thus $ixsum(\mathcal{N}(v)) = (ixsum_0 + low(\mathcal{N}(v))) \bmod n$. This completes the computation of $smmry(\mathcal{N}(v)))$.

(3) Let $\mathcal{N}(v) = (b_0, ..., b_{n-1})$. The $d+1$ indices i for which $b_i = 1$ are found as $ixsum(\mathcal{N}(v)) - ixsum(\mathcal{N}(u)) \bmod n$ for the $d+1$ choices of u as a predecessor of v.

(4) For a predecessor u of v, $\mathcal{N}(u)$ is found by flipping the bit indexed by $(ixsum(\mathcal{N}(v)) - ixsum(\mathcal{N}(u))) \bmod n)$ from 1 to 0 in $\mathcal{N}(v)$. $\square$

It follows from lemma 3.5 that it suffices in the orientation algorithm to send the summary of node label instead of the full label, and hence the algorithm can be implemented with messages of $O(\log N)$ bits. As the messages are used to assign different labels to $\Omega(n)$ links, the information in the messages cannot be compressed below $O(\log n)$ bits.

3.2. Named Hypercubes

The algorithm to orient leader hypercubes can be preceded by an election algorithm (cf. the construction of theorem 2.3) and then yields an orientation algorithm for named networks with properties summarized in the following theorem.

Theorem 3.6 *There exists a deterministic algorithm to orient named hypercubes, which exchanges the asymptotically optimal number of $O(E)$ messages.*

An alternative algorithm is obtained when extinction is applied directly to algorithm 7/8. Denote, as in subsection 2.2.1., by *LNA* algorithm 7/8 and by *NNA* the algorithm obtained when extinction is applied. Cf. theorem 2.6, algorithm *NNA* has a worst case message complexity which is bounded by $N \times 2E$, which is $n4^n$. In this section it will be shown that the worst case message complexity of algorithm *NNA* is actually bounded by $n3^n$. The proof is due to Anneke A. Schoone.

Define the *face* of the hypercube *spanned by* two nodes w and v, denoted $face(u, v)$, as the set of nodes "between" w and v.

$$face(w, v) = \{u \; : \; d(w, u) + d(u, v) = d(w, v)\}$$

The face spanned by two nodes at distance d forms a d–dimensional hypercube itself. The same face is spanned by each pair of opposite nodes in this sub–hypercube.

Lemma 3.7 *The n–dimensional hypercube has 3^n faces.*

Proof. For each w there are $\binom{n}{d}$ nodes v at distance d of w, and each of these v defines a different face containing w of dimension d. However, each face of dimension d is found for 2^d different choices of w (and a suitable v), so the number of faces of dimension d is $(2^n \times \binom{n}{d})/2^d = 2^{n-d} \times \binom{n}{d}$. Thus the total number of faces is $\sum_{d=0}^{n} 2^{n-d} \times \binom{n}{d} = (1+2)^n = 3^n$. □

For the analysis of algorithm *NNA* cost is charged to the number of times a processor exits the receive loop of phase 1. If processor v does so in the execution of *LNA* initiated by w, one unit of cost is charged to $face(w, v)$.

Lemma 3.8 *Each face gets charged at most one cost unit.*

Proof. If processor v exits the receive loop of phase 1 in the execution of *LNA* which is initiated by w, then processor w has the largest name of all processors in $face(w, v)$. This is because all processors in the face must forward the messages carrying w's name. As only one processor w in the face has the largest name (in the face), and the same face is not spanned by w and a node other than v, the lemma follows. □

Theorem 3.9 *Algorithm NNA sends at most $n3^n$ messages in the worst case.*

Proof. In algorithm *LNA* each processor sends n messages, all of them after the waiting in phase 1 has terminated. Thus the number of messages sent in algorithm *NNA* is bounded by n times the number of cost units charged. The proof is completed using lemmas 3.7 and 3.8. □

3.3.   Anonymous Hypercubes

The algorithm in subsection 3.1. can be combined with the election algorithm for anonymous networks in subsection 2.2.1., because the number of nodes is known. This proves the following result.

Theorem 3.10 *There exists a randomized algorithm to orient anonymous hypercubes, which terminates with probability 1.*

4.   The Orientation of Tori

In this section the problem of finding orientations for a torus is studied. It will be shown that deterministic algorithms for the orientation of leader and named tori exist, and that anonymous tori can be oriented by a randomized algorithm if and only if the size of the torus is known to the processors. For $n = 4$, the $n \times n$ torus is isomorphic to the 4–dimensional hypercube. An algorithm to orient it is easily obtained by application of the algorithm to orient the hypercube, followed by a local relabeling based on a processor's node label. The case $n = 3$ is simply ignored. In this section $n \times n$ tori are considered for $n \geq 5$, for a reason which will become clear in the next paragraph.

The orientation problem will be solved in two stages. The first stage computes a *consistent prelabeling*, and the second stage computes the orientation. The first stage is necessary because in torus networks it is in general *not* possible to extend the labeling of a single processor to a global orientation. In an oriented torus the *up* and *down* neighbor of one processor are at distance 2 of each other, and there exists *one* path of length 2 between them, provided $n \geq 5$. The same holds for the *right* and *left* neighbor. Each processor has pairs of neighbors which are at distance 2 of each other, for which there exist *two* paths of length 2 between these nodes (see figure 9). It follows that a labelling which assigns the

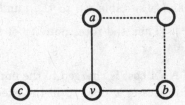

Figure 9. Neighbors of a node in the torus.

labels *up* and *down* to processors forming such a pair cannot be extended to an orientation.

The first stage of the algorithm divides the four links of each processor into two pairs, with the property that the links of one pair must have opposite labels in an orientation.

Definition 4.1 *A prelabeling $\mathcal{P}$ of the torus is an assignment in each node of labels from the set $\{hori, \; verti\}$ to the links of that node, such that each label is used twice.*
A prelabeling $\mathcal{P}$ is consistent if for all nodes v and neighbors u and w of v, $\mathcal{P}_v(u) = \mathcal{P}_v(w)$ implies that there exists one path of length 2 between u and w.

When a consistent prelabeling is available, a node may label the *verti* links with *up* and *down* and the *hori* links with *left* and *right*, and this labeling can be extended to an orientation. When a prelabeling is given, the *opposite* of a link is the single link with the same label, and the *perpendicular* links are the two links with different label.

4.1.   Named Tori

On named tori both stages can be performed by deterministic algorithms.

Computing a Prelabeling. The algorithm to compute a consistent prelabeling in a named network is given as algorithm 11. Each processor sends its name to each neighbor and each neighbor forwards the name one step further. Thus, the name of each processor is transmitted through 16 links, and each processor receives 16 messages (4 through each link). Of the 16 messages received, 8 contain names which are received only once, and 4 contain names which are received twice, but through different links (see figure 10). Two links via

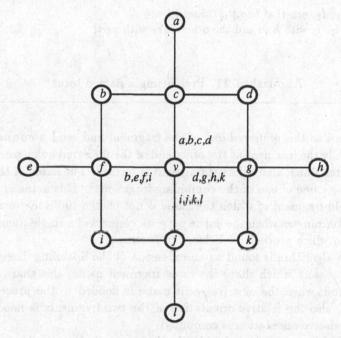

Figure 10. The messages received by processor v.

which the same name is received are perpendicular; so, when a processor has received its 16 messages a consistent prelabeling can be computed. The names are first sent in a $\langle \mathbf{one}, n \rangle$ message, and forwarded in a $\langle \mathbf{two}, n \rangle$ message. The names received in $\langle \mathbf{two}, n \rangle$ messages are stored in sets bag_v for each link.

Theorem 4.2 *There exists a deterministic algorithm to compute a consistent prelabeling on a named torus, which exchanges $16N$ messages.*

Computing an Orientation. An orientation can be computed by an algorithm based on the Spanning Tree algorithm by Gallager, Humblet, and Spira [9]. A brief description of this algorithm follows. During the execution of the algorithm the network is partitioned into *fragments*, each with a *fragment name*. Initially, each fragment consists of a single node, and the name of the fragment is the name of the node.

During the execution fragments are enlarged because fragments combine and form new, larger fragments. To this end the processors in a fragment cooperate to select one link which

```
begin forall links l do bag_v[l] := ∅ ;
      forall l do send ⟨one, name_v⟩ via l ;
      rcvd_v := 0 ;
      while rcvd_v < 16 do
          begin receive msg via link l ; rcvd_v := rcvd_v + 1 ;
                (* It is a ⟨one, n⟩ or ⟨two, n⟩ message *)
                if msg is a ⟨one, n⟩ message
                    then forall k ≠ l do send ⟨two, n⟩ via k
                    else bag_v[l] := bag_v[l] ∪ {n}
          end ;
      find l_1, l_2 such that bag_v[l_1] ∩ bag_v[l_2] = ∅ ;
      label l_1, l_2 with hori and the other links with verti
end .
```

Algorithm 11. Prelabeling a named torus.

leaves the fragment as the *preferred link* of the fragment and send a **connect** message via this link. Eventually the fragment at the other end of the preferred link agrees to connect the two fragments, after which a new, larger fragment is formed. The name of the new fragment is chosen to be the name of one of the combining fragments[2]. This name is flooded towards all nodes in the old fragment of which the name is not chosen to be the new name.

The algorithm terminates when the entire network consists of a single fragment. The name of the fragment to which processor v belongs is $frname_v$.

The orientation algorithm is found as an extension of the Spanning Tree algorithm. It is ensured, that processors which share the same fragment name, also share the same orientation. To this end, when the new fragment name is flooded to the processors that must update $frname_v$, also the relative orientation of the two fragments is flooded. It must be shown how this relative orientation is computed.

The combining of fragments is embedded in the protocol given in algorithm 12. Assume node v in fragment F answers the **connect** message of node u in fragment G with an **answer** message, where the combined fragment will have the name (and orientation) of fragment F. Processor v includes in the answer the label of the link over which it is sent, and this defines for u the new label of the link over which the message is received, as well as the opposite link. It remains to find the correct orientation of the two perpendicular links. To do this (see figure 13), v sends over one link l perpendicular to link (v, u) a message $⟨\textbf{dir1}, \pi_v[l]⟩$, which is forwarded by the receiving node as a $⟨\textbf{dir2}, \pi_v[l]⟩$ message. Processor u sends a $⟨\textbf{dirreq}⟩$ message via the two links perpendicular to link (u, v). A processor which receives both a $⟨\textbf{dir2}, ll⟩$ and a $⟨\textbf{dirreq}⟩$ message, replies to the $⟨\textbf{dirreq}⟩$ message with a $⟨\textbf{dirans}, ll⟩$ message. Thus u receives an answer to one of its $⟨\textbf{dirreq}⟩$ messages, which gives the orientation of the links perpendicular to (u, v).

To distinguish between the messages of different invocations of the connect protocol, all messages are tagged with the fragment names of F and G (not shown in figure 13). The

---

[2]In [9] it occurs that a new name is chosen for a new fragment, but the algorithm can easily be modified so as to use an existing name for the new fragment.

For processor v:
    send $\langle$answer$, \pi_v[l]\rangle$ via l ; (* to u *)
    send $\langle$dir1$, \pi_v[k]\rangle$ via one link k perpendicular to l

For processor u:
    receive $\langle$answer$, ll\rangle$ via l ; (* from v *)
    $\sigma[l] := oppos(ll)$; (* The opposite direction *)
    $\sigma[oppos(l)] := ll$;
    send $\langle$dirreq$\rangle$ via the two links perpendicular to l ;
    receive $\langle$dirans$, kk\rangle$ via link k ;
    $\sigma[k] := kk$; $\sigma[oppos(k)] := oppos(kk)$
    (* Now σ is the permutation to be applied to all
                 link labels in the fragment. *)

For all other processors:
    when a $\langle$dir1$, ll\rangle$ message is received via link l:
        send $\langle$dir2$, ll\rangle$ via the two links perpendicular to l

    when a $\langle$dir2$, ll\rangle$ message is received via link l
                and a $\langle$dirreq$\rangle$ message via link k:
        send $\langle$dirans$, ll\rangle$ via link k

Algorithm 12. Fragment combine protocol.

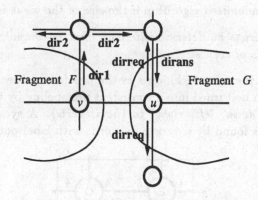

Figure 13. Extra messages in the connecting procedure.

connect protocol to combine two fragments exchanges 6 messages each time two fragments are combined, and as exactly $N-1$ merges take place, the message complexity of the orientation protocol exceeds the complexity of the underlying algorithm by $6N-6$ messages.

Thus the complexity of the second stage is $O(N \log N)$, which exceeds the complexity of the first stage in order of magnitude.

Theorem 4.3 *There exists a deterministic algorithm for the orientation of named tori, which exchanges $O(N \log N)$ messages in the worst case.*

4.2.   Leader Tori

Computing a Prelabeling.   A preorientation can be deterministically computed only by a computation starting from the leader. This computation could start by applying the naming algorithm (algorithm 3/4), followed by algorithm 11.

Theorem 4.4 *There exists a deterministic algorithm to compute a consistent prelabeling on a leader torus, which exchanges* $2E + N - 1 + 16N = 21N - 1$ *messages.*

Computating an Orientation.   As the computation of a consistent prelabeling includes the assignment of names, stage 2 can be performed as for named tori, which would cost $O(N \log N)$ messages. Using the same ideas as for the connect protocol, algorithm 12, it is possible to give an algorithm which exchanges only $O(N)$ messages. The details of this algorithm are left as an exercise for the reader.

Theorem 4.5 *There exists a deterministic algorithm for the orientation of leader tori, which exchanges* $O(N)$ *messages.*

4.3.   Anonymous Tori

Although in an anonymous network a consistent prelabeling can be computed (by a randomized algorithm), it is impossible to compute an orientation, even by use of a randomized algorithm, when N is not known.

Computing a Prelabeling.   A consistent prelabeling can be computed in an anonymous torus, but only by a randomized algorithm if the size of the torus is even.

Theorem 4.6 *There exists no deterministic algorithm to compute a consistent prelabeling for an anonymous torus of even size.*

Proof. The proof uses the same techniques as the proofs in subsection 2.4.. A labeling is a pre–prelabeling if it can be turned into a consistent prelabeling by the application of a fixed function ρ_0 from {*up, down, left, right*} to {*hori, verti*}. A symmetric labeling which is not a pre–prelabeling is found by covering the torus with label patterns as in figure 14. In

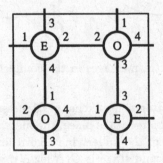

Figure 14. A symmetric labeling which is not a pre–preorientation.

this labeling, the even nodes (E) must label links 1 and 2 the same, while the odd nodes (O) must assign the same label to links 2 and 4.   □

A consistent prelabeling can be computed by a randomized algorithm which is an extension of algorithm 11. Processors cannot send their name, but instead draw a random number (in the range $[1, ..., M]$, say) and send this number together with a phase number (initially 1). Processors receiving 12 $\langle \mathbf{two}, n, p \rangle$ messages, but not carrying four numbers twice and four numbers once, reply by sending $\langle \mathbf{refuse}, n, p \rangle$ messages. These messages are sent back to the processors from which the number n originated and causes them to draw a new number in the next phase.

The probability that a "collision" occurs in a processor can be made small by choosing M large. The precise formulation of the algorithm, as well as the analysis of its expected message complexity is left to the reader.

Theorem 4.7 *There exists a randomized algorithm to compute a consistent prelabeling for an anonymous torus.*

Computing an Orientation. It has been established in subsection 2.4. that anonymous tori cannot be oriented by deterministic algorithms. The results presented so far suffice to construct a randomized algorithm for the orientation of tori when the size of the network is known. To this end, algorithms 5, 3/4, and the algorithm sketched in subsection 4.1. can be combined.

Theorem 4.8 *There exists a randomized algorithm for the orientation of anonymous tori, when the number of processors is known.*

The main result of this subsection is to prove that no such algorithm exists when the size of the torus is not known. The proof relies on techniques similar to those used by Itai and Rodeh [11] to establish that no (randomized) algorithm exists to compute the size of a anonymous ring network. An execution leading to a correct result on a (small) torus is finite, and hence it has a positive probability of being "accidently simulated" by a fragment of a larger torus. If this occurs in two different parts of the larger torus, processes may terminate with incompatible orientations, and this may happen with an arbitrarily large probability.

Theorem 4.9 *There exists no (randomized) algorithm for the orientation of tori when the number of processors is not known.*

Proof. Assume there exists an algorithm A that is able to compute an orientation in an

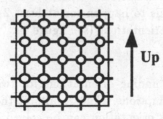

Figure 15. Algorithm A terminates with an orientation on a small torus.

$n_0 \times n_0$ torus T_0 (see figure 15). That is, there exists an execution Ex of A on the $n_0 \times n_0$ torus in which every processor terminates, and the resulting labeling is an orientation. Define a message chain as a series of messages $(M_1, M_2, ..., M_k)$, such that M_{i+1} was sent by the processor that received M_i, and was sent only after the receipt of M_i. Let the longest message chain in Ex have length L.

Next consider a torus T_1 of size $n_1 \times n_1$ with $n_1 > 2L + 1$. The l–$neighborhood$ of processor

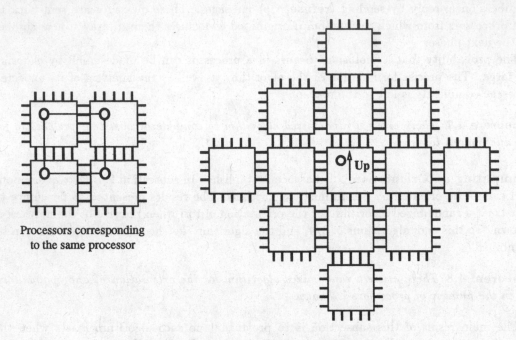

Processors corresponding
to the same processor

Figure 16. A subset of the processors simulates Ex.

v is the set of processors with distance at most l to v. Processor (i, j) in T_1 *corresponds* to processor $(i \bmod n_0, j \bmod n_0)$ in T_0. In execution Ex, all processors of T_0 take finitely many steps, and in particular draw a random number only finitely often. Thus, there is an $\epsilon > 0$ such that for each processor v_0 of T_1 the probability that all processors in the L–neighborhood of v_0 draw the same numbers as the corresponding processor in T_0 draw in Ex is at least ϵ. If this happens there is an execution of A on T_1 in which processor v_0 terminates after executing exactly the same steps as in execution Ex (see figure 16).

The size of T_1 can be chosen large enough to have an arbitrarily high probability that this occurs for at least one processor v_0. The size of T_1 can be chosen large enough to have an arbitrarily high probability of this to happen for at least 2 processors v_0 and v_1, where v_0 and v_1 terminate with different orientations (see figure 17.   □

5.   Final Remarks

In this chapter the problem of finding orientations for two network topologies has been studied under three model assumptions. The results of the study can be summarized as follows. The problem of network orientation can be solved by a deterministic algorithm in leader or named networks. The problem cannot be solved by a deterministic algorithm in anonymous networks. In anonymous networks the problem can be solved by a randomized algorithm if the size of the network is known (which is the case for hypercubes), and cannot be solved by a randomized algorithm when the size is not known. The results derived for

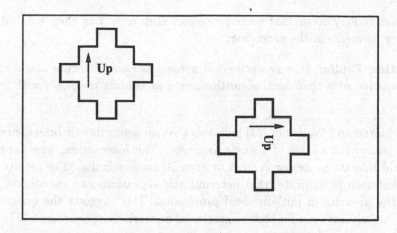

Figure 17. Processors terminate with inconsistent labelings.

the orientation of cliques [30] fit into this scheme as well.

These results are in accordance with know results in the area of distributed computing, cf. figure 18. Named networks can simulate leader networks (theorem 2.3) and vice versa (theorem 2.2). Anonymous networks can simulate leader networks with a randomized algorithm when the network size is known (theorem 2.11), but not when the size is unknown.

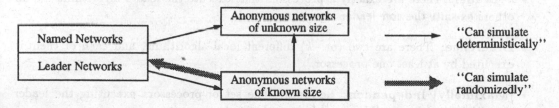

Figure 18. Leader, named and anonymous networks can simulate each other.

5.1. Dependency of other assumptions

In this chapter the solvability of the orientation problem was studied as a function of the required *symmetry* of the solution. The solvability may as well be studied as a function of other parameters.

5.1.1. Fault–Tolerance

In this chapter is was assumed that the network were *reliable*, that is, processors and links do not fail. Algorithms research in the past decade has frequently addressed the question if processors can be coordinated in systems where processors can fail, for example, according to one of the following fault models.

- **Initially Dead Processors:** It may occur that some processors do not execute a single instruction of their local algorithm.

- **Crashes:** It may occur that some processors stop executing their local algorithm at arbitrary moments in the execution.

- **Byzantine Faults:** It may occur that some processors execute steps which are in disaccordance with their local algorithm, such as sending messages with wrong information.

A result of Moran and Wolfstahl [21] indicates that no deterministic orientation algorithm exists that is resilient to a crash of a single processor. This leaves open, whether randomized solutions could tolerate processor crashes or even Byzantine faults. The results of Fischer, Lynch, and Peterson [8] indicate, that deterministic algorithms can coordinate non–trivial decisions in the presence of initially dead processors. This suggests the question whether deterministic algorithms exist for the orientation of networks in the presence of initially dead processors.

5.1.2. Refined Symmetry Assumptions

In this chapter only three different symmetry assumptions were considered, namely that all local algorithms are different (named networks), all local algorithms are identical (anonymous networks), or all local algorithms except one are identical (leader networks). Different assumptions about the symmetry are possible.

- k–**Leader:** There are exactly k processors that execute the leader algorithm, and all others execute the non–leader algorithm.

- **Difference:** There are two (or: k) different local algorithms, and each of them is executed by at least one processor.

- **[Maximally] Independent Leaders:** The set of processors executing the leader algorithm constitute a [Maximal] Independent set.

For each of these symmetry assumptions it can be investigated whether the class of computable functions is [strictly] included in or [strictly] includes the functions computable by leader or anonymous networks.

Open Question 5.1 *Fit the computational power of these symmetry assumptions in figure 18.*

5.1.3. Synchronism Assumptions

In this chapter *asynchronous systems* were considered. In these systems there is no bound on the time necessary to perform one operation, and no bound on the time between sending an receiving a message. A different model, which has frequently been used for the development of distributed algorithms, is that of *synchronous systems*. In synchronous systems bounds are known both on the time to perform one instruction and on the message delay time. The following four models can be distinguished.

- **Fully Asynchronous Networks:** The model that is considered in this chapter.

- **Archimedean Networks:** Bounds on the relative speeds of components do exist; they can be very rough, however, and need not be known to the processors; see Vitanyi [32].

- **Asynchronous Bounded Delay Networks:** Processing time within a processor is assumed to be neglictible, an upper bound is known on the message delay, and processors have clocks that run at the same speed (barring a very small drift); see, e.g., Korach et al. [13].

- **Fully Synchronous Networks:** Processors execute their local algorithm in discrete rounds, and a message sent in round i is received *before* the receiver executes round $i + 1$.

A lot of research has addressed the influence of synchronism assumptions on the functions that are computable, and the efficiency with which they can be computed.

The Power of Synchronism. *Stronger synchronism assumptions do not increase the class of functions computable by reliable networks.* This statement follows from the existence of so–called "synchronizer" algorithms, implementing fully synchronous networks on networks satisfying a weaker assumption. Awerbuch [2] proposed a synchronizer for fully asynchronous networks, and his "α–synchronizer" can be used even for anonymous (but reliable) networks. A more efficient algorithm (in terms of messages exchanged by the synchronizer) was presented by Korach et al. [13] for Asynchronous Bounded Delay Networks.

The Efficiency of Synchronism. *Stronger synchronism assumptions allow more efficient algorithms.* This statement can be illustrated by some results on the complexity of electing a leader on a named ring network. It was shown (by various authors, e.g., Pachl et al. [23]) that on an asynchronous ring at least $\Omega(N \log N)$ messages must be exchanged. Vitanyi [32] has demonstrated that on an Archimedean ring $O(N)$ messages suffice to elect a leader. The implicit constant hidden in the big–Oh notation depends on the ratio between the various upper and lower bounds on the relative speeds of components. Bodlaender and Tel [4] have shown, that on a synchronous ring $O(N)$ messages suffice, each message can be of $O(1)$ bits, and this is regardless of whether the processors know N or not.

A striking example of the efficiency that can be obtained from synchronism is the surprizing result that in a synchronous system any message M can be transmitted using $O(1)$ bits. This can be done by "coding M in time", namely, sending a **start** message and M time units later a **stop** message. The receiver obtains M by measuring the time between the receipt of the two messages; see, e.g., [4].

Fault–Tolerance and Synchronism. *Stronger synchronism assumptions are able to tolerate larger classes of faults in unreliable networks.* In a landmark chapter, Fischer et al. [8] have shown that no non–trivial agreement can be deterministically reached between processors in an asynchronous network in the possible presence of a single crash fault. On the other hand, Lamport et al. [17] have shown that in a synchronous system agreement can be reached even in the presence of (up to almost $N/3$) Byzantine faults. These results show that no deterministic synchronizer algorithm exists for fully asynchronous systems where processor crashes may occur. The implementation of fault–tolerant systems usually relies on the availability of clocks and an upper bound on message delays (the Asynchronous Bounded Delay assumption). The fault–tolerant synchronization of clocks (see Ramanathan *et al.* [24] for an overview article) is an important step in the implementation of a fully synchronous network.

5.2.   Other Topologies

In this chapter the orientation problem was studied for hypercubes and tori. Orientations of cliques can also be defined and orientation algorithms are given by Tel [30] for leader, named, and anonymous cliques. The problem can similarly be defined for other network topologies, such as shuffles, cube connected cycles, or multi dimensional grids. Orientations can easily be defined for these specific topologies, as was done for cliques, hypercubes, and tori.

Kranakis and Krizanc [16] define *Cayley networks* as follows. Let $\mathcal{G}$ be a (finite) group generated by $\{g_1, \ldots, g_k\}$. The Cayley network of $\mathcal{G}$ is the graph $G = (V, E)$ where $V = \mathcal{G}$ and $E = \{(x, y) \mid \exists i \, : \, x = g_i y \vee y = g_i x\}$. The network topologies considered in this chapter are special cases of Cayley networks, obtained by substituting for $\mathcal{G}$ groups with a relatively simple structure. More complicated groups give rise to different network topologies. Cayley networks can be naturally oriented by defining $\mathcal{O}_x(g_i x) = i$ and $\mathcal{O}_{g_i x}(x) = \bar{\imath}$. The related orientation problems may give rise to complicated algorithms, utilizing a large collection of algorithmical ingredients.

It is not clear whether the notion of orientations can be generalized to more general classes of topologies, for example, the class of all regular graphs. Orientations of planar graphs can be defined naturally. A labeling of a planar graph is an assignment in each node v of numbers from 1 to dgr_v to the edges of v. A labeling is an orientation if there exists a planar embedding of the graph, such that for each node the link labels increase in clockwise order.

Open Question 5.2 *Develop algorithms for the orientation of planar networks.*

5.3.   Termination and Termination Detection

This subsection discusses two different notions of termination, namely *processor termination* and *message termination*. Message terminating algorithms are simpler to design and can compute a larger class of functions. A brief discussion of the *termination detection problem* is included.

Processor and Message Termination.   The results in this chapter are derived for *processor terminating* algorithms. In these algorithms eventually a system configuration is reached in which all processors are in a terminated state. (Such a configuration is reached in all executions of a deterministic algorithm, and with probability 1 in a randomized algorithm.) In such a state, a processor is unable to execute further steps of the algorithm, and the values of its variables in that state are the output of the problem.

An algorithm is *message terminating* if eventually a configuration is reached where no further step of the algorithm can be taken, *i.e.*, all processors are either in a terminated state, or waiting to receive but there are no messages in the channels. (Such a configuration is reached in all executions of a deterministic algorithm, and with probability 1 in a randomized algorithm.) In a waiting state a processor is able to receive a message of the algorithm, which

```
        var a_v, b_v : integer ; (* Input, result *)

        begin b_v := a_v ;
                forall links k do send ⟨b_v⟩ via k ;
                while true do
                    begin receive ⟨b⟩ ;
                        if b > b_v then
                            begin b_v := b ;
                                forall links k do send ⟨b_v⟩ via k
                            end
                    end
            end
        end .
```

Algorithm 19. Computing the maximum in an anonymous network.

would change the value of its variables. In a message terminated configuration such a message will of course never arrive, but message termination is a property of the global configuration and is unobservable to a single processor. Hence a processor is not aware that its variable have converged to their final values (the "output" of the algorithm).

It has turned out, that message terminating algorithms are often simpler to design and verify, because aspects related to process termination can be ignored.

The Power of Termination.   Itai and Rodeh [11] have shown that in anonymous networks message terminating algorithms are able to compute a larger class of fuctions that processor terminating algorithms. An illustration of this result is found by considering the following problem. Each processor v in an anonymous network of unknown size has an input a_v, and it is required to compute in each processor the maximum over all inputs.

This computation can be carried out by a (deterministic) message terminating algorithm as stated in the following theorem.

Theorem 5.3 *Algorithm 19 terminates after exchanging at most NE messages. When the algorithm terminates, $b_v = \max_w a_w$ for each processor v.*

The proof is left as an exercise. On the other hand, the following impossibility result can be shown by methods similar to those used in the proof of theorem 4.9.

Theorem 5.4 *There exists no (randomized) processor terminating algorithm to compute the maximum of the inputs in an anonymous network of unknown size.*

Corollary 5.5 *The class of functions computable by message terminating algorithms is strictly larger than the class of functions computable by processor terminating algorithms, for anonymous networks of unknown size.*

Proof. That the first class includes the second class follows because a processor terminating algorithm is also message terminating. The strictness follows from the previous two theorems. □

Termination Detection. Just like algorithms for leader networks can be used for named networks by the application of an election algorithm, message terminating algorithms can be made processor terminating by the application of a *termination detection* algorithm. A termination detection algorithm runs concurrently with an arbitrary message terminating algorithm. When the latter algorithm reaches a message terminated configuration, the former algorithm eventually detects this and sends a terminate message to all processors.

The design of termination detection algorithms has received a lot of attention during the past decade. There do exist termination detection algorithms for leader networks (Dijkstra and Scholten [7]) and named networks (Tan and Van Leeuwen [28]). The existence of a termination detection algorithm for anonymous networks of known size follows from the results in this chapter or [29]. Corollary 5.5 implies that no termination detection algorithm exists for anonymous networks of unknown size.

Acknowledgements. The members of the Utrecht Distributed Algorithms Group are acknowledged for their stimulating discussions of the subject. I want to thank Anneke Schoone for her proof of theorem 3.9 and Petra van Haaften and Hans L. Bodlaender for their careful proofreading.

References

[1] Angluin, D., *Local and Global Properties in Networks of Processors*, in: *Proc. of the 12th ACM Symp. on Theory of Computing*, 1980, pp. 82-93.

[2] Awerbuch, B., *Complexity of Network Synchronization*, Journal of the ACM 32 (1985) 804–823.

[3] Beame, P.W., H.L. Bodlaender, *Distributed Computing on Transitive Networks: The Torus*, Tech. Rep. RUU-CS-88-31, University of Utrecht, Utrecht, 1988.

[4] Bodlaender, H.L., G. Tel, *Bit–Optimal Election in Synchronous Rings*, Inf. Proc. Lett. 36 (1990) 53–56. (This chapter appears in [31].)

[5] Bouabdallah, A., M. Naimi, *Parallel Assignment to Distinct Identities in an Arbitrary Network*, Report, Université de Besançon, 1989.

[6] Chang, E., R. Roberts, *An Improved Algorithm for Decentralized Extrema Finding in Circular Arrangements of Processes*, Comm. of the ACM 22 (1979) 281–283.

[7] Dijkstra, E.W., C.S. Scholten, *Termination Detection for Diffusing Computations*, Inf. Proc. Lett. 11 (1980) 1–4.

[8] Fischer, M.J., N.A. Lynch, M.S. Paterson, *Impossibility of Distributed Consensus with One Faulty Process*, Journal of the ACM 32 (1985) 374–382.

[9] Gallager, R.G., P.A. Humblet, P.M. Spira, *A Distributed Algorithm for Minimum–Weight Spanning Trees*, ACM Trans. on Prog. Lang. and Systems 5 (1983) 67-77.

[10] Israeli, A., M. Jalfon, *Uniform Self–Stabilizing Ring Orientation*, Information and Computation 1991.

[11] Itai, A., M. Rodeh, *Symmetry Breaking in Distributive Networks*, Proc. of Symposium on Theory of Computing, 1981, pp. 150–158.

[12] Korach, E., S. Moran, S. Zaks, *Tight Upper and Lower Bounds for Some Distributed Algorithms for a Complete Network of Processors*, Proc. of 3rd Conf. on Principles of Distributed Computing, 1984, pp. 199–207.

[13] Korach, E., G. Tel, S. Zaks, *Optimal Synchronization of ABD Networks*, in: F.H. Vogt (ed.), *Concurrency 88*, Lecture Notes in Computer Science, vol. 335, Springer Verlag, 1988, pp. 277–291. (This chapter appears in [31].)

[14] Korfhage, W., E. Gafni, *Orienting a Unidirectional Torus Network*, Manuscript.

[15] Kranakis, E., D. Krizanc, *Computing Boolean Functions on Anonymous Hypercube Networks*, Tech. Rep. CWI, Amsterdam, 1990.

[16] Kranakis, E., D. Krizanc, *Computing Boolean Functions on Cayley Networks*, Tech. Rep. CWI, Amsterdam, 1990.

[17] Lamport, L., R. Shostak, M. Pease, *The Byzantine Generals Problem*, ACM Trans. on Programming Languages and Systems 4 (1982) 382–401.

[18] Loui, M.C., T.A. Matsushita, D.B. West, *Election in Complete Networks with a Sense of Direction*. Inf. Proc. Lett. 22 (1986) 185–187 and I.P.L. 28 (1988) 327.

[19] Matias, Y., Y. Afek, *Simple and Efficient Election Algorithms for Anonymous Networks*, in: J.C. Bermond, M. Raynal (eds), *Distributed Algorithms*, LNCS 392, Springer Verlag, 1989, pp. 183-194.

[20] Mattern, F., *Verteilte Basisalgorithmen*, Springer Verlag, Informatik Fachberichte 226, 1989.

[21] Moran, S., Y. Wolfstahl, *Extended Impossibility Results for Asynchronous Complete Networks*, Information Processing Letters 26 (1987) 145–151.

[22] Peterson, G.L., *Efficient Algorithms for Elections in Meshes and Complete Networks*, Tech. Rep. TR-140, Univ. of Rochester, Rochester, 1985.

[23] Pachl, J., E. Korach, D. Rotem, *Lower Bounds for Distributed Maximum Finding Algorithms*, Journal of the ACM 31 (1984) 905–918.

[24] Ramanathan, P., K.G. Shin, R.W. Butler, *Fault–Tolerant Clock Synchronization in Distributed Systems*, IEEE Computer (October 1990) 33–42.

[25] Santoro, N., *Sense of Direction, Topological Awareness, and Communication Complexity*, ACM SIGACT News 16 (Summer 1984) 50–56.

[26] Syrotiuk, V., J. Pachl, *A Distributed Ring Orientation Problem*, in: J. van Leeuwen (ed.), *Distributed Algorithms*, Springer Verlag LNCS 312, 1987, 332–336.

[27] Schieber, B., M. Snir, *Calling Names on Nameless Networks*, in: *Proc. of the ACM Symp. on Principles of Distributed Computing*, 1989, pp. 319-328.

[28] Tan, R.B., J. van Leeuwen, *General Symmetric Distributed Termination Detection*, Technical Report RUU–CS–86–2, Dept. of Computer Science, Utrecht University, 1986.

[29] Tel, G., *Total Algorithms*, Algorithms Review 1 (1990) 13–42. (This chapter appears in [31].)

[30] Tel, G., *Network Orientation*, Technical Report RUU–CS–91–8, Dept. of Computer Science, Utrecht University, 1991.

[31] Tel, G., *Topics in Distributed Algorithms*, Cambridge International Series on Parallel Computation, vol. 1, Cambridge University Press, 1991.

[32] Vitanyi, P.M.B., *Time–Driven Algorithms for Distributed Control*, Tech. Rep. CS–R8510, CWI, Amsterdam, 1985.

Chapter 12

Special Purpose Parallel Computing

W F McColl *

Abstract

A vast amount of work has been done in recent years on the design, analysis, implementation and verification of special purpose parallel computing systems. This chapter presents a survey of various aspects of this work. A long, but by no means complete, bibliography is given.

1. Introduction

Turing [365] demonstrated that, in principle, a single general purpose sequential machine could be designed which would be capable of efficiently performing any computation which could be performed by a special purpose sequential machine. The importance of this universality result for subsequent practical developments in computing cannot be overstated. It showed that, for a given computational problem, the additional efficiency advantages which could be gained by designing a special purpose sequential machine for that problem would not be great.

Around 1944, von Neumann produced a proposal [66, 389] for a general purpose stored-program sequential computer which captured the fundamental principles of Turing's work in a practical design. The design, which has come to be known as the "von Neumann computer", has served as the basic model for almost all sequential computers produced from the late 1940s to the present time. As noted in [163], "The paper by Burks, Goldstine and von Neumann ([66]) was incredible for the period. Reading it today, one would never guess this landmark paper was written more than 40 years ago, as most of the architectural concepts seen in modern computers are described there." For an account of the principles of modern general purpose sequential (i.e. von Neumann) computer design, see e.g. [163]. For sequential computation, the stability of the von Neumann model has permitted the development, over the last three decades, of a variety of high level languages and compilers. These have, in turn, encouraged the development of a large and diverse software industry producing portable applications software for the wide range of von Neumann machines available, from personal computers to large mainframes. The stability of the underlying model has also allowed the development of a robust complexity theory for sequential computation and a set of algorithm design and software development techniques of wide applicability.

No single model of parallel computation has yet come to dominate developments in parallel computing in the way the von Neumann model has dominated sequential computing [135,

---

*This chapter was written while the author was a Visiting Scientist at NEC Research Institute, Princeton, USA.

375, 376]. Instead we have a variety of models such as VLSI circuits, systolic arrays and distributed memory multicomputers, in which the careful exploitation of network locality is crucial for algorithmic efficiency, and some models such as the PRAM in which there is no notion of network locality whatsoever. In this chapter we will be concerned with the locality-based models. In the related chapter [272] we consider locality-independent models and examine the prospects they offer for achieving the goal of a robust general purpose parallel computing framework, comparable to that provided for sequential computing by the von Neumann model.

2.   Network Locality

In the 1970s it became clear [211, 280, 355] that developments in VLSI technology would permit, not only the design of cheaper and faster general purpose sequential computers, but also the design of cost-effective special purpose parallel systems for computationally intensive problems. In [279], it was shown that the basic principles of VLSI design could be understood at a level somewhat above that of device physics. The publication of [279] had an immediate and profound impact. A large number of computer scientists were encouraged to think about the design and analysis of algorithms for implementation, not as programs to be run on a general purpose computer, but as special purpose hardware, for example, as custom VLSI chips or as systolic arrays.

In the early 1980s the first distributed memory multicomputers began to appear, e.g. [170, 181, 339, 397]. These systems consisted of a set of general purpose microprocessors connected by a sparse communications network, e.g. an array, butterfly or hypercube. As each processor typically had its own private physical memory module, the most natural memory organisation in these early architectures was to have multiple private address spaces with explicit message passing by the programmer [168, 170, 187] for all non-local memory requests. In most of the early multicomputer systems, message passing was implemented using simple, store-and-forward communication, and hence was extremely slow for messages which had to pass through a number of intermediate processors before reaching the destination processor. The key to algorithmic efficiency in each of these types of system - VLSI chips, systolic arrays and multicomputers, is the careful exploitation of *network locality*. In the different types of system it manifests itself in different ways. In a VLSI system, a design with good network locality will have short wires, and hence will require less area. An efficient systolic algorithm will have a simple, regular structure and use only nearest neighbour communication. An efficient multicomputer algorithm will be one which minimises the distance that messages have to travel in the network by careful mapping of the virtual process structure onto the physical processor architecture. Of course, an efficient algorithm for, say, a hypercube multicomputer will not necessarily perform well when run on, for example, a 2D array multicomputer with the same number of processors.

The exploitation of network locality to achieve efficiency is the main idea which unites the various parallel algorithms which we describe in this chapter. We will use the generic term "special purpose" to refer to this type of parallel computing. It can be contrasted with the development of algorithms for what we will refer to as a "general purpose" system [272], i.e. one in which the costs of communication between pairs of processors in the system is essentially uniform for all pairs. Examples of general purpose architectures, in this sense, would be the PRAM or the bulk-synchronous parallel computer [375, 376]. If architectures which efficiently support such a uniform memory model can be realised then they will offer major advantages in simultaneously providing both architecture-independence in software and scalable parallel performance. However, as noted in the next section, there are a number of application areas in parallel computing, e.g. signal processing, where the special purpose approach is likely to continue to be the method of choice.

Significant motivation for the special purpose approach is often drawn from the fact that computation is a physical process and must therefore be carried out in physical 3D space. Some, e.g. [232, 233, 383, 384] argue that this is such a fundamental constraint that it should play a major role in determining the model of parallel computation to be used in algorithm design. While accepting the validity of these physical 3D space arguments, the advocate of a more network-independent general purpose approach (such as the current author) would argue that, first and foremost, a model must be mathematically robust if it is to find widespread acceptance as a basis for the design and analysis of algorithms. Two examples of mathematically robust models are the unit cost RAM for sequential computation and the PRAM for idealised parallel computation. Both have proven to be very appropriate for encouraging the development of a wide variety of algorithms and design techniques, although neither reflects the true costs of physical computation in a highly accurate way. The major disadvantage of adopting a physically based model is, however, that it is likely to accurately reflect the costs of only one technology. There is strong evidence that the various costs associated with the emerging optical technologies are likely to be quite different from those which apply with VLSI semiconductor technologies. We will return to this issue later in the chapter. Irrespective of one's opinion on the special purpose/general purpose issue, there can be no doubt that many of the special purpose designs produced in recent years are remarkable achievements in terms of the complex dynamic patterns of communication which are involved. The constraint of having to strive for network locality has, in many cases, resulted in algorithm designs of great elegance and ingenuity. The fact that many of the algorithms are indeed so intricate does, of course, indicate that it may be difficult for this style of "special purpose parallel programming" to become a mainstream activity in computing, as opposed to a niche.

3. Applications

Special purpose parallel systems are particularly appropriate in application areas where the goal of achieving the best possible performance is much more appropriate than that of achieving an architecture-independent design. In this section we briefly describe some of those areas.

The design of a high-performance special purpose system will often require the solution of a number of low level design problems such as efficient process mapping to minimise communication distances, or careful VLSI layout to minimise chip area. These extra difficulties in design can be justified in a number of situations. The most obvious one is where it is the only known way of achieving the required performance. Another is where the system is to form part of a high volume product, and therefore the extra design costs can be justified if they result in a system which is more cost-effective in performance when manufactured. Performance requirements come in a variety of forms. A robot control system may have strict real-time performance requirements which must be met, e.g. that the computation performed be completed in some given fraction of a second. Another example of a parallel computing application with a rather strict performance requirement is weather prediction. A prediction of the weather for a given day is only of value if it is produced before that day! For a third example of an area where achieving a given level of performance is crucial we need look no further than the design of computing systems themselves. Modern VLSI systems are amongst the most complex engineering designs ever produced. Even using the best algorithms known, the simulation of a VLSI circuit for the purpose of detecting errors in the design can take months on a supercomputer. In a highly competitive and fast moving industry such as the semiconductor industry, the time taken to complete such a simulation may seriously affect when the company can get the product onto the market, with poten- tially drastic consequences for sales. These three examples indicate the kinds of performance requirements which can justify the extra design difficulties associated with special purpose systems.

The "high volume" justification for special purpose design arises in application areas such as data compression and computer graphics where the market for a high-performance system is very large. It is likely that in the coming decade there will be major growth in the demand for "smart" consumer goods and user interface devices of all kinds. These are likely to be produced as application specific parallel architectures with similar characteristics to those described in this chapter.

As a general rule, special purpose systems tend to be developed in areas where the basic algorithmic techniques involved are reasonably stable and well understood. The relative inflexibility of the design process tends to rule out application areas where a wide variety of high level algorithmic approaches are possible, and those where the algorithms and data structures involved are complex, dynamic and irregular. An area such as signal processing would appear to be ideally suited to the special purpose approach, whereas, at the present time at least, a complex, knowledge based system would not appear to be, although some computationally intensive component of it might be. In the remainder of this section we list a number of application areas for which special purpose systems are particularly appropriate at the present time. The list is not meant to be exhaustive, but merely to indicate the wide range of areas.

Digital Signal Processing

For a combination of technical, economic and performance reasons, a large number of digital signal processing applications are appropriate for special purpose implementation. Many such systems have been produced in recent years for various kinds of filtering and transform computations [214, 217]. Filtering: FIR, IIR, Wiener, Kalman, 1D and 2D convolution and correlation, 1D and 2D interpolation and resampling, template matching [214, 320]. Transforms: FFT, Walsh-Hadamard, discrete cosine, Hough, Karhunen-Loeve [40, 43, 89, 214, 358]. Another important application area is radar signal processing.

Image Processing and Pattern Recognition

As in the case of digital signal processing, many image processing applications require only relatively simple algorithmic structures, although they need to be performed very rapidly on large data sets [212, 214, 304, 312]. Some examples of computationally intensive problems in this area are: restoration, reconstruction, enhancement and smoothing, edge and line detection, template matching, texture analysis, basic geometric operations, syntactic pattern recognition, scene analysis, low level computer vision. For almost a decade, the NASA

Goddard Space Flight Center has been successfully using a 128×128 processor MPP system [23] for image processing applications [352]. This array architecture was specifically design to handle such problems.

Linear Algebra

For many fundamental linear algebra computations, if one is dealing with dense matrices or sparse regular matrices then one can obtain very efficient special purpose designs through the exploitation of network locality based on the matrix structure. Examples of such computations are: matrix multiplication, LU factorisation, Cholesky factorisation, solution of general, tridiagonal and triangular linear systems, matrix inversion, iterative solution of linear systems (e.g. using the conjugate gradient method), singular value decomposition, eigenvalue problems, QR factorisation, least squares problems, recursive least squares, [34, 85, 131, 132, 136, 137, 160, 162, 182, 185, 306, 311, 318, 331, 378]. The volume of published literature on this topic is huge. A bibliography on parallel numerical algorithms which contains over 2000 entries, many of them concerned with dense linear algebra computations, was produced in 1989 [296]. A useful entry point to the field is the survey paper [132].

Unfortunately, many linear algebra computations arising in practical applications involve very large sparse matrices with no regular structure [80, 86, 105, 138, 159, 191]. The efficient parallel solution of linear systems of this kind is generally much more complex than in the case of dense matrices. It often requires a number of very intricate algorithms and data structures to achieve acceptable efficiency. An excellent account of the difficulties involved in producing efficient parallel algorithms for the problem of sparse Cholesky factorisation can be found in [159]. Efficient Cholesky factorisation of large sparse matrices arises in a considerable number of computationally intensive applications. For example, it is at the heart of most of the modern interior point approaches to large scale linear programming [79, 173]. The careful exploitation of network locality seems less likely to deliver substantial additional performance gains in the case of large sparse irregular matrices. A random mapping of processes to processors, based simply on the goal of load balancing, may provide performance comparable to the best that could be achieved by careful design based on network locality. A similar situation exists with respect to many graph theoretic problems. The difficulty of designing efficient parallel algorithms for large sparse irregular matrix and graph problems provides a major practical impetus to much of the current work aimed at producing a more network-independent, general purpose approach to parallel computing. In [139] it is noted that some shared memory is desirable in parallel sparse matrix computations.

Scientific Computation

In industries such as the aerospace industry, the modelling of very complex scientific phenomena, e.g. turbulence, is an integral part of the design process. At present, such modelling problems account for a large percentage of the total time spent on all parallel supercomputers in use around the world. The problem areas include the following: computational fluid dynamics, direct and iterative solution of PDEs [266], 2D and 3D Navier-Stokes equations, lattice gas methods [46, 76, 100, 124, 125], finite element and finite volume methods [185, 186], multigrid methods [70, 299], climate modelling, weather prediction.

Simulation

In recent years, a number of new efficient algorithms have been developed for performing complex n-body particle simulations arising in astronomy, where the particles are interacting in a gravitational field, and in molecular modelling, where they are interacting in a Coulombic field [21, 147, 148, 257, 347, 410]. The implementation of these new methods on special purpose parallel architectures has enabled simulations to be performed on a scale which would have been unthinkable until recently. There is considerable scope for further improvements in this direction. Discrete-event simulation is another area where special purpose systems are appropriate, in view of the very specific techniques, such as the Time Warp mechanism of lookahead and rollback, which are currently being used to achieve concurrency in such simulations [128, 129, 130, 287]. Monte Carlo simulation was originally developed by Fermi, von Neumann and Ulam to solve certain problems related to neutron transport. Since then it has been widely used in applications where the goal is to accurately reproduce the microscopic dynamics of some statistical physical system [155]. For example, in the electronics industry it is used to model transport in semiconductor devices and to perform process modelling. The Monte Carlo method is also frequently used for the numerical evaluation of multidimensional integrals for which no analytical solution can be obtained. As in the case of the n-body simulations, special purpose parallel architectures will open up the possibility of performing Monte Carlo simulations with a greatly increased number of points, yielding results of much greater accuracy.

Communications

Although the capacity of communication networks is increasing steadily, the demands being placed upon such networks is probably increasing more rapidly. The development of special purpose parallel devices which quickly compress and expand text [356], images, audio and video [361] for more efficient use of communication networks is likely to be a major activity in the next few years. Other special purpose communications devices which give high performance encoding and decoding for error correction, and encryption and decryption for data security [345] are also likely to be in big demand.

Computer Graphics and Computational Geometry

Three-dimensional medical imaging [353], computer-aided design and solid modelling systems [406], spatial databases and computational geometry [74, 370], robot motion planning, scientific data visualisation, realistic image synthesis [97, 127, 303], ray tracing [144], animation, virtual reality systems, multimedia systems, high-definition television etc.

Molecular Modelling

Drug design has until recently been conducted in a rather haphazard manner. In an attempt to make it more rational and scientific, major pharmaceutical companies and large medical and scientific research organisations are increasingly using advanced computer systems to calculate the structure and dynamics of large biological macromolecules (proteins, carbohydrates and nucleic acids) using molecular mechanics [271, 349], molecular dynamics [267, 271, 349, 379, 380], free energy calculations [22] and quantum mechanical methods

[134, 161, 167]. At present, even very simple molecular modelling calculations of this kind can take months on the fastest available commercial supercomputers. Special purpose parallel architectures can provide improvements of orders of magnitude in performance. Other computationally demanding molecular modelling applications include structure prediction from NMR data using distance geometry methods [51, 92, 158] and modelling of new materials.

VLSI Design

The design and simulation of VLSI circuits requires a number of specialised tools for problems such as layout and wire routing, design rule checking, logic verification, switch-level simulation and circuit simulation [142, 279, 396]. Each of these is a major computationally intensive problem. The size of VLSI circuits continues to increase rapidly, creating a growing demand for very high performance special purpose parallel systems for these tasks. In performing layout and wire routing [239, 369], one is typically aiming to minimise the area required for the circuit, as the size of a chip can significantly affect the yield obtained when it is fabricated. Optimisation techniques such as simulated annealing can often be used to produce layouts which are close to optimal [1, 2, 196, 381]. The purpose of design rule checking is to ensure that all geometric features laid out on each mask meet the size, spacing and overlap rules. These design rules are specific to the technology and fabrication process to be employed. The geometric computation performed by a design rule checker [190] is similar to that performed by a hidden-line algorithm in computer graphics. The various types of VLSI verification and simulation are as follows. In logic verification, the circuit is modelled as a set of gates and flip-flops and the task is to verify that the design meets a specification given in some formalism such as higher-order logic [87] or temporal logic [63] For a survey of approaches to logic verification, see [275] and various other papers in [276]. In switch-level simulation, each transistor is modelled as a voltage-controlled switch which can be in a small fixed number of states [18, 64, 202]. A circuit simulation is the most detailed type of analysis and is usually only applied to small parts of a circuit design. Such simulations are often performed to get accurate information on timing delays. A well known example of a circuit simulator is the program SPICE [385] which models circuits containing transistors. A simulator such as SPICE solves the set of nonlinear equations corresponding to the electrical behaviour of the components in the circuit (gate capacitances, electron mobilities etc.) and the topology of those components. Standard algorithms such as Newton-Raphson are used.

Speech Processing

Continuous speech recognition, dynamic programming methods (time warps)[126, 405], speech synthesis.

Computational Physics

Lattice-gauge theories and quantum chromodynamics (QCD) [29, 32, 99].

Game Playing

Progress in computer chess in recent years has largely been based on the exploitation of special purpose parallel architectures [107, 174, 175]. It seems probable that the first non-human World Chess Champion will be a special purpose parallel computing system.

Control

Industrial control, mobile robot control etc. [61, 62]

Database Systems

Text retrieval, pattern matching in protein and nucleic acid sequence databases (Human Genome Project) [15, 246, 271, 329], relational databases (fast SQL servers) [210, 244], on-line transaction processing etc.

Financial Modelling

The valuation of complex financial instruments that appear in the banking and insurance industries requires simulation of their cashflow behaviour in a volatile interest rate environment. These simulations can be very computationally intensive and can benefit enormously from parallel computing. The use of parallelism in the simulation of multiple paths of interest rates is relatively straightforward. To exploit parallelism in performing a path dependent calculation along each of the paths one can use techniques such as parallel prefix computation [44, 45, 218]. Using advanced parallel systems, Hutchinson and Zenios [179] have shown that it is possible to perform the valuation of a single mortgage-backed security in real time (1-2 seconds) and that the analysis of a portfolio of such securities can be performed very rapidly. In the future, special purpose parallel systems are likely to offer significant advantages to those engaged in activities such as real-time trading and planning in the face of uncertain interest rates.

4.   Technologies

Special purpose parallel systems can be realised using a wide variety of technologies. In this section we describe a number of those technologies.

4.1.   VLSI Systems

The design and fabrication of a custom VLSI circuit [142, 279, 396] is one approach to implementing a special purpose system. Since the publication of [279], the principles of VLSI design have become not only a mainstream part of electronics but also of computer science. A large number of new and interesting VLSI designs for basic problems in computer science have been produced as a result [24, 75, 238, 240, 357, 369, 394]. At present, VLSI is essentially a two dimensional technology. A VLSI circuit is formed from a small (fixed) number of two dimensional layers, the exact number of layers depending on the particular type of circuit, e.g. CMOS [396]. More advanced fabrication processes in the future may permit full three dimensional VLSI designs to be realised. Although such a technological advance may yield more efficient devices, it is not likely to dramatically change the principles of efficient VLSI design which have been developed in recent years. We would instead see our current concern for area efficiency in the two dimensional model being replaced by a corresponding concern for volume efficiency in the three dimensional model. In fact, some theoretical work in this direction has already been done [229, 305, 322]. The impact of a technological change such as the replacement of VLSI by free-space optical systems [113, 252] would, on the other hand, be a fundamental change, with profound implications for the design and analysis of algorithms.

In deciding whether to implement a special purpose parallel system as a custom VLSI chip one has to weigh the advantages against the disadvantages. The arguments in favour of a custom VLSI implementation are typically that one can obtain the highest possible performance by that means and/or that one will be able to manufacture the custom VLSI system more cheaply. The latter may be very significant if it is to form part of a high volume product. The major disadvantages of custom VLSI design and implementation is that it is a very costly and time consuming process, and that it results in a product which cannot easily be changed. Although a large number of interesting and detailed VLSI algorithm designs have been developed over the last decade, remarkably few of them have actually been realised as custom chips. The reason for this is, of course, that few organisations can justify the prohibitive costs of producing such a chip.

4.1.1. Field-Programmable Gate Arrays

In the last five years, companies such as Xilinx [407] and Algotronix [7] have started to offer an attractive alternative to custom VLSI implementation. A field-programmable gate array (FPGA) [7, 33, 108, 253, 290, 298, 345, 407] consists of a matrix of logic cells with switched interconnections between them. The interconnections are configured afresh whenever the equipment is started up, by a program downloaded to the chip. By appropriate setting of the switching points, the programmer can group and interconnect the gates into useful functions: counters, flip-flops, shift registers, clocks, multiplexers, buffers, NOR gates, XOR gates etc.

The first gate array devices appeared in the 1970s. They were developed to provide a middle ground between off-the-shelf chips and full custom designs. They are essentially rows and columns of logic gates overlaid with rows and columns of metal paths. Customisation takes place in the last steps of the fabrication process using a design specific mask. These mask-programmed gate arrays offer a very large number of gates to work with. However, they suffer from the same problems as custom chips, they are expensive to produce and cannot be changed. Another approach is the programmable logic device. These are often structured as an array of AND gates with their outputs feeding into an array of OR gates. The earliest of these were programmed by electrically selecting and destroying fuses on the chip, leaving the desired interconnections intact. Later devices were electrically reprogrammable using ultraviolet-light-erasable memory technology. Programmable logic devices typically offer far fewer gates than FPGAs or mask-programmed arrays.

Compared to the other approaches, FPGAs would appear to offer an excellent compromise between flexibility and performance. As more powerful high-level design tools for FPGAs are developed [253, 298], the use of such arrays is likely to grow substantially in application areas where the volumes are insufficient to justify implementation either as a custom VLSI chip or as a mask-programmed gate array. FPGAs will also provide an unprecedented opportunity for computer scientists to pursue the development of high performance implementations of their parallel algorithms without requiring the services of a VLSI fabrication facility. We can look forward to a number of exciting new VLSI systems emerging as a consequence of this new found freedom.

4.1.2. Self-Timed and Delay-Insensitive Circuits

The complexity of custom VLSI systems has reached the point where the design time and design cost can greatly exceed the fabrication time and fabrication cost. Moreover, most VLSI systems designed today are monolithic and cannot easily be modified or improved [354]. A significant factor giving rise to this design difficulty and inflexibility is the synchronous nature of such systems. In recent years, a number of researchers have been investigating the possibilities of designing alternative forms of VLSI systems, such as self-timed and delay-insensitive circuits, which are not subject to the limitations imposed by the traditional clocked-logic framework [109, 262, 263, 338, 354, 368]. The use of delay-insensitive circuits, for example, can greatly simplify design at the system level as correct timing and control of operations can be achieved without explicit consideration by the system designer of circuit and interconnection delays, or of clock generation and distribution between components of the system. Only the sequences of operations to be performed need to be considered, not the times for performing each operation; operations are initiated after their predecessors are completed, not after some fixed and independently determined time. Such an approach offers the opportunity to build up complex systems by hierarchical composition from simpler ones, as in the case of modern software development methodologies. The resulting system designs are easier to modify and improve, in order to meet changing requirements or to take advantage of developments in VLSI technology. As in the case of FPGAs, the development of formal design methodologies and high-level design tools will result in self-timed and delay-insensitive circuits being used more and more as a means of implementing application specific VLSI designs.

4.2. Systolic Algorithms and Architectures

The concept of a "systolic array" was introduced by Kung and Leiserson in [211] where they describe the VLSI implementation of some matrix computations. In an outstanding paper, published slightly later [207], Kung discussed the key architectural issues involved in designing high performance special purpose parallel systems, and showed convincingly that the systolic approach offered an excellent means of producing such systems. A major problem in the design of special purpose parallel architectures is the input/output bottleneck. The systolic approach makes extensive use of pipelining, so that a large number of operations are performed on an input before it is output again. By increasing the ratio of computation to input/output in this way, a more balanced parallel design can be achieved which has no bottleneck at any point. Since those early papers, a whole subfield of parallel computing has developed, based around the concept of systolic computation, see e.g. [149, 206, 214, 231, 250, 258, 268, 277, 279, 291, 308, 309, 317]. Systolic array designs, and the related wavefront designs [213, 214], can be implemented in a variety of different ways. Depending on the application area and the performance requirements, they can be realised as custom VLSI systems, as FPGAs, or as programs to be run on a multicomputer. The wide range of applications for which the systolic approach is appropriate, has also motivated the development of programmable systolic machines.

4.2.1. Programmable Systolic Architectures

A group at Carnegie Mellon University, headed by H T Kung, started the development of a programmable systolic computer called Warp in 1984 [11]. Warp is a systolic array computer consisting of a linearly connected set of cells. Each cell contains a high performance programmable processor, a large local memory, and high bandwidth communications channels to adjacent cells in the linear array. The first ten-cell prototype was completed in 1986 and delivery of production machines started in 1987. A large number of computationally intensive application programs have been developed for the Warp architecture using the language W2 [11]. The applications include low-level vision for robot navigation, image processing, signal processing, scientific computing, magnetic resonance imagery, radar and sonar simulation, graph algorithms. The Warp project demonstrated the feasibility of programmable, high performance systolic array computers. In a successor project, Intel and Carnegie Mellon University have been developing the iWarp parallel architecture [27, 49, 50, 208]. Although based on the original Warp design, iWarp has added much more flexibility in the types of communication that can be efficiently supported. In particular, non-neighbour communication can be performed without involving programs at intervening cells. Also, iWarp architectures can handle intercell communication patterns which are quite different from the hardware interconnnect in the system, using techniques such as logical channels and wormhole routing. Unlike Warp, the iWarp design is probably best viewed as a modern general purpose multicomputer design with some special features to support the important class of systolic parallel computations.

4.3. Cellular Automata

The remarkable success of von Neumann's work on general purpose sequential computing has tended to link his name very strongly with the idea of sequential computation in the minds of many. However, he was also, in many ways, the major pioneer in parallel computing.

In the late 1940s, von Neumann began to develop a theory of automata. He envisaged a systematic theory which would be both mathematical and logical in form, and which would contribute in an essential way to our understanding of natural systems (natural automata) as well as to our understanding of both analog and digital computers (artificial automata). By the time of his premature death in February 1957, he had made major contributions in a variety of areas related to this general programme. He had developed the basic theory of self-reproducing cellular automata [388], demonstrated that reliable systems could be constructed from unreliable components [386], and had started to examine the structure and function of neural systems [387]. In this section we describe some of the achievements of von Neumann and others in the area of cellular automata, and discuss the significance of the model for the field of special purpose parallel computation. An up to date account of work on the development of reliable systems, stemming from his work in [386], can be found in [302]. The topic of neural systems will be briefly discussed at the end of the chapter.

Influenced by the work of Turing [365] and others on the theory of automata and universal computing machines, von Neumann set himself the goal of producing a system which would be capable of self-reproduction. In his early studies of this problem he explored a continuous model of self-reproducing automaton based on a system of nonlinear partial differential equations. He also pursued the idea of a kinematic automaton which could, using a description of itself, proceed to mechanically assemble a duplicate from available parts. When he found it difficult to provide the rigorous and explicit rules and instructions needed to realise such an automaton, he redirected his efforts towards a model of self-reproducing automata based on an array of computing elements. [The idea of using such a parallel array had been suggested to him by S Ulam.] He eventually succeeded in designing a self-reproducing two dimensional cellular automaton [388], although the design he produced was extremely complex. It required around 200,000 computing elements, each of which could be in one of 29 states. [A *cellular automaton* consists of a set of identical cells arranged in a regular lattice structure with connections between each cell and its neighbours in the lattice. At a given time step $t + 1$, the new state of each cell is computed in parallel as a function of the state of the cell and its neighbours at time t.] The complexity of von Neumann's design stemmed largely from the fact that he had tried to design not only a self-reproducing system but also one which would be a universal computing machine, equivalent in power to a Turing machine. Later work by Codd [83] produced a self-reproducing universal computing machine which required just 8 states per cell. Although simpler than von Neumann's, Codd's machine is still as complex as a modern digital computer. As noted by Langton [220], universality is a sufficient condition for self-reproduction, however it is not a necessary condition. In his paper, Langton [220] describes a very simple self-reproducing cellular automaton which is not based on the idea of a universal computing machine. Following the work of von Neumann, a great deal of work was done in the 1960s on the theoretical aspects of various types of cellular automata, see [65, 402].

In 1970, J H Conway produced a particularly interesting cellular automaton which he called "Life". Life is a two state cellular automaton on an infinite two dimensional grid. Each cell is either on or off, and the simple Life rule is the following. *If two of the eight nearest neighbours are on, then don't change. If three are on, then turn on. Otherwise, turn off.* Life may be thought of as describing a population of organisms, developing in time under the effect of counteracting propagation and extinction tendencies. A live cell will remain alive only when surrounded by two or three live neighbours, otherwise, it will feel either "overcrowded" or "too lonely" and will die. A dead cell will come to life when surrounded by exactly three live neighbours. Thus birth is induced by the meeting of three "parents". Conway's "Game of Life" was extensively reported by Martin Gardner in his widely read Scientific American column [133] and caught the attention of scientific amateurs and professionals all over the world. As a result, the incredible properties of various Life forms such as blinkers, gliders, glider guns, puffer trains, Catherine wheels, traffic lights and so on, became familiar to a large number of people, many of whom would otherwise have had little interest in cellular automata. A definitive account of these various forms can be found in [31] where it is also shown that Life can be used to construct a universal computing machine and, hence, can also be used to achieve self-replication. It is remarkable that a two state cellular automaton with such a simple rule can produce such complex phenomena. A number of three dimensional variants of Life have been studied by Bays [28]. A description of a one dimensional universal cellular automaton can be found in [245].

In the early 1980s, a number of researchers began to study cellular automata as models of complex dynamical systems and, more generally, as an alternative to differential equations in modelling physical phenomena [112, 259, 363, 382, 402]. Researchers such as Toffoli and Margolus have also produced various special purpose parallel machines for the simulation of cellular automata models [260, 261, 362, 364]. These machines provide performance at least several orders of magnitude greater than with a sequential computer, for a comparable cost. They have been used for a variety of physical modelling problems, including computing time correlations, self-diffusion, thermalisation, reflection and refraction, flow tracing, diffusion-limited aggregation, Ising spin systems, annealing, erosion, genetic drift, and spatial reactions. For details, see [261, 364]. As noted in [261], the advantages of using a special purpose parallel architecture optimised for cellular automata simulations are so great that for large scale cellular automata experiments, it would be absurd to use any other type of system. In terms of its impact on the development of special purpose parallel computing systems, one of the most important results of this research on "digital physics" has been the development of lattice gas methods for fluid flow problems.

4.3.1. Lattice Gas Computers

Partial differential equations have conventionally formed the basis of mathematical models of physical systems such as fluids. Only in rather simple circumstances can exact solutions to such equations be found. Most studies of fluid dynamics must therefore be based on digital calculations, which use discrete approximations to the original partial differential equations.

In recent years, an important class of cellular automata, called lattice gas automata, have been successfully used to model a variety of physical systems traditionally modelled by partial differential equations. Although the idea of using discrete methods such as cellular automata for modelling PDEs has been around for along time, the actual statement that cellular automata techniques could be used to approximate the solution of hydrodynamic PDEs was first discovered in August 1985 by Frisch, Hasslacher and Pomeau. For a description of the derivation, which assumes the validity of the Boltzmann equation, see [125]. The original demonstration by Frisch, Hasslacher and Pomeau of the validity of the lattice gas approach applied only to low-velocity incompressible flows near equilibrium. Since then, a huge amount of work has been carried out on the lattice gas method, and the range of applications for which the approach can be used is increasing steadily, see [46, 76, 100, 124, 364, 402].

One of the main reasons for the surge of interest in lattice gas methods has been the simple, regular and massively parallel nature of such computations and the prospects that offers for constructing special purpose lattice gas computers. Various designs for lattice gas architectures have been produced in the last few years [96, 204, 261]. Studies of related issues such as the problem of input/output complexity in lattice gas computations [203, 295] have also been carried out. Special purpose lattice gas architectures are likely to be the only way of achieving the performance required by researchers working on three dimensional fluid flow problems using these methods. A good indication of the requirements of such researchers can be seen in the target performance parameters in [96] for a dedicated lattice gas computer for the mid 1990s. They call for the design of a system capable of performing three dimensional incompressible hydrodynamics with flexible boundary conditions. It should have some flexibility in the possible rule sets for the lattice gas, have a high input/output rate, have around 10^{11} lattice sites (or cells), and should perform about 6×10^{15} site updates per second in total. It is unlikely that anything other than a very specialised system could come close to achieving these requirements.

Over the past few years, the technology for manipulating and observing material on an atomic scale has advanced at an astonishing pace. Although moving individual atoms is still essentially a laboratory game, laying down thin films of atoms has become serious business. By controlling precisely the structure and composition of layers of materials only an atom or two thick, scientists are demonstrating that they can program the electronic characteristics they want into a compound. Scientists have also succeeded in producing a variety of exotic quantum devices: two dimensional quantum wells, one dimensional quantum wires, and recently zero dimensional quantum dots [90, 143]. These developments open the way for a number of exciting new electronic and optical devices which would be much smaller, faster and more highly parallel than anything available today. Several researchers are currently working on techniques to produce two dimensional arrays of quantum dots. As each such dot can have multiple energy levels, it can, in principle, replace a number of conventional transistors. The physical structure of such an array should also allow adjacent quantum dots to communicate in certain ways. Arrays of this kind may, in the coming years, provide the means of developing quantum dot cellular automata machines of incredible computing power [90]. The exploration of array designs which permit quantum dot coupling of various kinds has only just begun. We can look forward some interesting possibilities for special purpose parallel computing systems from this work.

When Richard Feynman addressed the annual meeting of the American Physical Society on 29th December 1959, electrical engineers were struggling with the problems of fitting a few components on a chip. Nevertheless, Feynman, in a visionary lecture, described some of the opportunities for technology which would eventually emerge when single atoms and molecules could be manipulated. The text of his lecture was originally published as [114]. Feynman described techniques for developing computers with wires that were between 10 and 100 atoms in diameter, and circuits which were a few thousand angstroms across. He described the physics which would apply to circuits consisting of only a few atoms, and showed that such devices would present completely new opportunities for design. Feynman's remarkable ideas had little impact during the 1960s and 1970s, as the technology available in those years was far too primitive to permit the investigation of such structures. However, in the 1980s a number of researchers started to explore the possibilities of "nanotechnology", pursuing many of the ideas that he had originally proposed. Quantum dots are just one example of the kinds of interesting nanotechnologies that we can expect to emerge as a basis for the implementation of future special purpose parallel systems. In the next section we turn our attention away from exotic technologies and towards the mainstream.

4.4.   Multicomputers

Most of the practical work in the last decade on the design of highly parallel algorithms has been carried out with a view to implementation on some particular distributed memory multicomputer architecture. By a multicomputer we mean a set of computing elements connected by a sparse communications network, e.g. an array or a hypercube. Each computing element consists of a general purpose microprocessors and its private physical memory module. A number of such multicomputer systems have been commercially available from companies in the United States and Europe since the mid 1980s. In such a system, memory is organised in terms of multiple private address spaces with explicit message passing by the programmer [168, 170, 187] for all non-local memory requests. In most of the early systems

[170, 181, 339, 397], message passing was implemented using simple, store and forward communication, and hence was extremely slow for messages which had to pass through a number of intermediate processors before reaching the destination processor. In some of the later ones, techniques such as logical channels and wormhole routing have been used to improve the performance of non-local communication [224, 340, 341]. However, in those systems there is still a substantial advantage to be gained by designing algorithms which require only local communication. The key to algorithmic efficiency in multicomputer systems is, therefore, the careful exploitation of network locality. An efficient multicomputer algorithm will be one which minimises the distance that messages have to travel in the interconnection network by careful design of the virtual process structure in the algorithm so that it maps efficiently onto the physical structure of the machine. Despite the difficulties of programming such systems, and the architecture dependence of the resulting software, a large number of interesting new high performance parallel algorithms have been developed for multicomputer architectures of various kinds. Although most of these algorithms have been oriented towards MIMD multicomputers, there has also been a significant amount of work on the more restricted class of SIMD machines [15, 23, 29, 116, 166, 304, 352, 399, 410]. Locality based algorithms have been developed for all kinds of interconnection network structures. For an introduction to this area, see e.g. [34, 123, 185, 224]. The following is a short list of some of the more common network structures for which such algorithms have been produced: arrays [224, 292, 335, 360], trees and Sneptrees [165, 242, 264], pyramids [5, 284, 351], the mesh of trees structure [178, 224], fat trees [232, 233], hypercubes [70, 80, 93, 152, 153, 162, 182, 224, 266, 312, 404], the cube connected cycles architecture [224, 307], butterflies [224] and various shuffle exchange and de Bruijn graphs [224, 350].

4.5. Optical Systems

In previous sections we have considered a number of technologies which are convenient for the development of parallel systems in which network locality must be exploited to achieve efficiency. These include VLSI systems, systolic architectures, cellular automata machines, and multicomputers based on message passing. In this section we turn our attention to optical systems, which, among other things, may provide a means of achieving highly efficient non-local communication in parallel systems.

Since the invention of the laser in 1960, optical computing has offered the prospect of systems with much greater parallelism and communications power than one could obtain through the use of electronics [30, 113]. It now seems likely that in the 1990s this prospect will finally become a reality. One can identify three distinct areas in which optical systems may have an important impact in the coming years. The first is simply as a more efficient communications technology, particularly for irregular and non-local communication. The second is as a means of achieving very high performance application specific systems by directly exploiting the capabilities of optical technology at the algorithmic level. The third is in the development of all optical general purpose digital computers, in which the logic gates, memory elements etc. are implemented using optical devices. We will briefly discuss these three uses of optical technology in the following sections. A good general introduction to optical systems, written from a computer science perspective, can be found in [113].

4.5.1.   Optical Communication

Various kinds of communication systems are used in parallel architectures - buses [10, 101, 140, 272, 313, 375, 376], crossbars [113, 157, 334], networks [113, 300] etc. There are a number of reasons why optical technologies provide a more appropriate basis for the implementation of such systems than electronic technologies do. They include the following.

High bandwidth.

High speed of propagation. Electronic signals propagate approximately two orders of magnitude slower than light, because of the capacitance of electronic conductors.

Absence of interference. Electrons interact strongly with each other, through the Coulombic force. Therefore, electronic wires must be kept some distance apart, so as to prevent crosstalk. Photons, on the other hand, do not interact with each other. Beams of light carrying information can even cross each other without any problem. This absence of interference enables much greater density and parallelism to be achieved through the use of optics.

Dynamic reconfiguration. The interconnection pattern of an optical communication system can be dynamically changed in a way which would be difficult or impossible in electronics.

There are two basic approaches to the physical implementation of optical communication systems (i) the use of optical fibres as waveguides, and (ii) the use of free space. For communication over reasonably long distances it is necessary to conduct the light to wherever it should go. This can be done by using an optical fibre as a waveguide for the light. The propagation of light in (bent) optical fibres is controlled by ensuring the total internal reflection of the beam inside the fibre. The use of such fibre optic systems for long distance communication is already quite common in local area networks. In an application specific optical device or an all optical digital computer, the communication distances may be sufficiently short that it is more appropriate to simply allow the beams of light carrying information to cross in the free space between the various elements. [For engineering reasons it may be more appropriate to use a transparent material instead of free space. Nevertheless, we will refer to it as a free space interconnection.] The main advantage of this kind of free space interconnection is that one can more fully utilise the three dimensions of space. Free space interconnections can be implemented using various kinds of devices such as holographic elements and lenslet arrays. For details, see [113].

4.5.2.   Special Purpose Parallel Computing with Optical Primitives

Special purpose optical systems can be divided into two classes (i) those that deal with image and signal processing, and (ii) those that deal with numerical computation. In image and signal processing systems we take an input beam of light, manipulate it, and produce an output beam of light. These systems exploit various optical phenomena, such as the ability to perform two-dimensional Fourier transforms. Optical numerical processors do not manipulate beams of light in that way, rather they deal with arrays of numbers, represented by multiple points of light. While many of these special purpose optical systems are analog in nature, this is not always the case; a number of systems which use digital encodings in order to improve accuracy have also been proposed.

The basic elements of optical computing systems are as follows. The light sources are semiconductor LEDs (light emitting diodes) or lasers. Light beams can be manipulated using various kinds of optical devices, e.g. beam splitters, gratings, lenses, and polarisers. In particular, lenses can be used to form a light distribution that is the Fourier transform of another light distribution. The intensity of a light beam can be detected by a photodiode, and the intensity distribution in an image can be captured by an array of such detectors.

Images are naturally thought of in terms of optical systems and light beams. Various image processing functions may be carried out directly on the image by application specific optical systems, with no need for sampling, quantisation etc. In such direct image processing systems, the input data is a two-dimensional analog light distribution. As the light beam traverses the various optical elements it is manipulated, and at the end of the process an output light distribution is produced. Some examples of "computations" which can be performed in this way include Fourier transforms, spatial filtering, cross correlation, deconvolution, Radon transforms, and synthetic aperture radar imaging. Direct signal processing systems are similar to these image processing systems, the main difference is that the data is a one-dimensional temporal signal, rather than a two-dimensional spatial image. Optical signal processors are useful for the kinds of computations performed in radar systems.

Light intensities (or amplitudes) may be used to represent numerical values in an analog manner, rather than the usual digital representation. With an analog optical representation, the basic arithmetic operations are trivial: addition is done by combining beams of light, and multiplication by the modulation of beams of light. Various important linear algebra and matrix operations can be simply and efficiently performed using these primitives [16, 20, 68, 113, 243]. An interesting example of the use of such systems is given in [111] where they show how an optical matrix-vector multiplier can be used iteratively to efficiently simulate the Hopfield model [172] of neural networks. Analog optical methods can also be used for the solution of certain types of partial differential equations [113].

In [19, 110, 315] several interesting new theoretical models of optical computation have been proposed, which capture, in a simple and mathematically tractable form, the costs involved in computing with electro-optical devices. A number of efficient algorithms for those models have been developed, and are described in the papers. These models provide an appropriate starting point for the development of a robust complexity theory which will help guide the future design of special purpose optical systems for important applications.

4.5.3. Digital Optical Computers

The goal of developing an all optical general purpose digital computer has been pursued for many years [53, 113, 176, 251, 252, 395]. Although much progress has been made in demonstrating that the various components required for such a system can indeed be realised as optical devices, it is still not clear whether such systems will ever outperform their electronic counterparts. A good discussion of the prospects for all optical systems is given in [113], which also describes the various techniques which can be used to design optical logic elements, arithmetic units, memory systems etc.

5. VLSI Systems

VLSI models of parallel computation have been extensively studied in the last decade. The two main characteristics of such models are *finite resolution* and *quasi planarity*. The finite resolution property stems from the fact that a component on a VLSI chip, i.e. a gate or a wire, takes a finite amount of space and cannot be made arbitrarily small. The fabrication technology used will determine the minimum feature size which can be achieved. The quasi planarity property follows from the fact that a VLSI chip is composed of a small fixed number of layers. The precise number depends on the technology used. It can be as small as two or as large as about thirty. However, it is always fixed, i.e. it does not grow with the size of the circuit.

The goal of VLSI algorithm design is to produce an algorithm which, when embedded in such a quasi planar structure, optimises certain complexity measures such as area and time. A large number of efficient VLSI algorithms have been obtained for important problems. The upper bounds on complexity obtained from those algorithms have also, in many cases, been closely matched by lower bounds. Most of the lower bounds have been established by simply considering the required communication of data between the various components on the chip, and to a large extent ignoring the details of the computation. This shows, in a very convincing way, that in the design of VLSI systems, it is the efficient communication of information within the chip which is the dominant concern.

Several different VLSI models have been proposed and studied. The following description is intended to capture the main features of those models. A VLSI chip is a synchronous Boolean circuit with feedback, i.e. a sequential machine. All gate actions take place in parallel each clock cycle. Gates and wire segments are laid out on ν layers, where ν is fixed and at least two. Each layer is a convex region of the plane, partitioned into a rectilinear arrangement of square cells of side $\lambda > 0$ (Manhattan geometry). Each gate, input port and output port occupies a single cell, and each gate computes some two-argument Boolean function. Each wire consists of a connected set of straight line segments of cells. The segments of two distinct wires cannot lie in adjacent cells. The time for a signal to propagate along a wire is independent of the length of the wire. (This assumption is perhaps the most controversial of those we will describe. If one takes account of the resistances of wires, then one is led to a model in which the time for a signal to propagate is proportional to the length of the wire. This model is considered in [75]. If one also takes into account the capacitive and inductive properties of wires, then one is led to a model in which the propagation time is quadratic in the length of the wire.) The input and output ports are on the boundary of the chip. The input/output behaviour of the chip is defined by a schedule giving the times and locations for inputs and outputs. The schedule is oblivious, i.e. it is the same for all possible values of the inputs. Inputs are supplied only once.

The main complexity measures considered are the chip *area A* and the computing *time T*. For A we measure the number of λ^2 units on a layer, for T we take the number of clock cycles spent in the computation. Since synchronous circuits can be pipelined, another important complexity measure in some contexts, is the *period P*. A pipelined circuit can receive input to a new problem instance to be solved before it has completed the solution of the previous one. P is the number of clock cycles between the first input cycle of two consecutive problem instances. Besides area, time and period, the *switching energy E* is another complexity measure of interest in some VLSI chip computations [240]. Every cell is said to consume one unit of switching energy whenever it changes its state from 0 to 1, or vice versa, in a clock cycle. The total switching energy E consumed by a chip in the course of a computation is closely related to the heat dissipation of the chip for that computation. The various complexity measures A, T, P and E can be combined in a number of ways to form composite complexity measures which capture the various tradeoffs which are possible in the design of VLSI algorithms. The most widely studied of such composite measures is AT^2, which captures an important tradeoff between area and time in VLSI computations.

In 1979, Thompson [357] introduced the above VLSI model of computation and demonstrated that, for the problem of computing the Fast Fourier Transform (FFT) on n inputs, the chip area A and time T must satisfy $AT^2 = \Omega(n^2)$. In the two or three years following the publication of [357], the goal of establishing AT^2 lower bounds for other important problems was pursued by a large number of researchers, and many such results were obtained using "crossing sequence" or information flow arguments. Following this work, Savage [332] observed that, in fact, a number of those results could have been obtained as a fairly direct consequence of earlier results on the existence of small separators in planar graphs [248, 249], and on the simulation of sequential machines by combinational circuits without feedback loops [330]. We will describe how AT^2 lower bounds can be established in this way. Before doing so, we need to define the notion of a Boolean circuit [106, 394], and of a planar circuit [106].

Definition 5.1 *Let $B = \{0, 1\}$, $B_{n,m} = \{f : B^n \to B^m\}$, and $X_n = < x_1, x_2, \ldots, x_n >$ be a set of formal arguments. A <u>Boolean circuit</u> for $f \in B_{n,m}$ is a directed acyclic graph with n input nodes (in-degree 0) $I_1, I_2, \ldots, I_n$ where I_i is associated with x_i, and m output nodes $O_1, O_2, \ldots, O_m$ where O_i corresponds to the ith output function f_i. Every node, other than the input nodes, corresponds to a gate. Gates have in-degree two and compute some function $g \in B_{2,1}$ of their left and right inputs. Let π be a finite region of the plane bounded by a simple closed curve γ. A <u>planar Boolean circuit</u> for $f \in B_{n,m}$ is a Boolean circuit embedded on the surface π with no crossing edges. The input nodes and output nodes must be on the boundary γ, and should appear in the cyclic order $< I_1, I_2, \ldots, I_n, O_m, O_{m-1}, \ldots, O_1 >$.*

Definition 5.2 *The <u>size</u> of a circuit or planar circuit is the total number of gates. For $f \in B_{n,m}$, let $C(f)$ denote minimum size of any circuit for f and $PC(f)$ denote minimum size of any planar circuit for f. For the various VLSI complexity measures A, T, AT, AT^2 etc., we will use the same convention, e.g. $AT^2(f)$ will denote the minimum AT^2 complexity of any VLSI chip for f.*

Theorem 5.3 (Savage [332]) *For all $f \in B_{n,m}$, $C(f) = O(AT(f))$*

Proof. This is a restatement of an earlier result by Savage [330]. It is obtained by constructing a Boolean circuit for f from T copies of a VLSI chip for f. A stack of T copies of the chip is formed, and where loops exist on the chip in flip-flops, the loops are broken and the signals fed to the corresponding position on the chip above. A Boolean circuit of size $O(AT)$ is thus created that computes the same function as the chip   □

We can also relate circuit size and planar circuit size in the following way.

Theorem 5.4 *For all $f \in B_{n,m}$, $PC(f) = O((C(f))^2)$*

For a proof of Theorem 5.4, see [4] or [273]. By combining Theorems 5.3 and 5.4 we can show that $PC(f)$ is at most $A^2T^2(f)$. Savage [332] showed that the following stronger results could be obtained.

Theorem 5.5 (Savage [332]) *For all* $f \in B_{n,m}$, $PC(f) = O(AT^2(f))$ *and* $PC(f) = O(A^2T(f))$

The proof of these two upper bounds is again based on the idea of making T copies of the chip, breaking loops, and feeding signals between the copies. However, to achieve planarity, one must ensure that wires do not overlap and that at most one pair of wires cross at a point. In the AT^2 upper bound this is done by expanding the chip area by a factor of T in each dimension, and then stacking the copies with an incremental diagonal shift proportional to λ. Two-input two-output planar crossover circuits [249, 269] can then be used to produce the planar circuit. In the A^2T upper bound, the T copies of the chip are placed side by side in the plane, and crossings on the chip and those created by the wires connecting them are replaced by crossovers to produce a planar circuit. For more details, see [332].

For almost all Boolean functions, tight bounds on the various VLSI complexity measures can be easily obtained.

Theorem 5.6 *For all* $f \in B_{n,1}$, *the following upper bounds can be simultaneously achieved,* $A(f) = O(2^n)$, $T(f) = O(n)$ *and* $P(f) = O(1)$.

Proof. Let $f_{ij} = f(x_1, x_2, \ldots, x_{n-2}, i, j)$ and note that $f = (((f_{11} \wedge x_{n-1}) \vee (f_{01} \wedge \bar{x}_{n-1})) \wedge x_n) \vee (((f_{01} \wedge x_{n-1}) \vee (f_{00} \wedge \bar{x}_{n-1})) \wedge \bar{x}_n)$. This definition yields the recursive VLSI layout for f shown in Figure 1.

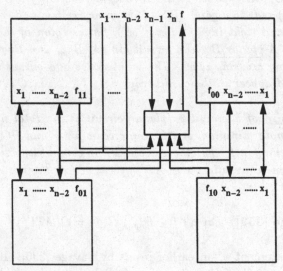

Figure 1. A universal VLSI chip

This layout establishes the bounds stated in the theorem. We have $A(f) \leq 4A(f_{ij}) + O(n^2)$ which yields $A(f) = O(2^n)$, and $T(f) \leq T(f_{ij}) + O(1)$ which gives $T(f) = O(n)$. The construction can also be used in a pipelined manner to give $P(f) = O(1)$ □

The bounds in Theorem 5.6 are tight for most Boolean functions.

Theorem 5.7 *For almost all* $f \in B_{n,1}$, $A(f) = \Omega(2^n)$ *and* $T(f) = \Omega(n)$.

The lower bound on area can be established by noting that the number of distinct chips with area a is at most c^a for some constant c. Since there are 2^{2^n} distinct functions in $B_{n,1}$, the lower bound follows [201]. A stronger result, showing that for almost all $f \in B_{n,1}$, $PC(f) = \Theta(2^n)$, is established in [270]. The lower bound on time in Theorem 5.7 follows from the well known lower bound on the circuit depth of almost all Boolean functions [106, 394].

Although we have tight bounds on the VLSI complexity of almost all Boolean functions, our real interest is, of course, in the complexity of specific functions of practical importance. Lower bounds on the VLSI complexity of specific Boolean functions can be established in a number of ways. We will now describe two simple lower bounds which can be obtained from a consideration of the input/output limitations and of the memory limitations of VLSI chips.

We begin by showing a simple input/output based lower bound. Let $COUNT^{(n)} \in B_{n,\log n}$ denote the Boolean function corresponding to the problem of computing the $(\log n)$-bit binary sum of n Boolean inputs.

Theorem 5.8 $AT^2(COUNT^{(n)}) = \Omega(n \log n)$

Proof. Consider a VLSI chip which has area a and computes $COUNT^{(n)}$ in t clock cycles. If n/q is the maximum number of bits input in any one clock cycle, then we must have $a \geq n/q$ and $t \geq q + \log(n/q)$, since a tree from n/q input ports to an output port must have area at least n/q and height at least $\log(n/q)$. Therefore, at^2 must be at least $\min\{nq + 2n\log(n/q) + (n/q)\log^2(n/q)\}$, where q ranges from 1 to n. This gives $AT^2(COUNT^{(n)}) = \Omega(n \log n)$ since the minimum is obtained for $q \approx \log n$ □

A reasonably efficient VLSI implementation of $COUNT^{(n)}$ can be obtained in the following way. We divide the inputs into k blocks, each of size n/k. $COUNT^{(n/k)}$ is computed for each block using a serial counter (area $\log(n/k)$, time n/k). The resulting k numbers, each $\log(n/k)$ bits, are then added using a balanced binary tree of full adder chains (area $k \log^2 n \log(n/k)$, time $\log k + \log(n/k)$). Choosing $k \approx (n/\log n)$, we obtain a construction with area $O(n \log n \log\log n)$ and time $O(\log n)$.

We now show how the memory limitations of VLSI chips can be used to prove lower bounds. Let $SORT^{(n,k)} \in B_{nk,nk}$ denote the Boolean function corresponding to the problem of sorting n k-bit binary numbers. Let X^i, $1 \leq i \leq n$, denote the ith input number and x_p^i, $1 \leq p \leq k$, denote the pth most significant bit of X^i, i.e. $X^i = \sum_{p=1}^{k} x_p^i * 2^{k-p}$. Let Y^i, $1 \leq i \leq n$, denote the ith output number and define y_p^i in the same way as x_p^i.

Theorem 5.9 $A(SORT^{(n,k)}) = \Omega(n)$ *for* $k > \log n$.

Proof. We first show that every x_k^i must be input before any y_k^j is output. If not, then there must be some r, s, such that y_k^r is output before, or when, x_k^s is input. Excluding X^s, let $r - 1$ of the input numbers be 0, and $n - r$ of them be 1. Let $x_s^i = 0$ for all $i < k$. If $y_k^r = 1$, then let $x_k^s = 0$ and note that y_k^r is incorrect. Similarly for $y_k^r = 1$.

Let $\alpha_{a_1,a_2,\ldots,a_n}$, $a_i \in \{0,1\}$, denote the chip input where, for all $1 \leq i \leq n$, the $(k-1)$-bit number $< x_1^i, x_2^i, \ldots, x_{k-1}^i >$ has the value $i - 1$, and $x_k^i = a_i$. Consider the behaviour of the chip on the family of 2^n inputs $\alpha_{a_1,a_2,\ldots,a_n}$. At the clock cycle just before the first least significant bit y_k^j is output, we know that every x_k^i must have been input, and that, henceforth, all inputs will be the same. We also know that for input $\alpha_{a_1,a_2,...,a_n}$, $y_k^i = a_i$, since the k-bit input numbers X^i are already sorted. If the area of the chip is less than n then there must be two distinct inputs $\alpha_{a_1,a_2,...,a_n}$ and $\alpha_{b_1,b_2,...,b_n}$ in the family of 2^n, for which the state of the circuit is identical. Since all further inputs are the same, all y_k^i outputs will be the same. Contradiction. Hence, the area must be at least n $\qquad\qquad\square$

The lower bounds in Theorems 5.8 and 5.9 are based on input/output and memory properties of VLSI computations. Stronger results can, in many cases, be obtained through an analysis of the information flow requirements of such computations [357]. In the remainder of this section we describe a number of lower bound results based on this approach. We begin by demonstrating a lower bound on the AT^2 VLSI complexity of $SORT^{(n,k)}$

Theorem 5.10 $AT^2(SORT^{(n,k)}) = \Omega(n^2)$ for $k > \log n$.

Proof. (Note. In proving the theorem we do not make use of our assumption that all input and output ports are on the boundary of the chip.) Suppose the chip looks like Figure 2, a rectangle of height h and width w. We assume, without loss of generality, that $h \le w$.

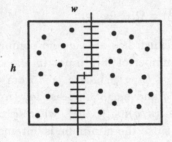

Figure 2. Bisection of VLSI chip

Let us focus, as we did in Theorem 5.9 on the least significant output bits. These bits are output at ports located at various points on the chip, as indicated in Figure 2. If as many as $n/3$ of them are output from the same port then $T \ge n/3$, and the theorem follows immediately. If no single port emits $n/3$ of the bits, then we can bisect the chip by a line, as in Figure 2, which runs between the cells and runs vertically, except possibly for a single jog of one cell width, and for which at least $n/3$ of the least significant output bits are emitted on each side of the line. To determine such a line we slide it from left to right, until the first point at which $n/3$ of the bits are output to the left of the line. If no more than $2n/3$ are output to the left we are done. If not, we start from the top and consider places to jog the line back one cell width to the left. Since no single cell outputs $n/3$ of the bits, we can always find a suitable place to jog the line. There, we will have between $n/3$ and $2n/3$ of the least significant output bits on each side. Now assume, without loss of generality, that at least half of the least significant input bits are read on the left of the line, and let us, by renumbering bits, if necessary, assume that these are $x_k^1, x_k^2, \ldots, x_k^{n/2}$. Suppose also that least significant output bits $y_k^{i_1}, y_k^{i_2}, \ldots, y_k^{i_{n/3}}$ are output on the right. Using an argument very similar to that used in the proof of Theorem 5.9 we can easily pick values for bits other than the least significant ones, so that for all $1 \le j \le n/3$, $y_k^{i_j} = x_k^j$. Therefore, at least $n/3$ bits must cross the line for the chip to correctly compute the outputs. The maximum number of bits which can cross the line in one clock cycle is $h + 1$ (h horizontal and one vertical, at the jog). It follows that $(h + 1)T \geq n/3$. Since we assumed $h \leq w$, we have both $hT = \Omega(n)$ and $wT = \Omega(n)$. Therefore, $hwT^2 = \Omega(n^2)$ which proves the theorem since $hw = A$ $\qquad\qquad\qquad\qquad\qquad\qquad\qquad\qquad\qquad\qquad\qquad\qquad\qquad\qquad\qquad\qquad$ □

Theorem 5.10 is proved for the (geometric) VLSI model introduced at the start of the section. However, as noted earlier, AT^2 lower bounds can, in fact, be established in a graph theoretic setting as lower bounds on planar circuit size. An important result in the area of computational complexity is the following planar separator theorem.

Theorem 5.11 (Lipton and Tarjan [248]) *Let G be any n-vertex planar graph with non-negative vertex costs summing to no more than one. Then the vertices of G can be partitioned into three sets A, B, C such that no edge joins a vertex in A with a vertex in B, neither A nor B has total vertex cost exceeding $2/3$, and C contains no more than $2\sqrt{2}\sqrt{n}$ vertices.*

Let $BC^{(n)} \in B_{2n,2n-1}$ denote the Boolean function corresponding to the problem of computing the convolution of two n-bit Boolean sequences, $IM^{(n)} \in B_{2n,2n}$ denote the Boolean function corresponding to the problem of computing the product of two n-bit integers, and $MM^{(n)} \in B_{2n^2,n^2}$ denote the function corresponding to the problem of computing the product of two $n \times n$ Boolean matrices. Using the planar separator theorem, Lipton and Tarjan [249] proved the following lower bounds on planar circuit size.

Theorem 5.12 $PC(BC^{(n)}) = \Omega(n^2)$, $PC(IM^{(n)}) = \Omega(n^2)$ and $PC(MM^{(n)}) = \Omega(n^4)$

These results are established by showing that in any planar circuit for Boolean convolution (integer multiplication, matrix multiplication) there must be an information flow of $\Omega(n)$ bits ($\Omega(n)$, $\Omega(n^2)$ bits respectively) from the input nodes to the output nodes. Any separator must therefore be of size $\Omega(n)$ ($\Omega(n)$, $\Omega(n^2)$ resp.) and thus by Theorem 5.11, any planar circuit must be of size $\Omega(n^2)$ ($\Omega(n^2)$, $\Omega(n^4)$ resp.). From Theorem 5.5 it follows that the lower bounds in Theorem 5.12 are also lower bounds on the AT^2 complexity and the A^2T complexity of those functions. We now describe two simple VLSI chip constructions which show that the lower bounds in Theorem 5.12 for Boolean convolution and matrix multiplication are quite close to the best possible.

Let $X = < x_{n-1}, x_{n-2}, \ldots, x_0 >$ and $Y = < y_{n-1}, y_{n-2}, \ldots, y_0 >$ be two n-bit sequences. The Boolean convolution $BC^{(n)}(X,Y)$ of X and Y is the sequence Z of functions $< z_{2n-2}, z_{2n-3}, \ldots, z_0 >$ where $z_i = \bigvee_{j\geq 0} x_j \wedge y_{i-j}$. A simple recursive construction based on divide and conquer can be used to compute $BC^{(n)}(X,Y)$. Let X_0 denote the subsequence of values x_i in X where $i < n/2$, and $X_1 = X - X_0$. Define Y_0 and Y_1 similarly. Let Z_k, $0 \leq k \leq 3$, denote the subsequence of values z_j in Z, where $kn/2 \leq i < (k+1)n/2$. If we compute $BC^{(n/2)}(X_i, Y_j)$ for all $i, j \in \{0, 1\}$ then the required sequences Z_k for the computation of $BC^{(n)}(X,Y)$ can be obtained from those subcomputations, by computing various disjunctions, see Figure 3.

For the recursive geometric layout shown in Figure 3, let H_n denote the vertical height of the whole circuit for $BC^{(n)}(X,Y)$, and W_n denote the horizontal width. Then we have $H_n \leq 4W_{n/2}$ and $W_n \leq H_{n/2} + O(n)$, which gives $H_n = O(n \log n)$ and $W_n = O(n \log n)$. Therefore, the area A_n of the construction is $O(n^2\log^2 n)$. For time, we have $T_n \leq T_{n/2} + O(1)$ which yields $T_n = O(\log n)$. Therefore, this simple construction shows that $AT^2(BC^{(n)}) = O(n^2\log^4 n)$.

Let A and B be two $n \times n$ Boolean matrices. The product $MM^{(n)}(A,B)$ of A and B is the $n \times n$ matrix C, where $c_{ij} = \bigvee_{k=1}^{n} a_{ik} \wedge b_{kj}$. To produce a VLSI chip for $MM^{(n)}$ we can again

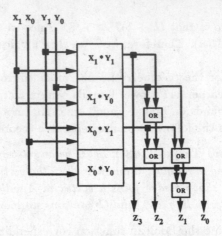

Figure 3. VLSI chip for convolution

use a recursive divide and conquer strategy, this time on partitioned matrices. To compute C, we partition each of the matrices A and B into four $(n/2) \times (n/2)$ submatrices, compute eight products on those submatrices, and then form disjunctions of the resulting matrices, see Figure 4.

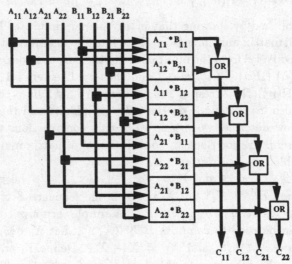

Figure 4. VLSI chip for matrix multiplication

For the layout shown in Figure 4, we can again let H_n denote the vertical height of the whole circuit for $MM^{(n)}(A, B)$, and W_n denote the horizontal width. This time we have $H_n \leq 8W_{n/2}$ and $W_n \leq H_{n/2} + O(n^2)$, which gives $H_n = O(n^2)$ and $W_n = O(n^2)$. Therefore, the area A_n of the construction is $O(n^4)$. For time, we again have $T_n \leq T_{n/2} + O(1)$ which gives $T_n = O(log\ n)$. Therefore, we have shown that $AT^2(MM^{(n)}) = O(n^4 log^2 n)$. In the next section we will describe a systolic algorithm for matrix multiplication which can be realised as a VLSI chip with area $O(n^2)$ and time $O(n)$. This systolic design shows that the lower bound in Theorem 5.12 for matrix multiplication is, in fact, optimal.

The AT^2 lower bounds which follow from Theorem 5.12 are for multiple output functions and assume that the inputs are read once only. Under this read once condition, lower bounds of the form $AT^2 = \Omega(n^2)$, where n is the number of inputs, have been obtained for a large number of important multiple output functions. They include Fourier transforms [357, 358], sorting [359], integer multiplication [3, 56, 249], matrix multiplication [249, 331], matrix inversion [331], transitive closure of a Boolean matrix [331], integer powers and reciprocals [332] and various transitive functions [390].

In [408], Yao introduced a general framework for the analysis of the communication complexity of problems. Informally, the communication complexity of a function f is the minimum amount of information that has to be exchanged between two cooperating processors that each have a partial knowledge of the input, and that want to aid each other in computing f [81, 184, 408]. In the VLSI context, one can think of the communicating processors as the two halves of the chip, when divided by a bisecting line as in Figure 2. The communication complexity corresponds to the minimum possible information flow between the two halves. Using the approach of communication complexity analysis, a number of lower bounds on the AT^2 complexity of single output Boolean functions have also been established [6, 227, 238, 240, 332, 333, 348]. The functions include graph isomorphism [409], evaluation of propositional formulae [54], recognition of a context-free language [54, 247], pattern matching [247], testing integer factorisation [247], testing matrix factorisation [332] and testing whether one matrix is the transitive closure of another [332]. In fact, Savage [332] shows that a lower bound can be obtained for every predicate (single output Boolean function) associated with a multiple output function for which such lower bound results have been derived. An excellent account of the methods used for establishing lower bounds on the VLSI complexity of predicates can be found in [238] and [240].

VLSI chips that can read inputs at multiple times and places have been considered in [194, 333, 409]. Yao [409] studied the function $x + y * z$, for integers over a finite field F. He showed that if a compact binary representation of F is used, then the lower bound $AT^2 = \Omega(n^2)$ holds for $n = log_2 | F |$. If no limit on the redundancy of the representation is prescribed, then he shows that we must have $AT^2 = \Omega(n^{4/3})$. Kedem and Zorat [194] show that, for the cyclic shift function on n inputs, $AT^2 = \Omega((n/\mu)^2)$ when inputs are read μn times. Savage [333] establishes lower bounds on the complexity of matrix multiplication and related problems such as LU decomposition, for the multiple read model.

The design of efficient VLSI algorithms for important problems has been widely studied over the last decade. A good general introduction to this area can be found in [369]. Some examples of the kinds of problems which have been investigated are: addition [55, 57], multiplication [3, 56, 282], division [281, 283], square root [281], convolution [26], Fourier transform [358], counting [84], sorting [41, 42, 88, 223, 359], merging [25], dictionaries [14, 297], graph computations [154, 183] and regular expressions [118]. Although many "paper designs" for VLSI systems have been produced, relatively few of these have actually been implemented as chips. The main reason has been the prohibitive time and cost of custom VLSI design and fabrication. As noted earlier in the chapter, the availability of field-programmable gate arrays will, in the future, enable many such designs to be realised quickly and cheaply.

In our consideration of VLSI systems we have emphasised efficiency considerations, and have demonstrated that there is now a well developed theory to guide the design of efficient VLSI circuits. There has also been much work, in recent years, on the development of techniques for the formal verification of VLSI systems. For an appreciation of the various approaches in this area see, for example, [87, 275, 276, 346].

6.   Systolic Algorithms and Architectures

In [207], Kung has persuasively argued the case for the design of parallel algorithms which carefully balance the input/output, communication and processing in parallel computations to avoid bottlenecks and hence increase throughput. Since the appearance of the early papers by Kung and his colleagues, a whole subfield of parallel computing has developed, based around the concept of systolic computation. In this section we will describe several simple systolic algorithms, and then briefly discuss some of the more general issues involved in the field of systolic computation. A systolic parallel algorithm typically has the following properties

- operations are pipelined to balance input/output, communication and processing

- there are only a few types of simple cells

- data and control flows are simple and regular

- only local communication is required

- computation proceeds synchronously

The synchronous property is not an essential feature and, indeed, many asynchronous systolic (or wavefront) algorithms have been developed [214, 215].

6.1.   Convolution

In [207], Kung presents a family of systolic designs for the convolution problem. The k-*convolution problem* is defined as follows. Given a sequence of weights $W =< w_0, w_1, \ldots, w_{k-1} >$ and an input sequence $X =< x_0, x_1, x_2, \ldots >$, compute the output sequence $Y =< y_{k-1}, y_k, y_{k+1}, \ldots >$, where $y_i = \sum_{j=0}^{k-1} a_j * x_{i-j}$. The k-convolution problem is representative of a wide class of computations which are well suited to systolic designs. The problem can be viewed as a problem of combining two data streams, W and X, in a certain manner (for example, as in the above equation) to form a resultant data stream Y. This type of computation is common to a number of problems such as filtering, pattern matching, correlation, interpolation, polynomial evaluation, (including discrete Fourier transforms), and polynomial multiplication and division. For example, if multiplication and addition are interpreted as comparison and conjunction respectively, then the convolution problem becomes the pattern matching problem [121]. In computing the k-convolution, each input x_i must be multiplied by each of the k weights in W. If the x_i is input separately from memory for each multiplication then, for large k, memory bandwidth will become a bottleneck, preventing a high performance solution. A systolic algorithm resolves this input/output bottleneck by making multiple use of each x_i fetched from the memory.

   Kung [207] describes two systolic designs for the convolution problem in which each of the inputs in X is simultaneously broadcast to all the cells in the systolic array. Such global data communication, although convenient, requires the use of a bus or some kind of tree network. As the number of cells increases, these bus or network structures will themselves become a bottleneck, limiting the performance which can be achieved. Noting this fact, Kung then describes four further systolic designs for the convolution problem, all of which require no global data communications whatsoever. Potentially, these four designs can be scaled to an arbitrarily large number of cells without loss of efficiency. We will now briefly describe two of these four designs. In both of them, each of the cells in the array is associated with a weight in W. In one, the inputs and results move in opposite directions. In the other, the inputs and results move in the same direction, but at different speeds.

Let $[m \ldots n]$ denote the sequence of integers $< i \mid m \leq i \leq n >$ and $[m \ldots]$ denote $< i \mid m \leq i >$. par endpar will be used to denote parallel iteration over a set, and seq endseq will be used to denote sequential iteration over a sequence. The k-convolution problem can be solved by the following parallel program.

```
par i ∈ [(k−1)...]
yᵢ := 0;
   seq j ∈ [0...(k−1)]
yᵢ := yᵢ + (w_{k−1−j} * x_{i+j−k+1})
   endseq
endpar
```

We will use this program as the basis for our systolic design. We begin by introducing an extra index for the y variables, which enables us to replace the assignments by equalities. This yields the following set of definitions (or single assignment program).

For all $i \geq k - 1$, $0 \leq j \leq k - 1$,
$$y_i^k = 0$$
$$y_i^j = y_i^{j-1 \ (mod \ (k+1))} + (w_{k-1-j} * x_{i+j-k+1})$$

The k-convolution problem then corresponds to the computation of y_i^{k-1}. From this set of definitions, we can obtain a linear systolic parallel algorithm for the computation of the y values, in which each y_i^j is computed in cell P_{k-1-j} during phase $i + j - k + 1$ of the computation. In this way we can avoid having to broadcast the weights in W (they can be held at the corresponding cell), and the propagation of y values requires only local communication between each cell P_{k-1-j} and its neighbours P_{k-2-j} and P_{k-j}. However, the algorithm still requires broadcasting of $x_{i+j-k+1}$ to all cells during phase $i + j - k + 1$. To eliminate this broadcasting we can redefine the values in the following way.

For all $i \geq k - 1$, $0 \leq j \leq k - 1$, $l \geq 0$,
$$x_l^l = x_l$$
$$y_i^k = 0$$
$$x_l^{l+j+1} = x_l^{l+j}$$
$$y_i^j = y_i^{j-1} + (w_{k-1-j} * x_{i+j-k+1}^{2i+j-2(k-1)})$$

Now if we compute y_i^j and $x_{i+j-k+1}^{2i+j-2(k-1)}$ in cell P_{k-1-j} during phase $2i + j - 2(k - 1)$ then we have a fully localised algorithm with only nearest neighbour communication. This algorithm can now be directly implemented on a linear systolic array with bidirectional dataflow. The systolic array consists of a linear array of k computation cells P_i, $0 \leq i < k$, and a "host" cell P_k which supplies input and receives output. For each $0 \leq i \leq k$, we have a unidirectional channel t_i from P_i to P_{i-1}, and a unidirectional channel b_i from P_{i-1} to P_i. (Note. All cell and channel indices are taken modulo $(k + 1)$.) At the start of the computation, the host cell inputs the values $x_0, x_1, x_2, \ldots$ to the array, on alternate clock cycles, using channel b_0. These values are propagated through the array, on successive clock cycles, using the b channels. Once x_0 arrives at P_{k+1}, the host begins to input zero values to the array, corresponding to $y_{k-1}^k, y_k^k, y_{k+1}^k, \ldots$, on alternate clock cycles, using the channel t_k. The array of cells P_i, $0 \leq i \leq k-1$, now perform the computation given by the above definition. Each cell P_i inputs an x value on b_i, a y value on t_{i+1}, and computes the new y value. At the next clock cycle, it outputs the x value on b_{i+1} and the new y value on t_i. The set of even numbered cells and the set of odd numbered ones compute on alternate cycles. The resulting y_i^{k-1} values are returned to the host using channel t_0.

In our second systolic design for k-convolution, the inputs and results move in the same direction, but at different speeds. The design is based on the following parallel program.

```
par i ∈ [(k − 1)...]
y_i := 0;
seq j ∈ [0...(k − 1)]
y_i := y_i + (w_j * x_{i-j})
endseq
endpar
```

As before, we introduce an extra index for the y variables, and replace the assignments by equalities. This yields the following set of definitions.

For all $i \geq k-1$, $0 \leq j \leq k-1$,
$$y_i^k = 0$$
$$y_i^j = y_i^{j-1 \ (mod \ (k+1))} + (w_j * x_{i-j})$$

The k-convolution problem then corresponds to the computation of y_i^{k-1}. From this set of definitions, we can obtain a linear systolic parallel algorithm for the computation of the y values, in which each y_i^j is computed in cell P_j during phase $i+j-k+1$ of the computation. We again avoid having to broadcast the weights in W by holding them at the corresponding cell and, as before, the propagation of y values requires only local communication between each cell P_j and its neighbours P_{j-1} and P_{j+1}. The movement of x values is simpler in this design. The x values need only be input to P_0 and then propagated from P_i to P_{i+1} during every alternate phase of the computation. This algorithm can be directly implemented on a linear systolic array with unidirectional dataflow. The systolic array again consists of a linear array of k computation cells P_i, $0 \leq i < k$, and a "host" cell P_k which supplies input and receives output. For each $0 \leq i \leq k$, we have a unidirectional channel t_i from P_{i-1} to P_i, and a unidirectional channel b_i from P_{i-1} to P_i. (Again, all cell and channel indices are taken modulo $(k+1)$.) At the start of the computation, the host cell inputs the values $x_0, x_1, x_2, \ldots$ to the array, on successive clock cycles, using the channel b_0. These x values are then propagated from P_i to P_{i+1}, on every second clock cycle, using the b channels. When x_{k-1} is due to be input, the host begins to input input zero values to the array, corresponding to $y_{k-1}^k, y_k^k, y_{k+1}^k, \ldots$, on successive clock cycles, using the channel t_0. The array of cells P_i, $0 \leq i \leq k-1$, now perform the computation given by the above definition. At time step s, each cell P_i inputs an x value on b_i, a y value on t_i, and computes the new y value. At the next clock cycle, it outputs the new y value on t_{i+1}, and outputs on b_{i+1} the x value which it received at time step $s - 1$. Therefore, the y values travel through the array at twice the speed of the x values. The resulting y_i^{k-1} values are returned to the host using channel t_k.

6.2. Sequence Comparison

Let $X_m = x_1 x_2 \ldots x_m$ and $Y_n = y_1 y_2 \ldots y_n$ be two sequences. The sequence comparison problem is the problem of determining the minimum number of insertions and deletions required to change X_m into Y_n. We assume that each insertion or deletion costs 1. Very large instances of this problem arise in the area of molecular biology where the strings correspond to nucleic acid sequences [329]. The edit distance is a measure of the similarity of the two sequences When $m = 0$ we have $Cost(X_m, Y_n) = n$. Similarly, $n = 0$ gives $Cost(X_m, Y_n) = m$. If $m > 0$, $n > 0$ then we have

$$Cost(X_m, Y_n) \leq Cost(X_{m-1}, Y_{n-1}) \qquad \text{if} \quad x_m = y_n$$

$$Cost(X_m, Y_n) \leq 1 + Cost(X_{m-1}, Y_n) \qquad [\text{delete } x_m]$$

$$Cost(X_m, Y_n) \leq 1 + Cost(X_m, Y_{n-1}) \qquad [\text{insert } y_n]$$

Using dynamic programming we can tabulate the values of $Cost$ in a straightforward way. As an example, consider the computation of $Cost(DEFINE, DESIGN)$.

	∅	D	E	F	I	N	E
∅	[0]	1	2	3	4	5	6
D	1	[0]	1	2	3	4	5
E	2	1	[0]	[1]	2	3	4
S	3	2	1	[2]	3	4	5
I	4	3	2	3	[2]	3	4
G	5	4	3	4	[3]	4	5
N	6	5	4	5	4	[3]	[4]

The number below x_i and to the right of y_j is $Cost(X_i, Y_j)$. The chain of bracketed numbers indicate that we should perform the following sequence of edits to change DEFINE into DESIGN: Delete F, insert S, insert G, delete E. The sequence comparison problem can, therefore, be solved by the following parallel program, where $c_{i,j}$ corresponds to $Cost(X_i, Y_j)$.

```
par i ∈ [0...n]
c_{0,i} := i
endpar
par i ∈ [0...m]
c_{i,0} := i
endpar
seq d ∈ [0...(m+n)]
par i ∈ [min{0, d-m}...min{d, n}]
c_{i,d-i} := min{c_{i,d-i-1}, c_{i-1,d-i}} + 1;
if x_i = y_{d-i} then c_{i,d-i} := min{c_{i,d-i}, c_{i-1,d-i-1}}
endpar
endseq
```

From this program we can easily obtain a linear systolic array algorithm with bidirectional dataflow for the sequence comparison problem. In this systolic array, $c_{i,d-i}$ is computed in cell P_{2i-d} during phase d of the computation. The algorithm requires at most $O(m+n)$ cells and runs in time $O(m+n)$. The following is an informal outline of the construction. The two sequences are compared as they pass through the array moving in opposite directions. Each processor P_k has input and output channels (In.L,Out.L) to the processor on the left, P_{k-1}, and similar channels (In.R,Out.R) to the processor on the right, P_{k+1}. We input the sequences $y_1 \, 1 \, y_2 \, 2 \, y_3 \, 3 \cdots y_n \, n$ and $x_1 \, 1 \, x_2 \, 2 \, x_3 \, 3 \cdots x_m \, m$ sequentially from the left and right respectively. Once the sequences have been input to the array, the computation proceeds with each processor repeatedly performing the following set of operations every two time steps.

Step 1:   In.R(x_i);
In.L(y_j);
Bool:=($x_i = y_j$);
Out.R(y_j);
Out.L(x_i);

Step 2:   In.R($c_{i,j-1}$);
In.L($c_{i-1,j}$);

$$c_{i,j} = minimum \begin{cases} c_{i,j-1} + 1 \\ c_{i-1,j} + 1 \\ c_{i-1,j-1} \;\; if \; Bool \end{cases}$$

Out.R($c_{i,j}$);
Out.L($c_{i,j}$);

A simple inductive argument shows that the matrix of edit distances has the property that horizontally and vertically adjacent pairs of values always differ by 1. Because of this property it is sufficient to keep the remainder modulo 4 of the matrix entry. If we implement the above systolic algorithm but keep only such remainders then we can still reconstruct the true value of the edit distance from either of the two sequences of values $c_{m,1}, c_{m,2}, \ldots, c_{m,n}$ and $c_{1,n}, c_{2,n}, \ldots, c_{m,n}$ which are output by the array $(c_{i,j} = Cost(X_i, Y_j) \bmod 4)$ since

$$c_{m,0} = m \quad , \quad (c_{m,i} = c_{m,i-1} - 1) \vee (c_{m,i} = c_{m,i-1} + 1)$$

$$c_{0,n} = n \quad , \quad (c_{i,n} = c_{i-1,n} - 1) \vee (c_{i,n} = c_{i-1,n} + 1)$$

In matching nucleic acid sequences (four letter alphabet) we need only two bits per character and, as we have seen, two bits per value. This greatly reduces the communication and storage costs and significantly improves performance. Nucleic acid sequence databases are already growing in size at an astonishing rate. The Human Genome Project promises to further accelerate this growth. Special purpose parallel architectures for pattern matching and database searching, such as those described, will be crucial to future developments in this area.

6.3.   Molecular Modelling

Molecular modelling is one of the most important practical applications of parallel architectures. Ab initio methods [134, 161, 167] are based on quantum-mechanical calculations of molecular structure. The computation times required for such calculations, even with highly parallel architectures, are at present prohibitive for all but the smallest molecules. However, as the power of parallel machines increases we can expect a much wider use of this approach.

At present, most calculations of the structure and dynamics of proteins, carbohydrates and nucleic acids are carried out using molecular mechanics [271, 349], molecular dynamics [267, 271, 349, 379, 380] and free energy [22] techniques. These methods adopt a force field approach to calculating the potential energy of a molecule in a given conformation. The *AMBER* force field [349] is quite typical. Let $i \Leftrightarrow j$ denote the (symmetric) relation that atom i is bonded to atom j. Then in *AMBER* the potential energy is calculated as a sum of the following types of term.

- Bond energies for all i, j, $i \Leftrightarrow j$

- Angle energies for all i, j, k, $(i \Leftrightarrow k) \wedge (k \Leftrightarrow j)$

- Torsional energies for all i, j, k, l, $(k \Leftrightarrow i) \wedge (i \Leftrightarrow j) \wedge (j \Leftrightarrow l)$

- Coulombic potential for all i, j, $(i \nLeftrightarrow j)$

- Lennard-Jones potential for all i, j, $(i \nLeftrightarrow j)$

- Hydrogen bonding term for all i, j, $(i \nLeftrightarrow j)$

The problem of calculating the potential energy of a molecular conformation is similar in many ways to the sequence comparison problem. They are both instances of "all pairs" computations [347]. For any such computation, a linear systolic array provides a convenient pattern of dataflow. In the case of the potential energy calculation we simply pass one copy of the atomic coordinates and bond information of the structure past another in the array. When the coordinate and bond information for atom i meets that for atom j, we execute the following program.

```
if              i ⇔ j          then   calculate bond term;
                                       for all k, l, (k ⇔ i) ∧ (i ⇔ j) ∧ (j ⇔ l),
                                       calculate torsional terms;

elseif  (i ⇔ k) ∧ (k ⇔ j)      then   calculate angle energy;

                                else   calculate Coulombic energy;
                                       calculate Lennard-Jones potential;
                                       calculate hydrogen bonding term;
```

Let $d_{i,j}$ denote the distance between atoms i, j. The contributions from the Lennard-Jones and hydrogen bonding terms rapidly decline with increasing $d_{i,j}$ and can safely be neglected beyond a certain predefined cut-off distance. Unfortunately, the Coulombic potential does not decline quickly, and it is the calculation of these Coulombic terms for all non-bonded pairs which dominates the energy calculation for large molecules. For a molecule with n atoms, where n is very large, one can use various multipole methods [21, 147, 148, 410] to compute these Coulombic terms using only $o(n^2)$ operations, although the dataflow involved is rather more complex than for the simple systolic algorithm, which uses $O(n^2)$ operations.

6.4. Matrix Multiplication

Consider the problem of multiplying two $n \times n$ matrices A, B to produce C. The definition of matrix multiplication provides us with the following parallel program.

```
par < i, j > ∈ [1...n]²
cᵢⱼ := 0;
seq k ∈ [1...n]
cᵢⱼ := cᵢⱼ + (aᵢₖ * bₖⱼ)
endseq
endpar
```

By adding an extra index to the c variables, we can replace the assignments by equalities, obtaining the following set of definitions.

For all $i, j, k \in [1 \ldots n]$

$c_{ij}^0 = 0$

$c_{ij}^k = c_{ij}^{k-1} + (a_{ik} * b_{kj})$

Implementing this definition as a systolic array would require the a and b values to be broadcast. To avoid this, we can add an extra index to those variables, and redefine the matrix product computation in the following way.

For all $i, j, k \in [1 \ldots n]$

$a_{ik}^0 = a_{ik}$

$b_{kj}^0 = b_{kj}$

$c_{ij}^0 = 0$

$a_{ik}^j = a_{ik}^{j-1}$

$b_{kj}^i = b_{kj}^{i-1}$

$c_{ij}^k = c_{ij}^{k-1} + (a_{ik}^j * b_{kj}^i)$

The graph of functional dependencies corresponding to this set of definitions is shown in Figure 5 for $n = 3$.

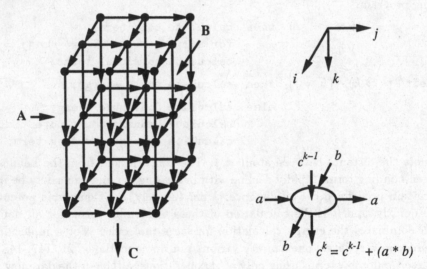

Figure 5. Dataflow for matrix multiplication

This graph shows the dataflow for a three dimensional parallel computation of matrix product. The algorithm requires volume $O(n^3)$ and runs in time $O(n)$. By projecting this graph in one of the three dimensions we can obtain a two dimensional systolic algorithm which requires area $O(n^2)$ and runs in time $O(n)$. For $n = 3$, the algorithm obtained by projecting in the k-direction is shown in Figure 6.

Each cell P_{ij} in the $n \times n$ array is associated with the computation of c_{ij}. The A matrix is input from the left and moves from left to right. The B matrix is input from the top and moves from top to bottom. (The D elements denote timing delays.) At each clock cycle, P_{ij} performs the computation $c_{ij} := c_{ij} + (a_{ik} * b_{kj})$. At the end of the computation, P_{ij} holds the final value of the inner product c_{ij}. The detailed timing and channel requirements

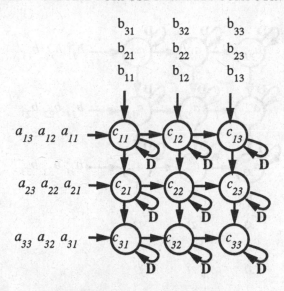

Figure 6. Projection in k-direction

are as follows. $Program_{ij}$ is implemented on processor $P_{i,j}$ in an $n \times n$ array of processors corresponding to the elements of C.

Program$_{ij}$

Time step 0   : $c_{ij} := 0;$

Time step $i + j + t - 2, 0 < t \leq n$: $\text{Input}(a_{it}, b_{tj});$
                                                                       $c_{ij} := c_{ij} + (a_{it} * b_{tj});$
                                                                       $\text{Output}(a_{it}, b_{tj});$

To ensure the correct synchronous dataflow we need to do the following. Provide a communication channel from $P_{i,j}$ to $P_{i,j+1}$ and from $P_{i,j}$ to $P_{i+1,j+1}$, supply a_{ij} as input to processor $P_{i,1}$ at time $i + j - 1$, and supply b_{ij} as input to processor $P_{1,j}$ at time $i + j - 1$. At time step $3n - 1$ the product matrix C is stored in the $n \times n$ processor array and can be output using the communication channels. The algorithm obtained by projecting in the j-direction is shown in Figure 7.

Each cell P_{ij} is associated with element a_{ij} from matrix A. The B matrix is input from the right and moves from right to left. The inner product c_{ij} is computed by the cells in column i, and is output at the bottom of the column. The algorithm obtained by projecting in the i-direction is very similar to the one obtained by projecting in the j-direction although, this time, each cell P_{ij} is associated with element b_{ij} from matrix B and the A matrix is input from the left. These three systolic algorithms can be implemented as VLSI chips which compute the Boolean matrix multiplication function in area $O(n^2)$ and time $O(n)$. Combining this upper bound with the lower bound in Theorem 5.12 we obtain

Theorem 6.1 $AT^2(MM^{(n)}) = \Theta(n^4)$

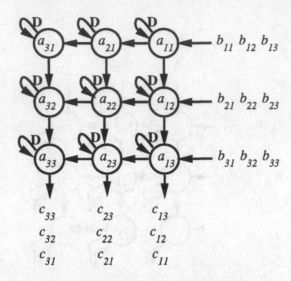

Figure 7. Projection in j-direction

6.5.   LU Decomposition

Another very important problem in linear algebra is LU decomposition. We now show how to derive systolic algorithms for this problem. We begin by describing the standard recursive algorithm for the LU decomposition of an $n \times n$ nonsingular matrix A [91]. For $n = 1$ the problem is trivial since we can take $L = I$ and $U = A$. For $n > 1$, we break A into four parts:

$$A = \begin{pmatrix} a_{11} & a_{12} & \cdots & a_{1n} \\ a_{21} & a_{22} & \cdots & a_{2n} \\ \vdots & \vdots & \ddots & \vdots \\ a_{n1} & a_{n2} & \cdots & a_{nn} \end{pmatrix}$$

$$= \begin{pmatrix} a_{11} & w^T \\ v & \hat{A} \end{pmatrix}$$

where v is an $(n-1)$-column vector, w^T is an $(n-1)$-row vector, and $\hat{A}$ is an $(n-1) \times (n-1)$ matrix. Then, using elementary matrix algebra, we can factor A as

$$A = \begin{pmatrix} 1 & 0 \\ v/a_{11} & I_{n-1} \end{pmatrix} \begin{pmatrix} a_{11} & w^T \\ 0 & \hat{A} - vw^T/a_{11} \end{pmatrix}$$

The 0's in the first and second matrices of the factorisation are row and column vectors, respectively, of size $n-1$. The term vw^T/a_{11}, formed by taking the outer product of v and w and dividing each element of the result by a_{11}, is an $(n-1) \times (n-1)$ matrix, which conforms in size to the matrix $\hat{A}$ from which it is subtracted. The resulting $(n-1) \times (n-1)$ matrix $\hat{A} - vw^T/a_{11}$ is called the *Schur complement* of A with respect to a_{11}. We can now apply the technique recursively to find the LU decomposition of the Schur complement $\hat{A} - vw^T/a_{11}$. Let $\hat{A} - vw^T/a_{11} = \hat{L}\hat{U}$ where $\hat{L}$ is lower triangular and $\hat{U}$ is upper triangular. Then we have

$$A = \begin{pmatrix} 1 & 0 \\ v/a_{11} & \hat{L} \end{pmatrix} \begin{pmatrix} a_{11} & w^T \\ 0 & \hat{U} \end{pmatrix}$$

$$= LU$$

thereby providing our LU decomposition. (Note that because $\hat{L}$ is lower triangular, so is L, and because $\hat{U}$ is lower triangular, so is U.) Transforming this tail recursion to an iteration we obtain the following parallel program.

```
seq k ∈ [1...n]
u_kk := a_kk;
par
par i ∈ [(k+1)...n]
l_ik := a_ik/u_kk
endpar
par j ∈ [(k+1)...n]
u_kj := a_kj
endpar
endpar
par < i, j > ∈ [(k+1)...n]²
a_ij := a_ij - (l_ik * u_kj)
endpar
endseq
```

From this program we can produce the following set of definitions.

For all $1 \leq k < i, j \leq n$,

$$
\begin{aligned}
u_{kk} &= a_{kk} \\
l_{ik} &= a_{ik}^{(k-1)}/u_{kk} \\
u_{kj} &= a_{kj}^{(k-1)} \\
a_{ij}^{(k)} &= a_{ij}^{(k-1)} - (l_{ik} * u_{kj})
\end{aligned}
$$

For $n = 4$, the horizontal sections of the corresponding dataflow graph are shown in Figure 8. (All vertical dataflow is downwards.)

By localising the broadcasts we obtain the following modified set of definitions.

For all $1 \leq k \leq i, j \leq n$,

$$
\begin{aligned}
u_{k,k,k} &= a_{k,k,k-1} \\
l_{i,j,k} &= a_{i,j,k-1}/u_{i,j,k} \text{ if } j = k, \ l_{i,j-1,k} \text{ otherwise.} \\
u_{i,j,k} &= a_{i,j,k-1} \text{ if } i = k, \ u_{i-1,j,k} \text{ otherwise.} \\
a_{i,j,k} &= a_{i,j,k-1} - (l_{i,j,k} * u_{i,j,k})
\end{aligned}
$$

where $a_{i,j,0} = a_{ij}$.

The revised dataflow is shown in Figure 9.

As in the case of matrix multiplication, we can obtain two dimensional systolic algorithms by projecting this dataflow graph in various ways. For $n = 4$, the algorithm obtained by projecting in the i-direction is shown in Figure 10.

In this design, the cells correspond to the u_{kj} values. The matrix A is input from the top, the l values are output from the left, and the u values are held in the array at the end of the computation. An alternative symmetric projection is suggested by the pattern of dataflow in Figure 9. We sketch this symmetric projection for the case $n = 4$ in Figure 11.

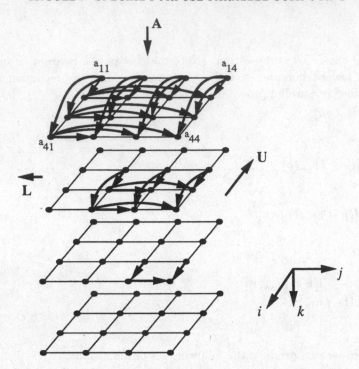

Figure 8. Horizontal dataflow for LU decomposition

The MA cells perform the multiply-and-add operation, those marked ∗ perform multiplication, the one marked / performs division, and those which are unmarked simply pass data. Each channel has an associated delay element for correct timing. For a detailed description of these systolic arrays, see [214].

6.6.　Algebraic Path Problem

A *closed semiring* is an algebraic structure $(S, \oplus, \otimes, I_\oplus, I_\otimes)$ with the following properties:

$\oplus$ is a commutative monoid ($\oplus$ satisfies the closure, associative, commutative properties, and has identity element $I_\oplus$).

$\otimes$ is a monoid ($\otimes$ satisfies the closure, associative properties, and has identity element $I_\otimes$).

$\oplus$ is idempotent.

$\otimes$ is right and left distributive over $\oplus$.

For all $s \in S$, $s \otimes I_\oplus = I_\oplus$.

Let $G = (V, A)$ be a directed graph on $\mid V \mid = n$ vertices, in which each $< i, j > \in A$ has an associated weight $s_{ij} \in S$. Define an $n \times n$ matrix M of weights m_{ij} corresponding to the arcs of G: $m_{ij} = s_{ij}$ if $< i, j > \in A$, $I_\oplus$ otherwise. The *Algebraic Path Problem (APP)* is to compute $M^* = \bigoplus_{k=0}^{\infty} M^k$ where matrix product is defined in terms of the two operations $\oplus$ and $\otimes$. (M^0 is the identity matrix with diagonal elements $I_\otimes$). M_{ij}^* gives the "sum" of the

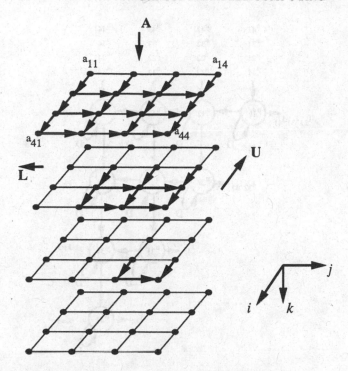

Figure 9. LU decomposition without broadcasting

weights of all directed paths from i to j where the weight of a path is the "product" of the weights of the arcs.

The APP is a problem of major importance in a wide variety of areas and has been extensively studied in recent years. A number of instances of the APP are described in [272]. They include a number of important problems on graphs such as transitive closure [393], shortest paths [117] and the minimum cost spanning tree problem [255]. Noting that node i is connected to node j by a directed path if and only if it is connected by a directed path of length $\leq n - 1$, we have

$$
\begin{aligned}
M^* &= \bigoplus_{k=0}^{n-1} M^k \\
&= (M^0 \oplus M)^{n-1} \\
&= (M^0 \oplus M)^{2^l} \text{ for } 2^l \geq n - 1
\end{aligned}
$$

Therefore, to obtain an efficient parallel algorithm for the computation of the APP on matrix M we need only set the main diagonal to $I_\otimes$ and repeatedly square the resulting matrix until we have a sufficiently large power. For an $n \times n$ matrix M, $O(\log n)$ squarings will be sufficient. We have seen that matrix multiplication, and hence matrix squaring, can be performed in time $O(n)$ on a systolic array of area $O(n^2)$. Therefore, this approach gives us a way of solving the APP in time $O(n \log n)$ on a systolic array of area $O(n^2)$. The systolic method which we will now describe, shows that time $O(n)$ and area $O(n^2)$ can be achieved.

The APP can be solved using the algorithm of Floyd [117]. Translated into our notation, Floyd's algorithm corresponds to the following parallel program.

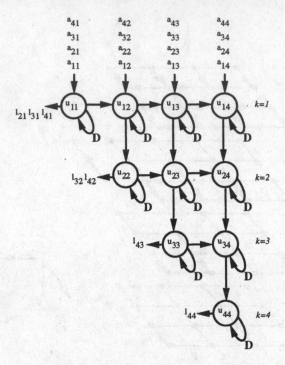

Figure 10. Projection in i-direction

```
seq k ∈ [1...n]
par < i,j > ∈ [1...n]²
m_ij := m_ij ⊕ (m_ik ⊗ m_kj)
endpar
endseq
```

Replacing the assignments by equalities we obtain the following definitions.

For all $1 \leq i,j,k \leq n$,

$$m_{ij}^{(0)} = m_{ij}$$
$$m_{ij}^{(k)} = m_{ij}^{(k-1)} \oplus (m_{ik}^{(k-1)} \otimes m_{kj}^{(k-1)})$$

By localising the broadcasts we obtain the following modified set of definitions.

For all $1 \leq i,j,k \leq n$,

$$m_{i,j,0} = m_{ij}$$
$$r_{i,j,k} = m_{i,j,k-1} \text{ if } j = k, r_{i,j+1,k} \text{ if } j < k, r_{i,j+1,k} \text{ otherwise}$$
$$c_{i,j,k} = m_{i,j,k-1} \text{ if } i = k, c_{i+1,j,k} \text{ if } i < k, c_{i-1,j,k} \text{ otherwise}$$
$$m_{i,j,k} = m_{i,j,k-1} \oplus (r_{i,j,k} \otimes c_{i,j,k})$$

The c and r variables propagate values along columns and rows respectively. The dataflow graph corresponding to these definitions is shown in Figure 12.

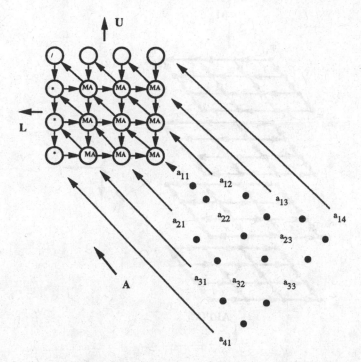

Figure 11. Symmetric i, j, k projection

The pattern of dataflow suggests that we should renumber the nodes, replacing each index (i, j, k) by $((i - k) \bmod n, (j - k) \bmod n, k)$. Having reindexed the nodes in this way, we can then project in the k-direction to obtain the two dimensional array shown in Figure 13.

All that now remains is to eliminate the spiral connections and the long connection between the m_{11} and m_{nn} nodes. Noting that $m_{i,k,k} = m_{i,k,k-1}$ and $m_{k,j,k} = m_{k,j,k-1}$ one can show that these connections can be eliminated to yield the systolic design shown in Figure 14.

A detailed account of this construction can be found in [216].

6.7.   Other Applications

We have described some of the basic problems for which efficient systolic algorithms are known. Over the last decade, a large and diverse range of important applications have been shown to benefit from the systolic approach [120, 121, 150, 205, 207, 211, 213, 214, 258, 268, 276, 277, 279, 291, 309, 317]. The application areas which have been investigated include the following.

Integer and polynomial arithmetic [58, 59, 60]: Multiplication, division, GCD.

Signal and image processing [207, 212, 214, 217, 237, 320]: Filtering, convolution, Fourier transforms, image segmentation.

Linear algebra [137, 214, 311, 317]: Matrix multiplication and inverse, triangularisation, solution of linear systems, LU decomposition, QR decomposition, singular value decomposition.

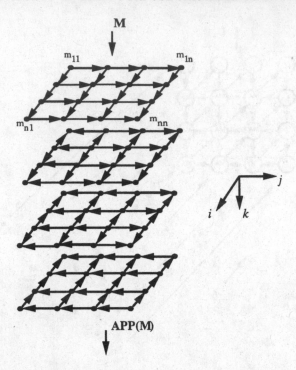

Figure 12. Horizontal dataflow for APP

Computational geometry [13, 74, 78, 95, 190, 370]: Convex hull, contour, visibility, triangulation, proximity, VLSI design rule checking.

Speech processing [126, 405]

Combinatorial algorithms [150, 216, 241, 316, 317, 321, 325]: Dynamic programming, transitive closure, shortest paths.

String processing [12, 73, 122, 180, 246, 271, 319, 356]: String matching, string comparison, longest common subsequence, regular expressions, parsing, data compression.

Data structures [151, 210, 219, 230, 244, 347]: Stacks, priority queues, counters, sorting, set operations, relational databases.

6.8.   Systolic Design

Research work in the field of systolic computation over the last decade has not been exclusively concerned with the problem of designing efficient systolic algorithms. It has addressed a whole range of important issues, including

- design and analysis of new, efficient systolic algorithms [207, 258, 317]

- complexity issues in systolic computation [149]

- direct implementation of systolic arrays using custom VLSI, FPGAs, or wafer scale integration [225]

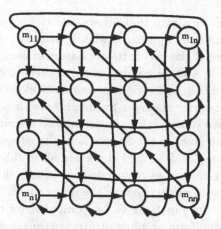

Figure 13. Projection in k-direction

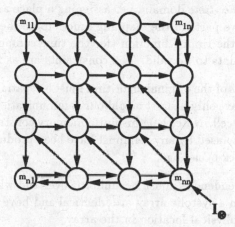

Figure 14. Systolic design for APP

- fault tolerance [209, 225]

- automatic synthesis of systolic designs from high level specifications [67, 72, 77, 177, 189, 214, 236, 250, 288, 308, 309, 310, 311, 314, 326, 346]

- automatic conversion of semi-systolic systems, involving broadcasting or unbounded fan-in, into pure systolic systems with no global data communication [234, 403]

- development of specification and programming languages for systolic computation [69, 77, 221, 346, 391]

- verification of systolic designs [71, 72, 77, 164, 346]

- investigation of asynchronous designs and wavefront arrays [213, 214, 215, 277]

- development of programmable systolic architectures [11, 27, 49, 50, 208]

A major emphasis has been placed on the formal synthesis of systolic designs. In this chapter we have described most of the systolic designs informally, using pictures. In order to be able to specify and derive designs in a way that allows one to reason about their correctness, one requires a much more rigorous approach, with appropriate formal notations. This is particularly important in view of the very intricate nature of many of these designs in terms of communication, timing etc. A large number of researchers have investigated this formal synthesis and verification problem, and various design methodologies have been proposed for its solution. We now briefly describe the main techniques used in several of these approaches. A typical situation is where one starts with an initial parallel algorithm that computes a set of functions at all points in some *index space*, for example, the integer lattice points in a subset of Euclidean space. The examples described above are all of this form. If the algorithm is given as a simple loop program (set of recurrence equations) then the ranges of the loop (ranges of equation indices, respectively) define the index space. The body of the loop (set of equations, resp.) defines the functions to be computed by the cell. Given an initial specification in the form of a uniform or affine recurrence equation [192, 311, 314, 326], or in a form that can be easily transformed into one, the synthesis problem reduces to mapping the original index space to a *space-time* domain, i.e. assigning a place and time to each point in the original domain. The two parts of the mapping function are the allocation function (for the space component) and the timing function (for the time component). Such a mapping must satisfy certain constraints to be valid. The constraints are as follows.

- The data dependencies of the original algorithm must be spatially and temporally local, since systolic arrays have only nearest neighbour communication (spatial locality) and a finite memory in each cell. Note that this finite memory constraint mandates temporal locality, since the value used by any cell must have been produced by a neighbour only a finite number of clock cycles ago.

- The transformed dependencies must be uniform over the whole space-time domain, since the processors in a systolic array are identical and have similar interconnections independent of their physical location in the array.

- The mapping must be bijective, i.e. distinct points in the index space must be mapped to distinct points in the space-time domain. If not, the computations from two distinct points in the problem domain would be scheduled on the same cell at the same time, giving rise to a conflict.

- The time component must preserve the dependencies of the original index space, i.e. if a computation is scheduled at some point, then the computation of each of its arguments must be scheduled earlier.

- The space component of the transformed dependencies must correspond to nearest neighbour connections.

For a description of the various methods used to produce such space-time mappings see, for example, [67, 250, 311, 314, 326].

The design, analysis, implementation and verification of systolic systems is a major area of activity within the field of special purpose parallel computing, and rightly so. It is perhaps the most mature subfield in the area, having its own languages, compilers, formal design methodologies and verification methods. Researchers in systolic computation have also succeeded in producing an impressive collection of interesting and efficient algorithms for a wide range of important problems. The early arguments of Kung [207] in support of the systolic approach have undoubtedly been shown, by the experience of the last few years, to have been justified.

7. Cellular Automata

Differential equations form the mathematical basis for most current models of natural systems. Cellular automata may be considered as an alternative, and in some respects, complementary basis for mathematical models of nature. Whereas differential equations are suitable for systems with a small number of continuous degrees of freedom, evolving in a continuous manner, cellular automata describe the behaviour of systems with large numbers of discrete degrees of freedom. Although cellular automata are simple mathematical systems they can exhibit very complex behaviour. The book by Toffoli and Margolus [364] and the collections of papers in [112] and [402] provide a wealth of information on the theoretical and practical aspects of cellular automata.

In a simple case, a cellular automaton consists of a line of cells or sites, each with value 0 or 1. The sequence of site values is the "configuration" of the cellular automaton. These values are updated synchronously in parallel in a sequence of discrete time steps, according to a fixed rule. Denoting the value of a site at position i by a_i, a simple rule gives its new value as $a_i^{(t+1)} = f(a_{i-1}^{(t)}, a_i^{(t)}, a_{i+1}^{(t)})$. Here f is a Boolean function which specifies the rule. In general, the sites in a cellular automaton may have any finite number k of possible values. The rules for updating these sites may depend on values up to any finite distance r away. In addition, the cellular automaton sites may be arranged not on a line, but on a regular lattice in any number of dimensions. Many of the generic features of behaviour are however largely unaffected by such additional flexibility. Cellular automata have a number of basic defining characteristics.

Discrete in space. They consist of a discrete grid of spatial cells or sites

Discrete in time. The value of each cell is updated in a sequence of discrete time steps.

Discrete states. Each cell has a finite number of possible values.

Homogeneous. All cells are identical, and are arranged in a regular array.

Synchronous updating. All cell values are updated in synchrony, each depending on the previous values of neighbouring cells.

Deterministic rule. Each cell value is updated according to a fixed, deterministic rule.

Spatially local rule. The rule at each site depends only on the values of a local neighbourhood of sites around it.

Temporally local rule. The rule for the new value of a site depends only on values for a fixed number of preceding steps (usually just one step)

Each of these characteristics represents a simplifying feature in the basic construction of cellular automata. They make many kinds of analysis and simulation much easier. But they yield few, if any, restrictions on overall cellular automaton behaviour. While each cell is discrete, collections of large numbers of cells may, for example, show effectively continuous behaviour.

It is a common occurrence in nature for a large number of similar elements (e.g. molecules, animals) to interact in such a way as to exhibit large-scale phenomena not present in the individual elements. A simple example is a gas: molecules that individually obey rather simple collision laws give rise to collective behaviour that can be quite varied and complex, including sound waves, vortices, and turbulence. What is interesting from a modelling viewpoint is that substantially the same macroscopic behaviour can be obtained starting from "individuals" that are much simpler than real molecules, namely, the cells of a cellular automaton. Only certain features (such as, in this case, conservation of particles and of momentum) manage to make their effects felt all the way up to the macroscopic level; the others become irrelevant on a sufficiently large scale. This phenomenology was originally observed in physics, but analogous effects have been noted in other fields, such as biology and economics, where the interacting individuals may be much more complex than gas molecules. As was the case with gases, the essential aspects of these collective phenomena can generally be reproduced by cellular automata because they possess the essential feature of locality of interaction among a large number of similar individuals.

Cellular automata provide exactly computable models for various physical phenomena and large-scale correlations that result from very simple short-range interactions. In doing so, they provide a third alternative to the classical dichotomy between models that are solvable exactly (by analytical means) but are very stylised, and models that are more realistic but can only be solved approximately (by numerical means).

7.1.   Lattice Gas Computers

In hydrodynamics we are chiefly interested in situations where different parts of a fluid move with respect to one another, and with respect to solid obstacles, at velocities that are much smaller than than that of sound. In this limit, and neglecting external forces such as gravity, any density differences equalise themselves in a negligible time and the fluid can be treated as incompressible. Even when these simplifications apply, the phenomenology of fluids can be enormously varied. Depending on the speed of the main flow, the size and shape of the obstacles, and the viscosity of the fluid, one can have laminar flow, vortices, turbulence etc. In this context the relevant variable is the *velocity* V (a vector) of flow at different points, and the relevant parameter is the *viscosity* ν of the fluid. The behaviour of the fluid is governed by the *Navier-Stokes* equation

$$\frac{\partial V}{\partial t} + (V\nabla)V = -\frac{1}{\rho}\nabla p + \nu\nabla^2 V$$

where p is the pressure and ρ is the (constant) density. This is a *nonlinear* differential equation, and, except for special cases, one must make recourse to numerical methods in order to find its solution for given initial and boundary conditions. Much computer time around the world is devoted to the numerical solution of such hydrodynamical problems.

In recent years various lattice gas cellular automata have been developed for the solution of fluid flow problems in hydrodynamics. We will briefly describe two of these automata. The first, which we will call HPP, was introduced in [156], and operates on a two dimensional orthogonal lattice. The second, FHP, was first described in [125], and operates on a two dimensional hexagonal lattice. It turns out that, on a macroscopic scale, the gases described by HPP obey the 2D Navier-Stokes equation approximately; and those described by FHP obey this equation exactly.

The HPP gas was originally formulated as follows. Consider an orthogonal lattice consisting of sites connected by north, south, west, and east links. There are four kinds of particles, one for each direction, and a site can be occupied by at most one particle of each kind (exclusion principle) Thus, there can be up to four particles per site. The updating is done with a two-step cycle. At step 0 each particle moves along a link from its current site to the adjacent site corresponding to its direction; at step 1 particles are shuffled within each site in the following way. If there are, at that site, exactly two particles which have come in from opposite directions, say north and south, then they are replaced by a west/east pair; otherwise nothing changes. As was mentioned, the behaviour of the HPP model departs from the Navier-Stokes equation. The various isotropy problems etc. associated with the HPP model are solved in the FHP model. It uses six kinds of particles; i.e. there are six directions of travel, with a 60° angle from one to the next. The lattice is a hexagonal one, and each site can contain up to six particles (one of each kind). As in the HPP model, collisions are defined so as to conserve energy (number of particles) and momentum. A simple version of the FHP rule has a collision occur whenever the momentum at a site is zero. If there is no collision, all particles go straight. If there is a collision, all particles at that site are deflected 60° clockwise (or counterclockwise) from the path they were following.

Three dimensional regular lattices do not have enough symmetry to ensure macroscopic isotropy [98, 125]. A suitable four dimensional structure was described in [98]. It is a face centered hypercubic (FCHC) lattice, defined as the set of signed integers (x_1, x_2, x_3, x_4) such that $x_1 + x_2 + x_3 + x_4$ is even. Each node is connected by links of length $\sqrt{2}$ to the 24 nearest neighbours, which have exactly two coordinates differing by ±1. To model three dimensional fluids and maintain the required isotropies, we can define a pseudo-four-dimensional model [98] as the three dimensional projection of an FCHC model with unit periodicity in the x_4 direction.

Since the appearance of [125], lattice gas methods have been used to study 3D Navier-Stokes (NS) flow, 2D convective NS flow, 2D and 3D two-phase NS flow with interfacial surface tension, and various linear and nonlinear diffusion equations. The collection of papers in [100] provides an excellent account of the research work which has been carried out in recent years on lattice gas computation. See also [46, 76, 124, 364, 402].

By definition, cellular automata are highly parallel, highly regular, and require only local communication. This means that cellular automata machines can be easily scaled to arbitrarily large sizes with no loss of efficiency, as in the case of systolic arrays. In a previous section we described the kind of performance that a researcher working on three dimensional fluid flow using lattice gas methods is likely to require by the mid 1990s [96]. As noted there, it is unlikely that anything other than a very specialised system could come close to achieving those requirements. Therefore, we can expect to see the emergence of various new cellular automata and lattice gas architectures over the next few years. At one end of the spectrum, such systems might be based on standard VLSI devices such as FPGAs. At the other end, they may be based on exotic new technologies such as arrays of quantum dots.

The study of cellular automata and lattice gas computation is in many respects only just beginning. It will probably be many years before we have an understanding of the theory and applications of cellular automata and lattice gases comparable to that which we have today for differential equations. The availability of very powerful special purpose parallel systems for performing those computations will ensure that we continue to strive for such an understanding.

8.   Multicomputers

A distributed memory multicomputer can be thought of as having p processor-memory pairs located at distinct vertices of a p-vertex graph. Each processor can send packets to, and receive packets from, processors at adjacent vertices in the graph. Each edge of the graph can transmit one packet of information in unit time, and has a queue for storing packets that have to be transmitted along it. A number of such multicomputer systems have been commercially available from companies in the United States and Europe since the mid 1980s. In such a system, memory is organised in terms of multiple private address spaces with explicit message passing by the programmer [168, 170, 187] for all non-local memory requests. Despite the difficulties of programming such systems, and the architecture dependence of the resulting software, a large number of interesting new high performance parallel algorithms have been developed for multicomputer architectures of various kinds. Detailed accounts of the theoretical aspects of multicomputers can be found in [185, 224, 226, 227]. For an account of some of the more practical issues involving multicomputers see, for example, [17, 34, 94, 185, 340, 341, 342]. In this chapter we will limit ourselves to discussing some of the general theoretical issues concerning such systems.

A large number of graphs have been proposed as interconnection networks for such multi-computers. Two important parameters of any such graph are its *degree*, i.e. the maximum number of edges incident at any vertex, and its *diameter*, i.e. the maximum distance between any pair of vertices, where the distance between two vertices is the length of a shortest path between them. If implemented using conventional VLSI technology, a graph with low degree is likely to have advantages in terms of physical packaging. The advantage of using a graph with small diameter is, of course, that it will permit a packet to be sent quickly between any two vertices in the network. Another important property of any such graph is its bisection width. The *bisection width* of a graph is the minimum number of edges that have to be removed in order to partition the graph into two parts where the numbers of vertices differ by at most one. The bisection width of a network is often a critical factor in determining the speed with which a multicomputer can perform a computation. This is due to the fact that for many problems, the data contained in, or computed by, one half of the machine may be needed by the other half before the computation can be completed. A fourth property of any such graph, closely related to the bisection width, is the *area* required for its layout in the VLSI model of section 5.

Theorem 8.1 (Thompson [357]) *Any VLSI layout of a graph with bisection width B and degree at most four requires area $\Omega(B^2)$.*

Proof. Suppose the graph can be laid out in a rectangle of height h and width w, as in Figure 2 (section 5). By an argument very similar to that used in the proof of Theorem 5.10, we can show that there is a line which partitions the layout into two parts where the numbers of vertices differ by at most one, and which runs vertically between the cells, except possibly for a single jog of one cell width. By the definition of the bisection width B, the number of edges crossing the line is at least $B-1$ (at most one edge may cross the horizontal segment). Thus, the height of the layout must be at least $B-1$. Similarly, the width of the graph must be at least $B-1$. Therefore, the area must be at least $(B-1)^2$. (Note that Theorem 8.1 can be trivial, as in the case of a disconnected graph.) $\square$

We have now listed four important properties of any graph proposed for the interconnection network of a multicomputer: degree, diameter, bisection width, and area. For our fifth, and final, property we note that ease of programming and avoidance of bottlenecks both suggest that a useful feature for any such graph is that it should look isomorphic from any vertex, i.e. it should be vertex transitive [39]. Let $G = (V, E)$ be an undirected graph, where V is the set of vertices and E is the set of edges. An automorphism of G is a permutation p of V such that $(v_1, v_2) \in E$ holds if and only if $(\pi(v_1), \pi(v_2)) \in E$. The set of all automorphisms with the operation of composition forms a group acting on V. For example, for the complete graph K_p on p vertices, the group of automorphisms is the symmetric group S_p since any permutation of vertices preserves adjacency. (The empty graph on p vertices also admits S_p.) A graph is *vertex transitive* if it admits a group of automorphisms acting transitively on the vertices [39]. (A permutation group (H, V) is *transitive* if there is only one orbit in the action of H on V. We can check this by picking an element $v \in V$ and looking for elements of H taking v to every other element in V.) There is also a related property of *edge transitivity* but, for simplicity, we will not pursue that notion here. Various graphs on p vertices which might be considered as interconnection networks, are listed in Table 1, together with information on their degree, diameter, bisection width, area, and vertex transitivity.

Detailed descriptions of these various graphs can be found in [38, 48, 145, 146, 222, 224, 227, 228, 231, 232, 233, 240, 289].

Name	Degree	Diameter	Bisection Width	Area	VT?
1D array (ring)	2	$p/2$	2	$\Theta(p)$	yes
Complete binary tree	3	$2 \log p$	1	$\Theta(p)$	no
Shuffle-exchange	3	$2 \log p$	$\Theta(p/\log p)$	$\Theta(p^2/\log^2 p)$	no
Cube-connected-cycles	3	$(5/2) \log p$	$\Theta(p/\log p)$	$\Theta(p^2/\log^2 p)$	yes
2D mesh of trees	3	$2 \log p$	$\Theta(p^{1/2})$	$\Theta(p \log^2 p)$	no
3D mesh of trees	3	$2 \log p$	$\Theta(p^{2/3})$	$\Theta(p^{4/3})$	no
1D multigrid	4	$4 \log p$	$O(\log p)$	$\Theta(p)$	no
2D array (toroidal)	4	$\Theta(p^{1/2})$	$\Theta(p^{1/2})$	$\Theta(p)$	yes
Tree of meshes	4	$\Theta(p^{1/2}/\log^{1/2} p)$	$\Theta(p^{1/2}/\log^{1/2} p)$	$\Theta(p \log p)$	no
Fat tree	4	$\Theta(\log p)$	$O(p^{1/2}/\log p)$	$\Theta(p)$	no
Butterfly (wrapped)	4	$2 \log p$	$\Theta(p/\log p)$	$\Theta(p^2/\log^2 p)$	yes
de Bruijn graph	4	$\log p$	$\Theta(p/\log p)$	$\Theta(p^2/\log^2 p)$	no
Complete quadtree	5	$\log p$	2	$\Theta(p)$	no
X-Tree	5	$2 \log p$	$\Theta(\log p)$	$\Theta(p)$	no
2D multigrid	6	$3 \log p$	$\Theta(p^{1/2})$	$\Theta(p)$	no
3D array (toroidal)	6	$\Theta(p^{1/3})$	$\Theta(p^{2/3})$	$\Theta(p^{4/3})$	yes
Twin butterfly (wrapped)	8	$2 \log p$	$\Theta(p/\log p)$	$\Theta(p^2/\log^2 p)$	no
Pyramid	9	$\log p$	$\Theta(p^{1/2})$	$\Theta(p)$	no
Complete 2^k-ary tree	$2^k + 1$	$2 \log_k p/k$	2^{k-1}	$O(4^k p)$	no
Hypercube	$\log p$	$\log p$	$p/2$	$\Theta(p^2)$	yes
$(p^{1/2})$-deg. random graph	$p^{1/2}$	2	$\Theta(p^{3/2})$	$\Theta(p^3)$	no
Complete graph (K_p)	$p - 1$	1	$\Theta(p^2)$	$\Theta(p^4)$	yes

Table 1.

If our interconnection network is to be implemented using VLSI technology then, ideally, we would like it to have low degree, low diameter, high bisection width and low area, and also to be vertex transitive. The reason so many networks have been proposed in the last decade is that, of course, these desirable features, to some extent, conflict with one another. The constant bisection width of rings and trees tends to rule them out of serious consideration. (Although multicomputers with more powerful connectivity are often used as rings to implement one dimensional systolic algorithms [271].) Graphs with degree higher than about $log\ p$ tend to be ruled out for multicomputer networks on grounds of packaging. (Although Valiant [374] has suggested ($p^{1/2}$)-degree random graphs as a biologically plausible structure for certain types of neural networks.) The multigrids, X-Tree and pyramid have been suggested as appropriate for applications in numerical computation, image processing and computer vision [5, 284, 351]. They do, indeed, appear to be well suited to such applications. However, for a broader class of computations, some of which require a large amount of simultaneous non-local communication, the exponentially decreasing bisection width as we move up from the base of the 2D multigrid or pyramid to the top level, is likely to be a severely limiting factor. Arrays have been widely proposed as the best general structure for multicomputers, and a number of practical designs are based on arrays. The main advantage of the 2D and 3D arrays are their simplicity, and the fact that they can be easily implemented as physical VLSI systems. 2D arrays have optimal $\Theta(p)$ VLSI area and 3D arrays have optimal $\Theta(p)$ VLSI *volume*. The main disadvantage of arrays, for computations requiring a large amount of non-local communication, is their high diameter. (Although, again, they are very appropriate for implementing systolic algorithms, and others which require only local communication [224, 335, 360].) We now briefly discuss some of the properties of the remaining graphs in the table. The shuffle-exchange, cube-connected-cycles, butterfly and de Bruijn graphs have very similar properties. We will refer only to the butterfly. Various fat tree designs have been proposed. They are all essentially improvements of Leighton's original tree of meshes graph [222]. For that reason, we will not explicitly consider the original tree of meshes graph further here. The 2D and 3D mesh of trees differ only in terms of their dimension. We will consider only the 2D mesh of trees. We thus have reduced our list of candidates to those shown in Table 2.

Name	Degree	Diameter	Bisection Width	Area	V.T. ?
2D mesh of trees	3	$2\ log\ p$	$\Theta(p^{1/2})$	$\Theta(p\ log^2 p)$	no
Fat tree	4	$\Theta(log\ p)$	$O(p^{1/2}/log\ p)$	$\Theta(p)$	no
Butterfly (wrapped)	4	$2\ log\ p$	$\Theta(p/log\ p)$	$\Theta(p^2/log^2 p)$	yes
Twin butterfly (wrapped)	8	$2\ log\ p$	$\Theta(p/log\ p)$	$\Theta(p^2/log^2 p)$	no
Hypercube	$log\ p$	$log\ p$	$p/2$	$\Theta(p^2)$	yes

Table 2.

Leiserson [232] has argued that, in the design of interconnection networks, a major goal should be to achieve *area universality* in the two dimensional VLSI model, or *volume universality* in the three dimensional VLSI model. An area universal network is one which, for a given area A, can simulate any other network of comparable area, with only $O(log\ A)$ slowdown (at least with high probability.) It is well known that a p-processor hypercube can efficiently simulate any fixed degree p-processor network. We need only realise an h-relation, where h is the degree of the network. This can be done in $O(log\ p)$ steps on a hypercube for any $h \leq log\ p$ [376]. If, however, we normalise by area instead of by number of processors, we see that an area A hypercube cannot simulate all area A networks efficiently. For example, since an area A hypercube (butterfly) has only $\Theta(A^{1/2})$ ($\Theta(A^{1/2}\ log\ A)$ respectively) processors (see above table), it cannot simulate a 2D array with area A, which has $\Theta(A)$ processors (see table) in any polylogarithmic time. Leiserson has established the following theorem.

Theorem 8.2 *The fat tree is an area universal network for the two dimensional VLSI model, and a volume universal network for the three dimensional VLSI model.*

For details of the proof of Theorem 8.2, see [145, 227, 232]. The design and analysis of efficient algorithms for the fat tree is considered in [233]. Theorem 8.2 suggests that if one plans to implement a p-processor interconnection network in VLSI, then, for large p, one should implement a fat tree rather than a butterfly or a hypercube, despite the fact that it lacks the attractive property of being vertex transitive. (Note. The interconnection network for the latest Connection Machine architecture, the CM5, is based on a fat tree.)

We have seen that butterflies and hypercubes cannot be efficiently implemented using VLSI technology, i.e. without having long wires for some of the edges in the network. However, optical communication systems [30, 113] offer the prospect of a dramatic improvement in the efficiency with which such networks can be implemented. In [313], Rao shows that a simple (and possibly cheap) optical interconnection architecture based on wavelength division multiplexing can be used to solve the VLSI wiring problem. He considers various routing problems on a $p^{1/2} \times p^{1/2}$ 2D array of processors, where the processors on each row of the array are connected by an optical bus, and the processors on each column of the array are also connected by such a bus. We thus have $2p^{1/2}$ buses, each of length $p^{1/2}$. Each bus uses *wavelength division multiplexing (WDM)* [101] to support simultaneous communication between many disjoint pairs of processors on the same bus. This communications architecture will be referred to as the p processor *mesh of buses (MOB)*. The idea of using a mesh of buses for interconnection was proposed by Wittie [401], and as a basis for optical interconnection networks by Dowd [101]. To solve the VLSI wiring problem we need only consider the simplest MOB in which the optical buses have fixed transmitters and receivers at each processor, i.e. where the transmitters and receivers are initially set (off-line) to achieve a certain communication pattern, e.g. a hypercube or a butterfly, and then remain fixed as that pattern is used. The first result shows that all networks can be emulated on the MOB with an efficiency related to the degree of the network.

Theorem 8.3 *Any p processor network N of degree d can be emulated on a p processor MOB so that (i) there are $O(d)$ transmitters/receivers per processor, and (ii) each edge in N is realised by a path of length at most three in the MOB.*

By an edge in the MOB we mean a channel on one of the buses, and by a path we mean a sequence of such edges. For networks such as the cube-connected-cycles, butterfly and hypercube we can do even better.

Theorem 8.4 *A p processor cube-connected-cycles or butterfly network can be emulated on a p processor MOB so that (i) there are $O(1)$ transmitters/receivers per processor, and (ii) each edge in the cube-connected-cycles is realised by a single edge in the MOB.*

Theorem 8.5 *A p processor hypercube network can be emulated on a p processor MOB so that (i) there are $O(\log p)$ transmitters/receivers per processor, and (ii) each edge in the hypercube is realised by a single edge in the MOB.*

Theorems 8.4 and 8.5 follow directly from standard VLSI layouts of those networks.

The mesh of trees network has been extensively studied in recent years. In Chapter 2 of [224], Leighton describes a large number of parallel algorithms which can be efficiently implemented on the two dimensional mesh of trees architecture. The problems include packet routing, sorting, matrix-vector multiplication, Jacobi relaxation, pivoting, convolution, convex hull, integer multiplication, powering, division, root finding, minimum cost spanning tree, connected components, transitive closure, shortest paths, maximum matching, breadth-first search, and evaluation of straight line programs. He also shows that various matrix problems such as matrix multiplication, inversion, decomposition and powering can be efficiently solved on the three dimensional mesh of trees.

The hypercube family of graphs (hypercube, butterfly, shuffle-exchange, cube-connected-cycles, de Bruijn graph) have also been widely studied. In Chapter 3 of [224], Leighton describes various parallel algorithms which can be efficiently implemented on the hypercube family. The problems include packet routing, sorting, and computing the discrete Fourier transform. He also describes a number of more general results concerning the hypercube family, including the following two theorems.

Theorem 8.6 *A p-processor hypercube can simulate any $O(p)$-processor array, binary tree, mesh of trees, X-Tree, or pyramid, with only a small constant factor slowdown.*

A hypercube algorithm is said to be *normal* if only one dimension of hypercube edges is used at any step, and if consecutive dimensions are used in consecutive steps. There are many important examples of hypercube algorithms that are normal. For instance, all of the mesh of trees algorithms described in Chapter 2 of [224] can be implemented in a normal form on the hypercube.

Theorem 8.7 *For a normal hypercube algorithm, the fixed degree members of the hypercube family (p-processor butterfly, shuffle-exchange, cube-connected-cycles, de Bruijn graph) can simulate the computation of the p-processor ($(\log p)$-degree) hypercube with only constant slowdown.*

Theorem 8.7 is a very powerful result since those fixed degree graphs have a factor of $\log p$ fewer edges than the hypercube. It is, however, known that for the general problem of packet routing, the hypercube is more powerful than the fixed degree members of the family, since one can realise a $O(\log p)$-relation on the hypercube in only $O(\log p)$ steps [376]. Therefore, for the packet routing problem at least, the much greater communications bandwidth afforded by the higher degree is an advantage.

The multibutterfly family of graphs, of which the twin butterfly is a member, is another family of interconnection networks which has been receiving attention recently. In [228, 371] it is shown that a simple deterministic packet routing algorithm can be used to realise a 1-relation in $O(\log p)$ steps on a multibutterfly. The multibutterfly is a randomly wired, bounded degree network based on the butterfly. An important feature of multibutterflies is that they have powerful expansion properties. In addition to permitting fast deterministic packet routing, such expander graphs also have very strong fault tolerance properties.

Finally, we mention two graphs of rather more specialised interest, the Sneptree and the polymorphic array. Many important computational problems have an inherent tree structure. For example, algorithms for game tree evaluation, functional expression evaluation, branch and bound search, and divide and conquer often give rise to tree structures, where the nodes of the tree represent computational tasks to be performed and the edges of the tree represent the required communication. For such computations, we would like to have an interconnection network onto which we could embed any tree in a way that balanced the computational load on each processor, and kept the communication local. In addition, we would like to be able to do the embedding dynamically. This is because, for many such applications (e.g. game tree evaluation, branch and bound search), the structure of the tree will change significantly during the course of the computation. In Chapter 3 of [224] it is shown that a binary tree can be efficiently embedded, in a dynamic manner, in a hypercube of comparable size. The Sneptree [165, 242, 264, 265] is another convenient network for dynamic tree embeddings. A Sneptree can be regarded as the degree-regular closure of a complete binary tree in much the same way as the ring is the degree-regular closure of a 1D array. A *k-level Sneptree* is a directed complete binary tree of $2^k - 1$ vertices, with arcs directed towards the leaves, augmented with 2^k arcs directed out of the leaves, such that each vertex has four incident arcs, two directed in and two directed out. The root and the leaves of the underlying binary tree of a Sneptree are called the root and leaves of the Sneptree as well. Of the two outgoing arcs of a vertex, one is called the left arc and the other the right arc, whilst the vertex pointed to by the left (right) arc of a vertex is said to be the left (right) child of that vertex. There are many possible ways to connect the 2^k augmented arcs. We can directly embed any complete binary tree T onto any Sneptree S by simply mapping the root of T onto the root of S, and mapping the left and right child of any vertex $t \in T$ onto the left and right child, respectively, of the vertex in S to which t is mapped. This embedding is efficient, i.e. achieves good load balancing and locality. For the problem of embedding a binary tree $\hat{T}$ which is not a complete binary tree, onto a Sneptree S, we can use exactly the same simple mapping technique. However, in this case, the distribution of vertices from $\hat{T}$ over the vertices of S will, of course, be strongly affected by the particular interconnection pattern of the Sneptree. A detailed treatment of Sneptrees can be found in [165]. A flexible network for 2D array computations is provided by the polymorphic array [115]. A *p-vertex polymorphic array* is a regular, degree four graph, which has a two dimensional VLSI layout in which all edges have constant length. It, therefore, requires only $O(p)$ area. Any 2D array (of any shape or size) can be directly mapped onto a polymorphic array, as in the case of the Sneptree. The resulting embedding preserves locality, and is guaranteed to balance the load on each processor to within an additive $O(log\ p)$ term of the best possible.

For more on the VLSI layout of networks, on the efficient embedding of one network in another, and on the demonstration of work-preserving emulations of one network by another, see [35, 36, 37, 38, 47, 52, 146, 165, 171, 185, 199, 200, 222, 224, 226, 227, 231, 240, 289, 323, 336, 372, 384].

9. Intelligent Systems

The remarkable phenomenon of human thought has interested philosophers since the time of Plato and Aristotle and a large number of physical and metaphysical explanations of thinking and, more generally, of the relationship between mind and body, have been proposed down through the centuries. In the past one hundred years, there have been major advances in neurobiology, psychology and computing. The developments in neurobiology and psychology have provided us with a detailed, but by no means complete, understanding of the structure and function of the various parts of the brain [343]. Progress in computing, and more particularly in the area of artificial intelligence [400], has shown that many of the "higher level" problem solving capabilities of the human brain can be performed by computing systems. In spite of these advances, a number of the central philosophical questions, such as "can a machine think?", continue to generate heated debates amongst both philosophers and scientists [82, 102, 119, 301, 337, 366, 367]. An examination of the arguments put forward in such debates would suggest that, as in the case of many interesting philosophical questions, the issues are unlikely to ever be completely resolved, and certainly not by progress in science and technology alone.

Soon after the first digital computers were developed, a number of researchers began to explore the possibility of designing computing systems which would be capable of "intelligent" behaviour, i.e. would exhibit behaviour which would hitherto have required human intelligence. From the time of the earliest papers on artificial intelligence, there have been two distinct approaches to achieving the general goal of intelligent computing systems. We will refer to these as the symbolic computation approach and the neural networks approach. In very general terms, those pursuing the symbolic computation approach, whether from the logicist [294] or the "knowledge is all there is" [235] schools, have been concerned with developing advanced computing systems which can perform "complex" problem solving tasks (e.g. chess playing, theorem proving, medical diagnosis, chemical structure analysis, constraint satisfaction, rule-based deduction) without particular regard to how those tasks might be carried out in the human brain. Those pursuing the neural networks approach, on the other hand, have traditionally been more concerned with directly modelling the kinds of complex physical processes that might be occurring in the brain when one is performing "simple" tasks such as vision or basic pattern recognition [8, 9, 172, 188, 195, 274, 285, 324, 327, 344, 398, 400]. In the neural networks approach there has been a much greater emphasis on the importance of training/learning. Over the last few years, in addition to the work which has been carried out on the engineering of learning systems (in the field of neural networks) and on the understanding of human learning (in computational neuroscience), a large amount of work has been done on the computational complexity of various aspects of machine learning [188, 193, 293, 373, 377].

The enthusiasm for each of these two approaches (symbolic computation, neural networks) has fluctuated over the years, as new computing technologies have been developed and as different types of applications have been explored [104, 286]. In the last few years, a third bottom-up perspective on the development of intelligent systems, which we might call the "embedded computation" approach, has been strongly promoted within the artificial intelligence community. In this approach there is much greater emphasis on the importance of situatedness and embodiment [61, 62, 197, 198, 254, 392], as in the philosophy of Heidegger [103]. These three approaches to the problem of developing intelligent systems emphasise the need for different types of special purpose parallel computing systems. With symbolic computation one requires high performance systems for combinatorial searching, mechanised reasoning etc. With neural networks one requires large collections of relatively simple automata. In the case of embedded computation, as exemplified by the robots developed by Brooks and his colleagues [61, 62], one requires small, powerful on-board distributed systems for various tasks such as sensing, navigation, planning, reaction and learning.

Much of the experimental work on neural networks so far has been concerned with the goal of emulating "high level" cognitive skills such as problem solving or language. Our current understanding of how such activities are performed in the human nervous system is not, however, particularly well developed. In contrast to this, there has been, in recent years, a major increase in our knowledge of the human visual and auditory systems, due to the emergence of new experimental techniques in neuroscience and psychology. Detailed physiological studies have given us a picture of the mapping of the visual field onto the visual cortex, and similar information is available for many important auditory areas. For simpler life forms, even more is known. For example, it is known that a fly eye contains about 24,000 visual receptors, and four layers of neurons between the photoreceptors at the input level and motoneurons at the output level (see reference in [343]). Over the last few years, Mead and his colleagues [256, 278, 328] have been developing a variety of new analog VLSI systems which aim to emulate the performance of living systems in certain well understood areas of neural computation. They have developed motion sensors [278], silicon models of the retina [256, 278] and inner ear [278], and models of pattern generators in simple invertebrate systems [328].

The development of various kinds of "intelligent" systems, based on special purpose parallel architectures, is likely to be a major area of activity in the coming decade.

Acknowledgements

I would like to thank Les Valiant and Bill Gear for providing the opportunity for me to spend my sabbatical leave from Oxford at NEC Research Institute, and to my colleagues at NECI for providing such a stimulating environment in which to work.

References

[1] E Aarts, F de Bont, E Habers, and P van Laarhoven. Parallel implementations of the statistical cooling algorithm. *Integration, The VLSI Journal*, 4:209–238, 1986.

[2] E H L Aarts and J H M Korst. Boltzmann machines as a model for parallel annealing. *Algorithmica*, 6(3):437–465, 1991.

[3] H Abelson and P Andreae. Information transfer and area-time tradeoffs for VLSI multiplication. *Communications of the ACM*, 23(1):20–23, January 1980.

[4] A Aggarwal. On simulation and interrelations between Boolean and VLSI circuits. In *Proc. 21st Annual Allerton Conference*, pages 258–265, 1983.

[5] A Aggarwal. A comparative study of x-tree, pyramid and related machines. In *Proc. 25th Annual IEEE Symposium on Foundations of Computer Science*, pages 89–99, 1984.

[6] A V Aho, J D Ullman, and M Yannakakis. On notions of information transfer in VLSI circuits. In *Proc. 15th Annual ACM Symposium on Theory of Computing*, pages 133–139, 1983.

[7] Algotronix Limited. *CAL 1024 Datasheet*. Algotronix Limited, 1990.

[8] J A Anderson, A Pellionisz, and E Rosenfeld, editors. *Neurocomputing 2: Directions for Research*. MIT Press, Cambridge, MA, 1990.

[9] J A Anderson and E Rosenfeld, editors. *Neurocomputing: Foundations of Research*. MIT Press, Cambridge, MA, 1988.

[10] R J Anderson and G L Miller. Optical communication for pointer based algorithms. Technical Report CRI 88-14, University of Southern California, 1988.

[11] M Annaratone, E Arnould, T Gross, H T Kung, M Lam, O Menzilcioglu, and J A Webb. The Warp computer: Architecture, implementation and performance. *IEEE Transactions on Computers*, C-36(12):1523–1538, December 1987.

[12] A Apostolico and A Negro. Systolic algorithms for string manipulations. *IEEE Transactions on Computers*, 33(4):361–363, April 1984.

[13] T Asano and H Umeo. Systolic algorithms for computing the visibility polygon and triangulation of a polygonal region. *Parallel Computing*, 6:209–216, 1988.

[14] M J Atallah and S R Kosaraju. A generalized dictionary machine for VLSI. *IEEE Transactions on Computers*, 34(2):151–155, 1985.

[15] M J Atallah and S McFaddin. Sequence comparison on the Connection Machine. *Concurrency: Practice and Experience*, 3(2):89–107, April 1991.

[16] R A Athale and J N Lee. Optical processing using outer product concepts. *Proceedings of the IEEE*, 72(7):931–941, July 1984.

[17] W C Athas and C L Seitz. Multicomputers: Message-passing concurrent computers. *IEEE Computer*, 12(8):9–24, August 1988.

[18] M L Bailey. How circuit size affects parallelism. *IEEE Transactions on Computer-Aided Design*, 11(2):208–215, February 1992.

[19] R Barakat and J H Reif. Lower bounds on the computational efficiency of optical computing systems. *Applied Optics*, 26:1015–1018, 1987.

[20] R Barakat and J H Reif. Polynomial convolution algorithm for matrix multiplication with application for optical computing. *Applied Optics*, 26(14):2707–2711, July 1987.

[21] J Barnes and P Hut. A hierarchical $O(n \, log \, n)$ force calculation algorithm. *Nature*, 324:446–449, 1986.

[22] P A Bash et al. Free energy calculations by computer simulation. *Science*, 236:564–568, 1987.

[23] K E Batcher. Design of a massively parallel processor. *IEEE Transactions on Computers*, C-29(9):836–840, September 1980.

[24] G M Baudet. Design and complexity of VLSI algorithms. In J W de Bakker and J van Leeuwen, editors, *Foundations of Computer Science IV, Part 1: Algorithms and Complexity, Mathematical Centre Tracts 158*, pages 49–74. Mathematisch Centrum, Amsterdam, 1983.

[25] G M Baudet and W-C Chen. Area-time tradeoffs for merging. In P Bertolazzi and F Luccio, editors, *VLSI: Algorithms and Architectures*, pages 61–68. North Holland, 1984.

[26] G M Baudet, F P Preparata, and J Vuillemin. Area-time optimal VLSI circuits for convolution. *IEEE Transactions on Computers*, 32(7):684–688, July 1983.

[27] B Baxter, G Cox, T Gross, H T Kung, D O'Hallaron, C Peterson, J Webb, and P Wiley. Building blocks for a new generation of application-specific computing systems. In J A B Fortes, S Y Kung, K W Przytula, and E E Swartzlander Jr, editors, *Proc. IEEE International Conference on Application Specific Array Processors, Princeton, New Jersey*, pages 190–201. IEEE Press, 1990.

[28] C Bays. Candidates for the game of life in three dimensions. *Complex Systems*, 1(3):373–400, June 1987.

[29] J Beetem, M Denneau, and D Weingarten. GF11 - a supercomputer for scientific applications. In *Proc. 12th Annual International Symposium on Computer Architecture*, 1985.

[30] T E Bell. Optical computing: A field in flux. *IEEE Spectrum*, 23(8):34–57, August 1986.

[31] E R Berlekamp, J H Conway, and R K Guy. *Winning Ways For Your Mathematical Plays. Volume 2: Games in Particular*. Academic Press, 1982.

[32] C Bermond, M C Ogilvie, T A DeGrand, C E DeTar, S A Gottlieb, A Krasnitz, R L Sugar, and D Toussaint. Studying quarks and gluons on MIMD parallel computers. *The International Journal of Supercomputer Applications*, 5(4):61–70, Winter 1991.

[33] P Bertin, D Roncin, and J Vuillemin. Introduction to programmable active memories. In J McCanny, J McWhirter, and E Swartzlander, editors, *Systolic Array Processors*, pages 301–309. Prentice Hall, 1989.

[34] D P Bertsekas and J N Tsitsiklis. *Parallel and Distributed Computation - Numerical Methods*. Prentice Hall, 1989.

[35] S N Bhatt, F Chung, F T Leighton, and A L Rosenberg. Optimal simulations of tree machines. In *Proc. 27th Annual IEEE Symposium on Foundations of Computer Science*, pages 274–282, 1986.

[36] S N Bhatt, F R K Chung, J W Hong, F T Leighton, and A L Rosenberg. Optimal simulations by butterfly networks. In *Proc. 20th Annual ACM Symposium on Theory of Computing*, pages 192–204, 1988.

[37] S N Bhatt, F R K Chung, F T Leighton, and A L Rosenberg. Efficient embeddings of trees in hypercubes. *SIAM Journal on Computing*, 21(1):151–162, February 1992.

[38] S N Bhatt and F T Leighton. A framework for solving VLSI graph layout problems. *Journal of Computer and System Sciences*, 28(2):300–343, 1984.

[39] N L Biggs. *Algebraic Graph Theory*. Cambridge University Press, Cambridge, UK, 1974.

[40] G Bilardi, S W Hornick, and M Sarrafzadeh. Optimal VLSI architectures for multidimensional DFT. In *Proc. 1st Annual ACM Symposium on Parallel Algorithms and Architectures*, pages 265–272, 1989.

[41] G Bilardi and F P Preparata. A minimum area VLSI network for $O(\log n)$ time sorting. *IEEE Transactions on Computers*, 34(4):336–343, April 1985.

[42] G Bilardi and F P Preparata. Area-time lower bound technique with application to sorting. *Algorithmica*, 1(1):65–91, 1986.

[43] G Bilardi and M Sarrafzadeh. Optimal discrete Fourier transform in VLSI. In P Bertolazzi and F Luccio, editors, *VLSI: Algorithms and Architectures*, pages 79–89. North Holland, 1984.

[44] G E Blelloch. Prefix sums and their applications. Technical Report CMU-CS-90-190, School of Computer Science, Carnegie Mellon University, November 1990.

[45] G E Blelloch. *Vector Models for Data-Parallel Computing*. MIT Press, Cambridge, MA, 1990.

[46] B M Boghosian. Lattice gases. In E Jen, editor, *1989 Lectures in Complex Systems. Proc. 1989 Complex Systems Summer School, Santa Fe, New Mexico*, pages 293–324. Addison-Wesley, 1990.

[47] S H Bokhari. On the mapping problem. *IEEE Transactions on Computers*, 30:207–212, 1981.

[48] B Bollobás. *Random Graphs*. Academic Press, 1985.

[49] S Borkar et al. iWarp: An integrated solution to high-speed parallel computing. In *Proc. Supercomputing '88*, pages 330–339, November 1988.

[50] S Borkar et al. Supporting systolic and memory communication in iWarp. In *Proc. 17th Annual International Symposium on Computer Architecture*, pages 70–81. IEEE Press, 1990.

[51] W Braun and N Go. Calculation of protein conformations by proton-proton distance constraints - A new efficient algorithm. *Journal of Molecular Biology*, 186:611–626, 1985.

[52] G Brebner. Relating routing graphs and two-dimensional grids. In P Bertolazzi and F Luccio, editors, *VLSI: Algorithms and Architectures*, pages 221–231. North Holland, 1984.

[53] K-H Brenner, A Huang, and N Streibl. Digital optical computing with symbolic substitution. *Applied Optics*, 25(18):3054–3060, September 1986.

[54] R P Brent and L M Goldschlager. Some area-time tradeoffs for VLSI. *SIAM Journal on Computing*, 11(4):737–747, November 1982.

[55] R P Brent and H T Kung. The chip complexity of binary arithmetic. In *Proc. 12th Annual ACM Symposium on Theory of Computing*, pages 190–200, 1980.

[56] R P Brent and H T Kung. The area-time complexity of binary multiplication. *Journal of the ACM*, 28(3):521–534, 1981.

[57] R P Brent and H T Kung. A regular layout for parallel adders. *IEEE Transactions on Computers*, C–31(3):260–264, March 1982.

[58] R P Brent and H T Kung. Systolic VLSI arrays for linear time GCD computation. In *VLSI83*. IFIP, 1983.

[59] R P Brent and H T Kung. Systolic VLSI arrays for polynomial GCD computation. *IEEE Transactions on Computers*, 33(8):731–736, August 1984.

[60] R P Brent and H T Kung. A systolic algorithm for integer GCD computation. In K. Hwang, editor, *Proc. 7th IEEE Symposium on Computer Arithmetic*, pages 118–125, 1985.

[61] R A Brooks. Intelligence without reason. In J Mylopoulos and R Reiter, editors, *Proc. 12th International Joint Conference on Artificial Intelligence*, pages 569–595. Morgan Kaufmann, San Mateo, CA, 1991.

[62] R A Brooks. Intelligence without representation. *Artificial Intelligence*, 47(1-3):139–159, January 1991.

[63] M C Browne, E M Clarke, D L Dill, and B Mishra. Automatic verification of sequential circuits using temporal logic. In C J Koomen and T Moto-oka, editors, *Computer Hardware Description Languages and Their Applications, Seventh International Conference, Tokyo*, pages 98–113. North Holland, 1985.

[64] R E Bryant. A switch-level model and simulator for MOS digital systems. *IEEE Transactions on Computers*, C-33(2):160–177, February 1984.

[65] A W Burks, editor. *Essays on Cellular Automata.* University of Illinois Press, 1970.

[66] A W Burks, H H Goldstine, and J von Neumann. *Preliminary discussion of the logical design of an electronic computing instrument. Part 1, Volume 1.* The Institute of Advanced Study, Princeton, First edition, 28 June 1946. Second edition, 2 September 1947. Report to the U.S. Army Ordnance Department. Also appears in *Papers of John von Neumann on Computing and Computer Theory*, W Aspray and A Burks, editors. Volume 12 in the Charles Babbage Institute Reprint Series for the History of Computing, MIT Press, 1987, 97-142.

[67] P R Cappello and K Steiglitz. Unifying VLSI array design with linear transformations of space-time. *Advances in Computing Research*, 2:23–65, 1984. Jai Press Inc.

[68] D Casasent. Acoustooptic linear algebra processors: Architectures, algorithms, and applications. *Proceedings of the IEEE*, 72(7):831–849, July 1984.

[69] P Caspi, D Pilaud, H Halbwachs, and J A Plaice. LUSTRE: A declarative language for programming synchronous systems. In *Proc. 14th Annual ACM Symposium on Principles of Programming Languages*, pages 178–188, 1987.

[70] T F Chan and Y Saad. Multigrid algorithms on the hypercube multiprocessor. *IEEE Transactions on Computers*, C-35:969–977, 1986.

[71] K M Chandy and J Misra. Systolic algorithms as programs. *Distributed Computing*, 1(3):177–183, 1986.

[72] K M Chandy and J Misra. *Parallel Program Design: A Foundation.* Addison-Wesley, 1988.

[73] J Chang, O Ibarra, and M Palis. Parallel parsing on a one–way array of finite–state machines. *IEEE Transactions on Computers*, C–36(1):64–75, January 1987.

[74] B Chazelle. Computational geometry on a systolic chip. *IEEE Transactions on Computers*, 33(9):774–785, September 1984.

[75] B Chazelle and L Monier. A model of computation for VLSI with related complexity results. *Journal of the ACM*, 32(3):573–588, July 1985.

[76] H Chen, S Chen, G D Doolen, and W H Matthaeus. Lattice-gas models for multiphase flows and magnetohydrodynamics. In E Jen, editor, *1989 Lectures in Complex Systems. Proc. 1989 Complex Systems Summer School, Santa Fe, New Mexico*, pages 389–399. Addison-Wesley, 1990.

[77] M C Chen. A parallel language and its compilation to multiple processor machines or VLSI. In *Proc. 13th Annual ACM Symposium on Principles of Programming Languages*, pages 131–139, 1986.

[78] Y-A Chen, Y-L Lin, and L-W Chang. A systolic algorithm for the k-nearest neighbors problem. *IEEE Transactions on Computers*, 41(1):103–108, January 1992.

[79] Y-C Cheng, D J Houck Jr, J-M Liu, M S Meketon, L Slutsman, R J Vanderbei, and P Wang. The AT&T KORBX system. *AT&T Technical Journal*, 68(3):7–19, May/June 1989.

[80] E Chu and A George. Sparse orthogonal decomposition on a hypercube multiprocessor. *SIAM Journal on Matrix Analysis and Applications*, 11:453–465, 1990.

[81] J I Chu and G Schnitger. The communication complexity of several problems in matrix computation. *Journal of Complexity*, 7:395–407, 1991.

[82] P M Churchland and P S Churchland. Could a machine think?   *Scientific American*, 262(1):32–37, January 1990.

[83] E F Codd. *Cellular Automata*. Academic Press, 1968.

[84] B Codenotti and G Lotti. A note on the VLSI counter. *Information Processing Letters*, 22:193–195, April 1986.

[85] B Codenotti, G Lotti, and P Romani. VLSI implementation of iterative methods for the solution of linear systems. *Integration, The VLSI Journal*, 3:211–221, 1985.

[86] B Codenotti and F Romani. A compact and modular VLSI design for the solution of general sparse linear systems. *Integration, The VLSI Journal*, 5:77–86, 1986.

[87] A Cohn and M Gordon. A mechanised proof of correctness of a simple counter. In K McEvoy and J V Tucker, editors, *Theoretical Foundations of VLSI Design*, volume 10 of *Cambridge Tracts in Theoretical Computer Science*, pages 65–96. Cambridge University Press, Cambridge, UK, 1990.

[88] R Cole and A Siegel. On information flow and sorting: New upper and lower bounds for VLSI circuits. In *Proc. 26th Annual IEEE Symposium on Foundations of Computer Science*, pages 208–221, 1985.

[89] J M Cooley and J W Tukey. An algorithm for the machine calculation of complex fourier series. *Mathematics of Computation*, 19(90):297–301, 1965.

[90] E Corcoran. Diminishing dimensions. *Scientific American*, 263(5):122–131, November 1990.

[91] T H Cormen, C E Leiserson, and R L Rivest. *Introduction to Algorithms*. MIT Press, Cambridge, MA, 1990.

[92] G M Crippen. *Distance Geometry and Conformational Calculations*. John Wiley and Sons, 1981.

[93] R Cypher and C G Plaxton. Deterministic sorting in nearly logarithmic time on the hypercube and related computers. In *Proc. 22nd Annual ACM Symposium on Theory of Computing*, pages 193–203, 1990.

[94] W J Dally. Network and processor architecture for message-driven computers. In R Suaya and G Birtwistle, editors, *VLSI and Parallel Computaion*, pages 140–222. Morgan Kaufmann, San Mateo, CA, 1990.

[95] F Dehne, J-R Sack, and N Santoro. Computing on a systolic screen: Hulls, contours and applications. In J W de Bakker, A J Nijman, and P C Treleaven, editors, *PARLE - Parallel Architectures and Languages Europe, Vol.1: Parallel Architectures, LNCS Vol. 258*, pages 121–133. Springer-Verlag, 1987.

[96] A Despain, C E Max, G D Doolen, and B Hasslacher. Prospects for a lattice-gas computer. In Doolen et al. [100], pages 211–218.

[97] P M Dew, R A Earnshaw, and T R Heywood, editors. *Parallel Processing for Computer Vision and Display*. Addison-Wesley, 1989.

[98] D d'Humiéres, P Lallemand, and U Frisch. Lattice gas models for 3D hydrodynamics. *Europhysics Letters*, 4(2):291–297, 1986.

[99] H-Q Ding. Simulating lattice QCD on a Caltech/JPL hypercube. *The International Journal of Supercomputer Applications*, 5(2):73–80, Summer 1991.

[100] G D Doolen, U Frisch, B Hasslacher, S Orszag, and S Wolfram, editors. *Lattice Gas Methods for Partial Differential Equations. A Volume of Lattice Gas Reprints and Articles, Including Selected Papers from the Workshop on Large Nonlinear Systems, Los Alamos, August 1987*, volume IV of *Santa Fe Institute Studies in the Sciences of Complexity*. Addison-Wesley, 1990.

[101] P W Dowd. High performance interprocessor communication through optical wavelength division multiple access channels. In *Proc. 18th Annual International Symposium on Computer Architecture*, pages 96–105, 1991.

[102] H L Dreyfus. *What Computers Can't Do: A Critique of Artificial Reason*. Harper and Row, 1972.

[103] H L Dreyfus. *Being In The World: A commentary on Heidegger's Being and Time, Division I*. MIT Press, Cambridge, MA, 1991.

[104] H L Dreyfus and S E Dreyfus. Making a mind versus modeling a mind: Artificial intelligence back at a branch point. *Daedalus*, 117(1):15–43, 1988.

[105] I S Duff, A M Erisman, and J K Reid. *Direct Methods for Sparse Matrices*. Oxford University Press, Oxford, UK, 1986.

[106] P E Dunne. *The Complexity of Boolean Networks*. Academic Press, 1988.

[107] C Ebeling. Flexible hardware for computing complex evaluation functions. Technical Report 91-07-03, Department of Computer Science, University of Washington, July 1991.

[108] C Ebeling, G Borriello, S A Hauck, D Song, and E A Walkup. TRIPTYCH: A new FPGA architecture. Technical Report 91-09-05, Department of Computer Science, University of Washington, September 1991.

[109] J C Ebergen. A formal approach to designing delay-insensitive circuits. *Distributed Computing*, 5(3):107–119, 1991.

[110] M M Eshaghian, D K Panda, and V K Prasanna Kumar. Resource requirements for digital computations on electrooptical systems. *Applied Optics*, 30(8):928–935, March 1991.

[111] N H Farhat, D Psaltis, A Prata, and E Paek. Optical implementation of the Hopfield model. *Applied Optics*, 24(10):1469–1475, May 1985.

[112] D Farmer, T Toffoli, and S Wolfram, editors. *Cellular Automata. Proceedings of an Interdisciplinary Workshop, Los Alamos, 7-11 March 1983*. North Holland, 1984.

[113] D G Feitelson. *Optical Computing. A Survey for Computer Scientists*. MIT Press, Cambridge, MA, 1988.

[114] R P Feynman. There's plenty of room at the bottom. *Engineering and Science*, February 1960.

[115] A Fiat and A Shamir. Polymorphic arrays: A novel VLSI layout for systolic computers. In *Proc. 25th Annual IEEE Symposium on Foundations of Computer Science*, pages 37–45, 1984.

[116] P M Flanders, R L Hellier, H D Jenkins, C J Pavelin, and S van den Berghe. Efficient high-level programming on the AMT DAP. *Proceedings of the IEEE*, 79(4):524–536, April 1991.

[117] R W Floyd. Algorithm 97: Shortest path. *Communications of the ACM*, 5(6):345, 1962.

[118] R W Floyd and J D Ullman. The compilation of regular expressions into integrated circuits. *Journal of the ACM*, 29(2):603–622, 1982.

[119] J A Fodor and Z W Pylyshyn. Connectionism and cognitive architecture: A critical analysis. *Cognition*, 28:3–72, 1988.

[120] F Fogelman Soulie, Y Robert, and M Tchuente. *Automata Networks in Computer Science: Theory and Applications*. Manchester University Press, 1987.

[121] M J Foster and H T Kung. The design of special purpose VLSI chips. *IEEE Computer*, 13:26–40, 1980.

[122] M J Foster and H T Kung. Recognizing regular languages with programmable building blocks. In J.P. Gray, editor, *VLSI 81*, pages 75–84. Academic Press, 1981.

[123] G C Fox, M A Johnson, G A Lyzenga, S W Otto, J K Salmon, and D W Walker. *Solving Problems on Concurrent Processors: Volume 1. General Techniques and Regular Problems.* Prentice Hall, 1988.

[124] U Frisch, D d'Humiéres, B Hasslacher, P Lallemand, Y Pomeau, and J P Rivet. Lattice gas hydrodynamics in two and three dimensions. *Complex Systems*, 1:649–707, 1987.

[125] U Frisch, B Hasslacher, and Y Pomeau. Lattice gas automata for the Navier-Stokes equation. *Physical Review Letters*, 56:1505–1508, 1986.

[126] P Frison and P Quinton. Systolic architectures for connected speech recognition. In R De Mori and C Y Suen, editors, *New Systems and Architectures for Automatic Speech Recognition and Synthesis, NATO ASI Series Vol. F16*, pages 145–167. Springer-Verlag, 1985.

[127] H Fuchs, J Poulton, J Eyles, T Greer, J Goldfeather, D Ellsworth, S Molnar, and G Turk. Pixel-Planes 5: A heterogeneous multiprocessor graphics system using processor-enhanced memories. *Computer Graphics*, 23(4):79–88, July 1989.

[128] R M Fujimoto. The virtual time machine. In *Proc. 1st Annual ACM Symposium on Parallel Algorithms and Architectures*, pages 199–208, 1989.

[129] R M Fujimoto. Parallel discrete event simulation. *Communications of the ACM*, 33(10):30–53, October 1990.

[130] R M Fujimoto, J-J Tsai, and G C Gopalakrishnan. Design and evaluation of the rollback chip: Special purpose hardware for Time Warp. *IEEE Transactions on Computers*, 41(1):68–82, January 1992.

[131] K A Gallivan, M T Heath, E Ng, J M Ortega, B W Peyton, R J Plemmons, C H Romine, A H Sameh, and R G Voigt. *Parallel algorithms for matrix computations*. SIAM Press, 1990.

[132] K A Gallivan, R J Plemmons, and A H Sameh. Parallel algorithms for dense linear algebra computations. In *Parallel algorithms for matrix computations*, K A Gallivan, M T Heath, E Ng, J M Ortega, B W Peyton, R J Plemmons, C H Romine, A H Sameh and R G Voigt, pages 1–82. SIAM Press, 1990.

[133] M Gardner. The fantastic combinations of John Conway's new solitaire game 'Life'. *Scientific American*, 223(4):120–123, April 1970.

[134] Gaussian Inc. Documentation on Gaussian 86 and Gaussian 88. Technical report, Gaussian Inc., Gaussian Inc., 4415 Fifth Avenue, Pittsburgh, PA 15213, 1988.

[135] C W Gear, editor. *Computation and Cognition. Proceedings of the First NEC Research Symposium*. SIAM Press, 1991. Panel Session - The Future of Parallelism, pages 153-168.

[136] G A Geist and C H Romine. LU factorization algorithms on distributed memory multi-processor architectures. *SIAM Journal on Scientific and Statistical Computing*, 9:639–649, 1988.

[137] W. Gentleman and H. Kung. Matrix triangularization by systolic arrays. In *Proc. SPIE 298, Real-time Signal Processing IV*, pages 19–26, 1981.

[138] A George, M T Heath, J Liu, and E Ng. Sparse Cholesky factorization on a local-memory multiprocessor. *SIAM Journal on Scientific and Statistical Computing*, 9(2):327–340, March 1988.

[139] A. George and E. Ng. Some shared memory is desirable in parallel sparse matrix computations. *SIGNUM Newsletter*, 23(2):9–13, 1988.

[140] M Gereb-Graus and T Tsantilas. Efficient optical communication in parallel computers. In *Proc. 4th Annual ACM Symposium on Parallel Algorithms and Architectures*, 1992.

[141] A M Gibbons and P Spirakis, editors. *Lectures on Parallel Computation. Proc. 1991 AL-COM Spring School on Parallel Computation*. Cambridge International Series on Parallel Computation. Cambridge University Press, Cambridge, UK, 1992.

[142] L A Glasser and D W Dobberpuhl. *The Design and Analysis of VLSI Circuits*. Addison-Wesley, 1985.

[143] G Graff. Materials scientists put the squeeze on electrons. *Science*, 254:1306–1307, 29th November 1991.

[144] S A Green and D J Paddon. A highly flexible multiprocessor solution for ray tracing. *The Visual Computer*, 6(2):62–73, March 1990.

[145] R I Greenberg and C E Leiserson. Randomized routing on fat-trees. In *Proc. 26th Annual IEEE Symposium on Foundations of Computer Science*, pages 241–249, 1985.

[146] R I Greenberg and C E Leiserson. A compact layout for the three-dimensional tree of meshes. *Applied Mathematics Letters*, 1(2):171–176, 1988.

[147] L Greengard. *The Rapid Evaluation of Potential Fields in Particle Systems*. MIT Press, Cambridge, MA, 1988.

[148] L Greengard and W D Gropp. A parallel version of the fast multipole method. Research Report YALEU/DCS/RR-640, Department of Computer Science, Yale University, August 1988.

[149] J Gruska. Systolic architectures, systems and computations. In T Lepistö and A Salomaa, editors, *Proc. 15th International Colloquium on Automata, Languages and Programming. LNCS Vol.317*, pages 254–270. Springer-Verlag, 1988.

[150] L J Guibas, H T Kung, and C D Thompson. Direct VLSI implementation of combinatorial algorithms. In C L Seitz, editor, *Proc. Caltech Conference on VLSI*, pages 509–525, 1979.

[151] L J Guibas and F M Liang. Systolic stacks, queues, and counters. In P Penfield Jr, editor, *Proc. MIT Conference on Advanced Research in VLSI*, pages 155–164, January 1982.

[152] J L Gustafson. Development of parallel methods for a 1024-processor hypercube. *SIAM Journal on Scientific and Statistical Computing*, 9(4):609–638, July 1988.

[153] J L Gustafson. Reevaluating Amdahl's Law. *Communications of the ACM*, 31(5):532–533, May 1988.

[154] S E Hambrusch and J Simon. Solving undirected graph problems on VLSI. *SIAM Journal on Computing*, 14:527–544, 1985.

[155] J M Hammersley and D C Handscomb. *Monte Carlo Methods*. Methuen, 1964.

[156] J Hardy, Y Pomeau, and O de Pazzis. Time evolution of a two-dimensional model system. I. Invariant states and time correlation functions. *Journal of Mathematical Physics*, 14:1746, 1973.

[157] A Hartmann and S Redfield. Design sketches for optical crossbar switches intended for large scale parallel processing applications. *Optical Engineering*, 29(3):315–327, 1989.

[158] T F Havel, I D Kuntz, and G M Crippen. The theory and practice of distance geometry. *Bulletin of Mathematical Biology*, 45(5):665–720, 1983.

[159] M T Heath, E Ng, and B W Peyton. Parallel algorithms for sparse linear systems. In *Parallel algorithms for matrix computations*, K A Gallivan, M T Heath, E Ng, J M Ortega, B W Peyton, R J Plemmons, C H Romine, A H Sameh and R G Voigt, pages 83–124. SIAM Press, 1990.

[160] M T Heath and C H Romine. Parallel solution of triangular systems on distributed memory multiprocessors. *SIAM Journal on Scientific and Statistical Computing*, 9:558–588, 1988.

[161] W J Hehre, L Radom, P v.R Schleyer, and J A Pople. *Ab Initio Molecular Orbital Theory*. John Wiley and Sons, 1986.

[162] C S Henkel and R J Plemmons. Recursive least squares on a hypercube multiprocessor using the covariance factorization. *SIAM Journal on Scientific and Statistical Computing*, 12(1):95–106, January 1991.

[163] J L Hennessy and D A Patterson. *Computer Architecture: A Quantitative Approach*. Morgan Kaufmann, San Mateo, CA, 1990.

[164] M Hennessy. Proving systolic systems correct. *ACM Transactions on Programming Languages and Systems*, 8(3):344–387, 1986.

[165] P Hilbers. *Processor Networks and Aspects of the Mapping Problem*, volume 2 of *Cambridge International Series on Parallel Computation*. Cambridge University Press, Cambridge, UK, 1991.

[166] W D Hillis. *The Connection Machine*. MIT Press, Cambridge, MA, 1985.

[167] A Hinchliffe. *Ab Initio Determination of Molecular Properties*. Adam Hilger, 1987.

[168] C A R Hoare. *Communicating Sequential Processes*. Prentice Hall, 1985.

[169] C A R Hoare, editor. *Developments in Concurrency and Communication.* University of Texas Year of Programming Institute on Concurrent Programming. Addison-Wesley, 1990.

[170] C A R Hoare. The transputer and occam: A personal story. *Concurrency: Practice and Experience*, 3(4):249–264, August 1991.

[171] J W Hong, K Mehlhorn, and A L Rosenberg. Cost trade-offs in graph embeddings, with applications. *Journal of the ACM*, 30:709–728, 1983.

[172] J J Hopfield. Neural networks and physical systems with emergent collective computational abilities. *Proceedings of the National Academy of Science*, 79(8):2554–2558, April 1982.

[173] E Housos, C C Huang, and J M Liu. Parallel algorithms for the AT&T KORBX system. *AT&T Technical Journal*, 68(3):37–47, May/June 1989.

[174] F-H Hsu. Large-scale parallelization of alpha-beta search: An algorithmic and architectural study with computer chess. Ph.D. Thesis. Technical Report CMU-CS-90-108, School of Computer Science, Carnegie Mellon University, February 1990.

[175] F-H Hsu, T Anantharaman, M Campbell, and A Nowatzyk. A grandmaster chess machine. *Scientific American*, 263(4):44–50, October 1990.

[176] A Huang. Architectural considerations involved in the design of an optical digital computer. *Proceedings of the IEEE*, 72(7):780–786, July 1984.

[177] C Huang and C Lengauer. The derivation of systolic implementations of programs. *Acta Informatica*, 24:595–632, 1987.

[178] M D A Huang. Solving some graph problems with optimal or near-optimal speedup on mesh-of-trees networks. In *Proc. 26th Annual IEEE Symposium on Foundations of Computer Science*, pages 232–240, 1985.

[179] J M Hutchinson and S A Zenios. Financial simulations on a massively parallel Connection Machine. *The International Journal of Supercomputer Applications*, 5(2):27–45, Summer 1991.

[180] O H Ibarra, T Jiang, and H Wang. String editing on a one-way linear array of finite-state machines. *IEEE Transactions on Computers*, 41(1):112–118, January 1992.

[181] INMOS Limited. *Transputer Reference Manual.* Prentice Hall, 1988.

[182] I C F Ipsen and E R Jessup. Solving the symmetric tridiagonal eigenvalue problem on the hypercube. *SIAM Journal on Scientific and Statistical Computing*, 11(2):203–229, March 1990.

[183] J Ja'Ja'. The VLSI complexity of selected graph problems. *Journal of the ACM*, 31:377–391, 1984.

[184] J Ja'Ja' and P Kumar. Information transfer in distributed computing with application to VLSI. *Journal of the ACM*, 31:150–162, 1984.

[185] S L Johnsson. Communication in network architectures. In R Suaya and G Birtwistle, editors, *VLSI and Parallel Computaion*, pages 223–389. Morgan Kaufmann, San Mateo, CA, 1990.

[186] S L Johnsson and K K Mathur. Data structures and algorithms for the finite element method on a data parallel supercomputer. *International Journal on Numerical Methods in Engineering*, 29(4):881–908, 1990.

[187] G Jones and M Goldsmith. *Programming in occam 2*. Prentice Hall, 1988.

[188] J S Judd. *Neural Network Design and the Complexity of Learning*. MIT Press, Cambridge, MA, 1990.

[189] A Kaldewaij and M Rem. The derivation of systolic computations. *Science of Computer Programming*, 14:229–242, 1990.

[190] R Kane and S Sahni. A systolic design rule checker. In *Proc. 21st Annual IEEE Design Automation Conference*, pages 243–250, 1984.

[191] N Karmarkar. A new parallel architecture for sparse matrix computation based on finite projective geometries. In *Proc. Supercomputing 91*, pages 358–369. IEEE Press, 1991.

[192] R M Karp, R E Miller, and S Winograd. The organization of computations for uniform recurrence equations. *Journal of the ACM*, 14:563–590, 1967.

[193] M Kearns. *The Computational Complexity of Machine Learning*. MIT Press, Cambridge, MA, 1990.

[194] Z M Kedem and A Zorat. On relations between input and communication/computation in VLSI. In *Proc. 22nd Annual IEEE Symposium on Foundations of Computer Science*, pages 37–44, 1981.

[195] T Khanna. *Foundations of Neural Networks*. Addison-Wesley, 1990.

[196] S Kirkpatrick, C D Gelatt Jr, and M P Vecchi. Optimization by simulated annealing. *Science*, 220(4598):671–680, May 1983.

[197] D Kirsh. Foundations of AI: The big issues. *Artificial Intelligence*, 47(1-3):3–30, January 1991.

[198] D Kirsh. Today the earwig, tomorrow man? *Artificial Intelligence*, 47(1-3):161–184, January 1991.

[199] R Koch, F T Leighton, B M Maggs, S B Rao, and A L Rosenberg. Work-preserving emulations of fixed-connection networks. In *Proc. 21st Annual ACM Symposium on Theory of Computing*, pages 227–240, 1989.

[200] S R Kosaraju and M J Atallah. Optimal simulations between mesh-connected arrays of processors. In *Proc. 18th Annual ACM Symposium on Theory of Computing*, pages 264–272, 1986.

[201] M Kramer and J van Leeuwen. The VLSI complexity of Boolean functions. In E Börger et al., editors, *Logic and Machines: Decision Problems and Complexity, LNCS Vol.171*, pages 397–407, 1984.

[202] S A Kravitz, R E Bryant, and R A Rutenbar. Massively parallel switch-level simulation: A feasibility study. *IEEE Transactions on Computer-Aided Design*, 10(7):871–894, July 1991.

[203] S D Kugelmass, R Squier, and K Steiglitz. Performance of VLSI engines for lattice computations. *Complex Systems*, 1(5):939–965, October 1987.

[204] S D Kugelmass and K Steiglitz. A scalable architecture for lattice-gas simulations. *Journal of Computational Physics*, 84:311–325, 1989.

[205] H T Kung. Let's design algorithms for VLSI systems. In *Proc. Caltech Conference on Very Large Scale Integration*, pages 65–90, 1979.

[206] H T Kung. The structure of parallel algorithms. *Advances in Computers*, 19:65–112, 1980.

[207] H T Kung. Why systolic architectures? *IEEE Computer*, 15(1):37–46, January 1982.

[208] H T Kung. New opportunities in multicomputers. In C W Gear, editor, *Computation and Cognition. Proceedings of the First NEC Research Symposium*, pages 1–21. SIAM Press, 1991.

[209] H T Kung and M S Lam. Fault-tolerance and two-level pipelining in VLSI systolic arrays. *Journal of Parallel and Distributed Computing*, 1(1):32–63, 1984.

[210] H T Kung and P L Lehman. Systolic (VLSI) arrays for relational database operations. In *Proc. ACM SIGMOD International Conference on Management of Data*, pages 105–116, 1980.

[211] H T Kung and C E Leiserson. Systolic arrays (for VLSI). In I S Duff and G W Stewart, editors, *Sparse Matrix Proceedings*, pages 256–282. SIAM Press, 1978.

[212] H T Kung and J A Webb. Mapping image processing operations onto a linear systolic array. *Distributed Computing*, 1(4):246–257, 1986.

[213] S Y Kung. On supercomputing with systolic/wavefront array processors. *Proceedings of the IEEE*, pages 867–884, July 1984.

[214] S Y Kung. *VLSI Array Processors*. Prentice Hall, 1988.

[215] S Y Kung, K S Arun, R J Gal-Ezer, and D B Bhaskar Rao. Wavefront array processor: Language, architecture, and applications. *IEEE Transactions on Computers*, 31(11):1054–1065, November 1982.

[216] S Y Kung, S-C Lo, and P S Lewis. Optimal systolic design for the transitive closure and the shortest path problems. *IEEE Transactions on Computers*, C-36(5):603–614, May 1987.

[217] S Y Kung, H J Whitehouse, and T Kailath, editors. *VLSI and Modern Signal Processing*. Prentice Hall, 1985.

[218] R E Ladner and M J Fischer. Parallel prefix computation. *Journal of the ACM*, 27(4):831–838, October 1980.

[219] H-W Lang, M Schimmler, H Schmeck, and H Schréder. Systolic sorting on a mesh-connected network. *IEEE Transactions on Computers*, 34(7):652–658, July 1985.

[220] C G Langton. Self-reproduction in cellular automata. In Farmer et al. [112], pages 135–144.

[221] H Le Verge, C Mauras, and P Quinton. The ALPHA language and its use for the design of systolic arrays. *Journal of VLSI Signal Processing*, 3(3):173–182, September 1991.

[222] F T Leighton. *Complexity Issues in VLSI: Optimal Layouts for the Shuffle-Exchange Graph and Other Networks*. MIT Press, Cambridge, MA, 1983.

[223] F T Leighton. Tight bounds on the complexity of parallel sorting. *IEEE Transactions on Computers*, 34(4):344–354, April 1985.

[224] F T Leighton. *Introduction to Parallel Algorithms and Architectures: Arrays, Trees, Hypercubes*. Morgan Kaufmann, San Mateo, CA, 1992.

[225] F T Leighton and C E Leiserson. Wafer-scale integration of systolic arrays. *IEEE Transactions on Computers*, C-34, No.5:448–461, May 1985.

[226] F T Leighton and C E Leiserson. Advanced parallel and VLSI computation. Research Seminar Series MIT/LCS/RSS 7, Laboratory for Computer Science, Massachusetts Institute of Technology, December 1989.

[227] F T Leighton, C E Leiserson, and M Klugerman. Theory of parallel and VLSI computation. Research Seminar Series MIT/LCS/RSS 10, Laboratory for Computer Science, Massachusetts Institute of Technology, January 1991.

[228] F T Leighton and B M Maggs. Expanders might be practical: Fast algorithms for routing around faults on multibutterflies. In *Proc. 30th Annual IEEE Symposium on Foundations of Computer Science*, pages 384–389, 1989.

[229] F T Leighton and A L Rosenberg. Three-dimensional circuit layouts. *SIAM Journal on Computing*, 15:793–813, 1986.

[230] C E Leiserson. Systolic priority queues. In *Proc. Caltech Conference on Very Large Scale Integration*, pages 199–214, 1979.

[231] C E Leiserson. *Area-Efficient VLSI Computation*. MIT Press, Cambridge, MA, 1983.

[232] C E Leiserson. Fat-trees: Universal networks for hardware-efficient supercomputing. *IEEE Transactions on Computers*, C–34(10):892–901, October 1985.

[233] C E Leiserson and B M Maggs. Communication-efficient parallel algorithms for distributed random-access machines. *Algorithmica*, 3:53–77, 1988.

[234] C E Leiserson and J Saxe. Retiming synchronous circuitry. *Algorithmica*, 6(1):5–35, 1991.

[235] D B Lenat and E A Feigenbaum. On the thresholds of knowledge. *Artificial Intelligence*, 47(1-3):185–250, January 1991.

[236] C Lengauer, M Barnett, and D G Hudson. Towards systolizing compilation. *Distributed Computing*, 5(1):7–24, 1991.

[237] C Lengauer and J Xue. A systolic array for pyramidal algorithms. *Journal of VLSI Signal Processing*, 3(3):237–257, September 1991.

[238] T Lengauer. The communication complexity of VLSI circuits. In *Proc. AMS Symposium in Applied Mathematics 31*, pages 59–82, 1985.

[239] T Lengauer. *Combinatorial Algorithms for Integrated Circuit Layout*. Teubner-Wiley Series of Applicable Theory in Computer Science. Teubner/Wiley, 1990.

[240] T Lengauer. VLSI theory. In J van Leeuwen, editor, *Handbook of Theoretical Computer Science: Volume A, Algorithms and Complexity*, pages 835–868. North Holland, 1990.

[241] G-J Li and B W Wah. Systolic processing for dynamic programming problems. In D DeGroot, editor, *Proc. IEEE International Conference on Parallel Processing*, pages 434–441. IEEE Press, 1985.

[242] P P Li and A J Martin. The sneptree - a versatile interconnection network. In *Proc. 1986 IEEE International Conference on Parallel Processing*, pages 20–27, 1986.

[243] Y-Z Liang and H K Liu. Optical matrix-matrix multiplication method demonstrated by the use of a multifocus hololens. *Optics Letters*, 9(8):322–324, August 1984.

[244] Y-C Lin and F-C Lin. A family of systolic arrays for relational database operations. In W Moore, A McCabe, and R Urquhart, editors, *Systolc Arrays*, pages 191–200, 1986.

[245] K Lindgren and M G Nordahl. Universal computation in simple one-dimensional cellular automata. *Complex Systems*, 4:299–318, 1990.

[246] R J Lipton and D P Lopresti. A systolic array for rapid string comparison. In H. Fuchs, editor, *1985 Chapel Hill Conference on Very Large Scale Integration*, pages 363–376. Computer Science Press, 1985.

[247] R J Lipton and R Sedgewick. Lower bounds for VLSI. In *Proc. 13th Annual ACM Symposium on Theory of Computing*, pages 300–307, 1981.

[248] R J Lipton and R E Tarjan. A planar separator theorem. *SIAM Journal on Applied Mathematics*, 36(2):177–189, April 1979.

[249] R J Lipton and R E Tarjan. Applications of a separator theorem. *SIAM Journal on Computing*, 9:615–627, 1980.

[250] B Lisper. *Synthesis of Synchronous Systems by Static Scheduling in Space-Time*. Springer-Verlag, 1989. LNCS Vol.362.

[251] A W Lohmann. What classical optics can do for the digital optical computer. *Applied Optics*, 25(10):1543–1549, May 1986.

[252] A Louri. Three dimensional optical architecture and data parallel algorithms for massively parallel computing. *IEEE Micro*, 11(2):24–27,65–82, April 1991.

[253] W Luk and I Page. Parametrising designs for field-programmable gate arrays. In W Moore and W Luk, editors, *FPGAs. Proc. International Workshop on Field Programmable Logic and Applications, Oxford, 1991*, pages 284–295. Abingdon EE&CS Books, UK, 1991.

[254] P Maes, editor. *Designing Autonomous Agents: Theory and Practice from Biology to Engineering and Back*. MIT Press, Cambridge, MA, 1990.

[255] B M Maggs and S A Plotkin. Minimum-cost spanning tree as a path-finding problem. *Information Processing Letters*, 26:291–293, 1988.

[256] M A Mahowald and C A Mead. The silicon retina. *Scientific American*, 264(5):76–82, May 1991.

[257] J Makino, T Ito, T Ebisuzaki, and D Sugimoto. Grape: A special-purpose computer for n-body problems. In J A B Fortes, S Y Kung, K W Przytula, and E E Swartzlander Jr, editors, *Proc. IEEE International Conference on Application Specific Array Processors, Princeton, New Jersey*, pages 180–189. IEEE Press, 1990.

[258] S Manohar. Systolic architectures: A critical survey. Technical Report CS-86-05, Department of Computer Science, Brown University, March 1986.

[259] N Margolus. Physics-like models of computation. In Farmer et al. [112], pages 81–95.

[260] N Margolus and T Toffoli. Cellular automata machines. *Complex Systems*, 1(5):967–993, October 1987.

[261] N Margolus and T Toffoli. Cellular automata machines. In Doolen et al. [100], pages 219–249.

[262] A J Martin. Compiling communicating processes into delay insensitive VLSI circuits. *Distributed Computing*, 1(4):226–234, 1986.

[263] A J Martin. Programming in VLSI: From communicating processes to delay-insensitive circuits. In Hoare [169], pages 1–64.

[264] A J Martin and J L A van de Snepscheut. Networks of machines for distributed recursive computations. Computing Science Note CS 8502, Department of Computing Science, University of Groningen, 1985.

[265] A J Martin and J L A van de Snepscheut. An interconnection network for distributed recursive computations. *IEEE Transactions on Computers*, 39(11):1393–1395, November 1990.

[266] O A McBryan and E F Van De Velde. Hypercube algorithms and implementations. *SIAM Journal on Scientific and Statistical Computing*, 8(2):s227–s287, March 1987.

[267] J A McCammon and S C Harvey. *Dynamics of Proteins and Nucleic Acids*. Cambridge University Press, Cambridge, UK, 1987.

[268] J McCanny, J McWhirter, and E Swartzlander, editors. *Systolic Array Processors*. Prentice Hall, 1989.

[269] W F McColl. Planar crossovers. *IEEE Transactions on Computers*, 30(3):223–225, March 1981.

[270] W F McColl. Planar circuits have short specifications. In K Mehlhorn, editor, *2nd Annual Symposium on Theoretical Aspects of Computer Science, LNCS Vol. 182*, pages 231–242, 1985.

[271] W F McColl. Parallel algorithms and architectures. In G A van Zee and J G G van de Vorst, editors, *Parallel Computing 1988, Shell Conference, LNCS Vol. 384*, pages 1–22. Springer-Verlag, 1989.

[272] W F McColl. General purpose parallel computing. This volume.

[273] W F McColl, M S Paterson, and B H Bowditch. Planar acyclic computation. *Information and Computation*, 90(2):178–193, February 1991.

[274] W S McCulloch and W H Pitts. A logical calculus for the ideas immanent in nervous activity. *Bulletin of Mathematical Biophysics*, 5:115–133, 1943.

[275] K McEvoy and J V Tucker. Theoretical foundations of hardware design. In K McEvoy and J V Tucker, editors, *Theoretical Foundations of VLSI Design*, volume 10 of *Cambridge Tracts in Theoretical Computer Science*, pages 1–62. Cambridge University Press, Cambridge, UK, 1990.

[276] K McEvoy and J V Tucker, editors. *Theoretical Foundations of VLSI Design*, volume 10 of *Cambridge Tracts in Theoretical Computer Science*. Cambridge University Press, Cambridge, UK, 1990.

[277] J G McWhirter and J V McCanny. Systolic and wavefront arrays. In J V McCanny and J C White, editors, *VLSI Technology and Design*, pages 253–299. Academic Press, 1987.

[278] C A Mead. *Analog VLSI and Neural Systems*. Addison-Wesley, 1989.

[279] C A Mead and L A Conway. *Introduction to VLSI Systems.* Addison-Wesley, 1980.

[280] C A Mead and M Rem. Cost and performance of VLSI computing structures. *IEEE Journal on Solid State Circuits*, SC-14(2):455–462, 1979.

[281] K Mehlhorn. AT^2-optimal VLSI integer division and square rooting. *Integration, The VLSI Journal*, 2:163–167, 1984.

[282] K Mehlhorn and F P Preparata. Area-time optimal VLSI integer multiplier with minimum computation time. *Information and Computation*, 58(1-3):137–156, July/August/September 1983.

[283] K Mehlhorn and F P Preparata. Area-time optimal division for $T = \Omega((\log n)^{1+\epsilon})$. *Information and Computation*, 72(3):270–282, March 1987.

[284] R Miller and Q F Stout. Data movement techniques for the pyramid computer. *SIAM Journal on Computing*, 16(1):38–60, February 1987.

[285] M Minsky and S Papert. *Perceptrons: An Introduction to Computational Geometry.* MIT Press, Cambridge, MA, 1969.

[286] M Minsky and S Papert. *Perceptrons: An Introduction to Computational Geometry.* MIT Press, Cambridge, MA, third edition, 1988. Epilog: The New Connectionism, pages 247-280.

[287] J Misra. Distributed-discrete event simulation. *ACM Computing Surveys*, 18(1):39–65, March 1986.

[288] D I Moldovan. On the design of algorithms for VLSI systolic arrays. *Proceedings of the IEEE*, 71(1):113–118, 1983.

[289] B Monien and I H Sudborough. Comparing interconnection networks. In M P Chytil, L Janiga, and V Koubek, editors, *Proc. 13th Symposium on Mathematical Foundations of Computer Science. LNCS Vol.324*, pages 138–153, 1988.

[290] W Moore and W Luk, editors. *FPGAs. Proc. International Workshop on Field Programmable Logic and Applications, Oxford, 1991.* Abingdon EE&CS Books, UK, 1991.

[291] W Moore, A McCabe, and R Urquhart, editors. *Systolic Arrays.* Adam Hilger, 1987.

[292] D Nassimi and S Sahni. Bitonic sort on a mesh-connected parallel computer. *IEEE Transactions on Computers*, 28(1):2–7, 1979.

[293] B K Natarajan. *Machine Learning: A Theoretical Approach.* Morgan Kaufmann, San Mateo, CA, 1991.

[294] N J Nilsson. Logic and artificial intelligence. *Artificial Intelligence*, 47(1-3):31–56, January 1991.

[295] M H Nodine, D P Lopresti, and J S Vitter. I/O overhead and parallel VLSI architectures for lattice computations. *IEEE Transactions on Computers*, 40(7):843–852, July 1991.

[296] J M Ortega, R G Voigt, and C H Romine. A bibliography on parallel and vector numerical algorithms. In *Parallel algorithms for matrix computations*, K A Gallivan, M T Heath, E Ng, J M Ortega, B W Peyton, R J Plemmons, C H Romine, A H Sameh and R G Voigt, pages 125–197. SIAM Press, 1990.

[297] T Ottmann, A L Rosenberg, and L J Stockmeyer. A dictionary machine (for VLSI). *IEEE Transactions on Computers*, 31:892–897, 1982.

[298] I Page and W Luk. Compiling occam into field-programmable gate arrays. In W Moore and W Luk, editors, *FPGAs. Proc. International Workshop on Field Programmable Logic and Applications, Oxford, 1991*, pages 271–283. Abingdon EE&CS Books, UK, 1991.

[299] V Pan and J H Reif. Compact multigrid. *SIAM Journal on Scientific and Statistical Computing*, 13(1):119–127, January 1992.

[300] R Paturi, D-T Lu, J E Ford, S C Esener, and S H Lee. Parallel algorithms based on expander graphs for optical computing. *Applied Optics*, 30(8):917–927, March 1991.

[301] R Penrose. *The Emperor's New Mind: Concerning Computers, Minds, and the Laws of Physics*. Oxford University Press, Oxford, UK, 1989.

[302] N J Pippenger. Developments in "The synthesis of reliable organisms from unreliable components". In J Glimm, J Impagliazzo, and I Singer, editors, *The Legacy of John von Neumann. Proc. of Symposia in Pure Mathematics*, volume 50, pages 311–324. American Mathematical Society, 1990. Proc. Summer Research Institute on the Legacy of John von Neumann, Hofstra University, May 29-June 4, 1988.

[303] M Potmesil and E M Hoffert. The Pixel Machine: A parallel image computer. *Computer Graphics*, 23(3):69–78, 1989.

[304] J L Potter. Image processing on the Massively Parallel Processor. *IEEE Computer*, 16(1):62–67, January 1983.

[305] F P Preparata. Optimal three-dimensional VLSI layouts. *Mathematical Systems Theory*, 16:1–8, 1983.

[306] F P Preparata and J Vuillemin. Area-time optimal VLSI networks for multiplying matrices. *Information Processing Letters*, 11(2):77–80, 1980.

[307] F P Preparata and J Vuillemin. The Cube-Connected Cycles: A versatile network for parallel computation. *Communications of the ACM*, 24(5):300–309, 1981.

[308] P Quinton. The systematic design of systolic arrays. In F Fogelman Soulie, Y robert, and M Tchuente, editors, *Automata Networks in Computer Science Theory and Applications*, pages 229–260. Manchester University Press, 1987.

[309] P Quinton and Y Robert. *Systolic Algorithms and Architectures*. Prentice Hall, 1991. Translated by Iain Craig.

[310] P Quinton and V Van Dongen. The mapping of linear recurrence equations on regular arrays. *Journal of VLSI Signal Processing*, 1:95–113, 1989.

[311] S V Rajopadhye. Systolic arrays for LU-decomposition: An application of formal synthesis techniques. *International Journal of Computer Aided VLSI Design*, 3(1):69–90, 1991.

[312] S Ranka and S Sahni. *Hypercube Algorithms for Image Processing and Pattern Recognition*. Springer-Verlag, 1990.

[313] S B Rao. Properties of an interconnection architecture based on wavelength divsion multiplexing. Technical Report TR-92-009-3-0054-2, NEC Research Institute, Princeton, January 1992.

[314] S K Rao and T Kailath. Regular iterative algorithms and their implementations on processor arrays. *Proceedings of the IEEE*, 76(2):259–282, March 1988.

[315] J H Reif and A Tyagi. Efficient parallel algorithms for optical computing with the DFT primitive. In K V Nori and C E Veni Madhavan, editors, *Proc. 10th Conference on Foundations of Software Technology and Theoretical Computer Science. LNCS Vol.472*, pages 149–160. Springer-Verlag, 1990.

[316] T Risset and Y Robert. Synthesis of processor arrays for the algebraic path problem: Unifying old results and deriving new architectures. *Parallel Processing Letters*, 1(1):19–28, 1991.

[317] Y Robert. Systolic algorithms and architectures. In F Fogelman Soulié, Y Robert, and M Tchuente, editors, *Automata Networks in Computer Science: Theory and Applications*, pages 187–228. Manchester University Press, 1987.

[318] Y Robert. *The Impact of Vector and Parallel Architectures on the Gaussian Elimination Algorithm*. Manchester University Press, 1990.

[319] Y Robert and M Tchuente. A systolic array for the longest common subsequence problem. *Information Processing Letters*, 21:191–198, October 1985.

[320] Y Robert and M Tchuente. An efficient systolic array for the 1D recursive convolution problem. *Journal of VLSI and Computer Systems*, 1(4):398–408, 1986.

[321] Y Robert and D Trystram. An orthogonal systolic array for the algebraic path problem. *Computing*, 39:187–199, 1987.

[322] A L Rosenberg. Three-dimensional VLSI: A case study. *Journal of the ACM*, 30:397–416, 1983.

[323] A L Rosenberg. On validating parallel architectures via graph embeddings. In S K Tewksbury, B W Dickinson, and S C Schwartz, editors, *Concurrent Computations - Algorithms, Architecture, and Technology*, pages 99–115. (Proc. 1987 Princeton Workshop on Algorithm, Architecture and Technology Issues for Models of Concurrent Computation), Plenum Press, 1988.

[324] F Rosenblatt. The perceptron: a probabilistic model for information storage and organization in the brain. *Psychological Review*, 65(6):386–408, 1958.

[325] G Rote. A systolic array algorithm for the algebraic path problem (shortest paths; matrix inversion). *Computing*, 34:191–219, 1985.

[326] V P Roychowdhury and T Kailath. Study of parallelism in regular iterative algorithms. In *Proc. 2nd Annual ACM Symposium on Parallel Algorithms and Architectures*, pages 367–376, 1990.

[327] D E Rumelhart and J L McClelland. *Parallel Distributed Processing: Explorations in the Microstructure of Cognition. Volumes 1 and 2*. MIT Press, Cambridge, MA, 1986.

[328] S Ryckebusch, J M Bower, and C A Mead. Modeling small oscillating biological networks in analog VLSI. In D S Touretzky, editor, *Advances in Neural Information Processing I*, pages 384–393. Morgan Kaufmann, San Mateo, CA, 1989.

[329] D Sankoff and J B Kruskal, editors. *Time Warps, String Edits, and Macromolecules: The Theory and Practice of Sequence Comparison*. Addison-Wesley, 1983.

[330] J E Savage. Computational work and time on finite machines. *Journal of the ACM*, 19(4):660–674, 1972.

[331] J E Savage. Area-time tradeoffs for matrix multiplication and related problems. *Journal of Computer and System Sciences*, 22(2):230–242, April 1981.

[332] J E Savage. Planar circuit complexity and the performance of VLSI algorithms. In H T Kung, B Sproull, and G Steele, editors, *VLSI Systems and Computations*, pages 61–68. Computer Science Press, 1981. (Expanded version appears as INRIA Report No.77 (1981).).

[333] J E Savage. The performance of multilective VLSI algorithms. *Journal of Computer and System Sciences*, 29:243–273, 1984.

[334] A A Sawchuk, B K Jenkins, C S Raghavendra, and A Varma. Optical crossbar networks. *IEEE Computer*, 20(6):50–60, 1987.

[335] C P Schnorr and A Shamir. An optimal sorting algorithm for mesh connected computers. In *Proc. 18th Annual ACM Symposium on Theory of Computing*, pages 255–263, 1986.

[336] E Schwabe. On the computational equivalence of hypercube-derived networks. In *Proc. 2nd Annual ACM Symposium on Parallel Algorithms and Architectures*, pages 388–397, 1990.

[337] J R Searle. Is the brain's mind a computer program? *Scientific American*, 262(1):26–31, January 1990.

[338] C L Seitz. System timing. In *Introduction to VLSI Systems*, C A Mead and L A Conway, chapter 7, pages 218–262. Addison-Wesley, 1980.

[339] C L Seitz. The Cosmic Cube. *Communications of the ACM*, 28(1):22–33, January 1985.

[340] C L Seitz. Concurrent architectures. In R Suaya and G Birtwistle, editors, *VLSI and Parallel Computaion*, pages 1–84. Morgan Kaufmann, San Mateo, CA, 1990.

[341] C L Seitz. Multicomputers. In Hoare [169], pages 131–200.

[342] C L Seitz, W C Athas, W J Dally, R Faucette, A S Martin, S Mattison, C D Steele, and W-K Su. *Message-Passing Concurrent Computers: Their Architecture & Programming*. Addison-Wesley, 1989.

[343] T J Sejnowski, C Koch, and P S Churchland. Computational neuroscience. *Science*, 241:1299–1306, 9th September 1988.

[344] T J Sejnowski and C R Rosenberg. NETtalk: A parallel network that learns to read aloud. Technical Report JHU/EECS-86/01, 32pp, Electrical Engineering and Computer Science, Johns Hopkins University, 1986. Also appeared as *Parallel networks that learn to pronounce english text* in Complex Systems, Volume 1, Number 1, February 1987, pages 145-168.

[345] M Shand, P Bertin, and J Vuillemin. Hardware speedups in long integer multiplication. In *Proc. 2nd Annual ACM Symposium on Parallel Algorithms and Architectures*, pages 138–145, 1990.

[346] M Sheeran. Describing and reasoning about circuits using relations. In K McEvoy and J V Tucker, editors, *Theoretical Foundations of VLSI Design*, volume 10 of *Cambridge Tracts in Theoretical Computer Science*, pages 263–298. Cambridge University Press, Cambridge, UK, 1990.

[347] Z-C Shih, G-H Chen, and R C T Lee. Systolic algorithms to examine all pairs of elements. *Communications of the ACM*, 30(2):161–167, February 1987.

[348] A Siegel. Aspects of information flow in VLSI circuits. In *Proc. 18th Annual ACM Symposium on Theory of Computing*, pages 448–459, 1986.

[349] U C Singh et al. AMBER Version 3.0 - Assisted Model Building with Energy Refinement. Manual, University of California, 1986.

[350] H S Stone. Parallel processing with the perfect shuffle. *IEEE Transactions on Computers*, C-20(2):153–161, 1971.

[351] Q F Stout. Algorithm-guided design considerations for meshes and pyramids. In M.J.B. Duff, editor, *Intermediate-Level Image Processing*, pages 149–165. Academic Press, 1986.

[352] J P Strong. Computations on the Massively Parallel Processor at the Goddard Space Flight Center. *Proceedings of the IEEE*, 79(4):548–558, April 1991.

[353] M R Stytz, G Frieder, and O Frieder. Three-dimensional medical imaging: Algorithms and computer systems. *ACM Computing Surveys*, 23(4):421–499, December 1991.

[354] I E Sutherland. Micropipelines. *Communications of the ACM*, 32(6):720–738, June 1989.

[355] I E Sutherland and C A Mead. Microelectronics and computer science. *Scientific American*, 237(3):210–228, September 1977.

[356] C D Thomborson and B W-Y Wei. Systolic implementation of a move-to-front text compressor. In *Proc. 1st Annual ACM Symposium on Parallel Algorithms and Architectures*, pages 283–290, 1989.

[357] C D Thompson. Area-time complexity for VLSI. In *Proc. 11th Annual ACM Symposium on Theory of Computing*, pages 81–88, 1979.

[358] C D Thompson. Fourier transforms in VLSI. *IEEE Transactions on Computers*, 32(11):1047–1057, November 1983.

[359] C D Thompson. The VLSI complexity of sorting. *IEEE Transactions on Computers*, 32(12):1171–1184, 1983.

[360] C D Thompson and H T Kung. Sorting on a mesh connected computer. *Communications of the ACM*, 20(4):263–271, 1977.

[361] M Tinker. DVI parallel image compression. *Communications of the ACM*, 32(7):844–851, July 1989.

[362] T Toffoli. CAM: A high-performance cellular-automaton machine. In Farmer et al. [112], pages 195–204.

[363] T Toffoli. Cellular automata as an alternative to (rather than an approximation of) differential equations in modelling physics. *Physica*, 10D:117, 1984.

[364] T Toffoli and N Margolus. *Cellular Automata Machines*. MIT Press, Cambridge, MA, 1987.

[365] A M Turing. On computable numbers, with an application to the Entscheidungsproblem. *Proceedings of the London Mathematical Society. Series 2*, 42:230–265, 1936. Corrections, *ibid.*, 43 (1937), 544-546.

[366] A M Turing. Computing machinery and intelligence. *Mind*, 59:433–460, 1950.

[367] A M Turing. Intelligent machinery. In B Meltzer and D Michie, editors, *Machine Intelligence 5*, pages 3–23. Edinburgh University Press, 1970.

[368] J T Udding. A formal model for defining and classifying delay-insensitive circuits and systems. *Distributed Computing*, 1(4):197–204, 1986.

[369] J D Ullman. *Computational Aspects of VLSI*. Computer Science Press, 1984.

[370] H Umeo and T Asano. Systolic algorithms for computational geometry problems: A survey. *Computing*, 41:19–40, 1989.

[371] E Upfal. An O(log N) deterministic packet-routing scheme. *Journal of the ACM*, 39(1):55–70, January 1992.

[372] L G Valiant. Universality considerations in VLSI circuits. *IEEE Transactions on Computers*, 30(2):135–140, 1981.

[373] L G Valiant. A theory of the learnable. *Communications of the ACM*, 27(11):1134–1142, 1984.

[374] L G Valiant. Functionality in neural nets. In *Proc. AAAI-88 Seventh American Association for Artificial Intelligence National Conference, St Paul, Minnesota*, volume 2, pages 629–634. Morgan Kaufmann, San Mateo, CA, August 1988.

[375] L G Valiant. A bridging model for parallel computation. *Communications of the ACM*, 33(8):103–111, 1990.

[376] L G Valiant. General purpose parallel architectures. In J van Leeuwen, editor, *Handbook of Theoretical Computer Science: Volume A, Algorithms and Complexity*, pages 943–971. North Holland, 1990.

[377] L G Valiant. A view of computational learning theory. In C W Gear, editor, *Computation and Cognition. Proceedings of the First NEC Research Symposium*, pages 32–51. SIAM Press, 1991.

[378] E F Van de Velde. Experiments with multicomputer LU-decomposition. *Concurrency: Practice and Experience*, 2(1):1–26, March 1990.

[379] W F van Gunsteren. The role of computer simulation techniques in protein engineering. *Protein Engineering*, 2(1):5–13, 1988.

[380] W F van Gunsteren and H J C Berendsen. Algorithms for macromolecular dynamics and constraint dynamics. *Molecular Physics*, 34(5):1311–1327, 1977.

[381] P J M van Laarhoven and E H L Aarts. *Simulated Annealing: Theory and Applications*. D.Reidel, 1987.

[382] G Y Vichniac. Simulating physics with cellular automata. In Farmer et al. [112], pages 96–116.

[383] P M B Vitányi. Locality, communication, and interconnect length in multicomputers. *SIAM Journal on Computing*, 17(4):659–672, August 1988.

[384] P M B Vitanyi. A modest proposal for communication costs in multicomputers. In S K Tewksbury, B W Dickinson, and S C Schwartz, editors, *Concurrent Computations - Algorithms, Architecture, and Technology*, pages 203–216. (Proc. 1987 Princeton Workshop on Algorithm, Architecture and Technology Issues for Models of Concurrent Computation), Plenum Press, 1988.

[385] A Vladimirescu and S Liu. The simulation of MOS integrated circuits using SPICE2. Electronics Research Laboratory Memo UCB/ERL-M80/70, Electronics Research Laboratory, University of California at Berkeley, October 1980.

[386] J von Neumann. *Probabilistic Logics and the Synthesis of Reliable Organisms from Unreliable Components*. California Institute of Technology, 1952. Lectures delivered at California Institute of Technology, 4-15 January 1952, with notes by R S Pierce.

[387] J von Neumann. *The Computer and the Brain*. Yale University Press, 1958. Silliman Lectures, Yale University, Spring Term 1956.

[388] J von Neumann. *Theory of Self-Reproducing Automata*. University of Illinois Press, 1966. Edited and completed by A W Burks.

[389] J von Neumann. *First draft of a report on the EDVAC*. Moore School of Electrical Engineering, University of Pennsylvania, 30 June 1945. Contract No. W-670-ORD-4926 between the United States Army Ordnance Department and the University of Pennsylvania. Reprinted in *Papers of John von Neumann on Computing and Computer Theory*, W Aspray and A Burks, editors. Volume 12 in the Charles Babbage Institute Reprint Series for the History of Computing, MIT Press, 1987, 17-82.

[390] J Vuillemin. A combinatorial limit to the computing power of VLSI circuits. *IEEE Transactions on Computers*, 32(3):294–300, March 1983.

[391] W W Wadge and E A Ashcroft. *Lucid, The Dataflow Programming Language*. Academic Press, 1985.

[392] P Wallich. Silicon babies. *Scientific American*, 265(6):124–134, December 1991.

[393] S Warshall. A theorem on Boolean matrices. *Journal of the ACM*, 9(1):11–12, 1962.

[394] I Wegener. *The Complexity of Boolean Functions*. John Wiley and Sons, 1987.

[395] L C West. Picosecond integrated optical logic. *IEEE Computer*, 20(12):34–46, December 1987.

[396] N H E Weste and K Eshraghian. *Principles of CMOS VLSI Design - A Systems Perspective*. Addison-Wesley, 1985.

[397] C Whitby-Strevens. The transputer. In *Proc. 12th Annual International Symposium on Computer Architecture*, pages 292–300, 1985.

[398] B Widrow and M E Hoff. Adaptive switching circuits. In *Institute of Radio Engineers, Western Electronic Show and Convention, Convention Record, Part IV*, pages 96–104. IRE, New York, August 1960.

[399] N B Wilding, A S Trew, K A Hawick, and G S Pawley. Scientific modelling with massively parallel SIMD computers. *Proceedings of the IEEE*, 79(4):574–585, April 1991.

[400] P H Winston. *Artificial Intelligence*. Addison-Wesley, third edition, 1992.

[401] L D Wittie. Communication structures for large networks of microcomputers. *IEEE Transactions on Computers*, C-30(4):264–273, April 1981.

[402] S Wolfram. *Theory and Applications of Cellular Automata (including selected papers 1983-1986)*, volume 1 of *Advanced Series on Complex Systems*. World Scientific, 1986.

[403] Y Wong and J-M Delosme. Transformation of broadcasts into propagations in systolic algorithms. *Journal of Parallel and Distributed Computing*, 14(2):121–145, February 1992.

[404] J Woo and S Sahni. Hypercube computing: Connected components. *The Journal of Supercomputing*, 3(3):209–234, September 1989.

[405] D Wood. A survey of algorithms and architecture for connected speech recognition. In R De Mori and C Y Suen, editors, *New Systems and Architectures for Automatic Speech Recognition and Synthesis, NATO ASI Series Vol. F16*, pages 233–248. Springer-Verlag, 1985.

[406] J R Woodwark. A multiprocessor architecture for viewing solid models. *Displays*, 5(2):97–103, April 1984.

[407] Xilinx Inc. *The Programmable Gate Array Data Book*. Xilinx Inc., 1991.

[408] A C-C Yao. Some complexity questions related to distributive computing. In *Proc. 11th Annual ACM Symposium on Theory of Computing*, pages 209–213, 1979.

[409] A C-C Yao. The entropic limitations on VLSI computations. In *Proc. 13th Annual ACM Symposium on Theory of Computing*, pages 308–311, 1981.

[410] F Zhao and S L Johnsson. The parallel multipole method on the Connection Machine. *SIAM Journal on Scientific and Statistical Computing*, 12(6):1420–1437, November 1991.

Chapter 13

General Purpose Parallel Computing

W F McColl *

Abstract

A major challenge for computer science in the 1990s is to determine the extent to which general purpose parallel computing can be achieved. The goal is to deliver both scalable parallel performance and architecture independent parallel software. (Work in the 1980s having shown that either of these alone can be achieved.) Success in this endeavour would permit the long overdue separation of software considerations in parallel computing, from those of hardware. This separation would, in turn, encourage the growth of a large and diverse parallel software industry, and provide a focus for future hardware developments.

In recent years a number of new routing and memory management techniques have been developed which permit the efficient implementation of a single shared address space on distributed memory architectures. We also now have a large set of efficient, practical shared memory parallel algorithms for important problems. In this chapter we discuss some of the current issues involved in the development of systems which support fine grain concurrency in a single shared address space. The chapter covers algorithmic, architectural, technological, and programming issues.

1. Introduction

The general purpose sequential computer is ubiquitous in contemporary society. A major challenge for computer science in the 1990s is to produce a credible framework which would allow parallel computing to develop in a way which would result in it eventually replacing sequential computing, not only in specific scientific and engineering applications, but in all areas.

> *Can parallel computing become the mainstream, rather than the interesting (and in some cases, important) sideshow that it is at present?*

At present, it is not commercially attractive to develop parallel software since the number of machines in use is small and current parallel software has to be extremely architecture dependent to achieve efficiency.

> *How can we bootstrap the parallel software industry?*

In this chapter we will attempt to address these issues and suggest some solutions. The first question which needs to be addressed is the following:

---

*This chapter was written while the author was a Visiting Scientist at NEC Research Institute, Princeton, USA.

What should be the main driving force in future parallel computing developments?

There are three obvious candidates - hardware, software, or some kind of intermediate computational model. We will argue below that having an intermediate model as the main driving force offers the best hope for progress from our present position. First, let us consider the alternatives.

For most of the 1980s, low level hardware considerations have been the main driving force in parallel computing. Rapid progress in VLSI technology has permitted the development of a wide variety of distributed memory multicomputer architectures [29, 130, 232, 233, 234, 235, 236, 274]. These systems consist of a set of general purpose microprocessors connected by a sparse network, e.g. array, butterfly or hypercube. The relatively low speed and capacity of such networks forces the programmer to think in terms of a model in which one has multiple private address spaces connected in some complex way, e.g. in a hypercube structure, with explicit message passing by the programmer [124, 125, 135] for all non-local memory requests. The key to algorithmic efficiency in such systems is the careful exploitation of network locality. By minimising the number of nodes through which a message has to travel one can substantially improve efficiency. Despite the programming difficulties inherent in this approach, a large amount of scientific and technical applications software has been developed for such systems. In positive terms, this work has demonstrated conclusively that for many important applications, scalable parallel performance can be achieved in massively parallel systems [112, 113], despite the reservations expressed by Amdahl [20]. However, in this message passing approach, most of the effort in software development tends to be devoted to the various low level process mapping activities which need to be performed to achieve efficiency. Besides being extremely tedious in many cases, this usually produces software which cannot easily be adapted to another architecture. In a world of rapidly changing parallel architectures, this architecture-dependence has proved to be a major weakness, and it has inhibited the growth of the field beyond the area of scientific research.

An alternative approach, which has been extensively pursued by computer science researchers in the last decade, is to make software the driving force. A variety of approaches of this kind have been investigated. They differ in terms of the type of programming language considered, e.g. functional [39, 126, 127] , single assignment, logic, mostly functional, and in the computational model which they adopt, e.g. graph reduction, rewriting, dataflow. However, they share a number of similarities, particularly in comparison to the framework proposed in this chapter. One example of this approach is where one starts by noting that a high level functional language [39, 126, 127] (if properly used) can often expose a large amount of implicit parallelism in a computational problem. The decision to work with a functional language, for reasons of architecture-independence, naturally leads to a decision to adopt, say, graph reduction as the model of parallel computation. The technological (hardware) goal is then to develop a scalable massively parallel architecture for graph reduction [210, 211]. This "software first" approach has a great deal of merit given that hardware is changing rapidly and that the cost and time required to produce software makes architecture-independence in software a major goal. Unfortunately, however, the amount of progress which has been made on the development of efficient parallel architectures for graph reduction, dataflow or rewriting has not been particularly impressive so far, despite much effort. The experiences of the last decade suggest that, in the pursuit of efficiency, it is often necessary to compromise some of the elegance and simplicity of such approaches.

To a large extent, this has already happened in dataflow implementations of functional languages, e.g. the implementation of Id [199] on Monsoon [206]. Modern dataflow architectures [128, 129, 200, 201, 206] are in many important respects quite close to those described in this chapter. For example, they must achieve latency tolerance through multithreading since, in the dataflow model, memory accesses are *split transactions* [201]. (In the dataflow model, a read may be requested before the value is computed.)

The third alternative is to have some model of parallel computation as the driving force. Around 1944, von Neumann produced a proposal [49, 269] for a general purpose stored-program sequential computer which captured the fundamental principles of Turing's work [249] in a practical design. The design, which has come to be known as the "von Neumann computer", has served as the basic model for almost all sequential computers produced from the late 1940s to the present time. As noted in [120], "The paper by Burks, Goldstine and von Neumann ([49]) was incredible for the period. Reading it today, one would never guess this landmark paper was written more than 40 years ago, as most of the architectural concepts seen in modern computers are described there." For an account of the principles of modern general purpose sequential (i.e. von Neumann) computer design, see e.g. [119, 120, 208]. For sequential computation, the stability of the von Neumann model has permitted the development, over the last three decades, of a variety of high level languages and compilers. These have, in turn, encouraged the development of a large and diverse software industry producing portable applications software for the wide range of von Neumann machines available, from personal computers to large mainframes. The stability of the underlying model has also allowed the development of a robust complexity theory for sequential computation, and a set of algorithm design and software development techniques of wide applicability. General purpose sequential computing based on the von Neumann model has developed vigorously over the last four decades. The widespread adoption of the model has not proved to be a harmfully constraining influence, in fact, it has been quite the reverse. A variety of hardware approaches have flourished within the framework provided by the model. The stability it has provided has been invaluable for the development of the software industry.

No single model of parallel computation has yet come to dominate developments in parallel computing in the way the von Neumann model has dominated sequential computing [84, 258, 259].

Can we identify a robust model of parallel computation which offers the prospect of achieving the twin goals of general purpose parallel computing - scalable parallel performance and architecture-independent parallel software?

Success in this endeavour would permit the long overdue separation of software and hardware considerations in parallel computing. This separation would, in turn, encourage the growth of a large and diverse parallel software industry, and provide a focus for future hardware developments.

The achievement of these goals would have profound consequences for the future development of both the computing industry and the academic subject of computer science. Given this fact, one might suspect that this issue would be central to much of the current research in parallel computing. However, at present, relatively little work is being done with these goals directly in mind. Much of the practical work in massively parallel computing today is concerned with the development of scientific applications software, without particular regard for the development of a credible strategy which would permit portability of that software as new architectures appear.

The current situation in parallel computing is remarkably chaotic when compared with that of sequential computing. With no agreed model to provide a focus for technological innovation, parallel hardware suppliers continue to develop, and attempt to market, systems with widely differing characteristics. Those people with the unenviable task of choosing a parallel system for their organisation are faced with the prospect of investing substantial resources in the purchase of such a machine, and in the development of software for it, only to find that the software quite quickly becomes obsolete.

At the present time, the MFLOP performance of the processors used in parallel systems is increasing rapidly. Unfortunately, this is not being matched by corresponding increases in communications performance. This rising imbalance is likely to further increase the difficulty of achieving architecture-independence in software. An important general message of the results in this chapter is that architecture-independence is more likely to be achieved in those parallel systems which invest more substantially in communications performance than in processor performance. It is striking that few of the commercial parallel systems being produced today seem to reflect this basic idea.

The current chaos in parallel computing has led many to conclude that the answer to the above question, on the prospects for agreement on a model, is no. Advocates of "heterogeneous parallel computing" [163] take as their starting point the idea that no convergence on a model is likely to take place. They argue that a wide variety of designs which are to some extent "special purpose" will continue to be produced and marketed, and that the primary function of parallel computing should be to develop languages and communications networks for the coordination of these ensembles of devices. It is again striking that many in computing have already accepted the inevitability of this rather pessimistic scenario, especially as no serious theoretical impediments to the achievement of the goals of general purpose parallel computing have yet been identified, despite much effort to find them. One can contrast this with the situation in complexity theory where the ideas of NP-completeness have demonstrated in a precise way that many desirable goals in terms of algorithmic performance, for problems in AI, scheduling, optimisation etc. are unlikely to be achievable and that we must, in some way, limit our expectations. There is no compelling evidence that general purpose parallel computing, as described above, cannot be achieved. We can be reasonably confident that, as future hardware developments alone fail to significantly increase the market for parallel systems, the manufacturers of those systems will see it as in their interests to seek convergence on a model, rather than to seek to avoid it. A major goal for computer science today is to develop the ideas and techniques which will provide the required solutions when that change in thinking comes about.

In this chapter we will describe one possible way forward for parallel computing, based on the bulk synchronous parallel (BSP) model of computation [258]. Although this approach has many strengths, we would not want to argue that it is the only viable approach. Two alternatives, which merit serious consideration, are the actor model [9, 10] and the dataflow model [128, 129, 199, 200, 206]. The most fundamental difference between these two approaches and the BSP model is that they both have at their core the idea of local (usually pairwise) synchronisation events, whereas the BSP model, as well as various PRAM [80, 89, 149, 224, 259, 266] and data parallel models [43, 123], have the idea of global barrier synchronisation as the basic mechanism. Another significant difference is that in the BSP, PRAM and data parallel approaches there is usually tight control of ordering and scheduling by the programmer. In contrast, a major attraction of the dataflow approach is that the programmer is freed from consideration of such issues. Although we have stressed the differences between these various approaches, there is reason to believe that, at the architectural level, the BSP, PRAM, actor and dataflow models will require a number of similar mechanisms for efficient implementation, in particular, high performance global communications, uniform memory access, and multithreading to hide network latencies.

It is perhaps not unreasonable to summarise the current situation with respect to these various approaches as follows. Work on the actor and dataflow models is much more highly developed in the areas of programming languages and methodologies than it is in the area of algorithm design, analysis and complexity. In contrast, for the BSP and PRAM models we have a highly developed set of techniques for the design and analysis of algorithms, but we do not yet have an established framework for the programming of such systems.

2.   Idealised Parallel Computing

Various idealised shared memory models of parallel computation have been used in the study of parallel algorithms and their complexity. Three such models are the PRAM, the circuit, and the comparison network. In this section we describe these models, and give a number of simple examples of efficient shared memory parallel algorithms which can be implemented on them. Most of the circuits and comparison networks described can be translated into PRAM algorithms in a straightforward manner. We also discuss various ways in which the efficiency of shared memory parallel algorithms can be measured. The class $\mathcal{NC}$ has, over the past decade, provided a very simple and robust framework for the classification of problems in $\mathcal{P}$, in terms of their parallel time complexity on a PRAM. A large number of important problems have been shown to lie in $\mathcal{NC}$, i.e. to be solvable on a PRAM in polylogarithmic time using a polynomial number of processors. Other problems have been shown to be $\mathcal{P}$-complete, i.e. to have no $\mathcal{NC}$ algorithm unless $\mathcal{P} = \mathcal{NC}$. The class $\mathcal{NC}$ and the notion of $\mathcal{P}$-completeness have allowed major advances to be made in our theoretical understanding of shared memory parallel algorithms and their complexity. However, as we now move forward to the point of developing parallel architectures based on the PRAM model, we require a rather more refined complexity theory which takes account of the amount of work done by a parallel algorithm. We describe an approach due to Kruskal, Rudolph and Snir [161] which captures this idea in a convenient way. At the end of the section, we discuss the communication complexity of PRAM algorithms. We describe various results showing tradeoffs between the time required for a parallel computation and the total number of messages which must be sent. Such results may provide a theoretical basis for the future development of software tools which efficiently schedule shared memory parallel algorithms for implementation on distributed memory architectures.

2.1.   The PRAM

A *parallel random access machine (PRAM)* [80, 83, 149, 266, 276] consists of a collection of processors which compute synchronously in parallel and which communicate with a common global random access memory. In one time step, each processor can do (any subset of) the following - read two values from the common memory, perform a simple two-argument operation, write a value back to the common memory. There is no explicit communication between processors. Processors can only communicate by writing to, and reading from, the common memory. The processors have no local memory other than a small fixed number of registers which they use to temporarily store the argument and result values. In a *Concurrent Read Concurrent Write (CRCW) PRAM*, any number of processors can read from, or write to, a given memory cell in a single time step. In a *Concurrent Read Exclusive Write (CREW) PRAM*, at most one processor can write to a given memory cell at any one time. In the most restricted model, the *Exclusive Read Exclusive Write (EREW) PRAM*, no concurrency is permitted either in reading or in writing. The CRCW PRAM model has a large number of variants which differ in the convention they adopt for the effect of concurrent writing. Three simple examples of such conventions are: two or more processors can write so long as they write the same value, one of the processors attempting to write will succeed but the choice of which one will succeed will be made nondeterministically, the lowest numbered processor will succeed (assuming some appropriate numbering.) In other CRCW models [221] one might have the possibility of concurrent writing in which the memory location is updated to the sum of the written values, or to the minimum of the written values.

As a simple example of a CREW PRAM computation, consider the problem of computing $ab + ac + bd + cd$ from inputs a, b, c, d. Let $p_i t_j$ denote the computation performed by processor i at time step j. Then we have

$$p_1 t_1 \; : \quad b + c \Rightarrow x$$
$$p_1 t_2 \; : \quad a * x \Rightarrow y$$
$$p_2 t_2 \; : \quad x * d \Rightarrow z$$
$$p_1 t_3 \; : \quad y + z \Rightarrow \text{result}$$

The complexity of a PRAM algorithm is given in terms of the number of time steps and the maximum number of processors required in any one of those time steps. The above example requires three time steps and two processors.

From the perspective of this chapter, the most important characteristic of the PRAM model is that it is a 1-level memory (or shared memory) model, i.e. all of the memory locations are uniformly far away from all of the processors, the processors have no local memory and there is no kind of memory hierarchy based on ideas of network locality. These simplifying properties of the PRAM model have made it extremely attractive as a robust model for the design and analysis of algorithms.

2.2.   Circuits

A *circuit* [77, 270, 272] is a directed acyclic graph with n input nodes (in-degree 0) corresponding to the n inputs to the problem, and a number of *gates* (in-degree 2) corresponding to two-argument functions. In a Boolean circuit, the gates are labelled with one of the binary Boolean functions $NAND, \wedge, NOR, \vee, \rightarrow, \oplus$ etc. In a typical arithmetic circuit, the input nodes are labelled with some value from $\mathbb{Q}$, the set of rational numbers, and the gates are labelled with some operation from the set $\{+, -, *, /\}$. The size of a circuit is the number of gates

Let g_i denote the function computed by gate i. Then we have the following arithmetic circuit for $ab + ac + bd + cd$.

$$g_1 \; = \; b + c$$

$$g_2 = a * g_1$$
$$g_3 = g_1 * d$$
$$g_4 = g_2 + g_3$$

An example of a Boolean circuit is the following, which computes the two binary digits $<d_1, d_0>$ of $x_1 + x_2 + x_3$.

$$g_1 = x_1 \wedge x_2$$
$$g_2 = x_1 \oplus x_2$$
$$g_3 = g_2 \wedge x_3$$
$$g_4 = g_2 \oplus x_3 \ (= d_0)$$
$$g_5 = g_1 \vee g_3 \ (= d_1)$$

The parallel complexity of a circuit is the depth of the circuit, i.e. the maximum number of gates on any directed path. The parallel complexity of both of the above examples is three.

2.3. Comparison Networks

It is well known that $\Theta(n \ log \ n)$ binary comparisons are necessary and sufficient to sort n elements drawn from an arbitrary totally ordered set. The lower bound follows from a simple information theoretic argument. The matching upper bound can be obtained, e.g. by a simple recursive mergesort algorithm. A convenient model for the investigation of the parallel complexity of comparison problems such as sorting, merging and selection is the comparison network [32, 66, 155]. Comparison networks have the attractive property that they are oblivious (as are circuits). An *oblivious algorithm* is one in which the sequence of operations performed is independent of the input data.

A *comparison element* is a two-input two-output device which computes the minimum $min(x, y)$ and the maximum $max(x, y)$ of its inputs x, y. In an *n-line comparison network*, the n inputs $<x_1, x_2, \ldots, x_n>$ are presented on the n lines and at each successive level of the network at most $n/2$ disjoint pairs of lines are put through comparison elements. After each level, the n lines carry the inputs in some permuted order. The *size* of a comparison network is the number of elements.

If we let l_i denote level i and (j, k) denote a comparison element connecting lines j, k, then the following is a comparison network of size five which sorts four elements

$$l_1 : \{(1, 2), (3, 4)\}$$
$$l_2 : \{(1, 3), (2, 4)\}$$
$$l_3 : \{(2, 3)\}$$

i.e. if we present the inputs $<x_1, x_2, x_3, x_4>$ on the four lines then after these three levels of comparison elements the values will appear on the lines in sorted order.

The parallel complexity of a comparison network is simply the *depth* of the network, i.e. the number of levels.

2.4.   Addition

Let $ADD_n(x_1, \ldots, x_n) = \sum_{i=1}^{n} x_i$ where $x_i \in \mathbb{Q}$. A circuit of depth $\lceil log_2 n \rceil$ for ADD_n can easily be obtained by constructing a balanced binary tree of $+$-gates, with n leaves corresponding to the arguments $x_1, \ldots, x_n$. This corresponds to an $n/2$ processor PRAM algorithm with complexity $\lceil log_2 n \rceil$ The optimality of this construction, in terms of depth, follows from the functional dependency of ADD_n on each of its n arguments. If we now define $OR_n(x_1, \ldots, x_n) = \bigvee_{i=1}^{n} x_i$ where $x_i \in \{0, 1\}$, then we have a very similar problem to that of computing ADD_n. We can easily obtain a PRAM algorithm of complexity $\lceil log_2 n \rceil$ and a Boolean circuit of depth $\lceil log_2 n \rceil$ for OR_n. That this circuit depth is optimal follows from functional dependency. However, as Cook and Dwork [64] observed, there is rather more to the question of the PRAM complexity of OR_n. If we allow concurrent write, then OR_n can be computed in one parallel step in an obvious way; processor i reads x_i from memory location i and if $x_i = 1$ it writes a 1 into location 0. Cook and Dwork [64] show that even on an EREW PRAM, OR_n can be computed in less than $\lceil log_2 n \rceil$ steps. They derive an upper bound of $(0 \cdot 72) log_2 n$ on the number of steps required. However, they also show that a lower bound of $\Omega(log_2 n)$ holds, and thus only a constant factor improvement is possible.

2.5.   Polynomial Evaluation

Let $P_n(a_0, a_1, \ldots, a_n, x) = \sum_{i=0}^{n} a_i x^i$ where $a_i, x \in \mathbb{Q}$. The standard sequential algorithm for polynomial evaluation is *Horner's Rule* where to calculate P_n we successively compute

$$
\begin{aligned}
p_n &= a_n \\
p_i &= (p_{i+1} * x) + a_i \quad for \ \ i = n-1, n-2, \ldots, 1, 0.
\end{aligned}
$$

Then $P_n = p_0$. The sequential complexity of polynomial evaluation has been studied for many years. It is known that $2n$ arithmetic operations are required to evaluate a general polynomial of degree n, given by its coefficients [46]. Thus, in terms of sequential complexity, Horner's Rule is optimal. However, it is very unsuitable for parallel computation since at every step in the computation the immediately preceding subresult is required. If instead, we evaluate each term $a_i x^i$ of the polynomial independently, in parallel, using a balanced binary tree of $*$-gates, and we then sum the values of the terms using a balanced binary tree of $+$-gates then we have a circuit of depth $2\lceil log_2(n+1) \rceil$. This circuit is *exponentially better*, in terms of depth, than a circuit based on Horner's Rule, although the number of gates (sequential complexity) is now $O(n^2)$ rather than $O(n)$. The $2\lceil log_2(n+1) \rceil$ upper bound can be further improved to $log_2 n + O(\sqrt{log_2 n})$ by using a simple recursive parallel algorithm due to Munro and Paterson [198] which splits the polynomial into consecutive blocks of terms and factors out the appropriate power of x. Kosaraju [157] has shown that the algorithm of Munro and Paterson is optimal, in terms of circuit depth, for polynomial evaluation.

2.6.   Prefix Sums

Let $x_1, x_2, \ldots, x_n$ be a set of values and $\circ$ be an associative operation on that set. The *prefix sums problem* is to compute $p_i = x_1 \circ x_2 \circ \cdots \circ x_i$ for all $1 \leq i \leq n$. The straightforward method yields a circuit of size $n - 1$ but its depth is also $n - 1$. By computing each p_i independently we can obtain a circuit of size $O(n^2)$ and depth $\lceil log_2 n \rceil$. An important result of Ladner and Fischer [165] shows that the prefix sums problem can be computed by a circuit of size $O(n)$ and depth $O(log\ n)$. This construction can be applied to produce small fast parallel circuits for a variety of important problems, including n-bit addition, n-bit multiplication, and Boolean sorting. It can also be used for the efficient parallel simulation of finite state automata. We will describe the application of parallel prefix computation to the problem of n-bit addition.

A binary number $<a_{n-1}, a_{n-2}, \ldots, a_0> \in \{0,1\}^n$ represents the value $\sum_{i=0}^{n-1} a_i * 2^i$. Given two n-bit binary numbers $X = <x_{n-1}, x_{n-2}, \ldots, x_0>$ and $Y = <y_{n-1}, y_{n-2}, \ldots, y_0>$, the *n-bit addition problem* is to compute the $(n+1)$-bit representation $Z = <z_n, z_{n-1}, \ldots, z_0>$ of $X + Y$.

In the normal "school method" we first compute $z_0 = x_0 \oplus y_0$ and the initial carry bit $c_0 = x_0 \wedge y_0$. We then use $n - 1$ full adders to compute z_i, c_i from x_i, y_i and c_{i-1}. Finally, we let $z_n = c_{n-1}$. This method yields a circuit of size $O(n)$ and depth $O(n)$. The prefix method consists of three stages:

Stage 1: Compute $u_j = x_j \wedge y_j$, $v_j = x_j \oplus y_j$ for all $0 \leq j < n$.

Stage 2: Compute the carry bits c_j for all $0 \leq j < n$.

Stage 3: Compute the outputs. $z_0 = v_0$, $z_j = v_j \oplus c_{j-1}$ for all $1 \leq j < n$, $z_n = c_{n-1}$.

Stages 1 and 3 can both be carried out in linear size and constant depth, therefore we need only consider Stage 2. Let $A_{(u,v)}(c) = u \vee (v \wedge c)$ for $c \in \{0,1\}$. Then we have

$$c_i = A_{(u_i,v_i)} \circ A_{(u_{i-1},v_{i-1})} \circ \cdots \circ A_{(u_0,v_0)}(0)$$

where $\circ$ denotes function composition. Since $(u_j, v_j) \in \{(0,0), (0,1), (1,0)\}$ and

$$A_{(0,0)} \circ A_{(u,v)} = A_{(0,0)}$$
$$A_{(0,1)} \circ A_{(u,v)} = A_{(u,v)}$$
$$A_{(1,0)} \circ A_{(u,v)} = A_{(1,0)}$$

it follows that the operation $\circ$ on sets of functions $A_{(u_j,v_j)}$ is associative. Therefore, we can use a prefix circuit to compute all the carry bits c_i. We need only design a circuit for the operation $\circ$. Let $A_{(u,v)} = A_{(u_2,v_2)} \circ A_{(u_1,v_1)}$. Then $(u, v) = (u_2 \vee (u_1 \wedge v_2), v_1 \wedge v_2)$ and therefore we can construct a subcircuit of size three and depth two for the operation $\circ$. We have shown that n-bit addition can be realised by a Boolean circuit of size $O(n)$ and depth $O(log\ n)$.

In functional programming [39], the second-order function *scan* corresponds to the prefix sums computation. The above mentioned results, and the work of Blelloch [41, 42, 43] and others, have shown it to be a parallel primitive of extremely wide applicability.

2.7. Matrix Multiplication

Let A, B be two $n \times n$ matrices of rational numbers. Then the product of A, B is an $n \times n$ matrix C, where $c_{i,j} = \sum_{k=1}^{n} a_{i,k} * b_{k,j}$. The exact determination of the sequential complexity of matrix multiplication is a major open problem in the field of computational complexity [62, 202, 247]. At the present time, the best known algorithm (asymptotically, as $n \to \infty$) requires only $O(n^{2.376})$ arithmetic operations [65] as opposed to the standard $O(n^3)$ which follows from the definition. No lower bound larger than the trivial $\Omega(n^2)$ is known.

In contrast, determining the shared memory parallel complexity of matrix multiplication is trivial. We can evaluate each $c_{i,j}$ term independently, in parallel, by a balanced binary tree of depth $\lceil log_2 n \rceil + 1$. Functional dependency shows this bound for $c_{i,j}$ to be optimal and so we have an optimal time bound for parallel matrix multiplication on the idealised PRAM and circuit models [number of processors $= O(n^3)$]. The simplicity of this solution is entirely attributable to the fact that in the PRAM and circuit models, the complexity and cost of communication is completely ignored. Those who have developed and implemented algorithms for distributed memory architectures over the last decade know, of course, that on such architectures the issue of managing communication is the dominant one.

2.8.   Linear Recurrences

The parallel evaluation of recurrences was discussed in the mid 1960s by Karp, Miller and Winograd [148]. Let us first consider the computation of the very simple recurrence which defines Fibonacci numbers. The mth Fibonacci number f_m is given by the second order linear recurrence

$$
\begin{aligned}
f_0 &= 0 \\
f_1 &= 1 \\
f_m &= f_{m-1} + f_{m-2} \quad for \ m \geq 2
\end{aligned}
$$

This definition can be directly translated into an arithmetic circuit with $m - 1$ gates (and depth $m - 1$) which successively computes $f_2, f_3, \ldots, f_m$. As in the case of Horner's Rule we have a circuit with no direct parallel speedup. If instead, we use the unconventional definition

$$
(f_{m-1} \ f_m) \ = \ (f_0 \ f_1) \begin{pmatrix} 0 & 1 \\ 1 & 1 \end{pmatrix}^{m-1}
$$

then we see immediately that f_m can be calculated by an arithmetic circuit of *size and depth* $O(log_2 m)$ if we compute the matrix power efficiently by repeated squaring.

The above result for Fibonacci numbers is a special case of the following more general result by Greenberg et al. [108] on the parallel evaluation of kth order linear recurrences. If we have $F = (f_0 \ f_1 \ \cdots \ f_{k-1})$ and $f_m = \sum_{j=1}^{k} a_{k-j} * f_{m-j}$ for $m \geq k$, then $(f_{m-k+1} \ \cdots \ f_m) = F * M^{m-k+1}$ where M is the $k \times k$ matrix

$$
\begin{pmatrix} 0 \cdots 0 & a_0 \\ & a_1 \\ I & \vdots \\ & a_{k-1} \end{pmatrix}
$$

and therefore the parallel complexity of computing f_m is at most $O(log_2 k \cdot log_2(m - k))$.

For a practical application of this result we consider the problem of solving linear systems. Let B be an $n \times n$ non-singular, lower triangular matrix, and $\underline{c}$ be an n-element vector. In solving the linear system $B\underline{x} = \underline{c}$ by 'back substitution' we use the recurrence $x_i = (c_i - \sum_{j=1}^{i-1} b_{i,j} * x_j)/b_{i,i}$ for $1 \leq i \leq n$. If we let $x_i = 0$ for $i < 1$ then we can rewrite this recurrence in the form $(x_i \; x_{i-1} \; \ldots \; x_{i-n+1} \; 1) \; = \; (x_{i-1} \; x_{i-2} \; \ldots \; x_{i-n} \; 1) * M_i$ where

$$M_i = \begin{pmatrix} -\frac{b_{i,i-1}}{b_{i,i}} & & & & \\ \vdots & & & & \\ -\frac{b_{i,1}}{b_{i,i}} & & I & & 0 \\ 0 & & & & \\ \vdots & & & & \\ 0 & & & & \\ \hline 0 & 0 & \cdots\cdots\cdots & 0 & 0 \\ \frac{c_i}{b_{i,i}} & 0 & \cdots\cdots\cdots & 0 & 1 \end{pmatrix}$$

Therefore we can design an arithmetic circuit of depth $O(log^2 n)$ which solves $B\underline{x} = \underline{c}$ to obtain $\underline{x}$. This circuit corresponds to a PRAM algorithm with parallel time $O(log^2 n)$ and number of processors $O(n^4)$. In contrast, a direct PRAM implementation of back substitution would have parallel time $O(n)$, but would require only $O(n)$ processors.

2.9. Merging

Let $<x_1, x_2, \ldots, x_m>$ and $<y_1, y_2, \ldots, y_n>$ be two sorted sequences. The *merging problem* is to produce a single sorted sequence consisting of the $m+n$ elements. This can, of course, be performed by a simple sequential algorithm which uses at most $m+n-1$ binary comparisons. We will describe two efficient parallel comparison networks for merging, both due to Batcher [32, 155]. The two techniques are known as odd even merging and bitonic sorting.

In odd-even merging, we merge the "odd sequences" $<x_1, x_3, x_5, \ldots>$ and $<y_1, y_3, y_5, \ldots>$, obtaining $<v_1, v_2, v_3, \ldots>$; and merge the "even sequences" $<x_2, x_4, x_6, \ldots>$ and $<y_2, y_4, y_6, \ldots>$, obtaining $<w_1, w_2, w_3, \ldots>$. (These two merges are performed in parallel). Finally, we apply comparison elements to the pairs $(w_1, v_2), (w_2, v_3), (w_3, v_4), \ldots$ to complete the merging.

This recursive method yields the following upper bounds:

$$\begin{aligned} size(n) &\leq 2 * size(n/2) + O(n) \\ &= O(n \; log \; n) \end{aligned}$$

$$\begin{aligned} depth(n) &\leq depth(n/2) + 1 \\ &\leq \lceil log_2 n \rceil \end{aligned}$$

A sequence $<z_1, z_2, \ldots, z_p>$ is *bitonic* if and only if $z_1 \geq \cdots \geq z_k \leq \cdots \leq z_p$ for some $1 \leq k \leq p$. An *n-line bitonic sorter* is a comparison network which will sort any bitonic sequence of length n. Merging can be performed by sorting the bitonic sequence $<x_m, x_{m-1}, \ldots, x_1, y_1, y_2, \ldots, y_n>$. Noting that any subsequence of a bitonic sequence is bitonic, it follows that we can construct an n-line bitonic sorter by first sorting the two bitonic subsequences $<z_1, z_3, \ldots>$ and $<z_2, z_4, \ldots>$ in parallel, and then applying comparison elements to the pairs $(z_1, z_2), (z_3, z_4), \ldots$ to complete the sort. This alternative method yields essentially the same upper bounds on size and depth as odd-even merging. It does, however, have some advantages in terms of simplicity of description. A bitonic sorter with 2^n lines numbered $0, 1, 2, \ldots, 2^n - 1$ can be defined (nonrecursively) in the following way:

Lines i, j are compared on level k if and only if i, j differ only in their k^{th} most significant bit.

It is quite easy to prove that both the size and depth of these merging networks are optimal to within a constant factor [155]. This shows that, for the problem of merging, comparison networks are much less powerful than general (adaptive) algorithms, at least when one compares the total number of comparisons performed. As we shall see in the next section, this does not apply in the case of the related problem of sorting.

2.10.   Sorting

An n-line sorting network can be constructed recursively using either of the efficient merging networks described above [32, 155]. To sort the set $x_1, x_2, \ldots, x_n$ we first (recursively) sort the two subsets $x_1, x_2, \ldots, x_{n/2}$ and $x_{(n/2)+1}, x_{(n/2)+2}, \ldots, x_n$ in parallel. The two sorted sequences can then be combined using one of the above merging networks of size $O(n \log n)$ and depth $O(\log n)$. This yields the following upper bounds for sorting n elements by a comparison network.

$$
\begin{aligned}
size(n) &\leq 2 * size(n/2) + O(n \log n) \\
&= O(n \log^2 n)
\end{aligned}
$$

$$
\begin{aligned}
depth(n) &\leq depth(n/2) + \log n \\
&= O(\log^2 n)
\end{aligned}
$$

From 1968 until 1983 this was the best known oblivious sorting algorithm. In 1983, Ajtai, Komlós and Szemerédi [11] succeeded in producing a remarkable n-line sorting network of size $O(n \log n)$ and depth $O(\log n)$, both of which are of course asymptotically optimal. A more efficient version, which improves the constant factors involved, has since been produced by Paterson [207]. Although the constant factors are still too large to make the networks competitive with those obtained from, say, odd-even merging, this is a result of major theoretical significance as it shows that for the important problem of sorting, adaptive algorithms are not (asymptotically) more powerful than oblivious ones.

2.11.   Selection

The tth selection problem is to determine the t largest elements in a set of size n. In this section we describe the design of some fast parallel comparison networks for this problem. When $t \approx n/2$, we cannot do significantly better than using an $O(n \log n)$ size, $O(\log n)$ depth sorting network [11] since any comparison network which determines the median of n elements must have size $\Omega(n \log n)$ [155]. We shall be concerned with the case where t is fixed as $n \to \infty$.

The following construction is due to Yao [277]. To produce a tth selection network of small depth we use a construction called a (t, n)-eliminator. Let $f(t, n)$ be a function which satisfies $f(t, n) \geq t$. A (t, n)-eliminator is a comparison network with the following property: Of the n output lines there are $f(t, n)$ designated lines among which the largest t elements are found. We now show how to construct a family $E(t, n)$ of (t, n)-eliminators.

First, we consider the case where $t = 1$. $E(1, 2)$ is simply a comparison element. An n-line $E(1, n)$ is recursively defined as follows: The first level consists of the elements $(1, n), (2, n -$

$1), (3, n-2), \ldots$. The rest of the network is simply an $E(1, n/2)$ network on lines $(n/2) + 1, (n/2) + 2, \ldots, n$. A simple analysis shows that

$$depth(E(1, n)) \;=\; \lceil log_2 n \rceil$$

$$f(1, n) \;=\; 1$$

For $t > 1$, an n-line $E(t, n)$ is recursively defined as follows: The first level again consists of the elements $(1, n), (2, n-1), (3, n-2), \ldots$. The rest of the network consists of an $E(\lfloor t/2 \rfloor, \lfloor n/2 \rfloor)$ network on lines $1, 2, \ldots, \lfloor n/2 \rfloor$ and an $E(t, \lceil n/2 \rceil)$ network on the remaining lines. For $t = 2$, we obtain

$$depth(E(t, n)) \;\leq\; max\{depth(E(t, n/2)), (log\ n) - 1\} + 1$$
$$\leq\; \lceil log_2 n \rceil$$

$$f(2, n) \;\leq\; f(2, n/2) + 1$$
$$=\; O(log\ n)$$

and, in general, for any fixed $t \geq 2$,

$$depth(E(t, n)) \;\leq\; \lceil log_2 n \rceil$$

$$f(t, n) \;=\; O((log\ n)^{\lfloor log_2 t \rfloor})$$

To obtain a fast parallel comparison network for the tth selection problem we simply compose appropriately sized eliminator networks. Applying $E(t, n)$ to the n input lines gives a set of $n_1 = f(t, n) \approx (log\ n)^{log\ t}$ lines on which the t largest elements are now known to lie. We can then apply an $E(t, n_1)$ to reduce the number of lines to $n_2 = f(t, n_1)$, and an $E(t, n_2)$ to further reduce it to $n_3 = f(t, n_2)$. The depth of the network at this stage of the construction is $log\ n + log\ n_1 + log\ n_2 = log\ n + log\ t\ loglog\ n + O(logloglog\ n)$ and the number of lines has been reduced to $O((logloglog\ n)^{log\ t})$. This is sufficiently small that we can now use, for example, a sorting network on those lines to complete the computation of the t largest elements. This gives a tth selection network of total depth $log\ n + log\ t\ loglog\ n + O(logloglog\ n)$.

2.12. Algebraic Path Problem

A *closed semiring* is an algebraic structure $(S, \oplus, \otimes, I_\oplus, I_\otimes)$ with the following properties:

$\oplus$ is a commutative monoid ($\oplus$ satisfies the closure, associative, commutative properties, and has identity element $I_\oplus$).

$\otimes$ is a monoid ($\otimes$ satisfies the closure, associative properties, and has identity element $I_\otimes$).

$\oplus$ is idempotent.

$\otimes$ is right and left distributive over $\oplus$.

For all $s \in S$, $s \otimes I_\oplus = I_\oplus$.

Let $G = (V, A)$ be a directed graph on $\mid V \mid = n$ vertices, in which each $<i, j> \in A$ has an associated weight $s_{ij} \in S$. Define an $n \times n$ matrix M of weights m_{ij} corresponding to the arcs of G: $m_{ij} = s_{ij}$ if $<i, j> \in A$, $I_\oplus$ otherwise. The *Algebraic Path Problem (APP)* is to compute $M^* = \bigoplus_{k=0}^\infty M^k$ where matrix product is defined in terms of the two operations $\oplus$ and $\otimes$. (M^0 is the identity matrix with diagonal elements $I_\otimes$). M_{ij}^* gives the "sum" of the weights of all directed paths from i to j where the weight of a path is the "product" of the weights of the arcs.

The APP is a problem of major importance in a wide variety of areas and has been extensively studied in recent years. Some examples of instances of the APP are the following:

Problem	S	$\oplus$	$\otimes$	$I_\oplus$	$I_\otimes$
Connectivity (trans. closure) [271]	$\{false, true\}$	or	and	$false$	$true$
Generation of regular language	$\{words\}$	$\cup$	$\cdot$	$\emptyset$	$empty\ word$
Max. capacity path	$\mathbb{R}^+ \cup \infty$	max	min	0	∞
Path with min. number of arcs	$\mathbb{N} \cup \infty$	min	$+$	∞	0
Shortest paths [82]	$\mathbb{R} \cup \infty$	min	$+$	∞	0
Max. reliability path	$\{a \mid 0 \leq a \leq 1\}$	max	$*$	0	1
Min. cost spanning tree [181]	$\mathbb{R}^+ \cup \infty$	min	max	∞	0

The APP also finds application in areas such as parsing and logic programming, and can be used as the basis of fast parallel algorithms for matrix inversion. Like the prefix sums computation, it is a remarkably versatile second-order function.

Noting that node i is connected to node j by a directed path if and only if it is connected by a directed path of length $\leq n - 1$, we have

$$
\begin{aligned}
M^* &= \bigoplus_{k=0}^{n-1} M^k \\
&= (M^0 \oplus M)^{n-1} \\
&= (M^0 \oplus M)^{2^l} \text{ for } 2^l \geq n - 1
\end{aligned}
$$

Therefore, to obtain an efficient shared memory parallel algorithm for the computation of the APP on matrix M we need only set the main diagonal to $I_\otimes$ and repeatedly square the resulting matrix until we have a sufficiently large power. For an $n \times n$ matrix M, this method yields a circuit of depth $O(log^2 n)$ or, equivalently, a PRAM algorithm of time complexity $O(log^2 n)$ (Number of processors $= O(n^3)$ if we use the standard matrix multiplication algorithm).

Consider the problem of topologically ordering the n vertices of a directed acyclic graph, i.e. assigning a number to each of the vertices such that there is no path from a vertex to a lower numbered one. There are several efficient sequential algorithms for this problem in which one successively numbers vertices from 1 to n. It is perhaps not immediately clear how one would shortcut this iterative process to achieve an algorithm which produces such an ordering in $o(n)$ parallel time. However, this problem can be solved in a straightforward way using the fast parallel APP algorithm. We can simply compute the connectivity or transitive closure of the dag using the parallel APP algorithm with (or, and), and then sort the vertices by their in-degree in the closure. If there is a directed path from i to j in the dag, then j will have a higher in-degree than i in the closure.

The minimum cost spanning tree problem is another one which has simple, efficient sequential algorithms, e.g. the algorithms of Kruskal and Prim [66], but for which it is not immediately clear that it has a fast parallel algorithm. As noted above, Maggs and Plotkin [181] observed that if the weights of the edges in the graph are distinct, then the minimum cost spanning tree is precisely the set of edges $<i, j>$ in the graph for which $M_{ij} = M_{ij}^*$ where we compute the APP with (min, max). [If the distinct weights property does not apply, then a simple modification can be made to the weights to achieve it.]

2.13.   Expression Evaluation

Consider the problem of evaluating a given (binary tree) expression for a particular set of values of the arguments. We have seen previously that particular expressions, such as Horner expressions corresponding to polynomials, can be evaluated by a PRAM or circuit in a number of steps logarithmic in the size (number of leaves) of the expression. What about the evaluation of an arbitrary tree expression? A basic technique in the field of circuit complexity is *tree restructuring* [48, 77, 157, 196, 214, 272]. The technique was developed to show that every function (Boolean or arithmetic) which can be represented by an expression of size s can also be represented by a circuit of depth $O(log\ s)$. One disadvantage of using this tree restructuring approach as a means of fast parallel expression evaluation on a PRAM is that it requires the calculation of appropriate points for tree splitting. When the cost of performing this tree splitting is taken into account the parallel complexity becomes $O(log^2 s)$ rather than $O(log\ s)$. If instead one uses *parallel tree contraction* [3, 30, 88, 190, 191, 192], then the $O(log\ s)$ parallel time bound can be achieved. Fast parallel tree contraction on a PRAM is another technique of very wide applicability.

2.14.   The Class $\mathcal{NC}$

We have described a number of parallel algorithms for the PRAM, circuit and comparison network models. The circuits and comparison networks given can be directly transformed into corresponding PRAM algorithms. These idealised models have provided a robust framework for the investigation of parallel algorithms and their complexity [26, 54, 61, 62, 63, 80, 87, 89, 149, 223, 224, 266, 270]. One outcome of this work has been the development of an extensive set of results concerning $\mathcal{NC}$, the class of computational problems which can be solved on a PRAM by a deterministic algorithm in polylogarithmic time using only a polynomial number of processors. A major open problem in theoretical computer science is to determine whether $\mathcal{P}$, the class of polynomial time computable problems, is contained in $\mathcal{NC}$. If this were shown to be true then it would imply that every problem which had a fast (polynomial time) sequential algorithm also had a fast (polylogarithmic time), efficient (polynomial number of processors) parallel algorithm. Over the last decade, a large number of important problems in $\mathcal{P}$ have been shown to also lie in $\mathcal{NC}$. The following list of such problems is by no means complete.

> **Evaluation of expressions and programs** [87, 88, 89, 103, 106, 149, 158, 185, 189, 193, 224, 261]: Tree restructuring, tree contraction, expression evaluation, evaluation of straight-line algebraic programs of polynomial degree over a commutative semiring, evaluation of straight-line programs corresponding to dynamic programming algorithms, context-free recognition, parallel simulation of finite state automata, circuit value problem for planar monotone circuits, evaluation of set expressions.

Logic [79, 143, 185, 224, 251]: Term matching, term equivalence, evaluation of DATALOG logic programs with the polynomial-fringe property.

Sets [27, 60, 149, 166, 224, 264]: Sorting, selection, set operations, constructing Huffman trees.

Sequences and strings [57, 80, 87, 149, 216, 224, 229]: Prefix sums, merging, sequence comparison (string edit problem), string matching, recognising shuffle of two strings , longest common substring, finding squares in a string, pattern matching for d-dimensional patterns.

Lists [22, 23, 55, 56, 57, 80, 89, 149, 224]: List ranking.

Arithmetic [17, 18, 33, 77, 149, 213, 270, 272] : n-bit integer arithmetic (addition, multiplication, division), linear recurrences, polynomial arithmetic (evaluation, multiplication, division, GCD), evaluation of elementary functions (exp, ln, sin, etc.).

Matrices [47, 67, 80, 149, 224, 270]: Matrix multiplication, determinant, rank, inverse, solution of linear system, Cholesky factorisation.

Graphs [28, 58, 68, 80, 89, 92, 99, 101, 133, 149, 151, 162, 178, 224, 230, 240, 248]: Algebraic path problem (transitive closure, shortest paths, minimum cost spanning tree, topological ordering of dag), transitive reduction, connected components, biconnectivity, triconnectivity, Euler tours, ear decomposition, maximal independent set, symmetry breaking, lowest common ancestors, planarity, tree isomorphism, bipartite perfect matching, minimal elimination ordering.

Combinatorial optimisation [15]: Fixed dimension linear programming.

Geometry [8, 224, 278]: Convex hull in two and three dimensions, Voronoi diagrams and proximity problems, detecting segment intersections, triangulating a polygon, point location.

A number of interesting and important randomised $\mathcal{NC}$ algorithms have also been produced [5, 91, 150, 176, 197, 217, 225, 226] for graph problems such as depth-first search, constructing a perfect matching, maximum cardinality matching, maximum $s - t$ flow, planar graph isomorphism, and subtree isomorphism, and for various problems in computational geometry.

An exciting development over the last few years has been the development of a large number of new deterministic [35, 36, 37] and randomised [96, 117, 266] parallel algorithms for important problems, which achieve nearly-constant time on a CRCW PRAM. The problems include hashing [31, 94, 96, 97, 183, 184], dictionary (insert, delete, query operations) [96], integer sorting [38, 115, 183, 184, 218, 219], integer chain sorting [96, 115, 116], space allocation [96, 116], linear approximate compaction [96, 105, 183], estimation [96, 116], load balancing [93, 96, 116], leaders election [95, 96, 116, 184], generation of random permutations [183], 2-ruling set [55, 96, 105, 183], all nearest-smaller-values [35], approximate sum [96], efficient simulation of Maximum PRAM model on Tolerant PRAM model [95, 96, 117, 184]. These new algorithmic techniques provide a theoretical framework for the future development of tools which would automate a number of tedious aspects of practical parallel computation, such as processor allocation [94, 96, 105, 183] and memory allocation [147].

2.15. $\mathcal{P}$-Completeness

Using techniques analogous to those used in sequential computation to establish $\mathcal{NP}$-completeness, a number of problems in $\mathcal{P}$ have been shown to be $\mathcal{P}$-complete. A computational problem Π is $\mathcal{P}$-complete if and only if $\Pi \in \mathcal{P}$ and $(\Pi \in \mathcal{NC} \Rightarrow \mathcal{P} \subseteq \mathcal{NC})$. The $\mathcal{P}$-complete problems are, in a sense, those in $\mathcal{P}$ for which it is hardest to obtain a fast, efficient PRAM algorithm. Showing that any one of them was in $\mathcal{NC}$ would imply that all problems in $\mathcal{P}$ had fast, efficient PRAM algorithms. The first $\mathcal{P}$-complete problems were established in the early 1970s [136, 137, 164]. Two recently published lists of such problems [110, 194] together contain around 250 problems. Those interested in $\mathcal{P}$-completeness results are strongly encouraged to consult [110]. Two very simple $\mathcal{P}$-complete problems are the following.

Subset Closure
Given: A finite set X, a binary operation o on X, a subset $S \subseteq X$, and an element $x \in X$.
To determine: Whether x is contained in the smallest subset of X which contains S and is closed under o.

Monotone Circuit Value Problem [102]
Given: A single-output Boolean circuit with $\{\wedge, \vee\}$ gates, and a set of values for the inputs.
To determine: The output.

Some other examples of $\mathcal{P}$-complete problems are:

Evaluation of expressions and programs [102, 182, 245]: Planar circuit value problem, arithmetic circuit value problem, type inference, deadlock detection.

Logic [78, 143, 279]: Unification, propositional Horn clause satisfiability, path systems, context-free grammar membership.

Algebra: Finite algebra, generalised word problem, subgroup equality, subgroup isomorphism, group rank.

Arithmetic [146]: Iterated mod.

Matrices [262]: Gaussian elimination with partial pivoting.

Graphs [104]: Maximum flow, lexicographically first maximal independent set, lexicographically first maximal path, lexicographically first depth-first search ordering, high degree subgraph, minimum degree elimination order.

Combinatorial optimisation [75, 154]: Linear programming, linear inequalities, first fit decreasing bin packing, nearest neighbour travelling salesman heuristic, two-player game.

Geometry [25]: Plane sweep triangulation, visibility layers.

Some simple examples of problems in $\mathcal{P}$ which are not currently known to be in $\mathcal{NC}$ or to be $\mathcal{P}$-complete are the following:

Integer GCD
Given: Two n-bit positive integers a, b.
To determine: $GCD(a, b)$

Relative Primeness
Given: Two n-bit positive integers a, b.
To determine: Whether a, b are relatively prime.

Stable Marriage
Given: n men and n women plus a list of marital preferences for each person.
To determine: n marriages that will stand the test of time.

Ray Tracing
Given: A set of n mirrors of lengths $l_1, l_2, \ldots, l_n$ and their placements, a source S and the trajectory of a single beam emitted from S, a designated mirror M.
To determine: If M is hit by the beam. At the mirrors the angle of incidence of the beam equals the angle of reflection.

Serna and Spirakis [237, 238, 239] have investigated the extent to which solutions to important $\mathcal{P}$-complete problems such as linear programming, maximum flow and high degree subgraph can be approximated by fast, efficient PRAM algorithms if $\mathcal{P} \neq \mathcal{NC}$.

2.16.   Parallel Efficiency

Matrix multiplication and the algebraic path problem are two fundamental computational problems which have fast $\mathcal{NC}$ algorithms. A large number of important problems in $\mathcal{P}$ can be shown to be in $\mathcal{NC}$ by a reduction to one of these two problems. (In the case of reductions to the APP, these are usually reductions to the transitive closure instance of that problem.) Unfortunately, many of the parallel algorithms so produced are extremely inefficient in terms of the number of processors required. For example, many problems on graphs with v vertices and e edges can be solved sequentially in time $O(v + e)$ or $O((v \ log \ v) + e)$. For a number of these problems, one can obtain a parallel algorithm with time complexity $O(log^2 v)$, but the algorithm requires $M(v)$ processors, where $M(v)$ is the sequential complexity of $v \times v$ matrix multiplication. As noted earlier, the best known upper bound on $M(v)$ is $O(v^{2.376})$ [65] and we know that it cannot be less than proportional to v^2. Thus we have a number of fast PRAM algorithms for which the processor-time product is much greater than the time required to solve the problem by a sequential algorithm. To produce fast practical parallel algorithms for such problems we must avoid the brute force use of matrix multiplication and transitive closure on dense matrices. This difficulty has come to be known as the *matrix multiplication / transitive closure bottleneck*. It is particularly serious in applications where one is dealing with highly sparse matrices or graphs. In such cases, by embedding the problem in one involving dense matrices one may produce a theoretically fast algorithm, but it is unlikely to be of much practical value. In the last few years, substantial progress has been made on overcoming this bottleneck. A number of important new PRAM algorithms for sparse matrix and graph problems have been developed which are very efficient in their use of processors [68, 98, 99, 100, 114, 132, 144, 160, 162, 203, 244, 252].

As we have seen, the robustness of the PRAM model and the class $\mathcal{NC}$ has permitted the development of a rich theory of parallel algorithms and their complexity. However, the above considerations show that a naive preoccupation with $\mathcal{NC}$ may not result in efficient parallel algorithms for practical implementation. Probing $\mathcal{NC}$ further, it is not even clear that the class captures the informal notion of "problems which are amenable to parallel solution". Vitter and Simons [268] have shown that some $\mathcal{P}$-complete problems may be solved by parallel algorithms which are in a very reasonable sense, efficient. On the other hand, a problem such as searching an ordered list, which runs in logarithmic sequential time, is in $\mathcal{NC}$, irrespective of the existence of efficient parallel algorithms for that problem. In fact, searching does not admit efficient parallel algorithms.

As noted in [263], efficiency is a prime consideration in the design of parallel algorithms: one would like to solve a problem roughly p times faster when using p processors. This consideration is missing from the definition of $\mathcal{NC}$, instead the emphasis of $\mathcal{NC}$ theory is simply on the development of parallel algorithms which have polylogarithmic time complexity. In [161], Kruskal, Rudolph and Snir develop an alternative set of complexity classes for PRAM computations, and demonstrate that they provide an equally robust framework for studying parallel algorithms and complexity, but one which is more relevant in the context of practical parallel computing. Their emphasis is much more on the performance of a parallel algorithm relative to the best known sequential algorithm for the same problem. In describing the approach of [161] we will use the following notation. For a given problem, $S(n)$ will denote the sequential running time, $T(n)$ the parallel running time, and $P(n)$ the number of processors.

One very weak requirement, in terms of parallel performance, would be that the parallel algorithm demonstrate some unbounded speedup, i.e. $lim_{n\to\infty}T(n)/S(n) = 0$. A parallel algorithm for which $T(n) = O(n/loglog\ n)$ when $S(n) = O(n)$ would satisfy this condition. That kind of small improvement is unlikely to be sufficient in many cases. We are more likely to want to claim that a significant reduction in running time can be achieved through the use of parallelism, i.e. that $T(n)$ is a fast decreasing function of $S(n)$. The two obvious choices for such a function are captured in the following definition.

Definition 2.1 *A parallel algorithm is* polynomially fast *if* $T(n) = O(S(n)^\epsilon)$ *for some* $\epsilon < 1$, *and it is* polylogarithmically fast *if* $T(n) = O(log^k S(n))$ *for some fixed* k.

Reduction in running time has a cost. The number of processors must increase as fast as the speedup; generally it increases faster. The *inefficiency* of a parallel algorithm is the ratio $T(n) * P(n)/S(n)$, i.e. the ratio between the time-processor product for the parallel algorithm and the number of operations performed by the sequential algorithm.

Definition 2.2 *A parallel algorithm has* constant inefficiency *if* $T(n) * P(n) = O(S(n))$, *it has* polylogarithmically bounded inefficiency *if* $T(n) * P(n) = O(S(n)\ log^k S(n))$ *for some fixed* k, *and it has* polynomially bounded inefficiency *if* $T(n) * P(n) = O(S(n)^k)$ *for some fixed* k.

Six interesting classes can be obtained by combining the two requirements on speedup with these three constraints on inefficiency.

	Polylog Fast	Poly Fast
Constant Ineff.	**ENC** (Efficient, NC fast)	**EP** (Efficient, Parallel)
Polylog Ineff.	**ANC** (Almost efficient, NC fast)	**AP** (Almost efficient, Parallel)
Poly Ineff.	**SNC** (Semi efficient, NC fast)	**SP** (Semi efficient, Parallel)

Kruskal, Rudolph and Snir [161] classify a large number of important problems within this framework.

ENC: Sorting, merging, selection, prefix sums, polynomial evaluation, expression evaluation, fast Fourier transform, connected and biconnected components of dense graphs.

EP: Various dense graph computations (strongly connected components, single source shortest paths, minimum cost spanning tree, directed graph reachability), monotone circuit value problem.

ANC: Connectivity and biconnectivity of sparse graphs with $e = O(v)$ edges.

SP: Depth-first search of undirected graphs, weighted bipartite matching, flows in $0 - 1$ networks.

2.17.   Communication Complexity

In discussing the complexity of PRAM algorithms we have used the two standard complexity measures, namely parallel time complexity and number of processors. For the circuit model, parallel time complexity corresponds to the depth of the directed acyclic graph (dag), and for the comparison network model it corresponds to the number of levels in the network. In this section we consider the communication complexity of PRAM algorithms in a simplified setting first proposed by Papadimitriou and Ullman [204].

We model the computational problem to be solved as a dag, with nodes corresponding to the functions computed and arcs corresponding to functional dependencies. In most practical situations, the development of an appropriate dag is a major part of the algorithm design process but, for simplicity, we will assume it is fixed and given. Our problem is to efficiently schedule the dag on a p processor parallel system which may have a large local memory at each processor, i.e. to assign each node of the dag to one or more processors in the system which will compute that node. (As we shall see, allowing more than one processor to compute the same node can sometimes save communication at no expense in terms of parallel time.) A schedule must satisfy the constraint that a node can only be computed at a given time step if its predecessors have been computed in previous time steps. We will use t to denote the total number of time steps required for a schedule.

Communication complexity is captured in the following way. If node v depends on node u, i.e. there is an arc from u to v in the dag, and u, v are computed in distinct processors then that arc is said to be a communication arc. The communication complexity c of a given schedule is simply the number of communication arcs in the dag. This measure captures an important practical cost in the implementation of parallel algorithms on a multiprocessor system, i.e. the total message traffic generated.

Example. Consider the (2×2 diamond) dag on vertices $\{v_{0,0}, v_{0,1}, v_{1,0}, v_{1,1}\}$ which has the four arcs $\{<v_{0,0}, v_{0,1}>, <v_{0,1}, v_{1,1}>, <v_{0,0}, v_{1,0}>, <v_{1,0}, v_{1,1}>\}$. This can be scheduled in the following way on two processors P_0, P_1.

t	P_0	P_1
1	$v_{0,0}$	
2	$v_{0,1}$	$v_{1,0}$
3	$v_{1,1}$	

giving a schedule with $c = 2, t = 3$. The alternative schedule

t	P_0	P_1
1	$v_{0,0}$	$v_{0,0}$
2	$v_{0,1}$	$v_{1,0}$
3	$v_{1,1}$	

yields $c = 1, t = 3$ and gives an example showing that allowing more than one processor to compute a node can reduce communication

Our main interest is in the tradeoff between parallel time and communication. First we note that for some simple dags there is no real issue concerning the best way to trade communication for time. For example, consider a complete binary tree on n nodes. If we schedule the tree on p processors, $p > 1$, then we must have $t \geq n/p$. As each processor, other than the one which computes the root, must compute a node value required by some other processor, we have also $c \geq p - 1$. Thus, we have $ct = \Omega(n)$. This lower bound for the communication-time product can be easily achieved by a schedule.

A more interesting dag is the diamond. The *diamond dag* is an $n \times n$ square mesh rotated 45 degrees, where the children of each node are the nodes immediately to the southeast and southwest, if they exist. More formally, it is the dag on n^2 nodes $\{v_{i,j} \mid 0 \leq i, j \leq n - 1\}$ where there is an arc from $v_{i,j}$ to $v_{i,j+1}$ and from $v_{i,j}$ to $v_{i+1,j}$, where those nodes exist. The diamond dag arises in a number of important dynamic programming algorithms. It turns out that the diamond does not share with the binary tree the nice property that the best lower bounds on time and communication can be simultaneously achieved. Rather, there is a lower bound on the product ct that is stronger than what is implied by the best lower bounds on c and t individually.

If we schedule an $n \times n$ diamond on p processors, $p \leq n$, then we must have $t \geq n^2/p$. This lower bound on parallel time is easily matched by a fast "stripes" schedule in which processor $k, 0 \leq k \leq p - 1$, computes nodes $v_{i,j}$, for all $kn/p \leq i \leq ((k+1)n/p) - 1$ and $0 \leq j \leq n - 1$. For this schedule we have $c = O(np)$. Now, let us consider a lower bound on communication. If we divide the nodes of the dag evenly among the $p > 1$ processors, then each will compute n^2/p nodes, and it is not hard to show that there must be among the arcs on the nodes computed by any one of these p processors at least $(n^2/p)^{1/2} = n/p^{1/2}$ communication arcs. Thus, we have $c = \Omega(np^{1/2})$. This lower bound on communication is easily matched by a schedule in which each processor computes a contiguous $(n/p^{1/2}) \times (n/p^{1/2})$ subdiamond of the dag, but for this method we have a rather higher parallel time of $O(n^2/p^{1/2})$. We have described two distinct parallel schedules for the $n \times n$ diamond, and have shown that one of them optimises time, while the other optimises communication. For both of these schedules we have $ct = O(n^3)$. Papadimitriou and Ullman [204] have shown that this bound on the communication-time product is, in fact, optimal to within a constant factor. This result demonstrates that there is an important tradeoff between communication and parallel time for the scheduling of the diamond dag on a multiprocessor. Papadimitriou and Ullman also studied a tradeoff between parallel time and communication delay for the diamond dag. The *communication delay* d of a scheduled dag is defined to be the maximum number of communication arcs on any directed path in the dag. In [204] it is shown that for the $n \times n$ diamond, $(d + 1)t = \Omega(n^2)$.

A number of other interesting communication-time tradeoff results have been obtained. Klawe and Paterson (see [204]) have shown a $ct = \Omega(n^4)$ lower bound for the dag where the children of node $v_{i,j}$ are all the nodes $v_{k,j}$ where $i < k$, and all the nodes $v_{i,l}$ where $j < l$. This dag arises in many important dynamic programming problems, and can be computed in $O(n^3)$ sequential time. Andivahis [24] has improved this tradeoff result to $c^2 t = \Omega(n^7)$. Jayasimha and Loui [131] show a $ct = \Omega(n^3)$ tradeoff for a dag that corresponds to the solution of a triangular system of linear equations. Afrati et al. [4] show that the problem of finding, for a given dag, a schedule which minimises time, and also minimises communication as a secondary criterion, is $\mathcal{NP}$-complete, even if the dag is a tree, and the number of processors to be used is either given or open (the problem can be solved in polynomial time if the amount of communication is fixed.) Papadimitriou and Yannakakis [205] develop a polynomial algorithm which, for any dag, calculates within a factor of two the optimum weighted sum $t + \tau d$, for any τ, when no bound on the number of processors is specified. In [140], it is shown that if τ is a fixed integer, then a dynamic programming approach can be used to obtain a polynomial time algorithm for solving the scheduling problem exactly.

Aggarwal, Chandra and Snir [7] have studied a model called the *local memory PRAM*, or *LPRAM*, which also captures both the communication and computation requirements of PRAM algorithms in a convenient way. An LPRAM is a CREW PRAM in which each processor is provided with an unlimited amount of local memory. Processors can simultaneously read from the same location in the global memory, but two or more are not allowed to simultaneously write into the same location. The input variables are initially available in the global memory, and the outputs must also be eventually there. The multiprocessor is a synchronous MIMD machine. In order to model the communication delay and computation time, it is convenient to restrict the machine such that, at every time step, the processors do one of the following:

In one communication step, a processor can write, and then read a word from global memory.

In a computation step, a processor can perform a simple operation on at most two values that are present in its local memory.

A computation is represented as a dag, and a schedule for a dag consists of a sequence of computation steps and communication steps. At a computation step each processor may evaluate a node of the dag; this evaluation can only take place at a processor when its local memory contains the values corresponding to all of the incoming arcs. After the computation step is completed the values for the outgoing arcs are held in the local memory. At a communication step, any processor may write into the global memory any value that is presently in its local memory, and then it may read into its local memory a value from the global memory.

Example. Consider the nine-node dag with arcs $\{<a,c>, <a,d>, <a,e>, <a,f>, <b,c>,$ $<b,d>, <b,e>, <b,f>, <c,g>, <d,g>, <e,h>, <f,h> <g,r>, <h,r>\}$. This can be scheduled to run on a four processor LPRAM in five communication steps and three computation steps as follows.

Comm. step 1 : P_1, P_2, P_3, P_4 read a.
Comm. step 2 : P_1, P_2, P_3, P_4 read b.
Comp. step 1 : P_1, P_2, P_3, P_4 compute c, d, e, f respectively.
Comm. step 3 : P_2, P_4 write d, f respectively. P_1, P_3 read d, f respectively.

Comp. step 2 : P_1 computes g, P_3 computes h.
Comm. step 4 : P_3 writes h, P_1 reads it.
Comp. step 3 : P_1 computes r.
Comm. step 5 : P_1 writes r.

The dag can also, for example, be computed on a two processor LPRAM in four communication steps and four computation steps, or on a single processor LPRAM in three communication steps and seven computation steps. Note that the minimum communication delay (number of communication steps) and the minimum computation time (number of computation steps) may not be achievable by the same schedule.

Aggarwal, Chandra and Snir [7] show that two $n \times n$ matrices can be multiplied in $O(n^3/p)$ computation time and $O(n^2/p^{2/3})$ communication delay using p processors, for $p \le n^3/log^{3/2}n$, and that these bounds are optimal. They also show that any algorithm which uses only binary comparisons and sorts n elements requires a communication delay of $\Omega((n\ log\ n)/(p\ log\ (n/p)))$ for $1 \le p \le n$, and also that this lower bound can be achieved by an algorithm with $O((n\ log\ n)/p)$ computation time. Other problems considered include computing an n-point FFT graph, computing binary trees, and computing the diamond dag.

3. Special Purpose Parallel Computing

We noted in the introduction to this chapter that no single model of parallel computation had yet come to dominate developments in parallel computing in the way the von Neumann model has dominated sequential computing [84, 258, 259]. Instead we have a variety of models such as VLSI systems, systolic arrays and distributed memory multicomputers, in which the careful exploitation of network locality is crucial for algorithmic efficiency. In the different types of system it manifests itself in different ways. In a VLSI system, a design with good network locality will have short wires, and hence will require less area. An efficient systolic algorithm will have a simple, regular structure and use only nearest neighbour communication. An efficient multicomputer algorithm will be one which minimises the distance that messages have to travel in the network by careful mapping of the virtual process structure onto the physical processor architecture. Of course, an efficient algorithm for, say, a hypercube multicomputer will not necessarily perform well when run on, for example, a 2D array multicomputer with the same number of processors. We will use the generic term "special purpose" to refer to this type of parallel computing.

In the related chapter [187], we describe a number of aspects of the work which has been done in recent years on the design, analysis, implementation and verification of special purpose parallel computing systems. The volume of published material on these topics is huge. A long, but by no means complete, bibliography is given at the end of [187]. Special purpose parallel systems are particularly appropriate in application areas where the goal of achieving the best possible performance is much more important than that of achieving an architecture-independent design. Some examples of such areas are: digital signal processing (filtering, transforms), image processing, computer vision, mobile robot control, particle simulation, cellular automata / lattice gas computations, dense matrix computations, communications and cryptography, speech recognition, computer graphics, game playing. For more examples, see [187].

The range of possible technologies for the development of such systems is extensive, varied, and growing. The following is a representative sample of those in use today.

VLSI systems (custom VLSI chips, field-programmable gate arrays)

Systolic architectures (application specific arrays, programmable systolic architectures)

Cellular automata machines

Multicomputers (2D and 3D arrays, pyramids, fat trees, hypercubes, butterflies etc.)

Neural systems (VLSI neural networks, analog VLSI systems)

On the technological horizon we have the prospects of various exotic, massively parallel systems such as lattice gas machines, quantum dot arrays, and various types of optical and holographic systems.

We will not pursue the fascinating world of special purpose parallel computing further in this chapter. We simply note that, in the next few years, we will probably start to see a much sharper distinction between the two fields of special purpose parallel computing and general purpose parallel computing than at present. Those primarily concerned with achieving the maximum possible performance for a specific application (at any cost?) are likely to move more and more towards highly specialised architectures and technologies in the pursuit of performance gains. In contrast, those for whom it is important to achieve architecture-independence and portability in their designs, will increasingly seek a robust and lasting framework within which to develop their designs. In the remainder of this chapter we will describe some ideas which have as their goal, the development of such a robust framework. As we shall see, the use of advanced technologies such as optics may also have an important role to play in achieving the communications performance required for efficient general purpose parallel computing systems. In this setting, the model is the central driving force and the optical hardware is simply one possible means of implementing the model. This can be contrasted with work on the development of special purpose optical parallel systems, where one directly exploits the capabilities of optical technology at the algorithmic level to produce, for example, very high performance image processing systems, signal processors, or neural networks.

4.   General Purpose Parallel Computing

We have seen that an idealised model of parallel computation such as the PRAM can provide a robust framework within which to develop techniques for the design, analysis and comparison of parallel algorithms. A major issue in theoretical computer science since the late 1970s has been to determine the extent to which the PRAM and related models can be efficiently implemented on physically realistic distributed memory architectures. A number of new routing and memory management techniques have been developed which show that efficient implementation is indeed possible in many cases. In this section we describe some of the results which have been obtained, and discuss their significance for the future of general purpose parallel computing. Before doing so, we will give an *informal* description of what we mean by a general purpose parallel computer (GPPC).

A GPPC consists of a set of general purpose microprocessors connected by a communications network. The memory is fully distributed, with each processor having its own physically local memory module. The GPPC supports a single address space across all processors by allocating a part of each module to a common global memory system. Each processor thus has access to its own private address space of local variables, and to the global memory system. The purpose of the communications network is simply to support non-local memory accesses in a *uniformly efficient* way through message routing. By uniformly efficient, we mean that the time taken for a processor to read from, or write to, a non-local memory element in another processor-memory pair should be independent of which physical memory module the value is held in. The algorithm designer / programmer should not be aware of any hierarchical memory organisation based on the particular physical interconnect structure currently used in the communications network. Instead, performance of the communications network should be described only in terms of its global properties, e.g. the maximum time required to perform a non-local memory operation, and the maximum number of such operations which can simultaneously be in the network at any time.

A GPPC, as described, differs from a PRAM in that it has a two-level memory organisation. Each processor has its own physically local memory; all other memory is non-local and accessible at a uniform rate. In contrast, the PRAM has a one-level memory organisation; all memory in a PRAM is non-local. The GPPC and PRAM models are similar to the extent that they both have no notion of network locality. The GPPC differs from most current distributed memory multicomputers, e.g. hypercubes, in having no exploitable network locality, but is similar in that it is constructed as a network of processor-memory pairs. One formal model which would correspond reasonably closely to the (informally defined) GPPC would be a distributed memory multicomputer with full connectivity, i.e. with an interconnection structure corresponding to the complete graph [147]. Another is the bulk-synchronous parallel computer [258] which we will describe later in the chapter.

Our purpose in giving this informal description of what we mean by a general purpose parallel computer is simply to describe, in very general terms, the main characteristics that we would expect any such computer to have. We have placed emphasis on the communication / memory organisation of such a machine. However, to support a coherent global memory it would also be necessary to provide support for features such as processor synchronisation.

The efficient implementation of a single address space on a distributed memory architecture requires an efficient method for the distributed routing of read and write requests, and of the replies to read requests, through the network of processors. In the following section we show how the idea of randomising can be used to produce an efficient distributed routing scheme for this problem.

4.1.   Randomised Routing

A distributed memory multicomputer can be thought of as having p processor-memory pairs located at distinct nodes of a p-node graph. Each processor can send packets to, and receive packets from, processors at adjacent nodes in the graph. Each edge of the graph can transmit one packet of information in unit time, and has a queue for storing packets that have to be transmitted along it.

A large number of graphs have been proposed as interconnection networks for such multicomputers. Two important parameters of any such graph are its *degree*, i.e. the maximum number of edges incident at any node, and its *diameter*, i.e. the maximum distance between any pair of nodes, where the distance between two nodes is the length of a shortest path between them. If implemented using conventional VLSI technology, a graph with low degree is likely to have advantages in terms of physical packaging. The advantage of using a graph with small diameter is, of course, that it will permit a packet to be sent quickly between any two nodes in the network. (The constraints of VLSI technology and, more generally, of three dimensional space, imply that some low diameter networks cannot be realised without having long wires. We will return to this wiring problem later in the chapter and show how optics may provide a solution.) Some of the graphs which have been proposed as interconnection networks on p nodes are listed in the following table, together with their degree and diameter.

Name	Degree	Diameter
1D array (ring)	2	$p/2$
Shuffle-exchange	3	$2 \log p$
Cube-connected-cycles	3	$(5/2) \log p$
2D mesh of trees	3	$2 \log p$
3D mesh of trees	3	$2 \log p$
2D array (toroidal)	4	$\Theta(p^{1/2})$
Butterfly (wrapped)	4	$2 \log p$
de Bruijn graph	4	$\log p$
3D array (toroidal)	6	$\Theta(p^{1/3})$
Pyramid	9	$\log p$
Hypercube	$\log p$	$\log p$

A large amount of work has been done in recent years on the development of efficient routing methods for such networks [167, 168, 169, 171, 259], on the efficient embedding of one network in another [122, 134, 167, 168, 169, 227], and on the demonstration of work-preserving emulations of one network by another [156, 167, 168, 231]. We will focus our attention here on the routing problem.

We consider the problem of packet routing on a p-processor network. Let h-relation denote the routing problem where each processor has at most h packets to send to various points in the network, and where each processor is also due to receive at most h packets from other processors. We are interested in the development of distributed routing methods in which the routing decisions made at a node at some point in time are based only on information concerning the packets that have already passed through the node at that time. In the nondistributed case where global information is available everywhere, the problem of routing is easier and well understood.

Let us first consider deterministic methods for distributed routing. We define a routing method to be *oblivious* if the path taken by each packet is entirely determined by its source and destination. (Note that the use of the term oblivious here is slightly different from its use in the context of comparison networks or circuits.) It is known [45, 142] that, for a 1-relation no deterministic oblivious routing method can do better than $\Omega(p^{1/2}/d)$ time steps, in the worst case, for any degree d graph. The most obvious examples of deterministic oblivious approaches are greedy methods in which one sends all packets to their destination by a shortest path through the network. For 1-relations, the performance of greedy routing on a butterfly can be summarised as follows. All 1-relations can be realised in $O(p^{1/2})$ steps, which, as we have observed, is an optimal worst case bound for any such fixed degree network. A large number of 1-relations which arise in practical parallel computation, e.g. the bit-reversal permutation and the transpose permutation, provably require $\Theta(p^{1/2})$ steps. What about the "average case"? Define a *random* 1-*mapping* to be the routing problem where each processor has a single packet which is to be sent to a random destination. Greedy routing of a random 1-mapping on a butterfly will terminate in $O(log\ p)$ steps. Moreover, the fraction of all random 1-mappings which do not finish in $O(log\ p)$ steps is incredibly small, despite the fact that most of the 1-relations which seem to arise in practice do not finish in this time. We can probably conclude from these results that "typical" routing problems, in a practical sense, is a rather different concept from "typical" routing problems in a mathematical sense. The performance of greedy routing on a hypercube is very similar to the case of the butterfly. All 1-relations can be realised in $O(p^{1/2}/log\ p)$ steps, which is an optimal worst case bound for any $log\ p$ degree network. For the average case, where each packet has a random destination, greedy routing will terminate in $O(log\ p)$ steps. In the case of the hypercube, there are exponentially many shortest paths for a greedy method to choose from, but even randomising among these choices still gives no better than $O(p^{\alpha})$, $\alpha > 0$, steps for many 1-relations.

Another possible approach to deterministic routing is to use a sorting network of low depth. For example, from Batcher's odd-even merge sorting network [32, 155] we can obtain an interconnection network by associating each line in the sorting network with a node in the interconnection network, and each comparison element in the sorting network with an edge in the interconnection network. In this way, we can obtain a p-node graph of degree $O(log^2 p)$ and diameter $O(log^2 p)$. Any 1-relation routing problem can be realised in $O(log^2 p)$ steps by using the associated sorting network as a means of "sorting" the packet addresses. Note that this method is deterministic and requires no queueing. By using the sorting network of Ajtai, Komlos and Szemeredi [11], or its refinement by Paterson [207], we can improve this result to obtain degree, diameter, and number of time steps $O(log\ p)$. However, the complex structure of the networks involved, and the very large constant factors hidden in the $O(log\ p)$ bounds, rule out this approach as a practical option, at least for the present time.

We have seen that for the butterfly and hypercube, the performance of greedy routing on random 1-mappings is much better than on "worst case 1-relations", such as the bit-reversal permutation in the case of the butterfly. Around 1980, Valiant made the simple and striking observation that one could achieve efficient distributed routing, in terms of worst case performance, if one could reduce a 1-relation to something like the composition of two random 1-mappings. The resulting technique which emerged from this observation has come to be known as *two-phase randomised routing* [12, 167, 212, 253, 256, 257, 259, 260]. Using this approach, a 1-relation is realised by initially sending each packet to a random node in the network, using a greedy method. From there it is forwarded to the desired destination, again by a greedy method. Both phases of the routing correspond closely to the realisation of a random 1-mapping. Extensive investigation of this method, in terms of the number of steps required, size of buffers required etc., has shown that it performs extremely well, both in theory and in practice. The main theoretical results which follow from the use of randomised routing are summarised in the following two theorems.

Theorem 4.1 *With high probability, every 1-relation can be realised on a p processor cube-connected-cycles, butterfly, 2D array and hypercube in a number of steps proportional to the diameter of the network.*

For the fixed degree networks in Theorem 4.1, this result is essentially optimal. For the $(log\ p)$-degree hypercube, the following stronger result can be obtained.

Theorem 4.2 *With high probability, every* $(\log p)$-*relation can be realised on a* p *processor hypercube in* $O(\log p)$ *steps.*

Proofs of Theorems 4.1 and 4.2 can be found in [259]. Randomised routing can also be used to achieve good worst case performance on networks such as the shuffle-exchange graph [12] and fat trees [109, 172].

An interesting alternative to using randomised routing on a standard, well defined network such as a butterfly, is to use *deterministic routing on a randomly wired network.* In [170, 254] it is shown that a simple deterministic routing algorithm can be used to realise a 1-relation in $O(\log p)$ steps on a randomly wired, bounded degree network known as a multibutterfly. An important feature of multibutterflies is that they have powerful expansion properties. In addition to permitting fast deterministic routing, such expander graphs [13, 14, 16, 141, 177, 255] also have very strong fault tolerance properties.

The techniques and results that we have described for various types of randomised routing show convincingly that for the problem of routing h-relations at least, there are a variety of theoretically and practically efficient methods which can be used. In order to show that we can efficiently simulate a shared address space on a distributed memory architecture we also need to show that we can deal with the problem of "hot spots", i.e. where a large number of processors simultaneously try to access the same memory module.

4.2.   Hashing

In theoretical terms, one very effective method of uniformly distributing memory references is to hash the single address space. The hash function has, of course, to be efficiently computable. Hash functions for this purpose have been proposed and analysed by Mehlhorn and Vishkin [188]. They suggest using an elegant class of functions with some provably desirable properties: the class of polynomials of degree $O(\log p)$ in arithmetic modulo m, where p is the number of processors and m is the total number of words in the shared address space. As in the case of randomised routing, the idea of hashing the address space in this way has been subjected to extensive scrutiny in terms of both its theoretical and its practical performance. All of the available evidence suggests that it works extremely well in both respects. In fact, even constant degree polynomial hash functions, e.g. degree two, seem to work well in practice. (Recent results [73, 74] show that linear hash functions have certain limitations, at least in a theoretical sense, but that cubic hash functions work well. The results also suggest that quadratic hash functions may have some shortcomings.) One additional advantage of using a hashed address space is that we do not need then to resort to randomising to avoid bottlenecks in packet routing, simple deterministic methods will suffice.

Detailed technical accounts of the role of hashing in achieving efficient general purpose parallel computing can be found in [145, 147, 220, 221, 242, 258, 259]. We will mention only the following two results which demonstrate that distributed memory architectures can efficiently simulate PRAMs. Let $EPRAM(p, t)$ [$CPRAM(p, t)$, $HYPERCUBE(p, t)$, $COMPLETE(p, t)$] denote the class of problems which can be solved on a p processor EREW PRAM [CRCW PRAM, hypercube, completely connected network, respectively] in t time steps.

Theorem 4.3 (Valiant [259])
With high probability, $EPRAM(p \log p, t/\log p) \subseteq HYPERCUBE(p, t)$.

Theorem 4.4 (Karp, Luby and Meyer auf der Heide [147])
With high probability, $CPRAM(p \log \log p \log^* p, t) \subseteq COMPLETE(p, t \log \log p \log^* p)$.

Theorems 4.3 and 4.4 show that PRAM algorithms with a degree of parallel slackness can be implemented on distributed memory architectures in a way which is optimal in terms of the processor-time product.

Definition 4.5 *An m processor algorithm, when implemented on an n processor machine, where $n \leq m$, is said to have a* parallel slackness *factor of m/n for that machine.*

Parallel slackness is an idea of fundamental importance in the area of general purpose parallel computing. If parallel algorithms and programs are designed so that they have more parallelism than is available in the machine, then the available parallel slackness can be effectively exploited to hide the kind of network latencies one finds in distributed memory architectures. The only requirement is that the processors provide efficient support for multithreading and fast context switching [44, 228]. Latency tolerance via multithreading is likely to be more effective on large scale general purpose parallel computing systems than the use of complex caching schemes for latency reduction [111, 175].

The idea of exploiting parallel slackness can even be carried over into the area of sequential computing. Much effort in recent years has been devoted to the development of complex heuristic techniques for the efficient prefetching of values from memory in sequential computations [50, 139, 195]. A radical alternative to this approach is, instead, to design parallel algorithms for implementation on sequential machines. The parallel slackness of the algorithm can then be exploited to achieve efficient prefetching. For more on this topic, see [265].

We have seen then that by achieving a degree of parallel slackness in program designs one can provide significant opportunities for the effective scheduling of those programs, by the programmer or by a compiler, to hide the various kinds of latencies which arise in both sequential and parallel computing. This idea of exploiting parallel slackness, or overdecomposition, is not new. It was, for example, a central idea in the early HEP parallel architecture [243], and has been used in its successors, Horizon and Tera [19]. In recent years it has come to be recognised as crucial, not only for efficient implementation of PRAM like models [147, 258, 259], but also for dataflow models [201]. The prospects for "autoparallelising" sequential code, which may be regarded as the extreme opposite of this approach, appear very bleak indeed.

The above analysis strongly supports the general principle that one should aim, at all times, to produce algorithms and programs which have more parallelism in them than is available in the machine (subject, of course, to the kinds of constraints on parallel efficiency which were discussed earlier in the chapter.) In the future we can expect to see the development of a variety of programming languages for general purpose parallel computing. A clear message from our discussion is that such languages must permit, and indeed encourage, the development of programs which demonstrate a high degree of fine grain concurrency.

4.3.   Combining

In the previous sections we have been concerned with the problems of implementing the weakest PRAM model, the EREW PRAM, on a distributed memory architecture. In practical parallel programming it is often convenient to permit concurrent access to a memory location, as in the CRCW PRAM model. An important practical case is that of broadcasting, where all processors simultaneously require the value of a single memory location.

One approach to the implementation of concurrent memory access is to use combining networks [107], i.e. networks that can combine and replicate messages in addition to delivering them in a point-to-point manner. The Fluent machine of Ranade [220, 221] provides an excellent example of how a CRCW PRAM can be efficiently implemented on a distributed memory architecture equipped with a combining network. The interconnection network of the Fluent machine is a butterfly. Let $CBUTTERFLY(p,t)$ denote the class of problems which can be solved on a p processor butterfly with a combining network in t time steps.

Theorem 4.6 (Ranade [221])
With high probability, $CPRAM(p,t) \subseteq CBUTTERFLY(p, t \log p)$.

The theorem is established by showing that a p-processor Fluent machine can emulate a p-processor CRCW PRAM with only a slowdown of $O(\log p)$, i.e. each parallel step of the PRAM requires at most $O(\log p)$ steps on the Fluent machine, with high probability. The size of buffers required at each node of the network is constant. The following is a very brief account of the main ideas used in the emulation. The address space of the PRAM is hashed onto the memory modules of the Fluent machine using a hashing function chosen at random from a $(\log n)$-universal class of hash functions [53, 273]. Suppose several processors wish to read the same memory location at the same time. Each one sends a message to the appropriate memory module along some path in the network. These paths will intersect to form a tree and there is, therefore, no need to send more than one request along any branch of the tree. A request simply waits at each node until (i) another request to the same destination arrives on the other input to the node, in which case the node combines the two and forwards the result along the tree, or (ii) the node determines that no future requests arriving on the other input will have the same destination. By always transmitting messages in sorted order of their destinations, and using "ghost messages" where necessary, one can achieve the above emulation result.

Concurrent access to shared variables in the Fluent machine is based on the multiprefix primitive. It has the form $MP(A, v, \oplus)$ where A is a shared variable, v is a value, and $\oplus$ is a binary associative operator. At any time step a processor can execute a multiprefix operation, with the constraint that if processors P_i and P_j execute $MP(A, v_i, \oplus_i)$ and $MP(A, v_j, \oplus_j)$, then $\oplus_i = \oplus_j$. The semantics of the multiprefix operation is defined as follows.

Definition 4.7 *At time step T, let $P_A = \{p_1, p_2, \ldots, p_k\}$ be the set of processors referring to variable A, such that $p_1 < p_2 < \cdots < p_k$. Suppose that $p_i \in P_A$ executes instruction $MP(A, v_i, \oplus)$. Let a_0 be the value of A at the start of time step T. Then, at the end of time step T, processor p_i will receive the value $a_0 \oplus v_1 \oplus \cdots \oplus v_{i-1}$ and the value of variable A will be $a_0 \oplus v_1 \oplus \cdots \oplus v_k$.*

Thus, when a set of processors perform a multiprefix operation on a common variable, the result is the same as if a single prefix operation were performed with the processors ordered by their index.

A parallel architecture which is very close in design to the Fluent machine is currently under construction at the University of Saarbrücken [1, 2].

Valiant [258] has investigated the extent to which concurrent access to shared variables can be provided without the use of combining networks. Working with the BSP model, he has shown that if one has enough parallel slackness, then one can support concurrent accesses in software on networks which have only point-to-point communication, with only constant slowdown, by using fast integer sorting methods. In the next section we describe the BSP model of parallel computation proposed by Valiant.

4.4.   The BSP Model

For a detailed account of the model, and of the various routing and hashing results which can be obtained for it, the reader is referred to [258]. We concentrate here on presenting a view of (i) how a bulk-synchronous parallel architecture would be described, and (ii) how it would be used.

A *bulk-synchronous parallel (BSP) computer* consists of the following:

a set of processor-memory pairs

a communications network that delivers messages in a point-to-point manner

a mechanism for the efficient barrier synchronisation of all, or a subset, of the processors

There are no specialised combining, replication or broadcasting facilities. If we define a time step to be the time required for a single local operation, i.e. a basic operation on locally held data values, then the performance of any BSP computer can be characterised by the following four parameters:

p = number of processors

s = processor speed, i.e. number of time steps per second

l = synchronisation periodicity, i.e. minimal number of time steps between successive synchronisation operations

g = (total number of local operations performed by all processors in one second) / (total number of words delivered by the communications network in one second)

The parameter l is related to the network latency, i.e. to the time required for a non-local memory access in a situation of continuous message traffic. The parameter g corresponds to the frequency with which non-local memory accesses can be made; in a machine with a higher value of g one must make non-local memory accesses less frequently. More formally, g is related to the time required to realise h-relations in a situation of continuous message traffic; g is the value such that an h-relation can be performed in gh steps.

A BSP computer operates in the following way. A computation consists of a sequence of parallel *supersteps*, where each superstep is a sequence of steps, followed by a barrier synchronisation at which point any memory accesses take effect. During a superstep, each processor has a set of programs or threads which it has to carry out, and it can do the following:

perform a number of computation steps, from its set of threads, on values held
locally at the start of the superstep

send and receive a number of messages corresponding to non-local read and write
requests

The complexity of a superstep S in a BSP algorithm is determined as follows. Let L be the
maximum number of local computation steps executed by any process or during S, h_1 be the
maximum number of messages sent by any processor during S, and h_2 be the maximum number of messages received by any processor during S. The cost of S is then $max\{l, L, gh_1, gh_2\}$
time steps. (An alternative is to charge $max\{l, L + gh_1, L + gh_2\}$ time steps for superstep
S. The difference between these two costs will not, in general, be significant.)

The use of the parameters l and g to characterise the communications performance of
the BSP computer contrasts sharply with the way in which communications performance is
described for most distributed memory architectures on the market today. We are normally
told many details about local network properties, e.g. the number of communications channels per node, the speed of those channels, the graph structure of the network etc. The way
in which such descriptions emphasise local properties of the network, rather than its global
properties, reflects the fact that most of those machines are designed to be used in a way
where network locality is to be exploited. Those customers who have highly irregular problems, for which such exploitation is much more difficult, are often much less impressed by
such machines when they are told about the global performance of the network in situations
where network locality is not exploited.

A major feature of the BSP model is that it lifts considerations of network performance
from the local level to the global level. We are thus no longer particularly interested in
whether the network is a 2D array, a butterfly or a hypercube, or whether it is implemented
in VLSI or in some optical technology. Our interest is in global parameters of the network,
such as l and g, which describe its ability to support non-local memory accesses in a uniformly
efficient manner. As an aside, we note that it might be an interesting and instructive exercise
to benchmark the various parallel architectures available today, in terms of such global
parameters.

In the design and implementation of a BSP computer, the values of l and g which can be
achieved will depend on (i) the capabilities of the available technology, and (ii) the amount
of money that one is willing to spend on the communications network. As the computational
performance of machines, i.e. the performance captured by p and s, continues to grow, we
will find that to keep l and g low it will be necessary to continually increase our investment
in the communications hardware as a percentage of the total cost of the machine. A central
thesis of the BSP and PRAM approaches to general purpose parallel computing is that
if these costs are paid, then parallel machines of a new level of efficiency, flexibility, and
programmability can be obtained.

On the basis of Theorems 4.1 and 4.2 we might expect to be able to achieve the following
values of l and g for a p processor BSP computer, by using the network shown.

Network	l	g
2D Array	$O(p^{1/2})$	$O(p^{1/2})$
Butterfly	$O(log\ p)$	$O(log\ p)$
Hypercube	$O(log\ p)$	$O(1)$

These estimates are based entirely on the asymptotic degree and diameter properties of the graph. In a practical setting, the use of techniques such as wormhole routing [69, 167, 234, 235], rather than store and forward routing, would also have a significant impact on the values of l and g which could be achieved.

When g is small, e.g. $g = 1$, the BSP computer corresponds closely to a PRAM, with l determining the degree of parallel slackness required to achieve optimal efficiency. For a BSP computer of this kind, i.e. with a low g value, we can use hashing to achieve efficient memory management [258]. The case $l = g = 1$ corresponds to the idealised PRAM, where no parallel slackness is required.

In designing algorithms for a BSP computer with a high g value, we need to achieve a measure of *communication slackness* by exploiting thread locality in the two-level memory, i.e. we must ensure that for every non-local memory access we request, we are able to perform approximately g operations on local data. To achieve architecture independence in the BSP model, it is therefore appropriate to design parallel algorithms which are parameterised not only by n, the size of the problem, and p, the number of processors, but also by l and g. The following example of such an algorithm appears in [258]. The problem is the multiplication of two $n \times n$ matrices A, B on $p \leq n^2$ processors. The standard $O(n^3)$ sequential algorithm is adapted to run on p processors as follows. Each processor computes an $(n/p^{1/2}) \times (n/p^{1/2})$ submatrix of $C = A.B$. To do so it will require $n^2/p^{1/2}$ elements from A and the same number from B. For each processor we thus have a computation requirement of $O(n^3/p)$ operations, since each inner product requires $O(n)$ operations, and a communications requirement of $O(n^3/p)$ for the number of non-local reads, since $p \leq n^2$. If we assume that both A and B are distributed uniformly amongst the p processors, with each processor receiving $O(n^2/p)$ of the elements from each matrix, then the processors can simply replicate and send the approprate elements from A and B to the $2p^{1/2}$ processors requiring them. Therefore, we also have a communications requirement of approximately $n^2/p^{1/2} = O(n^3/p)$ for messages sent. We thus have a total parallel time complexity of $O(n^3/p)$, provided $l = O(n^3/p)$ and $g = O(n/p^{1/2})$. An alternative algorithm, given in [7], that requires fewer messages altogether, can be implemented to give the same optimal runtime, with g as large as $O(n/p^{1/3})$ but with l slightly smaller at $O(n^3/p \log n)$.

The BSP model can be regarded as a generalisation of the PRAM model which permits the frequency of barrier synchronisation to be controlled. By capturing the network performance of a BSP computer in global terms using the values l and g, the model enables us to design algorithms and programs which are parameterised by those values, and which can therefore be efficiently implemented on a range of BSP architectures with widely differing l and g values. It therefore provides a solution to the problems posed at the start of the chapter. We have a simple and robust model which permits both scalable parallel performance and a high degree of architecture independence in software. Its simplicity also offers the prospect of our being able to develop a coherent framework for the design and analysis of parallel algorithms.

5.   Optical Communication

Simple arguments can be used to show that various low diameter networks, such as the butterfly and the hypercube, cannot be implemented using VLSI technology without having long wires for some of the edges in the network. This has led some to conclude that such networks should be replaced by networks such as fat trees [172, 173] which are more efficient, in the VLSI model [174, 250, 267], in terms of their use of area or volume.

In this section we show that optical communication systems [34, 81] offer the prospect of a dramatic improvement in the efficiency with which non-local communication can be achieved. We show that a simple (and possibly cheap) optical interconnection architecture based on wavelength division multiplexing can be used (a) to solve the above mentioned VLSI wiring problem, and (b) to implement an extremely simple and efficient form of randomised optical routing. The results presented in this section are due, in this form, to Rao [222], although most of them are reinterpretations, in terms of optical communication, of known results in the theory of parallel computation. The power of optical communication has also been investigated in [21, 86, 118, 209, 258, 259].

Rao [222] considers various routing problems on a $p^{1/2} \times p^{1/2}$ 2D array of processors, where the processors on each row of the array are connected by an optical bus, and the processors on each column of the array are also connected by such a bus. We thus have $2p^{1/2}$ buses, each of length $p^{1/2}$. Each bus uses *wavelength division multiplexing (WDM)* [76] to support simultaneous communication between many disjoint pairs of processors on the same bus. This communications architecture will be referred to as the p processor *mesh of buses (MOB)*. The idea of using a mesh of buses for interconnection was proposed by Wittie [275], and as a basis for optical interconnection networks by Dowd [76].

5.1.   Solving The VLSI Wiring Problem

To solve the VLSI wiring problem we need only consider the simplest MOB in which the optical buses have fixed transmitters and receivers at each processor, i.e. where the transmitters and receivers are initially set (off-line) to achieve a certain communication pattern, e.g. a hypercube, and then remain fixed as that pattern is used. The first result shows that all networks can be emulated on the MOB with an efficiency related to the degree of the network.

Theorem 5.1 *Any p processor network N of degree d can be emulated on a p processor MOB so that (i) there are $O(d)$ transmitters/receivers per processor, and (ii) each edge in N is realised by a path of length at most three in the MOB.*

By an edge in the MOB we mean a channel on one of the buses, and by a path we mean a sequence of such edges. Theorem 5.1 is a consequence of the following well known results: (a) any such degree d network has $O(d)$ perfect matchings, (b) each perfect matching corresponds to a 1-relation, and (c) by Hall's Theorem, all 1-relations can be routed (off-line) in a 2D array by permuting the packets of the rows, then permuting the packets of the columns, and then finally permuting the packets of the rows again. For details of the proof of part (c), see [167]. For networks such as the cube-connected-cycles and the hypercube we can do even better.

Theorem 5.2 *A p processor cube-connected-cycles network can be emulated on a p processor MOB so that (i) there are $O(1)$ transmitters/receivers per processor, and (ii) each edge in the cube-connected-cycles is realised by a single edge in the MOB.*

Theorem 5.3 *A p processor hypercube network can be emulated on a p processor MOB so that (i) there are $O(\log p)$ transmitters/receivers per processor, and (ii) each edge in the hypercube is realised by a single edge in the MOB.*

Theorems 5.2 and 5.3 follow directly from standard VLSI layouts of those networks.

5.2. Randomised Optical Routing

We now consider a model of optical communication corresponding to the case where the buses in the MOB have tunable transmitters at each processor. Unlike the previous model, we are now able to dynamically change (on-line) the destination on the bus to which a processor can send a message. The model of computation is as follows. At any step, a processor can send a message directly to any other processor on the same bus. A message is successfully received if it was the only message sent to that destination in the step. A processor which successfully receives a message sends back an acknowledgement. (A single bus version of this optical model was investigated in [21].) We now describe a very simple randomised method for routing 1-relations on a MOB with tunable transmitters, which Rao [222] credits to Leighton and Maggs. The method proceeds in rounds, where each round consists of the following sequence of steps.

1. Each processor with a message sends it to a randomly selected position in its row bus.

2. Each processor that successfully received a message in step 1 forwards it using its column bus to the correct destination row for that message.

3. Each processor that successfully receives a message from step 2 forwards it using its row bus to the correct destination for that message.

4. For each message that was successfully received in step 3, an acknowledgement is sent to its source along the path it took. (It is easy to show that an acknowledgement gets back to any processor whose message was successfully sent to its destination.)

5. When a processor receives an acknowledgement, it does not send the message in later rounds.

Theorem 5.4 *With high probability, the above method will route any 1-relation in $O(\log \log p)$ steps on a MOB.*

The $O(\log \log p)$ upper bound is easily established as follows. Each round takes six communication steps. The probability of a given message colliding with another in the first round is less than $1/e$. If we have p/l messages left at the start of some round, then no more than about p/l^2 of them will be unsuccessful in that round. Therefore, after k rounds we will have no more than about p/e^{2^k} of them left, and thus $O(\log \log p)$ rounds will be sufficient. On a completely connected optical network with the same collision rules, the problem of routing a 1-relation can be trivially completed in one step, whereas the above method requires $O(\log \log p)$ steps on the MOB. For the problem of routing h-relations, where h is at least logarithmic in p, Rao [222] has established the following powerful result.

Theorem 5.5 *With high probability, any h-relation, with $h \geq \log p$, can be routed in $O(h)$ steps on a MOB.*

Therefore, for such larger h-relations, the MOB is as powerful as a completely connected network! For the case where $1 < h < \log p$, much less is known. In particular, no constant time method is known for routing a 2-relation on a completely connected optical network.

6.   Challenges

In the previous sections we have seen that there are a variety of theoretically and practically efficient solutions to the problem of supporting a single address space on a distributed memory architecture. We have also seen that there are a large number of efficient, practical shared memory algorithms for important problems. In this section we briefly describe some of the main issues which need to be addressed in the future in order to continue the development of this framework for general purpose parallel computing based on fine grain concurrency in a shared address space.

6.1.   Architecture

Most distributed memory architectures are based on conventional microprocessors [119, 120, 208]. We need alternative processor designs which can support a very large number of lightweight threads simultaneously, and can provide fast context switching, message handling, address translation, hashing etc. [44, 69, 71, 130, 274]. If such designs are not produced then we may find that the processors, and not the communications network, will be the bottleneck in the system.

We need to continue to develop improved networks for communication [69, 76, 170, 209, 222] and synchronisation [40, 138, 159]. There is currently great emphasis in parallel computing on various "Grand Challenge" applications in science and engineering. While not doubting the importance of these applications, we would suggest that perhaps the most important challenge for parallel architectures at the present time is to develop systems for which global "inefficiency parameters", such as l and g in the BSP model, are as low as possible. We have observed that the use of optical technologies may prove to be extremely important in this respect. In focusing our attention on the reduction of global parameters such as l and g, we should note that it may not necessarily be cost-effective to try to obtain the extreme case of the PRAM, where l and g are both 1. At any given point in time, the capabilities and economics of the technologies available will determine the most cost-effective values of such parameters. An important advantage of the BSP model [258] over the PRAM [1, 2, 221] is that it provides an architecture-independent framework which allows us to take full advantage of whichever values of l and g are the most cost-effective at a given point in time.

Large general purpose parallel computer systems will inevitably suffer hardware faults of various kinds during their operation. We need to develop efficient techniques which can provide a degree of fault tolerance for processors, memories, and communications links. An interesting approach to this problem is to use the idea of information dispersal [179, 180, 215], where a space efficient redundant encoding of data is used to provide secure and reliable storage of information, and efficient fault tolerant routing of messages. Other approaches to the problems of fault tolerance are described in [152, 153, 241].

6.2.   Algorithms

Although the potential for automating memory management via hashing is a major advantage of the BSP model, the BSP algorithm designer may wish to retain control of memory management in the two-level memory to achieve higher efficiency, e.g. on a BSP computer with a high value of g. A systematic study of bulk-synchronous algorithms remains to be done. Some first steps in this direction are described in [85, 258].

We need to continue to investigate the effects of hashing on the algorithmic performance achievable for important computational problems. There is already some theoretical evidence to confirm what one might intuitively expect, namely that any negative effects of hashing on algorithmic performance are much less dramatic on problems involving complex sparse irregular data structures, than they are on problems involving simple regular data structures. It is likely that future developments in most scientific and engineering applications will involve problems on large sparse irregular matrices and graphs, much more than on dense matrices and graphs. It is, therefore, likely that the advantages, in terms of programming simplicity, of using hashing will increasingly outweigh any disadvantages. We need to continue to develop fast, processor efficient parallel algorithms for sparse matrix and graph computations.

6.3.   Languages and Software

The PRAM model was developed to facilitate the study of parallel algorithms and their complexity. In that context it has proved to be extremely useful. However, as we have pursued the design and implementation of parallel architectures based on the PRAM model, it has become clear that we have no well developed framework for the programming of such architectures. This can be contrasted with other approaches to general purpose parallel computing such as the actor and dataflow models, where there has been an intensive effort to develop a programming framework, although rather less on the investigation of parallel algorithms and their complexity. It is vital for the success of the approach described in this chapter that we develop programming languages and methodologies for the kinds of parallel architectures proposed. Of the various challenges mentioned, this is perhaps the most important, and in many respects the most difficult one. The apparent unwillingness of many programmers of parallel machines to use anything other than minor variants of the sequential languages FORTRAN and C is widely perceived to be a major impediment to the continuing development of parallel computing. Another impediment is, of course, the "dusty decks" of old FORTRAN codes which many organisations are unwilling, or unable, to abandon. Many new parallel programming languages have been proposed and rejected over the last decade or so. Nevertheless, we must continue to seek a programming model which will provide a means of achieving the architecture-independence sought, while permitting scalable parallel performance on the kinds of architectures described. Some preliminary work in this direction can be found in [186]. It is to be hoped that as such a programming framework is developed we will also be able to provide a strategy for the migration of the dusty decks to the new architectures.

7.   Other Approaches

A large number of approaches are currently being proposed as the basis of a framework for general purpose parallel computing. In this chapter, the case for the BSP/PRAM approach has been presented. In this section we will briefly mention some of the other approaches.

Perhaps the most conservative of the alternatives is SIMD or data parallelism. Although a number of interesting algorithms have been developed for such architectures [41, 42, 43, 123, 246] , the model does not appear to be sufficiently general, even when extended to its SPMD form.

Another conservative approach is simply to continue with architectures based on message passing across a fixed set of channels [124, 125, 135]. Although such a model is adequate for the development of many special purpose parallel systems, and for low level systems programming, it does not appear to offer enough in terms of architecture-independence.

An approach related to message passing which appears to be more attractive is the actor model [9], which we might think of as message passing using names rather than a fixed set of channels. The names are first class objects and can be passed in messages. The graph of possible interactions between actors can thus change dynamically. The actor model provides a convenient framework for concurrent object-oriented programming [10]. Dally has developed an interesting parallel architecture, called the J-Machine [69, 70, 72], which supports the actor model.

The dataflow model has evolved considerably over the last decade. Modern designs for dataflow architectures [128, 129, 200, 201, 206] emphasise the importance of ideas such as efficient multithreading and the exploitation of parallel slackness, in the same way as the PRAM architectures do. There are, of course, major differences between the two approaches in terms of synchronisation control, scheduling control etc. It is not yet clear whether the freedom which the dataflow model offers the programmer has a cost to be paid in terms of scalable parallel performance.

Other approaches to general purpose parallel computing which have been suggested in recent years include asynchronous PRAMs [59, 90], block PRAMs [6], hierarchical PRAMs [121], tuple space [51, 52], graph reduction [210, 211], rewriting, and shared virtual memory.

8.   Conclusion

The goals of general purpose parallel computing are to achieve both scalable parallel performance and architecture-independent parallel software. Despite much effort to find them, no serious theoretical impediments to the achievement of these goals have yet been found. We have argued that the bulk-synchronous parallel computer is a robust model of parallel computation which offers the prospect of achieving both requirements. The main challenge at the present time is to develop an appropriate programming framework for the BSP model.

Two other models which appear to offer the required architecture-independence are the actor and dataflow models. Unlike the BSP and PRAM models, which have global barrier synchronisation as the basic mechanism, these two models have at their core the idea of local, usually pairwise, synchronisation events. It is not yet clear whether these two models can offer the same scalability in parallel performance as we have demonstrated can be obtained for the BSP model. It is also unclear at present whether they can offer a convenient framework for the investigation of parallel algorithms and their complexity. Nevertheless, by virtue of their attractiveness in programming terms, they merit serious consideration.

Although we have stressed the differences between these various approaches, there is reason to believe that, at the architectural level, the BSP, PRAM, actor and dataflow models will require a number of similar mechanisms for efficient implementation; in particular, high performance global communications, uniform memory access, and multithreading to hide network latencies.

Acknowledgements

I would like to thank Les Valiant for the numerous discussions we have had, over the last few years, on the development of a framework for general purpose parallel computing. The idea of exploiting bulk synchrony in parallel computation is due to him. I would also like to thank Les Valiant and Bill Gear for providing the opportunity for me to spend my sabbatical leave from Oxford at NEC Research Institute, and to my colleagues at NECI for providing such a stimulating environment in which to work.

References

[1] F Abolhassan, J Keller, and W J Paul. On the cost-effectiveness and realization of the theoretical PRAM model. Research Report 09/1991, Fachbereich Informatik, Universität des Saarlandes, Saarbrücken, 1991.

[2] F Abolhassan, J Keller, and W J Paul. On the cost-effectiveness of PRAMs. In *Proc. 3rd IEEE Symposium on Parallel and Distributed Processing*, pages 2–9, 1991.

[3] K Abrahamson, N Dadoun, D G Kirkpatrick, and T Przytycka. A simple parallel tree contraction algorithm. *Journal of Algorithms*, 10:287–302, 1989.

[4] F Afrati, C H Papadimitriou, and G Papageorgiou. Scheduling DAGs to minimize time and communication. In J H Reif, editor, *VLSI Algorithms and Architectures. 3rd Aegean Workshop on Computing (AWOC 88). LNCS Vol.319*, pages 134–138. Springer-Verlag, 1988.

[5] A Aggarwal and R J Anderson. A random NC algorithm for depth first search. *Combinatorica*, 8(1):1–12, 1988.

[6] A Aggarwal, A K Chandra, and M Snir. On communication latency in PRAM computations. In *Proc. 1st Annual ACM Symposium on Parallel Algorithms and Architectures*, pages 11–21, 1989.

[7] A Aggarwal, A K Chandra, and M Snir. Communication complexity of PRAMs. *Theoretical Computer Science*, 71:3–28, 1990.

[8] A Aggarwal, B Chazelle, L Guibas, C O'Dunlaing, and C Yap. Parallel computational geometry. In *Proc. 26th Annual IEEE Symposium on Foundations of Computer Science*, pages 468–477, 1985.

[9] G Agha. *Actors: A Model of Concurrent Computation in Distributed Systems*. MIT Press, Cambridge, MA, 1986.

[10] G Agha. Concurrent object-oriented programming. *Communications of the ACM*, 33(9):125–141, September 1990.

[11] M Ajtai, J Komlós, and E Szemerédi. Sorting in C log N parallel steps. *Combinatorica*, 3:1–19, 1983.

[12] R Aleliunas. Randomized parallel communication. In *Proc. 1st Annual ACM Symposium on Principles of Distributed Computing*, pages 60–72, 1982.

[13] N Alon. Eigenvalues and expanders. *Combinatorica*, 6(2):83–96, 1986.

[14] N Alon. Eigenvalues, geometric expanders, sorting in rounds, and Ramsey Theory. *Combinatorica*, 6:207–219, 1986.

[15] N Alon and N Megiddo. Parallel linear programming in fixed dimension almost surely in constant time. In *Proc. 31st Annual IEEE Symposium on Foundations of Computer Science*, pages 574–582, 1990.

[16] N Alon and V D Milman. Eigenvalues, expanders and superconcentrators. In *Proc. 25th Annual IEEE Symposium on Foundations of Computer Science*, pages 320–322, 1984.

[17] H Alt. Comparing the combinational complexities of arithmetic functions. *Journal of the ACM*, 35(2):447–460, April 1988.

[18] H Alt. On the efficient parallel evaluation of elementary functions. Technical Report B 90-03, Institut für Informatik, Freie Universität Berlin, March 1990.

[19] R Alverson, D Callahan, D Cummings, B Koblenz, A Porterfield, and B Smith. The Tera computer system. In *Proc. International Conference on Supercomputing. ACM SIGARCH Computer Architecture News, Vol.18 No.3*, pages 1–6. ACM Press, 1990.

[20] G M Amdahl. Validity of the single processor approach to achieving large scale computing capabilities. In *Proc. AFIPS Spring Joint Computer Conference 30*, pages 483–485, 1967.

[21] R J Anderson and G L Miller. Optical communication for pointer based algorithms. Technical Report CRI 88-14, University of Southern California, 1988.

[22] R J Anderson and G L Miller. A simple randomized parallel algorithm for list-ranking. *Information Processing Letters*, 33(5):269–273, 1990.

[23] R J Anderson and G L Miller. Deterministic parallel list ranking. *Algorithmica*, 6(6):859–868, 1991.

[24] D Andivahis. Time-communication tradeoff in multiprocessing systems. Diploma Dissertation, National Technical University of Athens, Athens, Greece, 1984. (In Greek).

[25] M J Atallah, P Callahan, and M T Goodrich. P-complete geometric problems. In *Proc. 2nd Annual ACM Symposium on Parallel Algorithms and Architectures*, pages 317–326, 1990.

[26] M J Atallah, R Cole, and M T Goodrich. Cascading divide-and-conquer: A technique for designing parallel algorithms. In *Proc. 28th Annual IEEE Symposium on Foundations of Computer Science*, pages 151–160, 1987.

[27] M J Atallah, M T Goodrich, and S R Kosaraju. Parallel algorithms for evaluating sequences of set-manipulation operations. In J H Reif, editor, *VLSI Algorithms and Architectures (3rd Aegean Workshop on Computing, AWOC 88), LNCS Vol. 319*, pages 1–10. Springer-Verlag, 1988.

[28] M J Atallah and U Vishkin. Finding Euler tours in parallel. *Journal of Computer and System Sciences*, 29(3):330–337, July 1984.

[29] W C Athas and C L Seitz. Multicomputers: Message-passing concurrent computers. *IEEE Computer*, 12(8):9–24, August 1988.

[30] I Bar-On and U Vishkin. Optimal parallel generation of a computation tree form. *ACM Transactions on Programming Languages and Systems*, 7, No.2:348–357, April 1985.

[31] H Bast and T Hagerup. Fast and reliable parallel hashing. In *Proc. 3rd Annual ACM Symposium on Parallel Algorithms and Architectures*, pages 50–61, 1991.

[32] K E Batcher. Sorting networks and their applications. In *Proc. AFIPS Spring Joint Computer Conference*, pages 307–314, 1968.

[33] P W Beame, S A Cook, and H J Hoover. Log depth circuits for division and related problems. *SIAM Journal on Computing*, 15(4):994–1003, November 1986.

[34] T E Bell. Optical computing: A field in flux. *IEEE Spectrum*, 23(8):34–57, August 1986.

[35] O Berkman, D Breslauer, Z Galil, B Schieber, and U Vishkin. Highly parallelizable problems. In *Proc. 21st Annual ACM Symposium on Theory of Computing*, pages 309–319, 1989.

[36] O Berkman, J Ja'Ja', S Krishnamurthy, R Thurimella, and U Vishkin. Some triply-logarithmic parallel algorithms. In *Proc. 31st Annual IEEE Symposium on Foundations of Computer Science*, pages 871–881, 1990.

[37] O Berkman and U Vishkin. Recursive *-tree parallel data-structure. In *Proc. 30th Annual IEEE Symposium on Foundations of Computer Science*, pages 196–202, 1989.

[38] P C P Bhatt, K Diks, T Hagerup, V C Prasad, T Radzik, and S Saxena. Improved deterministic parallel integer sorting. *Information and Computation*, 94(1):29–47, September 1991.

[39] R S Bird and P Wadler. *Introduction to Functional Programming*. Prentice Hall, 1988.

[40] Y Birk, P B Gibbons, J L C Sanz, and D Soroker. A simple mechanism for efficient barrier synchronization in MIMD machines. Research Report RJ 7078, IBM Research, October 1989. Also appears in Proc. 1990 IEEE International Conference on Parallel Processing, Volume II Software, pages 195-198.

[41] G E Blelloch. Scans as primitive parallel operations. *IEEE Transactions on Computers*, 38(11):1526–1538, November 1989.

[42] G E Blelloch. Prefix sums and their applications. Technical Report CMU-CS-90-190, School of Computer Science, Carnegie Mellon University, November 1990.

[43] G E Blelloch. *Vector Models for Data-Parallel Computing*. MIT Press, Cambridge, MA, 1990.

[44] B Boothe and A Ranade. Improved multithreading techniques for hiding communication latency in multiprocessors. In *Proc. 19th Annual International Symposium on Computer Architecture*, 1992. To appear.

[45] A Borodin and J E Hopcroft. Routing, merging, and sorting on parallel models of computation. *Journal of Computer and System Sciences*, 30(1):130–145, February 1985.

[46] A Borodin and I J Munro. *The Computational Complexity of Algebraic and Numeric Problems*. American Elsevier, 1975.

[47] A Borodin, J von zur Gathen, and J E Hopcroft. Fast parallel matrix and GCD computations. *Information and Computation*, 52:241–256, 1982.

[48] R P Brent. The parallel evaluation of general arithmetic expressions. *Journal of the ACM*, 21, No.2:201–206, April 1974.

[49] A W Burks, H H Goldstine, and J von Neumann. *Preliminary discussion of the logical design of an electronic computing instrument. Part 1, Volume 1*. The Institute of Advanced Study, Princeton, First edition, 28 June 1946. Second edition, 2 September 1947. Report to the U.S. Army Ordnance Department. Also appears in *Papers of John von Neumann on Computing and Computer Theory*, W Aspray and A Burks, editors. Volume 12 in the Charles Babbage Institute Reprint Series for the History of Computing, MIT Press, 1987, 97-142.

[50] D Callahan, K Kennedy, and A Porterfield. Software prefetching. In *Proc. 4th International Conference on Architectural Support for Programming Languages and Operating Systems*, pages 40–52, 1991.

[51] N Carriero and D Gelernter. How to write parallel programs: A guide to the perplexed. *ACM Computing Surveys*, 21(3):323–358, September 1989.

[52] N Carriero and D Gelernter. *How to write parallel programs: a first course*. MIT Press, 1990.

[53] J L Carter and M N Wegman. Universal classes of hash functions. *Journal of Computer and System Sciences*, 18(2):143–154, April 1979.

[54] R Cole and U Vishkin. Deterministic coin tossing and accelerating cascades: Micro and macro techniques for designing parallel algorithms. In *Proc. 18th Annual ACM Symposium on Theory of Computing*, pages 206–219, 1986.

[55] R Cole and U Vishkin. Deterministic coin tossing with applications to optimal parallel list ranking. *Information and Computation*, 70(1):32–53, 1986.

[56] R Cole and U Vishkin. Approximate parallel scheduling. Part 1: The basic technique with applications to optimal parallel list ranking in logarithmic time. *SIAM Journal on Computing*, 17:128–142, 1988.

[57] R Cole and U Vishkin. Faster optimal parallel prefix sums and list ranking. *Information and Computation*, 81(3):334–352, June 1989.

[58] R Cole and U Vishkin. Approximate parallel scheduling. II. Applications to logarithmic-time optimal parallel graph algorithms. *Information and Computation*, 92(1):1–47, 1991.

[59] R Cole and O Zajicek. The APRAM: Incorporating asynchrony into the PRAM model. In *Proc. 1st Annual ACM Symposium on Parallel Algorithms and Architectures*, pages 169–178, 1989.

[60] R J Cole. An optimally efficient selection algorithm. *Information Processing Letters*, 26(6):295–299, January 1988.

[61] S A Cook. The classification of problems which have fast parallel algorithms. In M Karpinski, editor, *Proc. Conference on Foundations of Computation Theory, LNCS Vol. 158*, pages 78–93, 1983.

[62] S A Cook. An overview of computational complexity. *Communications of the ACM*, 26(6):400–408, 1983.

[63] S A Cook. A taxonomy of problems with fast parallel algorithms. *Information and Computation*, 64((1-3)):2–22, 1985.

[64] S A Cook and C Dwork. Bounds on the time for parallel RAM's to compute simple functions. In *Proc. 14th Annual ACM Symposium on Theory of Computing*, pages 231–233, 1982.

[65] D Coppersmith and S Winograd. Matrix multiplication via arithmetic progressions. In *Proc. 19th Annual ACM Symposium on Theory of Computing*, pages 1–6, 1987.

[66] T H Cormen, C E Leiserson, and R L Rivest. *Introduction to Algorithms*. MIT Press, Cambridge, MA, 1990.

[67] L Csanky. Fast parallel matrix inversion algorithms. *SIAM Journal on Computing*, 5(4):618–623, December 1976.

[68] E Dahlhaus and M Karpinski. An efficient parallel algorithm for the minimal elimination ordering (MEO) of an arbitrary graph. In *Proc. 30th Annual IEEE Symposium on Foundations of Computer Science*, pages 454–459, 1989.

[69] W J Dally. Network and processor architecture for message-driven computers. In R Suaya and G Birtwistle, editors, *VLSI and Parallel Computation*, pages 140–222. Morgan Kaufmann, San Mateo, CA, 1990.

[70] W J Dally, A Chien, S Fiske, W Horwat, J Keen, M Larivee, R Lethin, P Nuth, and S Wills. The J-Machine: A fine-grain concurrent computer. In G X Ritter, editor, *Proc. Information Processing 89*, pages 1147–1153. Elsevier Science Publishers, B. V., 1989.

[71] W J Dally et al. The Message-Driven Processor. In *Proc. Hot Chips III Symposium*, 1991.

[72] W J Dally and D S Wills. Universal mechanisms for concurrency. In E Odijk, M Rem, and J-C Syre, editors, *Proc. PARLE 89: Parallel Architectures and Languages Europe. LNCS Vol.365*, pages 19–33. Springer-Verlag, 1989.

[73] M Dietzfelbinger. On limitations of the performance of universal hashing with linear functions. Forschungsbereich Nr. 84, Fachbereich 17, Universität-GH Paderborn, June 1991.

[74] M Dietzfelbinger, J Gil, Y Matias, and N Pippenger. Polynomial hash functions are reliable. In *Proc. 19th International Colloquium on Automata, Languages and Programming, LNCS*. Springer-Verlag, 1992.

[75] D Dobkin, R J Lipton, and S Reiss. Linear programming is log-space hard for P. *Information Processing Letters*, 8:96–97, 1979.

[76] P W Dowd. High performance interprocessor communication through optical wavelength division multiple access channels. In *Proc. 18th Annual International Symposium on Computer Architecture*, pages 96–105, 1991.

[77] P E Dunne. *The Complexity of Boolean Networks*. Academic Press, 1988.

[78] C Dwork, P C Kanellakis, and J Mitchell. On the sequential nature of unification. *Journal of Logic Programming*, 1:35–50, 1984.

[79] C Dwork, P C Kanellakis, and L J Stockmeyer. Parallel algorithms for term matching. *SIAM Journal on Computing*, 17(4):711–731, August 1988.

[80] D Eppstein and Z Galil. Parallel algorithmic techniques for combinatorial computation. *Ann. Rev. Comput. Sci.*, 3:233–283, 1988.

[81] D G Feitelson. *Optical Computing. A Survey for Computer Scientists*. MIT Press, Cambridge, MA, 1988.

[82] R W Floyd. Algorithm 97: Shortest path. *Communications of the ACM*, 5(6):345, 1962.

[83] S Fortune and J Wyllie. Parallelism in random access machines. In *Proc. 10th Annual ACM Symposium on Theory of Computing*, pages 114–118, 1978.

[84] C W Gear, editor. *Computation and Cognition. Proceedings of the First NEC Research Symposium*. SIAM Press, 1991. Panel Session - The Future of Parallelism, pages 153-168.

[85] A V Gerbessiotis and L G Valiant. Direct bulk-synchronous parallel algorithms. Technical Report TR-10-92, Aiken Computation Laboratory, Harvard University, 1992. To appear in *Proc. 3rd Scandinavian Workshop on Algorithm Theory*, July 8-10, 1992. LNCS, Springer-Verlag.

[86] M Gereb-Graus and T Tsantilas. Efficient optical communication in parallel computers. In *Proc. 4th Annual ACM Symposium on Parallel Algorithms and Architectures*, 1992 (to appear).

[87] A M Gibbons and W Rytter. *Efficient Parallel Algorithms*. Cambridge University Press, Cambridge, UK, 1988.

[88] A M Gibbons and W Rytter. Optimal parallel algorithms for dynamic expression evaluation and context-free recognition. *Information and Computation*, 81:32–45, 1989.

[89] A M Gibbons and P Spirakis, editors. *Lectures on Parallel Computation. Proc. 1991 AL-COM Spring School on Parallel Computation*. Cambridge International Series on Parallel Computation. Cambridge University Press, Cambridge, UK, 1992.

[90] P B Gibbons. A more practical PRAM model. In *Proc. 1st Annual ACM Symposium on Parallel Algorithms and Architectures*, pages 158–168, 1989.

[91] P B Gibbons, R M Karp, G L Miller, and D Soroker. Subtree isomorphism is in random NC. In J H Reif, editor, *VLSI Algorithms and Architectures. 3rd Aegean Workshop on Computing (AWOC 88). LNCS Vol.319*, pages 43–52. Springer-Verlag, 1988.

[92] P B Gibbons, R M Karp, V Ramachandran, D Soroker, and R E Tarjan. Transitive reduction in parallel via branchings. Technical Report CS-TR-171-88, Department of Computer Science, Princeton University, July 1988.

[93] J Gil. Fast load balancing on a PRAM. In *Proc. 3rd IEEE Symposium on Parallel and Distributed Processing*, pages 10–17, 1991.

[94] J Gil and Y Matias. Fast hashing on a PRAM - designing by expectation. In *Proc. 2nd Annual ACM-SIAM Symposium on Discrete Algorithms*, pages 271–280, 1991.

[95] J Gil and Y Matias. Leaders election without a conflict resolution rule - Fast and efficient randomized simulations among CRCW PRAMs. In *Proc. 1st Latin American Informatics Symposium*, 1991.

[96] J Gil, Y Matias, and U Vishkin. Towards a theory of nearly constant time parallel algorithms. In *Proc. 32nd Annual IEEE Symposium on Foundations of Computer Science*, pages 698–710, 1991.

[97] J Gil, F Meyer auf der Heide, and A Wigderson. Not all keys can be hashed in constant time. In *Proc. 22nd Annual ACM Symposium on Theory of Computing*, pages 244–253, 1990.

[98] J R Gilbert and H Hafsteinsson. Parallel solution of sparse linear systems. In R Karlsson and A Lingas, editors, *Proc. 1st Scandinavian Workshop on Algorithm Theory. LNCS Vol. 318*, pages 145–153. Springer-Verlag, 1988.

[99] A V Goldberg, S A Plotkin, and G E Shannon. Parallel symmetry-breaking in sparse graphs. *SIAM Journal of Discrete Mathematics*, 1(4):434–446, November 1988.

[100] M Goldberg and T Spencer. Constructing a maximal independent set in parallel. *SIAM Journal of Discrete Mathematics*, 2(3):322–328, August 1989.

[101] M Goldberg and T Spencer. A new parallel algorithm for the maximal independent set problem. *SIAM Journal on Computing*, 18(2):419–427, April 1989.

[102] L M Goldschlager. The monotone and planar circuit value problems are log space complete for P. *ACM Sigact News*, 9(2):25–29, 1977.

[103] L M Goldschlager. A space efficient algorithm for the monotone planar circuit value problem. *Information Processing Letters*, 10(1):25–27, February 1980.

[104] L M Goldschlager, R A Shaw, and J Staples. The maximum flow problem is log space complete for P. *Theoretical Computer Science*, 21:105–111, 1982.

[105] M T Goodrich. Using approximation algorithms to design parallel algorithms that may ignore processor allocation. In *Proc. 32nd Annual IEEE Symposium on Foundations of Computer Science*, pages 711–722, 1991.

[106] M T Goodrich and S R Kosaraju. Sorting on a parallel pointer machine with applications to set expression evaluation. In *Proc. 30th Annual IEEE Symposium on Foundations of Computer Science*, pages 190–196, 1989.

[107] A Gottlieb, R Grishman, C P Kruskal, K P McAuliffe, L Rudolph, and M Snir. The NYU Ultracomputer - Designing an MIMD, shared-memory parallel machine. *IEEE Transactions on Computers*, 32:75–89, 1983.

[108] A C Greenberg, R E Ladner, M S Paterson, and Z Galil. Efficient parallel algorithms for linear recurrence computation. *Information Processing Letters*, 15(1):31–35, August 1982.

[109] R I Greenberg and C E Leiserson. Randomized routing on fat-trees. In *Proc. 26th Annual IEEE Symposium on Foundations of Computer Science*, pages 241–249, 1985.

[110] R Greenlaw, H J Hoover, and W L Ruzzo. A compendium of problems complete for P. Technical Report TR 91-05-01, Department of Computer Science, University of Washington, June 1991.

[111] A Gupta, J Hennessy, K Gharachorloo, T Mowry, and W-D Weber. Comparative evaluation of latency reducing and tolerating techniques. In *Proc. 18th Annual International Symposium on Computer Architecture*, pages 254–263, 1991.

[112] J L Gustafson, G R Montry, and R E Benner. Development of parallel methods for a 1024-processor hypercube. *SIAM Journal on Scientific and Statistical Computing*, 9(4):609–638, July 1988.

[113] J L Gustafson. Reevaluating Amdahl's Law. *Communications of the ACM*, 31(5):532–533, May 1988.

[114] T Hagerup. Optimal parallel algorithms on planar graphs. *Information and Computation*, 84(1):71–96, January 1990.

[115] T Hagerup. Constant-time parallel integer sorting. In *Proc. 23rd Annual ACM Symposium on Theory of Computing*, pages 299–306, 1991.

[116] T Hagerup. Fast parallel space allocation, estimation and integer sorting. Technical Report 03/1991, Max-Planck-Institut für Informatik, Saarbrücken, April 1991.

[117] T Hagerup. The log-star revolution. In *Proc. Annual Symposium on Theoretical Aspects of Computer Science*, 1992.

[118] A Hartmann and S Redfield. Design sketches for optical crossbar switches intended for large scale parallel processing applications. *Optical Engineering*, 29(3):315–327, 1989.

[119] J Hennessy. VLSI processor architecture. *IEEE Transactions on Computers*, C-33(11):1221–1246, December 1984.

[120] J L Hennessy and D A Patterson. *Computer Architecture: A Quantitative Approach*. Morgan Kaufmann, San Mateo, CA, 1990.

[121] T H Heywood. A practical hierarchical model of parallel computation. Technical Report SU-CIS-91-39, School of Computer and Information Science, Syracuse University, November 1991.

[122] P A J Hilbers. *Processor Networks and Aspects of the Mapping Problem*, volume 2 of *Cambridge International Series on Parallel Computation*. Cambridge University Press, Cambridge, UK, 1991.

[123] W D Hillis and G L Steele Jr. Data parallel algorithms. *Communications of the ACM*, 29(12):1170–1183, December 1986.

[124] C A R Hoare. *Communicating Sequential Processes*. Prentice Hall, 1985.

[125] C A R Hoare. The transputer and occam: A personal story. *Concurrency: Practice and Experience*, 3(4):249–264, August 1991.

[126] P Hudak. Concept, evolution, and application of functional programming languages. *ACM Computing Surveys*, 21(3):359–411, 1989.

[127] P Hudak, S Peyton Jones, and P Wadler, editors. Report on the Programming Language Haskell - A Non-Strict, Purely Functional Language. Version 1.1 , 1991.

[128] R A Iannucci. Toward a dataflow/von Neumann hybrid architecture. In *Proc. 15th Annual International Symposium on Computer Architecture*, pages 131–140, 1988.

[129] R A Iannucci. *Parallel Machines: Parallel Machine Languages*. Kluwer Academic Publishers, 1990.

[130] INMOS Limited. *Transputer Reference Manual*. Prentice Hall, 1988.

[131] D N Jayasimha and M C Loui. The communication complexity of parallel algorithms. Technical Report CSRD 629, University of Illinois at Urbana-Champaign, 1986.

[132] D B Johnson and P Metaxas. Connected components in $O(lg^{3/2} \mid V \mid)$ parallel time for the CREW PRAM. In *Proc. 32nd Annual IEEE Symposium on Foundations of Computer Science*, pages 688–697, 1991.

[133] D B Johnson and P Metaxas. Optimal algorithms for the vertex updating problem of a minimum spanning tree. In *Proc. 6th International Parallel Processing Symposium*, pages 306–314. IEEE Press, 1992.

[134] S L Johnsson. Communication in network architectures. In R Suaya and G Birtwistle, editors, *VLSI and Parallel Computaion*, pages 223–389. Morgan Kaufmann, San Mateo, CA, 1990.

[135] G Jones and M Goldsmith. *Programming in occam 2*. Prentice Hall, 1988.

[136] N D Jones and W T Laaser. Complete problems for deterministic polynomial time. *Theoretical Computer Science*, 3:105–117, 1977.

[137] N D Jones, Y E Lien, and W T Laaser. New problems complete for nondeterministic log space. *Mathematical Systems Theory*, 10:1–17, 1976.

[138] H F Jordan. A special purpose architecture for finite element analysis. In *Proc. IEEE International Conference on Parallel Processing*, pages 263–266, 1978.

[139] N P Jouppi. Improving direct-mapped cache performance by the addition of a small fully-associative cache and prefetch buffers. In *Proc. 17th Annual International Symposium on Computer Architecture*, pages 364–373, 1990.

[140] H Jung, L Kirousis, and P Spirakis. Lower bounds and efficient algorithms for multiprocessor scheduling of dags with communication delays. In *Proc. 1st Annual ACM Symposium on Parallel Algorithms and Architectures*, pages 254–264, 1989.

[141] N Kahale. Better expansion for Ramanujan graphs. In *Proc. 32nd Annual IEEE Symposium on Foundations of Computer Science*, pages 398–404, 1991.

[142] C Kaklamanis, D Krizanc, and T Tsantilas. Tight bounds for oblivious routing in the hypercube. *Mathematical Systems Theory*, 24:223–232, 1991.

[143] P C Kanellakis. Logic programming and parallel complexity. Technical Report CS-86-23, Department of Computer Science, Brown University, October 1986.

[144] M Y Kao and P N Klein. Towards overcoming the transitive-closure bottleneck: Efficient parallel algorithms for planar digraphs. In *Proc. 22nd Annual ACM Symposium on Theory of Computing*, pages 181–192, 1990.

[145] A Karlin and E Upfal. Parallel hashing - An efficient implementation of shared memory. *Journal of the ACM*, 35(4):876–892, 1988.

[146] H J Karloff and W L Ruzzo. The iterated mod problem. *Information and Computation*, 80(3):193–204, March 1989.

[147] R M Karp, M Luby, and F Meyer auf der Heide. Efficient PRAM simulation on a distributed memory machine. In *Proc. 24th Annual ACM Symposium on Theory of Computing*, 1992. To appear.

[148] R M Karp, R E Miller, and S Winograd. The organization of computations for uniform recurrence equations. *Journal of the ACM*, 14:563–590, 1967.

[149] R M Karp and V Ramachandran. Parallel algorithms for shared-memory machines. In J van Leeuwen, editor, *Handbook of Theoretical Computer Science: Volume A, Algorithms and Complexity*, pages 869–941. North Holland, 1990.

[150] R M Karp, E Upfal, and A Wigderson. Constructing a perfect matching is in random NC. *Combinatorica*, 6:35–48, 1986.

[151] R M Karp and A Wigderson. A fast parallel algorithm for the maximal independent set problem. *Journal of the ACM*, 32(4):762–773, October 1985.

[152] Z M Kedem, K V Palem, A Raghunathan, and P G Spirakis. Combining tentative and definite executions for very fast dependable parallel computing. In *Proc. 23rd Annual ACM Symposium on Theory of Computing*, pages 381–390, 1991.

[153] Z M Kedem, K V Palem, and P G Spirakis. Efficient robust parallel computations. In *Proc. 22nd Annual ACM Symposium on Theory of Computing*, pages 138–148, 1990.

[154] G A P Kindervater, J K Lenstra, and D B Shmoys. The parallel complexity of TSP heuristics. *Journal of Algorithms*, 10:249–270, 1989.

[155] D E Knuth. *Sorting and Searching*, volume 3 of *The Art of Computer Programming*. Addison-Wesley, 1973.

[156] R Koch, F T Leighton, B M Maggs, S B Rao, and A L Rosenberg. Work-preserving emulations of fixed-connection networks. In *Proc. 21st Annual ACM Symposium on Theory of Computing*, pages 227–240, 1989.

[157] S R Kosaraju. Parallel evaluation of division-free arithmetic expressions. In *Proc. 18th Annual ACM Symposium on Theory of Computing*, pages 231–239, 1986.

[158] S R Kosaraju. On the parallel evaluation of classes of circuits. In K V Nori and C E Veni Madhavan, editors, *Proc. 10th Conference on Foundations of Software Technology and Theoretical Computer Science. LNCS Vol.472*, pages 232–237. Springer-Verlag, 1990.

[159] C P Kruskal, L Rudolph, and M Snir. Efficient synchronization on multiprocessors with shared memory. *ACM Transactions on Programming Languages and Systems*, 10(4):579–601, 1988.

[160] C P Kruskal, L Rudolph, and M Snir. Techniques for parallel manipulation of sparse matrices. *Theoretical Computer Science*, 64:135–157, 1989.

[161] C P Kruskal, L Rudolph, and M Snir. A complexity theory of efficient parallel algorithms. *Theoretical Computer Science*, 71:95–132, 1990.

[162] C P Kruskal, L Rudolph, and M Snir. Efficient parallel algorithms for graph problems. *Algorithmica*, 5:43–64, 1990.

[163] H T Kung. New opportunities in multicomputers. In C W Gear, editor, *Computation and Cognition. Proceedings of the First NEC Research Symposium*, pages 1–21. SIAM Press, 1991.

[164] R E Ladner. The circuit value problem is log space complete for P. *ACM Sigact News*, 7(1):18–20, 1975.

[165] R E Ladner and M J Fischer. Parallel prefix computation. *Journal of the ACM*, 27(4):831–838, October 1980.

[166] L L Larmore and T M Przytycka. Parallel construction of trees with optimal weighted path length. In *Proc. 3rd Annual ACM Symposium on Parallel Algorithms and Architectures*, pages 71–80, 1991.

[167] F T Leighton. *Introduction to Parallel Algorithms and Architectures: Arrays, Trees, Hypercubes*. Morgan Kaufmann, San Mateo, CA, 1992.

[168] F T Leighton and C E Leiserson. Advanced parallel and VLSI computation. Research Seminar Series MIT/LCS/RSS 7, Laboratory for Computer Science, Massachusetts Institute of Technology, December 1989.

[169] F T Leighton, C E Leiserson, and M Klugerman. Theory of parallel and VLSI computation. Research Seminar Series MIT/LCS/RSS 10, Laboratory for Computer Science, Massachusetts Institute of Technology, January 1991.

[170] F T Leighton and B M Maggs. Expanders might be practical: Fast algorithms for routing around faults on multibutterflies. In *Proc. 30th Annual IEEE Symposium on Foundations of Computer Science*, pages 384–389, 1989.

[171] F T Leighton, B M Maggs, and S B Rao. Universal packet routing algorithms. In *Proc. 29th Annual IEEE Symposium on Foundations of Computer Science*, pages 256–269, 1988.

[172] C E Leiserson. Fat-trees: Universal networks for hardware-efficient supercomputing. *IEEE Transactions on Computers*, C–34(10):892–901, October 1985.

[173] C E Leiserson and B M Maggs. Communication-efficient parallel algorithms for distributed random-access machines. *Algorithmica*, 3:53–77, 1988.

[174] T Lengauer. VLSI theory. In J van Leeuwen, editor, *Handbook of Theoretical Computer Science: Volume A, Algorithms and Complexity*, pages 835–868. North Holland, 1990.

[175] D Lenoski, J Laudon, K Gharachorloo, W-D Weber, A Gupta, J Hennessy, M Horowitz, and M S Lam. The Stanford Dash Multiprocessor. *IEEE Computer*, 25(3):63–79, March 1992.

[176] A Lingas and M Karpinski. Subtree isomorphism is NC reducible to bipartite perfect matching. *Information Processing Letters*, 30(1):27–32, January 1989.

[177] A Lubotzky, R Phillips, and P Sarnak. Ramanujan graphs. *Combinatorica*, 8(3):261–277, 1988.

[178] M Luby. A simple parallel algorithm for the maximal independent set problem. *SIAM Journal on Computing*, 15(4):1036–1053, November 1986.

[179] Y-D Lyuu. Fast fault-tolerant parallel communication and on-line maintenance using information dispersal. In *Proc. 2nd Annual ACM Symposium on Parallel Algorithms and Architectures*, pages 378–387, 1990.

[180] Y-D Lyuu. *Information Dispersal and Parallel Computation.* Cambridge International Series on Parallel Computation. Cambridge University Press, Cambridge, UK, 1992. To appear.

[181] B M Maggs and S A Plotkin. Minimum-cost spanning tree as a path-finding problem. *Information Processing Letters*, 26:291–293, 1988.

[182] H G Mairson. Type inference for the simply-typed lambda calculus is complete for PTIME: Proof by computer program, 1991. Article on TYPES mailing list.

[183] Y Matias and U Vishkin. Converting high probability into nearly-constant time, with applications to parallel hashing. In *Proc. 23rd Annual ACM Symposium on Theory of Computing*, pages 307–316, 1991.

[184] Y Matias and U Vishkin. On parallel hashing and integer sorting. *Journal of Algorithms*, 12:573–606, 1991.

[185] E W Mayr. Theoretical aspects of parallel computation. In R Suaya and G Birtwistle, editors, *VLSI and Parallel Computaion*, pages 85–139. Morgan Kaufmann, San Mateo, CA, 1990.

[186] W F McColl. Phase: A programming language for general purpose parallel computing. Technical report, NEC Research Institute, Princeton, 1992. (In preparation).

[187] W F McColl. Special purpose parallel computing. In Gibbons and Spirakis [89].

[188] K Mehlhorn and U Vishkin. Randomized and deterministic simulations of PRAMs by parallel machines with restricted granularity of parallel memories. *Acta Informatica*, 21:339–374, 1984.

[189] G L Miller, V Ramachandran, and E Kaltofen. Efficient parallel evaluation of straight-line code and arithmetic circuits. *SIAM Journal on Computing*, 17(4):687–695, August 1988.

[190] G L Miller and J H Reif. Parallel tree contraction and its application. In *Proc. 26th Annual IEEE Symposium on Foundations of Computer Science*, pages 478–489, 1985.

[191] G L Miller and J H Reif. Parallel tree contraction. Part I: Fundamentals. In S Micali, editor, *Randomness and Computation. Vol.5*, pages 47–72. JAI Press, 1989.

[192] G L Miller and J H Reif. Parallel tree contraction. Part 2: Further applications. *SIAM Journal on Computing*, 20(6):1128–1147, December 1991.

[193] G L Miller and S H Teng. Dynamic parallel complexity of computational circuits. In *Proc. 19th Annual ACM Symposium on Theory of Computing*, pages 254–263, 1987.

[194] S Miyano, S Shiraishi, and T Shoudai. A list of P-Complete problems. RIFIS Technical Report RIFIS-TR-CS-17, Research Institute of Fundamental Information Science, Kyushu University, October 1989.

[195] T Mowry and A Gupta. Tolerating latency through software-controlled prefetching in shared-memory multiprocessors. *Journal of Parallel and Distributed Computing*, 12:87–106, 1991.

[196] D E Muller and F P Preparata. Restructuring of arithmetic expressions for parallel evaluation. *Journal of the ACM*, 23:534–543, 1976.

[197] K Mulmuley, U V Vazirani, and V V Vazirani. Matching is as easy as matrix inversion. *Combinatorica*, 7:105–113, 1987.

[198] I J Munro and M S Paterson. Optimal algorithms for parallel polynomial evaluation. *Journal of Computer and System Sciences*, pages 189–198, 1973.

[199] R S Nikhil. Id - Language Reference Manual. Version 90.1. Computation Structures Group Memo 284-2, Laboratory for Computer Science, Massachusetts Institute of Technology, July 1991.

[200] R S Nikhil and Arvind. Can dataflow subsume von Neumann computing? In *Proc. 16th Annual International Symposium on Computer Architecture*, pages 262–272, 1989.

[201] R S Nikhil, G M Papadopolous, and Arvind. *t: A killer micro for a brave new world. Computation Structures Group Memo 325, Laboratory for Computer Science, Massachusetts Institute of Technology, July 1991.

[202] V Pan. *How to Multiply Matrices Faster. LNCS Vol.179*. Springer-Verlag, 1984.

[203] G E Pantziou, P G Spirakis, and C D Zaroliagis. Efficient parallel algorithms for shortest paths in planar graphs. In J R Gilbert and R Karlsson, editors, *Proc. 2nd Scandinavian Workshop on Algorithm Theory. LNCS Vol.447*, pages 288–300. Springer-Verlag, 1990.

[204] C H Papadimitriou and J D Ullman. A communication-time tradeoff. *SIAM Journal on Computing*, 16(4):639–646, August 1987.

[205] C H Papadimitriou and M Yannakakis. Towards an architecture-independent analysis of parallel algorithms. *SIAM Journal on Computing*, 19(2):322–328, 1990.

[206] G M Papadopolous and K R Traub. Multithreading: A revisionist view of dataflow architectures. In *Proc. 18th Annual International Symposium on Computer Architecture*, pages 342–351, 1991.

[207] M S Paterson. Improved sorting networks with $O(\log N)$ depth. *Algorithmica*, 5(1):75–92, 1990.

[208] D A Patterson. Reduced instruction set computers. *Communications of the ACM*, 28(1):8–21, January 1985.

[209] R Paturi, D-T Lu, J E Ford, S C Esener, and S H Lee. Parallel algorithms based on expander graphs for optical computing. *Applied Optics*, 30(8):917–927, March 1991.

[210] S Peyton-Jones and D Lester. *Implementing Functional Languages*. Prentice Hall, 1992.

[211] S L Peyton Jones. Parallel implementation of functional programming languages. *The Computer Journal*, 32(2):175–186, 1989.

[212] N J Pippenger. Parallel communication with limited buffers. In *Proc. 25th Annual IEEE Symposium on Foundations of Computer Science*, pages 127–136, 1984.

[213] N J Pippenger. The complexity of computations by networks. *IBM Journal of Research and Development*, 31(2):235–243, March 1987.

[214] F P Preparata and D E Muller. Efficient parallel evaluation of Boolean expressions. *IEEE Transactions on Computers*, 25:548–549, 1976.

[215] M O Rabin. Efficient dispersal of information for security, load balancing, and fault tolerance. *Journal of the ACM*, 36(2):335–348, April 1989.

[216] M O Rabin. Optimal parallel pattern matching through randomization. In *Proc. Sequences 91 Conference*, 1991.

[217] S Rajasekaran and J H Reif. Randomized parallel computation. In S K Tewksbury, B W Dickinson, and S C Schwartz, editors, *Concurrent Computations - Algorithms, Architecture, and Technology. Proc. 1987 Princeton Workshop on Algorithms, Architecture and Technology Issues for Models of Concurrent Computation*, pages 181–202. Plenum Press, 1988.

[218] R Raman. The power of collision - Randomized parallel algorithms for chaining and integer sorting. In *Proc. 10th Conference on Foundations of Software Technology and Theoretical Computer Science, LNCS Vol.472*, pages 161–175. Springer-Verlag, 1990.

[219] R Raman. Optimal sub-logarithmic time integer sorting on a CRCW PRAM. Technical report, 1991. Submitted for publication.

[220] A G Ranade. How to emulate shared memory. In *Proc. 28th Annual IEEE Symposium on Foundations of Computer Science*, pages 185–194, 1987.

[221] A G Ranade. Fluent parallel computation. Ph.D. Thesis, Department of Computer Science, Yale University, May 1989.

[222] S B Rao. Properties of an interconnection architecture based on wavelength division multiplexing. Technical Report TR-92-009-3-0054-2, NEC Research Institute, Princeton, January 1992.

[223] J H Reif. Depth first search is inherently sequential. *Information Processing Letters*, 20(5):229–234, 1985.

[224] J H Reif, editor. *Synthesis of Parallel Algorithms*. Morgan Kaufmann, San Mateo, CA, 1992. To appear.

[225] J H Reif and S Sen. Randomization in parallel algorithms and its impact on computational geometry. In H Djidjev, editor, *Proc. International Symposium on Optimal Algorithms. LNCS Vol.401*, pages 1–8. Springer-Verlag, 1989.

[226] J H Reif and S Sen. Optimal randomized parallel algorithms for computational geometry. *Algorithmica*, 7(1):91–117, 1992.

[227] A L Rosenberg. On validating parallel architectures via graph embeddings. In S K Tewksbury, B W Dickinson, and S C Schwartz, editors, *Concurrent Computations - Algorithms, Architecture, and Technology*, pages 99–115. (Proc. 1987 Princeton Workshop on Algorithm, Architecture and Technology Issues for Models of Concurrent Computation), Plenum Press, 1988.

[228] R H Saavedra-Barrera, D E Culler, and T von Eicken. Analysis of multithreaded architectures for parallel computing. In *Proc. 2nd Annual ACM Symposium on Parallel Algorithms and Architectures*, pages 169–178, 1990.

[229] A Saoudi, M Nivat, C Pandu Rangan, R Sundaram, and G D S Ramkumar. A parallel algorithm for recognizing the shuffle of two strings. In *Proc. 6th International Parallel Processing Symposium*, pages 112–115, 1992.

[230] B Schieber and U Vishkin. On finding lowest common ancestors: Simplification and parallelization. In J H Reif, editor, *VLSI Algorithms and Architectures. 3rd Aegean Workshop on Computing (AWOC 88). LNCS Vol.319*, pages 111–123. Springer-Verlag, 1988.

[231] E Schwabe. On the computational equivalence of hypercube-derived networks. In *Proc. 2nd Annual ACM Symposium on Parallel Algorithms and Architectures*, pages 388–397, 1990.

[232] C L Seitz. Concurrent VLSI architectures. *IEEE Transactions on Computers*, 33:1247–1265, 1984.

[233] C L Seitz. The Cosmic Cube. *Communications of the ACM*, 28(1):22–33, January 1985.

[234] C L Seitz. Concurrent architectures. In R Suaya and G Birtwistle, editors, *VLSI and Parallel Computation*, pages 1–84. Morgan Kaufmann, San Mateo, CA, 1990.

[235] C L Seitz. Multicomputers. In C A R Hoare, editor, *Developments in Concurrency and Communication*, University of Texas Year of Programming Institute on Concurrent Programming, pages 131–200. Addison-Wesley, 1990.

[236] C L Seitz, W C Athas, W J Dally, R Faucette, A S Martin, S Mattison, C D Steele, and W-K Su. *Message-Passing Concurrent Computers: Their Architecture & Programming*. Addison-Wesley, 1989.

[237] M Serna. Approximating linear programming is log-space complete for P. *Information Processing Letters*, 37(4):233–236, February 1991.

[238] M Serna and P Spirakis. The approximability of problems complete for P. In H Djidjev, editor, *Proc. International Symposium on Optimal Algorithms. LNCS Vol.401*, pages 193–204. Springer-Verlag, 1989.

[239] M Serna and P Spirakis. *The Parallel Approximability of Hard Problems*. Cambridge International Series on Parallel Computation. Cambridge University Press, Cambridge, UK, 1992. To appear.

[240] Y Shiloach and U Vishkin. An $O(\log n)$ parallel connectivity algorithm. *Journal of Algorithms*, 3:57–67, 1982.

[241] A A Shvartsman. Achieving optimal CRCW PRAM fault-tolerance. *Information Processing Letters*, 39(2):59–66, 1991.

[242] A Siegel. On universal classes of fast high performance hash functions, their time-space tradeoff, and their applications. In *Proc. 30th Annual IEEE Symposium on Foundations of Computer Science*, pages 20–25, 1989.

[243] B J Smith. Architecture and applications of the HEP multiprocessor computer system. In T F Tao, editor, *SPIE (Real Time Signal Processing IV)*, volume 298, pages 241–248. Society of Photo-Optical Instrumentation Engineers, August 1981.

[244] T H Spencer. More time-work tradeoffs for parallel graph algorithms. In *Proc. 3rd Annual ACM Symposium on Parallel Algorithms and Architectures*, pages 81–93, 1991.

[245] P Spirakis. The parallel complexity of deadlock detection. *Theoretical Computer Science*, 52((1,2)):155–163, 1987.

[246] G L Steele Jr and W D Hillis. Connection Machine Lisp: Fine-grained parallel symbolic processing. In *Proc. ACM Conference on Lisp and Functional Programming*, pages 279–297, 1986.

[247] V Strassen. Gaussian elimination is not optimal. *Numerische Mathematik*, 13:354–356, 1969.

[248] R E Tarjan and U Vishkin. An efficient parallel biconnectivity algorithm. *SIAM Journal on Computing*, 14(4):862–874, 1985.

[249] A M Turing. On computable numbers, with an application to the Entscheidungsproblem. *Proceedings of the London Mathematical Society. Series 2*, 42:230–265, 1936. Corrections, *ibid.*, 43 (1937), 544-546.

[250] J D Ullman. *Computational Aspects of VLSI*. Computer Science Press, 1984.

[251] J D Ullman and A van Gelder. Parallel complexity of logical query programs. *Algorithmica*, 3:5–42, 1988.

[252] J D Ullman and M Yannakakis. High-probability parallel transitive-closure algorithms. *SIAM Journal on Computing*, 20(1):100–125, February 1991.

[253] E Upfal. Efficient schemes for parallel communication. *Journal of the ACM*, 31:507–517, 1984.

[254] E Upfal. An O(log N) deterministic packet-routing scheme. *Journal of the ACM*, 39(1):55–70, January 1992.

[255] L G Valiant. Graph-theoretic properties in computational complexity. *Journal of Computer and System Sciences*, 13:278–285, 1976.

[256] L G Valiant. A scheme for fast parallel communication. *SIAM Journal on Computing*, 11(2):350–361, 1982.

[257] L G Valiant. Optimality of a two-phase strategy for routing in interconnection networks. *IEEE Transactions on Computers*, c-32(9):861–863, September 1983.

[258] L G Valiant. A bridging model for parallel computation. *Communications of the ACM*, 33(8):103–111, 1990.

[259] L G Valiant. General purpose parallel architectures. In J van Leeuwen, editor, *Handbook of Theoretical Computer Science: Volume A, Algorithms and Complexity*, pages 943–971. North Holland, 1990.

[260] L G Valiant and G J Brebner. Universal schemes for parallel communication. In *Proc. 13th Annual ACM Symposium on Theory of Computing*, pages 263–277, 1981.

[261] L G Valiant, S Skyum, S Berkowitz, and C Rackoff. Fast parallel computation of polynomials using few processors. *SIAM Journal on Computing*, 12(4):641–644, November 1983.

[262] S Vavasis. Gaussian elimination with pivoting is P-complete. *SIAM Journal of Discrete Mathematics*, 2(3):413–423, 1989.

[263] U Vishkin. Synchronous parallel computation - a survey. Technical Report 71, Courant Institute, New York University, April 1983.

[264] U Vishkin. An optimal parallel algorithm for selection. *Advances in Computing Research*, 4:79–86, 1987.

[265] U Vishkin. Can parallel algorithms enhance serial implementation? Technical Report UMIACS-TR-91-145, Institute for Advanced Computer Studies, University of Maryland, 1991.

[266] U Vishkin. Structural parallel algorithmics. In J Leach Albert, B Monien, and M Rodriguez Artalejo, editors, *Proc. 18th International Colloquium on Automata, Languages and Programming, LNCS Vol.510*, pages 363–380. Springer-Verlag, 1991.

[267] P M B Vitanyi. A modest proposal for communication costs in multicomputers. In S K Tewksbury, B W Dickinson, and S C Schwartz, editors, *Concurrent Computations - Algorithms, Architecture, and Technology*, pages 203–216. (Proc. 1987 Princeton Workshop on Algorithm, Architecture and Technology Issues for Models of Concurrent Computation), Plenum Press, 1988.

[268] J S Vitter and R A Simons. New classes for parallel complexity: A study of unification and other complete problems for P. *IEEE Transactions on Computers*, C-35(5):403–418, May 1986.

[269] J von Neumann. *First draft of a report on the EDVAC*. Moore School of Electrical Engineering, University of Pennsylvania, 30 June 1945. Contract No. W-670-ORD-4926 between the United States Army Ordnance Department and the University of Pennsylvania. Reprinted in *Papers of John von Neumann on Computing and Computer Theory*, W Aspray and A Burks, editors. Volume 12 in the Charles Babbage Institute Reprint Series for the History of Computing, MIT Press, 1987, 17-82.

[270] J von zur Gathen. Parallel arithmetic computations: A survey. In *Proc. Mathematical Foundations of Computer Science1986, LNCS Vol. 233*, pages 93–112. Springer-Verlag, 1986.

[271] S Warshall. A theorem on Boolean matrices. *Journal of the ACM*, 9(1):11–12, 1962.

[272] I Wegener. *The Complexity of Boolean Functions*. John Wiley and Sons, 1987.

[273] M N Wegman and J L Carter. New hash functions and their use in authentication and set equality. *Journal of Computer and System Sciences*, 22(3):265–279, 1981.

[274] C Whitby-Strevens. The transputer. In *Proc. 12th Annual International Symposium on Computer Architecture*, pages 292–300, 1985.

[275] L D Wittie. Communication structures for large networks of microcomputers. *IEEE Transactions on Computers*, C-30(4):264–273, April 1981.

[276] J C Wyllie. The complexity of parallel computations. Ph.D. Thesis, Department of Computer Science, Cornell University, 1981.

[277] A C-C Yao. Bounds on selection networks. *SIAM Journal on Computing*, 9(3):566–582, August 1980.

[278] C K Yap. What can be parallelized in computational geometry? In A Albrecht, H Jung, and K Mehlhorn, editors, *Parallel Algorithms and Architectures, LNCS Vol. 269*, pages 184–195, 1987.

[279] H Yasuura. On parallel computational complexity of unification. In *Proc. International Conference on Fifth Generation Computers*, pages 235–243, 1984.

Chapter 14

Complexity Models for All-Purpose
Parallel Computation

Andrew Chin

Abstract

The advent of general-purpose parallel computation raises new issues in algorithm design and memory management. The PRAM model, for decades the centerpiece of parallel complexity theory, is no longer sufficient for investigating these issues. Very recently, many realistic alternative models of parallel computation have been proposed in the literature, with the goal of bridging the gap between theory and practice.

This chapter illustrates the role of these new models. Several realistic aspects of parallel computation excluded from the PRAM model, and the alternative models which have been advanced to incorporate them, are described. One of these models, the Block PRAM, is discussed in more detail. Complexity results for the Block PRAM are presented which show that list ranking is asymptotically more difficult than prefix sums, and that universal hashing can be performed without destroying data locality in shared memory.

In recent years, the complexity theory research community has shown how major obstacles to massive parallelism can be overcome through careful hardware and software design. Techniques such as randomized routing [36], universal hashing [5] and robust computation [18, 20, 21] can provide a reliable environment for the design of portable, scalable, efficient and correct parallel algorithms. The challenge of realizing such an environment is of considerable interest to supercomputer manufacturers, because portable software is essential if parallel computation is to gain widespread acceptance.

In return, the emergence of general-purpose parallel computation [28] presents important challenges to the complexity theory of parallel algorithms. Although the PRAM model has been prominent in the development of a parallel complexity theory, it fails to represent the time complexities of interprocessor communication, asynchrony and hardware failure. More accurate complexity models, if appropriately defined, can identify new techniques for the efficient implementation of PRAM algorithms. Furthermore, they can show how existing special-purpose algorithmic techniques can be exploited on future general-purpose parallel architectures, raising the prospect of *all-purpose parallel computation*.

This chapter surveys the potential contribution of these new parallel complexity models to efficient parallel computation. (An understanding of the PRAM model is assumed; see e.g. [14].) The remainder of this chapter is organized as follows. Section 1 describes several features of parallel computation that are not accounted for by the PRAM model. Section 2 compares and contrasts several parallel complexity models which have been proposed as more realistic alternatives to the PRAM model. One of these models, the Block PRAM, is particularly useful for modeling *locality of reference,* which we discuss in more detail. Section 3 uses the two most fundamental PRAM algorithms—prefix sums and list ranking—to illustrate the importance of locality of reference to fast parallel computation. Section 4 describes *locality-preserving hashing,* which may allow good locality of reference to be exploited in general-purpose parallel computation. Section 5 concludes with research objectives which will support the goal of all-purpose parallel computation.

1.   Obstacles to the PRAM model

As a shared-memory model of parallel computation, the PRAM model does not accurately represent the state of the art in supercomputing. At present, the most feasible approach to building massively parallel computers is with physically distributed memory. However, a distributed-memory parallel computer with a fixed interconnection network can *simulate* shared memory in the following way. The aggregate of the local memory elements is taken to be the shared memory. To write into a shared memory location, a processor sends the data to the location's host processor through the network. To read a shared memory location, a processor sends a request to the location's host processor, which sends back a reply.

To support this simulation, algorithms have been developed for routing messages around hypercubes, butterflies, meshes and related networks so that with high probability, all messages arrive at their destinations in time proportional to the diameter of the network. These algorithms, based on the technique of two-phase *randomized routing* due to Valiant [36], have been refined most recently to tolerate a large number of failures in wires and switches [16, 34] and to support block pipelining [3, 24]. However, these algorithms only support permutation routing problems, in which a processor can send or receive only one message at a time. Since each processor is responsible for many memory locations, it is possible at any given time that some processors may be severely overloaded with communication activities, delaying the entire computation. This situation, known as contention, can be prevented using two complementary techniques, message *combining* [33] and memory *hashing* [5]. A choice of protocols for message routing/combining and memory management on a given multiprocessor network is often referred to as a *PRAM simulation* or *PRAM emulation* for that network.

Using hashing, combining, and a greedy routing algorithm, Ranade [35] has shown that a multiprocessor consisting of p processors connected by a $\log p$-level[1] butterfly network of message-combining switches can simulate one step of a $p \log p$-processor CRCW PRAM in $O(\log p)$ time with high probability. In other words, such a multiprocessor would be able to provide asymptotically optimal ($\Theta(p)$) speedup for any CRCW algorithm with sufficient (at least $\Omega(p \log p)$) logical parallelism.

It follows from this and similar PRAM simulation results that machines can be built which behave similarly to the PRAM model. However, it does not seem likely that the PRAM itself will be realized in the foreseeable future. The many obstacles to realizing the PRAM model are well-documented in the parallel complexity literature and include:

1. Communication latency. Distinct processors working together on the same problem will need to communicate from time to time. In present-day machines, this communication must take place through a physical network and is subject to considerable delay. The asymptotic cost of this delay is difficult to define. Ultimately, any network of processors

---

[1]In this chapter, all logarithms are binary.

must be constructed in a three-dimensional world, and the physical diameter of any network of p processors must be $\Omega(p^{1/3})$. Currently, however, routing of signals at the nodes of an interprocessor network takes much longer than propgagation of signals along the wires, and so it may be argued that the $\Omega(\log p)$ lower bound on the graph-theoretic diameter of bounded-degree networks more accurately represents the time complexity of communication. Future supercomputers may even exploit optical communication to produce networks with $O(1)$ graph-theoretic diameter [26]. However, it is likely that an access to a non-local memory location will continue to take longer—and be more difficult to control—than a local computation. It will therefore continue to be difficult to realize the PRAM model, which performs local computations and shared-memory accesses both in unit time.

2. Contention and congestion. In current large-scale parallel computers, the memory resource is contained in "modules" or "banks." Each module contains many memory locations, and each is capable of serving only a constant number of requests during each time step. The modules are connected to the processors by way of a physical network, and each link in the network is capable of transmitting only a constant amount of data during each time step. (For example, the machine may consist of a network of processor-memory units, or *processing elements.*) Contention results when the accesses during a time step require a module to serve too many requests, and congestion occurs when a link or node is required to transmit too much data. Excessive accesses and transmissions must be serialized, or staggered to take place over several time steps. Unless contention and congestion are managed, they may well dominate the actual running time of a theoretically efficient algorithm [33]. Since the PRAM model does not restrict memory access patterns, PRAM algorithms need not, and generally do not, account for the possibility of contention and congestion.

3. Arbitrary pipelining. In distributed-memory multiprocessing, it may be desirable for a processor to access many non-local memory locations in succession. The time required for *pipelining,* or performing such a sequence of accesses, appears to depend on physical locality. If the memory locations are contiguous, communication latency is incurred for accessing the first location, but subsequent locations can be accessed very rapidly. This phenomenon, known as *block pipelining,* has been observed on a wide range of architectures for more than ten years. In an ideal world, however, the lack of physical locality would not greatly affect the pipelining rate, and the PRAM model proceeds under the optimistic assumption of *arbitrary pipelining.*

4. Asynchrony. It has long been observed in parallel computation [22, 40] that machine specifications provide very limited information about machine behavior in practice. Intricate characteristics of the input data and the real-time activities of the operating system can cause great variations in processing speed. The machine specifications themselves may be subject to complicated kinds of alteration, as components are replaced and upgraded. The unpredictable variation of processor speeds relative to one another causes difficulty in specifying and debugging algorithms. For example, synchronization is necessary to execute any imperative communication instruction, because communication between two processors occurs precisely when one processor performs an action (e.g. writes into a shared memory location, sends a message) that the other later detects (e.g. reads the shared memory location, receives the message). To guarantee this ordering of events, some synchronization control mechanism is necessary. Since synchronization is a kind of interprocessor communication, it is subject to latency. However, processors in the PRAM model run synchronously without incurring additional delay.

5. Hardware failure. It is a fundamental principle of engineering that the larger and more complex a system is, the more likely it is to fail. In a parallel computer with many thousands of processing elements and communication paths, the possibility of failure is a serious obstacle to achieving the correctness and complexity specifications of any given parallel program. Clearly, we should not proceed with designing parallel algorithms and programs under the assumption that improvements in technology will eliminate the threat of failure. However, since failure is excluded from the PRAM model, PRAM algorithms need not, and generally do not, account for the possibility of failure.

2.   Realistic parallel complexity models

As we have seen, the PRAM model omits many important realistic aspects of parallel computation. Of course, the importance and usefulness of the PRAM model in parallel complexity theory is precisely due to these omissions. By using this powerful, idealized model of computation, algorithm designers have been able to focus on the logical, algorithmic and mathematical issues of solving problems in parallel. However, the PRAM model becomes less useful when programmers undertake to implement parallel algorithms efficiently on distributed-memory multiprocessors, and even on machines dedicated to PRAM simulation. Models of parallel computation which more closely represent actual machine behavior can provide more accurate measurements of complexity, creating significant new opportunities for improved performance.

As of this writing, the number of parallel complexity models proposed in the literature continues to grow, as researchers continue to glean insights from the Cartesian product of model assumptions. This work will have considerable importance to the practice of parallel computation, but only so long as these models remain robust and simple. For example, soon after the appearance of Ranade's result, several attractive complexity models were designed to represent the performance of dedicated PRAM simulations. These models are robust and simple because PRAM simulations promise asymptotically predictable machine behavior. Among the most significant of these realistic parallel complexity models are:

1. **Latency models.** In the PRAM model, an access to a location in the shared memory takes unit time. By modifying this time charge, Aggarwal, Chandra and Snir [1, 2] have extended the PRAM model to account for communication latency.

- The *Local-Memory PRAM* model [2] is defined to be a CREW PRAM in which communication and computation steps are counted separately.

- The *Block PRAM* model [1] is an EREW PRAM in which each access to a block of b contiguous locations in the shared memory takes time $l + b$, where l is a parameter representing latency; typically, $1 \leq l \leq p$. Several variations on this model have been suggested.

  - The *Arbitrary Block PRAM* model [15] is an EREW PRAM in which each access to any b shared memory locations with no data interdependencies takes time $l + b$. This is an arbitrary pipelining version of the Block PRAM.

  - The *Message-Passing Block PRAM* model [1] consists of p processing elements which communicate by exchanging messages. A processor can send or receive only one message at a time, and a message of length m is transferred in time $l + m$.

- The *Fixed-Size Block PRAM* model [1] is a Block PRAM which restricts accesses to the shared memory to blocks of fixed size l.

- The *Faulty Block PRAM* model [6] is a Block PRAM in which accesses to each location in the shared memory may result in an error with probability ϕ, where ϕ is a parameter representing failure.

2. Asynchronous models.
In the PRAM model, all processors run synchronously. By allowing the processors to run asynchronously, Cole and Zajicek [11, 12, 41], Nishimura [32], Martel, Park and Subramonian [27], Gibbons [15] and Valiant [38] have extended the PRAM model in various directions.

- The *APRAM* model of Cole and Zajicek [11, 12, 41] measures computation time in "rounds." A round is the time required for each processor to execute at least one instruction; i.e, time is measured according to the slowest processor clock. The time for each processor to execute an instruction varies according to some probability distribution, typically binomial.

- The model of Nishimura [32] measures computation time as the maximal number of steps taken by any processor. The actual order of execution of the instructions by processors is chosen uniformly at random from the space of all possible sequences of steps.

- The model of Martel, Park and Subramonian [27] measures *work*, or the total number of instructions (including wait steps) executed by all processors. The time for each processor to execute an instruction is arbitrary and unbounded.

- The *Asynchronous PRAM* models of Gibbons [15] measures time as the maximal number of steps taken by any processor. The cost of wait steps is subsumed in the cost $B(x)$ of synchronizing x processors. (A synchronization step is required between a write by one processor to a shared memory location and a read by a different processor to the same location.) There may also be a charge d for communication latency, imposed as in the Arbitrary Block PRAM model. (Typically, $2 \leq d \leq B(x) \leq p$.) Gibbons introduces four models—Phase PRAM, Phase LPRAM, Subset PRAM and Subset LPRAM—each with EREW, CREW and CRCW variants. The "phase" models require all-processor synchronization ($x = p$); the "subset" models allow any value of x, $2 \leq x \leq p$. The PRAM models do not charge for latency; the LPRAM models do.

- Unlike the other asynchronous models, processors in the *Bulk-Synchronous Parallel* (BSP) model of Valiant [37] communicate by message-passing; there is no shared memory. The cost of wait steps is subsumed in the cost L of synchronizing up to p processors. There is an explicit cost s for communication latency. There is also a parameter $g \geq 1$ representing the pipelining rate, so that the time required for a processor to send and receive h messages is $s + gh$. (The assumption of arbitrary pipelining is equivalent to setting $g = O(1)$.) The *XPRAM* [38] is a version of the BSP which requires all-processor synchronization.

3. Failure models. In the PRAM model, all processors run without stopping throughout the execution of an algorithm. Kanellakis and Shvartsman [18] and Kedem, Palem, Raghunathan and Spirakis [20, 21] consider a version of the CRCW PRAM model in which some processors may fail by stopping during an execution (and may later restart). The complexity measure of interest is work, or the total number of instructions performed by all of the working processors.

4. Contention and congestion models. Mehlhorn and Vishkin [29] consider a *Module Parallel Computer,* in which the memory is taken to be stored in modules with constant bandwidth. Leiserson and Maggs [25] introduce the *Distributed Random Access Machine,* a message-passing multiprocessor where the maximum flow of messages across a cut in the network is used as a complexity measure.

Note that some models cross the boundaries of the above classification. The Faulty Block PRAM incorporates communication failures, and the LPRAM and BSP models account for communication latency.

Some general remarks can be made about the power of these models.

- Since message-passing can be simulated by shared memory, the EREW Phase LPRAM is stronger than the XPRAM (with $g = 1$), and the Block PRAM is stronger than the message-passing Block PRAM.

- A parallel computation is *oblivious* if, when executed on all inputs of the same size, the operations executed and memory locations accessed on each processor during each time step are the same. For oblivious computations, message-passing can simulate shared memory by adapting a technique of Vishkin and Wigderson [39]. Therefore, for oblivious computations, the EREW Phase LPRAM is asymptotically equivalent to the XPRAM (with $g = 1$) [8], and the Block PRAM is asymptotically equivalent to the message-passing Block PRAM [1].

- By adapting the information dispersal algorithm of Rabin [34], a Faulty Block PRAM can probabilistically simulate a Fixed-Size Block PRAM [6].

- Since a synchronous model does not charge for synchronization, the arbitrary Block PRAM is stronger than the EREW Phase LPRAM. In the reverse direction, T steps of a Block PRAM (p, l) can be simulated by $O(BT/l)$ steps of an EREW Phase LPRAM with pl/B processors, latency l and barrier synchronization cost $B = B(p)$ [15].

The reader should refer to the cited papers for more specific information about each of the models. In most cases, the papers provide algorithms for particular problems, and show how to simulate general PRAM computations on their weaker models with asymptotically optimal (or near-optimal) efficiency.

3.   Locality of reference and algorithm design

The remainder of this chapter focuses on the Block PRAM model of Aggarwal, Chandra and Snir [1]. We believe that block pipelining is likely to remain the most accurate theoretical description of access times to virtual shared memory for the foreseeable future.[2] This

---

[2]Block pipelining also has strong support from recent theoretical algorithms for bit-serial routing on hypercube and butterfly networks [3, 24].

situation raises interesting issues about algorithm design and memory management.

Consider the following two problems:

1. Prefix sums. Let $\oplus$ be an associative binary operation with identity 0 that may be computed sequentially in $O(1)$ time. The *prefix sums* $\oplus$ computation takes an array $A = (a_0, a_1, a_2, \ldots, a_{n-1})$ and returns the array $(a_0, a_0 \oplus a_1, a_0 \oplus a_1 \oplus a_2, \ldots, a_0 \oplus a_1 \oplus a_2 \oplus \cdots \oplus a_{n-1})$.

2. List ranking. A *linked list* of n elements consists of two arrays $A[1 \ldots n]$ and $S[1 \ldots n]$. A is called the *data array* and S is called the *pointer array*. The first element in the list, called the *head*, is stored in $A(1)$. For $1 \leq i \leq n-1$, if the i-th element of the list is stored in $A(j)$, then the $(i+1)$-th element of the list is stored in $A(S(j))$. Given a linked list (A, S), the *list ranking* problem is to compute the equivalent array B. That is, compute $B[1 \ldots n]$ such that $B(i) = A(S^{(i-1)}(1))$.

Prefix sums and list ranking are widely considered to be the most fundamental PRAM algorithms. The prefix sums procedure has been implemented as a time-saving primitive on the Connection Machine with applications to algorithms in graph theory, computational geometry and numerical analysis [4]. List ranking is used in standard parallel algorithms for graph connectivity and ear decomposition. Optimal $O(n/p + \log n)$ time EREW PRAM algorithms are known for both prefix sums [23] and list ranking [10]. However, it has been observed that in practical experience, list ranking appears to be a more difficult problem, so that the list ranking procedure should be replaced with prefix sums whenever possible [13, 30]. Using the Block PRAM, we can confirm this intuition.

Definition.

An algorithm for list ranking is *shortcut-based* if in its execution on a list (A, S):

- For each element $A(i)$, some processor executes a *shortcut* step:
  $S(S^{-1}(i)) \leftarrow S(i)$
  Remove $A(i)$
  (Note that S, the array of pointers, changes during the algorithm.)

- No two consecutive elements $A(i)$, $A(S(i))$ are shortcut in parallel.

It is an open question whether list ranking can even be performed correctly by an algorithm that is not essentially shortcut-based.

Theorem 3.1. [9]

On a Block PRAM with p processors and latency l,

- The time complexity of the prefix sums $\oplus$ computation is $\Theta(n/p + l \log n / \log l)$.

- The time complexity of any shortcut-based list ranking algorithm is $\Omega(\min(nl/p, n \log p/(p \log(2n/pl))))$ for $pl \leq n$.

For illustration, on a Block PRAM with $p = n/\log n$ processors and latency $l = \log p$, the complexity of prefix sums is $\Theta(\log^2 n / \log \log n)$ and the complexity of list ranking is $\Theta(\log^2 n)$. This result indicates that prefix sums has better locality of reference than list ranking, and that on large-scale multiprocessors which exhibit block pipelining, we should expect that the prefix sums computation can be performed much more quickly than the list ranking computation.

4.   Locality of reference and memory management

An appealing solution to the problem of contention in PRAM simulation is to assign random logical addresses to the memory locations according to some *hash function*. The probability of each particular mapping of memory accesses to modules is exactly the same; so that with high probability, the physical distribution of memory accesses is nearly uniform, regardless of the pattern of addresses specified in the algorithm. However, hashing completely at random is not practical. Hash functions must be capable of being computed quickly and specified in relatively little space, so that a processor can efficiently evaluate the hash function for all of its memory accesses.

Universal families of hash functions were introduced by Carter and Wegman [5] as a practical way to use randomized hashing. The hash function to be used is chosen randomly from a universal family consisting of functions that are easy to specify and compute.

Definition.
   The performance of a universal class of hash functions is expressed in terms of its *independence*. A family F of hash functions with domain D and range R is said to be $(h)_\mu$-*wise independent* if for all $y_1, \ldots, y_h \in R$ and all distinct $x_1, \ldots, x_h \in D$, $|\{f \in F : f(x_i) = y_i, i = 1, \ldots, h\}| \leq \mu |F|/|R|^h$. (It is understood that $h \geq 2$ and $\mu \geq 1$. When μ is omitted we understand $\mu = 1$.)   □

For any set of h memory addresses, the probability that a hash function randomly chosen from F maps them to modules in a particular pattern is approximately the same as if the hashing had been done completely at random. The number h is a parameter of the family and is a measure of its *performance*, or *independence*. High-performance families can be used to avoid contention, with high probability, in PRAM simulations [1, 29, 38]. Lower-performance families (with $h = 2$) have been adequate so far in practice [37], although extra care in choosing parameters for the family can be necessary [31].

   A perceived drawback to using hashing in PRAM simulations is that the natural locality of reference in a problem (e.g. prefix sums) might be destroyed, resulting in a loss of performance [17]. It is possible to address this problem by showing that it is possible to perform universal hashing on the shared memory of a Block PRAM quickly and without significantly degrading locality of reference. (By "performing hashing," we mean performing a sequence of copying instructions on memory locations which effect the desired mapping.) This issue is of interest in several contexts.

   1.   **All-purpose parallel computation.** Locality of reference is a central issue in the design and analysis of special-purpose algorithms; i.e., those designed for particular network topologies. It has been viewed as less important in general-purpose parallel computation because the target model, the PRAM, was able to support arbitrary pipelining. However, the availability of locality-preserving hashing for block-pipelining multiprocessors should motivate the development of PRAM algorithms which exploit locality of reference. The Block PRAM is an appropriate model for this research, which should aim to remove the dichotomy between problem solving techniques for special-purpose and general-purpose parallel computation.

   2.   **Simulations between theoretical models.** In order for a Block PRAM to simulate a uniform shared memory model such as the PRAM, the memory addresses are hashed. The Block PRAM complexity of hashing corresponds to the complexity of moving between

arbitrary- and block-pipelining characterizations of communication latency.

3. Programmer-controlled hashing. The prevailing vision of general-purpose parallel computers [37] is that the network topology should be hidden, but that the programmer should retain control of memory management, including the decision whether or not to hash the shared memory. This decision should take into account the complexity of hashing, as well as the extent to which the algorithm exploits locality.

4. Automatic hashing. Even if the shared memory is always hashed, it will still be necessary to change the hash function from time to time [31, 35]. Rehashing is required, for example, if a particular hash function proves ineffective in preventing contention during a given computation.

5. Partially hashed shared memory. In certain shared-memory designs, some of the memory address space will be hashed and some left unhashed [15]. The Block PRAM complexity of hashing is important in determining the possible benefits to this approach, and the cost of changing the partition.

6. Input/output. Files will read into (and out from) the shared memory in unhashed form and will need to be hashed (and unhashed).

We will say that a universal family F of hash functions is *locality-preserving* for a particular Block PRAM algorithm if that algorithm runs equally quickly in hashed and unhashed shared memory for all hash functions in F (up to a constant factor).

Definition.

Let $\mathcal{A}$ be a Block PRAM algorithm with time bound $T(n, l, p)$ which uses at most $S(n, l, p)$ shared memory locations. Let F be a universal family of hash functions from $[1 \ldots S(n, l, p)]$ to $[1 \ldots S(n, l, p)]$. Then F is *locality-preserving* for $\mathcal{A}$ if, for any $f \in F$, f can be performed and inverted by a Block PRAM on $S(n, l, p)$ consecutive locations in shared memory in time $O(T(n, l, p))$. □

Assuming that a locality-preserving hash function has been used, a Block PRAM can exploit locality in hashed shared memory as follows. First, the memory space is unhashed; next, the Block PRAM algorithm is executed; and finally, the memory space is rehashed. The algorithm uses at most $S(n, l, p)$ shared memory locations; without loss of generality these can be consecutive. The definition of locality preservation implies that the unhashing and rehashing do not dominate the complexity of the algorithm.

Theorem 4.1. [7]

- Let $\mu > 0$ be a constant, let F be a universal family of 2_μ-wise independent hash functions and let f be chosen at random from F. Then performing f requires expected time $\Omega(n \log \min(n/l, n/p)/p \log(2n/lp))$ for $lp \leq n$; and $\Omega(l + l \log \min(l, p)/\log(2lp/n))$ for $lp > n$.

- Let $n = 2^k$ and identify $N = [1 \ldots n]$ with the set of 0-1 vectors of length k (most significant bit first). Let M be the set of nonsingular $k \times k$ 0-1 matrices. Let $f_A(x) = Ax \bmod 2$. Define $\mathcal{H} = \{f_A : A \in M\}$. Then $\mathcal{H}$ is a $2_{4.06}$-wise independent universal family of hash functions from N to N, and any member of $\mathcal{H}$ can be performed and inverted in time $O((n \log \min(n/l, n/p))/(p \log(2n/lp)))$ for $lp \leq n$; and $O(l + l \log \min(l, p)/\log(2lp/n))$ for $lp > n$.

Our results show that $\mathcal{H}$ has the best locality-preserving properties possible for a universal family of hash functions, and in particular, $\mathcal{H}$ is locality-preserving for the prefix sums computation. In fact, the Block PRAM complexity of $\mathcal{H}$ turns out to be asymptotically the same as the complexity of transposing square matrices.

5.   Conclusions

For some time to come, locality of reference is likely to remain a central issue in the design of general-purpose parallel computers and the implementation of portable parallel software. The Block PRAM model provides a useful complexity theory for this study and may motivate problem-solving that unites the fields of general-purpose and special-purpose parallel computation. The theory also appears to have intrinsic combinatorial interest.

The need for realistic models of parallel computation such as the Block PRAM model comes from the central concern of complexity theory: improved performance in large-scale computation. By modeling the supercomputers of the future accurately and robustly, we are likely to discover fundamental and applicable techniques for both hardware and software design.

The results mentioned in this chapter leave much scope for improvement. Our lower bound for list ranking does not preclude an efficient Block PRAM algorithm using fewer processors. Our results for hashing could be extended or improved for families with higher degrees of independence. It would also be desirable to learn more about relationships between the independence and locality of hash families. Future work in these areas would constitute significant progress towards providing for the exploitation of locality in general-purpose parallel computation.

Acknowledgements. I wish to thank W. F. McColl for many helpful comments.

References

[1] A. Aggarwal, A. K. Chandra and M. Snir, "On communication latency in PRAM computations," *Proc. First Annual ACM Symp. on Parallel Algorithms and Architectures*, 1989, 11–21.

[2] A. Aggarwal, A. K. Chandra and M. Snir, "Communication complexity of PRAMs," *Theor. Comput. Sci.* **71** (1990), 3–28.

[3] W. Aiello, T. Leighton, B. Maggs and M. Newman, "Fast algorithms for bit-serial routing on a hypercube," *Proc. 2nd Annual ACM Symp. on Parallel Algorithms and Architectures*, 1990, 55–64.

[4] G. E. Blelloch, *Vector Models for Data-Parallel Computing*, Cambridge, Mass.: MIT Press, 1990.

[5] J. L. Carter and M. N. Wegman, "Universal classes of hash functions," *J. Comput. Syst. Sci.* **18** (1979), 143–154.

[6] A. Chin, "Latency hiding for fault-tolerant PRAM computation," in: *Proc. Int. Conf. on Sets, Graphs and Numbers* (D. Miklos, ed.), Amsterdam: North-Holland, to appear.

[7] A. Chin, "Locality-preserving hash functions for general purpose parallel computation," *Algorithmica*, submitted.

[8] A. Chin, "On the equivalence of asynchronous parallel models of computation," in preparation.

[9] A. Chin and W. F. McColl, "Virtual shared memory: algorithms and complexity," *Inf. Comput.*, to appear.

[10] R. Cole and U. Vishkin, "Approximate parallel scheduling. Part I: The basic technique with applications to optimal parallel list ranking in logarithmic time," *SIAM J. Comput.* **17** (1988), 128–142.

[11] R. Cole and O. Zajicek, "The APRAM: incorporating asynchrony into the PRAM model," *Proc. First Annual ACM Symp. on Parallel Algorithms and Architectures*, 1989, 169–178.

[12] R. Cole and O. Zajicek, "The expected advantage of asynchrony," *Proc. 2nd Annual ACM Symp. on Parallel Algorithms and Architectures*, 1990, 85–94.

[13] H. Gazit, G. L. Miller and S. H. Teng, "Optimal tree contraction in the EREW model," *Proc. Princeton Workshop on Algorithm, Architecture and Technology Issues for Models of Concurrent Computation*, New York: Plenum Press, 1987, 139–156.

[14] A. M. Gibbons and W. Rytter, *Efficient Parallel Algorithms*, Cambridge, England: University of Cambridge Press, 1988.

[15] P. B. Gibbons, "The Asynchronous PRAM: a semi-synchronous model for shared memory MIMD machines," Ph. D. thesis, University of California at Berkeley, 1989.

[16] J. Håstad, T. Leighton and M. Newman, "Fast computation using faulty hypercubes," *Proc. 21st Annual ACM Symp. on Theory of Computing*, 1989, 251–263.

[17] T. Heywood and S. Ranka, "A practical hierarchical model of parallel computation: the model," Technical Report SU-CIS-91-06, Syracuse University, Syracuse, N.Y., 1991.

[18] P. Kanellakis and A. Shvartsman, "Efficient parallel algorithms can be made robust," *Proc. 8th Annual ACM Symp. on Principles of Distributed Computing*, 1989, 211–222.

[19] R. M. Karp and V. Ramachandran, "Parallel algorithms for shared-memory machines," in: *Handbook of Theoretical Computer Science* (J. van Leeuwen, ed.), Amsterdam: North-Holland, 1990, 869–942.

[20] Z. M. Kedem, K. V. Palem and P. G. Spirakis, "Efficient robust parallel computations," *Proc. 22nd Annual ACM Symp. on Theory of Computing*, 1990, 138–148.

[21] Z. M. Kedem, K. V. Palem, A. Raghunathan and P. G. Spirakis, "Combining tentative and definite executions for very fast dependable parallel computing," *Proc. 23rd Annual ACM Symp. on Theory of Computing*, 1991.

[22] H. T. Kung, "Synchronized and asynchronous parallel algorithms for multiprocessors," in: *Algorithms and Complexity: New Directions and Recent Results* (J. F. Traub, ed.), New York: Academic Press, 1976, 153–200.

[23] R. E. Ladner and M. J. Fischer, "Parallel prefix computation," *J. ACM* **27** (1980), 831–838.

[24] F. T. Leighton and C. G. Plaxton, "A (fairly) simple circuit that (usually) sorts," *Proc. 31st Annual IEEE Symp. on Foundations of Computer Science*, 1990.

[25] C. E. Leiserson and B. M. Maggs, "Communication-efficient parallel algorithms for distributed random-access machines," *Algorithmica* **3** (1988), 53–77.

[26] E. S. Maniloff, K. M. Johnson and J. Reif, "Holographic routing network for shared-memory parallel computers," Technical Report CSE-89-8, University of California at Davis, 1989.

[27] C. Martel, A. Park and R. Subramonian, "Optimal asynchronous algorithms for shared memory parallel computers," Technical Report CSE-89-8, University of California at Davis, 1989.

[28] W. F. McColl, "General-purpose parallel computation," this volume.

[29] K. Mehlhorn and U. Vishkin, "Randomized and deterministic simulations of PRAMs by parallel machines with restricted granularity of parallel memories," *Acta Inf.* **21** (1984), 339–374.

[30] G. L. Miller, "Are pointer-based parallel algorithms realistic?" in: *Opportunities and Constraints of Parallel Computing* (J. L. C. Sanz, ed.), New York: Springer-Verlag, 1989, 85.

[31] J. K. Mullin, "A caution on universal classes of hash functions," *Inform. Process. Lett.* **37** (1991), 247–256.

[32] N. Nishimura, "Asynchronous shared memory parallel computation," *Proc. Second Annual ACM Symp. on Parallel Algorithms and Architectures*, 1990, 76–84.

[33] G. F. Pfister and V. A. Norton, " 'Hot spot' contention and combining in multistage interconnection networks," *Proc. Int. Conf. on Parallel Processing*, 1985, 790–797.

[34] M. O. Rabin, "Efficient dispersal of information for security, load balancing and fault tolerance," *J. ACM* **36** (1989), 335–348.

[35] A. G. Ranade, "How to emulate shared memory," *Proc. 28th Annual IEEE Symp. on Foundations of Computer Science*, 1987, 185–194.

[36] L. G. Valiant, "A scheme for fast parallel communication," *SIAM J. Comput.* **11** (1982), 350–361.

[37] L. G. Valiant, "A bridging model for parallel computation," *Comm. ACM* **33** (1990), 103–110.

[38] L. G. Valiant, "General purpose parallel architectures," in: *Handbook of Theoretical Computer Science* (J. van Leeuwen, ed.), Amsterdam: North-Holland, 1990, 943–971.

[39] U. Vishkin and A. Wigderson, "Dynamic parallel memories," *Inf. Control* **56** (1983), 174–182.

[40] H. A. G. Wijshoff, "A phenomenology of current parallel computers," this volume.

[41] O. Zajicek, "The APRAM: a model for asynchronous parallel computation," Ph. D. thesis, New York University, 1990.

Chapter 15

Implementing Sparse BLAS Primitives on Concurrent/Vector Processors: a Case Study

Harry A.G. Wijshoff

Abstract

In this chapter we study the design and implementation of sparse BLAS primitives on concurrent/vector processors. Sparse computations are not only dependent on the architecture, but also on the problem instance, e.g., the structure of the sparsity pattern of a matrix. This fact increases the complexity of sparse matrix computations considerably. In fact no systematic approach in implementing sparse codes for concurrent/vector processors is proposed yet. In this chapter we layout a generic strategy for designing and implementing sparse BLAS primitives on concurrent/vector processors. The implementation of the primitive sparse matrix times a number of dense vectors will be handled in detail and essentially three different implementations of this primitive will be given. We show that each of these implementations have their own advantages/disadvantages depending on the architecture and the problem instance. These trade offs are verified by experiments on the Alliant FX/8 and the FX/80.

1. Sparse BLAS Kernels

With the increasing complexity of writing efficient codes for novel super/parallel architectures, scientific software packages are getting more and more based on highly efficiently implemented basic computational primitives. This development started with the definition of Basic Linear Algebra Subroutines primitives [4]. These primitives were defined for dense computations and consisted out of vector-vector linear algebra routines, such as sdot, saxpy, etc. In order to exploit the features of parallel/super computers and to obtain fast implementations of the BLAS primitives a need for higher level BLAS primitives arose. This need was temporarily satisfied by the introduction of BLAS2 primitives [5] which consisted of vector-matrix linear algebra routines, e.g., rank-1 updates, matrix vector multiply, etc.. However with the introduction of parallel/super computers enrusted with hierarchical memory systems, e.g. the Alliant series, the CRAY 2 and the CEDAR architecture etc., the implementation of the BLAS2 primitives did not allow enough flexibility to achieve reasonable performance on these machines. So, BLAS3 routines were introduced on which blocking techniques could be employed [7]. The BLAS3 routines consist out of, e.g., Matrix times Matrix, Matrix plus Scalar times Matrix, Rank-k Updates. Both the BLAS, BLAS2 and the BLAS3 primitives were defined for dense computations.

Whereas the development of these BLAS primitives for dense computations evolved rather strongly and received a lot of attention in the literature lately, for sparse computations the opposite is true. This is mainly caused by the fact that the computational complexity of sparse computations on parallel/super computers is not very well understood, and that there are no paradigms developed for implementing sparse computations on these architectures. The only direct effort for defining BLAS routines for sparse computations was done by Dodson and Lewis [3], who proposed a sparse extension to the dense BLAS primitives. They did not go into great detail with respect to the implementation of these primitives, though. Contrary to dense computations the performance of sparse computations is not only dependent on the underlying architecture but also on the problem instance. This fact is reflected by, for instance, the numerous studies of the amount of fill-in created during a Gaussian elimination of a sparse matrix, because the amount of fill-in created is directly correlated to the number of operations to be performed. In the context of vector/parallel computers these issues have to be reconsidered again, because the performance of sparse matrix computations on vector/parallel architectures cannot be measured by operation counts merely. So is it, for instance, doubted whether fill-in should be considered as important for sparse matrix computations. The performance of sparse matrix computations on these architectures is determined by the occurrence of indirect addressing in the code, the vectorizing/parallelizing capabilities of the compiler, the irregularity of data transfers, the exploitation of data-locality, and the number of operations per data element, next to the operation counts.

A drawback of the sparse BLAS routines as proposed by Dodson and Lewis is that these primitives do not allow enough manipulation possibilities to achieve an efficient implementation on today's parallel/super computers. For instance, consider a sparse triad:

$$y(i) = y(i) + d(i) * x(a(i)), i = 1, N,$$

then the only optimizations possible are a splitting of this loop into consecutive sub-loops which can be run concurrently in vector mode if a GATHER instruction on the x vector is issued. This, however, induces an extra vector load of the address vector $a(i)$, and, because the GATHER instruction is mostly implemented as a memory-register operation, the triad operation $y(i) + d(i) * x(a(i))$ does not overlap with a memory-register transaction. So, we can see that the sparse triad primitive runs on an Alliant FX/8 at a rate of approximately 3 Mflops (double precision), which is about 5% of the performance achieved in some of the dense computations [7], see also [12].

The above leads us to conclude, that in order to obtain efficient implementations of sparse codes one should turn to primitives, which are of a larger granularity than one-dimensional BLAS routines (e.g. for dense computations these were the BLAS3 primitives). However, this gives rise to the problem of identifying/classifying these primitives for sparse computations. Actually, it is questionable whether sparse matrix computations can be viewed as consisting out of a number of higher level primitives. After all the components of a sparse matrix computation code, interact strongly with each other. For instance, in a solver for systems of linear equations, the handling of fill-in determines the storage format of the matrix which directly influence the reordering used in the code, and the choice of a pivoting strategy influences both the fill-in handling as the reordering. The complexity of such a code, however, should not prevent us from trying to identify crucial components with respect to the amount of the computation spend. It is not within the scope of this chapter to identify all the higher level primitives for sparse computations. We would rather like to mention some candidates for these primitives: Sparse Matrix times Sparse Matrix, Sparse Matrix times Vector, Sparse Matrix times Dense Matrix, n-Diagonal Sparse Matrix times Vector, Triangular Solve (Back

Substitution), and Sparse Rank-k Update. These primitives cannot be viewed as standing alone. For each primitive the data storage format used for the sparse matrix (matrices) determines the implementation and performance of the primitive. So, different versions of each primitive based on different storage formats have to be implemented.

In this chapter we will consider the implementation of the the Sparse Matrix times Dense Matrix and also Sparse Matrix times Vector, which is a special case of the former one, in detail. We will use for convenience's sake the denotations SpMxM and SpMxV for these two primitives. The primitive SpMxM derives, for instance, from an iterative method to obtain the eigenvalue vectors of a sparse matrix. At each iteration the iteration matrix is multiplied with the approximates of the eigenvectors. The primitive SpMxV is the crucial component, with respect to performance, in most iterative solvers.

In section 3. we layout a design strategy for the implementations of SpMxM and SpMxV for concurrent/vector processors with a hierarchical memory system. We discuss successively how to cope with different types of data access, data locality, irregularity of the computation and parallelization. Essentially four different implementations of the SpMxM and SpMxV primitive will be proposed. The viability of these implementations will be studied in section 4.. The performance and trade-offs of these implementations are verified on both the Alliant FX/8 and the FX/80 architecture. Further we examine the efficiency of Fortran coded implementation versus assembler coded implementation. In the last section we will summarize the results obtained and give some conclusions.

2. Data Storage Formats for Sparse Matrices

In order to obtain efficient implementations for sparse computations several distinct stage formats are in use for sparse matrices. For naming conventions we use n for the number of rows, (respectively, columns[1]) and nnz for the number of non-zeros in the matrix. Some of the most common ones are:

Coordinate Scheme This storage schemes stores only the non-zeros of a sparse matrix as collection of 3-tuples (i, j, x), where i is the row number j is the column number and x is the value. Because there is no order assumed on this collection of tuples, this scheme can be very useful in sparse routines which affect the non-zero pattern of the matrix, such as creating fill-in or reordering a sparse matrix. However there are two major drawbacks with this scheme. First of all the storage requirements are $2 * nnz$ integers and nnz reals. Secondly each access of a subset of the matrix, e.g. a row, requires a search through the whole collection of tuples. The latter one can be facilitated by maintaining an order on the tuples, but then the flexibility is lost of this storage scheme.

Sparse Row(Column)-wise Format This scheme is based on linked lists, and actually consists out of three arrays, value(1:nnz), index(1:nnz), and pointer(n). The value array contains all the non-zero entries, the index array contains the corresponding column entry of each non-zero, and the pointer array points to the beginning of each row in the value and index array. The advantage of this scheme is that the storage

---

[1]Throughout this chapter it is assumed that the sparse matrices are square. This is done to ease the presentation. However, the results obtained can be translated to non-square matrices in a straightforward manner

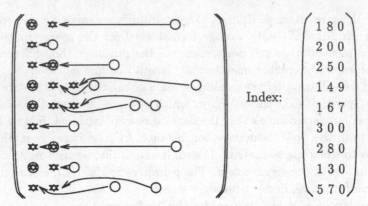

Figure 1. The extended column scheme.

requirements are minimized, and the access of rows needs only a lookup of the pointer array to obtain the row boundaries, followed by a direct fetch from the value array. Note that accessing columns of the matrix can give some problems. Gustavson [9], for that reason, proposed an extended form of the sparse row-wise format by adding two additional arrays one which is the equivalent of the index array but than for columns, and another which is a pointer array for the columns. A disadvantage is that the scheme is not as flexible as the coordinate scheme, so, for instance, if fill-in is created during, e.g., Gaussian Elimination, then some form of garbage collection has to be provided or an additional work space has to be used, which can magnify the storage requirements considerably.

Full Array Storage As in dense computations the sparse matrix could be stored fully, including the zero entries. Although the storage requirements are extensive for the whole matrix, for subsets of the matrix this can be very useful. For instance, if a submatrix is almost dense obtained either on input or in the process of Gaussian Elimination, then expanding the submatrix to a full matrix can be very cost effective in the sense that indirect addressing can be omitted in the code. Also related to this issue is the "clique" storage scheme.

For our results we shall also make use of another storage scheme, **Extended Column Scheme**, which actually derives from the "jagged diagonal" presentation of sparse matrices [11], see also [2]. Our scheme does not impose an ordering restriction on the diagonal elements, however. So this storage scheme actually is obtained by shifting all the non-zeros of each row to the left, in order to get a rectangular, almost dense matrix. The density of the resulting matrix depends on the distribution of non-zeros over the rows. Further we need together with the resulting value array an index array which indicates the column index of each value. Thus the resulting data structure consists essentially out of two rectangular arrays: value($1:n,1:max$) of reals and index($1:n,1:max$) of integers, with max the maximal over the number of non-zero entries per row. See figure 1. As different storage schemes are better suited for different pieces of codes, and different problem instance, sparse codes mostly comprise several storage schemes and part of the codes consists out of mapping one storage scheme into another.

3. Design Issues for the Primitive SpMxM (SpMxV)

In this section we will describe four possible implementations of the SpMxM primitive. First it should be noted that the the product of a sparse $N_1 \times N_2$ matrix A and a dense $N_2 \times N_3$ matrix B takes

$$nnz.N_3 \qquad \text{multiplications and}$$
$$(nnz - N_1).N_3 \qquad \text{additions,}$$

or, a total of

$$(2.nnz - N_1).N_3 \qquad \text{arithmetic steps,}$$

with nnz the number of non-zero entries in the matrix A, if each row of A contains at least one non-zero element. Thus, the computational complexity is independent of the dimension N_2. This fact directly indicates a problem when implementing this primitive on a vector architecture. In order to have a efficient implementation of this primitive the representation of the sparse matrix A should be made independent of the dimension N_2 and this introduces irregularity in the computation. The minimalization of this irregularity is an important mean to obtain a good performance. One way of achieving this is to choose a suitable data representation of the sparse matrix.

Another problem is formed by the relative small number of operations per data element. Compare the computational complexity of this primitive with the dense equivalent. The product of a dense $N_1 \times N_2$ matrix A and a dense $N_2 \times N_3$ matrix B takes a total of $(2.N_2 - 1).N_1.N_3$ steps. This amounts into an average of $\frac{(2.N_2-1).N_1.N_3}{(N_1+N_3).N_2}$ operations per data element. For the primitive SpMxM this number is $\frac{(2.nnz-N_1).N_3}{nnz+N_2.N_3}$. So, if we take the ratio of the first number over the latter one, we get

$$\frac{(2.N_2 - 1).N_1.N_3}{(N_1 + N_3).N_2} \cdot \frac{nnz + N_2.N_3}{(2.nnz - N_1).N_3} = \frac{N_2 - 1}{\frac{nnz}{N_1} - 1} \cdot \frac{\frac{nnz}{N_2} + N_3}{N_1 + N_3}$$

$$\approx \frac{1 + \frac{N_2.N_3}{nnz}}{1 + \frac{N_3}{N_1}}$$

$$\approx \frac{N_1.N_2}{nnz}.$$

Because the number of non-zero entries in a sparse matrix are expected to be small compared with the dimensions of the matrix, and in most cases a constant times the dimension N_1, the ratio is considerably large. This indicates that the exploitation of a hierarchical memory system as is done for the dense matrix multiplication by blocking techniques [7], is not as easy realizable for the SpMxM primitive. In this section we will discuss four implementation issues for the SpMxM primitive: the different types of data accesses, the exploitation of data locality, the handling of the irregularity of the computation and the parallelization of this primitive. All four issues are strongly related to each other, but we try to handle them as separately as possible in the next subsections.

3.1. Different Types of Data Access

In vector/concurrent architecture with a hierarchical memory system we have essentially two different types of data access: vector access and scalar access. For the primitive SpMxM we can think of two possible ways of realizing these vector accesses. One realization is based upon the row/columns of matrix A and/or B, and the other realization is obtained by extending each row (column) of A to a full row (column) by shifting all the non-zero entries of A to the top (to the right), see also the extended column storage scheme of the previous section. The following table depicts which combinations of these accesses makes sense for the implementation of SpMxM:

A B	scalar	row	column	ext. row	ext. column
scalar	X		X		
row	X				
column		X			X

So, for instance the implementation of row-A/column-B is given by:

$$\text{for } i \text{ from 1 to } N_2$$
$$\quad \text{for } j \text{ from 1 to } N_3$$
$$\quad\quad C(i,j) = \text{dotproduct}(A(i,*), B(ind(*),j))$$
$$\quad \text{endfor}$$
$$\text{endfor}$$

The scalar-A/scalar-B version is certainly implementable but does not exploit the vector capabilities of the architecture under investigation. This leaves us with four different types of implementation for SpMxM. Note that, because of the condensed storage format mostly used in representing the sparse matrix A (see previous section), the rows and columns of A and B do not necessarily reflect "complete" rows and columns. So we have that: the rows of the scalar-A/row-B version are complete, hence of length N_3, the columns of the row-A/column-B version are indexed and of length the number of non-zero entries in the corresponding row of A, the columns of the column-A/scalar-B version are complete in the sense that they reflect a complete column of A, the extended columns in the ext. column-A/column-B version are more than complete in the sense that they contain non-zero entries of A from a certain number of columns, and the columns of B are indexed.

3.2.   The Exploitation of Data Locality

Another important implementation issue is the exploitation of data locality. By this we mean the ability to keep data in the highest level of a system, e.g., vector registers and/or cache/local memory, for as long as possible during a computation. The performance can be significantly enhanced by exploiting the data-locality on a architecture with a hierarchically structured memory system, as was clearly pointed out in [7, 8]. The data locality of a computation is largely determined by the distance between re-usage of data. So, when this distance for a particular set of data is large, it is likely the case that during the computation the need for other data forces this set of data to be moved out of registers/cache/local memory in between fetches. As already was pointed out in the beginning of this section we have to be very careful when considering the re-usage of data in sparse computational primitives. In case of the product of a sparse $N_1 \times N_2$ matrix A and a dense $N_2 \times N_3$ matrix B the number of operations for each element a_{ij} is $\approx 2.N_3$, and for each element b_{ij} the number of non-zero entries in column i of A.

In general the concept of data locality is mainly applied to fetching operands from memory, however, we would like to point out:

NOTE DATA LOCALITY CAN BE EXPLOITED IN BOTH FETCHING DATA AND STORING DATA.

The latter form of data locality will be explained in the next discussion. With respect to the four versions of SpMxM we can make the following observations.

Observation 3.2.1 *In the* scalar-A/row-B *version we have two possible forms of data locality.*
(i) As many consecutive operations as possible are performed on each row of B. *This results in maximally n consecutive operations with n equal to the average number of non-zero entries per column of A.*
(ii) As many consecutive operations as possible are performed for each row in the resulting matrix. This results in maximally n consecutive operations with n equal to the average number of non-zero entries per row of A.

For simplicity's sake we will refer to the first optimization as version 1A and the later one as version 1B. Note that the numbers n in *(i)* and *(ii)* are equal for the case that A is a square matrix. The resulting codes are:

Version 1A:
```
        for each row B(i) of B
            for each scalar a(j) of column i of A
                C(j) = C(j) + a(j)*B(i)
                #C(j) is the j-th row of the result matrix#
            endfor
        endfor
```

Version 1B:
```
        for each row C(i) of C #the result matrix#
            for each scalar a(j) of row i of A
                C(i) = C(i) + a(j)*B(j)
                #B(j) is the j-th row of B#
            endfor
        endfor
```

Version 1B demonstrates data locality in storing data (each row of C in this case). Note further that both code fragments are triply nested DO-loops (or 4-tuple loops if vector operations are not allowed) when implemented in Fortran. So, a reasonable restructuring compiler should be able to perform the transformation from version 1A into version 1B and visa versa automatically.

Observation 3.2.2 *In the* row-A/column-B *version we have two possible forms of data-locality.*
(i) As many consecutive operations as possible are performed on each row of A. *This results in maximally $\approx 2.N_3$ consecutive operations.*

(ii) As many consecutive operations as possible are performed on each column of B. *This results in maximally* $2.N_1$ *consecutive operations.*

Call the first optimization version 2A and the second one version 2B. Note further that, although the number of consecutive in version 2B appears to be high, each column of B is indexed by a row of A. So per element of each column of B the actual number of consecutive operations is much lower. The implementation of version 2A can be found on page 410, the resulting code for version 2B can simply be obtained by a loop interchange on version 2A.

Observation 3.2.3 *In the* column-A/scalar-B *version we have two possible forms of data-locality.*
(i) As many consecutive operations as possible are performed on each column of A. *This results in maximally* $\approx 2.N_3$ *consecutive operations.*
(ii) As many consecutive operations as possible are performed for each column of the result matrix. This results in maximally $2.N_2$ *consecutive operations.*

Call the two versions as described in this observation version 3A and version 3B. Version 3B is actually a repetition of an implementation of SpMxV. The resulting codes are:

Version 3A:
```
        for each column A(i) of A
            for each scalar b(j) of row i of B
                C(j) = C(j) + b(j)*A(i)
                #C(j) is the j-th column of the result matrix#
            endfor
        endfor
```

Version 3B:
```
        for each column C(i) of C #the result matrix#
            for each scalar b(j) of column i of B
                C(i) = C(i) + b(j)*A(j)
                #A(j) is the j-th column of A#
            endfor
        endfor
```

Observation 3.2.4 *In the* ext. column-A/column-B *version we have three possible forms of data locality.*
(i) As many consecutive operations as possible are performed on each extended column of A. *This results in maximally* $\approx 2.N_3$ *consecutive operations.*
(ii) As many consecutive operations as possible are performed for each column of B. *This results in maximally* n *consecutive operations with* n *equal to the average number of non-zero entries per row of* A.
(iii) As many consecutive operations as possible are performed for each column of the result matrix. This results in the same implementation as (ii).

Because the third version is essentially the same as the second version, this observation gives us two version version 4A and version 4B.

Version 4A:

```
for each extended column A(i) of A
    for each column B(j) of B
        C(j) = C(j)+B(j)*A(i)
        #C(j) is the j-th column of the result matrix#
    endfor
endfor
```

Version 4B:

```
for each column B(i) of B
    for each extended column A(j) of A
        C(i) = C(i)+B(i)*A(j)
        #C(i) is the i-th column of the result matrix#
    endfor
endfor
```

Although the strategies introduced in the previous observations appear to be rather successful, they have an unwanted side effect: forcing part of the data to be kept in registers could increase the distance of re-usage for other parts of the data, henceforth, the other part of the data cannot be kept in a high level of the architecture. For clarifying this trade-off, let us look at version 1A. In the innermost loop of this code we have to fetch $C(j)$ and to store each newly computed $C(j)$ for each iteration. Further each stored $C(j)$ is used again only after n iterations of the innermost loop, with n equal to the number of non-zero entries on the i-th column of A. So, we can conclude that if the data locality in the rows of B increases, the data locality in the rows of C decreases. This can nullify all the performance gain achieved by this strategy. This tendency can be generally observed when exploiting data locality.

NOTE THE EXPLOITATION OF DATA LOCALITY FOR ONE PART OF THE DATA CAN DECREASE THE DATA LOCALITY FOR ANOTHER PART.

A way of overcoming this penalty is to use some kind of blocking technique for exploiting data locality. Blocking techniques are used in dense computations in order to achieve best performance on a hierarchical memory system [8]. These blocking techniques differ slightly from our notion of blocking. By blocking we mean that the innermost loop of a nested loop is not iterated for a maximal number of times, but only in chunks of a certain length. So if we look at the following generic doubly nested loop:

```
for i from 1 to N
    for j from 1 to M
        ........
    endfor
endfor
```

then after blocking this loop becomes:

```
for k from 1 to M/BL
    for i from 1 to N
```

for j from $(k-1) * BL + 1$ to $k * BL$

....

    endfor

  endfor

 endfor

Suppose for simplicity's sake that we are fetching one operand in the innermost loop which profits from the data locality in the unblocked version, for instance $B(i)$ in version 1A. Let T_l be the time spend by fetching that operand from register/cache/local memory and let T be the additional time needed for one iteration of the innermost loop. Further, let the difference of fetching data from register/cache/local memory versus fetching data from main memory be of a factor of k. Then the relative performance loss due to the blocking is approximately:

$$\frac{T_{\text{original}} - T_{\text{blocking}}}{T_{\text{original}}} = \frac{BL.T + BL.T_l - BL.T - k.T_l - (BL - 1).T_l}{BL.(T + T_l)}$$

So, the loss of performance in % of the execution time is:

$$\frac{1 - k}{BL(1 + T/T_l)}.100\%.$$

So, if BL is reasonable large compared with the difference in access time this performance is reduced to an acceptable value. The advantage of blocking is that other parts of the data could profit from data locality as well. So, if we apply blocking to, for instance, version 1A, then the distance in re-usage of $C(j)$ decreases from n to BL. By choosing BL carefully this forces the $C(j)$'s to be kept in register/cache/local memory. In general we have that the relative performance loss/gain due to blocking is approximately:

$$\frac{BL.T_l + BL.k.T_m - k.T_l - (BL - 1).T_l - k.T_m - (Bl - 1).T_m}{BL.(T + T_l + k.T_m)}.100\%,$$

where T_m is the spend by fetching the second operand, and T the time of one iteration of the innermost loop minus T_l and T_m. By putting T_l equal to T_m we get as performance loss/gain:

$$\frac{(k - 1).(BL - 2)}{(k + 1 + T/T_l).BL}.100\%.$$

So, we can conclude that for blocksizes greater than 2 we will gain performance. The effect of blocking is depicted in figure 2.

 This concept of blocking can be applied throughout version 1A, version 1B, version 2A, ... , and version 4B as the reader easily can verify. The following table shows the reduction in non-local data streams for each of the versions if blocking is applied successfully:

Version	1A	1B	2A	2B	3A	3B	4A	4B
# Datastreams								
Originally	3	3	3	3	4	4	5	5
Before Blocking	2	2	1	3*	2	4*	3	3*
After Blocking	1*	1*	1*	1*	2*	2*	1*	1*

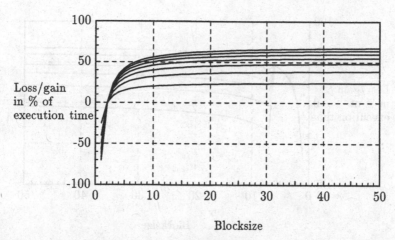

Figure 2. Performance trade-off for blocking, ratio $T/T_l = 1$, $k = 2, 3, ..., 8$.

The entries in this table which are suffixed by a * indicate a non-optimal reduction of the data streams caused by the occurrence of indirect addressing. To clarify this consider version 4B. Originally, for each operation a column of C, an extended column of A, the index for this column of A, and an indexed column of B had to be fetched and the column of C had to be stored. This totals to 5 data streams per operation. In the code fragment of version 4B can be seen that the columns of C can be kept locally. However, because each column of B is indexed by the corresponding index array of each column of A, this is not possible for the columns of B. So the number of data streams is reduced to 3. After blocking is applied the code fragment looks like:

```
for k from 1 to M/BL
#M is the maximum number of non-zero entries in a row of A#
     for each column B(i) of B
          for the ((k − 1) ∗ BL + 1)-th to the (k ∗ BL)-th
          extended column A(j) of A
               C(i) = C(i)+B(i)*A(j)
               #C(i) is the i-th column of the result matrix#
          endfor
     endfor
endfor
```

In this code fragment the extended columns of A with their corresponding index arrays can be kept locally. For each column of B, however, a separate fetch has still to be performed. This gives 1 non-local data stream per operation.

The re-usage of the columns of B in the code fragment mentioned above is dependent on the index array given by the columns of the sparse matrix A. This did not give any a-priory mean for keeping the columns of B locally. However, depending on the nature of the index arrays, or the sparsity pattern of A, there could still be some gain to achieve. On an architecture, which has a hierarchical memory system, elements of each column of B could be kept

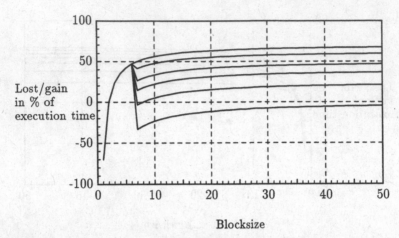

Figure 3. Second order blocking effect, ratio $T/T_l = 1$, $k = 8$, $k1 = 1, 2, 3, 4, 6, 8$.

in cache/local memory, if the sparsity pattern of the matrix A is such that for consecutive extended columns of A a non-trivial set of the row indices overlap. This is the case, for instance, when the sparse matrix is banded and the fill-in percentage within the band is high. Vector registers can mostly not be exploited in this manner. Call this a second order data locality effect. See also section 4.1.. Second order data locality can also occur when an algorithm lends itself perfectly for exploiting data locality, but the amount of data is too large to be kept within vector registers.

NOTE IN A HIERARCHICAL MEMORY SYSTEM WHICH COMPRISES A SUFFI-CIENT NUMBER OF LEVELS A SECOND ORDER DATA-LOCALITY EFFECT CAN OCCUR WHEN THE DATA AMOUNT TO BE KEPT LOCALLY IS TOO LARGE OR WHEN INDIRECTION PROHIBITS THE EXPLOITATION OF DATA IN ONE LEVEL.

So the curves of figure 2 reflect the ideal case when there is enough storage space to keep all the data local. In figure 3 the case were blocking is successful up to blocksize 6 is depicted after that a drop can been seen which reflects the curve for a smaller factor k: k_1. The formula for this case of performance loss/gain is:

$$\frac{k_1(BL - 1) - k - BL + 2}{(k_1 + 1 + T/T_l).BL}.100\%.$$

Note that there can also occur third, fourth, .. order blocking effect depending on the number of levels a certain hierarchical memory systems comprises.

The whole discussion so far was concerned with reducing the number of data streams. However, as was mentioned above, the amount of data to be kept locally can prohibit the exploitation of data locality in the sense that there is not enough space on one particular level to store it away. This is particularly the case on the highest level which provides mostly a limited number of vector register of a certain length. A way of overcoming this problem is to reduce not only the number of data streams but also the length of the data streams.

Again blocking can be used to reduced the length of the data streams. In order to distinguish the two different ways of blocking we will call the latter one vertical blocking.

NOTE VERTICAL BLOCKING REDUCES THE AMOUNT OF DATA TO BE KEPT LOCALLY.

Previous studies did not distinguish between the two forms of blocking. To our opinion this distinction is essential in order to obtain a better understanding of the implications of data-locality. Whereas both blocking techniques try to decompose a DO-loop in chunks of a certain length (the vector operations in the innermost loop bodies are DO-loops themselves actually), the vertical blocking is constrained to the vector processing capabilities of an architecture. Implementations of vertical blocking can be found in sections 3.4. and 4..

3.3. The Irregularity of the Computation

As already was pointed out in section 2 sparse matrices are mostly stored in a condensed form in order to reduce storage requirements and redundant operations. This introduces address vectors and indirect addressing which complicates coding considerably. Although most architectures nowadays provide fast GATHER and SCATTER primitives, the programmer should realize that indirect addressing still requires an extra address load which can strain the memory/cache bandwidth. Moreover, indirect addressing causes data streams to be irregular which on its turn can cause more memory bank conflicts or less exploitation of the cache line, see [12]. In addition, the presence of indirect addressing and/or using a condensed storage format for a sparse matrix influences the loop boundaries and the vector lengths of the operations, which become dependent on the sparsity structure of the matrix. In order to keep the discussion transparent, these issues were left out of consideration in the previous subsection. In this subsection each of these effects will be studied and their impact on the blocking and performance of the proposed versions for the SpMxM primitive will be pointed out.

Observation 3.3.1 *A condensed storage format for the sparse matrix A will cause indirection in:*
− *the B-array in version 2A/B*
− *the C-array in version 3A/B*
− *the B-array in version 4A/B*

Note that the indirection in version 2A/B and 3A/B differs essentially from the indirection of the B-array in version 4A/B. This is due to the fact that in version 4A/B an extended column format is used instead of a sparse row/column-wise format. So the C-array in version 4A/B is not indirect addressed, because an extended column of A is mostly full. Because the address array of each indirect addressing is correlated with the A matrix, there is a significant difference between the A versions and the B versions. In all three A versions the outer loops iterate through the rows/columns of A whereas the inner loops do not. In the B versions this is just the other way around. This means that in the B versions both a fetch of the values of a row of A as a fetch of the index array has to be performed for each iteration of the innermost loop, whereas in the A versions only the values of a row of A have to be fetched for each iteration. The performance of the A versions will, therefore, likely to be better. However if a blocking strategy is applied this will be doubly effective for the B versions.

Observation 3.3.2 *A condensed storage format for the sparse matrix* A *will affect the loop boundaries of:*
- *the innermost loop in* version 1A/B
- *the outermost loop in* version 4A
- *the innermost loop in* version 4B

This implies that for version 1A/B and version 4B blocking is constrained to the loop boundary. So, the choice of the blocksize BL is limited to the maximal number of iterations of the innermost loop. For each of these version this number is dependent on the average number of non-zero entries per row/column of the sparse matrix and can, therefore, be rather small. On the other hand, as the blocksize can be chosen to be the number of available vector registers which for most architecture is also limited to a small number, this could still be sufficient for applying blocking. For version 4A only the outermost loop is affected by indirect addressing. Whereas this has no consequences for blocking except that blocking could be more successful because the re-usage distance of the data referenced in the innermost loop is reduced, the possibility for parallelization of this version is reduced, see the next subsection.

Observation 3.3.3 *A condensed storage format for the sparse matrix* A *will affect the vector length of the operations in:*
- *version 2A/B*
- *version 3A/B*

Reduction of the vector length of the operations can nullify the gain obtained by vectorizing the code. This is especially apparent when the vector length is small compared with the length of the vector registers. In this case the larger start-up time of vector operations can outweight the slower scalar operations. Because both in version 3A/B and in version 4A/B the vector length is determined by the average number of non-zero entries per row/column of the sparse matrix the vector length is likely to be small. Note that the strength of the extended column format is reflected by the fact that the vector length of operations in version 4A/B are not affected.

If we summarize all the effects of using a condensed storage format for the sparse matrix, we obtain the following table:

Version / Effect	1A	1B	2A	2B	3A	3B	4A	4B
Ind. Addr.			X	X	X	X	X	X
Inner Lp. Bnd.	X	X						X
Outer Lp. Bnd.							X	
Vector Length			X	X	X	X		

3.4.   Parallelization

Parallelization can be easily established for the versions introduced in the previous subsection, as each version actually constitutes a loop of depth 4 to 5 depending on whether vertical blocking is applied. If vertical blocking is applied the generic loop body looks like:

```
for k from 1 to M1/BL1
    for i from 1 to M
        for h from 1 to M2/BL2
            for j from (k − 1) * BL1 + 1 to k * BL1
                for l from (h − 1) * BL2 + 1 to h * BL2
                    ........
                end for
            end for
        endfor
    endfor
endfor
```

where N is the number of iterations of the original outer loop, $M1$ the number of iterations of the original inner loop, $M2$ the length of the data streams, and $BL2$ the blocksize of the vertical blocking. The corresponding values of N, $M1$ and $M2$ for each of the versions are given in the following table:

Version Value	1A	1B	2A	2B	3A	3B	4A	4B
M	N_2	N_1	N_1	N_3	N_2	N_3	$*$	N_3
$M1$	$*$	$*$	N_3	N_1	N_3	N_2	N_3	$*$
$M2$	N_3	N_3	$*$	$*$	$*$	$*$	N_1	N_1

The sparse matrix is N_1 by N_2 and the dense matrix is N_2 by N_3. The $*$ entries indicate the values which are dependent on the sparsity pattern of the matrix, see the previous subsection. Note that the h-loop can also occur in between the k- and i-loop or before the k-loop. Either one of these places give no significant difference in the flow of the computation.

Observation 3.4.1 *If the lengths of data streams are sufficiently large the l-loop can be parallelized and the need for vertical blocking can be eliminated.*

Recall that vertical blocking is mostly applied for the highest level of a hierarchical memory system, or, in other words, for efficiently managing vector registers. As most architectures supply distinct sets of vector registers for different processors, by parallelizing the l-loop the storage capacity of the vector registers is multiplied by the number of processors. So depending on the number of processors and the length of the data streams the need for vertical blocking can disappear.

The parallelization of the h-loop does not require any communication and/or synchronization between the processors, except for version 2A/B. In version 2A/B the results of the parallelized dotproducts have to be gathered, which can introduce a slight overhead. Further the granularity of the parallelism for this loop should be at least the length of the vector registers, otherwise the vector registers are not fully exploited. In some cases, however, finer granularity may still be worthwhile.

Observation 3.4.2 *The parallelization of the j-loop should be avoided as it destroys the data-locality.*

This observation directly follows from the discussion in the previous subsection.

Observation 3.4.3 *The i-loop can be parallelized without any restrictions.*

These observations leave us with two significant parameters: M and $M2$ for considering parallelization. Let n be the average number of non-zero entries per row/column of the sparse matrix, and let $N_1 = N_2 (= N)$. Further, write m for N_3. Then we have that the potential parallelism for versions 1A/B, 4B is $N.m$, for versions 2A, 3A and 4A is $N.n$, and for versions 2B and 3B is $n.m$. So, if, for instance, we have the SpMxV primitive which is a special case of the SpMxM primitive than the potential for parallelism is almost reduced to zero for the version 2B and 3B especially if the matrix has only a small average number of non-zeros per row.

4.   The Implementation of the Primitive SpMxM (SpMxV)

The implementation of the primitive SpMxM on a particular architecture requires next to the considerations as described before a more detailed account for the peculiarities of the architecture, the expressional power of the programming language, the (optimizing) compiler and the code generator. Generally it is assumed that when implementing dense BLAS primitives, the compilation of a Fortran coded primitive does not generate a sufficiently efficient implementation. In this section we will study these issues for two different architectures: the Alliant FX/8 and FX/80, and we will analyze the impact on the efficiency of the implementations for the two architectures. Each version will be treated separately in the following subsections. Because of the poor data-locality of version 3A/B, see the table on page 414, and the fact that the vector length depends on the sparsity pattern, see the table on page 418, version 3A/B is not considered here.

The Alliant FX/8 architecture comprises up to 8 vector processors, strongly connected with each other via a concurrency control bus. Each of the 8 processors has floating point pipelines for addition, multiplication and division, and 8 vector registers which can contain 32 64-bit words. Further gather and scatter instructions are implemented. The cycle-time is 85 ns, which gives rise to a theoretical peak performance of 96 Mflops for 8 processors. The processors are connected through a crossbar switch to a shared cache, which consists out of four interleaved quadrants. The maximal bandwidth of the crossbar switch is 47 Mword/s. The size of the cache is 4x4K 64-bit words. Cache and main memory are connected via the main memory bus, which has a maximal bandwidth of 23.5 Mword/s. Main memory is organized into four interleaved banks, each of size of 1 Mword (64-bit) up to 8 Mword. For more detailed information, see [1].

Experimental results are obtained by using a banded arbitrary sparse matrix generator, which has as parameters the dimension (ranging from 400 to 4000), the average number of non-zero entries per row (ranging from 3 to 30) and the bandwidth (ranging from 15 to 60). Further arbitrary sparse matrices are generated. The # of vectors denotes the width of the dense matrix throughout this section.

4.1.   Version 2A/B: The Dotproduct Version

The implementation which seems to be the most obvious for the SpMxM primitive is the one which makes use of a fast dotproduct:

```
KERNEL1
        do i=1, n
```

```
        k1 = pointer(i)
        k2 = pointer(i+1)-1
        do j=0, m-1
           result(i,j) =
+          dotproduct(value(k1:k2),rhs(index(k1:k2),j))
        end do
     end do
```

The storage scheme chosen is the sparse row-wise format, see section 2. Further rhs$(1{:}n,1{:}m)$ represents the dense matrix and result$(1{:}n,1{:}m)$ represents the resulting matrix. This implementation reflects version 2A and sweeps through the algorithm by rows of A (value(k1:k2) and index(k1:k2), see section 3.1.). With optimization turned off the FX/Fortran compiler (version 4) generates for the innermost loop essentially the following code:

```
label_j:
label_h:
                   .
                   .
                   .
        vmove    @vector,v1       | 1
        vmove    @vector,v2       | 2
        vadd     v2,d0,v2         | 3
        vgathr   @vector,v2,v2    | 4
        vdot     v1,v2,fp0        | 5
        fmove    fp0, @scalar     | 6
                   .
                   .
        vcnt32   label_h          | 7
                   .
                   .
        ble  label_j
```

As can be seen the available data locality is not exploited at all: for each iteration three times a vector fetch (lines 1, 2 and 4), and one scalar store (line 6) has to be performed. Note that the number of data streams can theoretically be reduced to 1 (table on page 414). This is partly caused by the fact that the length of the vectors is not known at compile time. This causes the code generator to generate a vcnt32 loop (line 7), so that the vectors are cut in pieces of length 32 to fit the vector register length. As already was pointed out in section 3.2. vertical blocking can be applied to resolve this problem. When this is done on the Fortran level the code generator will still not keep the two vectors in registers, however the length of the loop bodies are shortened. This reduces the overhead of each iteration which makes the code more efficient. Further the resulting code allows some hand optimizing, by which we were able to reduce the number of vector fetches for each iteration to 1. The optimization was obtained by modifying the assembler object code such that value(k1:k2) and index(k1:k2) are explicitly kept in vector registers. By further manipulation of the Fortran code, e.g. explicitly copying the blocked vectors in a temporary array and loop unrolling, we were able to force the code generator to generate only one vector fetch per loop iteration. However, the additional overhead created by these manipulations appears to nullify any gain obtained by

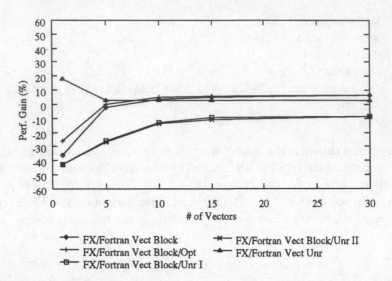

Figure 4.   Performance gain over FX/Fortran Vect (FX/8–double), dimension 3600, nnzero/row 30, bandwidth 1800.

reducing the number of data streams. In figure 4 the performance gain is shown on the Alliant FX/8 for the blocked Fortran code (Vect Block), the hand optimized code (Vect Block Opt) and the manipulated Fortran code (Vect Block/Unr I and II) over the initial Fortran code, all three running in vector mode and concurrency turned off. Another technique commonly used to enhance the efficiency of a code is loop unrolling. The performance gain of loop unrolling (of depth 5) is also depicted in figure 4. The performance gains obtained by these optimizations seems to be rather disappointing. This is mainly caused by the fact that only one CE out of 8 is active so the cache/memory bandwidth is not stressed enough to achieve a lot of performance gain by reducing the number of data streams. Further the vector start-up time of the dot-product and register-register operations is rather high on the Alliant FX/8 (these start-up times are shortened for the Alliant FX/80), which causes the overhead for each loop iteration to be considerably high. However, as will see later on in concurrent mode these optization can yield up to 40% performance gain.

When optimizing is turned on the FX/Fortran compiler will optimize this code by parallelizing the j-loop. That this is not a optimal way of implementing this code follows from observation 3.4.2. Thus the data locality of value(k1:k2) and index(k1:k2) is destroyed. In figure 5 the speedup of this implementation on an Alliant FX/8 is depicted versus the performance of this code when concurrency is prohibited. The Alliant FX/8 is configured with 8 processors. So we observe that, even when the number of vectors (the width of the dense matrix) is large enough, the maximal speedup achieved is approximately 6. It is in fact impossible to force only the outerloop to be parallelized in the above code fragment when using FX/Fortran. A loop interchange is also not too advantageously, because both k1 and k2 are dependent on the loop index i. This is reflected in the table on page 414. The only way of achieving parallelism in the outer loop in FX/Fortran is to put the loop body in a subroutine, which then is concurrently called. The resulting speedup is depicted in figure 6 for both a blocked Fortran version with a concurrent call to the loop body (CnCall Block), and a version obtained by explicitly optimizing the object code of the code generator (CnCall Block Opt). The optimization was obtained by modifying the assembler object code such that value(k1:k2) and index(k1:k2) are explicitly kept in vector registers. The innermost loop of the resulting object code for this optimized version essentially looks like:

```
        vmove    @vector,v5
        vmove    @vector,v6

label_1:
        .
        .

        vadd     v6,d2,v1         | 1
        vgathr   @vector,v1,v2    | 2
        vdot     v5,v2,fp1        | 3

        fmove    fp1,@scalar      | 4
        .

        bles label_1
```

The speedup is impressive, especially, because each iteration of the loop involves a call to a subroutine. This means that for the dotproduct exploiting data-locality can yield significant efficiency when the code is parallelized.

The resulting code is so efficient that a assembler coded version of SpMxM shows only a slight gain in performance, see figure 7. The assembler coded version of SpMxM is referred to as Dotproduct. Note, however, that the optimized code is not produced by the code generator of FX/Fortran solely. So from this cannot be concluded that assembler implementations of sparse BLAS primitives are not worthwhile.

The problems as described above are different for CEDAR-Fortran. CEDAR-Fortran is a super-set of FX/Fortran developed at CSRD for the CEDAR system [10], which runs under the Xylem operating system. Implementations of CEDAR Fortran and Xylem are currently running on both the Alliant systems and a prototype of the CEDAR system. Because of the more expressive power of CEDAR-Fortran (e.g. CEDAR-Fortran allows different types of DO-loop structures: CDOALL, CDOACROSS, SDOALL, etc.), the SpMxM primitive can be coded as follows.

```
        cdoall i=1, nrow
        integer*4 k, k1, k2, h, j, jj, proc
        loop
           proc = extract_vpn()
           k1 = pointer(i)
           k2 = pointer(i+1)-1
           k  = (k2-k1+1)/32
C*******Split k2-k1 up into pieces of 32****************
           do j=0, k-1
              h = k1+j*32
              hvalue(1:32,proc)=value(h:h+31)
```

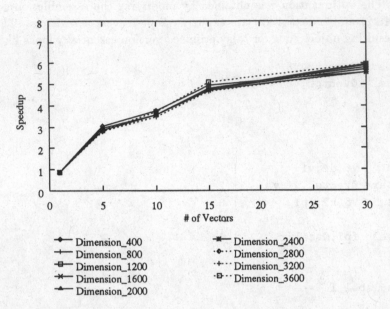

Figure 5.   Speedup of FX/Fortran Conc/Vect over FX/Fortran Vect (FX/8–double), nnzero/row 15, bandwidth 30.

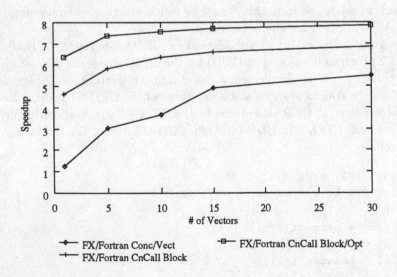

Figure 6.   Speedup over FX/Fortran Vect Block/Opt (FX/8–double), dimension 3600, nnzero/row 30, bandwidth 30.

```
            hrowind(1:32,proc)=rowind(h:h+31)
            do jj=0, nx-1
               result(i+jj*nrow) =
    +          dotproduct(hvalue(1:32,proc),
    +             rhs(hrowind(1:32,proc)+jj*nrow))
            end do
         end do
C*******Handle the remainder****************************
         h = k2-k1+1-k*32
         if (h.ne.0) then
            hvalue(1:h,proc)=value(k1+k*32:k2)
            hrowind(1:h,proc)=rowind(k1+k*32:k2)
            do jj=0, nx-1
               result(i+jj*nrow) =
    +          dotproduct(hvalue(1:h,proc),
    +             rhs(hrowind(1:h,proc)+jj*nrow))
            end do
         end if
      end cdoall
```

This code implements a blocked version with a concurrent outerloop, such that each iteration is scheduled on an available processor of the Alliant system or on an available processor of one of the CEDAR clusters. The CDOALL constructs forces the CEDAR-Fortran compiler to parallelize the loop, and the C routine extract_vpn yields the virtual processor ID in order to ensure that the local copies hvalue and hrowind are distinct for different processors. In figure 8 the performance of this CEDAR-Fortran on an Alliant FX/8 is depicted versus the blocked blocked FX/Fortran implementation using a CnCall. So, we see that in this case CEDAR-Fortran does not only allow more explicit control of the parallelization of DO-loops but yields also a slightly more efficient implementation. With respect to this it is important to mention that the code generators were the same for both FX/Fortran and CEDAR-Fortran.

In all implementations of version 2A described above each iteration of the most innermost loop does a fetch of rhs(hrowind( )) (and of hrowind( ) and hvalue( ), in case the code is not hand optimized). This means that the performance of this implementation on an Alliant system, is also dependent on the indirection behavior of hrowind( ). As reusage of data within a short time interval can guarantee that the data is kept in cache the access time of (hrowind( )) is dependent on how many elements of hrowind( ) match with each other in successive iterations. This was also described in section 3.2. as second order data locality. So, for instance if the sparse matrix has only a limited bandwidth, then the elements referenced by hrowind is reduced to only a slice of length twice the bandwidth, and access of rhs( ) should be faster than for an arbitrary sparse matrix. In figure 8 this second order effect of data locality is shown for the case of banded matrices. It is noticeable that the performance degradation is consistently 48-51% for all 6 implementations. This can be explained by the fact that the bandwidth of the memory bus in between cache and memory decreases linearly, when the number of data streams increases, see also [6].

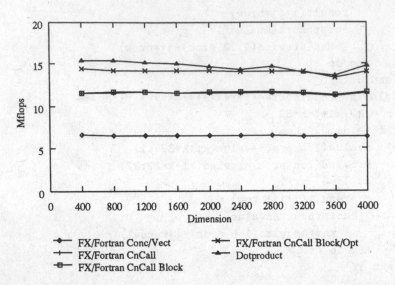

Figure 7. Varying the dimension (FX/8–double), nnzero/row 30, bandwidth 30, # of vectors 10.

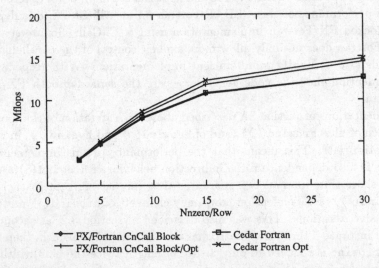

Figure 8. Varying the nnzero/row (FX/8–double), dimension 3600, bandwidth 30, # of vectors 30.

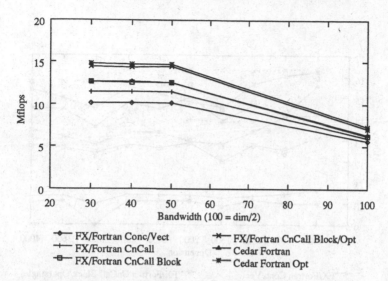

Figure 9. Varying the bandwidth (FX/8–double), dimension 3600, nnzero/row 30, # of vectors 30.

The floating point arithmetic pipelines in the Alliant systems are all 64 bits wide, so there should be no real difference in performance when using double precision or single precision floating point operations. This can be seen from figure 9 where the performance is depicted for the different versions of SpMxM for varying dimension both for single precision and double precision floating point operations. However, for the second order data-locality effect we see some difference. The performance of the single precision versions do not drop as much (approximately 40%) when second order effect data-locality cannot be exploited (see figure 10). This is caused by the fact that on the Alliant systems this performance loss is determined by the bandwidth of the memory bus, which in case of single precision numbers is higher than for double precision numbers, see also [6].

The Alliant FX/80 differs from the Alliant FX/8 in essentially, the floating point pipelines: startup times are reduced and chime rates of certain register-register operations are also reduced, the larger cache size, and the VME bus connecting the IP's (the Interactive Processors) to the input/output devices instead of a multi-bus. The Alliant FX/80 we used for our experiments had not a standard configuration, but a multi-bus for the IP interface instead of a VME bus. Because of the faster floating point pipelines we see a significant performance increase of about 30-60% in case second order data-locality can be exploited, see figure 11. However, as soon as this is not the case the performance drops to about the same performance as on the Alliant FX/8. This is caused by the fact that both the Alliant FX/80 and the Alliant FX/8 have the same cache-memory bus. It is important to note that the performance of the different versions of SpMxM relate to each other in the same way as on the Alliant FX/8, see figure 12. Overall we can say that, except for the assembler coded version, the Cedar Fortran implementation is the fastest implementation of SpMxM, closely followed by the FX/Fortran implementation with the CnCall.

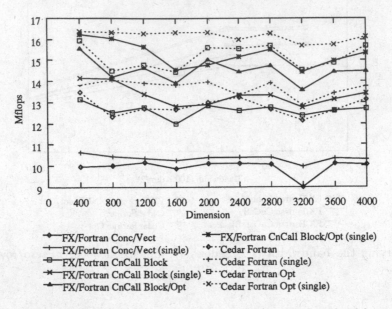

Figure 10. Varying the dimension (FX/8–double), nnzero/row 30, bandwidth 30, # of vectors 30.

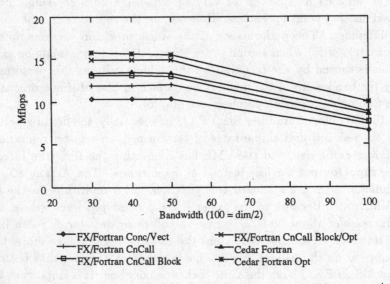

Figure 11. Varying the bandwidth (FX/8–double), dimension 3600, nnzero/row 30, # of vectors 30.

4.2. Version 1A/B: The Triad Version

For the implementation of version 1A/B we have chosen for an assembler coded version. Recall that version 1A demonstrates data locality in fetching data whereas version 1B utilize data locality in storing data (observation 3.3.1). Because storing data is more costly than fetching data on most architectures an implementation of version 1B is clearly superior to an implementation of version 1A. For version 1B we have in fact two versions, the first one, called **triadc**, having the dense matrix stored column by column, and the second version, **triadr**, row by row. Recall that access types for version 1 are scalars for the sparse matrix and rows for the dense matrix. Because Fortran stores a matrix column-wise, the second version actually works on the transposed of the dense matrix. This causes the row accesses to be vector accesses of stride 1 rather than stride "the number of rows". The two versions are essentially the same and their innermost loop look like:

```
          fmove    @scalar,fp0        | 1
          vmul     @vector,fp0,v0     | 2
Kloop:
          .
          .
          .
          fmove    @scalar,fp0        | 3
          vmuad    fp0,@vector,v0,v0  | 4
          .
          .
          .
          jle      Kloop
          vmove    v0,a5@             | 5
```

The only difference between triadc and triadr is that the vmul and vmuad operations are performed with stride N_1 versus stride 1. As we can see the innermost loop of these two implementations is much simpler than the ones we obtained for the version 2A implementation. This is mainly caused by the fact that the indirection is hidden in the scalar loads (lines 1 and 3), so the need for explicit gathers is eliminated. In fact for each vector access two operations on the accessed data can be performed, which gives a high potential for good performance. However, as also can be concluded from the tables on page 418 and 419, the vectorlength in the triadc and triadr implementations is determined by the number of vectors, and the number of iterations of the Kloop is dictated by the number of non-zero elements of a row of the sparse matrix. So, in case the sparse matrix is multiplied with only one vector all the vector operations in the triadc and triadr implementation are of length 1, or in other words triadc and triadr turn out to be scalar codes, see figure 13.   On the other hand, if the number of vectors is large enough (e.g. in the order of the length of the vector register), the performance of the triadr can increase considerably. For certain values of the average number of non-zeros per row and the number of vectors the performance of this implementation of SpMxM actually approximates the performance of the dense BLAS3 implementation of the matrix-matrix multiply on the Alliant FX/8/80. We observed performance rates of up to 35 Mflop on an Alliant FX/8 and up to 55 on the Alliant FX/80, when the number of vectors and the average number of non-zeros is equal to 30. This is not very surprising as the triadr implementation resembles the dense BLAS3 implementations of the matrix times matrix primitive.

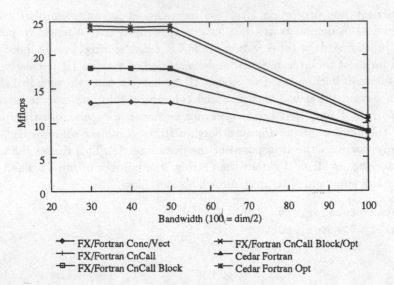

Figure 12. Varying the bandwidth (FX/80–double), dimension 8000, nnzero/row 30, # of vectors 30.

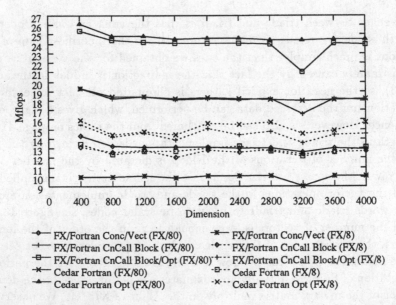

Figure 13. Comparing FX/80–double and FX/8–double, nnzero/row 30, bandwidth 30, # of vectors 30.

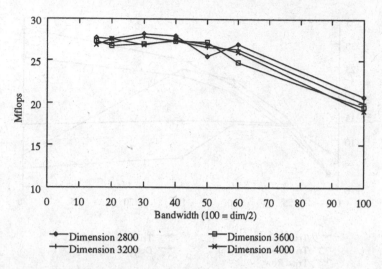

Figure 14. Varying the bandwidth for Triad Row (FX/8–double), nnzero/row 30, # of vectors 30.

In figure 14 the performance is depicted of the triadr, triadc and the dotproduct version (the assembler coded implementation of version 2A) for increasing number of vectors. Of the triadc and triadr also the performance of the single arithmetic implementations are given. It can be observed that on the Alliant FX/8 the performance of the triadr is already paying off when the number of vectors is larger than 5 to 10 depending on the average number of non-zeros per row. Furthermore the striding in the triadc version destroys all the performance gain obtained for larger numbers of vectors. If we look at the difference in performance of single precision versus double precision, then we see a non-negligible difference. This difference in performance is explained by the fact that for the double precision implementations the exploitation of cache becomes harder as the amount of data involved is higher than for the single precision implementations. In addition the start-up times for the vmuad (triad) instructions is significantly smaller than the start-up time for the dotproduct instruction, which makes this effect more noticeable.

The second order data locality effect, which we observed for the version 2A/B implementations in the previous subsection, also occurs for this implementation of SpMxM. In figure 15 the performance of triadr is depicted as a function of the bandwidth of the sparse matrix. As can be seen the performance drops significantly as the bandwidth increases.

Concluding we can say that, when the number of vectors is larger than 5-10, the triadr implementation on an Alliant FX/8/80 is superior over the version 2A implementations. For a small number of vectors and specifically for the case we have a sparse matrix times vector multiplication this is not the case.

4.3. Version 4A/B: The Extended Triad Version

Version 4A and version 4B essentially differ with respect to the loop boundaries of the inner and outer loop, recall the table on page 419. In version 4B the inner loop boundary is determined by the number of non-zero per rows of the sparse matrix, whereas in version 4A the inner loop boundary is always equal to the number of vectors. Because the performance is

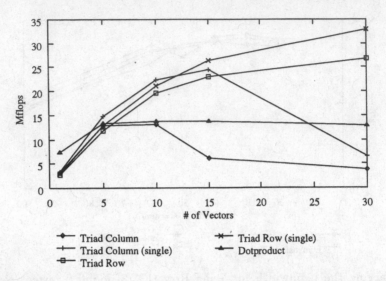

Figure 15. Varying # of vectors (FX/8–double), dimension 4000, nnzero/row 30, bandwidth 30.

mostly dictated by the inner loop, version 4B is not as good a candidate for implementation as version 4A. Further in version 4A (and version 4B) the vectorlength of the vector operations is not dependent on the sparsity structure, or number of vectors, as was the case in versions 1A and 2B. The assembler coded implementation of version 4A essentially looks like:

```
          .
          .
          .
      vmove    @vector,v0
      vmove    @vector,v7
      vgathr   @vector,v0,v1
      vmul     v7,v1,v1
      vgathr   @vector,v0,v2
      vmul     v7,v2,v2
      vgathr   @vector,v0,v3
      vmul     v7,v3,v3
          .
          .
          .
Kloop:
          .
          .
          .
      vmove    @vector,v0
      vmove    @vector,v7
      vgathr   @vector,v0,v6
      vmul     v7,v6,v6
      vadd     v6,v1,v1
      vgathr   @vector,v0,v6
      vmul     v7,v6,v6
```

```
vadd     v6,v2,v2
vgathr   @vector,v0,v6
vmul     v7,v6,v6
vadd     v6,v3,v3
.

.
jmp      Kloop
.

.
vmove    v1,@vector
vmove    v2,@vector
vmove    v3,@vector
```

Note that unrolling is necessary for the implementation of version 4A. This is because of the fact that the number of non-local data streams before blocking and after blocking decreases with 2, see the table on page 414. So, in order to exploit blocking optimally the vector registers have to be arranged as a temporary two dimensional storage space. This causes the degree of unrolling to be limited to the number of vector registers minus 2. So, for instance on an Alliant FX architecture the maximal degree of unrolling is 5. In the code fragment only unrolling up to three is depicted. Further the degree of unrolling is dependent on the number of vectors.

The performance of the extended triad on the Alliant FX architectures is the most stable one among the implementations described in the previous subsections. This is caused by the fact that the vectorlength of the operations is only dependent on the number of rows of the sparse matrix which is generally large enough to guarantee a sufficient utilization of the vector operations. Even the second order data-locality effect does have a smaller impact on the performance than in the other implementations. This is caused by the fact that the number of vector register–register operations is larger than the number of vector memory–register operations (see the code fragment above). So the performance of this implementation is highly determined by the speed of vector register–register operations, see also section 5.. The only dependency which influences the performance is the dependency of the degree of unrolling on the number of vectors. In figure 16 the performance of the extended triad implementation on the Alliant FX/8 is depicted with varying number of vectors. As can be seen the performance drops each time slightly if the number of vectors is a multiple of 5 plus one or two. This is because the degree of unrolling on the Alliant FX/8 is limited to 5, see above. Figures 17 and 18 show the stable performance of the extended triad implementation for varying average non-zero entries per row of the sparse matrix and varying number of vectors. ¿From figure 17 can also be observed that, if the number of vectors is small, i.e. smaller than 10, and especially in the case of SpMxV, the performance of this implementation is clearly superior over all implementations considered thus far, see also section 5..

5.   Summary and Conclusions

As can be concluded from section 4. the performance of the different implementations of SpMxM vary significantly for different values of the dimension of the sparse matrix, the bandwidth, the average number of non-zero entries per row of the sparse matrix, and the width of the dense matrix (# of vectors). In table 1 the performance range of all implemen-

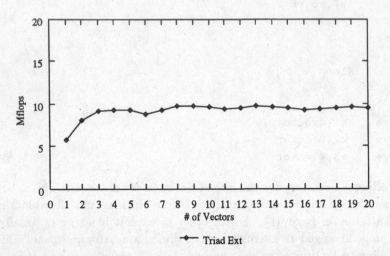

Figure 16. Varying # of vectors for Triad Ext (FX/8–double), dimension 3600, nnzero/row 30, bandwidth 30.

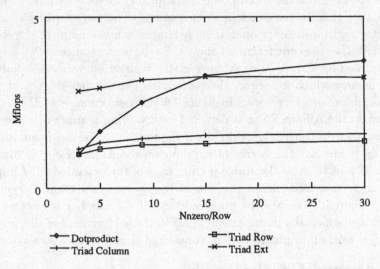

Figure 17. Varying the nnzero/row (FX/8–double), dimension 4000, bandwidth 30, # of vectors 1.

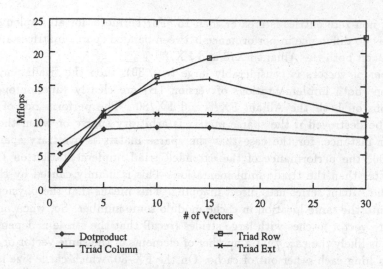

Figure 18. Varying # of vectors (FX/8–double), dimension 4000, nnzero/row 9, bandwidth 30.

	FX/8	FX/80	Dependent on
FX/Fortran Conc/Vect	0.1–10	0.1–14.5	Avp, Nx, Bndw
FX/Fortran CnCall	2–12	2–17	Avp, Nx, Bndw
FX/Fortran CnCall Block	1–13.5	1.5–19.5	Avp, Nx, Bndw
FX/Fortran CnCall Block/Opt	1–15.5	1.5–26	Avp, Nx, Bndw
Cedar Fortran	1–13.5	1.5–19.5	Avp, Nx, Bndw
Cedar Fortran Opt	1–15.5	1.5–26	Avp, Nx, Bndw
Dotproduct	2–15.5	2.5–23	Avp, Nx, Bndw
Triad Column	2–28	4–47	Avp, Nx, Bndw, Dim
Triad Row	2–31	4–50	Avp, Nx, Bndw
Triad Ext	5–11.5	8–20	Nx

Table 1. The performance range and the dependencies of the different implementations. (Avp (3-30) means average number of non-zero entries per row, nx means the number of vectors (1-30), bndw means the bandwidth (10-50), and Dim (400-4000) means the dimension.)

tations on both the Alliant FX/8 and FX/80 is depicted. Further, for each implementation the parameters, on which its performance is dependent, are given. There is not a best implementation of the SpMxM primitive for all cases. We can extract some general information from these curves, though.

For the case of sparse matrix times one vector (SpMxV) the extended triad implementation (an implementation of version 4A) together with the dotproduct implementation (an implementation of version 2A) achieve clearly the best performance on both the Alliant FX/8 and FX/80. The extended triad is superior over all other implementation if the average number of non-zero entries is smaller or equal to 15 (e.g. for average number of non-zero entries equal to 5 the extended triad is at least twice as fast as any other implementation). The dotproduct implementation is performing better than the other implementations if the average number of non-zero entries is greater than 15. Furthermore, for all implementations of SpMxV there is no difference in performance between banded sparse matrices and arbitrary sparse matrices on both the Alliant FX/8 and FX/80.

If the number of vectors is considerably large (e.g. 30), then the triadr and the triadc implementation (both implementations of version 1B) are clearly superior over all other implementations on both the Alliant FX/8 and FX/80. The performance of the triadc, however, can be destroyed if the sparse matrix is arbitrary sparse or when the dimension increases. For instance, for the case that the sparse matrix is arbitrary sparse and has dimension 4000, the performance of the extended triad implementation on the FX/8 is about 50% faster than the triadc implementation. This is mainly caused by the fact that the cache of the Alliant series uses direct mapping. This means that the physical addresses are mapped onto the same location in cache modulo some number. So, when in the case of triadc there are vector fetches with large strides (recall that the stride is dependent on the dimension), it is likely the case that a number of elements of the same vector or consecutive vectors are trashing each other out of cache. On the FX/80, which cache size is four times larger than the cache size of the FX/8, this effect is less significant.

The performance of all implementations on the FX/80 is about 50% better than on the FX/8. The relative performance of the implementations with respect to each other is the same for the FX/80 as for the FX/8, with one exception. The performance of the extended triad increases about 100% on the FX/80. This is because the computation of the extended triad implementation is dominated by vector register–register operations, which are much more efficient on the FX/80 than on the FX/8, see also section 4.3..

The main difference between banded sparse matrices and arbitrary sparse matrices is that the high performance for larger number of vectors cannot be sustained, when the dimension increases. Further the performance for arbitrary sparse matrices does not increase as much when the average number of non-zero entries per row increases. This is not the case for the extended triad implementation.

Concluding we can say that sparse BLAS implementations can speed up the performance of sparse computations considerably. So, in the case of the Alliant FX/8 (FX/80), on which the performance of unstructured sparse computations lies within the range of 0.1–10 Mflops, specialized higher order BLAS routines can speedup this performance to 5–30 (8–50) Mflops. The implementation of these BLAS routines is far from trivial, though. First sparse BLAS primitives cannot be viewed as standing alone. These primitives are dependent on the data format used for sparse matrices as well as on the code in which they are embedded. Secondly the parameters which determine the performance of the primitives have to be identified. Further, the number of these parameters causes the evaluation of the performance of sparse BLAS primitives to be very tedious. However, as was pointed out in this chapter the considerations made in section 3. carried through into the next sections very well. So, the design methodology of section 3. could alleviate some of the problems mentioned above.

Acknowledgements. The helpful comments and suggestions of K. Gallivan, Y. Saad and A. Sameh were very much appreciated.

References

[1] Alliant Computer Systems Corporation, *FX/Series Product Summary*, 1985.

[2] E. Anderson and Y. Saad, *Solving Sparse Triangular Linear Systems on Parallel Computers*, CSRD Report No. 794, Center for Supercomputing Research, University of Illinois at Urbana–Champaign, June 1988.

[3] D.S. Dodson and J.G. Lewis, *Proposed Sparse Extensions to the Basic Linear Algebra Subprograms*, SIGNUM newsletter, ACM, vol. 20, pp. 22-25 (1985).

[4] J. Dongarra, J. Bunch, C. Moler, and G.W. Stewart, *LINPACK User's Guide*, SIAM Publications, Philadelphia, 1979.

[5] J. Dongarra, J. DuCroz, S. Hammarling, and R. Hanson, *A Proposal for an Extended Set of Fortran Basic Linear Algebra Subprograms*, Technical Memo #41, Mathematics and Computer Science Division, Argonne National Laboratory, December 1984.

[6] K. Gallivan, D. Gannon, W. Jalby, A. Malony, and H. Wijshoff, *Behavioral Characterization of Multiprocessor Memory Systems: A Case Study*, CSRD Report No. 808, Center for Supercomputing Research, University of Illinois at Urbana–Champaign, September 1988. To appear in the proceedings of the 1989 ACM SIGMETRICS Conference on Measurement and Modeling of Computer Systems.

[7] K. Gallivan, W. Jalby, U. Meier, and A. Sameh, *The Impact of Hierarchical Memory Systems on Linear Algebra Algorithm Design*, International J. Supercomputer Applications, vol. 2, no. 1 (1988).

[8] D. Gannon, W. Jalby, and K. Gallivan, *Strategies for Cache and Local Memory Management by Global Program Transformation*, Journal of Parallel and Distributed Computing, vol. 5, pp. 587–616 (1988).

[9] F.G. Gustavson, *Two Fast Algorithms for Sparse Matrices: Multiplication and Permuted Transposition*, ACM Transactions on Mathematical Software, vol. 4, no. 3, pp. 250–269 (1978).

[10] M.D. Guzzi, *Cedar Fortran Programmer's Handbook*, CSRD Report No. 601, Center for Supercomputing Research, University of Illinois at Urbana–Champaign, June 1987.

[11] R. Melhem, *Parallel Solution of Linear Systems with Striped Sparse Matrices*, Parallel Computing, vol. 6, no. 3, pp. 165–184 (1988).

[12] Y. Saad and H. Wijshoff, *A Benchmark Package for Sparse Computations*, proceedings of the 1988 International Conference on Supercomputing, pages 500–509, ACM Press, New York, 1988.